THE FUTURE OF EUROPE: TOWARDS A TWO-SPEED EU?

The European Union is in crisis. Public unease with the project, problems with the euro and dysfunctional institutions give rise to the real danger that the European Union will become increasingly irrelevant just as its Member States face more and more challenges in a globalized world. Jean-Claude Piris, a leading figure in the conception and drafting of the EU's legal structures, tackles the issues head on with a sense of urgency and with candour. The book works through the options available in the light of the economic and political climate, assessing their effectiveness. By so doing, the author reaches the (for some) radical conclusion that the solution is to permit 'two-speed' development: allowing an inner core to move towards closer economic and political union, which will protect the Union as a whole. Compelling, critical and current, this book is essential reading for all those interested in the future of Europe.

JEAN-CLAUDE PIRIS served as the Legal Counsel of the Council of the EU and Director General of its Legal Service from 1988 to 2010. He is an Honorary French Conseiller d'Etat, a former diplomat at the UN and the former Director of Legal Affairs of the OECD. He was the Legal Adviser to the successive intergovernmental Conferences which negotiated and adopted the treaties of Maastricht, Amsterdam and Nice, the Constitutional Treaty and, finally, the Lisbon Treaty. He was also Senior Emile Noël Fellow and Straus Institute Fellow at New York University.

THE FUTURE OF EUROPE: TOWARDS A TWO-SPEED EU?

JEAN-CLAUDE PIRIS

CAMBRIDGE
UNIVERSITY PRESS

CAMBRIDGE UNIVERSITY PRESS
Cambridge, New York, Melbourne, Madrid, Cape Town,
Singapore, São Paulo, Delhi, Tokyo, Mexico City

Cambridge University Press
The Edinburgh Building, Cambridge CB2 8RU, UK

Published in the United States of America by Cambridge University Press, New York

www.cambridge.org
Information on this title: www.cambridge.org/9781107021372

First published 2012

Printed in the United Kingdom at the University Press, Cambridge

A catalogue record for this publication is available from the British Library

Library of Congress Cataloging in Publication data
Piris, Jean-Claude.
The future of Europe : towards a two-speed EU? / Jean-Claude Piris.
p.   cm.
Includes index.
ISBN 978-1-107-02137-2 (hardback)
1. European Union.   2. European Union – International cooperation.
3. European Union countries – Politics and government – 21st century.   I. Title.
KJE947.P49   2012
341.242′2 – dc23   2011042602

ISBN 978-1-107-02137-2 Hardback
ISBN 978-1-107-66256-8 Paperback

To my former colleagues in the Legal Service of the Council of the European Union, in recognition of their work and dedication

2011 could turn out to be the year that a multi-speed Europe starts to look more like a two-speed Europe, with an inner core impelled towards closer political and economic union by the need to rescue the single currency.

David Rennie, political editor, The Economist, 4 January 2011

Contents

Foreword

I recall it being said of a legendary former Director General of the Legal Service of the Commission of the European Union that it was as if the Commission had an extra Member. What, then, is one to say of the legendary former Director General of the Legal Service of the Council – the author of this study? That during his tenure it was as if the Council had an extra Member State? If power and influence were the measure, I would have no problem with such a statement as long as it was not a Malta or an Estonia that one had in mind, but one of the 'biggies': a France or a Germany or, perhaps, a United Kingdom. It is difficult to overstate the mark of Jean-Claude Piris on the fortunes of Europe. Cast your mind to any major development, challenge or crisis in recent Union history – whether the Charter of Fundamental Rights or the deliciously bureaucratically named Treaty on the Functioning of the European Union, and the large fingerprints of Jean-Claude Piris will be detected. Never at the forefront, but ever present. It is not only in Praxis that Piris has left his mark. Peruse the pages of the European literature and his writing stands out – it was quite laughable when he tried to hide behind a pseudonym: Justus Lipsius. The consummate political-legal fixer has not only a distinct style, direct with a touch of irony, but is refreshingly politically incorrect, compared with the typically smooth, Barbie-style spin-doctors of the European bureaucracy.

That Europe is in crisis – the travails of the euro actually mask how deep and structural the crisis runs – is a common place. Lisbon?, the Constitutional-Mountain-turned-into-Molehill-except-the-Mountain-was-a-Molehill-to-begin-with, is more the problem than a solution. If you wish to read one of the most incisive analyses of the current circumstance of Europe (grim), you will find it here. If you wish to read an equally incisive analysis of the various institutional options (grimmer), you will find that here too. But Piris is no Cassandra. You will also find one the most incisive analyses of the indispensability of the European construct for the future welfare of European citizens and their Member States. What, then, to do with the willing patient betrayed by the ageing organs? Where is the Viagra going to come from?

I would normally be inclined to say that the two-speed Europe solution is the refuge not only, like patriotism, of scoundrels (Bavarian Christian Social Union politicians trying to stop the Barbarians at the gate), but normatively and technically the scrapings from the bottom of the barrel. When you have nothing else to serve, *Europe à deux vitesses*, like ever-fresh, ever-stale crackers, is sure to be found in the pantry.

Normatively it seems preposterous. Europe has largely moved to majority voting. The minority is expected to follow the majority decision. That is democracy. But when the majority cannot get enough votes, or a minority cannot persuade enough adherents, you go it alone and, by way of koshering the pig, you call it *deux vitesses*. Technically, all previous attempts usually foundered because of their fracturing effect on the Single Market, still the signal achievement of Europe.

Piris is in a different category. At a minimum, he will make you rethink. He is not starry-eyed about the two-speed option, but shows some distinct political advantages, especially compelling, because situated in a vision of a united Europe. Two-speed, not two-tier: everyone is welcome to an upgrade when ready without the need for a gold or platinum card. The political case is accompanied by the legal machinery, sober and technical, which gives the project a purchase on gritty reality.

The two-speed Europe proposed here is not presented as a panacea, but as a vision rooted firmly in the ground, in which imagination and reality cohere in the best tradition of, might one say it, signal French contributions to Europe.

J. H. H. Weiler

Acknowledgements

This book was written during the academic year 2010–2011, while the author was a Senior Emile Noël Fellow at the Jean Monnet Center and a Fellow at the Straus Institute, New York University, for which he is very grateful to Professor Weiler.

The author thanks all his friends and colleagues, both in Europe and in the United States, lawyers, diplomats, scholars, civil servants, economists, political scientists, for countless and endless discussions, which have been helpful in the writing of this book.

The author thanks particularly Michael Bishop, who agreed to read the manuscript and improve the English language.

Last, but not least, the author thanks Patricia Hancq for her kind assistance and infinite patience.

Any mistakes are those of the author.

Introduction

The European Union (EU) is currently and simultaneously facing three huge challenges, which are making the present period the most serious crisis the EU has ever known.

First, there is an immediate and urgent problem, which already affects the stability of the EU and might even affect its survival if it is not solved rapidly: the acute crisis of the euro area. The imbalances in the EU's economic and monetary union (EMU), as it is conceived in the EU treaties, are serious. They will be difficult to correct as long as those Member States who have the euro as their currency remain the masters of their own budgetary and economic policies, as is allowed by the treaties. The process of giving huge loans to countries in need (Greece, Ireland and Portugal) might soon reach both its economic and political limits. Many economists think that no solution will be found without 'significantly increasing the degree of political union' according to Paul de Grauwe,[1] or what a Nobel prize-winner for economics (2001), Paul Krugman, calls 'a revised Europeanism'[2] and another Nobel prize-winner for economics (2008), Michael Spence, calls an inevitable 'greater centralization and political unification'.[3] Such a great leap forward would not only raise economic problems, but also political, institutional and legal ones.[4]

---

[1] Paul de Grauwe, 'The Governance of a Fragile Eurozone', Centre for European Policy Studies (CEPS), Brussels, 4 May 2011.
[2] 'Can Europe be saved?', *New York Times Magazine*, 16 January 2011.
[3] 'Five steps to fix the world', Newsweek, 31 January 2011.
[4] See also Martin Wolf, *Financial Times*, 1 June 2011: 'The eurozone, as designed, has failed . . . it has only two options: to go forwards towards a closer union or backwards towards at least partial dissolution. This is what is at stake.'

Second, this crisis is happening at a time when the trust in and enthusiasm of European public opinion for the EU is diminishing. This trust will hardly be regained with an EU programme that, based on the need to solve the euro area crisis, could be characterized as exclusively aimed at producing a reduction in social welfare, an increase in budgetary savings and stricter economic discipline. This will not only risk diminishing the trust of the public in the EU, but also open the way to populism, as elections in a number of EU countries have already shown. Therefore, one should think about a wider and more ambitious programme, able to give hope for the future.

Third, it is by no means obvious that the institutions of the EU, which are not working well, would be able to deliver such a programme with their present decision-making system. As a result of this dysfunctionality, the EU does not deliver enough internally and has become less relevant in the external world. This is all the more so as the EU now has twenty-seven Member States, each with different levels of economic development and extremely different needs. Yet its current decision-making process is based largely on the system of 'one-decision-fits-all', inherited from the time when the aim was to establish a uniform common market among the six rather homogeneous founding countries. The reforms made by the Treaty of Lisbon are not on the kind of scale that is necessary to solve these problems.

A priori, the three challenges referred to above cannot be met without substantively amending the current EU treaties, but this is opposed by many (if not all) Member States.[5] What if this leads to

---

[5] This opposition is led by the United Kingdom. When the 'EU Bill', put before Parliament by the UK Government on 11 November 2010, comes into force, it provides for the UK to hold a national referendum on nearly every proposed change of the EU treaties. This would include provisions of the treaties enabling the European Council or the Council to adopt changes to the treaties to switch decisions from unanimity to qualified majority vote in the Council (QMV). This is despite the fact that some of these so-called 'passerelles' provide for a six-month period during which any national parliament can oppose the proposal, and that some of these 'passerelles' already existed before the Lisbon Treaty. This is why, in the written personal evidence I gave to the House of Commons on 24 November 2010 (see House of Commons' website), I stressed that this 'could trigger a tendency among other Member States to circumvent this situation, either by engaging in enhanced cooperation among themselves without the participation of the UK, or by concluding intergovernmental agreements outside the framework of the EU'.

stagnation and a growing irrelevance of the EU? Would it be possible for the EU to continue on its present path, while developing further closer cooperation? The growing diversity of formulas adopted over the years by the EU in order to adapt itself to the heterogeneity of its members has helped, but without deeper reform, continuing on the current path will be difficult.

The purpose of this book is to examine all possible options for the future: first, a revision of the treaties; second, a continuation on the current path and, finally, to consider, particularly from a legal point of view, the possibility of a group of Member States, the composition of which would probably be based on that of the euro area, acting temporarily in closer cooperation in order to be able to progress, without changing the EU treaties. These states would develop common policies and actions before the other Member States, thus playing the role of an 'avant-garde'. The others would join them when willing and able to do so. The aim of the process would be to improve the working of the entire EU.

This concept has already been discussed in the past. However, the consequences of the euro area crisis and the need for the seventeen members of the euro area to advance towards more economic convergence make it necessary to revisit this issue, especially at a time when the Union is not working well and when its purpose has become unclear to many Europeans.

*

The Lisbon Treaty entered into force in December 2009 after eight years of gestation and a very difficult ratification process. After this painful period, one would have hoped that, thanks to its new treaty, the European Union would work more efficiently, and would be more visible and more active on the international scene.

However, since the treaty's entry into force, negative assessments have flooded in: 'The Death of the European Dream';[6] 'Europe is sleepwalking to decline';[7] 'Europe is a dead political project';[8] 'Is Europe heading for a meltdown';[9] 'Would Europe be condemned to

---

[6] Gideon Rachman, *Financial Times*, 18 May 2010.
[7] Timothy Garton Ash, *The Guardian*, 19 May 2010.   [8] Etienne Balibar, 26 May 2010.
[9] Edmund Conway, *Daily Telegraph*, 27 May 2010.

disappear?';[10] 'Can anything perk up Europe?';[11] 'Europe heads for irrelevance';[12] 'A loss in Europe's global influence';[13] 'Europe does not get how irrelevant it is becoming to the rest of the world';[14] 'The EU is agonizing';[15] 'The European Union as a Small Power';[16] 'Can Europe be saved?';[17] 'Five reasons why Europe is cracking'.[18]

Some recent events are equally disturbing, among them the European Union's fiasco at the end of the Climate Conference in Copenhagen in December 2009.[19] It was also a shock when, during the first six months of 2010, President Obama cancelled the planned summit between the United States and the EU. One may also mention 'the EU's debacle at the UN'.[20] This refers to the fact that on 14 September 2010 the EU lost its first battle to obtain an improved observer status at the General Assembly of the United Nations (UNGA). This was overcome, however, in a second battle eight months later.[21] One may add to that many announcements by various 'Cassandras' predicting that, due to the economic and financial crisis, the euro will collapse soon and that this will be followed by the disappearance of the EU itself!

[10] Alain Frachon, 'L'Europe serait-elle condamnée à disparaître?', *Le Monde*, 9 July 2010.
[11] Front page, *The Economist*, 10–16 July 2010.
[12] Philip Stephens, *Financial Times*, 10 September 2010.
[13] Wolfgang Munchau, *Financial Times*, 20 September 2010.
[14] Kishore Mahbubani, a former Singaporean diplomat, Dean of the Lee Kuan Yew School of Public Policy, University of Singapore, wrote in an article in *Time* magazine in March 2010: 'Europe just doesn't get it. It does not get how irrelevant it is becoming to the rest of the world' (quoted in *The Economist*, 9–15 October 2010, p. 63).
[15] Charles Kupchan, Professor of International Relations at Georgetown University, Washington, DC, former Director of European Affairs at the National Security Council (1993–4): 'L'UE est à l'agonie – pas une mort spectaculaire ni soudaine, non, mais une agonie si lente et si progressive qu'un jour prochain, les Américains, en portant nos regards de l'autre côté de l'Atlantique, découvriront peut-être que ce projet d'intégration européenne, qui allait de soi depuis un demi siècle, a cessé d'être', *Le Monde*, 14 October 2010.
[16] Title of a book by Asle Toje, *The European Union as a Small Power* (Basingstoke: Palgrave Macmillan, 2010).
[17] Paul Krugman, *New York Times Magazine*, 16 January 2011.
[18] José Ignacio Torreblanca, *El País*, 15 May 2011.
[19] The 15th Conference of Parties to the Framework Convention on Climate Change.
[20] Michael Emerson and Jan Wouters, 'The EU's Diplomatic Debacle at the UN. What else and what next?', Centre for European Studies, CEPS Commentary, Brussels, 1 October 2010.
[21] The EU finally obtained on 3 May 2011 the better status it was seeking from the United Nations General Assembly by a massive vote (180 in favour, 10 votes against and only 2 abstentions). This vote was quite important, as it did actually establish a new kind of observer in the UNGA.

Is it true that the EU is in such a desperate state? Despite the fact that reports of its agony are obviously exaggerated, some factors nevertheless incline one not to be excessively optimistic. To begin with, the Lisbon Treaty was supposed to give to the EU the means to speak with a more united and powerful voice in the world, and to act with more cohesion and more determination. This was expected due to some of the reforms brought by the treaty, such as a full-time President of the European Council, a High Representative of the Union for Foreign Affairs and Security Policy and the European External Action Service. At least on this point, and for the time being, one must recognize that it is a failure. Is this failure temporary, due to an inevitable period of adaptation, or is it going to be durable? Another issue is the adequacy of the EU's responses to the economic and financial crisis and the question of whether it would be able, together with its Member States, to stabilize the euro in an enduring way, as it was able to resist the first euro crisis which was surmounted in the spring of 2010. One may also draw attention to the fact that the 'Lisbon Strategy', which was supposed to make the EU one of the most advanced economies of the world within ten years (2000–2010), was not self-evidently successful.[22] Finally, the crisis has increased the natural tendency of Member State governments not to put efforts into strengthening the solidarity between them and to avoid the adoption of bold and courageous decisions which could make the EU stronger.

Against this background one may ask iconoclastic questions: will the EU still be necessary in the future? Will the EU still be useful for its Member States and their peoples? Should they fight to prevent it from slowly becoming irrelevant? An analysis of the situation of the Member States leads to a positive answer to these questions. Actually, at the beginning of the second decade of the twenty-first century the prospects for the future of most of the twenty-seven EU Member States, taken individually, do not look promising. Due to their small size, the alarming development of their demographic situation, their huge budget deficits and public debts, the scarcity of

---

[22] The Lisbon Strategy, adopted by the European Council in 2000, aimed at making the EU 'the most competitive and dynamic knowledge-based economy in the world, capable of sustainable economic growth with more and better jobs and greater social cohesion' by 2010. It was commented on as being a relative failure: see Charles Wyplosz, *Vox*, 12 January 2010 or Charlemagne, *The Economist*, 10 January 2010.

their energy resources, the often mediocre state of their economies, their insufficient investment in structural reforms necessary to prepare for the future, most of the EU's countries will find themselves in a difficult situation in the decades to come. They will need to cooperate or to act jointly through the EU to benefit from the better governance it brings in order to be able to continue to prosper and to defend their needs, interests and values in the world.

What if the EU was not able to help due to the limits set by the treaties to its powers and to its decision-making procedures?

In that case, and if it was impossible to revise the treaties substantively,[23] would the EU be condemned to slowly becoming irrelevant? Or would a temporary 'two-speed' help to open another way forward?

'Two-speed Europe' does not mean 'two-class Europe'

The hostility towards a 'two-speed Europe' is sometimes due to a lack of precision in the vocabulary and, therefore, to the confusion between a 'two-speed' and a 'two-class' (or 'two-tier') Europe. The two concepts must be distinguished.

'Two-speed' Europe means the development of closer cooperation among some Member States, pursuing objectives that are common to all EU Member States, as they are actually and precisely the objectives aimed at by the EU treaties. The idea is that the members of a smaller group would be both able and willing to go ahead

---

[23] At the time of writing three *ad hoc* revisions of the treaties have been 'promised', but they have not yet been formally decided and the procedure for their ratification has not been launched in the Member States. These revisions were promised during the ratification of the Lisbon Treaty: (a) in order to codify in a Protocol some 'guarantees' politically given to Ireland (see European Council Presidency Conclusions, 18/19 June 2009, doc.11225/1/09 REV 1); (b) in order to revert to the rule of one Commissioner per Member State, also promised at the same time to Ireland (same reference, as well as European Council Presidency Conclusions, 11/12 December 2008, doc.17271/1/08 REV 1); (c) in order to adopt a Protocol promised to the Czech Republic aimed at adding the name of the Czech Republic to those of Poland and the United Kingdom in the Protocol on the EU Charter of Fundamental Rights (European Council Presidency Conclusions, 29/30 October 2009). A fourth ad hoc revision has already been decided by the European Council on 25 March 2011 and the process of its ratification has been launched. It concerns, within the framework of the EMU, a modification of Article 136 TFEU, which is due to enter into force, after its ratification by the twenty-seven Member States, on 1 January 2013 (see the text of this amendment, p. 97).

immediately, while this would not be possible for all. The other Member States, each of them travelling at its own speed, would follow later. The differentiation between Member States would be temporary. In the past, transition periods and temporary derogations, frequently provided by accession treaties for new EU Member States, have been examples of such a concept. These periods have sometimes been quite long, but the derogations have been limited in time, at least in principle.[24] There are other examples, such as Article 27 of the Treaty on the Functioning of the EU (TFEU),[25] or the treaty articles on the consequences of the division of Germany.[26]

'Two-class' (or 'two-tier') Europe equally means closer cooperation within a group that would not include all EU Member States. However, that cooperation would aim at a permanent and irreversible separation between this group and the other EU Member States, which, because they would be perceived as structurally unable or politically and durably unwilling, would not be expected to follow later. In that case, the differentiation would therefore be conceived as a permanent one. That kind of concept will not be considered in this book.

---

[24] A number of exceptions to this principle do exist, such as for 'snuff' (Sweden), secondary houses (Denmark), the Åaland Islands (Finland), abortion (Ireland), defence (Denmark), the euro (Denmark and the United Kingdom), the Schengen acquis (Ireland and the United Kingdom), etc. Some of them will be explained later in more detail.

[25] According to that Article, which was previously Article 7c of the EECT, then 15 ECT: 'When drawing up its proposals . . . the Commission shall take into account the extent of the effort that certain economies showing differences in development will have to sustain for the establishment of the internal market and it may propose appropriate provisions. If these provisions take the form of derogations, they must be of a temporary nature and must cause the least possible disturbance to the functioning of the internal market.'

[26] Articles 98 and 107(2c) TFEU allow Germany to take measures compensating for the economic disadvantages caused by the division of Germany to the economy of certain areas affected by that division. These provisions, which have existed since the establishment of the European Economic Community in 1957, may be repealed five years after the entry into force of the Lisbon Treaty.

CHAPTER I

The continuing need for a strong European Union in the foreseeable future

MOST EU COUNTRIES FACE SIMILAR PROBLEMS, WHICH MAY NEGATIVELY INFLUENCE THEIR FUTURE

On the one hand, European countries have important advantages, which should allow them to continue to prosper

They have highly educated populations

On average, EU citizens enjoy a very good education system, which is obviously vital for economic development. Thus, a high proportion of children at the age of 4 in the EU (around 85 per cent) have the benefit of pre-primary educational institutions. Compulsory education lasts for nine or ten years in most EU countries, starting from the age of 5 or 6. Ratios used by statisticians show that the EU-27 average situation is better than in other developed countries (for example, Japan and the United States), be it pupil–teacher ratios or youth education attainment levels. More than three-quarters of all 18-year-olds within the EU-27 remained within the education system in 2007.

However, the situation is far from being perfect. The proportion of the population aged 25–64 in the EU-27 who had a tertiary education in 2008 was under 25 per cent. Some studies have established that 'an additional year of average school attainment raises productivity by 6.2 per cent and by a further 3.1 per cent in the long run through the contribution of faster technical progress'.[1] With rapidly

---

[1] Joint Report by the Economic Policy Committee and the Directorate-General for Economic and Financial Affairs of the European Commission, 8 October 2010, European Economy Occasional Papers No. 70.

ageing populations, raising the productivity of the labour force in European countries will increasingly become imperative in order to maintain standards of living. Therefore, the target aimed at by the EU with the 'European 2020 Strategy' is to increase the share of the population aged 30–34 who have completed tertiary education from 31 per cent to at least 40 per cent. In 2007, less than half the Member States, mostly among the EU-15, had already reached this target.[2] In comparison with the United States, the situation is not favourable: in 2007, the United States devoted 2.9 per cent of its GDP to education, compared with a mere 1.4 per cent for the EU as a whole; moreover, spending per student in the United States, including public and private contributions, is roughly double that of the EU.

These populations generally enjoy good living conditions and welfare

Favourable living conditions are vital for economic growth; they depend on a wide range of factors, which may be income-related or not. The factors that are not income-related include healthcare services, education and training opportunities and transport facilities – aspects that affect everyday lives and working conditions. The income-related indicators cover income, poverty and social exclusion. All factors and indicators show that the EU citizens enjoy a privileged situation in the world.

Social protection systems are highly developed in the EU: they protect people against the risks and needs associated with unemployment, parental responsibilities, sickness, healthcare, invalidity, the loss of a spouse or parents, old age, housing and social exclusion, etc. Social protection expenditure in the EU-27 averaged 26.9 per cent of GDP in 2006. It was more than 25 per cent in eleven of the EU-15, but less than 20 per cent in the Member States that had joined the EU since 2004, with the exception of Slovenia and Hungary, as well as being below this threshold in Ireland. Most expenditure on social benefits in the EU-27 is directed towards pensions, sickness and healthcare. Together these items accounted for close to 70 per cent

---

[2] European Policy Centre Issue Paper No. 61, October 2010: 'Skills and Education for Growth and Well-being in Europe 2020: Are We on the Right Path?'.

of the total EU-27 benefits in 2006. On top of the action of each Member State, the EU plays a coordinating role to ensure that people who move across borders continue to receive adequate protection.

EU citizens are well protected against illness and disease. The EU and its Member States have developed policies which include consumer protection (notably food safety), workplace safety, environmental and social policies, etc. This explains why the health status of the EU-27 citizens is very high and life expectancy at birth is one of the highest in the world. Other indicators also show that EU citizens enjoy more 'healthy life years' (also called 'disability-free life expectancy') than most people in the rest of the world. A number of indicators, such as expenditure on healthcare per inhabitant, the quality of healthcare services, the number of doctors per inhabitant, the number of hospital beds, the rate of serious accidents at work, etc., show that the EU Member States enjoy a privileged situation in the world.

Public infrastructure and services are excellent: in particular, the railway network for high-speed trains is one of the best in the world. The network of roads and motorways is also very dense and modern. In 2008, a majority (60 per cent) of households in the EU-27 had access to the Internet, and this figure was rapidly increasing (54 per cent in 2007). However, there are wide differences between the Member States, access being very high in the Netherlands, Finland and Sweden and quite low in some other countries, such as Bulgaria with 25 per cent.

EU Member States generally benefit from a good governance

As compared with the rest of the world, including, of course, comparable developed countries, governance, defined as the rules, processes and behaviour that affect the way in which public authority is exercised at the level of each EU Member State, particularly as regards openness, participation, accountability, effectiveness and coherence, looks to be at a top level and durable.

Voter turnout in national parliamentary elections is reasonably high. However, at the level of the Union, the turnout in elections for the European Parliament has tended to decline steadily and was only 43.3 per cent in the June 2009 elections.

The level of criminality is lower in EU countries than in comparable societies in the world, including (by far) the United States. During the period 2002 to 2007, general recorded crime in the EU was in decline.

In general, EU Member States, especially the EU-15, benefit from excellent administrative and judicial systems and strong economic and social cohesion in their populations. However, the fight against corruption and ensuring an efficient and independent judiciary system is not yet successful in some of the Member States.

Finally, one of the strengths of the EU countries is that they have decided to share their sovereignty in some areas in order to guarantee peace, stability and democracy within (and around) their borders, and to combine their efforts and be stronger in order to confront the economic, social and political challenges of the future: these are the aims of the European Union. Together the EU-27 are the largest exporters and the second-largest importers of services and goods in the world.[3] They are also the biggest donor of aid to developing countries.[4] If it were to be considered as a single entity, the EU would be a great economic power in the world.

On the other hand, most EU countries and peoples share a number of characteristics that make them different from the rest of the world and will make it more difficult for them to confront future challenges and competition

The small land area and size of population of EU countries, as well as the size of their economies, make it difficult for them to express their opinions forcefully and to defend their interests and values in the world, where their visibility and negotiating power are weak

Land surface
With its twenty-seven Member States, the EU covers only 2.8 per cent of the land surface of the world. As compared with the 17 million km²

---

[3] In 2007, 17.4 per cent of exports of goods and services in the world (versus 11.9 per cent for the United States) and 19 per cent of the imports (versus 19.6 per cent for the United States) (source: *Eurostat Yearbook*, 2010).

[4] More than 50 per cent of the aid in the world comes from the EU and its Member States, compared with 20 per cent from the United States (source: *Eurostat*, September 2009).

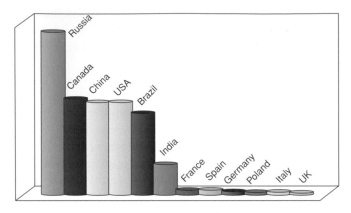

Figure 1.1 Land surface

of Russia, 10 million km² of Canada, 9.6 million km² each of China and the United States, 8.5 million km² of Brazil or 3.2 million km² of India, the EU countries are indeed in a quite different category! The largest of them are France (forty-third in the world) covering 0.55 million km², Spain 0.50 million km², Germany 0.35 million km², Poland 0.31 km², Italy 0.30 million km² and the United Kingdom 0.24 million km².

Population
The EU-27 comprises only 7 per cent of the world's population. Again, when compared with the 1,330 million inhabitants of China, the 1,148 million of India, the 304 million of the United States or the 196 million of Brazil, the EU countries are in a quite different category. The most populated of them are Germany (fifteenth in the world) with 82 million inhabitants, France with 64.35 million, the United Kingdom with 61.57 million, Italy with 60.05 million, Spain with 45.83 million and Poland with 38.14 million.

Gross domestic product
Despite only having 7 per cent of the world's population, the EU-27 generates almost 22 per cent of the world's wealth. Therefore, the comparison for gross domestic product (GDP) is less difficult, taking into account the fact that individual EU Member States are (still)

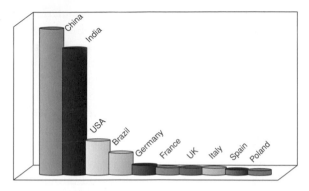

Figure 1.2 Population in 2010

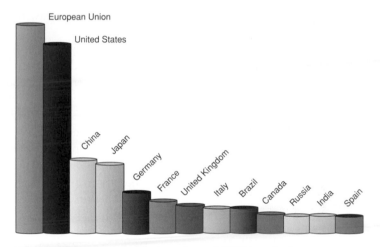

Figure 1.3 Countries by estimated GDP (nominal), 2010

among the richest in the world and that some of them rank on the same scale as the United States, China and Japan.

Negative demographic trends are a huge handicap for the future of EU Member States

While the number of the inhabitants of the EU-27 grew from 402 million in 1960 to 501 million in 2010, according to current trends the population of most EU countries will stagnate until 2035 and then decline. Moreover, the average age of the population will rapidly become higher. This rapid development will shrink the workforce and make it difficult to promote prosperity and sustain current generous social benefits. It will also make inevitable an increase in immigration, which is already one of the most acute socio-political problems in Europe.[5] The EU's population is now increasing only because of the number of immigrants and their high birth-rate. Moreover, the number of deaths will be higher than the number of births in the EU as early as 2015.[6] The EU-27 has one of the lowest fertility rates in the world (average 1.5 children per woman). At the same time, it enjoys the highest life expectancy in the world (around 75 years for men and 81 years for women). The negative balance resulting from that will increase more rapidly after 2020. Thus, the population of the most populated EU Member State, Germany, will decrease from 82 million in 2010 to 70.8 million in 2060.[7]

In Europe generally, the old-age dependency ratio (concerning people over 65 years of age) is expected to more than double within forty-five years, from 22 per cent in 2005 to 45 per cent in 2050. In particular, the dependency ratio concerning people aged over 80 will more than treble during the same period, reaching 15 per cent. Added to the youth-age dependency ratio (children under 15 years), the over-all demographic burden of the population outside the productive age (from 15 to 64 years) is going to increase by a factor of 1.5.

One of the consequences will be the difficulty of preserving the social security system, in particular pension schemes. It will obviously lead to an increase in the retirement age, but this will not be sufficient.[8]

---

[5] There were 20 million non-EU citizens in the EU-27 in 2007. The Commission gives an estimate of about 8 million additional immigrants living illegally in the EU. The difficulties in integrating Muslim immigrants is one of the major political problems in a number of EU countries, and has a strong influence on national elections (see, e.g., the Netherlands in June 2010, Sweden in September 2010, etc.).

[6] In 1960, the twenty-seven EU countries counted 8 million births for 4 million deaths; in 2009, these figures were, respectively, 5.4 and 4.8 million.

[7] 'Ageing Characterises the Demographic Perspectives of the European Societies', *Eurostat Report*. See also 'Europe in Figures', *Eurostat Yearbook*, 2010.

[8] See the 2005 United Nations population study, as well as Rainer Muenz, 'Aging and Demographic Change in European Societies: Main Streams and Alternative Policy Options', The World Bank, Discussion Paper No. 0703, March 2007. See also 'Tendances récentes de migrations internationales', OECD Report, 2010.

Currently (2011–2012), all EU Member States have budget deficits, and most have very large public debts accumulated over the years

The criteria[9] that were adopted when the rules of the euro area were established (i.e., less than 3 per cent of GDP for budget deficits, a maximum of 60 per cent of GDP for public debts) are no longer respected. Forced by the markets (where the interest rates for ten-year government bonds vary daily according to the trust enjoyed by individual countries on the market, from around 3 per cent for Germany to 20 per cent or more for Greece in 2010–2011), governments are applying massive cuts in their expenditure, while at the same time trying to increase their revenues. This is not always understood or accepted by the public, which sometimes perceives it, not as a social and economic necessity to preserve the well-being of future generations, but as a push from 'Brussels', the EU being seen as imposing straitjacket rules that are not equitable and unnecessary.

The majority of the EU Member States lack energy resources. Hence, their economies are dependent on massive imports of energy from third countries

The total gross energy consumption of the EU-27 in 2008 was the equivalent of 1,825 million tonnes of oil, 54 per cent of which was imported, mostly from Russia (33 per cent of the oil imported and 40 per cent of the gas) and from Norway (16 per cent and 23 per cent, respectively). The dependency is relatively low for some EU countries, such as Poland[10] (20 per cent) and the UK (21 per cent), but is very high for some others, such as Italy and Spain (around 80 per cent), Germany (60 per cent) and France (51 per cent).

According to some studies, if no action is taken the average EU energy dependency will increase to 65 per cent in 2030.[11] EU imports of gas are expected to increase from 57 per cent to 84 per cent by 2030, while imports of oil will climb from 82 per cent to 93 per cent.

Obviously, this carries both economic and political risks.[12]

---

[9] See Protocol No. 12 on the excessive deficit procedure attached to the EU treaties.
[10] With the difficulties entailed by the (still) significant use of coal in Poland.
[11] See 'Europe's Energy Portal', available at: www.energy.eu.
[12] See 'Communication from the Commission to the European Council and the European Parliament – An Energy Policy for Europe', January 2007, doc.COM 2007 1 final.

EU Member States make insufficient investment in
research and development

Research and development (R&D) is a driving force pushing growth
and job creation. As there are insufficient investments in R&D in
the EU, one direct consequence is a shrinking share of the world's
scientific and technical innovations. In a communication published
in 2000,[13] the Commission suggested aiming towards a 'European
Research Area', in which the funding of research activities would be
granted irrespective of national borders but according to the needs of
economic growth and employment. This 'European Research Area'
was made a central element of the Lisbon Strategy[14] for the years
2000–10, with the aim of investing 3 per cent of the EU's GDP
in R&D. However, between 2000 and 2005, instead of increasing,
the EU's overall R&D expenditure decreased slightly. During the
same period, R&D spending increased in Japan, South Korea and
China. While the share of GDP devoted to R&D was 1.77 per cent
for the EU-25 in 2005, it was 3.40 per cent for Japan (2006), 2.99
per cent for South Korea and 2.67 per cent for the United States
(2007).[15] Gross domestic expenditure on R&D in the EU-27 in 2007
was €228,681 million, the equivalent of 85 per cent of the US figure.
Despite the fact that the number of researchers in the EU-27 increased
by 22.5 per cent between 2000 and 2007, the number of full-time
equivalent (FTE) researchers in the business enterprise sector was
only 662,000 in the EU-27, compared with 1,135,000 in the United
States.

   In October 2010, the Commission warned that the EU was facing
an 'innovation emergency', and that competition with the rest of the
world made it increasingly urgent to stimulate the private sector's
R&D expenditure. The calculation of the Commission is that if the
3 per cent target is reached in 2020, an estimated 3.7 million jobs
would be created. Some measures were taken at the level of the EU
in order to try and reach this aim, but the figure was still only around
1.8 per cent in 2010.

---

[13] 'Towards a European Research Area', European Commission, 2000.
[14] The 'Lisbon Strategy for Growth and Competitiveness' was agreed by the European Council
   in Lisbon on 23–24 March 2000.
[15] OECD, Main Science and Technology Indicators (2006).

A *weak entrepreneurial spirit*

The fact that the EU Member States have a very well protected population in terms of social welfare and that this population is ageing rapidly are two of the reasons explaining why the entrepreneurial spirit is weaker in the EU than in American or Asiatic countries. Other elements are the higher level of regulation of economic activities, the low degree of flexibility in the labour market, as well as the low mobility of workers. Historical factors might also play a role. In any case, the result is that the rate of creation of new enterprises and of creativity is lower in the EU than in all its major economic competitors in the world.

A *lack of competitiveness*

In a world where borders are more and more open to the flow of goods and services, EU countries are in a difficult situation due to the fact that they have secured a high protection of the environment and of consumers, and they have adopted generous social rules and benefits. This tends to make them less competitive than less regulated and protected societies.

As a result, the average economic growth of European countries is slow,[16] and Europe's share of the world's wealth is decreasing. For the first time in history, there is a fear that, for the European peoples, the future will not be as good as the present. In order to cope with their problems, European countries will need to cooperate on some issues and even have common international policies on others, such as:

- promoting better protection of the environment and the fight against climate change;
- acting to improve the regulation of competition and having an active role in world trade negotiations;
- fighting against international crime, human trafficking and the illegal drugs trade;
- acting to prevent war in the world;
- combating poverty and promoting democracy, human rights and equality between women and men;

---

[16] The forecasts for economic growth by the IMF for 2010 are 1 per cent for the EU, 2.7 per cent for the United States and 10 per cent for China.

- protecting minorities in Europe, thus avoiding tensions that could, as often in the past, give rise to violence and armed conflicts;
- coordinating better, in order to act effectively in case of international economic and financial crises; and
- acting in favour of the poorest regions of Europe through solidarity from the richest.

THE EU SHOULD HELP ITS MEMBER STATES TO FACE THEIR PROBLEMS MORE EFFECTIVELY IN THE FUTURE

From the beginning the EU (European Economic Community (EEC) and later the European Community (EC)) was established not only to try and end the scourge of war between European peoples, but also to help its Member States and their citizens to have better governance and to prosper economically.

The EU was established in order to help its Member States and, in principle, it has many advantages in order to be able to do that

- By finalizing the internal market (the four freedoms, i.e., movement of goods, services, capital and people): this is the first aim of the EU, that is, the EU market of 500 million consumers should be as open and transparent as a national one.
- By uniting to defend common interests in the world (trade, energy, immigration).
- By improving governance in its twenty-seven Member States through peer pressure, and by regulating economic and monetary union (the euro area), in particular for the seventeen Member States that have the euro as their currency.
- By together fighting terrorism, criminality (especially since the development, after the 1993 Maastricht Treaty, of what was called the 'third pillar', known as 'justice and home affairs', and now as 'freedom, security and justice') and international instability (through the development of the 'second pillar', that is, the Common Foreign and Security Policy (CFSP), after the same Treaty).
- Through sharing costs to establish common policies and to realize concrete projects (research and development, industry, defence,

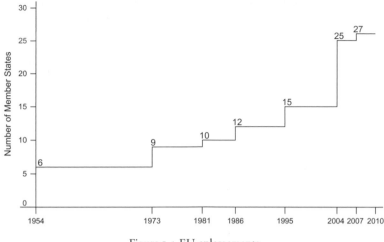

Figure 1.4 EU enlargements

etc.), allowing for more efficiency: this has not been an achievement of the EU as such, but of several intergovernmental or private undertakings (e.g., in the air and space industry).

- By having a more united and therefore stronger voice in the world.

However, several factors have contributed to the EU and its institutions becoming less effective and commanding less support among European peoples, such as:

- the imbalances contained in the Treaty;
- the growing dysfunctionalities of the institutions; and
- the fact that the identity and cohesiveness of the EU have become less obvious with the rapid and huge mutation of its 2004 and 2007 enlargements. As shown by Figure 1.4, the EU has nearly doubled in size from fifteen countries in 2004 to twenty-seven in 2007.

CHAPTER 2

An assessment of the present situation of the European Union

An assessment of the present situation shows that the European Union does not function well and that it is unable to solve its current fundamental problems.

Its political institutions suffer from weaknesses and deficiencies: this is the case for the Council, the Commission, the European Parliament (EP), as well as for the High Representative of the Union for Foreign Affairs and Security Policy (HR) and the European External Action Service (EEAS).

Its substantive policies are not successful enough, be it the internal market, monetary union in the euro area, defence or the matters covered by what used to be called 'the third pillar'.

Finally, the reforms of the Lisbon Treaty, although helpful, are not on the scale of what would be needed in order for the EU to be able to tackle its problems.

THE POLITICAL INSTITUTIONS SUFFER FROM DEFICIENCIES WHICH HAMPER THE FUNCTIONING OF THE EU

Neither the Council, the Commission, the European Parliament nor the HR and the EEAS are working today in an optimal way; far from it.

The difficult decision-making in the Council

As to the decision-making in the Council,[1] it is true that, and contrary to what most people think, the common agreement of the Member

---

[1] A system which has been described by Andrew Moravcsik as a 'cumbersome decision-making process constrained by super-majoritarian and unanimous decision-making' ('Federalism in the EU: Rhetoric and Reality', in Kalypso Nicolaïdis and Robert Howse (eds.), *The Federal*

States or unanimity in the Council is required for many important decisions, as shown by the list below.[2] However, after the successive enlargements of the scope of qualified majority vote (QMV) in the Single European Act and in the Maastricht, Amsterdam, Nice and Lisbon treaties, the decisions contained in this list concern issues that are very sensitive for the Member States, which, therefore, would be reluctant to accept their inclusion in the scope of QMV.

On institutional matters

- Accession of a new Member State (Treaty on European Union (TEU), Article 49).
- Determining the seats (Treaty on the Functioning of the EU (TFEU), Article 341) and the rules governing the languages (TFEU, Article 342) of the EU institutions.
- Composition of the European Parliament (TEU, Article 14(2), subparagraph 2), of the Economic and Social Committee (TFEU, Article 301) and of the Committee of the Regions (TFEU, Article 305).
- Appointment of judges and advocates general of the Court of Justice, of the General Court (TEU, Article 19(2), subparagraph 3) and of the specialized courts (TFEU, Article 257, subparagraph 4).
- Conferral of jurisdiction on the Court of Justice in disputes relating to the application of EU acts creating European intellectual property rights (TFEU, Article 262).
- System of own resources (TFEU, Article 311, subparagraph 3) and adoption of the multi-annual financial framework (TFEU, Article 312(2)).
- Flexibility clause (TFEU, Article 352, formerly TEC, Article 308).[3]

Vision: Legitimacy and Level of Governance in the USA and the EU (Oxford University Press, 2001), pp. 161–87, at p. 176.

[2] See Jean-Claude Piris, *The Lisbon Treaty* (Cambridge University Press, 2010), Appendix 3, pp. 386–97.

[3] The use of Article 352 will also require the adoption of a law in Germany, as had been requested by the German Constitutional Court in its judgment on the Lisbon Treaty of 30 June 2009 (2 be 2/08, 2 BvE5/08, 2 BvR 1010/08, 2 BvR1022/08, 2 BvR 1259/08, 2 BvR 182/09, Bundes Verfassungsgericht). On this judgment, see Franz C. Mayer, 'Rashomon in Karlsruhe – A Reflection on Democracy and Identity in the European Union', Jean Monnet Working Paper 05/10. See also Piris, *The Lisbon Treaty*, pp. 141–5 and 341–58.

- Association of the overseas countries and territories with the EU (TFEU, Article 203).
- Accession of the EU to the European Convention for the Protection of Human Rights and Fundamental Freedoms (TEU, Article 692 and TFEU, Article 218(8), subparagraph 2).

Of all these matters, only two issues would really deserve to be changed. The first is the appointment of the members of the courts, but this does not appear essential in the 'post-Lisbon' situation, with the TFEU, Article 255 Committee, which *de facto* has a powerful say in the choice of judges. The second is the adoption of the multi-annual budget, but TFEU, Article 312(2), subparagraph 2 allows the European Council, acting unanimously, to authorize the Council to decide by QMV.

On substantive matters

- Determination of the existence of a serious and persistent breach by a Member State of the EU's values (TEU, Article 7).
- Any decision in the field of foreign policy and defence (TEU, Articles 31 and 42(2)), including to proceed with enhanced cooperation (TFEU, Article 329(2), subparagraph 2).
- Conclusion of some international agreements concluded only on behalf of the EU (TFEU, Article 218(8), subparagraph 2), and of international agreements concluded on behalf of the EU, but containing some elements belonging to the Member States' competences and which therefore have to be concluded on their behalf also, even if most commitments to be undertaken in the international agreement belong to the competences of the EU ('mixed agreements').
- Some matters concerning commercial policy (TFEU, Article 207(4), subparagraph 2).
- Any decision concerning direct or indirect taxes (TFEU, Articles 113, 192(2)(a) and 194(3)).
- Measures concerning social security, with a few exceptions (TFEU, Articles 153(2), subparagraph 3 and 21(3)). In any case, provisions adopted in that area 'shall not affect the right of Member States to define the fundamental principles of their social security system and must not significantly affect the financial equilibrium thereof'.

- Addition of new rights for EU citizens (TFEU, Article 25).
- Actions to combat discrimination based on sex, racial or ethnic origin, religion or belief, disability, age or sexual orientation (TFEU, Article 19(1)).
- Most sensitive measures in the field of protection of the environment, in particular measures 'affecting' town and country planning, quantitative management of water resources or 'affecting, directly or indirectly', the availability of those resources, land use, with the exception of waste management, as well as measures 'significantly affecting' a Member State's choice between different energy sources and the general structure of its energy supply (see TFEU, Article 192(2)(b)).
- Most important measures in the field of energy, measures 'significantly affecting' a Member State's choice between different energy sources and the general structure of its energy supply or measures primarily of a fiscal nature (TFEU, Articles 192(2)(c) and 194(2)).
- Acts concerning family law (TFEU, Article 81(3)).
- Acts concerning some aspects of cooperation in criminal law and criminal procedure (TFEU, Articles 82(2), (3), 83(3), 86).
- Provisions concerning passports, identity cards, residence permits or any other such document (TFEU, Article 77(3)).
- Establishment of a European public prosecutor (TFEU, Article 86).
- Operational police cooperation (TFEU, Article 87(3), subparagraph 1).
- Measures setting out the conditions and limitations under which the competent judicial and police authorities of a Member State may operate in the territory of another Member State in liaison and in agreement with that Member State (TFEU, Article 89).

Some issues on this list certainly deserve discussion, for example, the provision on tax matters which has a very large scope, but all have the potential to raise sensitive problems.

In any case, the major problems in the Council's decision-making are not due to an excessive scope of application of the unanimity rule

First, where applicable, QMV requires a high threshold:
- until 31 October 2014 (and probably until 31 March 2017, as foreseen in Article 3(2) of Protocol No. 36 on Transitional Provisions),

the QMV required will remain the same as in the treaties before the Lisbon Treaty entered into force, that is, essentially based on weighted votes attributed to each Member State, as has always been the case before; however, since the Treaty of Nice, it is also required that the majority represents at least 62 per cent of the EU population;

- after 31 October 2014 or 31 March 2017, QMV will be based on a 'double majority' with two thresholds: at least 55 per cent of the number of the Member States and at least 65 per cent of the total population of the EU.

Such strict requirements are much more demanding than requirements for the adoption of legislation in any EU Member State.[4]

Second, the political culture in the Council is such that Member States always try to take into account the specific problems caused to one or some of them by any given proposed legislation. Consequently, they often try to avoid going to a vote and putting some of them in a minority.[5]

Third, under the Treaty provisions, the right of veto actually has two effects: not only does it allow the Member State exercising it not to adopt legislation or a decision that would cause problems for its economy, culture or values but, at the same time, it also forbids other Member States from going ahead and adopting the act in question, even if that would not harm the interests of the Member State exercising the veto.

Fourth, the simple fact that the number of participants is higher makes the decision-making longer, more cumbersome and more difficult. Actually, each Member State's representative tries to modify the legislative act proposed in such a way that his authorities will not

---

[4] See Moravcsik, already quoted, 'Federalism in the EU: Rhetoric and Reality', pp. 173–4: 'Political decisions in the EU are taken under rules that require unanimity or super-majoritarian support in order to reach a decision. This level of consensus, namely, support of representatives of between 70 per cent and 100 per cent of the weighted votes of territorial representations, depending on the particular issue, is far higher than in any existing national polity . . . Everyday EU legislation must secure approximately 70 per cent of the weighted votes of national ministers sitting in the Council of Ministers. This is a comparatively high standard, which severely limits potential legislative activity.'

[5] This has been symbolically reflected over the years by different political mechanisms, such as the 1966 so-called 'Luxembourg compromise', or the 1994 'Ioannina decision' and the 2009 'Ioannina-bis mechanism' (see Piris, *The Lisbon Treaty*, pp. 223–4).

have to revise their existing national legal provisions, or will have to revise them as little as possible.

Fifth, each of the twenty-seven Member States has different needs. As a consequence, it is difficult to adopt a decision on any matter, be it economic, social, environmental, judicial cooperation, etc. which could be apt to suit all the interests and needs of so many and such different countries. To begin with, the Council, as legislature, does not receive enough proposals or in any case substantive enough proposals, from the Commission. This is due to the fact that the Commission itself cannot agree on substantive proposals, at least in some matters, such as the area of freedom, security and justice, or on tax, social or environmental matters. Then, even if and when the Commission manages to reach a consensus on making a meaningful proposal (see below the difficulties for a Commission composed of one member per Member State to decide through a simple majority vote), the Council has difficulties in reaching the QMV or unanimity necessary to adopt the proposed act, because of the diverging views of its twenty-seven members.

The progressive weakening of the Commission

Most observers would agree that the Commission has gradually become weaker since the 1990s. This weakness is due to a number of factors, among which the major ones are probably its composition, as well as pressure from both the European Parliament and from the biggest Member States.

The political decision to go back to the composition of one Commissioner per Member State, if formally adopted, as has been politically promised to Ireland, would reinforce the two consequences such a composition has had already.

First, with enlargement, such a composition results in too high a number of Commissioners. Therefore, the Commission cannot work efficiently as a 'college', as it should do according to the Treaty, but forces its President to take the lead on all major subjects. Second, the principle of independence of Commissioners vis-à-vis their country of origin has become theoretical, which has serious consequences for the legitimacy of the decision-taking in the Commission, because all decisions may – in principle – be taken by a simple majority with one vote per Commissioner; consequently, if this rule were actually implemented, no decision could ever be made which would not suit the smaller Member States (i.e., on some institutional matters).

This is why the most important measure the Lisbon Treaty contains to increase the effectiveness of the Commission is the reduction of the number of Commissioners from one per Member State to two-thirds of the number of Member States, with a system of equal rotation. The treaty provides that this measure is to be applied from 1 November 2014 (TEU, Article 17(5)). In the meantime (i.e., until 31 October 2014), Article 17(4) of the TEU provides that the Commission should be composed of one national per Member State. However, after the failure of the first Irish referendum on the ratification of the Lisbon Treaty in June 2008, the European Council decided in December 2008 to abandon the planned reduction in the number of Commissioners in order to try to facilitate the success of a second referendum in Ireland. The political decision of the European Council will have to be legally implemented through a 'decision . . . in accordance with the necessary legal procedures'.[6]

A Commission with one Commissioner per Member State runs the risk of falling into 'intergovernmentalism', as Member States tend to identify 'their' Commissioner as 'their representative' in the Commission, who will defend their national interests. This runs contrary to the spirit and the letter of the treaties, which require that the Commission's members are to be independent from governments.[7] An 'intergovermentalist' trend would jeopardize the legitimacy of the Commission's decisions, since these decisions may be taken by a simple majority of fourteen Commissioners. In a borderline case, a majority of fourteen Commissioners could 'represent' only 12.65 per cent of the EU's population (adding together the population of the fourteen smallest Member States). Such a majority could easily outvote the six Commissioners who are nationals of the six largest Member States having more than 70 per cent of the EU's total population. This, of course, is completely theoretical. However, the argument might be used in order to weaken the legitimacy of the Commission's

---

[6] See paragraph 2 of the Presidency Conclusions (doc. 17271/1/08 REV 1), repeated in the Presidency Conclusions of the June 2009 European Council. The issue as to what are 'the necessary legal procedures' to be followed is disputed: see fn. 11, below.

[7] TEU, Article 17(3), subparagraphs 2 and 3.

decisions when it deals with politically sensitive dossiers (notably in the field of competition, merger control or state aid). Moreover, as demonstrated by Philippe de Schoutheete, a Commission composed in such a way makes it very difficult to vote, as a non-weighted vote would lack legitimacy. Therefore, decisions are always taken by consensus, which means that, with twenty-seven members, the Commission finds it difficult to take decisions.[8]

The truth is that the argument of legitimacy may also be used, and is actually used, in the other direction: as public opinion in the Member States tends to regard the EU as a classic international organization, they might feel 'unprotected' without one of the members of the Commission being of their nationality.

It should be recalled that, due to its difficult ratification in some Member States, the Lisbon Treaty did not enter into force on or before 1 November 2009 (i.e., before the end of the term of office of the 'Barroso I' Commission). Consequently, the Nice Treaty was to apply to the Commission that should have been appointed as from 1 November 2009. The Nice Treaty[9] had amended Article 213(1) of the TEC by providing that 'the number of Members of the Commission shall be less than the number of Member States'. The Treaty provided that 'as from the date on which the first Commission following the date of accession of the twenty-seventh Member State of the Union takes up its duties', that is, on 1 November 2009, the rule on the reduced Commission would apply. This entered into force on 1 January 2007 (i.e., from when the EU consisted of twenty-seven Member States) and the treaty did not provide any possibility of derogating from that rule. Therefore, the Council should have adopted, acting unanimously, a decision setting out the number of Commissioners and other 'implementation arrangements'[10] before 1 November 2009, that is, before the beginning of the mandate of the 'Barroso II' Commission. One may have thought that the solution found in Article 17(5) of the TEU (i.e., two-thirds of the number

---

[8] Philippe de Schoutheete, 'La crise et la gouvernance européenne', *Revue Politique Etrangère*, 1 (2009), 33–46.

[9] Article 4(2) of the Protocol on the enlargement of the EU, attached to the treaties by the Nice Treaty.

[10] The Commissioners were to be chosen 'according to a rotation system based on the principle of equality': see Article 4(3) of the Protocol on the enlargement.

of Member States) might have helped in that respect, but it would actually have been politically difficult to adopt it. In any case, this issue did not arise as the Council decided to wait for the entry into force of the Lisbon Treaty, which was going to happen within a reasonably short time.

For the future, before the end of the term of office of the 'Barroso II' Commission (i.e., before 31 October 2014), a legal decision will have to be adopted in order to provide that, in accordance with what was decided in December 2008 and confirmed in June 2009 by the European Council, the Commission will continue to be composed of one member per Member State.[11]

At this stage, it is interesting to recall the debate on the size and composition of the Commission that took place in the 2002/2003 Convention and in the 2003/2004 intergovernmental conference (IGC).

As mentioned above, the less populated Member States insisted on the need to be 'represented' by one of their nationals in the Commission in order for the Commission to be more legitimate. Not without reason, they argued that even if one of the larger Member States did

---

[11] See Presidency Conclusions, European Council, 11–12 December 2008 (paragraph 2, doc. 17271/1/08 REV 1) and Presidency Conclusions, European Council, 18–19 June 2009 (paragraph 2, doc. 11225/1/09 REV 1). The legal procedure to be followed is disputed. Some argue that a decision of the European Council would be sufficient, because of the phrase at the end of TEU, Art. 17(5), subparagraph 1, which reads: 'the Commission shall consist of a number of members . . . corresponding to two-thirds of the number of Member States, unless the European Council, acting unanimously, decides to alter this number'. However, according to others, including the author of this book, this legal interpretation is not correct, as this phrase should be read in its context. First, it should be read together with paragraph 4 (limiting until 31 October 2014, without exception, the composition of one Commissioner per Member State). Second, it should be read particularly together with the next subparagraph of paragraph 5, which sets out the conditions governing the principle of a reduced Commission (establishment of a strictly equal rotation system, reflecting the demographic and geographical range of all the Member States, which are developed in more detail in Art. 244 of the TFEU). Otherwise, Art. 244 of the TFEU would be deprived of any legal effect. Read in accordance with these texts, the phrase of paragraph 5, subparagraph 1 of Art. 17 of the TEU, therefore does not allow the European Council to depart from the very principle of a smaller Commission. The purpose and meaning of this sentence is to enable the European Council to further reduce the number of Commissioners when the EU is enlarged to include more Member States, so as to be able to keep a reasonable number of Commissioners. In other words, any decision of the European Council will have to respect both the treaty principle of the reduction in the number of the members of the Commission and the principle of a strictly equal rotation system. Declaration No. 10 confirms this interpretation: 'when the Commission no longer includes nationals of all Member States, the Commission should . . .' The debate on the number of Commissioners might come back on the occasion of future EU enlargements.

not have one of its nationals as a member of the Commission its interests could not be ignored, but that the same would not be necessarily true for the smaller Member States.[12] The larger Member States, for their part, insisted that the size of the Commission should be reduced, arguing that a Commission with twenty-seven members would not function effectively, that its members are not meant to represent the interests of the Member States and that a Commission reduced in size would be more efficient and more collegial.

This is why, trying to square the circle, the Convention suggested an innovative formula. According to that formula, one national from each Member State would have been a 'member of the Commission'. However, only some of these 'members' (then to be called 'the European Commissioners') would have had the right to vote in the Commission. The other 'members' (then to be called 'the Commissioners') would have participated in Commission meetings, but without the right to vote.[13]

This formula was rejected by the Member States during the 2003/2004 IGC.

After long discussions, a compromise was finally found, based on three elements:
- equality between states: the rotation between the Commissioners would apply on a strictly equal footing, regardless of the size of the population of the Member States. Each Member State would have one of its nationals appointed as a Commissioner for two out of three mandates of the Commission. The precise arrangements for this system of equal rotation would be established by a unanimous decision of the European Council. Each successive Commission would be composed so as to reflect satisfactorily the demographic and geographical range of all the Member States;
- progressivity: the new system would start to apply only with the Commission which would be appointed on 1 November 2014;
- package deal with the composition of the European Parliament: the less populated Member States obtained a guarantee that each state, whatever its population, would have a minimum of six seats in the European Parliament.

---

[12] Declaration No. 10 of the Lisbon Intergovernmental Conference (IGC) is meant to address these concerns.
[13] See Article 25(3) of the draft text as submitted by the Convention to the President of the European Council on 18 July 2003.

However, this compromise was set aside by the European Council in December 2008, which accepted the desire expressed by the Irish authorities in order to present the Lisbon Treaty for a second referendum of ratification with a better chance of success. Therefore, before the end of the term of office of the 'Barroso II' Commission (i.e., before 31 October 2014), a legal decision will have to be adopted in accordance with the treaty, in order to be applicable before the appointment of the next Commission.

Finally, since the resignation 'en masse' of the Santer Commission,[14] the Commission has been weakened by the European Parliament (EP). It is true that the treaty gives the EP the right to vote a motion of censure on the activities of the Commission (TFEU, Article 234). It is also a fact that, through the years, using this right as a means of pressure the EP has *de facto* acquired more powers than those legally conferred on it by the treaties. One illustration of this excessive domination of the Commission by the EP may be found in the so-called 'Framework Agreements', the adoption of which is imposed on the Commission by the EP at the beginning of each legislature. The last one in particular, concluded in October 2010, shows clearly how much the autonomy of the Commission and of its President are affected by the EP.[15] The principle of the treaty according to which the Commission is a college, that all decisions are taken by the college and that only the college as such is responsible to the Parliament has become theoretical. Every member of the Commission knows that his or her individual destiny is in the hands of the EP. Therefore, their independence is not protected and the 'inter-institutional balance' is no longer what is legally prescribed by the provisions of the treaties. The EP is constantly trying to influence the day-to-day work of the Commission in adopting implementing acts or in negotiating international treaties.

Moreover, Member States, especially the larger ones, put strong pressure on the Commission when their national interests are at stake. This is facilitated by the development of the Commission towards

---

[14] The resignation of all members of the Commission presided by Jacques Santer in 1999 was caused by pressure of the EP which, however, did not actually vote a motion of censure.
[15] See Joseph H. H. Weiler, 'Dispatch from the Euro Titanic: And the Orchestra Played On', Editorial, *European Journal of International Law*, 21(4) (2011).

a presidential system. In his search for consensus, the President of the Commission speaks directly to heads of state or government, whom he meets regularly in the European Council, rather than to 'their representative' in the Commission. As twenty-seven is a lot of people to speak with, he is led to speak more to the leaders of the biggest Member States, and tends to drop a possible proposal when it is opposed by one of them.[16]

The relative failure of the European Parliament

The EP often tries (with many successes), through pressure, to obtain new powers not conferred on it in the treaties. The tactic usually followed is to group together two or more files, the decision on some of which requires the consent or the co-decision of the EP in order to be adopted, whereas it has only the right to deliver a mere consultative opinion on the others. The EP then makes known that it will give its agreement on the first files only if and when the Council accepts its requests on the other files. This is common practice. It is a distortion of the treaties, as it tends to confer on the EP new powers that were not conferred on it in the treaties, therefore affecting the balance between the institutions.

Two recent examples might help in understanding this problem. During the autumn of 2010, several pieces of legislation were to be adopted by the EU on financial surveillance. According to the treaties, the EP had a co-decision power on some legislation and a merely advisory role for others. The EP requested and succeeded in having this considered as a package, thus obtaining more powers than those conferred on it in the treaties. Similarly, the adoption of the Council's Decision on the organization and functioning of the European External Action Service (EEAS) legally requires, under Article 27(3) of the TEU, a mere consultation of the EP. However, the functioning of the EEAS required amendments to the EU's Financial Regulation as well as to the EU's Staff Regulations, amendments for which the EP has a right of co-decision. The EP refused to give its agreement on those amendments until the Council agreed, through difficult negotiations, to some of the EP's wishes to amend the draft

---

[16] de Schoutheete, 'La crise et la gouvernance européenne'.

Decision on the EEAS. Thus, the EP informally obtained a right of co-decision on a matter on which it was clear that the authors of the treaties did not intend to confer such a right on it. Again, the resulting 'inter-institutional balance' was different from that which the treaties prescribed.

However, the success of the EP in gaining more powers does not mean that it has been equally successful in gaining strong democratic legitimacy. On the contrary, there are a number of reasons why the EP may be regarded as having, relatively, failed on this point.

'Relative failure' means, of course, that the EP is 'relatively successful'. The EU obviously benefits from an EP whose members are democratically elected. For example, the EP played a significant role in the case of the Directive on Services, and on the REACH Regulation.[17] In the future, with the new powers it obtained in the Lisbon Treaty, the EP will certainly help to re-balance the trend of the Council since the 9/11 attacks to adopt tough laws to fight terrorism without always fully respecting fundamental freedoms. The role of the EP in the area of freedom, security and justice, for which EU legislation is adopted by co-decision since the entry into force of the Lisbon Treaty, will be particularly important. Besides, it should also be recognized that its relative failure is to be mostly attributed not to the EP or the MEPs themselves, but rather to the very structure and essence of the EU. In any case, what follows should not be misinterpreted. The EP is an indispensable institution of the EU and nobody is suggesting that it should be abolished. While it does not contribute enough, what it does contribute is still better than if it did not exist!

However, the fact remains that, as explained in an article by Yves Meny,[18] with regard to the decision to have a directly elected EP, 'this major leap was not sufficient. In fact, the democratic deficit argument never raged as much as it did *after* the election of MEPs by universal suffrage. It might have been a necessary, but not a sufficient condition to fulfil the democratic requirements expected by Europe's

---

[17] Directive 2006/127 EC on Services in the Internal Market, 12 December 2006, and Regulation EC/1907/2006 on Registration, Evaluation, Authorization and Restriction of Chemicals (REACH), 18 December 2006.

[18] 'De la démocratie en Europe: Old Concepts and New Challenges', *Journal of Common Market Studies*, 41(1) (2002), 1–13.

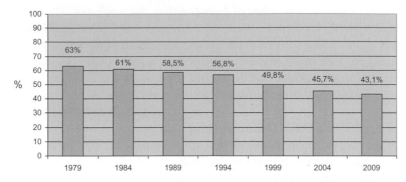

Figure 2.1 Turnout for elections to the European Parliament
Source: European Parliament

people, media and elites . . .' Member States decided, nevertheless, to increase the powers of the EP more and more in treaty after treaty. The results of these decisions have not been as positive as expected. The EP is still perceived as not bringing enough legitimacy to the EU.

In parallel with the increase of the powers of the EP, the turnout for the elections of its members has steadily decreased since 1979, the date of the first direct elections, from 63 per cent to 43 per cent thirty years later. This decline has been constant, at every election, as shown by Figure 2.1. In 2009, participation in elections in the most populated Member States was: 66.4 per cent in Italy; 44.3 per cent in Spain; 43 per cent in Germany; 40.49 per cent in France; 34.27 per cent in the United Kingdom; and 28.25 per cent in Poland.

One must also stress that distortions in the representation of the citizens of the EU in the EP are quite significant. Suffice it to say that a majority may be reached in a vote in the EP without any vote coming from the MEPs elected in the four biggest Member States, where 53.64 per cent of the total EU population lives,[19] because they have only 42 per cent of the seats.[20] Therefore, a majority in the EP may not respect the wishes of a majority of citizens of the EU.

---

[19] Germany, 16.32 per cent; France, 12.91 per cent; United Kingdom, 12.37 per cent; Italy, 12.04 per cent (official EU 2011 figures, *Eurostat*).
[20] The German Constitutional Court has seen in this distortion a sign of a structural democratic deficit (judgment 30 June 2009, Treaty of Lisbon).

Furthermore, a number of factors reflect the weak political legitimacy of the EP. Its members are more accountable to their political party than to their voters. In the EU, there is no government, nor a parliamentary majority to support a government. No one has the power to dissolve the EP before the end of the five-year duration of the legislature, whatever the circumstances. Member States wished to remain free to choose the arrangements for the elections to the EP, and they have often chosen proportional representation. A number of them have decided to organize elections in a single national constituency, but this does not allow the voters to know their MEP.

The main weakness of the EP is that, in Europe, the political game takes place at the national level. As explained by Chris Patten:[21] 'the EP's detachment from national political debates means that it has less political legitimacy than is desirable'. The national country of the voters is the place where, through political elections, they are able to choose their government, which is obviously not the case with the EP elections.[22]

Equally not attributable to the EP, is the fact that it does not deal with those issues that are the most important for voters, because these issues remain largely within the competences of the Member States, be it unemployment and the labour market, social security and public health, education and training, direct and indirect taxes, public services or decisions on foreign policy. Citizens know that decisions in these fields do not depend on their vote in EP elections, because they are essentially made at the national level.

In parallel with that, another issue is that the EP has, indirectly but effectively, through its power to adopt EU legislation, the power to oblige Member States to increase their public expenditure. At the same time, the treaty does not give any responsibility to the EP for finding the means to provide for the necessary corresponding resources.

---

[21] Chris Patten, *European Voice*, 4 June 2009.
[22] As Joseph H. H. Weiler put it: 'no one who votes in the European elections has a strong sense at all of affecting critical policy choices at the European level and certainly not of confirming or rejecting European governance', *The Constitution of Europe* (Cambridge, MA: Harvard University Press, 1999), p. 266.

Finally, as has already been stressed, the EP often tries to obtain more powers than those conferred on it in the treaties, powers which it regards as a basis to ask for more. This is, for example, the case when the EP tries to obtain powers in the process of adopting implementing rules, to the detriment of the Commission and of the Council, or when it tries to have a say in the decisions on the EU's own resources or in the conduct of international negotiations. This behaviour does not correspond to the distribution of powers legally provided for in the treaties and does not improve the political trust one may have in the EP.

On the whole, as Joseph H. H. Weiler put it in 1999: 'a system that enjoys formal legitimacy may not necessarily enjoy social legitimacy... democracy can be measured by the closeness, responsiveness, representativeness, and accountability of the governors to the governed'.[23] These conditions are not met in the case of the EP.

This is why there might now be an understanding among most political authorities of the twenty-seven Member States that enhancing further the EP's powers would not help to solve the EU's legitimacy problems, because these problems are not an issue of formal democracy. The EU's legitimacy derives to a large extent from the democratic legitimacy of the Member States themselves.[24] Some think that the role of national parliaments in the EU decision-making process should be increased. It is to be stressed that this could be done without amending the EU treaties.[25] This would be a (much needed) complement to the democratic control of the EU which is exercised by the EP.

---

[23] Weiler, *The Constitution of Europe*, p. 81.

[24] According to the former UK Prime Minister Tony Blair: 'The European Parliament is more directly democratic but it is more remote from people than their National Parliaments or their elected governments. The Council of Ministers is closer to people in the sense that the British Prime Minister is directly accountable to the British electorate in a very obvious way and yet, in terms of the European decisions we take, [the Council] is less directly democratic. That's the dilemma.' Cited in Moravcsik, 'Federalism in the EU: Rhetoric and Reality', p. 182.

[25] First, by each Government giving more information and more say to its Parliament, through systematic pre- and post-briefings of the sessions of the EU Council and of the European Council. Second, by collectively helping national parliaments to exercise their powers under the Lisbon Treaty, through giving them the means to organize a common secretariat, which might be an effective measure to coordinate better.

The difficult birth of the External Action Service

In order to take a major step forward in the field of external affairs, the Lisbon Treaty established a new 'triple-hatted'[26] High Representative of the Union for Foreign Affairs and Security Policy (HR) (TEU, Article 18(1)) and a European External Action Service (EEAS) (TEU, Article 27(3)). In order to allow the EU to progress on European Security and Defence Policy (ESDP), the treaty also provides for the possibility of a permanent structured cooperation between willing Member States 'whose military capabilities fulfil higher criteria' (TEU, Articles 42(6) and 46 and Protocol No. 10).

The probability is that these new provisions will take years before they produce actual positive results. At the time of writing (i.e., 18 months after the entry into force on 1 December 2009 of the Lisbon Treaty), the situation has not improved. The new HR, Baroness Catherine Ashton, has so many tasks that it is difficult for her to perform them all simultaneously. Moreover, being President of the Council at the same time as being Vice-President of the Commission entails difficulties. The mood among the foreign ministers of Member States is not very positive. Cooperation is not perfect, neither with them nor with the Commission. The difficulties that were foreseen[27] have been confirmed.

As far as the EEAS is concerned, the decision to establish its organization and functioning on the basis of Article 27(3) of the TEU was adopted on 26 July 2010,[28] but the task of actually establishing an efficient single external service is just beginning, and it will take years before being achieved. For now, the different services to be merged are still working in a number of different buildings in Brussels, and the unity and esprit de corps of the new service remain to be built up. For the external world and third countries, positive results are not yet apparent. On the contrary, quarrels over the delimitation of the respective competences of the EU and of the Member States and about the extent of the new powers of the EP in external affairs have

---

[26] The new HR took over the tasks of the ex-HR (Javier Solana), of the ex-Commissioner for External Affairs (Benita Ferrero-Waldner) and of the Minister of Foreign Affairs exercising the semestrial Presidency of the Council of Foreign Affairs.

[27] See Piris, *The Lisbon Treaty*, pp. 248–9.

[28] Council Decision 2010/427/EU, published EU OJ L 201/30, 3 August 2010.

been exacerbated. Difficulties have prevented the EU delegations in the world, particularly those accredited to international organizations, from speaking with one voice. Finally, defence ministers have decided that as far as the possibility of 'permanent structured cooperation' offered by the Treaty of Lisbon is concerned, the time is not ripe to begin implementing it.

Therefore, the tools given by the Treaty of Lisbon exist, but their concrete implementation is proving to be more difficult than was foreseen and, up to the time of writing, the relevance and strength of the EU in the world is generally seen as having diminished during the recent past.

THE EU'S SUBSTANTIVE POLICIES ARE NOT SUCCESSFUL ENOUGH

The internal market is far from being achieved

The aim of the internal market is to open the EU's internal borders to a free flow of goods, services, capital and workers in the same way as within a national market, but in a larger market of half a billion consumers. This aim is presented as having more or less been achieved, but the fact is that it is not complete, in particular, but not only, in the area of services.

According to the 2010 Report of Mario Monti to José Manuel Barroso on 'A New Strategy for the Single Market':[29]

The Single Market is Europe's original idea and unfinished business. In his Political guidelines for this Commission, President Barroso pointed to the gaps and 'missing links' that hamper the functioning of the Single Market. Echoing this orientation, the European Council of 26 March 2010 has agreed that the new Europe 2020 strategy should address 'the main bottlenecks . . . related to the working of the internal market and infrastructure'.

'Missing links' and 'bottlenecks' mean that, in many areas, the Single Market exists in the books, but, in practice, multiple barriers and regulatory obstacles fragment intra-EU trade and hamper economic initiative and

---

[29] See report by Professor Mario Monti, 'A New Strategy for the Single Market at the Service of Europe's Economy and Society', Report to the President of the European Commission José Manuel Barroso, 9 May 2010, available at: http://ec.europa.eu/bepa/pdf/monti.

innovation. In others, the potential for greater economic gains is frustrated by lack of physical and legal infrastructure or by absence of dialogue between administrative systems. The ITC revolution and rapid technological development add a third category to the list of missing pieces in the single market: sectors that did not exist when the single market was initially conceived, such as e-commerce, innovative services and eco-industries. These are the sectors which hold the largest growth and employment dividends for the future. They represent the new frontiers of the single market.

Relaunching the single market requires tackling the different challenges posed by missing links, bottlenecks and new frontiers. In some sectors, such as in the single market for goods, market integration reached a mature stage. Policy action can focus on 'market maintenance' through market monitoring, targeted regulatory intervention, simplification and reduction of compliance costs. In others, as in the case of services, Europe is still in a phase of 'market construction' that requires breaking down barriers to cross-border activity, cutting the dead wood of national administrative and technical barriers and overcoming corporatist resistances. In the new frontiers, Europe should harness the full range of single market tools to drive forward the construction of a digital and low-carbon resource efficient economy. The marginal gains from action in this area are the greatest. Turning the attention to the new frontiers is key to generate new momentum for and confidence in the single market as a priority for tomorrow's Europe.

However, no project to relaunch the single market will have the necessary political energy to succeed, if it fails to show citizens, consumers and SMEs that it works first and foremost for them.

On 27 October 2010, on the basis of the Monti Report, the Commission produced a Communication, 'Towards a Single Market Act. For a Highly Competitive Social Market Economy',[30] which introduces fifty possible proposals, some of which are:

- the EU patent;[31]
- the management of copyrights;
- an action plan against counterfeiting and piracy;

---

[30] Communication from the Commission to the European Parliament, the Council, the Economic and Social Committee and the Committee of the Regions, 'Towards a Single Market Act. For a Highly Competitive Social Market Economy. 50 Proposals for Improving our Work, Business and Exchanges with One Another', doc. COM (2010) 608, 27 October 2010.

[31] Hungary, as Presidency of the EU Council during the first semester of 2011, estimated that the direct cost of a 'fragmented' patent system adds up to 750 million euros of extra costs on EU business each year.

- the development of the internal market in services;
- the development of electronic commerce in the internal market;
- legislative reform of the standardization framework;
- measures intended to remove obstacles to the internal market on transport;
- an examination of the deficiencies of the internal market on services to business;
- legislative proposals on European public procurement legislation;
- a proposal on the introduction of a common consolidated corporate tax base;
- an examination of a possible fundamental review of the VAT system;
- a decision to ensure mutual recognition of e-indentification and e-authentification in the EU;
- measures on services of general interest;
- a legislative initiative to reform the systems for the recognition of professional qualifications;
- a legislative initiative on access to certain basic banking services;
- a proposed directive geared towards the creation of a single integrated mortgage market;
- a communication aimed at identifying and eliminating the tax obstacles still facing European citizens;
- an initiative on the use of alternative dispute resolution in the EU; and
- 'a more resolute policy to enforce the rules of the single market' (sic.!).

One thing seems to be missing from the Commission's list: to provide for appropriate measures to tackle the remaining obstacles to movement of workers within the internal market, not only with regard to differences in professional qualifications, but also in educational qualifications.

Another issue is that the internal market has been made possible by taking certain measures in order to prevent distortions of competition between the Member States. A number of directives and regulations have consequently been adopted with the aim of avoiding such distortions. However, differences in fiscal and social laws were not considered by all Member States as distortions of competition. Therefore, the treaty does not make harmonization in these matters a necessary condition for the achievement of the internal market, and the adoption of rules in these areas is almost always subject to unanimity voting in the Council. As a result, Member States have retained a large degree of freedom in those fields; hence, the tensions over what some call 'fiscal dumping' or 'social dumping', and the reactions to certain (questionable) judgments of the Court of Justice of the EU (such as *Viking* and *Laval*[32]). Again, this asymmetry – regarded by some as a normal area of competition between the Member States – is not easy to correct, because any solution would have to reconcile contradictory interests of the Member States. Moreover, possible decisions on such issues have to be underpinned by a strong democratic legitimacy on the part of the decision-makers, which is not obviously the case at the EU level.

Moreover, the Commission has sometimes been too weak in implementing rules on state aid, which are also distortions of competition.

On another issue, while the EU allows free movement of persons inside the external borders of its Member States, and rules and instruments regulating this freedom are decided in a 'federal' way, Member States have retained the power to grant their nationality to non-EU citizens, or to allow them to immigrate for long-term stays, which subsequently gives them complete freedom to move to any other Member State. Moreover, controls at the external borders of the Schengen area are left to the competent authorities of the Member States, and are not always implemented with the necessary rigour. The Commission has no effective means of controlling the behaviour of the Member States at their external borders.

Finally, the lack of sufficient cooperation in the area of energy is obvious, although it is urgently needed. Proposals have been presented recently by Jacques Delors, former President of the Commission, aiming in particular at establishing a 'European Energy Community'.[33] This is also one of the recent fifty possible proposals of the Commission: 'A Communication to contribute to the development of a fully operational internal energy market'. For the time

---

[32] Judgment of 11 December 2007, Case C-438/05 *Viking* [2007] ECR I-10806 and judgment of 18 December 2007, Case C-341/05 *Laval* [2007] ECR I-11845.

[33] 'Towards a European Energy Community: A Policy Proposal', *Notre Europe*, March 2010.

being, Member States are openly divided on this issue, quite obviously according to their short- or medium-term interests.

Monetary union is fragile because of its imbalances

These imbalances were well known from the beginning (negotiation of the 'Delors Report' and of the Maastricht IGC). At that time, some Member States refused to share powers over their budgetary and economic policies. They argued that the market would help to prevent any crisis and that, with the adoption of a 'Stability and Growth Pact', it would not be necessary to go further, especially since it was difficult to conceive a centralization of powers on such matters at the level of the EU.

These imbalances affect the relationship between the two parts of economic and monetary union: the economic part and the monetary part. The euro is the single currency of seventeen Member States (including Estonia since 1 January 2011), and it will probably become the currency of more of them in the future. There is an obvious link between the economic and the monetary parts if one wants to be sure that the euro remains stable while allowing for reasonable economic growth.

Presently, on one side, the euro is managed in a 'federal' way by the European Central Bank (ECB) and, on the other side, fiscal, budgetary and economic policies remain almost completely in the hands of the Member States.[34] Up to now, for this economic part the powers of the 'federal' centre have been, *de jure* or *de facto*, limited to recommendations which are not binding. As Angela Merkel, Federal Chancellor of Germany, stressed in her 'Humboldt Speech on Europe' in May 2009: 'The powers regarding budget, tax and social policy are held by the Member States for good reasons.' It is certainly an inescapable fact that there is a necessity for a direct link between these powers and an effective political legitimacy (i.e., the link between the voters and those who decide). Solving this asymmetry while keeping

---

[34] This imbalance is all the more striking since, as the EU budget represents only around 1 per cent of the total GNI of the EU, as compared with the approximately 47 per cent represented by the budget of the public authorities (national/regional/local) of its twenty-seven Member States (source: *Eurostat*), the EU does not have the budgetary means at its disposal which could help to deal with an economic and financial crisis.

the present political features of the EU presents an almost impossible
task. However, a monetary union which is based on loose rules on
budget/tax/economic governance will remain incomplete and unsus-
tainable, as the continuing financial crisis which began in 2009 is
demonstrating. Many efforts to resolve this have been, and continue
to be, made by the European Council and by the 'Task Force'[35]
under the presidency of Herman van Rompuy, by the Commission
under the presidency of Jose Manuel Barroso, by the ECB under
the presidency of Jean-Claude Trichet, by the Council of Ministers
of Economic and Financial Affairs ('ECOFIN') under the successive
six-monthly presidencies, and by the Euro Group under the presidency of Jean-Claude Juncker. It is to be hoped that these efforts will
continue to be tightly coordinated and that they will lead to measures
which are actually adopted and implemented and prove to be successful. Both the President of the ECB and a few Member States think that
the measures envisaged, even if they were all adopted swiftly, would
not be sufficient. Moreover, the limited revision of the treaty which
is needed by Germany[36] in order to be able to agree on the establishment of a permanent 'Mechanism' will have to be ratified before the
expiration of the temporary Mechanism in the spring of 2013.

Member States do not cooperate sufficiently in defence matters

There is no internal market for military equipment; there is no
opening of public procurement in this domain; there is not enough
cooperation in the armaments industry between the Member States.
Moreover, the way in which participation in EU military operations
works is that Member States that decide to participate with troops also
have to pay for their expenses.[37] Therefore, they 'pay twice' (men and
money), whereas the Member States that decide not to participate
with troops are also free not to contribute to their financing, even
though the military operations are carried out on behalf of the EU.
At the same time, defence budgets are being diminished in almost
all EU Member States; only two of them reach the 2 per cent GDP
threshold requested by NATO (Greece and the United Kingdom),

---

[35] Final Report by the Task Force, doc. 15302/10, 21 October 2010.   [36] See p. 97.
[37] According to the NATO principle: 'costs lie where they fall'.

while, in contrast, the United States spends about 5 per cent of its GDP annually on defence. In this area, the EU risks becoming rapidly irrelevant.[38]

The agreement signed by the two most powerful military powers of the EU, France and the United Kingdom, in November 2010 is a welcome sign that things might change in the future:[39] for the first time both states announced that they will cooperate over their nuclear deterrents (which will remain independent); they will agree on the timing of the deployment of their aircraft carriers; they will work together on the next generation of drones (unmanned air surveillance systems); and they will develop a rapid reaction force of 10,000 men, 5,000 of each nationality, trained to fight alongside each other on joint missions under a commander from either state.

The very slow progress of the former 'Third Pillar'

There are several factors that explain the very slow progress of the work done by the EU in the area of freedom, security and justice, despite this being an area where more cooperation between Member States, be it for regulating immigration, judicial cooperation in civil (including family law) and criminal law or police cooperation, could positively affect the daily lives of Europeans.

The first factor is that the Member States with a system of common law have great difficulties in accepting the rules and procedures which would better suit the other Member States. Despite the large-scale opt-outs obtained by the United Kingdom and Ireland (as well as Denmark), this is still a problem. The second factor is that in some Member States that acceded to the EU in 2004 and 2007 the judicial system is not up to the standard that would be necessary for other Member States to accept mutual recognition of judgments and other decisions of judicial authorities. Taking these two factors into account, one can understand why, in matters where unanimity was the rule, it was difficult to agree on legal texts.

With the Lisbon Treaty, a number of those matters, although not all, are now covered by QMV in the Council. Rules applicable to the former 'First Pillar' are now applicable to those matters, including

---

[38] See *The Economist*, 18–24 June 2011.   [39] See *Financial Times*, 3 November 2010.

the ordinary legislative procedure. The Lisbon Treaty should lead to better democratic accountability, taking into account the co-decision procedure with the EP and, in particular, the new powers conferred on national parliaments in this field by Article 12(c) of the TEU, Articles 69, 70, 85 and 88 of the TFEU and Article 7(2) of Protocol No. 2 on the application of the principles of proportionality and subsidiarity. Better protection of individual rights should also result from the treaty, given the fact that the Court of Justice will, in the future, have full jurisdiction in this field.[40]

However, on the one hand, QMV is not a panacea, because in this field it would be difficult to impose rules on Member States whose content they would disagree with.[41] On the other hand, unanimity remains applicable in a number of cases. Consequently, closer cooperation among some Member States will probably be unavoidable. That is why it has been made easier to authorize it in cases covered by unanimity through the 'brake–accelerator' mechanism.[42] In this policy area, more than in others, there will be no possibility of the EU progressing in future without, as mentioned in Article 67(1) of the TFEU, respecting 'the different legal systems and traditions of the Member States', therefore without providing for more differentiation. However, taking into account the situations of individual Member States might unfortunately lead to a complicated patchwork of different legislation being applied by groups of Member States, which would be different from one piece of legislation to another.

THE REFORMS OF THE LISBON TREATY WERE NOT ON THE SCALE THAT WAS NEEDED

The Lisbon Treaty entered into force on 1 December 2009. However, it already looks outdated.[43] Actually, it was conceived on the basis

---

[40] After the completion of a five-year transitional period and with a possible full 'opt-out' for the United Kingdom (see Title VII of Protocol No. 36 on Transitional Provisions).

[41] See on this issue the opinion of the German Constitutional Court in its judgment of 30 June 2009 on the Lisbon Treaty.

[42] See box below; see TFEU, Articles 82(3), subparagraph 2, 83(3), subparagraph 2, 86(1), subparagraph 3 and 87(3), subparagraph 3.

[43] See *El País*, 18 November 2010: 'El Tratado de Lisboa cumple un año, y ya está viejo'.

of the Laeken Declaration, which was adopted in 2001.[44] The treaty is mostly based on the work of the 2002/2003 Convention, which, before the huge enlargement of the EU in 2004 and 2007, drafted the failed so-called 'Constitution for Europe'.[45] Choosing this misleading label 'Constitution' was a political mistake, which was one of the causes of the failure of the Constitutional Treaty.[46] Partly because of this title, the Constitutional Treaty, and consequently the Lisbon Treaty – as it kept most of the reforms foreseen in the Constitutional Treaty – were seen as achieving a very substantial reform of the EU.

This was a misunderstanding. Far from being a political or legal revolution, the Lisbon Treaty's reforms were not on the scale of what was needed. They were insufficient. Consequently, the EU retains the same (heavy and cumbersome) decision-making process, with the same (unsatisfactory) elements that are supposed to bring it democratic support from EU citizens (i.e., essentially based on the EP).

The Treaty of Lisbon will allow some progress, but it has not put an end to the major imbalances which affect the Union.

The progress allowed by the Lisbon Treaty

Potential progress has been brought about by the Lisbon Treaty. The effective implementation of its reforms will depend on the political will of the Member States, as well as on the economic situation and on the action of some individual personalities. The most important of these reforms, which aim at strengthening the Union, its effectiveness and its legitimacy, but which do not provide for substantive extensions of powers, are discussed below.

---

[44] The 'Declaration of Laeken' was approved by the European Council as Annex I to the Presidency conclusions at its meeting in Laeken (Belgium) on 14–15 December 2001, doc. SN 300/1/01 REV 1.

[45] See Jean-Claude Piris, *The Constitution for Europe – A Legal Analysis* (Cambridge University Press, 2006).

[46] See my lecture at the Harvard Law School in May 1999, published under the title 'Does the European Union have a Constitution? Does it need one?', by Harvard Law School, Harvard Jean Monnet Working Paper No. 2000 and in *European Law Review*, 24(66) (December 1999).

The 'communitarization' of the former 'third pillar'

The improvements made to the freedom, security and justice (FSJ) provisions of the treaties lie mainly in the 'communitarization' of the former 'third pillar' through its incorporation into one Title of the TFEU covering the whole FSJ area. This brings a simpler and more consistent architecture. It also allows full parliamentary control (European and national) of measures that may affect every citizen, thus helping to guarantee better protection of the rights of individuals. It also means a more efficient decision-making procedure. There are more cases of QMV for taking decisions in the Council and more co-decisions with the European Parliament for the adoption of legal acts. However, QMV and co-decisions do not apply to a number of cases, such as family law, some forms of operational police cooperation or to the establishment of a European Public Prosecutor's Office.

This reform should help more decisions to be taken in order to enhance the level of security within a border-free EU, while respecting individual rights. This should also allow full control by the Commission, the Court of Justice and national courts over the implementation of these legal acts by the Member States, which should lead to a better level of implementation. The treaty also allows a 'fast-track' to authorize closer cooperation among some Member States: the so-called 'Brake–Accelerator' Mechanism.

Box 2.1: The 'Brake–Accelerator' Mechanism

In order to accompany the switch to QMV in the Council on decisions in the sensitive area of judicial cooperation in criminal matters, the Lisbon Treaty has introduced a new procedure, with two elements:

- the first is a so-called *'emergency brake'* system, which allows a Member State that considers that a draft legislative act 'would affect fundamental aspects of its criminal justice system' to bring the matter to the European Council, in which case the co-decision procedure is suspended. After discussion, and if there is a consensus, the European Council, within four months, is to refer the draft back to the Council, which terminates the suspension of the procedure (see TFEU, Articles 82(3), subparagraph 1 and 83(3), subparagraph 1);

- the second is a so-called '*accelerator*', which is designed to avoid a stalemate. If, within this four-month period, there is still disagreement in the European Council but at least nine Member States wish to establish an enhanced cooperation on the basis of the draft act in question, they will notify the European Parliament, the Council and the Commission accordingly and the enhanced cooperation will automatically apply between them, thus by-passing some of the preliminary steps that are normally required under the enhanced cooperation procedure and hence 'accelerating' the procedure (see TFEU, Articles 82(3), subparagraph 2 and 83(3), subparagraph 2). See also the '*fast track*' provided by Articles 86(1), subparagraph 3 and 87(3), subparagraph 3 of the TFEU.

This mechanism might lead to enhanced cooperation among groups of Member States, the composition of which might be different from one legislative act to another.

A significant increase of the powers of the European Parliament in the legislative and international areas

The trend to find a solution to the so-called 'democratic deficit' through the extension of the powers of the European Parliament has continued, despite the fact that the previous increases in its powers have not given the expected results.

At the same time, the national parliaments of the Member States have for the first time been given the opportunity of being active on the EU political scene (TEU, Article 12), and even to intervene directly in the EU legislative process in order to control the application of the principle of subsidiarity (TEU, Article 12(b) and Protocols 1 and 2, respectively, on the role of national parliaments in the EU and on the application of the principles of subsidiarity and proportionality). Besides, the treaty provides citizens with the possibility of suggesting new legislation (TEU, Article 11(4)). Finally, some provisions aim at improving the possibility of 'civil society' (associations, etc.) being better informed so as to allow it to play a role (TEU, Article 11(a), (b), (c)).

The establishment of two new offices

The first new office is a full-time President of the European Council. Herman van Rompuy, who at the time of the entry into force of the Lisbon Treaty was Prime Minister of Belgium, was elected as the first President of the European Council with a mandate for two and a half years, renewable once.[47]

The second office is a full-time High Representative of the Union for Foreign Affairs and Security Policy. Catherine Ashton, who at that time was Commissioner for EU External Trade, was appointed to the office for five years. This office makes her, at the same time, President of the EU Council of Ministers for Foreign Affairs and one of the Vice-Presidents of the European Commission.

If effective and well coordinated with the President of the Commission, these two new figures, who, like him, are political figures independent from the national authorities of a Member State, could strengthen considerably 'the centre' of the EU. They might, together with the other institutions and bodies that have 'federal' characteristics, become decisive actors in the development and progress of EU policies. This should, in principle, result in better visibility of the EU on the international scene. However, no one knows how this will work in the future. In particular, as several figures have emerged as 'would-be rivals' they could fight against each other and decrease the influence of the EU institutions. At the time of writing, rivalries between institutions have proven to be real on several issues concerning the way in which the new provisions of the Lisbon Treaty should be implemented and have not yet been completely resolved. The aim of having the EU speaking with one voice on the international scene, or at least delivering a unified message, which was one of the aims of the Treaty, has not yet been achieved. Disputes between the Commission and the Member States on the limits between the external competences of the EU and those of the Member States have been exacerbated.

---

[47] See Tony Barber, 'The Appointments of Herman van Rompuy and Catherine Ashton', *Journal of Common Market Studies*, 48 (2010), 55–67.

*The treaty contains a new definition and method of calculation of
QMV in the Council (which will be fully applicable in 2014 at the
earliest and, more probably, only in 2017)⁴⁸ and a moderate extension of
its scope of application. This goes in the direction of a better democratic
legitimacy for the decisions taken by the Council, either on its own or in
co-decision with the European Parliament, especially as the new method
of calculation will take more account of the actual number of
inhabitants in order to determine the number of votes conferred on the
representative of each Member State in the Council.*

*The Lisbon Treaty puts at the forefront the values on which the
Member States have based the EU (TEU, Article 2).⁴⁹ It also takes two
important symbolic steps: first, by giving the Charter of Fundamental
Rights of the EU the same legal value as the treaties (TEU, Article
6(1)); and, second, by laying down an obligation for the EU to accede to
the European Convention for the Protection of Human Rights and
Fundamental Freedoms (ECHR) (TEU, Article 6(2)).*

*The treaty does not change very much the general provisions for
enhanced cooperation among some Member States, except for the specific
cases of security and defence (with the 'permanent structured
cooperation' of Articles 42(6) and 46 of the TEU)⁵⁰ and of the former
'third pillar' (with the 'brake–accelerator' mechanism).*

*Finally, after the entry into force of the Lisbon Treaty the division of
substance between the two treaties, the new TEU and the Treaty on the
Functioning of the EU (TFEU), brings more clarity than the division
that existed between the former TEU and the Treaty establishing the
European Community (TEC). The current TEU contains the general*

---

[48] See Protocol No. 36 on Transitional Provisions.

[49] Article 2 of the TEU on the Union's values is not only a political and symbolic statement, it also has concrete legal effects. First, it is a condition which a European state has to respect in order to be allowed to apply for membership: 'Any European State which respects the values referred to in Article 2 and is committed to promoting them may apply to become a member of the Union' (TEU, Art. 49). Second, serious breaches of these values by a Member State may lead to the suspension of some of its rights resulting from Union membership (TEU, Art. 7).

[50] During an informal meeting of the ministers of defence in Ghent, Belgium on 24 September 2010 it was decided not to implement these provisions immediately.

provisions applying to the EU, its values and objectives, its basic principles, the definition of its powers, the procedure for revising the treaties and the main characteristics of its institutions and a description of their powers. For its part, the TFEU contains the legal bases that give the EU and its institutions the power to act, while delimiting and setting limits to those powers. It is true that the result of the Lisbon IGC is difficult to read and that there are inconsistencies (the main one being the location of the provisions on Common Foreign and Security Policy (CFSP) in the TEU and not in the TFEU).[51] On the whole, it does represent a certain progress as far as clarity is concerned. Thus, a reading of the 'consolidated' TEU on its own might be enough for the 'man in the street' to understand what the EU is about and how it functions in a reasonably short text (fifty-five articles in thirty pages).

By taking on the reforms envisaged in the failed 'Constitution for Europe', the Lisbon Treaty therefore contains some potential improvements for the effectiveness of the EU. It allows it to adopt legal acts more easily in certain areas, albeit not very numerous and important, except in the former 'third pillar'. The EU does not gain substantive new competences, if any. It obtains better tools, which could allow it to be more active and visible on the international scene. It remains to be seen whether and how these tools will be used in the future.

Nevertheless, these main characteristics, accompanied by some other changes, do not bring about enough improvements, and the EU remains affected by major imbalances. These imbalances, some of which are due to the fact that the Union remains a classic international organization in some areas, while working in a federal way in others, may be a cause of instability, as they make it difficult for the EU to work effectively in a sustainable way.

The imbalance concerning EMU has not been solved. However, it is true that Article 136 of the TFEU allows the euro area's members to take measures to strengthen the coordination and surveillance of their budgetary discipline and to set out economic policy guidelines.

---

[51] This was demanded by some delegations, especially the British one, in order to stress the fact that CFSP remains a separate 'pillar' in the EU, governed by rules different from those applicable to the other areas of action of the EU.

The imbalance concerning the EU's political legitimacy is also very difficult to resolve. The EP has not been fully successful. As more competences to adopt legislation were transferred by the Member States to the EU, this reduced the powers of national parliaments, which did not pay sufficient attention to the legislative work being done in Brussels, while most governments did not involve them in EU matters, aiming to have more liberty to act on their own. The growing distrust of citizens concerning the EU is partially due to this lack of political legitimacy. The powers attributed by the Lisbon Treaty to national parliaments, especially for controlling the application of the principle of subsidiarity by the EU institutions, will probably be too weak to provide an actual solution to this problem.

The third imbalance is between the decision-making system of the EU and the fact that it has a membership of twenty-seven states, each with extremely different needs. The essential elements of the EU system basically remain the same for a Union of twenty-seven as they were in 1957 for a Community of six. The system provides for the adoption of one identical decision to be implemented by all twenty-seven ('one-decision-fits-all'), as the 'enhanced cooperation' mechanism has hardly ever been used. This is inadequate and inefficient, and has not been resolved by the Lisbon Treaty despite the specific provisions adopted with regard to some areas of the former 'third pillar' and for defence.

Therefore, on the whole, the implementation of the Lisbon Treaty, even after a normal period of adaptation, will probably not deliver what is needed to allow the EU-27 to work effectively and with the support of its citizens.

ASSESSMENT OF THE PRESENT SITUATION OF THE EU: CONCLUSIONS

(1) The depth of the EU's current crisis, and the difficulty in solving it, is due to the fact that the EU is simultaneously confronted with three fundamental issues: the crisis due to the euro area's imbalances; the political gap between the EU and public opinion; and the dysfunctionality of the decision-making.

(2) Given the deficiencies and weaknesses of the EU institutions, the insufficient results of the EU substantive policies and the wide

differences between the economic and social needs and political desires of its twenty-seven Member States, the reforms of the Lisbon Treaty are not on the scale that is needed.

Against this background, several options could be examined for the future:

Among those, one should consider as the first priority options permitting all twenty-seven Member States to participate.

The first option would be to consider a revision of the EU treaties, which, in order to be effective, would have to be substantial (Chapter 3).

If this option appeared politically unrealistic, then another option would be to continue on the present path, which already provides many possibilities of differentiation, opt-outs and enhanced cooperation, while strengthening the efforts to solve the euro crisis and using the treaty's provisions on enhanced cooperation more frequently (Chapter 4).

If this is inadequate to solve the EU's present problems, then the option of a 'Two-speed Europe' should be considered, with a group of Member States playing the role of an 'avant-garde'. This option could be envisaged either in a 'softer' form (Chapter 5) or in a 'bolder' one (Chapter 6).

CHAPTER 3

First option: substantially revising the European Union treaties

If the assessment of the present situation in Chapter 2 is correct, it means that while Member States will in the future still be in need of the EU, the EU will not be able to help sufficiently, given its present institutional procedures and rules. The logical answer to this dilemma in theory looks obvious: in order to respond to those needs, it would be necessary to modify the present institutions, their procedures and decision-making processes, as well as to try and conceive a more legitimate democratic control. In order to be adequate and to answer effectively the serious present problems and deficiencies, the amendments to the treaties need to be sufficiently bold. In other words, they should take the shape of a substantive revision of the institutional provisions of the current treaties.

Such a revision would be based on the recognition that with twenty-seven heterogeneous members, and the prospect of welcoming Croatia in 2013 (1 July 2013 was chosen during the European Council session of 23–24 June 2011) and possibly Iceland later, the EU has become an entirely new entity. One may add that some or all of the other western Balkan countries might also join the EU, possibly in the 2020s (Albania, Bosnia-Herzegovina, the Former Yugoslav Republic of Macedonia (FYROM), Kosovo, Montenegro, Serbia). Some are also referring to Georgia,[1] Moldova and even Ukraine,[2]

---

[1] Thornike Gordadze, Vice-Minister of Foreign Affairs in Georgia declared in *Libération* on 11 September 2010 that 'Georgia has a vocation to be a Member of the European Union'.
[2] According to the *Wall Street Journal*, 20 September 2010, Ukraine's President Viktor Yanukovych said at the opening of the General Assembly of the United Nations in September 2010 that 'Ukraine is determined to join the European Union'.

while Turkey is actually negotiating accession now.[3] Such an entity
of thirty to thirty-five members could not work properly on the basis
of the present system, whose architecture and procedures remain
those that were originally conceived for six Member States that had
a comparable degree of economic development and the same political desire to integrate. In order to meet this challenge adequately,
one should be much more innovative and creative than were the
2003/2004 European Convention and the 2007 IGC on the Lisbon
Treaty.

The EU's decision-making system was built in the 1950s and aimed
at 'one-decision-fits-all'. The successive enlargements from six to
twenty-seven members have not been followed by the great and bold
reform that was necessary. The major elements of the EU system,
which should be designed to allow its institutions to take quick and
bold decisions, have basically remained the same. In the 1950s, the
founding states were close to each other, geographically, historically,
economically and politically. Their aim with the creation of the
European Economic Community (EEC) was clearly political: to put
an end to centuries of wars between their peoples and to build an
'ever closer Union'. The means used were to establish close economic
interdependence between them, through the realization of a common
market, which would be as uniform as possible and lead to closer
political links later.

The EU is now composed of twenty-seven very heterogeneous
countries, geographically, economically, historically and politically.

---

[3] According to some, including the author of this book, the accession of Turkey to the EU
does not look realistic and will probably not happen unless the EU changes drastically. This
is not linked to religion, as is shown by the fact that some Muslim countries will probably
accede to the EU in the future, such as Albania (70 per cent of its population is Muslim),
Bosnia-Herzegovina (60 per cent) or Kosovo (90 per cent). The first reason is that the
accession of Turkey would mean the mutation of the EU from a cohesive political entity into
an international organization grouping very heterogeneous states not sharing quite the same
fundamental values and the same historic roots. The second reason is that such an accession
would certainly prevent the EU institutions from developing the most important existing
EU policies: economic and social cohesion, the common agricultural policy, social policy,
the area of freedom, security and justice, foreign policy, etc. It is, however, obvious that a
fundamental aim of the foreign policy of the EU must be to keep Turkey, a great country
and a great civilization, as a friend, ally and partner as close as possible: 'all or nothing' is
not necessarily a good solution (see Christopher Caldwell, 'Why Turkey Sits Outside the
Tent', *Financial Times*, 31 July–1 August 2010 and Philip Stephens, 'West must offer Turkey
a Proper Seat', *Financial Times*, 17 June 2010).

The vision of a political aim is not shared by all twenty-one states that have acceded over the years. The aims of the EU now concern a large number of policies, both economic and political. While it was conceivable that uniform decisions would be reached concerning the internal market for six homogeneous countries, today it has become extremely difficult to reach uniform decisions that fit the needs and wishes of twenty-seven countries in a much larger array of issues and policies. Still, the system is based on unanimity for the most delicate matters, on a culture of consensus and on the adoption of one identical decision to be implemented by all twenty-seven. This results in difficulties because quick and bold decisions are needed in a world that is changing extremely rapidly. This is inadequate and inefficient and does not allow the EU to help its Member States to confront the challenges they are facing.

Further EU enlargement to the western Balkans will increase these difficulties, especially if carried out too quickly and without enough preparation in the acceding states, as it has sometimes been the case, at least in some areas and for some of the acceding states, with the enlargements of 2004 and 2007. The fact is that the enlargement of the EU was mostly seen and used as a foreign policy instrument, whereas it was obvious that it primarily had the consequence of transforming the EU itself.

Therefore, it is actually the entire institutional system that should be re-considered, be it the composition, role and independence of the Commission; the composition, role and powers of the European Parliament; the role to be given to the national parliaments; the composition of the Court of Justice and of the Court of Auditors, etc.

In the same innovative way, the decision-taking system should be thoroughly re-examined, the three aims being:

- that the EU should be able to take decisions rapidly;
- that these decisions should not always be obligatory for all Member States; and
- that there should be an improved democratic legitimacy.

Generalization of QMV in the Council, as advocated by the European Parliament and the Commission, is too simplistic and it would not be an appropriate solution to most problems. Therefore, the list of issues to be examined should be centred around the need to have more efficiency, more democratic legitimacy and more flexibility.

In order to increase efficiency, the following should be re-considered

- The nomination, composition, role and independence of the Commission: ideally, the Commission should be transformed into a very small institution, whose members would really be independent from their Member State of origin.
- The decision-making system in the Council.
- The means of controlling the implementation of EU decisions by Member States.
- The composition of other institutions and organs (Court of Justice, Court of Auditors).

In order to aim at a better democratic legitimacy of the EU, the following should be considered

- Possible reforms of the European Parliament: these reforms should address its composition, the establishment of the lists of candidates and the arrangements for the election of its members. They should also more explicitly focus the powers of the EP in order to prohibit any direct interference with the powers of the Commission to take implementing measures and to negotiate international agreements. Another important decision to be taken would be that, in a situation of enhanced cooperation, the EP members representing the people of a Member State that does not participate should not be allowed to take part in the deliberations and the votes concerning that case.
- A greater involvement of the national parliaments: their role and powers should be increased and their coordination at the EU level should be facilitated, with a secretariat and modern means of communication allowing them to consult each other concretely and to participate effectively in controlling respect for the principle of subsidiarity by the EU institutions and in the control of decisions taken by the Council in the area of foreign policy and in defence matters.

In order to have more flexibility the feasibility and suitability of a number of reforms should be considered as this issue is just as important as those above

- A reform of the mechanism of enhanced cooperation: if the Commission were not to be reformed so as to make it a very small institution, one needs to face up to reality. The reality, which everybody knows but which it is not politically correct to express, is that when there is one Commissioner per Member State, one of the aims pursued by such a rule is obviously that, *inter alia*, with his or her other tasks, each Commissioner takes care, within the Commission, of the interests of his or her country of origin. That being so, in the case of enhanced cooperation it is only logical that Commissioners who are nationals of a non-participating Member State should not participate in the deliberations of the Commission on the subject, should not be consulted on the substance of the proposal to be made by the Commission, and should not participate in discussions on that matter with the EP and the Council.

- Other ideas could be explored further. For example, building on the mechanism of the 'constructive abstention', which exists in the area of CFSP (TEU, Article 31(1))[4] or extending the scope of application of the so-called 'brake–accelerator' mechanism (see, e.g., TFEU, Article 82(3)) to a number of areas presently covered by unanimity voting in the Council. These two last ideas could be pursued, in particular, if it appeared that a thorough and substantive revision of the treaties were impossible. In such a case, one could think about a 'minimalist' revision, which would improve the decision-making system only in order to allow for more flexibility between the Member States. For example, a short new provision could generalize the procedure of constructive abstention. In cases where one or several members of the Council abstained from voting, their countries would not be obliged to apply the decision, but they would accept that the decision is a decision of the Union binding on all other Member States. The same exception as provided in Article 31(1), subparagraph 2 of the TEU would be applicable, so that the decision would not be adopted if the 'constructive abstentions'

---

[4] 'When abstaining in a vote, any member of the Council may qualify its abstention by making a formal declaration under the present subparagraph. In that case, it shall not be obliged to apply the decision, but shall accept that the decision commits the Union. In a spirit of mutual solidarity, the Member State concerned shall refrain from any action likely to conflict with or impede Union action based on that decision and the other Member States shall respect its position. If the members of the Council qualifying their abstention in this way represent at least one-third of the Member States comprising at least one-third of the population of the Union, the decision shall not be adopted.'

represent at least one-third of the Member States comprising at least one-third of the population of the Union. However, these limits could well be increased, for example, to a majority in both cases. Another exception should in any case be that such a mechanism would not be applicable to decisions in the area of the internal market or in areas in which the Union has an exclusive competence (see TFEU, Article 3).

Any revision of the Treaties requires the common agreement of all EU states. A number of people have criticized this rule and propose to amend it, which itself would legally require a revision of the treaties as the rule is incorporated in them. At least twice in the past both the EP and the Commission have nevertheless proposed ideas that, according to them, would have allowed this rule to be by-passed.

According to these suggestions, treaty amendments could enter into force even if not ratified by all Member States:

- On 14 February 1984, the EP adopted a resolution concerning a draft treaty establishing the EU (ECOJ, No. C 77, 19 March 1984). Article 82 of the draft treaty (known as the 'Spinelli draft') provided that:

  This Treaty shall be open for ratification by all the Member States of the European Communities. Once this Treaty has been ratified by a majority of the Member States of the Communities whose population represents two-thirds of the total population of the Communities, the governments of the Member States which have ratified shall meet at once to decide by common accord on the procedures by and the date on which this Treaty shall enter into force.

- On 4 December 2002, the text 'Penelope – Preliminary Draft of the Constitution of the European Union' was drafted and published on the initiative of the Commission by the Commission's services.[5] The text of the 'Draft Constitution' was accompanied by a separate Agreement on its entry into force 'in order to propose a solution to the problem – almost inextricable in law – of the situation which arises if a State refuses to ratify the new Treaty'. The solution proposed was the following (Articles 3 and 5 of the Agreement):

[5] Available at: http://europa.eu.int/futurum/comm/const051202.

Article 3: Before the date of entry into force of the Treaty on the Constitution, each Member State shall make a solemn declaration confirming the resolve of its people to continue to belong to the European Union. A Member State which is not in a position to make that solemn declaration shall leave the European Union on the date of entry into force of the Treaty on the Constitution. Relations between the Union and the Member State leaving it shall be governed by the agreement which will be concluded between them in accordance with Article 4.

Article 5: The Treaty on the Constitution shall enter into force on 1 January of the year following that in which this Agreement enters into force, provided that three-quarters of the Member States have made the solemn declaration referred to in Article 3.

- The special Agreement was to be subject to a different ratification procedure than the Treaty on the Constitution. It was supposed to enter into force even if not all Member States had ratified it, provided that at least five-sixths of the Member States did so.

It is obvious, however, that adopting amendments to the Treaties in such a way will never be accepted: revising the Constitutional Charter without the unanimous agreement of the constituent parts of an entity is the mark of a federation. The EU is not a federation. There is no government or parliament of the twenty-seven EU Member States that would accept such a rule, which obviously might jeopardize their vital interests. Imagine a majority of Member States wishing to give new powers to the EU in the area of defence, whereas some EU states are neutral, or to decide that the Schengen rules would be obligatory for all Member States, or that penal law would become an exclusive competence of the EU, etc. Such new treaty provisions could not be imposed on unwilling Member States. The option of having new treaty provisions applying to some Member States only, with the others continuing to apply the former treaty provisions, would be legally dubious, and in any case would not be acceptable by Member States. It is therefore clear that common agreement will, in the future, remain the rule for agreement on a revision of the Treaties.

Thus, at least at the time of writing, a substantive revision of the EU treaties looks politically implausible. There is a consensus among Member States not to launch a new saga that could become as painful and as risky as the one that was initiated by the 2001

Laeken Declaration and completed by the entry into force of the Lisbon Treaty in December 2009. It remains to be seen whether the realization of 'small' revisions of the treaties ('Irish guarantees', the Czech Protocol on the Charter, the composition of the Commission, the Franco-German request on EMU)[6] will give rise to a wider discussion on other possible revisions.

But would it be possible for the EU to try and continue to work on the basis of its current treaties? After all, these treaties, as will be shown in Chapter 4, allow for a number of possible differentiations between Member States.

[6] See Introduction, fn. 23.

Second option: continuing on the present path while developing further closer cooperation

In order to attain the objectives set out in the treaties, the EU institutions impose obligations on Member States on the basis of the competences that have been conferred on the EU. In areas where no such obligations are imposed, either because the EU does not have any power or because its institutions have decided not to use it, the Member States remain free to act and take decisions. In such a case, they might do this on their own or, if they so wish, in cooperation with other states that may also be EU members. Such a 'closer' cooperation is legally possible. It allows those Member States that want to cooperate together to progress on some issues or to develop some policies, whereas other EU Member States do not participate.

A number of Member States do practise closer cooperation in economic, industrial, military, cultural or other fields *outside* the EU institutional framework. The EU treaties do not forbid this so long as EU law is respected.

THE EU IS ALREADY WORKING IN A MULTI-SPEED WAY

Closer cooperation may also take place *within* the EU institutional framework, using the EU institutions and procedures, when the EU treaties explicitly provide for this possibility. In certain fields, the treaties themselves contain the rules and procedures organizing closer cooperation among some Member States (these cases are sometimes called 'in-built' cases of closer cooperation). In other fields, they provide the possibility for a group of Member States willing to do so to request an authorization to exercise closer cooperation on a case-by-case basis under certain conditions (this is called 'enhanced' cooperation). In specific cases, the treaties also allow one or several

Member States not to participate in a policy pursued within the EU framework (these cases are called 'opt-outs'). Opt-outs may be seen as a particular kind of enhanced cooperation, as they actually allow closer cooperation among Member States that are not opting out; however, in that case, all decisions taken legally are EU decisions and they become part of the *acquis* of the EU. Such an *acquis* will be binding on future Member States, whereas this is not the case for decisions taken in the framework of 'enhanced' cooperation.

Therefore, the reality is that the EU is already working at two speeds in some fields, in particular, in the two important fields of border controls ('Schengen') and of monetary policy (the euro), and at several speeds in other fields. This has allowed the EU to develop in a flexible way, taking into account the degree of economic development, the specific needs or the political wishes of its Member States.

Since this is already the case, one may wonder why talking about a 'two-speed Europe' is sometimes considered as provocative.

The main reason why using these words raises controversy is that they are not precise enough, and that consequently they are interpreted in different ways. In principle, they describe the different kinds of closer cooperation among some Member States as mentioned above. However, taken literally, a 'two-speed Europe', as opposed to a 'multi-speed' one (which better describes the reality of the EU today),[1] is to be interpreted as describing the same group of specific Member States cooperating together in all kinds of areas and policies

---

[1] A two-speed system exists for the euro as seventeen Member States are 'in' and ten are 'out', but the Schengen area is a different grouping (twenty-two EU Member States are 'in' and five are 'out'). Moreover, the United Kingdom, Denmark and Ireland have specific opt-outs as far as the area of freedom, security and justice is concerned, Denmark does not participate in activities having defence implications, etc. Countries not participating in this or that policy do not necessarily constitute 'a group', because they do not share the same concerns. The EU is not divided into two groups, but into several groupings of countries, which are different according to the areas concerned. Therefore, this situation might be described as 'a multi-speed Europe'. Alexander Stubb has defined this concept as 'the mode of differentiated integration according to which the pursuit of common objectives is driven by a core group of Member States which are both able and willing to pursue some policy areas further, the underlying assumption being that the others will follow later. In other words, the multi-speed approach signifies integration in which Member countries maintain the same policies and actions, not simultaneously, but at different times. The vision is positive in that, although admitting differences, the Member States maintain the same objectives which will be reached by all members in due time' ('A Categorization of Differentiated Integration', *Journal of Common Market Studies*, 34(2) (June 1996), 283–95 at 287.

('two-speed'), as opposed to different groupings of states cooperating in this or that specific area or policy ('multi-speed'). It is why there has been no actual 'two-speed' EU functioning up to now, because the members of the euro area are not the same as the members of the Schengen area. Moreover, the non-participating members do not constitute a 'group'.

The fears – or the suspicions – come from two quarters: a number of the less populated or less economically developed Member States, on the one side (not only among those that became members of the EU in 2004 and 2007, but also including, for example, Ireland and Portugal), and the United Kingdom and Poland, on the other side, and for other reasons. For the smaller Member States, as the number 'two' is used to qualify the number of 'speeds', this is interpreted as referring to a 'two-class Europe', some states travelling in the 'first class' and others in the 'second class', whereas everybody wants to travel in the best class. The fear of these Member States is both of being left behind, with less incentive to improve their own governance, and that the larger Member States could become 'more equal than the others' and impose their decisions on the others. As for the United Kingdom, this corresponds to the historic fear of being faced with an alliance between the two big continental powers, France and Germany. Poland probably shares the fears both of some smaller or less developed Member States and of the United Kingdom.

This is the basic reason why defiance, or even in some cases hostility, has always existed against any form of closer cooperation. This also explains why it has taken a long time for 'enhanced cooperation' to be enshrined in the treaties as a possibility to be developed within the EU institutional framework. This is also why, even after this recognition took place in 1999 with the entry into force of the Amsterdam Treaty, the procedure was used for the first time only at the end of 2010.

However, while the necessity of closer cooperation was less obvious for an Economic European Community composed of just six Member States with a rather homogeneous degree of economic and social development, this necessity looked more and more imperative when they admitted more Member States, with different economic needs and political aspirations.

Closer cooperation began with the 1957 Treaty of Rome

Even at the time of the signature of the Treaty of Rome establishing the EEC in 1957, when the Community was composed of a small number of states presenting significant similarities, economically, socially and politically, it was already admitted that, beyond their treaty obligations, some Member States, if they wished to do so, could cooperate in order to proceed faster than the others.

Thus, the aim of Article 233 of the EEC Treaty, successively renumbered, first as Article 306 of the EC Treaty,[2] now as Article 350 of the TFEU,[3] and which has kept the same wording since 1957, is to recall that cooperation among the Benelux countries may continue to exist and to develop:

The provisions of the Treaties shall not preclude the existence or completion of regional unions between Belgium and Luxembourg, or between Belgium, Luxembourg and the Netherlands, to the extent that the objectives of these regional unions are not attained by application of the Treaties.

Another example is the continued existence of the Nordic Council, which was established in 1952 to promote regional, economic and political cooperation between Denmark, Finland, Iceland, Norway and Sweden and which survived the accession of Denmark, and then of Finland and Sweden to the EU.[4]

Both the Benelux and the Nordic Council are regional organizations aiming at general cooperation between their members, but covering very different fields.

The 1957 Treaty of Rome also contained a number of provisions that provided differentiation among Member States, either by limiting the territorial scope of application of the treaty (overseas territories, etc.), by authorizing specific derogations (intra-German trade, the importation of bananas into Germany, safeguard clauses), or by requesting that the Commission should take into account the differences between the economic development of Member States when making proposals to establish the internal market. The treaties of

---

[2] Treaty establishing the European Community.
[3] Treaty on the Functioning of the European Union.
[4] See Declaration on Nordic Cooperation in the Act of Accession of Austria, Finland and Sweden to the EU, 1994, OJ C 241/392.

accession always contain some (in principle temporary) derogations for acceding states. In certain cases, these are quite long periods of transition (Spain for fisheries, Eastern and Central European Member States for freedom of movement of workers, etc.).

Speaking in general terms, there are obviously matters for which the treaties do not confer any competence on the EU. These matters therefore continue to be covered by the exclusive competences of the Member States. There are also matters for which the EU has potential powers, which its institutions have yet to decide to exercise or which they decided to exercise only in a partial manner. In all these cases, it remains legally possible for Member States to act, either through the adoption of national legislation or through the conclusion of international agreements, possibly with other EU Member States. These different cases can legally be described as 'external' cooperation between some Member States, that is, without making use of the EU institutions.

If and when some Member States wish to cooperate while making use of the EU institutions and procedures, they need the authorization of the other Member States, because EU institutions are 'common property'. In that case, one may speak about an 'internal' cooperation between Member States. Such authorization has sometimes been anticipated in the EU treaties.

Some observers tend to mix together these two kinds of cooperation, but they are legally different.

Therefore, one has to be careful in the use of the multiple expressions describing the political phenomenon of 'a Europe working at different speeds'. The vocabulary is very rich[5] but not very precise.[6] Some authors have helped to distinguish the different concepts:

---

[5] Alexander Stubb, in 'A Categorization of Differentiated Integration', made the following amazing enumeration: 'Two-speed, multi-speed, step-by-step, strengthened solidarity, graduated integration, hard core, variable integration, concentric circles, two-tier, multi-tier, multi-track, two-track, "swing wing", circles of solidarity, variable speed, imperial circles, pick-and-choose, overlapping circles, structural variability, opt-in, opt-out, opt-up, opt-down, bits-and-pieces, *ad libitum* integration, multi-level, two-level, restrained differentiation, flying geese, magnetic fields, hub-and-spoke and many circles, are a few examples of the rhetoric in English.'

[6] Eberhard Grabitz and Bernd Langeheine, 'Legal Problems Related to a Proposed "Two-Tier System" of Integration within the European Community', *Common Market Law Review* (1981), 33–48.

Charlemagne[7] and Justus Lipsius[8] did so, as, in a more developed and scientific manner, did Claus-Dieter Ehlermann[9] and Alexander Stubb.[10]

The Two Concepts of a 'Multi-Speed Europe'

At the price of some simplification, the different formulations of a 'multi-speed Europe' may be grouped into two broad concepts. In all cases, the principle is that, in a multi-speed Europe, the Member States would do the same things, but not necessarily at the same time or at the same pace. Therefore, this does not include the 'à la carte Europe' in which each Member State would retain a permanent and complete freedom of choice on whether or not to take part in the policies proposed.

The first concept is known under different formulations: it might be called a 'hard core group', a 'pioneer group', an 'avant-garde', a 'centre of gravity' or a 'two-speed Europe'

Under this approach, the intention is that all Member States will eventually take part in all the policies, but the calendar for doing so may vary in order to accommodate differences in political will or in economic development. The terminology aims at describing a group of EU Member States that decide, on the basis either of a political or of a legal agreement, to cooperate more closely in different areas in order to proceed faster than the other EU Member States. They would, of course, continue to be members of the EU and be obliged to fully respect their treaty obligations vis-à-vis the EU, its institutions and the other Member States, including the *acquis communautaire*. Despite having been predicted several times, such closer cooperation has never materialized. One of the difficult

---

[7] Charlemagne, 'L'équilibre entre les Etats Membres', *L'équilibre européen – Etudes rassemblées et publiées en hommage à Niels Ersbøll* (Secrétaire général du Conseil de l'Union européenne, 1994).

[8] Justus Lipsius, 'The 1996 IGC', *European Law Review*, 20(3) (1995), 235–67.

[9] Claus-Dieter Ehlermann, 'Differentiation, Flexibility, Closer Cooperation: the New Provisions of the Amsterdam Treaty', *European Law Journal*, 4(3), (September 1998), 246–70.

[10] Alexander Stubb, 'The Semantic Indigestion of Differentiated Integration', College of Europe, Bruges, 1995; 'Flexible Integration and the Amsterdam Treaty: Negotiating Differentiation in the 1996–1997 IGC', PhD thesis, London School of Economics, London, 1998.

questions it raises is whether the group would have to establish its own organs or if it could use the EU institutions, and, in either case, how this could be legally and politically achieved. Another difficulty would be the question as to what would be the actual areas to which closer cooperation would apply.

This first concept has been suggested by a number of politicians, mostly French and German, sometimes Italian or Belgian.

The first time the concept was mentioned was as early as 1974, when the European Community was composed of only nine Member States. This was in a speech given in November 1974 by Willy Brandt (Chancellor of Germany from October 1969 to May 1974) shortly after the end of his term as Chancellor.[11] The idea of having two or several speeds for the EC was formally presented in the 'Leo Tindemans Report' in 1975. Leo Tindemans was at that time Prime Minister of Belgium and had been asked by his eight colleagues at the Paris Summit of December 1974 to write a 'Report on the European Union', which was published on 19 December 1975.[12] The report was presented to the European Council in Luxembourg in April 1976. It presented the possibility of having a 'two-speed Europe', in terms which are so clear that they still deserve to be quoted today:

It is impossible at the present time to submit a credible programme of action if it is deemed absolutely necessary that in every case all stages should be reached by all the States at the same time. The divergence of their economic and financial situations is such that, were we to insist on this progress would be impossible and Europe would continue to crumble away. It must be possible to allow that:
- within the Community framework of an overall concept of European Union as defined in this report and accepted by the Nine,
- and on the basis of an action programme drawn up in a field decided upon by the common institutions, whose principles are accepted by all,
  (1) those States which are able to progress have a duty to forge ahead,
  (2) those States which have reasons for not progressing which the Council, on a proposal from the Commission, acknowledges as valid do not do so,
    – but will at the same time receive from the other States any aid and assistance that can be given them to enable them to catch the others up,

[11] Speech given on 19 November 1974 in Paris (see Europa-Archiv, 1975).
[12] This Report was published in the *Bulletin of the Commission*, No. 1, 1976.

  – and will take part, within the joint institutions, in assessing the
  results obtained in the field in question.

This does not mean Europe à la carte: each country will be bound by the
agreement of all as to the final objective to be achieved in common; it is
only the timescales for achievement which vary.

This system which accepts that there should temporarily be a greater
degree of integration between certain members is not without analogy in the
Community: Article 233 of the Treaty of Rome specifically provides for it in
the case of the Benelux countries and the Belgium–Luxembourg Economic
Union. The system could, as matters turn out, be of great assistance in
enabling the process of development of the Union to regain its momentum,
albeit imperfectly.

These ideas were not implemented.

In the 1990s, the idea reappeared in a forceful document published
in Germany by Karl Lamers and Wolfgang Schäuble.[13] A few years
later, in 2000, Joschka Fischer made his famous speech, 'From Confederation to Federation, Thoughts on the finality of the European
Integration' with the idea of a 'centre of gravity'.[14] The idea was also
referred to several times in France, both on the right of the political
spectrum by Edouard Balladur[15] and Jacques Chirac,[16] with the idea
of a 'pioneer group',[17] and on the left by Jean-Noël Jeanneney, Pascal

[13] *Reflections on European Policy – The Future Course of European Integration*, 1994, documents
of CDU – Bundesgeschäftsstelle. This gave rise to political disputes, as it was suggested that
the core group could be constituted only by five Member States, i.e., Benelux, France and
Germany, therefore even 'excluding' one of the six founding countries, Italy.

[14] 12 May 2000, at Humboldt University, Berlin, text available at: www.auswaertiges_amt.de.

[15] 1994, 'The Three Concentric Circles'. See the interview of the former French Prime Minister,
Edouard Balladur, in *Le Figaro*, 30 August 1994: 'l'Europe se diviserait en trois cercles concen-
triques. Le premier cercle comprendrait les pays ayant décidé d'avancer vers leur intégration
politique par coopération renforcée ou par un traité sur une Union politique européenne.
Le deuxième cercle comprendrait tous les pays du premier cercle et les autres pays de l'UE
actuelle, c'est-à-dire les pays qui voudraient poursuivre leur intégration économique dans
le cadre du traité UE, mais ne souhaiteraient pas participer à une intégration politique plus
poussée. Le troisième cercle comprendrait les pays des deux premiers cercles et les pays
européens qui voudraient rester en dehors du processus d'intégration tant économique que
politique et avoir seulement une coopération intergouvernementale avec les pays de l'UE.'
See also interview in *Le Monde*, 30 November 1994.

[16] 27 June 2000, speech at the Bundestag, and 13 December 2003, declaration in Brussels.

[17] See text of the 2000 speech, available at: www.elysee.fr/rech_htm, in particular: 'I would
like the pioneer group to be able to get to work on more effective coordination of economic policies, a strengthening of defence and security policy and increased effectiveness in
combating crime.' In 2003, President Chirac declared: 'I continue to think that it is a good
solution because it will provide an engine, an example. I think that it will allow Europe to

Lamy, Henri Nallet and Dominique Strauss-Kahn,[18] and by Jacques Delors in 1999[19] and 2000.[20]

On the opposite side, the concept of a 'two-speed Europe' has always been fiercely opposed by British commentators and journalists: see, for example, Charles Grant, director of the Centre for European Reform, in August 2001,[21] Heather Grabbe, also from the CER, in 2003[22] and Tony Barber in the *Financial Times* in 2009.[23] Actually, the concept is considered with even more alarm and hostility by British politicians than by British observers and journalists. This was the case, for example, when the UK's then Prime Minister, Tony Blair, decided in 2000 'to warn' (his German colleague Gerhard Schroeder) 'that the United Kingdom will not accept a two-speed Europe'.[24] Before him, his predecessor, John Major, expressed the same view in a speech made at Leyden University in 1994: 'I see a real danger in talk of "hard core" inner and outer circles, a two-tier Europe.'[25] The Government of Poland[26] and the authorities of Ireland and of Portugal have also expressed their reluctance over ideas going in the

move faster, further, and to work better, but I recognize that we have to be careful to avoid any segregation. We must not designate second-class countries.'

[18] 20 June 2001, *Le Monde*.

[19] 16 June 1999, hearing in the French Senate: Délégation du Sénat pour l'UE, Audition de Monsieur Jacques Delors sur la réforme des institutions européennes: 'Je crois nécessaire une initiative franco-allemande autour d'un projet. Les Etats intéressés pourraient la rejoindre. Elle prendrait la forme d'un traité particulier compatible avec les Traités européens. On peut imaginer divers domaines où cette formule pourrait s'appliquer: le rapprochement des fiscalités, la défense, l'énergie . . .'

[20] 'Europe needs an avant-garde, but . . .', *Centre for European Reform Bulletin*, No. 14, October/November 2000.

[21] 'France, Germany and a "Hard-Core" Europe', *Centre for European Reform Bulletin*, No. 19, 2001.

[22] 'The Siren Song of a Two-speed Europe', Centre for European Reform, 16 December 2003.

[23] 'Two-speed Europe is the Dog that doesn't Bark', *Financial Times*, 1 October 2009.

[24] Tony Blair, BBC News, 29 June 2000.

[25] Once again, one should stress that this is a mistake (voluntary or not): a 'two-speed Europe' is not the same as a 'two-tier Europe'. The former is temporary, all EU members being expected to go in the same direction and therefore being separated only for a given period, while the 'two-tier' or 'two-class Europe' gives the idea of a permanent division of Europe into two different groups of Member States.

[26] See Tony Barber: 'Poland expressed concern that efforts to improve the eurozone's economic governance should not turn non-euro area countries into second-class members of the EU', *Financial Times*, 9 June 2010. See also Gazeta Wyborcza, Warsaw, 17 June 2010, Thomas Bielicki, 'Poland and other "new" Member States of the EU will have to fight to avoid being consigned to a future second division' (one could make the same observation as the one made in the preceding footnote).

direction of a 'two-class' Europe, while not expressing themselves clearly on the idea of a temporary 'two-speed' Europe.

Some in the United Kingdom would rather favour an 'à la carte' concept,[27] in which, apart from a minimum of common policies (common trade policy, internal market, etc.), participation in other policies would remain optional on the basis of a unilateral decision of each Member State taken at its own discretion. This concept has been suggested by two former British prime ministers.[28] It will not be examined in this book as it appears to go in a direction that is opposed to the very basic principles on which the EU is built.

The second concept is also known by different expressions – 'flexibility', 'differentiation', 'variable geometry', 'voluntary cooperation' – and it has had the official description of 'enhanced cooperation' since its introduction into the EU treaties by the Treaty of Amsterdam

This concept differs substantially from the first one, because it does not imply a fixed composition of a group of Member States all cooperating together on different issues and matters.[29] It may be cooperation on a case-by-case basis, with different participants in each case. Therefore, it would lead to a 'multi-speed Europe'. This may happen on the basis of the rules provided in the treaties for enhanced cooperation, with some Member States making use of the EU institutions in order to adopt and implement legislation in a given area, while other Member States do not wish to participate. This may also happen outside the EU framework, without using its institutions.

THE PRESENT TREATIES AUTHORIZE SOME MEMBER STATES TO COOPERATE MORE INTENSIVELY IN SOME AREAS OR NOT TO PARTICIPATE IN IMPORTANT EU POLICIES

The present EU treaties contain:
- first, provisions establishing different cases of 'in-built' cooperation, meaning that it has already been decided in the treaty itself that

---

[27] Which, to complicate things further, is sometimes called 'variable geometry' by its partisans (see Charles Grant, 'Variable Geometry', *Prospect Magazine*, July 2005).

[28] Lady Thatcher and John Major (see, e.g., the 7 September 1994 speech of John Major at Leyden University).

[29] As in the above-mentioned formula suggested in 1974 by Willy Brandt and in 1975 in the Tindemans Report.

such cooperation will actually take place. This is the case for the Schengen area and the euro area, as well as for permanent structured cooperation (PSC) in the field of defence; these provisions are therefore already actually being implemented (except for the PSC where this is not yet the case); different 'opt-outs' allowing some Member States not to participate in some policies are also foreseen in the treaties and are actually being implemented;

- second, general provisions on 'enhanced cooperation', which may be used to allow some Member States, using the EU institutional framework, to cooperate in cases where the other Member States do not wish to do so; therefore, the decision to cooperate remains to be taken on a case-by-case basis; these general provisions were inserted in the treaty in 1997, with the Amsterdam Treaty, but they were used for the first time only in late 2010;

- third, other provisions allowing for different possibilities of differentiation between the Member States.

The treaty provides for significant cases of so-called 'in-built' enhanced cooperation

The description of this closer cooperation as 'in-built' (or 'predefined') means that this mechanism and the arrangements for it have been established once and for all in the treaties themselves. Therefore, it is no longer necessary to permit it on a case-by-case basis. Both the Schengen area and the euro area have been conceived as beginning with the participation of some Member States, but aiming at covering all EU Member States in the future. Legally, decisions adopted in these areas are part of the 'EU *acquis*'. Member States acceding to the Schengen area or to the euro area in the future will therefore have to respect them.

The Schengen area

The so-called 'Schengen cooperation'[30] aims at totally removing the checks on persons at internal borders and relies on use of the

---

[30] Schengen Cooperation was established by two Agreements in 1985 and 1990, both signed in the small Luxembourg town of Schengen. The first Agreement was signed on 14 June 1985, and the second, an Implementing Agreement, on 19 June 1990. They were concluded by five EU Member States (Belgium, France, Germany, Luxembourg and the Netherlands) and entered into force among them (plus Portugal and Spain) in March 1995. The five

'Schengen Information System'. After having begun outside the treaties, on the basis of an international agreement concluded by a few Member States and without making use of the EU institutions, it was later integrated into the EU treaties. Today, twenty-two states out of the twenty-seven EU members participate fully in Schengen cooperation. Participation in the Schengen area is subject to the state concerned having successfully undergone an evaluation procedure, notably on the quality and level of controls at external borders. For a Member State to be accepted as a participant, it requires a Council decision taken unanimously by the members representing the Member States that are already members of the Schengen area. Bulgaria and Romania have not yet been authorized by the Council to participate fully.[31] Cyprus does not fully participate because of its particular situation. Ireland and the United Kingdom are not willing to participate (see Protocol No. 19 on the Schengen *acquis* integrated into the framework of the EU). The United Kingdom has always been hostile to abandoning full control of its borders; Ireland cannot dissociate itself from the United Kingdom, as there are no controls at the borders between the two countries. Moreover, some third states have concluded agreements with the EU that allow them to participate (Iceland, Norway, Switzerland and, since April 2011, Liechtenstein).

The Schengen system was incorporated into the EU treaties by the Amsterdam Treaty, signed in 1997 and entered into force in 1999.

The same process was followed for some other matters. Before being integrated into the treaties as one of the most important

original members of Schengen were joined, through the conclusion of accession protocols, by Italy (November 1990), Portugal and Spain (June 1991), Greece (November 1992), Austria (April 1995), and Denmark, Finland and Sweden (December 1996). In December 1996, an Agreement was signed with two non-EU States, Iceland and Norway, which allowed them to join the Schengen area with the other Nordic countries in order to preserve the Nordic Passport Union. Following the EU enlargements of 2004 and 2007, the Schengen area was extended to Estonia, Lithuania, Latvia, Poland, the Czech Republic, Slovakia, Hungary, Slovenia and Malta. Two non-EU states joined the Schengen area later, Switzerland (2008) and Liechtenstein (2011). Therefore, by 2011 the Schengen area covered twenty-six states, twenty-two EU members and four non-EU members. The United Kingdom and Ireland may ask to participate on a case-by-case basis in measures adopted in the framework of Schengen cooperation. The Council decides on their request with the unanimity of the members of the Schengen area (Article 4 of Protocol No. 19 on the Schengen *acquis* integrated into the framework of the EU).

[31] See Chris Bryant and Stanley Pignal, 'Bloc's Newcomers Smart over Schengen Delay', *Financial Times*, 22 January 2011.

policies of the EU, the issue of a 'European judicial area' began with informal and intergovernmental discussions among a group of Member States. This happened with the creation of an informal group called 'TREVI'[32] in Rome in December 1975, mainly to discuss combating terrorism and, later, organized crime. This was also the case with the 'Pompidou' group, informally established by seven EC states (Belgium, France, Germany, Italy, Luxembourg, the Netherlands and the United Kingdom) to share experience in combating drug abuse and drug trafficking. Then, the idea of establishing a body dealing at EU level with police was launched in 1991. This idea was retained in the 1993 Maastricht Treaty, which established Europol, initially to cover drug trafficking and organized crime.

The same thing also happened with the Convention of Prüm, signed in May 2005 by seven member states (Austria, Belgium, France, Germany, Luxembourg, the Netherlands and Spain), on the exchange of police data such as DNA profiles, fingerprints and vehicle number plates,[33] and with the decision by four Member States (Belgium, France, Germany and Spain) to interconnect their criminal records as from 31 March 2006.[34] Both 'closer cooperations' began with only a few participating Member States. Both were later integrated into EU law.

This therefore proves that the development of some policies may begin with a group of Member States and later be enlarged to all Member States of the EU, when experience has demonstrated that it is useful and it is working. It is probably better to proceed this way, rather than trying immediately to adopt uniform legislation for all twenty-seven Member States, which turns out later to be very difficult to implement in the same way in all EU Member States.[35]

---

[32] 'TREVI' was both a French acronym for terrorism, radicalism, extremism and international violence and a reminder of its Roman birth-place (Fontana di Trevi).

[33] The Prüm Convention which strengthened cross-border police cooperation, particularly in combating terrorism and cross-border crimes, has been replaced by two 2008 Council Decisions (2008/615/JHA and 2008/616/JHA).

[34] This was taken over by the EU Framework Decision on the organization and content of the exchange between Member States of information extracted from criminal records, 26 February 2009 (2009/315/JHA) and the Decision of 6 April 2009 setting up the corresponding information technology system ECRIS (2009/316/JHA).

[35] The EU Council Framework Decision (2002/584/JHA) of 13 June 2002 on the European Arrest Warrant (OJ L 190 18 July 2002) could be quoted as an example, because

The euro area

As far as the euro is concerned, the point of departure was the opposite situation. The euro was conceived from the outset as becoming the currency of all EU Member States. In principle, all EU Member States must have the euro as their currency as soon as they fulfil all the conditions required by the treaty.[36] The other Member States are described in the treaty as 'Member States with a derogation' (see TFEU, Article 139(1)). This derogation is meant to be temporary. However, both Denmark (Protocol No. 16 on certain provisions relating to Denmark) and the United Kingdom (Protocol No. 15 on certain provisions relating to the United Kingdom) have been given, at their request, a permanent derogation. Denmark has announced its intention to proceed with the termination of its opt-out in the future; this would require a referendum in that country. Of the other twenty-five Member States, eight still have a derogation at the date of writing.[37] After a 'No' vote in a referendum on this issue, Sweden is voluntarily staying out.

The TFEU contains provisions that allow members of the euro area wide-ranging possibilities to develop policies and actions in the areas of budgetary and economic policies (Article 136), as well as to have a unified representation and to express common positions at international institutions and conferences (Article 138). The decisions taken are EU decisions and part of the *acquis*, even though they are adopted by, and obligatory for, only seventeen states out of the twenty-seven.

---

its implementation was confronted with many difficulties. This Decision aims at simplifying and expediting the proceedings and facilitating the enforcement of criminal convictions against a person in the territory of another EU Member State. The European Arrest Warrant has replaced formal extradition processes between the twenty-seven EU Member States. The 2002 Framework Decision has been amended by another Framework Decision (2009/299/JHA) adopted on 26 February 2009 (OJ L 81 March 27, 2009).

[36] Participation in the euro area is subject to fulfilling a number of conditions, including the independence of national central banks and the 'convergence criteria' relating to a high degree of price stability, a low budgetary deficit and the durability of limited fluctuation margins within the exchange rate mechanism (see in particular Article 140(1) of the TFEU and Protocol No. 13 on the convergence criteria).

[37] The seventeen Member States that have the euro as their currency are: Austria, Belgium, Cyprus, Finland, France, Germany, Greece, Ireland, Italy, Luxembourg, Malta, the Netherlands, Portugal, Slovakia, Slovenia, Spain, and, since 1 January 2011, Estonia.

Permanent structured cooperation in the field of defence

The Lisbon Treaty adds a new case of 'inbuilt enhanced cooperation', that is, 'permanent structured cooperation' in the field of defence (TEU, Articles 42(6) and 46). This cooperation is open to Member States 'whose military capabilities fulfil higher criteria and which have made more binding commitments to one another in this area with a view to the most demanding missions . . .' The criteria concerning military capabilities to be fulfilled are set out in Protocol No. 10 on permanent structured cooperation. The Council will decide on the establishment of such cooperation by QMV, while to launch enhanced cooperation in the other fields of CFSP requires unanimity. At the date of writing, the 'permanent structured cooperation' has not yet been launched. At an informal meeting in Bruges (Belgium) during the second semester of 2010, the ministers of defence of the twenty-seven Member States agreed not to proceed with launching it for the time being.

The treaties also allow some Member States to 'opt out' from some EU policies

The treaties provide other kinds of 'flexibilities', which have been added to them through Protocols in order to accommodate specific economic or legal difficulties (or political preferences) of this or that Member State, often by giving a state the right to 'opt out' from a given policy. This is the reason why some Member States, often the United Kingdom and Denmark ('the opt-out champions'),[38] do not participate in some of the most important EU common policies:

- Denmark (Protocol No. 22 on the position of Denmark), as well as Ireland and the United Kingdom (Protocol No. 21 on the position of the United Kingdom and Ireland), have specific positions regarding the area of freedom, security and justice, permitting them not to participate in a number of policies developed by the EU in this area. With the Treaty of Lisbon, the non-participation (opt-out)

---

[38] Formula borrowed from Rebecca Adler-Nissen, 'Behind the Scenes of Differentiated Integration: Circumventing National Opt-outs in Justice and Home Affairs', *Journal of European Public Policy*, 16(1) (January 2009), 62–80.

of Denmark now not only concerns judicial cooperation in civil matters, as was the case before, but also judicial cooperation in criminal matters and police cooperation.[39]

- It is also the case for the free movement of persons (TFEU, Article 26) and border checks (TFEU, Article 77) for Ireland and the United Kingdom (Protocol No. 20 on the application of certain aspects of Article 26 of the TFEU to the United Kingdom and Ireland).

- Denmark does not participate in the European Policy on Defence and Security (ESDP): see Article 5, subparagraph 1, Protocol No. 22 on the position of Denmark.

- Sweden has a derogation for the consumption of 'Snus' (a kind of chewing tobacco).[40]

- One may also add that, at the end of the negotiation of the Lisbon Treaty, the United Kingdom and Poland obtained a Protocol (No. 30) on the EU Charter of Fundamental Rights. This Protocol aims at 'clarifying the application of the Charter in relation to the laws and administrative action of Poland and of the United Kingdom and of its justiciability within Poland and within the United Kingdom'. It has been seen and called by many as an opt-out from the Charter. However, it will probably not have this effect.[41]

---

[39] See Jeannine Dennewald, 'The European Judicial Area after the Lisbon Treaty: State of Play and Perspectives of the Differentiated Integration' (text in French, abstract in English), *ERA Forum*, 11 (2010), 169–96.

[40] In its Accession Treaty of 1994, Sweden was permanently authorized to continue the consumption on its territory of 'snus' (snuff), despite it being illegal in the rest of the EU. The Swedish authorities considered it difficult to go to a referendum on the Accession Treaty without such a permanent derogation, due to the fact that around 10 per cent of the 8 million voters were 'snus' users. Another example of a permanent derogation is the prohibition on non-nationals (i.e. non-Danes) buying second homes in Denmark (Protocol No. 32 on the acquisition of property in Denmark added by the Maastricht Treaty). A third example is the special status agreed for the Åaland Islands on certain issues in the Accession Treaty of Finland in 1994. A fourth example is Protocol No. 35 on Article 40.3.3 of the Constitution of Ireland (which concerns the prohibition against abortion in Ireland). On these 'special cases', see comments by Deirdre Curtin, 'The Constitutional Structure of the Union: a Europe of Bits and Pieces', *Common Market Law Review*, 30 (1993), 17–69. See also Hervé Bribosia, 'Différenciation et avant-gardes au sein de l'UE, Bilan et perspectives du Traité d'Amsterdam', *Cahiers de droit européen*, 36(1/2) (2000), 57–115.

[41] See Piris, *The Lisbon Treaty*, pp. 160–3. See also the Report of the UK House of Lords (EU Committee) published 13 March 2008, vol. I, p. 102, paragraph 5.87: 'The Protocol is not an opt-out from the Charter. The Charter will apply in the UK, even if its interpretation may be affected by the terms of the Protocol.'

- In the field of the Common Foreign Security Policy, including the Common Security and Defence Policy (CFSP and CSDP), although the unanimity rule is the normal way to decide in the Council, there is always the possibility of the representative of any Member State making a so-called 'constructive abstention' (TEU, Article 31(1)). This is the possibility for a Member of the Council, when abstaining in a vote, to qualify his or her abstention by making a 'formal declaration'. This will result in the Member State in question not being obliged to apply the decision, although the decision will nevertheless be taken on behalf of the EU and commit the EU as such. If such 'constructive abstentions' represent at least one-third of the Member States comprising at least one-third of the EU's population, the decision cannot be adopted. At the date of writing, the constructive abstention has been used only once.[42]

As a result of the above observations, at least for Denmark and the United Kingdom, while they are full EU Member States, they are certainly not travelling at the same speed as the others in some areas.

THE TREATY CONTAINS GENERAL RULES ('ENABLING CLAUSES') DESIGNED TO ALLOW 'ENHANCED COOPERATION' TO BE APPLIED ON A CASE-BY-CASE BASIS AT THE REQUEST OF MEMBER STATES WHO ARE WILLING TO COOPERATE

The treaties, since their modification by the Amsterdam Treaty in 1999,[43] provide for rules designed to allow some Member States, using the EU framework and institutions, to cooperate further in cases where the other Member States do not wish to participate. This was done in order to take into account the fact that an EU of fifteen Member States could not always find a way to progress which would be acceptable to all of them, given the growing heterogeneity of economic and social interests, as well as the growing diversity of political

---

[42] By Cyprus, on the occasion of the adoption of Council Joint Action 2008/124/CFSP on the European Union Rule of Law Mission in Kosovo (EULEX Kosovo).

[43] The idea was initially suggested by Chancellor Helmut Kohl of Germany and President Jacques Chirac of France by a joint letter of 6 December 1995, followed by a joint letter of the foreign ministers of both countries, Kinkel and de Charette, on 17 October 1996.

preferences. These so-called 'flexibility' provisions represented one of the main features of the Amsterdam Treaty. However, this procedure was not used for many years, not until the end of 2010 in fact.[44] This was perhaps due to the strict conditions attached to launching it, which at that time raised doubts about the concrete possibility of doing so.[45] Actually, it was also due to political reasons, reflecting the desire of many Member States to avoid the establishment of a 'two-speed Europe', because they feared that this could one day be transformed into a 'two-class Europe', in which they might find themselves in the 'second class' and not the 'first class'.

Since the Amsterdam Treaty provisions were considered to be too restrictive, their amendment was considered, at least by some Member States, to be one of the priorities of the Intergovernmental Conference (IGC) which negotiated the Nice Treaty. As a result, the Nice Treaty made the procedure less cumbersome on a number of points:[46]

- The number of Member States necessary to initiate a case of enhanced cooperation was reduced from 'a majority' to the fixed figure of eight; in practice this did not change anything at that time as the EU comprised fifteen members in 2000, but it was a good signal for the future as this figure of eight was supposed to remain unchanged after the future enlargement of the EU, which was already envisaged at that time.
- The provision allowing for a request for enhanced cooperation to be blocked by a veto in the European Council was deleted, thus making it possible to launch a case of enhanced cooperation by QMV in the Council.
- The conditions to be respected were formulated in a somewhat less rigid and restrictive way, though remaining quite strict in substance: for instance, any case of enhanced cooperation must not 'undermine the internal market'.
- Enhanced cooperation remained impossible in defence matters.

---

[44] In two cases: the Directive on the law applicable to divorce and the proposal to create a European Patent.

[45] See Jean-Claude Piris and Giorgio Maganza, 'The Amsterdam Treaty: Overview and Institutional Aspects', *Fordham International Law Journal*, 22 (1999), esp. p. 546.

[46] Hervé Bribosia, 'Les Coopérations renforcées au lendemain du Traité de Nice', *Revue du droit de l'UE*, 1 (2001), 111–71.

It is to be stressed that, even after the entry into force of the Treaty of Nice in 2003, providing for the possibility of cases of enhanced cooperation with eight Member States only, the rule remained that all members of the European Parliament and all members of the Commission would continue to participate in the decision-making process in these cases, whatever their nationality and whatever the number of Member States involved.

This rule has also remained unchanged after the entry into force of the Lisbon Treaty in 2009. That treaty regroups the four sets of rules on enhanced cooperation of the past treaties (due to the structure in 'pillars')[47] into two sets of rules, the first one set out in the TEU for general governing principles (Article 20) and the second one in the TFEU for the specific arrangements (Articles 326–334). Some modifications have been made to the procedure:

- the whole area of CFSP, including defence, is now open to possible cases of enhanced cooperation;
- it is no longer possible to launch a so-called 'emergency brake' procedure, which allowed a Member of the Council to request that the issue of the authorization to be given to a specific case of enhanced cooperation be referred to the European Council in order to try and block it;
- a new and important 'passerelle' (TFEU, Article 333) will allow participants in a specific case of enhanced cooperation to decide unanimously in the Council that, within the framework of the development of their cooperation, the Council will be able to decide by QMV instead of unanimity (although this will not be possible for decisions having military or defence implications); they will also be able to decide to switch from a special legislative procedure to the ordinary legislative procedure (i.e., the Council in co-decision with the European Parliament);
- the procedure might be 'accelerated' in some cases, with regard to the approximation of certain aspects of criminal procedure (TFEU, Article 82(3)), the approximation of criminal offences and sanctions in certain areas of criminal law (TFEU, Article 83(3)), the establishment of the European Public Prosecutor's office (TFEU, Article

[47] Articles 27A–27E former TEU (CFSP), 40 and 40A former TEU (JHA), 43–45 former TEU (General rules), and 11 and 11A TEC (first pillar).

86(1)), and the adoption of measures concerning operational cooperation between authorities of police, customs and other specialized
law enforcement services in relation to the prevention, detection
and investigation of criminal offences (TFEU, Article 87(3)). This
means that in a case where one or several Member States prevent
the adoption of proposed measures, and if at least nine Member States wish to go ahead, the authorization to proceed will
immediately be deemed to have been granted and the provisions
on enhanced cooperation will automatically apply (see Box 2.1 in
Chapter 2).

However, the possible effect of these improvements will be somewhat
reduced by other new provisions providing for:

- a slight increase (from eight to nine) in the minimum number of
  participants necessary to launch a case of enhanced cooperation;
- the requirement of a unanimous vote in the Council for authorizing
  any case of cooperation in the area of CFSP, whereas the previous
  treaty allowed a decision by QMV for a case of enhanced cooperation which would simply aim at implementing CFSP decisions
  that had already been adopted beforehand;
- the requirement of the consent of the European Parliament, where
  all the members (from all Member States) have the right to
  vote, for launching any case of enhanced cooperation, even in
  cases in which the co-decision procedure does not apply, which
  would make the decision more difficult to take as compared with
  the previous treaty, under which the EP was consulted only in
  cases where the co-decision procedure was not applicable; this
  could make the decision to launch enhanced cooperation more
  difficult;
- the requirement of a Commission proposal (which has to be
  decided, as in all cases, by a simple majority of Commissioners
  originating from all Member States) for triggering enhanced cooperation in matters other than CFSP, including in cases concerning
  the former 'third pillar'.

Besides the above, the prevailing conditions of substance for
launching a case of enhanced cooperation have essentially remained
the same as before, which means that they are strict and numerous, but quite logical and necessary in order to protect the non-
participating states. They are described in particular in Article 326 of

the TFEU. Enhanced cooperation has to 'comply with the Treaties and Union law'. It 'shall aim to further the objectives of the EU, protect its interests and reinforce its integration process'. It 'shall be open at any time to all Member States' (TEU, Article 20(1)). It can intervene 'as a last resort, when it has been established that the objectives of such cooperation cannot be attained within a reasonable period by the Union as a whole' (TEU, Article 20(2)). It must 'not undermine the internal market or economic, social and territorial cohesion'. It must 'not constitute a barrier to or discrimination in trade between Member States' and not distort competition between them. Of course, there is no possibility of enhanced cooperation in areas covered by an exclusive competence of the EU (TFEU, Article 329(1)). Finally, 'any enhanced cooperation shall respect the competences, rights and obligations of those Member States which do not participate in it' (TFEU, Article 327).

Actually, obstacles to enhanced cooperation remain significant in the treaties, but they are due more to procedural requirements than to substantive ones. In order to launch a case of enhanced cooperation, it is not sufficient to respect fully the substantive conditions required by the treaties, but it is also necessary to have the support of:

- fourteen Commissioners out of twenty-seven;[48]
- an absolute majority of the European Parliament; and
- a qualified majority in the Council.

It is therefore clear that even a strong political will of nine Member States to go ahead and cooperate among themselves is not enough, as they would still have to obtain approval from all three EU political institutions.

In this context, one has to remember that the Commission has always been politically hostile to enhanced cooperation. For example, its official communication presented to the Constitutional Convention in 2002, 'A Project for the EU', showed this negative approach.

---

[48] A recent example shows that such a decision will not always be easy to reach in the Commission. After the failure of the Commission's proposal on a Regulation on the law of 'cross-borders' divorce in 2008, due to the negative vote of one Member of the Council (Sweden), ten Member States requested the Commission to launch an enhanced cooperation. The Commission ('Barroso I') refused: see *Bulletin Quotidien Europe*, 16 January 2009 and 23 January 2009. Finally, the following Commission ('Barroso II') agreed to present the proposal in March 2010.

One could also mention the December 2002 'Draft Constitution', nicknamed 'Penelope', which was prepared by Commission officials at the request of Romano Prodi, President of the Commission at that time,[49] and which did not contain any rule allowing for enhanced cooperation. Its ambition was to abolish unanimous voting for legislative matters in the Council. Therefore, any legislation would have been adopted by QMV in all areas, and the implementation of all legislation imposed on all Member States whatever their needs or interests!

One may explain this attitude of the Commission by the fact that it is afraid that the single institutional framework, and its own powers, might be affected by enhanced cooperation. Besides, one has also to take into account that smaller Member States, nationals of which form a majority in the Commission, have always been cautious about enhanced cooperation, especially when they are not among the richest countries of the EU. For these smaller states, the fear of being relegated to a 'second-class' Europe is still very much alive.

Up to now, this fear has been greater than the fear of seeing the EU become less efficient, less helpful and less relevant.

Finally, the procedure allowing for a case of enhanced cooperation was used for the first time at the end of 2010, that is, well after the enlargement to twenty-seven states between 2004 and 2007 and after the entry into force of the Lisbon Treaty in 2009, for a Directive on the law applicable to divorce.[50] The Council also gave its authorization for a second possible case in March 2011, for the creation of an EU patent, a project that had been pursued since the 1970s but that always failed, in particular on the issue of the languages in which the EU patent should be drawn up and translated; this authorization was requested by twenty-five Member States.[51]

---

[49] Commission, 'Contribution to a Preliminary Project of a Constitution of the EU', December 2002, available at: http://europa.eu.int/futurum/comm/const.

[50] Council Regulation 1259/2010 of 20 December 2010 implementing enhanced cooperation in the area of law applicable to divorce and legal separation, EU OJ L 343, 29 December 2010 (fourteen Member States are participating).

[51] Italy and Spain objected to the solution chosen by the Commission and approved by the EP and the Council. They think that this solution would give unfair advantages to the countries using the English, French and German languages. They seized the Court of Justice of the EU of the legality of the decision for the authorization on 30 May 2011.

Other possible cases allowing for differentiation between Member States

The treaties contain other provisions allowing Member States to decide not to participate in an action or policy. This is the case for the European Defence Agency (EDA): see Articles 42(3) and 45 of the TEU. Article 45(2) states in particular that: 'The European Defence Agency shall be open to all Member States wishing to be part of it.' This is also the case for supplementary research programmes. Article 184 TFEU states: 'In implementing the multi-annual framework programme, supplementary programmes may be decided on involving the participation of certain Member States only, which shall finance them subject to possible Union participation.'

In some cases, EU secondary law allows Member States to participate or not in EU operational programmes. This is, for example, the case for FRONTEX, the agency established in 2004: 'European Agency for the Management of Operational Cooperation at the External Borders of the Member States of the EU'.[52]

Generally speaking, as reflected in Protocol No. 25 on the exercise of shared competences, 'when the Union has taken action in a certain area, the scope of this exercise of competence only covers those elements governed by the Union act in question and therefore does not cover the whole area'. This means that outside of these elements – elements which form part of the EU *acquis* and on which Member States cannot adopt their own rules – Member States remain able to legislate nationally or to conclude agreements with other states in order to adopt common rules between them. Nothing in EU law prevents them from doing so; Protocol No. 25 confirms a rule that existed before the inclusion of that protocol in the treaties by the Lisbon Treaty.

Furthermore, in certain matters the treaty authorizes Member States to continue to legislate further, even in cases where the EU has adopted legislation. For example, it has always been the case that EU legislation adopted in the area of social policy 'shall not prevent any Member State from maintaining or introducing more stringent protective measures compatible with the Treaties' (TFEU, Article

---

[52] Council Regulation, 26 October 2004 (OJ L 349/1), modified by Council Regulation, 11 July 2007 (OJ L 199/30).

153(4)). Likewise, in the domain of the protection of the environment, 'The protective measures adopted pursuant to Article 192 shall not prevent any Member State from maintaining or introducing more stringent protective measures. Such measures must be compatible with the Treaties' (TFEU, Article 193). In another area, the responsibilities of Member States are fully safeguarded: 'This Title shall not affect the exercise of the responsibilities incumbent upon Member States with regard to the maintenance of law and order and the safeguarding of internal security' (TFEU, Article 72).

The formulation of specific EU secondary law itself often leaves Member States flexible as to its implementation.[53] It is true that, initially, the approach of the EC institutions as regards the exercise of their powers to harmonize national legislation in given areas was to aim at a total harmonization of the laws of the Member States.[54] This means that EC legislation could cover a whole area exhaustively. This had the consequence that Member States had no competence left as far as that area was concerned, the competence of the EC having become exclusive.

However, already at the beginning of the 1980s, the Commission had begun to limit some of its legislative proposals to a 'minimum' or a 'partial' harmonization. When, after the entry into force of the Single European Act in July 1987, QMV in the Council became the normal rule for adopting legislation concerning the internal market, Members of the Council pushed the Commission to aim systematically at partial harmonization.

At the same time, the Single European Act introduced into the treaty the possibility of a partial opt-out from a given harmonization, through the system established by Article 100A(4):

If, after the adoption of a harmonisation measure by the Council acting by a qualified majority, a Member State deems it necessary to apply national provisions on grounds of major needs referred to in Article 36, or relating to

---

[53] See Claus-Dieter Ehlermann, 'How Flexible is Community Law? An Unusual Approach to the Concept of "Two Speeds"', *Michigan Law Review*, 82(5/6); *Festschrift in Honor of Eric Stein* (April/May, 1984), pp. 1274–93.

[54] This was the period that was dominated by the 'unity narrative', used, for example, by the EC Court of Justice in its landmark judgment *Costa* v. *E.N.E.L.* (Case 6/64, 1964 ECR 1251): 'The executive force of Community law cannot vary from one State to another . . . without jeopardizing the attainment of the objectives of the Treaty.'

protection of the environment or the working environment, it shall notify the Commission of these provisions.

The Commission shall confirm the provisions involved after having verified that they are not a means of arbitrary discrimination or a disguised restriction on trade between Member States.

By way of derogation from the procedure laid down in Articles 169 and 170, the Commission or any Member State may bring the matter directly before the Court of Justice if it considers that another Member State is making improper use of the powers provided for in this Article.

This was the price to pay, especially at the request of Denmark, for accepting the principle of QMV in the Council for the establishment of the single market.

Even before the enlargement to fifteen Member States in 1995, some differentiation between the twelve Member States appeared to be more and more necessary, not only because of the increased objective economic differences between them, but also because of the growing divergence of their political aspirations.

It is at that time that the Maastricht Treaty, signed in 1992 and entered into force in 1993, provided for provisions on social policy that were legally binding only for eleven Member States, with the exception of the United Kingdom.[55] It was also the Maastricht Treaty that allowed Denmark and the United Kingdom not to participate in the final stage of monetary union.

The present treaties sometimes request that the Union (and, there-fore, its legislation) should respect the diversity of national systems or practice:

- Article 3 of the TEU (paragraph 3, subparagraph 4): 'It [the Union] shall respect its rich cultural and linguistic diversity, and shall ensure that Europe's cultural heritage is safeguarded and enhanced';
- Article 67(1) of the TFEU for the area of freedom, security and justice: 'The Union shall constitute an area of freedom, security and justice with respect for fundamental rights and the different legal systems and traditions of the Member States';
- Article 69 of the TFEU, also for that area: 'National Parlia-ments [shall] ensure that the proposals and legislative initia-tives . . . comply with the principle of subsidiarity . . .';

---

[55] The Labour Government of Tony Blair renounced this opt-out in 1997.

- Article 83(1) of the TFEU on judicial cooperation in criminal matters: 'The European Parliament and the Council may, by means of directives adopted in accordance with the ordinary legislative procedure, establish minimum rules concerning the definition of criminal offences and sanctions in the areas of particularly serious crime with a cross-border dimension . . .';
- see also Article 83(2) of the TFEU on the approximation of criminal laws and regulations: 'minimum rules . . .';
- Article 83(3) of the TFEU provides that if a Member State considers that a draft directive as referred to in Article 83(1) or (2) 'would affect fundamental aspects of its criminal justice system . . .', it may seize the European Council and prevent the adoption of the proposed act (however, this may give the possibility of enhanced cooperation among some other Member States, according to the 'brake–accelerator' mechanism);
- Article 151 of the TFEU on social policy: 'the Union and the Member States shall implement measures which take account of the diverse forms of national practices . . .';
- Article 152 of the TFEU: 'The Union recognizes and promotes the role of the social partners at its level, taking into account the diversity of national systems'; and finally
- Article 4(2) of the TEU provides in a general manner that the Union must respect the 'national identities' of the Member States, 'inherent in their fundamental structures, political and constitutional' and that 'it shall respect their essential State functions, including ensuring the territorial integrity of the State, maintaining law and order and safeguarding national security. In particular, national security remains the sole responsibility of each Member State.' These provisions were not in the treaties before their amendment by the Treaty of Lisbon.

On this basis, one could draw the following conclusions:
- the so-called 'in-built cooperations', which the highest decision-making authorities of the Member States decided to insert in the treaties, and which concern major and clear political purposes, allow willing Member States to cooperate among themselves and to take decisions, within the framework of the EU institutions, without being obliged to have the agreement of the other Member States;

- the 'enhanced cooperations', proposed in the treaties since 1999, but which remain to be decided on a case-by-case basis at the level of the EU institutions, have hardly ever been used. However, taking into account two recent cases,[56] could one hope that this might be a sufficient solution for the future? Unfortunately, this might not be the case, for the reasons given below.

WITH THE SUCCESSIVE EU ENLARGEMENTS, THE INTERESTS AND NEEDS OF THE MEMBER STATES HAVE BECOME VERY DIFFERENT, AND ARE SOMETIMES EVEN CONTRADICTORY

In particular, some of the Member States integrated into the EU in 2004 and in 2007 have very different needs and interests as compared with the others.

Some of them even have difficulties in implementing their duty to respect the *acquis*, that is, all legislation and decisions adopted by the EU in the past. This is more particularly the case as regards social rules and rules on the protection of the environment. The administrative structures, the quality of the bodies exercising controls and the quality of the judicial systems of some of the 'new' Member States are not up to the level that would be needed in order to guarantee control of a full implementation of the 90,000 pages of legislative *acquis*. Therefore, it is quite understandable that when new proposals are made in order to increase the standards or to improve the rules on the protection of workers, or of consumers or of the environment, the representatives of these countries, at least in the Council, tend to be reluctant and, consequently, to reduce the ambition. A different attitude would be surprising, as it would go against the interests of these countries. One has to add that, given the composition and weakness of the Commission, the ambition of its proposals is already quite weak before they are presented to the legislature, that is, the European Parliament and the Council.

The levels of economic development are very different from one Member State to another, as Table 4.1 shows.

---

[56] The case on the law applicable to 'cross-border' divorce and the potential case on the establishment of an EU patent.

Table 4.1 *GNP per capita at current market prices*

| | EU-27 = 100 | | | | | |
	2004	2005	2006	2007	2008	Euro 2008[a]
EU-27	100	100	100	100	100	25,100
Euro area	109	110	109	109	108	28,300
Belgium	121	119	118	118	115	32,200
Bulgaria	34	35	37	37	40	4,500
Czech Republic	75	76	78	80	80	14,200
Denmark	126	124	123	120	118	42,400
Germany	116	117	116	115	116	30,400
Estonia	57	61	65	68	67	12,000
Ireland	142	144	147	150	139	40,900
Greece	94	93	94	95	95	21,300
Spain	101	102	104	105	104	23,900
France	110	111	109	109	107	30,400
Italy	107	105	104	102	100	26,300
Cyprus	90	91	90	91	95	21,700
Latvia	46	49	53	58	56	10,200
Lithuania	51	53	56	60	61	9,600
Luxembourg	253	254	267	267	253	80,500
Hungary	63	63	64	63	63	10,500
Malta	77	78	77	78	76	13,800
Netherlands	129	131	131	131	135	36,200
Austria	127	124	124	124	123	33,800
Poland	51	51	52	54	58	9,500
Portugal	75	77	76	76	75	15,700
Romania	34	35	38	42	46	6,500
Slovenia	86	87	88	89	90	18,400
Slovakia	57	60	64	67	72	12,000
Finland	116	114	115	116	115	34,800
Sweden	125	120	121	122	121	35,400
United Kingdom	124	122	121	118	117	29,600

Source: 'Eurostat – Europe in Figures', Eurostat Yearbook, 2010.
[a] Extracted 14 January 2010.

Taking into account the figures available for the year 2009, and with 100 as the average index for the EU-27 GDP per capita, seven Member States were at least 35 per cent below that average and two of them were around 55 per cent below.[57] The graph reproduced in Figure 4.1 reflects this situation. As a comparison, for the United

[57] Source: *Eurostat*, GDP per capita, February 2011.

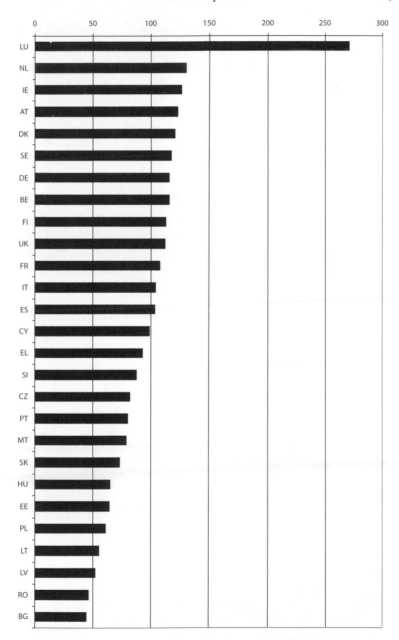

Figure 4.1 Index of GDP per inhabitant in the EU, 2009 (EU-27 average = 100)
Source: Eurostat

States in the same year no US State was below 30 per cent of the average national index.[58]

If one talks about external relations of the EU, whether it be for economic matters or justice and home affairs, the interests, attitudes and policies of some of the Central and Eastern EU Member States are, for historical and geographical reasons, different from those of the Western countries of the EU. This makes it all the more difficult to reach clear positions on some issues, when, for instance, it involves relations with Russia or Ukraine.

Decisions taken recently concerning the euro area

For the time being, the Euro Group has not used the legal possibilities offered by Article 136 of the TFEU. This is probably due to the fact that not all its members are ready to accept legally binding obligations in this very sensitive field. Therefore, they have instead adopted the 'Euro-Plus-Pact', which is described in Box 4.1 below.

THE 'EURO-PLUS-PACT': COOPERATION WITHIN OR OUTSIDE THE EU INSTITUTIONAL FRAMEWORK?

Box 4.1

As an illustration of the rapid shift towards a two-speed Europe, this box reproduces (and briefly comments on) the decisions taken by the heads of state or government of the euro area on 11 March 2011 ('Pact for the Euro') on the basis of informal suggestions that had been made by the French and the German delegations in the margins and on the occasion of the meeting of the February 2011 European Council. The 'Pact for the Euro' became the 'Euro-Plus-Pact' on the occasion of the 24–25 March 2011 European Council, when six EU Member States that are not members of the euro area also agreed to the Pact.[59]

---

[58] Source: US Department of Commerce, Bureau of Economic Analysis, GDP per State Statistics, November 2010.
[59] Bulgaria, Denmark, Latvia, Lithuania, Poland and Romania. Therefore, only four EU Member States have not accepted the Pact: the Czech Republic, Hungary, Sweden and the United Kingdom. However, it is not impossible that the Czech Republic and Sweden might decide to accept it in the future.

Annex I: The Euro-Plus-Pact

Stronger economic policy coordination for competitiveness and convergence

European Council Conclusions, 24–25 March 2011

This Pact has been agreed by the euro area Heads of State or government and joined by Bulgaria, Denmark, Latvia, Lithuania, Poland, Romania to strengthen the economic pillar of the monetary union, achieve a new quality of economic policy coordination, improve competitiveness, thereby leading to a higher degree of convergence. This Pact focuses primarily on areas that fall under national competence and are key for increasing competitiveness and avoiding harmful imbalances. Competitiveness is essential to help the EU grow faster and more sustainably in the medium and long term, to produce higher levels of income for citizens, and to preserve our social models. Other Member States are invited to participate on a voluntary basis.

This renewed effort for stronger economic policy coordination for competitiveness and convergence rests on four guiding rules:

(a) It will be *in line with and strengthen the existing economic governance* in the EU, while providing added value. It will be consistent with and build on existing instruments (Europe 2020, European Semester, Integrated Guidelines, Stability and Growth Pact and new macro-economic surveillance framework). It will involve a special effort going beyond what already exists and include concrete commitments and actions that are more ambitious than those already agreed, and accompanied with a timetable for implementation. These new commitments will thereafter be included in the National Reform and Stability Programmes and be subject to the regular surveillance framework, with a strong central role for the Commission in the monitoring of the implementation of the commitments, and the involvement of all the relevant formations of the Council and the Euro Group. The European Parliament will play its full role in line with its competences. Social partners will be fully involved at the EU level through the Tripartite Social Summit.

(b) It will be focused, action oriented and cover *priority policy areas that are essential for fostering competitiveness and convergence*. It will concentrate on actions where the competence lies with the Member States. In the chosen policy areas *common objectives will be agreed upon at the Heads of State or Government level. Participating Member States will pursue these objectives with their own policy-mix, taking into account their specific challenges.*

(c) *Each year, concrete national commitments will be undertaken by each Head of State or Government.* In doing so, Member States will take into account best practices and benchmark against the best performers, within Europe and vis-à-vis other strategic partners.

The implementation of commitments and progress towards the common policy objectives will be *monitored politically by the Heads of State or Government* of the euro area and participating countries on a yearly basis, on the basis of a report by the Commission. In addition, Member States commit to consult their partners on each major economic reform having potential spill-over effects before its adoption.

(d) Participating Member States are fully committed to the completion of the Single Market which is key to enhancing the competitiveness in the EU and the euro area. This process will be fully in line with the treaty. *The Pact will fully respect the integrity of the Single Market.*

Our goals

Participating Member States undertake to take all necessary measures to pursue the following objectives:

- foster competitiveness
- foster employment
- contribute further to the sustainability of public finances
- reinforce financial stability.

Each participating Member State will present the specific measures it will take to reach these goals. If a Member State can show that action is not needed on one or the other areas, it will not include it. The choice of the specific policy actions necessary to achieve the common objectives *remains the responsibility of each country, but particular attention will be paid to the set of possible measures mentioned below.*

Concrete policy commitments and monitoring

Progress towards the common objectives above will be politically monitored by the Heads of State or Government on the basis of a series of indicators covering competitiveness, employment, fiscal sustainability and financial stability. Countries facing major challenges in any of these areas will be identified and will have to commit to addressing these challenges in a given timeframe.

(a) Foster competitiveness

Progress will be assessed on the basis of *wage and productivity developments and competitiveness adjustment needs*. To assess whether wages are evolving in line with productivity, unit labour costs (ULC) will be monitored over a period of time, by comparing with developments in other euro area countries and in the main comparable trading partners. For each country, ULCs will be assessed for the economy as a whole and for each major sector (manufacturing, services, as well as tradable and non-tradable sectors). Large and sustained increases may lead to the erosion of competitiveness, especially if combined with a widening current account deficit and declining market shares for exports. Action to raise competitiveness is required in both by all countries, but particular attention will be paid to those facing major challenges in this respect. To ensure that growth is balanced and widespread in the whole euro area, specific instruments and common initiatives will be envisaged to foster productivity in regions lagging behind.

Each country will be responsible for the specific policy actions it chooses to foster competitiveness, but the following reforms will be given particular attention:

(i) respecting national traditions of social dialogue and industrial relations, measures to ensure costs developments in line with productivity, such as:
- review the wage setting arrangements, and, where necessary, the degree of centralisation in the bargaining process, and

the indexation mechanisms, while maintaining the autonomy of the social partners in the collective bargaining process;

- ensure that wages settlements in the public sector support the competitiveness efforts in the private sector (bearing in mind the important signalling effect of public sector wages).

(ii) measures to increase productivity, such as:

- further opening of sheltered sectors by measures taken at the national level to remove unjustified restrictions on professional services and the retail sector, to foster competition and efficiency, in full respect of the Community *acquis*;
- specific efforts to improve education systems and promote R&D, innovation and infrastructure;
- measures to improve the business environment, particularly for SMEs, notably by removing red tape and improving the regulatory framework (e.g., bankruptcy laws, commercial code).

(b) Foster employment

A well-functioning labour market is key for the competitiveness of the euro area. Progress will be assessed on the basis of the following indicators: long-term and youth unemployment rates, and labour participation rates.

Each country will be responsible for the specific policy actions it chooses to foster employment, but the following reforms will be given particular attention:

- labour market reforms to promote '*flexicurity*', reduce undeclared work and increase labour participation;
- life long learning;
- tax reforms, such as lowering taxes on labour to make work pay while preserving overall tax revenues, and taking measures to facilitate the participation of second earners in the work force.

(c) Enhance the sustainability of public finances

In order to secure the full implementation of the Stability and Growth Pact, the highest attention will be paid to:

Sustainability of pensions, health care and social benefits
This will be assessed notably on the basis of the sustainability gap indicators.[60] These indicators measure whether debt levels are sustainable based on current policies, notably pensions schemes, health care and benefit systems, and taking into account demographic factors.

Reforms necessary to ensure the sustainability and adequacy of pensions and social benefits could include:
- aligning the pension system to the national demographic situation, for example, by aligning the effective retirement age with life expectancy or by increasing participation rates;
- limiting early retirement schemes and using targeted incentives to employ older workers (notably in the age tranche above 55).

National fiscal rules
Participating Member States commit to translating EU fiscal rules as set out in the Stability and Growth Pact into national legislation. Member States will retain the choice of the specific national legal vehicle to be used, but will make sure that it has a sufficiently strong binding and durable nature (e.g., constitution or framework law). The exact formulation of the rule will also be decided by each country (e.g., it could take the form of a 'debt brake', rule related to the primary balance or an expenditure rule), but it should ensure fiscal discipline at both national and sub-national levels. The Commission will have the opportunity, in full respect of the prerogatives of national parliaments, to be consulted on the precise fiscal rule before its adoption so as to ensure it is compatible with, and supportive of, the EU rules.

(d) Reinforce financial stability

A strong financial sector is key for the overall stability of the euro area. A comprehensive reform of the EU framework for financial sector supervision and regulation has been launched.

In this context, Member States commit to putting in place national legislation for banking resolution, in full respect of the

---

[60] The sustainability gap is indicators agreed by the Commission and Member States to assess fiscal sustainability.

Community *acquis*. Strict bank stress tests, coordinated at EU level, will be undertaken on a regular basis. In addition, the President of the ESRB and the President of the Euro Group will be invited to regularly inform Heads of State or Government on issues related to macro-financial stability and macro-economic developments in the euro area requiring specific action. In particular, for each Member State, the level of private debt for banks, households and non-financial firms will be closely monitored.

In addition to the issues mentioned above, attention will be paid to *tax policy coordination*.

Direct taxation remains a national competence. Pragmatic coordination of tax policies is a necessary element of a stronger economic policy coordination in the euro area to support fiscal consolidation and economic growth. In this context, Member States commit to engage in structured discussions on tax policy issues, notably to ensure the exchange of best practices, avoidance of harmful practices and proposals to fight against fraud and tax evasion.

Developing a common corporate tax base could be a revenue neutral way forward to ensure consistency among national tax systems while respecting national tax strategies, and to contribute to fiscal sustainability and the competitiveness of European businesses.

The Commission has presented a legislative proposal on a common consolidated corporate tax base.

Concrete yearly commitments

In order to demonstrate a real commitment for change and ensure the necessary political impetus to reach our common objectives, each year participating Member States will agree at the highest level on a set of concrete actions to be achieved within 12 months. The selection of the specific policy measures to be implemented will remain the responsibility of each country, but the choice will be guided by considering in particular the issues mentioned above. These commitments will also be reflected in the National Reform Programmes and Stability Programmes submitted each year which will be assessed by the Commission, the Council, and the Euro Group in the context of the European Semester.

Annex II: Term sheet on the ESM

The European Council has decided to add to Article 136 of the Treaty the following paragraph:

The Member States whose currency is the euro may establish a stability mechanism to be activated if indispensable to safeguard the stability of the euro area as a whole. The granting of any required financial assistance under the mechanism will be made subject to strict conditionality.

Further to this decision, the European Council has agreed on the need for euro area Member States to establish a permanent stability mechanism: the European Stability Mechanism (ESM). The ESM will be activated by mutual agreement, if indispensable to safeguarding the financial stability of the euro area as a whole. The ESM will assume the role of the European Financial Stability Facility (EFSF) and the European Financial Stabilisation Mechanism (EFSM) in providing external financial assistance to euro-area Member States after June 2013.

Access to ESM financial assistance will be provided on the basis of strict policy conditionality under a macro-economic adjustment programme and a rigorous analysis of public-debt sustainability, which will be conducted by the Commission together with the IMF and in liaison with the ECB. The beneficiary Member State will be required to put in place an appropriate form of private-sector involvement, according to the specific circumstances and in a manner fully consistent with IMF practices.

The ESM will have an effective lending capacity of €500 billion. The adequacy of the lending capacity will be reviewed on a regular basis and at least every five years. The ESM will seek to supplement its lending capacity through the participation of the IMF in financial assistance operations, while non-euro area Member States may also participate on an ad hoc basis.

*

[The remainder of Annex II sets out the key structural features of the ESM.

Non-euro states may also participate on an ad hoc basis alongside the ESM in financial assistance operations for euro zone Members.

It is also provided that, if a dispute arises between a euro zone Member and the ESM in relation with the interpretation and application of the treaty which will establish the ESM, the Board of Governors (i.e., the Ministers of Finance of the Euro Group) will decide on the dispute. If the Member State concerned does not agree with this decision, the dispute will be submitted to the EU Court of Justice, in accordance with Article 273 TFEU.]

*

Finally, the ESM contribution key for the euro zone Members will be the following:

ESM contribution key based on the ECB key

Country	ISO	ESM key
Austria	AT	2.783
Belgium	BE	3.477
Cyprus	CY	0.196
Estonia	EE	0.186
Finland	FI	1.797
France	FR	20.386
Germany	DE	27.146
Greece	EL	2.817
Ireland	IE	1.592
Italy	IT	17.914
Luxembourg	LU	0.250
Malta	MT	0.073
Netherlands	NL	5.717
Portugal	PT	2.509
Slovakia	SK	0.824
Slovenia	SI	0.428
Spain	ES	11.904
Total	EA17	100.0

Note: The ESM key is based on the ECB capital contribution key.

Member States with a GDP per capita of less than 75% of the EU average will benefit from a temporary correction for a period of 12 years after their entry into the euro area.

This temporary correction will be three-quarters of the difference between GNI and ECB capital shares (effectively comprising of 75% of GNI share and 25% of ECB capital share) as follows: *ESM share = ECB key share – 0.75* (ECB key share – GNI share).*

The downwards compensation on those countries will be redistributed among all the other countries according to their ECB key share.

GNI and GDP per capita in 2010.

Remarks on the 'Euro-Plus-Pact'

The aim of the 'Euro-Plus-Pact' is obviously to establish stronger economic coordination among the states concerned to boost competitiveness and convergence in the euro area and also in the EU as a whole. It is presented as focusing on matters that belong to national powers and as fully respecting the integrity of the single market. The progress of participating countries will be measured against economic indicators to be verified by the Commission. Policies and measures are not described in very precise terms in the Pact. The intention is that it will be for each state to formulate and adopt them. This will not take the form of EU legal acts. As described by Herman van Rompuy, President of the European Council, their adoption will depend on the pressure of the markets, of the institutions and on 'a strong peer pressure'. In other words, the Pact is not a legally binding instrument for the participating states, and the implementing decisions will be taken in an intergovernmental way, by each of the participating Member States according to its own national legal requirements. The Commission will not have the power to seize the EU Court of Justice if one of those states does not fully respect its commitments. Therefore, one could say that the Pact is a form of cooperation that will mainly take place outside the EU institutional framework, not within it. And that will be the case even if a number of links are established with the EU institutions:

- the Pact will be discussed at the European Council;
- 'The European Parliament will play its full role in line with its competences';

- the annual commitments of each participating Member State will be included in its National Reform and Stability (or Convergence) Programme, which has to be drawn up in the framework of the implementation of Article 121 of the TFEU;
- these commitments will be subject to regular surveillance by the formations of the Council and the Euro Group and will be politically monitored every year by the heads of state or government of the euro area and of the other participating EU Member States;
- this will be done on the basis of a report by the Commission, which will be prepared on the basis of a series of indicators agreed upon for each of the four objectives of the Pact.

Therefore, the Pact and its implementation will be partly but not totally integrated within the EU's institutional framework. As such, all decisions will have to be taken by the common agreement of all participating states. The Pact will benefit from neither the control of the EU's institutions over national implementing measures, including the role of the Court of Justice of the EU, nor from the possibility of sanctions as provided by the treaty against Member States not implementing EU law correctly.

*

This chapter has shown that in order to try to cope with the growing heterogeneity of its Member States, the EEC and then the EC and the EU have developed, over the years from the Treaty of Rome in 1957 to the Treaty of Lisbon in 2009, a great variety of mechanisms, including differentiations, opt-outs, enhanced cooperation, two-speed systems, etc. This began early and has experienced a faster development over recent years, mostly in response to the pressure from some Member States that were reluctant to accept an increase in the EU's competences. Against this background, will it be possible for the European Union to work in a sufficiently efficient way by continuing on its current path? The assessment of the situation of the EU in Chapter 2 has shown that the present situation is not good, due particularly to the fact that the EU institutions are not working well. Nevertheless, one could imagine them working better in the future. To begin with, the Commission could be composed of fewer members than the number of the Member States, which would make it stronger, more independent and more efficient. As regards the EP, one would hope that a better coordination of the action of the Committees by the large political groups and a more reasonable interpretation and implementation of the Lisbon Treaty would help, in particular by not weakening the Commission. But this would still not be enough. It should also be accompanied by a number of measures capable of resolving the euro crisis. The EU institutions have done quite a lot already; in particular, the European Central Bank has demonstrated its economic and financial skills and its political strength. The measures to be adopted by the legislature in 2011 should enhance budgetary discipline in the Member States and broaden the surveillance of their economic policies, thus implementing the recommendations of the taskforce which was presided over by the President of the European Council, Herman van Rompuy. It is to be noted that this legislative package consists of six important texts on the surveillance and coordination of Member States' budgetary and economic policies, on modifying the rules on the excessive deficit procedure, on the enforcement of budgetary surveillance in the euro area, on the prevention and correction of macro-economic imbalances and on enforcement measures to correct those possible imbalances, and on requirements for the Member States' budgetary frameworks.[61]

It is hoped that all these measures, together with those adopted since the beginning of the crisis and taking into account the firm political determination shown by the European leaders, will convince the financial markets. If this were to be successful, a country such as Greece should again be able to obtain loans from the market at 'normal' interest rates. If this were to be achieved, it would mean that the present system of the euro area, based on a centralized monetary policy and on a high degree of decentralization of budgetary and economic policy, is viable, but on the strict condition that all euro members respect the common rules.

Therefore, the option described and commented in the present chapter cannot be discarded from a legal/institutional point of view. In order for it to work, it would need a lot of political will and greater discipline on the part of the Member States. The recent history of the EU does not incline one towards much optimism, but the current

---

[61] See Chapter 5, fn. 3.

crisis might give the necessary impulse to the political will. If this does not work, it would mean that the status quo is not a sustainable solution and that one should examine the possibility of going towards a 'two-speed Europe'.

The arguments in favour of a 'two-speed Europe'

Going towards a 'two-speed Europe' means that a number of Member States will proceed faster than the others. These other Member States would not constitute a group themselves, as each of them may decide to travel at its own pace or even refuse sometimes to go in a given direction. Therefore, the result would not literally be a 'two-speed Europe', but actually an 'avant-garde' proceeding more quickly than the other Member States.

Such a 'division' of the members of the EU, even if conceived as provisional, has always been resisted up to now, mainly for political reasons. However, if the situation in the future became such that the EU were forced either to take this way forward or to accept that its progress would be halted and possibly even begin to decline, the idea could and should be considered again.

Actually, today in 2011 one of the consequences of the euro crisis is that a 'two-speed Europe' is already establishing itself and strengthening, through the necessity for France, Germany and others to unite in order to save the euro. As David Rennie, the political editor of *The Economist* wrote on 4 January 2011: '2011 could turn out to be the year that a multi-speed Europe starts to look more like a two-speed Europe, with an inner core impelled towards closer political and economic union by the need to rescue the single currency'.

This is one of the reasons why the old concept of 'two-speed Europe' deserves to be carefully examined today, as a project whose legal feasibility deserves to be studied

It is an economic fact that the two branches of EMU must be re-balanced. It is also a fact that, in order to do that, it would be necessary to harmonize somewhat the budgetary and economic policies of those states that have the euro as their currency. Under the current treaties, those states are not legally obliged to do so. To amend the treaties on this issue is not acceptable today by the twenty-seven Member States, just as it was not acceptable in the past: this had already been proposed, discussed and refused before and during the negotiations on the Treaty of Maastricht. Therefore, one way forward might be for the euro area members or, if they could not agree, for those euro area members willing to do so, to find a solution where only *they* would accept such new obligations, outside the current EU treaties, and therefore without the need to amend them. This seems to be, at least from an *economic* point of view, a necessity. The aim of Chapters 5 and 6 of this book is to consider if this would be a *legally* correct way to proceed.

The imbalance of EMU is not the only reason the issue of the legal feasibility of a two-speed Europe should be carefully studied. Beyond the question of the euro, the fact remains that an EU composed of twenty-seven heterogeneous[62] Member States has proven that it is not able to function efficiently within its present legal framework and that it is not able to answer the needs, interests and wishes of all its Member States at the same time. The causes of this situation have already been explained.

A two-speed Europe might also help to try and regain the support of European citizens by presenting them with a bold and coherent political project. The cohesiveness and identity of the European project has not yet recovered after the 2004 and 2007 enlargements. Popular support has been decreasing. Launching an ambitious project for an 'avant-garde', on the condition that it would be clear and understandable, could inject more life and enthusiasm into the project, provide an ambitious aim for future generations, and give back its 'soul' to European integration. Given the fact that such a project would be open to all EU Member States, all EU citizens should be interested in it.

Moreover, things are linked together. How could citizens accept budgetary restrictions, tougher rules on the retirement age, less social

---

[62] See above. See also Jean Pisani-Ferry, 'Intégration à géométrie variable et organisation de la politique économique en Europe', *EURO*, 39 (1997), 27–33; see in particular the disparity of income per head (10 in the 1965 EC of six Member States, 19.5 in the EU-15 of 1995, and a prediction of 42.2 for a possible EU-28 in 2015).

benefits and austere economic and social policies if they perceive these measures to be a 'diktat' coming from Brussels and not accompanied by positive measures? Rather, these matters might be perceived differently if they were included in a wider political project offering more European integration and solidarity, as well as hope for the future. This could also be a possible means to fight against the trend towards populism that is threatening a number of European countries (in Belgium with the 'Vlaams Belang', in Denmark with the 'Danish People's Party', in Finland with the 'True Finns', in France with the 'Front National', in the Netherlands with the 'Freedom Party', in the United Kingdom with the 'National Party', in Sweden with the 'Sweden Democrats', etc.). This populist trend is a mix of nationalism, Euro scepticism and xenophobia.

However, the actual legal feasibility of a two-speed Europe does not seem, up to now and despite a good number of books and articles addressing the issue from a political point of view, to have been the subject of a serious, in-depth legal analysis,[63] despite the observation that 'a two-speed Europe would pose huge technical and judicial problems'.[64]

Two options look possible: a softer one and a bolder one.

For the softer one, the issue is to determine whether the closer cooperation which has begun among the euro area countries could develop further and better, without changing the treaties and without formally establishing a group through a legal instrument. In practice, this would mean that participating Member States would simply announce that they will work together within the existing legal framework and use all the possibilities that it offers.

For the bolder option, it would raise the question of whether the euro area's closer cooperation should be developed further, with more political visibility and more functional means, by legally establishing a group. This could be done through the adoption of an international legal instrument, which would, of course, have to be compatible

---

[63] One of the best legal articles written on the issue remains the article by Claus-Dieter Ehlermann, 'How Flexible is Community Law? An Unusual Approach to the Concept of "Two Speeds"'. However, this article was published in 1984, at a very different time in the history of European integration (at that time the EC was composed of ten Member States). Other references are given in Further reading.

[64] Grant, 'France, Germany and a "Hard-Core" Europe'.

with the EU's current treaties. Such an 'additional treaty' would legally bind the participating states to cooperate in a given number of fields. It would give them the opportunity of choosing both the legal framework within which this would be done and the specific procedures that would be applied.

The possible content and feasibility of these two options will be successively examined in Chapters 5 and 6.

CHAPTER 5

Third option: politically progressing towards a two-speed Europe

Under this option, a number of willing EU Member States, probably on the basis of the present composition of the euro area, would decide to go ahead and develop more intense cooperation in some areas, using all existing legal possibilities to do that. This would neither make it necessary to modify the current EU treaties nor to conclude a new international legal instrument. It could be publicly announced by a Political Declaration of the heads of state or government of the willing EU Member States.

It would depend on the political will of those states to decide to which matters their enhanced cooperation would apply. Decisions would have to be adopted in accordance with the rules of the treaties and *within* the EU institutional framework; on this basis, they could be adopted and implemented by the participating Member States only. Some cooperation could also possibly be developed *outside* the EU institutional framework, on the condition of fully respecting the EU treaties and EU law, as well as the rights of the non-participating Member States.

COOPERATION WITHIN THE EU'S INSTITUTIONAL FRAMEWORK

The point of departure could be that the willing Member States would meet to take the decision of principle to try to develop all existing possibilities offered by the EU treaties, including (but not limited to) matters concerning economic and monetary union. There are matters that would have to be excluded. First, the treaties exclude enhanced cooperation in areas of EU exclusive competences. Second, even in areas covered by shared competence, where enhanced cooperation is in principle possible, the treaties lay down a number of limitations in Articles 326–327 of the TFEU. Third, as far as CSDP is concerned, the TEU provides for specific rules, both in Article 45 on the European Defence Agency (EDA), and in Articles 42(6) and 46 and Protocol No. 10 on permanent structured cooperation (PSC).

As far as the euro area is concerned, and if the Group were to be composed of the euro area members

The Group could use extensively all potentialities offered by Article 136 of the TFEU

According to Article 136(1) of the TFEU, 'In order to ensure the proper functioning of economic and monetary union . . . the Council shall . . . adopt measures specific to those Member States whose currency is the euro.' Article 136(2) provides that 'only members of the Council representing Member States whose currency is the euro shall take part in the vote'. The Council will be able to take measures 'to strengthen the coordination and surveillance of their budgetary discipline' and 'to set out economic policy guidelines for them, while ensuring that they are compatible with those adopted for the whole of the Union and are kept under surveillance'. In other words, the scope of application of Article 136 is *extremely* wide, because many measures may be characterized as 'strengthening the coordination and surveillance' of the budgetary discipline of the states whose currency is the euro, or as 'setting out economic policy guidelines' for them. Measures adopted on the basis of Article 136 of the TFEU will legally be EU measures, thus becoming part of the EU *acquis.* Therefore, they will have to be applied by Member States that become members of the euro area in future. It might then be appropriate to adopt transitional measures to help them to adapt more easily, if such measures appear necessary.

The Euro Group, composed of the ministers of finance of the Member States of the euro area, has remained an informal group, even after the entry into force of the Lisbon Treaty. Thus, it does not have the power to adopt legal decisions, as reflected in Article 137 of the TFEU and especially in Article 1 of Protocol No. 14 on the Euro Group: 'The Ministers of the Member States whose

currency is the euro shall meet informally.' Therefore, any formal
decisions will continue to be taken by the Council in its plenary
composition of twenty-seven members but where, when deciding
on the basis of Article 136 of the TFEU, only the seventeen members of the Euro Group have the right to vote. However, it is clear
that during the meetings of the Euro Group, which are held just
before the meetings of the EU Council, common positions are prepared, to be presented later during the formal session of the Council.
Therefore, the seventeen members of the Euro Group might agree
beforehand on what they wish to be adopted on the basis of Article
136 of the TFEU. In accordance with the treaty, however, the proposal
will have to come from the Commission (composed of twenty-seven
members having the nationality of all twenty-seven Member States),
and all decisions that, according to the applicable provisions of the
Treaty, have to be taken on the basis of the ordinary legislative procedure will need the agreement of the European Parliament (composed of representatives elected in each of the twenty-seven Member
States).

Article 136 does therefore provide the possibility of the Council,
with only the seventeen members concerned having the right to vote,
deciding on the coordination of economic policies of the members
of the euro area.

*The Group could also decide to ensure a unified representation of the
euro area within international financial organizations and conferences
(including the IMF and the World Bank), using the potentialities
offered by Article 138 of the TFEU*

Article 138(1) of the TFEU provides that: 'In order to secure the
euro's place in the international monetary system, the Council, on a
proposal from the Commission, shall adopt a decision establishing
common positions on matters of particular interest for economic and
monetary union within the competent international financial institutions and conferences.' According to Article 138(2), 'The Council, on
a proposal from the Commission, may adopt appropriate measures
to ensure unified representation within the international financial
institutions and conferences.' Article 138(3) provides that in order to
adopt these decisions and measures, 'only members of the Council

representing Member States whose currency is the euro shall take part in the vote'. Again, the implementation of this Article may (potentially) have very substantial consequences.

Actually, the present practice followed by the EU and its Member States in these organizations or conferences is quite complicated. Moreover, it does not allow it to symbolize the unity of the EU countries in the presentation and defence of their common interests:

- in the annual meetings of the IMF and the World Bank (WB), all twenty-seven Member States and the Commission participate;
- in the IMF and WB Executive Boards, three Member States always participate (France, Germany and the United Kingdom), while the other Member States belong to groups of states (in which both EU states and non-EU states participate), which elect one of their members to participate; neither the EU nor the euro area are represented;
- in the G20 meetings at the level of ministers of finance, the EU is represented by the President of the ECOFIN Council and by the President of the European Central Bank, together with the ministers of France, Germany, Italy and the United Kingdom; in the G20 meetings at the level of heads of state or government, the EU is represented by the President of the European Council and by the President of the Commission, as well as the leaders of France, Germany, Italy and the United Kingdom; in recent meetings, the Netherlands and Spain were also represented;
- in the G8 meetings at the level of ministers of finance, the EU is represented by the President of the Euro Group, the President of the ECB and the member of the Commission responsible for economic and monetary affairs, together with the ministers of France, Germany, Italy and the United Kingdom; at the level of the heads of state or government, the President of the European Council and the President of the Commission represent the EU, together with the leaders of France, Germany, Italy and the United Kingdom.

It is entirely in the hands of the members of the euro area whether to bring this complicated situation to an end and to have a unified representation in the IMF and the WB instead, and indeed in all international financial institutions and conferences. Again, this will depend on a proposal by the Commission (twenty-seven members), but would not legally require either the agreement or the consultation of the European Parliament.

If the euro area countries decide to use fully the extensive potentialities offered by Articles 136 and 138 of the TFEU, this would entail a dramatic change of the EU. Actually, the establishment of a 'two-speed Europe' does not need any other legal text to become a reality. These texts already exist. They could be implemented at any time, should the political will exist. Besides, nothing would prevent the seventeen members of the euro area from deciding to have regular (annual or more frequent) meetings of their heads of state or government as part of a comprehensive set of measures aimed at reinforcing their economic cooperation, as they in fact did so on 11 March 2011.

Cooperation in the area of defence and security could be developed through the means listed below

- implementation of the 'permanent structured cooperation' (PSC) foreseen by the Lisbon Treaty (TEU, Articles 42(6) and 46 and Protocol No. 10 on PSC established by TEU, Article 42);
- participation in projects within the framework of the European Defence Agency (EDA) (TEU, Articles 42(3) and 45, in particular Article 45(2));
- participation in groups of Member States (which are willing and have the necessary capabilities), tasked by the Council to implement Council decisions for joint operations or tasks involving the use of civilian and military means (TEU, Article 44);
- other suggestions made together by France and Germany during the 2002–2003 European Convention.[1]

This does not mean that states participating in such cooperation would have either a common army or a common defence. It is also clear that each participating state will always keep its exclusive right to decide on any engagement of its armed forces in any circumstances.

---

[1] See document CONV422/02, 22 November 2002, 'Contribution by Mr Dominique de Villepin and Mr Joschka Fischer, members of the Convention, presenting Franco-German proposals for the European Convention in the field of European Security and Defence Policy'.

For the other areas covered by the TFEU, the Group could cooperate by using the general enhanced cooperation rules provided by the treaties

In the field of the former 'third pillar'

- In judicial cooperation in criminal matters, the Group could consider: the approximation of legislation and procedures; the adoption of directives laying down rules and procedures for ensuring recognition of judgments and judicial decisions and of measures to prevent and settle conflicts of jurisdictions, as well as measures to support the training of the judiciary and judicial staff and measures to facilitate cooperation between judicial or equivalent authorities in relation to proceedings in criminal matters and the enforcement of decisions (see TFEU, Article 82); the adoption of directives establishing 'minimum rules concerning the definition of criminal offences and sanctions in the areas of particularly serious crime with a cross-border dimension resulting from the nature or impact of such offences or from a special need to combat them on a common basis' (see TFEU, Article 83); the establishment of a European Public Prosecutor's office (see TFEU, Article 86(1)).
- In judicial cooperation in civil matters, especially concerning family law with cross-border implications, the field of possible cooperation is wide (law of contracts, marriage, divorce, adoption, succession, etc.), given the fact that families made up of different nationalities are becoming more frequent in the EU. One example is the Agreement of 4 February 2010 between France and Germany establishing an optional common matrimonial regime (during the marriage the spouses have a regime of separation of property, but after its dissolution each spouse is entitled to half the property acquired during the marriage).

In some specific areas of what used to be called the 'first pillar'

- Taxation: both direct and indirect taxation could be open to some possible approximation of national legislations. The field of possibilities is wide because this area has always been subject to unanimity in the Council, where divergences of views and of interests between Member States have resulted in few texts being adopted.

- Social policy: EU law does not prevent some Member States, if they so wish, from providing for higher standards of protection than those adopted in the EU, for instance, establishing a common minimum guaranteed salary, or harmonizing the age and conditions of retirement, etc.
- Environmental policy: the same observations as for social policy can be made. However, no measure could be envisaged among the participating states if it were to entail a distortion of competition with the other EU Member States.
- As regards public health, education, culture, civil protection, etc., areas where the EU cannot adopt legislation aimed at harmonizing national laws, the door is largely open for participating states, if they so desire, to approximate or coordinate their practices or their laws, to establish some projects in common in order to save money, to be more efficient and to obtain economies of scale or to further encourage cultural exchanges between their peoples.
- Immigration policy: the coordination of policies on the movement of persons and on the control of immigration would appear to be a priority, taking into account the influx of immigrants that will become inevitable in the future given the EU's demographic trends, and given the tensions already appearing between some EU countries on some occasions.[2]

By adopting procedural measures in the field of foreign policy

- In this field, the Group should refrain from taking any foreign policy decision that would distinguish it from the EU; therefore, only procedural measures should be aimed at, for instance, the organization of joint embassies or joint services for consulates, joint visits by foreign affairs ministers to third countries, temporary exchanges of diplomats or common training for diplomats, etc.
- Any of these measures should be preceded by giving information to and having consultation with the other EU Member States within the Council (see TEU, Articles 32–35).

[2] Such as between France and Italy in the spring of 2011, on the occasion of the illegal immigration of Tunisian nationals into the EU.

POSSIBLE ADDITIONAL COOPERATION OUTSIDE THE EU INSTITUTIONAL FRAMEWORK

On top of the possible cases of enhanced cooperation that would be developed inside the EU's institutional framework, the interested countries could also envisage measures to be taken outside this framework.

- The Member States of the euro area have already decided, at the height of the Greek debt crisis in May 2010, to set up a temporary (until 2013) European Financial Stability Facility (EFSF), through an international agreement. This agreement allows the EFSF to borrow cash on the market of up to €250 billion against up to €440 billion of joint euro area government guarantees, in order to help a euro area Member State that cannot properly finance itself on the market. This instrument has been used three times at the time of writing, to lend money to Greece (April 2010), to Ireland (end of 2010) and to Portugal (May 2011), without accepting liability or assuming the commitments of these Member States' authorities (in compliance with TFEU, Article 125(1)).

  On 25 March 2011, the European Council decided to amend Article 136 of the TFEU, at the request of Germany, to ensure without any legal doubt that this process is legally in accordance with obligations under the EU treaties and in particular with Article 125 of the TFEU (see the text of the amendment in Chapter 4). The entry into force of this amendment depends on its ratification by the twenty-seven EU Member States and is expected on 1 January 2013. The EFSF will be succeeded in 2013 by the European Stability Mechanism (ESM), which will also be established by a treaty between the euro area members. The ESM will in total hold €700 billion to shield the euro area from possible future debt crises. This will allow it an effective lending capacity of €500 billion. The adequacy of this capacity will be reviewed on a regular basis, and at least every five years, to determine whether it is still adequate to meet the potential financing needs of the members of the euro area.

- The group of participating states could also increase their cooperation aimed at strengthening the stability of the euro area, by choosing to continue on the intergovernmental path taken with the adoption of the 'Euro-Plus-Pact', for example, by adopting a gentleman's agreement on possible sanctions against those states that do not respect jointly agreed rules. They would do this if they decided that the system of sanctions based on the current treaties is insufficient.[3] They might therefore decide not to use the potentialities offered by Article 136 of the TFEU, in order to avoid legally binding requirements, the control of the Commission and of the Court of Justice, and formal approval by their respective national parliaments. In such a case, they could continue to take 'intergovernmental' decisions on rules concerning their national budget, limiting their budgetary deficit and their debt, as well as coordinating their economic policies and partially approximating their taxation system, in particular concerning corporate taxes. As long as they decided not to use Article 138 of the TFEU, they could also coordinate their positions in an informal way in international financial organizations and conferences, possibly on a case-by-case basis.

- Voluntary approximation of national legislation could be envisaged in fiscal, social and environmental policies, as long as it would not be possible (or desired) to apply the EU treaty's rules on enhanced cooperation. This could concern, for instance, the age of retirement, a minimum guaranteed salary, the abolition of the indexation of salaries to inflation or any other measures of harmonization that could be agreed by all participating states.

- Defence and security: the participating states could organize armament cooperation and some opening of defence procurement in order to consolidate their defence industries (personnel vehicles, transport of troops by air, helicopters, naval shipyards, etc.). Cooperation in this area already exists between a number of EU Member States:
  - within the framework of the Organization for Joint Armament Cooperation (OCCAR),[4] which was established in November 1996 by Belgium, France, Germany, Italy, Spain and the United

---

[3] Six important proposals for EU legislative acts ('on economic governance') are to be adopted by the EP and the Council. Four of these proposals include a reform of the EU Stability and Growth Pact, aimed at enhancing the surveillance of fiscal policies, introducing provisions on national fiscal frameworks and applying enforcement measures for non-compliant Member States more consistently and at an earlier stage (doc. 7960/11, ECOFIN Council, 15 March 2011).

[4] French acronym for Organization Conjointe de Coopération en Matière d'Armement.

Kingdom 'in order to enable a strengthening of the competitiveness of a European defence technological and industrial base';[5]
- as well as on the basis of the 'Letter of Intent/Framework Agreement' (actually an international agreement) signed in July 2000 by France, Germany, Italy, Spain, Sweden and the United Kingdom, which aims in particular at harmonizing rules related to defence procurement 'in order to facilitate the restructuring of the European Defence Industry'.

Cooperation could also be developed in operational defence projects, such as the Eurocorps, established in 1992 with armed forces from Belgium, France, Germany, Luxembourg and Spain, and the European Rapid Operational Force (Eurofor), established between France, Italy, Portugal and Spain, which is also the case for Euromafor in the field of naval forces. This would seem not to be possible for neutral EU Member States.
- The participating Member States could also envisage intergovernmental joint projects in the fields of energy, industry and research and development. Actually, many cooperations in these areas already exist between some EU Member States outside the EU framework: the European Space Agency (ESA);[6] the European Organization for the Exploitation of Meteorological Satellites (EUMETSAT, established in 1986, twenty-six Member States); the European Aeronautic Defence and Space Company (EADS) and its Airbus and Eurocopter companies; the European Organization for Nuclear Research (CERN), established in 1954 and in which twenty-eight states participate, including eighteen members of the EU; the European Higher Education Area (the Bologna Process); the European Patent Office, established in 1973, in which all EU Member States participate, as well as eight non-EU Members; EUREKA,[7] established in 1985, in which twenty-five EU Member States participate, as well as eleven other states.

---

[5] Without being a member, Turkey now participates in some activities of OCCAR, along with Finland, Luxembourg, the Netherlands, Poland and Sweden.

[6] The ESA, established in 1975, and in which eighteen states participate, including sixteen members of the EU, participates in the EU Galileo (navigation satellite system) and Copernicus (surveillance of the environment by satellite) projects.

[7] EUREKA was established in order to raise the productivity and competitiveness of industries in the participating Member States through funding research and development cooperation projects in the field of advanced technologies.

These fields of cooperation would have to be developed while at the same time respecting the EU treaties.

Feasibility and difficulties

• The participating states could adopt a Political Declaration in which they would commit themselves to participate in an agreed list of projects and areas of cooperation. One of the issues would be for them to decide whether to make a commitment to participating in *all* areas of the list or if it would be acceptable for any of them to opt out from a specific case or area.[8]

The key issue would probably be to require at least the participation of all members of the group in economic, taxation and budgetary policies, in order to be able to take measures necessary to strengthen and stabilize the euro area in a durable way. Not all participating states might be interested in participating in, for example, cultural, educational or health projects; in that case, cooperation in areas not agreed by all might be abandoned altogether. This would have the advantage of prohibiting opt-outs, which would ensure a coherent group and a more visible project, making it possible to present the group to the public in a clear way. One may also note that, according to this principle, and if participation in cooperation in defence matters were required to become a member of the group, some members of the euro area would not be able to qualify for that group without abandoning their neutrality or their policy of neutrality. Requesting participation in the Schengen area would cause further difficulties for Ireland, which also has a policy of neutrality, if it desired to participate in the group.

If each participating state remained free to choose the areas in which it participated, the project would be more flexible, but it would risk appearing as a patchwork, which would mean more complexity, an absence of political visibility and, therefore, less attraction to citizens. The coherence of the group would allow the political dimension of the project to be stressed, expressing the leap forward in more coordination and more solidarity that it would represent for the participating states.

---

[8] According to C. D. Ehlermann, in his 1995 article, 'the notion of a pre-established hard core implies (even if the hard core is potentially open) that its members commit themselves to participate in all new and additional ventures'.

- A possible weakness would appear if non-legally binding inter-governmental cooperation were exclusively followed, as this would result in less efficiency. Intergovernmental cooperation means the absence of EU decision-making procedures, the absence of control by the Commission and the Court of Justice of the EU on the implementation by the participating states of the decisions taken in common, and the absence of sanctions. As a result, measures would be more difficult to adopt, as this would require mutual agreement, and compliance with them would not be fully guaranteed, as there would not be any 'guardian' or 'sanction'. The way to avoid these difficulties would be to remain with decisions taken within the EU institutional framework. One has to recognize that this is not the way that was chosen with the adoption of the 'Euro-Plus-Pact' on 25 March 2011.

- Another weak point would be the functioning of the institutions. For a number of areas of enhanced cooperation, the EU institutions would obviously continue to play their role under the treaty, with their full composition as provided for in the treaties.

  That would not be the case for the Council, however. As soon as a particular case of enhanced cooperation has been decided, and even immediately in cases where there is 'inbuilt' cooperation, such as the Schengen and euro areas, the treaty provides that only participating Member States' representatives have the right to vote in the Council.

  This was considered by the authors of the treaties as quite natural in the case of the Council, where there is one member for each Member State, who has the task of defending the interests of the Member State which he or she represents.[9] However, this was not considered as appropriate in the case of the Commission because, even if there is one Commissioner per Member State, Commissioners are supposed to be independent of their state of origin. Of course, this is theoretical. Everybody knows that the political reality is different. This was illustrated, for example, by the

---

[9] See Article 20(2) of the TEU: 'The decision authorising enhanced cooperation shall be adopted by the Council . . . ' and, in order to adopt decisions to develop the cooperation, Article 20(3) states: 'All members of the Council may participate in its deliberations, but only members of the Council representing Member States participating in enhanced cooperation shall take part in the vote' (see also TEU, Article 330). The rule is the same for the Schengen area and for the euro area.

criticisms aimed at Lady Ashton that, due to her heavy schedule as the EU High Representative, she does not have the time to attend all the Commission's meetings. According to the British press, Lady Ashton should be defending the interests of the United Kingdom in the Commission. Actually, and to say the least, these views of the British press are probably shared not only by the national press of other countries, but also by some national political authorities.

In any case, this issue deserves to be discussed.

A case of enhanced cooperation may be launched when a minimum of nine Member States are willing to participate. This represents one-third of the twenty-seven Member States, and therefore one-third of the twenty-seven Commissioners. Any decision in the Commission must be taken at least by a simple majority (i.e., fourteen Commissioners). Let us take an example where there are ten Member States participating in a given case of enhanced cooperation. To be launched, this case must succeed in obtaining the agreement of a majority in the Commission, a majority in the Parliament and a qualified majority in the Council. Let us suppose that this is decided. Then, this particular case of enhanced cooperation will later have to be further developed. Let us imagine that there would be a need for the Commission to adopt a specific proposal that would be a subject of controversy among the Member States. Some of the seventeen Member States not participating in the cooperation might object to the proposal to be made by the Commission. The political risk is that their position might influence the Commissioners having the same nationality, who would then be reluctant to approve the proposal. In such a case, the proposal, which needs fourteen votes, might not secure these votes and might not be adopted by the Commission.

Therefore, there are convincing arguments in favour of changing the rules on this point, in order to allow only those Commissioners having the same nationality as the participating Member States to participate in votes when the aim is to develop a given case of enhanced cooperation involving those Member States only. That is why the institutional Committee of the European Parliament, in Article 46, subparagraph 3 of its 1994 draft report on the Constitution of the EU, often referred to as 'the Herman Draft', suggested that both the Members of the Commission and of the European

Parliament who are nationals of Member States not participating in the 'avant-garde' be excluded from deliberating and voting on issues concerning only the 'avant-garde':[10]

Member States which so desire may adopt among themselves provisions enabling them to advance further and more quickly towards European integration, provided that this process remains open at all times to any Member State wishing to join it and that the provisions adopted remain compatible with the objectives of the Union and the principles of its Constitution.

In particular, with regard to matters coming under Titles V and VI of the Treaty on European Union, they may adopt other provisions which are binding only on themselves.

Members of the European Parliament, the Council and the Commission from the other Member States shall abstain during discussions and votes on decisions adopted under these provisions.

The reasoning made for the Commission was, therefore, equally applied to the European Parliament.[11]

The fact remains that the rules concerning the arrangements for voting in the European Parliament and in the Commission, as defined in the current treaties, do not provide for any exception to the composition or voting rules of the European Parliament and of the Commission in cases of enhanced cooperation. Therefore, according to the treaty, all members of the European Parliament and all members of the Commission have the right to vote, not only to authorize new cases of enhanced cooperation, but also in all subsequent decisions to develop, modify or implement these cases. It is probable that there would not be unanimity among the twenty-seven Member States in favour of modifying the treaty on such an issue.

On the whole, a 'two-speed Europe' conceived as described in this 'soft option' would be far from being revolutionary. It would neither

[10] Article 46 of the 'Herman Draft': 'Resolution of 10 February 1994 on the Constitution of the EU', EU OJ C-61, 28 February 1994.

[11] In 1996, the 'Club of Florence' in *Europe: The Impossible Status Quo* (foreword by Jacques Delors), also proposed reserving the vote to MEPs elected in the Member States participating to the avant-garde, while a deliberation should take place in the plenary of the EP. See also C.-D. Ehlermann, 'Increased Differentiation or Stronger Uniformity', EUI Working Paper RSC 95/21, 1995. See also similar proposals made during the 1996 IGC in the draft provisions on enhanced cooperation, doc. CONF 3914/96, 24 September 1996. A majority in the EP has often opposed these proposals (see a number of resolutions in 1995, 1998, 2000, etc.).

entail any amendment to the treaties nor the adoption of a new treaty by the participating states. Obviously, its aims would not be to try and transform the EU into a federal state. It would simply allow the EU, as it is today, to work better without changing its characteristics, powers or rules. It would also allow the participating states to present their citizens with a complete, coherent and attractive project for their future, rather than limiting themselves to a list of measures for economic austerity, reduced social welfare and budgetary restraint.

However, the fact that the treaty procedures will not be changed and that, consequently, all members of the EP and the Commission would participate in the decision-making, would probably push the participating states to develop their cooperation towards an inter-governmental way, outside the institutional framework of the EU, as they began to do so with the 'Euro-Plus-Pact'. This would make their cooperation less efficient.

*

That is one of the reasons why one could envisage another option, a bolder one, in which an additional treaty would legally bind the participating states. This would have the advantage of better political visibility, which would be necessary in order to explain to the citizens the aim and content of this new step in European integration. It would also, and above all, have the advantage of allowing the organs, rules and procedures that would govern the development of this closer cooperation to be defined in an optimal way.

The institutional and legal feasibility of this last option has to be seriously considered and thoroughly examined. This is done in Chapter 6.

CHAPTER 6

Fourth option: legally building a two-speed Europe

Just like the preceding one, this option would consist in permitting some EU Member States, those that are willing and able, to cooperate together at a faster pace than the other Member States. One of the differences between the two options is that, in the second one, the group of participating states would be established legally, through the conclusion of an international agreement. This *additional treaty* would specify the rules and procedures under which the participating states would decide to cooperate together, while continuing to fully respect the EU treaties.

At first sight, the group could be expected to be composed on the basis of the list of the Member States that have already demonstrated their willingness to go ahead by participating in the euro area. Whether that would be not only a necessary, but also a sufficient, condition is a political issue which would have to be considered by the Member States concerned. Another major closer cooperation is, of course, the Schengen area, and participation in the Schengen area could also be considered as a political condition for acceding to the group by the states that would launch the project. Common views as regards defence issues could also be taken into account.

An additional treaty could be negotiated among the interested EU Member States in order to strengthen further and speed up their cooperation, while fully respecting their obligations under EU law and without harming the rights and interests of other EU Member States. This group would constitute a temporary 'avant-garde', which would remain open and welcome other Member States willing and able to join. The participating states should observe full transparency vis-à-vis the others and should offer to help those willing to join, so that they would be able to do so as soon as possible.

This option has many advantages, but it would also raise a number of difficult legal, institutional and political questions concerning:
- the substantive areas that could be subject to closer cooperation;
- the necessary institutional arrangements and their co-existence with those already existing in the EU;
- its feasibility, including its consistency with international law and EU law;
- how to organize effective controls guaranteeing the rights and interests of the non-participating EU Member States.

POSSIBLE SUBSTANTIVE CONTENT OF THE CLOSER COOPERATION AMONG PARTICIPATING STATES IN AN ADDITIONAL TREATY

The primary principle of an 'avant-garde' group would be that *all* participating states should be fully committed to participate in *all* areas of cooperation, no areas being optional. From a legal point of view, it would be possible to consider very wide potential areas of cooperation, as long as the proper functioning of the internal market and the *acquis communautaire*, as well as all the other rules of the treaties, would be respected. Despite these strict requirements, several important areas could be considered as possible 'candidates':[1]
- the economic component of economic and monetary union;
- security and defence policy;
- matters concerning what used to be called the 'third pillar' after the Maastricht Treaty, that is, cooperation in civil and criminal law, as well as, more generally, the rights of citizens;
- some specific areas of the former 'first pillar', that is, social policy, taxation policy, environmental protection not linked with the

---

[1] These areas could be compared with those which were advocated by Claus-Dieter Ehlermann in his 1995 article already quoted, 'Increased Differentiation or Stronger Uniformity' (EUI, 95/21, 1995): 'The economic component of EMU', 'The intensification of cooperation in the field of security and defence', 'The area of foreign policy', 'The third pillar' and 'Certain activities of the first pillar'; and by Jacques Delors in 2000, *Centre for European Reform Bulletin*, 14: 'The avant-garde should make a success of economic and monetary union, move ahead in economic policy coordination, and enlarge the area of social protection. It should be able to manage common actions in the sphere of foreign policy, and project military power. The avant-garde should create a common space for justice and security, arriving at a common approach to immigration.'

internal market, public health, culture and education, civil protection, etc.;

- some procedural aspects of the implementation of the EU's foreign policy.

The economic component of economic and monetary union

This is, of course, the area where the current EU treaties contain major imbalances and where a group of Member States already exists and cooperates within the euro area. Therefore, here lies the more fundamental reason as to why the idea of an additional treaty might be considered.

First, the group of participating states, if composed of the euro area countries, could use extensively all the possibilities offered by Articles 136 and 138 of the TFEU, as described in Chapter 5. On top of that, with an additional treaty the participating states could decide to take further legally binding commitments.

This is not the place to go into details on the substance of what such commitments might be. However, one may think about decisions having an important impact on the convergence of budgetary and economic policies and which would result in a closer solidarity among the participants, for example:

- stricter budgetary rules, accompanied by a close examination by peers of draft national budgets; the obligation to respect a maximum level of budgetary deficit could be made enforceable; the level of debt could be regulated (commitment to introduce an amendment into each national constitution?) and it could be controlled by an independent organ;
- these measures could be accompanied by harmonizing measures[2] concerning both fiscal legislation (e.g., through the creation of a common basis for the assessment of corporate taxes, which might be followed by a beginning of the harmonization of national laws) and social legislation (such as linking the age and conditions of retirement to current demographic trends or measures aimed at promoting labour mobility); participating states could agree to

---

[2] For example, see those contained in the 'Euro-Plus-Pact' agreed on 25 March 2011 (see Box 4.1).

invest a given percentage of their budget or of their GNP in research and development;

- participating states could establish a European debt agency[3] or some other mechanism that would help to establish more solidarity among the participating states;
- possible sanctions against participating states that did not respect these rules;
- any decision would be made subject to effective democratic control (see below).

Actually, a great step would be made in that direction if it were simply decided to make the 'Euro-Plus-Pact' adopted in March 2011 legally binding under the EU treaties. That might be less difficult to accept by participating States in the context of new institutional arrangements, as examined below.

Security and defence policy

This is an area where neither the EU treaties, nor other international commitments nor national constitutions (except for some of the neutral countries) present obstacles. The obstacles are the divergence of political opinions, the lack of political will and the lack of mutual trust between the Member States.[4] In the hypothesis that a group of states would trust each other enough to adopt the measures described above in the economic and monetary field, which would lead to more solidarity among them, it would seem logical that the same states (except for the neutral ones) should be able to adopt equally bold measures in this area as well, for example, on top of the possible cooperations referred to in the 'softer' option:

- organizing shared public procurement in the area of security and defence and planning future needs together in order to prepare such procurement;
- establishing a permanent civil–military planning and command headquarters for EU operations, as suggested by the foreign

[3] See the proposal made by Jean-Claude Juncker, Prime Minister and Treasury Minister of Luxembourg, and Giulio Tremonti, Minister of Economy and Finance of Italy, 'Euro-wide Bonds would Help to End the Crisis', *Financial Times*, 6 December 2010.
[4] See Antonio Missiroli, 'Pesc, Défense et Flexibilité', *Cahiers de Chaillot*, 38, (February 2000), Institute for Security Studies – Western European Union.

ministers of France, Germany and Poland (the so-called 'Weimar Triangle').[5] This would reduce the dependency of the EU on the five EU Member States that are presently able to provide operational headquarters;

- organizing battalions ready and able to leave for missions abroad at a given distance and for a given period of time, for instance, by joining existing cooperations in that field such as the Franco-German brigade, Eurocorps or Eurofor;
- making a commitment not to reduce their national defence budgets below a given threshold; this looks difficult in a period of budgetary restraint, but one has to take into account the possible 'disengagement' of the United States, at least from what they consider to be the EU's 'back-yard'. Some facts are a matter of concern: the United States spends more than $700 billion annually on its military (including the cost of the operations in Afghanistan and Iraq),[6] while the EU spends €200 billion.[7] The Secretary General of NATO, Anders Fogh Rasmussen, stressed in February 2011 that, in the past two years, the defence spending of NATO's European Member States has shrunk by $45 billion, and that while ten years ago the United States accounted for a little less than half of NATO member's total defence spending, today the US share is close to 75 per cent.[8] According to NATO statistics (reported by the French Ministry of Defence in its 'Annuaire Statistique' for 2010/2011), the United States spent 4.68 per cent of their GDP in their defence budget, while the expenses of the larger EU Member States were much lower: 2.40 per cent for the United Kingdom, 1.65 per cent for France, 1.11 per cent for Germany, 0.88 per cent for Italy and 0.87 per cent for Spain.

If some Member States accepted that they should go further than OCCAR and the Letter of Intent/Framework Agreement by launching joint programmes in weapons' research and development, they

---

[5] See Claudia Major, 'A Civil–Military Headquarters for the EU: the Weimar Triangle Initiative Fuels the Current Debate', *SWP Comments*, 31 December 2010, German Institute for International and Security Affairs.

[6] Richard N. Haas, 'The Age of Nonpolarity', *Foreign Affairs*, June 2008.

[7] Chris Patten, 'Pour un multilatéralisme efficace', *Le Monde*, 23 March 2010. Chris Patten stresses that these expenses are not well oriented, as 70 per cent of the troops of the EU Member States are not able to serve outside their national territory.

[8] *Financial Times*, 8 February, 2011.

would achieve economies of scale and strengthen their respective armament industries. Again, such options would not entail an EU army, an EU defence or EU decisions as to the engagement of troops.

Areas which were covered in the past by the former 'third pillar'

In this area, closer cooperation among some EU Member States would probably open the door to the possible adoption of legislation or harmonization of legislation, which has not been possible up to now due to the differences between the legal systems of the twenty-seven Member States (one example being the difference between common law and continental law), or due to the different levels of development of the judicial system.

Possible cooperation in this field would be the same as in the 'softer' option. On top of that, one could envisage possible new rights for citizens being adopted: provisions could be aimed at better equality of rights for citizens of other participating states, who have been living in a given participating state for a period of time to be determined, for example, the right to vote and to be a candidate in political elections (see TFEU, Article 25). Other measures aimed at favouring the mobility of EU citizens could also be imagined.

Participating Member States could also develop together common controls of their external borders. As the crisis of the Schengen area in 2011 has shown, there is an urgent need to act concretely in this domain, which appears to be impossible while it needs the agreement of the twenty-seven Member States.

For the other fields (former first pillar, foreign policy), possible cooperations would be the same as in the 'softer' option described in Chapter 5.

WOULD IT BE NECESSARY AND LEGALLY FEASIBLE TO CREATE A NEW INSTITUTIONAL FRAMEWORK DIFFERENT FROM THAT OF THE EU?

It would obviously be politically and legally better and more simple to avoid establishing new institutions or organs, as this might entail political tensions and legal difficulties.

It is therefore necessary to examine, for each of the EU institutions, if some of their roles and tasks would need, *mutatis mutandis*, to be exercised in the context of an additional treaty in which only some of the EU Member States participated. If this were to be the case, which bodies and organs could play this role? Would it be possible for the present EU institutions to do so? This would, in any case, make it legally necessary to obtain the authorization of all the twenty-seven EU Member States, but that does not look politically impossible.

However, it has already been stressed that, given that their composition is open to representatives or nationals of all twenty-seven EU Member States, the European Parliament and the Commission could hardly exercise their functions for a smaller group of states: could representatives or nationals of Member States not participating in a particular policy nevertheless continue to take part in the deliberations and decisions of the EU institutions aiming at defining that policy?

If the establishment of some new organs would therefore be difficult to avoid, this should at least be as light as possible and inspired by the EU's institutional framework, while trying to avoid its defects as much as possible. In any case, it would be essential that the authority of the Court of Justice of the EU is not affected.

A parliamentary organ different from the European Parliament

The first and absolute priority would be to establish the closer cooperation under effective and legitimate democratic control.

In order to do that, it would seem difficult to use the European Parliament acting in its full composition in the context of an additional treaty, because its members represent the peoples of the twenty-seven Member States.[9] As has already been stressed, this could lead to paradoxical cases in which MEPs from participating states would vote on a given proposed measure, but this measure would not be adopted because MEPs from non-participating Member States voted against it and thus prevent the necessary majority from being attained.

---

[9] In his 2000 article already mentioned (*CER Bulletin* 14), Jacques Delors favoured the creation of 'a special bicameral Parliament. The latter would consist of MEPs from avant-garde countries, and also deputies from the parliaments of those countries.'

A priori, it would look feasible to require the participation of only those MEPs representing the Member States that had ratified the additional treaty. This has been proposed several times in the past.[10] However, it might arguably be criticized as going against the letter and the spirit of the present treaty provisions on the EP. Article 10(2) of the TEU provides that 'citizens are directly represented at Union level in the European Parliament'. The mandate of MEPs is a European mandate, not a national one. Actually, there are a multitude of acts voted on in the EP that do not apply to all twenty-seven EU Member States (legal acts concerning fisheries, or mountain areas or specific kinds of industry, to take some obvious examples). It follows that it would probably be unavoidable to think about another type of parliamentary organ, without modifying the EU's current treaties, that is, to look outside the EP. If this were to be the case, the choice could be either to organize direct elections to a

[10] The formula of an 'EP with a variable geometry' has been suggested several times in the past by: (a) Claus-Dieter Ehlermann, 'Increased Differentiation or Stronger Uniformity', EUI Working Paper, Robert Schuman Center No. 95/21, European University Institute, 1995, p. 30 'no special rules have been laid down for the functioning of the EP in the context of radical "multi-speed" or "variable geometry" operations. In view of the increased powers of the EP in the Community's legislative process, this absence of special rules is not obvious. Members of the EP are of course not representatives of any government. But they express the opinions of the citizens of their country of origin. And it is in the end this country which does not participate in a certain policy or which is not bound by certain decisions. I am therefore inclined to join those which consider that members of the EP elected in a country which does not participate in a certain policy or which is not bound by certain decisions should not take part in the voting process. All members should however be entitled to participate in the debates, whatever the status of their country of origin may be. Whether this position is compatible with the EP's request that the EP as a whole should be responsible "for exercising control over those union policies which are pursued by a limited number of Member States on a temporary basis" is a matter of interpretation, as it depends on the exact meaning of the word "control"'; (b) the Club of Florence, *The Impossible Status Quo* (London: Palgrave Macmillan, 1997); and (c) during the 1996 IGC within the context of the draft provisions on enhanced cooperation, doc. CONF 3914/96, 24 September 1996: '3. Insofar as they are involved, Member States shall apply the acts and decisions necessary to the implementation of the cooperation action in which they are participating. This action shall be adopted pursuant to the relevant rules of the Treaty, except where the following provisions allow for a derogation: (a) only Members of the European Parliament elected in the Member States taking part in cooperation action shall take part in votes on Commission proposals requiring implementation of the procedure laid down in Article 189b, the required majority being calculated accordingly; (b) representatives of the Member States not taking part in the cooperation action in question shall not participate in Council decisions; the qualified majority in the Council shall be made up of two thirds of the votes of the Council members concerned; unanimity shall include only the Council members concerned.'

smaller European parliamentary organ or to turn towards national parliaments as a basis for establishing a new parliamentary organ. The history of the EU, that is, the relative failure of the EP, might favour the second solution, especially as an additional treaty would not create a new institutional organization, but would only establish new forms of cooperation among the participating states. Moreover, this would avoid the confusing creation of a new elected European parliamentary organ, whose members would be elected in a similar way as the MEPs.

If this choice were to be made, then the following two questions would have to be answered:

- how many parliamentary representatives should be attributed to each Member State?; and
- what would be the powers of this new Parliamentary Organ?

The first question would be difficult to answer, because a number of sensitive political criteria would have to be taken into account. For example, one might try to take into account the judgment of the German Constitutional Court of 30 June 2009 on the Lisbon Treaty, and try to avoid departing too far from the democratic principle of 'one man, one vote'.[11] The German Court stressed the fact that each MEP elected in Germany (the most populated Member State) represented as much as twelve times the number of citizens represented by an MEP elected in Malta (the least populated Member State). However, the court did not mention the facts that, first, in any federal or confederal organization, smaller entities are always over-represented and, second, that in the organs representing the governments, the number of votes given to the more populated states is always greater than the votes given to the smaller ones. One should always allow the less populated Member States to be adequately represented. Finally, one should also take into account the desirability of not establishing an organ with too many members. All these considerations could lead to the suggestion, for example, of a minimum of two members for the smallest participating state (in order that at least two political points of view may be represented for each country) and a maximum of forty for the biggest Member State. If the same comparison was made as above between a German and a Maltese parliamentarian, it

---

[11] See Chapter 2, fnn. 3 and 20.

would give a figure of about ten times instead of twelve, which would be a slight improvement towards a better democratic representation of the citizens.

As for the powers of this new parliamentary organ, it would seem simple and appropriate to confer upon it similar legislative powers to those that the EP has had in the EU since the entry into force of the Lisbon Treaty. On top of these powers, it might also seem appropriate to confer on it a power of legislative initiative, which could be shared with executive powers (see below).

The heads of state or government of the participating states, and members of their governments, could meet in parallel with the European Council and the EU Council

It would be difficult to envisage, in a plenary meeting of twenty-seven taking place in the EU framework, that only those prime ministers and ministers representing the participating states to an additional treaty would deliberate and decide on issues concerning them, and on the basis of another text than the EU treaties. It has in the past already been decided that if a Member State does not participate in a particular policy, it follows that the representatives of the government of that state should not take part in the Council's deliberations on that policy. This was the solution adopted for the United Kingdom in the Social Protocol, attached to the treaties by the Treaty of Maastricht in 1993, as well as for Denmark for defence policy, etc. Therefore, the establishment of new organs, parallel to the European Council and to the EU Council, would appear to be difficult to avoid.[12]

There would be no legal obstacle to two organs of this type being established, one at the level of the heads of state or government and the other one at the level of ministers. It would follow that both would have a specific presidency, different from the presently distinct presidencies of the European Council and of the Council of the EU. These presidents could be elected, for example, for a period of one or two years by the members representing the participating states from among themselves. The powers of the two organs could be similar,

---

[12] In his article already quoted, Jacques Delors suggested the establishment of 'a special Council of Ministers for the avant-garde countries'.

mutatis mutandis, to those of the European Council and the Council of the EU. It might seem appropriate that they could be given a (non-exclusive) power of legislative initiative, together with the parliamentary organ and with the administrative authority (see below). For the sake of simplicity, the weight of the votes of their members could be the same as those defined in the Lisbon Treaty, and be applicable without the transitional arrangements provided by that treaty and the so-called 'Ioannina arrangements'.[13] The frequency of their meetings could be the same as for the corresponding EU institutions; actually, they might be organized in parallel to those meetings ('back-to-back'), as is already the case for ministers of finance of the Euro Group (who meet before every session of the ECOFIN Council), and as has been the case for the heads of state or government of the seventeen members of the euro area, who met just after the European Council on 11 March 2011.

A new administrative authority distinct from the European Commission

In his article in October 2000,[14] Jacques Delors expressed the following opinion: 'I think the Commission could fulfil the same function that it does for the Union, since it is the guardian of the European interest.' One may disagree with that opinion, expressed by a former President of the Commission. A Commission composed of twenty-seven members, each with the nationality of one of the twenty-seven EU Member States, could hardly take decisions and play a decisive role for a group comprising only a fraction of those states. But the fact remains that its tasks, or at least some of the tasks conferred on it by the EU treaties, would have to be carried out within the cooperations to be initiated by an additional treaty. This could be, for instance, conferred upon an organ to be established in that treaty and which could be called the 'administrative authority'.

When trying to imagine how such an administrative authority could be conceived, one should take into account that the EU

[13] See Piris, *The Lisbon Treaty*, pp. 222–5.
[14] 'Europe needs an avant-garde, but...', *Centre for European Reform Bulletin*, 14 (October/November 2000).

Commission has become weaker over the years. We have already argued that two main factors had this effect:

- it is currently composed of one member per Member State; this has transformed the Commission into an inter-governmental body whose members cannot be fully independent from the government of the country of which they are a citizen; and
- the Commission is collectively responsible to the European Parliament, a power that the European Parliament has never formally used, but which it has often used (and abused) implicitly in practice to obtain, through pressure, powers that were not conferred upon it by the treaties.[15]

Therefore, if possible, these two features should not be retained for the administrative authority that could be established by an additional treaty.

Actually, the members of the administrative authority should not be seen as representing the governments or the peoples of the participating states. Their number should be adapted to the tasks to be fulfilled and should not be dependent on the number of participating states. Taking that into account, and in order to be more efficient and independent, this number could, for instance, be as low as five to seven. These members could be elected by the parliamentary organ, for example, from among the members of the governments of the participating states (or from among the members of their national parliaments). They could be elected for a fixed duration, for example, six years, and this period might be non-renewable, in order to strengthen their independence. In such case, however, in order to preserve continuity, it could be envisaged that two or three members could be elected for a second and final term, or that the first appointments could be for different durations.

The major task of the administrative authority would be to control the correct application by the participating states of the acts and measures adopted on the basis of the additional treaty, and, if needed, to bring infringement actions against those states before the administrative court.[16]

---

[15] Including the threat to transform its right of censure of the Commission (as a collective body) into a right of censure of each Commissioner considered individually.

[16] In the framework of the EEA, which is composed of the twenty-seven EU states and of three of the Member States of the EFTA (Iceland, Liechtenstein and Norway), this role is

An important issue would be to decide if the administrative authority should be put in charge of preparing legislative proposals, in the same way and with the same monopoly of initiative that the Commission has for the EU. If this task were not conferred on the administrative authority, because this would imply the need for too great human resources, the question would be to decide who would do it. Would it be possible to out-source this task to the government/administration of participating states on a rotation basis, or to obtain the authorization of the twenty-seven EU Member States that the EU Commission itself could be entrusted to do it (in that case, would it be with all its twenty-seven members or only the nationals of the participating states), or leave it to the administrative authority to receive help from the participating states[17] when needed? This last option might appear, at least at first sight, to be flexible, pragmatic and workable.

The participating states might envisage giving the administrative authority the power to launch legislative initiatives, but not as a monopoly right. It could share this power with the organs representing the governments and with the parliamentary organ.

The Court of Justice

It is obvious that the establishment of a specific new jurisdiction ought to be avoided if possible, because this could entail the risk of conflicts of interpretation with the Court of Justice of the EU. Therefore, the participating states could confer new tasks related to the additional treaty on the Court of Justice of the EU itself, if the other EU Member States and the court itself agreed.

If this was not possible, another option would be to create a new tribunal. In that case, it would be essential to avoid inconsistencies between the case law of this tribunal and the EU Court of Justice. This means that the case law of the new tribunal should not put into jeopardy the case law of the EU Court of Justice. Therefore, the new tribunal should be somehow linked to the case law of the EU

---

played by the EFTA 'Surveillance Authority', which brings infringement actions against an EFTA state before the EFTA Court.

[17] And also by the Commission, on condition of obtaining the authorization of the twenty-seven EU Member States.

Court of Justice, in the same way that the EFTA Court is. Thus, it should be obliged by a provision in the additional treaty, on the one hand, to fully respect the *previous* case law of the EU Court of Justice and, on the other hand, to take due account of the *future* case law of the EU Court. This is what is provided for by Article 3(2) of the 1992 Agreement between the EFTA States on the establishment of the EFTA Surveillance Authority and the EFTA Court of Justice ('Surveillance and Court Agreement').[18] With regard to the case law of the Court of Justice of the EU from the period before the signing of the EFTA Agreement, that is, 2 May 1992, the EFTA Court has to follow the rulings of the Court of the EU (Article 6 of the EFTA). As for the EU, 'Court judgments delivered after that date . . . have to be taken duly into account' by the EFTA Court.[19] If created, the new tribunal could be called the 'administrative tribunal'. As is already the case with the Court of Justice of the EU and of the EFTA Court, the new tribunal could be based in Luxembourg.

It would be appropriate that the number of members of this tribunal should be adapted to the tasks to be fulfilled, and not be dependent on the number of participating states. Therefore, this number could, for example, be limited to three or five. These members could be appointed by a simple majority vote by the heads of state or government of the participating states, for example, for a fixed duration of nine years, not renewable, in order to strengthen their independence. It would be essential that their appointment should be subject to a *positive* opinion of the panel established under Article 255 of the TFEU[20] (after authorization of all twenty-seven EU Member States). The first appointment could be for a different duration for

---

[18] Agreement between the EFTA states on the Establishment of a Surveillance Authority and a Court of Justice (SCA).

[19] On the EFTA Court, see: Carl Baudenbacher (President of that Court) 'The EFTA Court – An Example of the Judicialisation of International Economic Law', *European Law Review*, 28 (2003), 880–95 and 'The EFTA Court: An Actor in the European Judicial Dialogue', *Fordham International Law Journal* (2004–2005), 353–91; Thérèse Blanchet, 'Le succès silencieux de dix ans d'Espace économique européen: un modèle pour l'avenir avec d'autres voisins?', in Martin Johansson, Nils Wahl and Ulf Bernitz (eds.), *Liber Amicorum in Honour of Sven Norberg: A European for all Seasons* (Brussels: Bruylant, 2005).

[20] 'A panel shall be set up in order to give an opinion on candidates' suitability to perform the duties of Judge and Advocate-general of the Court of Justice and the General Court before the governments of the Member States make the appointments . . .'

some members in order to preserve continuity. The administrative tribunal could be in charge of controlling the correct application by the participating states of legislation/regulations adopted on the basis of the additional treaty. The administrative authority and the participating states should be able to seize the administrative tribunal. At first sight, there seems to be no need to have a system of preliminary rulings.

The Central Bank

The European Central Bank (ECB) will, of course, continue to exercise fully its role. The additional treaty would not change anything about that whatsoever. Therefore, there would be no need to have any corresponding organ.

The Court of Auditors

The participating states could confer on the Court of Auditors of the EU the task of controlling the accounts and the implementation of 'their' budget, which will necessarily be separate from the EU's budget. This is the simplest solution, but it would have to be accepted by all twenty-seven Member States.

If this was not possible, another option could be to establish a small organ of control, the number of its members being independent from the number of participating states and limited, for example, to three or five. The role of this organ would be similar to that of the EU's Court of Auditors. Its members could be appointed by a simple majority vote by the heads of state or government of the participating states for a fixed duration of nine years, not renewable, in order to strengthen their independence. Their appointment should be subject to a *positive* opinion given by the panel established on the basis of Article 255 of the TFEU (after authorization of the EU-27 Member States). The first appointment could be for a different duration for some members, in order to preserve some continuity.

A third option, which would be simpler than the second one, might be to confer the task of auditing the accounts to the participating states, on a rotating basis (see, e.g., the system used by the OECD).

The Economic and Social Committee and the Committee of the Regions

If it was desired that all or some legal acts should be submitted for consultation of the Economic and Social Committee or/and the Committee of the Regions of the EU, it could be decided that all members of the Economic and Social Committee and of the Committee of the Regions, who are not bound by any mandatory instructions and are independent in the performance of their duties (which are exclusively advisory) in the general interest of the Union, would take part in all discussions. This would be subject to an authorization by the twenty-seven Member States.

Budget and decision-making

All financial consequences entailed by the implementation of an additional treaty should be borne by the participating states only. In that context, participating states could consider whether this budget could be covered by actual 'own' resources, on the basis of the ideas expressed in 2010 by Mr Janusz Lewandowski, the Commissioner responsible for the EU budget, who has referred to different possibilities as far as the future own resources of the EU are concerned, such as a tax on financial transactions, on air transport, or on CO_2.

As to the decision-making system, consideration might be given to examining possible innovations, for example:

- sharing the legislative initiative between three organs: the Committee of Ministers, the administrative authority and the parliamentary organ;
- providing that legislative acts could be adopted through co-decision between the parliamentary organ and the Committee of Ministers, according to rules that would be identical, *mutatis mutandis*, to those provided for the EU in the Lisbon Treaty, except for the rule according to which the EU Council (i.e., the Committee of Ministers) needs unanimity in order to modify a proposal of the European Commission (i.e., the administrative authority);
- providing that all decisions could be taken through qualified majority voting by the Committee of Ministers, thus meaning that unanimity would no longer exist as a rule for adopting decisions;

- however, in that case, a distinction should be made between two categories of decisions. For the first category, participating states would not be obliged to implement decisions on which the minister representing them had voted negatively. For the second category, the acts adopted would be obligatory for all participating states, including those whose minister had voted against;
- providing, for the second category, that a 'strengthened' qualified majority would be required, for example, 80 per cent of the votes and 80 per cent of the population, a blocking minority being composed of at least three participating states.

FEASIBILITY

Would such an additional treaty be compatible with international law and EU law?

The conclusion of an additional treaty as described in this chapter would be compatible both with international law and with EU law.

Compatibility with international law

The 1969 Vienna Convention on the Law of Treaties, which largely reflects customary international law, does not prohibit the negotiation and conclusion of an additional treaty among some of the parties to a multilateral treaty (see, *a contrario*, Article 41). An additional treaty would not require the consent of the other EU Member States, on condition that their interests are not harmed and that the EU treaties as well as the EU law adopted on their basis remain fully applicable.

Compatibility with EU law

Similarly, nothing in EU law prevents two or more EU Member States from concluding new treaties between themselves, under the same conditions, that is, that they remain fully bound by their obligations under the EU treaties and that any amendment to the EU treaties may only be adopted by all EU members.

This has already been recognized in the past, as shown by Article 350 of the TFEU on the Benelux countries, by the Declaration[21] in

---

[21] Declaration 28, Act of Accession, 1994, OJ C 241/392.

the Act of Accession of Austria, Finland and Sweden on the Nordic Cooperation, or by the Treaty of 1963 between France and Germany.[22] These examples concern closer cooperation of a general nature. In addition, there are also examples of treaties organizing closer cooperation among a group of willing Member States in specific areas, such as the 1985 Agreement on 'Schengen cooperation' signed by only five EU Member States (Belgium, France, Germany, Luxembourg and the Netherlands).

Furthermore, some people have voiced a possible concern with regard to the application of the 'ERTA' case law[23] of the EU Court of Justice to the acts adopted by the participating states. However, this would not actually be problematic, as the ERTA case law comes into play if, and only if, the EU itself has an exclusive or exercised competence in a given area. The fact that a number of Member States exercise their national powers together has never entailed (and could not entail) any 'ERTA effect' for the EU.

Other observers thought that the right to pursue the objectives of the EU treaties belongs exclusively to the full EU membership and would be legally doubtful for a smaller group. However, this is not legally correct, as Protocol No. 25 shows, even in a case where the EU has begun to adopt acts in order to pursue an EU objective: 'when the Union has taken action in a certain area, the scope of competence only covers those elements governed by the Union act in question and therefore does not cover the whole area'.

Finally, the decision on the institutional arrangements in an additional treaty might result in setting up new organs, whose tasks would be comparable to those conferred in the EU treaties on the European Parliament and the Commission (the European parliamentary organ and the administrative authority). In that case, and as far as these new organs would be composed only of nationals from the participating states, this might be criticized as 'by-passing' the normal rules of the treaties. However, although one might well understand the political

---

[22] 'The Treaty of Elysée', signed in Paris, 22 January 1963 (see English text in *International Currency Review*, 23(3) (1996).
[23] Case 22/70, ERTA, *Commission* v. *Council* [1971] ECR 263. Under this case law, the EU has exclusive competence to enter into an international commitment if and to the extent that it has exercised its (internal or external) competence in the field concerned.

criticisms that such institutional arrangements might provoke, there would not be any ground for criticizing their legality. As long as a Member State remains free to act in a given area while respecting its legal obligations under the EU treaties, that Member State also has the right to join forces with other Member States willing to do so. Together, they have the right to organize their joint cooperation as they see fit, including by establishing their own institutional structures and organs and their own legal procedures and rules, it being understood that their closer cooperation will never be an obstacle to the EU institutions acting under the rules of the EU treaties, and that only these EU institutions will be competent to develop the *acquis* of the EU.

Therefore, it follows from this examination that there would be no legal obstacle to the conclusion of an additional treaty organizing closer cooperation between some of the EU Member States on matters to be determined by them, as long as they continue to be bound by all their obligations under the EU treaties.

How should the group's membership be composed?

The Member States concerned could decide on the composition of their group as they see fit, that is, on purely political criteria. They could also constitute their group by taking into account the willingness to proceed demonstrated by Member States in the past, that is, by aiming at those that had used the existing possibilities of closer cooperation already offered by the treaties, and especially and most probably by being a member of the euro area (which, at the time of writing, would temporarily include seventeen of the twenty-seven Member States).[24]

This would not mean that all Member States actually participating in the euro area at the time when the decision would be made would automatically participate in an additional treaty. Each state

---

[24] Other major cooperations foreseen in the treaty are the Schengen area (only one Member State, Ireland, is a member of the euro area but not of the Schengen area) and the 'permanent structured cooperation' (PSC) in the area of the Common Security and Defence Policy; however, this cooperation has not started at the time of writing. Five Member States are neutral or have a policy of neutrality: Austria, Finland, Ireland, Malta and Sweden.

would naturally be free to decide whether to participate or not, taking into account the conditions to be fulfilled, for example, through the acceptance of a minimum set of principles, or the measures to be agreed upon before the formal negotiation with regard to an additional treaty could start. One could imagine that tough conditions might be imposed on the convergence of budgetary and economic policies, reflecting the fact that, in parallel, the solidarity among participating states would probably be increased as compared with the present situation between the members of the euro area. Legally, the conditions formalized in an additional treaty, unless adopted later by the EU Council on the basis of Article 136 of the TFEU, will not be part of the *acquis* of the EU and, therefore, will not become binding for the Member States which join the euro area in the future.

One should also take into account the wise words used by Joschka Fischer in his famous 2000 speech:[25]

The question of which countries will take part in such a project, the EU founding members, the Euro-[11] members or another group, is impossible to answer today. One thing must be clear when considering the option of forming a centre of gravity: this avant-garde must never be exclusive but must be open to all Member States and candidate countries, should they desire to participate at a certain point in time. For those who wish to participate but do not fulfil the requirements, there must be a possibility to be drawn closer in. Transparency and the opportunity for all EU Member States to participate would be essential factors governing the acceptance and feasibility of the project. This must be true in particular with regard to the candidate countries. For it would be historically absurd and utterly stupid if Europe, at the very time when it is at long last reunited, were to be divided once again.

How to guarantee the rights and interests of the non-participating EU Member States?

Such a guarantee would certainly be necessary. It would naturally be required by the EU Member States not participating in the additional

---

[25] Speech by Joschka Fischer at Humboldt University, Berlin, 12 May 2000: 'From Confederation to Federation: Thoughts on the Finality of European Integration'. At that time, the Euro Group was composed of eleven Member States.

treaty, and it should be organized in such a way as to preserve the necessary mutual trust among all EU members.

In order to be effective, this guarantee should be accompanied by the control of organs which should fulfil three conditions:

- they should be trusted by the non-participating EU Member States;
- they would have a legal right of decision and of sanction acceptable to the participating states; and
- they would have recognized standing and authority.

This would lead to the conclusion that such control would have to be exercised by the European Commission and the EU Court of Justice themselves, acting with their full composition (twenty-seven members each), as they do to control the exercise of enhanced cooperation on the basis of Article 327 of the TFEU. One cannot imagine other organs able to satisfy the three conditions referred to above. The Commission or any EU Member State should be able to seize the Court of Justice of the EU of any infringement of the EU treaties and EU law by one participating state or by all of them collectively.

A decision organizing this control would have to be included in the provisions of the additional treaty. To this end, it would also need to be authorized by the twenty-seven EU Member States. Any authorization of this kind by the twenty-seven could be adopted by an intergovernmental decision taken by them in the margins of a meeting of the European Council or of the EU Council.

*

The establishment of new bodies to permit closer cooperation between some EU Member States would certainly be criticized as complicating the image of Europe and its visibility for the citizens.

First, however, the creation of a single 'avant-garde' would actually result in a simpler picture than the complicated 'patchwork' image of the present EU.

Second, and in any case, without the creation of new bodies, it would not be possible to achieve the project. An additional treaty would have to be ratified by the willing Member States only. If a revision of the current EU treaties were necessary, as would be the case if one wished to change the rules of the treaties on the participation of the Members of the European Parliament and of the Commission in the decision-making process in cases of enhanced cooperation (modification of Title IV of the TEU and of Part VI, Title III of the TFEU), it would have to be ratified by all twenty-seven EU Member States. This would be a non-starter and would put an end to the project.

Conclusion

The European Union is in crisis.

At the same time, with the support of its public opinion diminishing, it must try to solve the acute problems of the euro area, while its institutions are not working properly on the basis of their current rules and procedures.

Given the fact that the EU's Member States will need its help more than ever in the future, to face globalization, to preserve peace, security, safety and prosperity, to deal with their catastrophic demographic trends and their financial and economic problems, something has to be done in order to permit the EU to be able to help them more efficiently and with a better political legitimacy.

The first option, which would consist of substantively revising the EU treaties, looks unrealistic.

The second option, which would be to continue to work on the current path, might entail the risk either of a slow reduction in the ambitions of the EU, which could become a progressively less significant actor in the world and less able to help its Member States, or even of a splitting up of the EU in the case of divergences on how to solve a serious economic and financial crisis. However, this second option might be successful, as long as it were supported by quite a strong political will demonstrated both by the Member States and by the EU institutions. The implementation of the Lisbon Treaty with regard to the reduction in the number of members of the Commission could help to restore the strength, efficiency and independence of the Commission. A better respect of the treaty provisions by the European Parliament, especially as regards the powers of the Commission, would also be helpful to achieve a better balance between the institutions. Of paramount importance would obviously be the adoption and strict implementation of the legislative programme on budgetary and economic convergence. If all these conditions were met, then the EU might be able to prove to the world that a monetary union based on a centralized monetary policy and on decentralized budgetary and economic policies can be viable. On top of this, the provisions of the treaty, which have as their very aim to permit the EU to work with twenty-seven members, should no longer be ignored, but should be used whether it be through Articles 136 and 138 of the TFEU, permanent structured cooperation, constructive abstention or enhanced cooperation.

If this does not prove to be feasible, then the hypothesis of a 'two-speed Europe', probably based on the euro area, should be considered. Two options are legally possible, one softer, one bolder. Both will, of course, be criticized. The following criticisms would be raised:

- increasing complexity: this would be true without a unified 'avant-garde'; but if a substantial group of Member States accepted that they should go ahead together in all areas, establishing themselves as an 'avant-garde', this would, on the contrary, simplify the picture as compared with the present EU, which is becoming more and more divided into a patchwork of different sub-groups;
- creating an inner group imposing its political will on the others[1] or condemning the 'new' Member States to an 'inferior peripheral status':[2] this is not correct, as the members of the group will have to respect all EU decisions, which would continue to be taken according to the current rules, by the EU institutions in their present composition;
- dividing Eastern and Western countries: this would not be the case as candidates for the group might be, for instance, Estonia or Slovenia and, most probably within a few years, Poland and some others, while the United Kingdom or Sweden might wish to stay outside;
- establishing a federal European state: this is obviously out of the question, as the present characteristics of the EU would remain

---

[1] See Helen Wallace, 'Possible Future for the EU. A British Reaction', Jean Monnet Working Paper No. 7/00, 2000.

[2] See Jan Zielonka, 'Enlargement and the Finality of European Integration', Jean Monnet Working Paper No. 7/00, 2000.

the same, with no power or very little in the most important areas of state activities (the army, police, education, social security, public transport and public services in general, etc.),[3] with very small financial resources (around 1 per cent GDP, which represents a relative diminution since and despite the EU's enlargement from fifteen to twenty-seven Member States[4]), with very small powers of implementation (EU law is implemented by Member States' administrations[5]), and while any change of the EU treaties, whatever its importance, will always have to be agreed unanimously by all EU Member States' governments, as well as either by their parliaments or by a national referendum. *The purpose of the EU is to help and to strengthen its Member States, not to weaken and to abolish them.* Under both options, the EU will not become a state, which neither its Member States nor its citizens want. However, in order to allow the EU to be able to develop, in a sustainable way, common policies in some areas, or better cooperation in other areas, it might be necessary that an 'avant-garde' group pulls it forward for an interim period;

- difficulties for potential participating states to agree on a common list of areas in which they would find it acceptable to cooperate together: this would certainly be the most relevant and serious criticism. Would countries like Finland, Germany or the Netherlands agree with Greece, Ireland or Portugal on a common list of (legally

---

[3] See Andrew Moravcsik, 'The European Constitutional Settlement', *The World Economy*, 2008, pp. 157–82 at pp. 173–4: 'the European Superstate is an illusion . . . the EU, broadly speaking, does not tax, spend, implement, coerce or, in most areas, monopolise public authority. It has no army, police and intelligence capacity, and a minuscule tax base, discretion on spending, and administration. Many . . . areas remain essentially untouched by direct EU policy making, including taxation, fiscal policy, social welfare, health care, pensions, education, defence, active cultural policy, and most law and order.'

[4] See Chapter 2, fn. 34.

[5] The Commission has less than 13,000 officials in the 'A' grade (permanent and non-permanent staff included), while the number of citizens of the EU is more than 500,000,000. Ever since its origins, the EEC–EC–EU has been based on the 'principle of indirect administration', which reflects the fact that Member States do not wish to endow the EU with the large administrative infrastructure that would be necessary to enable it to implement EU legislation. It is only in exceptional cases that the Commission has the power to adopt implementing decisions. This system is reflected in Article 4(3) of the TEU, which obliges Member States to take 'any appropriate measure, general or particular, to ensure fulfilment of the obligations arising out of the Treaties or resulting from the acts of the institutions of the Union' (compare with Article 83 of the German Fundamental Law).

binding) social, fiscal and economic measures to be taken? Would Germany or Austria accept common endeavours in the military sphere or in EU penal legislation? The crux of the problem lies here. The political hypothesis is that the euro crisis might be such that it could oblige the euro Member States to adopt tough and legally binding measures. But these measures might be difficult for citizens in some countries to accept (see the present reactions, for example, in Greece or Finland), and could risk opening the door to populist political parties. According to such an hypothesis, interested governments might find it wiser to include those measures in a much wider project, providing more European integration and solidarity and hope for the future.

The world is changing more and more rapidly. Globalization is a reality. On the global scale, individual EU Member States are geographically small, economically fragile, and demographically in a declining and ageing trend. In the future, they will continue to need the EU to meet the huge challenges that they face in order to preserve their prosperity and their internal and external security, to maintain a safe environment, to organize better controlled immigration, etc. The EU must be able to help. However, with its present institutions and procedures, the EU is slow, heavy, not flexible enough, not able to adapt and decide rapidly. The current EU has difficulties, not only in resolving the crisis of the euro area, but also in completing the internal market and even implementing it correctly, or in ensuring full respect of the Schengen rules, in deciding on foreign policy matters, on cooperating in the defence field, etc.

The implementation of the Lisbon Treaty, even after a normal period of adaptation, will not deliver what is needed. The status quo and the system of 'one-decision-fits-all' are not satisfactory. Given the diversity of the interests and needs of its twenty-seven members, and the way its decisions are taken, this might lead to an EU taking fewer and too modest decisions and incorrectly implementing its past achievements.

Decreasing efficiency and relevance are not the only issues. The cohesiveness and identity of the EU has suffered from the huge and rapid enlargements of 2004 and 2007. European citizens, who no longer understand what the purpose of the EU is, what its political aims are and what its political borders will be, are tending to withdraw their support. The support of citizens and the political legitimacy of the EU have begun to decrease, particularly given the relative failure of the European Parliament. Regaining this support, while fighting populism, is a necessity. To do so, at the same time as taking difficult decisions in order to solve the euro crisis, to complete and implement the internal market and to respect Schengen, an ambitious project is needed. The EU should not be seen only as imposing less social benefits and more austere economic policies; it should offer a wider political project.[6]

Since the best-suited option, that is, a substantive revision of the treaties, is excluded politically, the time is approaching when the choice will be between the status quo, which might mean a diluted EU, slowly stagnating and becoming irrelevant, and an EU that accepts, as a temporary measure, more differentiation between its Member States. The fact is that a number of the twenty-seven Member States are not presently in a position to accept the measures that would be necessary in order to strengthen the EU and, in particular, to stabilize the euro area. Therefore, one has to try and find another feasible option, in which the euro area countries should probably lead.

The recognition and better organization of a temporary 'avant-garde' group, which is *de facto* already imposing itself in actuality, could allow for progressively reducing and eventually putting an end to some of the imbalances that affect the strength and effectiveness of the EU, and that have not been resolved by the Lisbon Treaty:

- for economic and monetary union, a better convergence of the budgetary and economic policies of the Member States concerned;
- favouring the mobility of EU citizens through recognizing new political and social rights and solving cross-border family law issues;
- in relation to the internal market, a reduction in the differences in tax and social policies;
- a correction to the asymmetry between the movement of persons across external and internal borders, as well as better organization and control of immigration and strict implementation of the Schengen rules;

---

[6] To quote the words of Joseph W. W. Weiler in his speech in Florence on 9 May 2011 on the occasion of the sixtieth anniversary of the Schuman Declaration: 'the ideal pursued, the destiny to be achieved, the Promised Land waiting at the end of the road'.

- full participation in the Common Security and Defence Policy and closer cooperation in public procurement in the sphere of defence; and
- last, but not least, the effective political democratic legitimacy of these policies could be improved through an increased role given to the national parliaments of participating states.

*

Short-term financial decisions will have to be taken to solve the current burning euro crisis. However, the need will remain to try to put an end to the structural imbalances of the EU, in order to prevent new crisis.

It is argued that this book shows that the legal difficulties of such an enterprise are not insurmountable. If there is a political will, institutional and legal solutions are available. As a 'softer' option, the interested Member States could simply choose to use all the possibilities offered by the current treaties. As a 'bolder' option, the adoption of an additional treaty, which would present many advantages, is legally feasible and not so complex as it appears at first sight.

This could open the way to the other Member States, which would be welcomed and helped to join when they are ready to do so. It would prepare for a future European Union of the twenty-seven and more, which, without aiming for federalism, would be more dynamic and effective, more legitimate, present and active in the external world and more responsive to the needs of Europeans in the decades to come.

Further reading

Adler-Nissen, Rebecca 2009. 'Behind the scenes of differentiated integration: circumventing national opt-outs in Justice and Home Affairs', *Journal of European Public Policy* 16 January:, 62–80.

Ahrens, Joachim, Renate Ohr and Götz Zeddies 2006. 'Enhanced Cooperation in an Enlarged EU', CEGE, Georg August Universität, Göttingen, Discussion Paper 53.

Allemand, Frédéric 2005. 'The Impact of the EU Enlargement on Economic and Monetary Union: What Lessons can be Learnt from the Differentiated Integration Mechanisms in an Enlarged Europe?', *European Law Journal* 5: 586–617.

Allemand, Michael and Clara Brandi Wohlgemuth 2007. 'Shall We Try New Methods to Make the EU-27 Work?', *FIP*, Paris, September.

Amato, Giuliano 2000. 'Un Coeur Fort pour l'Europe', Jean Monnet Working Paper No. 7/00.

Andreani, Gilles 2002. *What Future for Federalism?* London: Centre for European Reform.

Areilza Carvajal, José M. de and Alfonso Dastis Quecedo 1997. 'Flexibilidad y Cooperaciones Reforzadas: Nuevos Métodos para una Europa Nueva?', *Revista de Derecho Comunitario Europeo* 1: 9–28.

Barber, Tony 2009. 'Two-Speed Europe is the Dog that doesn't Bark', *Financial Times*, 1 October.

2010. 'Poland warns of Two-Speed Europe', *Financial Times*, 9 June.

Baudenbacher, Carl 2004. 'The EFTA Court – An Example of the Judicialisation of International Economic Law', *European Law Review* 28(6): 880–99.

2005. 'The EFTA Court – An Actor in the European Judicial Dialogue', *Fordham International Law Journal* 28: 353–91.

Beaumont, Paul, Carole Lyons and Neil Walker (eds.) 2002. *Convergence and Divergence in European Public Law?* Oxford: Hart Publishing.

Beneyto, José María 2009. *Unity and Flexibility in the Future of the European Union: The Challenge of Enhanced Cooperation*. Madrid: CEU Ediciones.

Blanchet, Thérèse 2005. 'Le succès silencieux de dix ans d'Espace économique européen: un modèle pour l'avenir avec d'autres voisins?', in Martin Johansson, Nils Wahl and Ulf Bernitz (eds.), *Liber Amicorum in Honour of Sven Norberg: A European for all Seasons*. Brussels: Bruylant, pp. 101–24.

Boele-Woelki, Katharina 2009. 'To Be, or Not to Be: Enhanced Cooperation in International Divorce Law within the European Union', *Victoria University Wellington, Law Review* 780: 779–92.

Bribosia, Hervé 2000. 'Différenciation et avant-gardes au sein de l'UE. Bilan et perspectives du Traité d'Amsterdam', *CDE* 1–2: 57–115.

2001. 'Les coopérations renforcées au lendemain du Traité de Nice', *Revue du droit l'Union européenne* 1: 111–71.

2004. 'Les coopérations renforcées et les nouvelles formes de flexibilité en matière de défense dans la Constitution européenne', *Revue du droit l'Union européenne* 4: 647–708.

Broberg, Morten 2011. 'The EU's Legal Ties with its Former Colonies – When Old Love Never Dies', DIIS Working Paper, Copenhagen.

Búrca, Gráinne de 2000. 'Differentiation within the "Core"?', in de Búrca and Scott (eds.), *Constitutional Change in the EU: From Uniformity to Flexibility?*, pp. 133–72.

Búrca, Gráinne de and Joanne Scott (eds.) 2000. *Constitutional Change in the EU: From Uniformity to Flexibility?* Oxford: Hart Publishing.

Burgorgue-Larsen, Laurence 2004. 'Le droit communautaire dans tous ses états ou les désordres du IN et du OUT', *Mélanges en hommage à Guy Isaac, '50 ans de droit communautaire'*. University of Toulouse, pp. 121–36.

Cameron, Fraser 2004. 'Widening and Deepening', in F. Cameron (ed.), *The Future of Europe: Integration and Enlargement*. London: Routledge.

Caracciolo, Lucio 2010. 'Are We Already in a Two-Speed Europe?', *La Repubblica*, Rome, 26 April.

Centre for Economic Policy Research 1995. 'Flexible Integration: Towards a More Effective and Democratic Europe', *Monitoring European Integration* 6, London: CEPR.

Charlemagne (alias: Christoffersen, Keller-Noëllet, Piris) 1995. 'L'Equilibre entre les Etats Membres', in *L'Equilibre européen. Etudes rassemblées et publiées en hommage à Niels Ersbøll, Secrétaire général du Conseil de l'UE*. Brussels: Council of the European Union.

Chevallier-Govers, Constance 2002. 'La création d'une police européenne grâce aux mécanismes de la coopération renforcée', in F. Hervouët and P. Norel (eds.), *La dynamique de la démarche communautaire dans la construction européenne*, vol. II. Paris: La documentation française, pp. 295–330.

Closa Montero, Carlos 2010. 'Differentiated Integration and Flexibility in the EU under the Lisbon Treaty', Real Instituto Elcano, Ari, April, pp. 1–6.

Club of Florence 1997. *Europe: The Impossible Status Quo*. London: Macmillan.

Commissariat General du Plan 2004. *Perspectives de la coopération renforcée dans l'UE*, Paris: La documentation française.

Common Market Law Review Editorial 2011. 'Enhanced Cooperation: A Union à taille réduite or à porte tournante', *Common Market Law Review* 48(2): 317–27.

Constantinesco, Vlad 1997. 'Les clauses de coopération renforcée', *Revue trimestrielle de droit européen*, 83(4): 751–67.

Crivat, Liliana 1997. *Mythes et réalités de l'intégration différenciée dans l'Union européenne*. European Institute, University of Geneva.

Curtin, Deirdre 1995. 'The Shaping of a European Constitution and the 1996 IGC: "Flexibility" as a Key Paradigm', *Aussenwirtschaft* 50(1): 237–51.

de Grauwe, Paul 2011. 'The Governance of a Fragile Eurozone', University of Leuven and Centre for European Political Studies (CEPS), Brussels, 4 May.

Dehousse, Renaud 2000. 'Rediscovering Functionalism', Jean Monnet Working Paper No. 7/00.

Delhey, Jan 2007. 'Do Enlargements Make the European Union Less Cohesive? An Analysis of Trust between EU Nationalities', *Journal of Common Market Studies* 45(2): 253–79.

Delors, Jacques 2000. 'Europe needs an avant-garde, but ...', *Bulletin of the Centre for European Reform*, 14.

Den Boer, Monica, Allan Guggenbühl and Sophie Vanhoonacker (eds.) 1998. *Coping with Flexibility and Legitimacy after Amsterdam*. Maastricht: EIPA.

Dennewald, Jeannine 2010. 'L'espace judiciaire européen au lendemain du Traité de Lisbonne: état des lieux et perspectives de l'intégration différenciée', *ERA Forum* 11: 169–96.

Deubner, Christian 1999. 'Enhanced Cooperation of EU Member States after Amsterdam. A New Tool to be Applied or to be Avoided?', Eben Hausen: SWP-KA 3108.

2000. 'Harnessing Differentiation in the EU. Flexibility after Amsterdam', A Report on Hearings with Parliamentarians and Officials in Seven European Capitals, European Commission Forward Studies Unit, Brussels.

Dudzik, Slawomir 2003. 'Enhanced Cooperation between EU Member States: An Opportunity or a Threat to Poland', in Adam Bodnar *et al.* (eds.), *The Emerging Constitutional Law of the European Union: German and Polish Perspectives*. Berlin: Springer, pp. 239–52.

Dyson, Kenneth and Martin Marcussen 2010. 'Transverse Integration in European Economic Governance: Between Unitary and Differentiated Integration', *Journal of European Integration*, 32(1): 17–39.

Dyson, Kenneth and Angelos Sepos (eds.) 2010. *Which Europe? The Politics of Differentiated Integration*. Basingstoke: Palgrave Macmillan.

Edwards, Geoffrey and Eric Phillipart 1997. 'Flexibility and the Treaty of Amsterdam: Europe's new Byzantium', CELS Occasional Paper No. 3.

Egeberg, Morten and Jarle Trondal 1999. 'Differentiated Integration in Europe: The Case of an EEA Country, Norway', *Journal of Common Market Studies* 33(1): 133–42.

Ehlermann, Claus Dieter 1984. 'How Flexible is Community Law? An Unusual Approach to the Concept of "Two Speeds"', *Michigan Law Review* 82: 1274–93.

  1995. 'Increased Differentiation or Stronger Uniformity', EUI Working Paper RSC, No. 95/21, European University Institute, Florence.

  1998. 'Differentiation, Flexibility, Closer Cooperation: The New Provisions of the Amsterdam Treaty', *European Law Journal* 4: 246–70.

Eliassen, Kjell A. and Nick Sitter 2002. 'Defence Procurement in the European Union', Norwegian School of Management, Oslo.

Epiney, Astrid 2000. 'Flexible Integration and Environment Policy in the EU – Legal Aspects', in K. Holzinger and P. Knoepfel (eds.), *Environmental Policy in a European Union of Variable Geometry? The Challenge of the Next Enlargement*. Basel: Helbing & Lichtenhahn Verlag, pp. 39–64.

Faegerlund, N. 1997. 'The Special Status of the Åaland Islands in the European Union', in L. Hannikainen and F. Horn (eds.), *Autonomy and Demilitarisation in International Law: The Åaland Islands in a Changing Europe*. The Hague: Kluwer Law International, pp. 189–256.

Fauchon, Pierre 2009. 'Rapport d'information du Sénat français sur les coopérations spécialisées: une voie de progrès de la construction européenne', *Sénat* 237: 1–54.

Fauchon, Pierre and François Sicard 2010. 'L'Europe des coopérations volontaires ou comment donner une nouvelle impulsion à l'Europe ... ', Fondation Robert Schuman, Paris.

Gaja, Giorgio 1998. 'How Flexible is Flexibility under the Amsterdam Treaty', *Common Market Law Review* 35: 855–70.

Grabbe, Heather 2003. 'The Siren Song of a Two-Speed Europe', Centre for European Reform, London.

Grabitz, Eberhard 1986. 'L'intégration différenciée de *lege ferenda*', in *L'Intégration différenciée*. Brussels: IEE.

Grabitz, Eberhard and Bernd Langeheine 1981. 'Legal Problems Related to a Proposed "Two-Tier System" of Integration within the European Community', *Common Market Law Review* 18: 33–48.

Grant, Charles 2001. 'France, Germany and a "Hard-Core" Europe', *Centre for European Reform Bulletin* 19.

2005. 'Variable Geometry', *Prospect Magazine*.

Guillard, Christine 2007. *L'intégration différenciée dans l'Union européenne*. Brussels: Bruylant.

Hanf, Dominik 2001. 'Flexibility Clauses in the Founding Treaties, from Rome to Nice', in B. de Witte, D. Hanf and E. Vos (eds.), *The Many Faces of Differentiation in the EU Law*. Antwerp: Intersentia, pp. 3–26.

Harlow, Carol 2001. 'Voices of Difference in a Plural Community. The Case for Legal Diversity Within the European Union', Harvard Jean Monnet Working Paper No. 3/00.

Harmsen, Robert 1994. 'A European Union of Variable Geometry. Problems and Perspectives', *Northern Ireland Legal Quarterly* 45(12): 109–33.

Harstad, Bard 2006. 'Flexible Integration? Mandatory and Minimum Participation Rules', *Scandinavian Journal of Economics* 108(4): 683–702.

Hedemann-Robinson, Martin 1999. 'The Area of Freedom, Security and Justice with Regard to the UK, Ireland and Denmark', in D. O'Keeffe and P. Twomey (eds.), *Legal Issues of the Amsterdam Treaty*. Oxford: Hart Publishing, pp. 271 ff.

Jensen, Christian B. and Jonathan B. Slapin 2010. 'Institutional Hokey-Pokey: the Politics of Multispeed Integration in the European Union', UCD Dublin Institute, DEI Working Paper No. 10-1, April.

Joerges, Christian, Yves Mény and Joseph H. H. Weiler (eds.) 2000. *What Kind of Constitution for what Kind of Polity? Responses to Joschka Fischer*. Florence: Robert Schuman Center for Advanced Studies, European University Institute.

Junge, Kerstin 1999. *Flexibility, Enhanced Cooperation and the Treaty of Amsterdam*. London: Kogan Page, European Dossier Series,

Kempe, Iris and Wim Van Meurs 2001. 'Towards a Multi-Layered Europe', in B. de Witte, D. Hanf and E. Vos (eds.), *The Many Faces of Differentiation in the EU Law*. Antwerp: Intersentia.

Kölliker, Alkuin 2001. 'Bringing Together or Driving Apart the Union? Towards a Theory of Differentiated Integration', *West European Politics* 24(4): 125–51.

2006. *Flexibility and European Unification: The Logic of Differentiated Integration*. Lanham, MD: Rowman & Littlefield.

Kortenberg, Helmut 1998. 'Closer Cooperation in the Treaty of Amsterdam', *Common Market Law Review* 35: 833–54.

Kowalski, Michael 2005. 'Comment on Daniel Thym – United in Diversity or Diversified in the Union?', *German Law Journal* 6(11): 1750–3.

Kurpas, Sebastian *et al.* 2006. 'From Threat to Opportunity – Making Flexible Integration Work', *European Policy Institutes Network*, Working Paper No. 15, September.

Lamoureux, François 2003. 'Projet de Constitution: de la nécessité d'organiser une "arrière-garde"', *Revue du droit l'Union européenne* 4: 807–11.

Leben, Charles 2000. 'A Federation of Nation States or a Federal State?', *Jean Monnet Working Paper* No. 7/00.

Lipsius, Justus (alias Jean-Claude Piris) 1995. 'The 1996 IGC', *European Law Review* 20(3): 235–67.

Louis, Jean-Victor 2001. 'Post-Scriptum: From Differentiation to the "Avant-Garde"', in de Witte, Hanf and Vos (eds.), *The Many Faces of Differentiation in EU Law*, pp. 379–89.

Maillet, Pierre 1995. 'Convergence et géométrie variable – L'organisation et le fonctionnement de l'Union européenne diversifiée est à repenser', *Revue du Marché Commun et de l'UE* 386: 145–59.

Maillet, Pierre and Dario Velo 1994. *L'Europe à Géométrie Variable – Transition vers l'Intégration*. Paris: Editions L'Harmattan.

Majone, Giandomenico 1996. *Regulating Europe*. London: Routledge.
　　2009. *Europe as the Would-Be World Power – The EU at Fifty*. Cambridge University Press.
　　2009. *Dilemmas of European Integration – The Ambiguities and Pitfalls of Integration by Stealth*. Oxford University Press.

Manin, Philippe 2008. 'La place de la diversité dans les traités sur l'Union européenne', in *Mélanges en l'honneur de Jean Charpentier: la France, l'Europe, le Monde*. Paris: Editions A. Pedone, pp. 395–408.

Manin, Philippe and Jean-Victor Louis (eds.) 1996. *Vers une Europe différenciée? Possibilité et limite*. Paris: Editions A. Pedone/TEPSA.

Marciali, Sébastien 2007. *La flexibilité du droit de l'Union européenne*. Brussels: Bruylant.

Martin, Philippe 1995. 'Free-Riding, Convergence, and Two-Speed Monetary Unification in Europe', *European Economic Review* 39: 1345–64.

Milner, F. and A. Kölliker 1999. 'How to Make Use of Closer Cooperation? The Amsterdam Clauses and the Dynamic of European Integration', European Commission Forward Studies Unit, Brussels.

Missiroli, Antonio 1998. 'Coopération renforcée et flexibilité dans le deuxième pilier: un parcours d'obstacles?', in G. Lenzs (ed.), *L'UEO à 50 ans*. Paris: Institut européen de sécurité de l'UEO, pp. 37–53.
　　1998. 'Flexibility and Enhanced Cooperation after Amsterdam: Prospects for CFSP and the WEU', *The International Spectator* 3: 101–18.

2000. 'CFSP, Defence and Flexibility', Chaillot Paper No. 38, WEU Institute for Security Studies, Paris.

Monar, Jörg 1997. 'Schengen and Flexibility in the Treaty of Amsterdam: Opportunities and Risks of Differentiated Integration in EU Justice and Home Affairs', in M. Den Boer (ed.), *Schengen, Judicial Cooperation and Policy Coordination*. Maastricht: EIPA, pp. 9–28.

1998. 'Justice and Home Affairs in the Treaty of Amsterdam: Reform at the Price of Fragmentation', *European Law Review* 23(4): 320–35.

2010. *'Europe 2020' Project. The Future of European Governance*. Bruges: College of Europe.

Moravcsik, Andrew 2001. 'Federalism in the European Union: Rhetoric and Reality', in Kalypso Nicolaïdis and Robert Howse (eds.), *The Federal Vision: Legitimacy and Levels of Governance in the USA and the EU*. Oxford University Press, pp. 161–87.

2008. 'The European Constitutional Settlement', *World Economy*, pp. 157–82.

Motoc, Iulia 2000. 'Europe and its Teleology: Is there a Central–Eastern Vision?', Jean Monnet Working Paper No. 7/00.

Neve, Jean-Emmanuel de 2007. 'The European Onion? How Differentiated Integration is Reshaping the EU', *Journal of European Integration* 29: 503–21.

Olsen, Johan P. 2000. 'How, Then, Does One Get There? An Institutional Response to Herr Fischer's Vision of a European Federation', Jean Monnet Working Paper No. 7/00.

Ott, Andrea 2007. 'A Flexible Future for the EU: The Way Forward or a Way Out?', in S. Blockmans and S. Prechal (eds.), *Reconciling the Deepening and Widening of the EU*. The Hague: T. M. C. Asser Press, pp. 133–56.

2009. 'EU Constitutional Boundaries to Differentiation: How to Reconcile Differentiation with Integration?', in A. Ott and E. Vos (eds.), *50 Years of EU Integration: Foundations and Perspectives*. The Hague: T. M. C. Asser Press, pp. 113–38.

Philippart, Eric 2003. 'A New Mechanism of Enhanced Cooperation for the Enlarged European Union', *Notre Europe, Research and European Issues* 22.

Philippart, Eric and Geoffrey Edwards 1999. 'The Provisions on Closer Cooperation in the Treaty of Amsterdam – Politics of Multi-Faceted Systems', *Journal of Common Market Studies* 37(1): 87–108.

Philippart, Eric and Monika Sie Dhian Ho 2000. 'From Uniformity to Flexibility – The Management of Diversity and its Impact on the EU System of Governance', in de Búrca and Scott (eds.), *Constitutional Change in the EU: From Uniformity to Flexibility?*, pp. 299–336.

2000. 'The Pros and Cons of Closer Cooperation in the EU: Argumentation and Recommendations', Netherlands Scientific Council for Government Policy, Working document No. W104, The Hague.

Pisani-Ferry, Jean 1995. 'L'Europe à géométrie variable: une analyse économique', *Politique étrangère*, pp. 447–65.

1997. 'Monetary Union with Variable Geometry', CEPS Paper No. 70, Brussels, October.

1997. 'Intégration à géométrie variable et organisation de la politique économique en Europe', *Euro* 39: 27–33.

Pons Rafols, Xavier 2001. 'Las Cooperaciones reforzadas en el Tratado de Niza', *Revista de Derecho Comunitario europeo* 9: 145–95.

Priban, Jiri 2009. 'The Self-Referential European Polity, its Legal Context and Systemic Differentiation: Theoretical Reflections on the Emergence of the EU's Political and Legal Autopoiesis', *European Law Journal* 15(4): 442–61.

Quermonne, Jean-Louis 1994. 'La différenciation dans l'UE: l'Europe à géométrie variable', Institut d'Etudes Européennes, Université Libre de Bruxelles.

Rennie, David 2011. 'A New Two-Speed Europe could leave Britain Behind', *The Guardian*, 4 January, available at www.guardian.co.uk.

Rossolillo, Giulia 2009. 'A "Federal Core" in a Wider European Union. How Could the Core be Founded? How Could the Institutions of the Core be Structured? How to Structure its Relations with the Institutions of the Wider Union?', *The Federalist* 51: 58–65.

Schoutheete, Philippe de 1990. 'The European Community and its Subsystems,' in W. Wallace (ed.), *The Dynamics of European Integration*. London: Pinter, pp. 108–11.

1999. 'Closer Cooperation: Political Background and Issues in the Negotiation', in J. Monar and W. Wessels (eds.), *The Treaty of Amsterdam*. London: Pinter.

Schrauwen, Annette (ed.) 2002. *Flexibility in Constitutions. Forms of Closer Cooperation in Federal and Non-Federal Settings*, post-Nice edn. Amsterdam: Hogendorp Centre for European Constitutional Studies.

Serre, Françoise de la 1999. 'Une Europe ou Plusieurs?', *Politique Etrangère* 1: 21–34.

Serre, Françoise de la and Helen Wallace 1997. 'Les Coopérations renforcées: une fausse bonne idée?', *Notre Europe, Etudes et Recherches* 2.

1997. 'Flexibility and Enhanced Cooperation in the European Union – Placebo rather than Panacea?', *Notre Europe, Research and Policy*, Paper No. 2, September.

Shaw, Jo 1998. 'The Treaty of Amsterdam: Challenges of Flexibility and Legitimacy', *European Law Journal* 4(1): 63–86.

1998. 'Flexibility and Legitimacy in the Domain of the Treaty establishing the European Community', in M. Den Boer, A. Guggenbühl and S. Vanhoonacker (eds.), *Coping with Flexibility and Legitimacy after Amsterdam*. Maastricht: IEAP, pp. 85–111.

2000. 'Relating Constitutionalism and Flexibility in the European Union', in de Búrca and Scott (eds.), *Constitutional Change in the EU: From Uniformity to Flexibility?*, pp. 337–58.

Stephens, Philip 2011. 'All Aboard for a Two-speed Europe', *Financial Times*, 11 February 2011.

Stubb, Alexander 1995. 'The Semantic Indigestion of Differentiated Integration: the Political Rhetoric of the pre-1996 IGC Debate', thesis, Department of Politics and Administration, College of Europe, Bruges.

1996. 'A Categorization of Differentiated Integration', *Journal of Common Market Studies* 34(2): pp. 283–95.

1998. 'Flexible Integration and the Amsterdam Treaty: Negotiating Differentiation in the 1996–1997 IGC', PhD thesis, London School of Economics.

2002. *Negotiating Flexibility in the European Union*. Basingstoke: Palgrave Macmillan.

Tekin, Funda and Wolfgang Wessels 2008. 'Flexibility within the Lisbon Treaty: Trademark or Empty Promise?', European Institute of Public Administration, EIPASCOPE, No. 1.

Thym, Daniel 2004. 'Asymmetry and European Constitutional Law', Abstract in English, *Ungleichzeitigkeit und Europäisches Verfassungsrecht*. Baden-Baden: Nomos.

2005. 'United in Diversity – The Integration of Enhanced Cooperation into the European Constitutional Order', *German Law Journal* 6(11): 1731–48.

2006. 'The Political Character of Supranational Differentiation', *European Law Review* 31(6): 781–99.

Tohidipur, Timo 2001. 'Expansion of Closer Cooperation as Contra-Indication to the Idea of European Integration: A Critique of Joschka Fischer's Speech and Giuliano Amato's Comment Thereon', *German Law Journal* 2.

Törö, Csaba 2005. 'The Latest Example of Enhanced Cooperation in the Constitutional Treaty: The Benefits of Flexibility and Differentiation in European Security and Defence Policy Decisions and their Implementation', *European Law Journal* 11(5): 641–56.

Tosato, Gian Luigi 2007. 'How to Relaunch Europe – The Reasons for Flexibility', *The International Spectator* 42(2): 249–60.

Tuytschaever, Filip 1998. 'L'incidence de la coopération renforcée sur les relations extérieures de la Communauté', in Y. Lejeune (ed.), *Le traité d'Amsterdam. Espoirs et déceptions*. Brussels: Bruylant.

1999. *Differentiation in European Union Law*. Oxford: Hart Publishing.

Usher, John A. 1997. 'Variable Geometry or Concentric Circles: Patterns for the European Union', *International and Comparative Law Quarterly* 46: 243–73.

1998. 'Flexibility and Enhanced Cooperation', in T. Heukels, N. Blokker and M. Brus (eds.), *The EU after Amsterdam – A Legal Analysis*. The Hague: Kluwer Law International, pp. 253–71.

2002. 'Enhanced Cooperation or Flexibility in the Post-Nice Era', in A. Arnull and D. Wincott (eds.), *Accountability and Legitimacy in the European Union*. Oxford University Press.

Van Raepenbusch, Sean and Dominik Hanf 2001. 'Flexibility in Social Policy', in de Witte, Hanf and Vos (eds.), *The Many Faces of Differentiation in EU Law*, pp. 65–81.

Vibert, Frank 1996. 'Structured Flexibility in the European Union', European Policy Forum, London, August.

Vigneron, Philippe and Maria R. Mollica 2000. 'La différenciation dans l'Union economique et monétaire', *Euredia* 2: 197–231.

Walker, Neil 1999. 'Flexibility within a Metaconstitutional Frame: Reflections on the Future of Legal Authority in Europe', Jean Monnet Center, NYU and European University Institute.

Wallace, Helen 2000. 'Flexibility: A Tool of Integration or a Restraint on Disintegration?', in Karlheinz Neunreither and Antje Wiener (eds.), *Amsterdam and Beyond: Institutional Dynamics and Prospects for Democracy*. Oxford University Press.

2000. 'Possible Futures for the European Union: A British Reaction', Jean Monnet Working Paper No. 7/00.

Warleigh, Alex 2001. *Flexible Integration – Which Model for the European Union?* London: Sheffield Academic Press.

Weatherill, Stephen 1999. 'If I'd Wanted You to Understand, I Would Have Explained it Better: What is the Purpose of the Provisions on Closer Cooperation Introduced by the Treaty of Amsterdam?', in D. O'Keefe and P. Twomey (eds.), *Legal Issues of the Amsterdam Treaty*. Oxford: Hart Publishing, pp. 21–41.

Weiler, Joseph H. H. 1999. *The Constitution of Europe – Do the New Clothes Have an Emperor? and other essays on European Integration*. Cambridge, MA: Harvard University Press.

Wilkinson, Michael 2002. 'Constituting Europe: Flexibility or Finalité', *Oxford Journal of Legal Studies* 1: 177–87.

Witte, Bruno de 2000. 'Old Flexibility', in de Búrca and Scott (eds.), *Constitutional Change in the EU: From Uniformity to Flexibility?*, pp. 31–58.

Witte, Bruno de, Dominik Hanf and Ellen Vos (eds.) 2001. *The Many Faces of Differentiation in EU Law*. Antwerp: Intersentia.

Zervakis, Peter 2006. '"Differentiated Integration": An Alternative Path to Classical Integration?', *The Federalist* 3: 205–13.

Zielonka, Jean 2000. 'Enlargement and the Finality of European Integration', Jean Monnet Working Paper No. 7/00.

Ziller, Jacques 2000. 'Flexibility in the Geographical Scope of EU Law: Diversity and Differentiation in the Application of Substantive Law on Member States Territories', in de Búrca and Scott (eds.), *Constitutional Change in the EU: From Uniformity to Flexibility?*, pp. 113–31.

Index

Index

An Introduction to
European Law

Written with exceptional clarity, simplicity and precision, this short
textbook provides a classic introduction to European law. Using a
clear structural framework, it guides students through the subject's
core elements and key issues, from the creation and enforcement of
European law to the workings of the internal market. Chapters are
enriched with figures and tables to clarify difficult topics and
illustrate relationships and processes, ensuring that students
understand even the most complex of concepts. The second edition
has been updated throughout, and includes an entirely new chapter
on the internal market for goods. Two new practical appendices offer
suggestions for further reading and guide readers through the
process of finding and reading EU Court judgments. A companion
website (accessible at www.schutze.eu) features full 'Lisbonized'
versions of the cases cited in the text, links to EU legislation,
downloadable figures and textbook updates.

Robert Schütze is Professor of European Law and Co-Director of the
Global Policy Institute at Durham University.

An Introduction to

European Law

Second edition

Robert Schütze

CAMBRIDGE
UNIVERSITY PRESS

CAMBRIDGE
UNIVERSITY PRESS

University Printing House, Cambridge CB2 8BS, United Kingdom

Cambridge University Press is part of the University of Cambridge.

It furthers the University's mission by disseminating knowledge in the pursuit of education, learning and research at the highest international levels of excellence.

www.cambridge.org
Information on this title: www.cambridge.org/9781107530324

© Cambridge University Press 2015

First published 2015

Printed in the United Kingdom by TJ International Ltd. Padstow Cornwall

A catalogue record for this publication is available from the British Library

ISBN 978-1-107-11181-3 Hardback
ISBN 978-1-107-53032-4 Paperback

In Memory of Boris Rotenberg: Debater, Dreamer, Traveller

Summary Contents

Contents

Illustrations

Tables

Acknowledgements

Thankful acknowledgements are made to Hart Publishing, Kluwer Law International, Oxford University Press, and Sweet & Maxwell for their kind permission to incorporate sections from previously published material. Parts I and II of this book originally drew on my *European Constitutional Law* (Cambridge University Press, 2012). In writing this small text, I am grateful to many a colleague and friend, and especially to Sinéad Moloney and Valerie Appleby of Cambridge University Press who have provided a truly wonderful and professional support for, respectively, the first and second edition of this book. The book is dedicated to a remarkable friend from my "EUI years": Boris Rotenberg, who died much too young.

Table of cases

Contents

1 European Court of Justice: cases (numerical)

2 European Court of Justice: cases (alphabetical)

3 General Court: cases (numerical)

4 Other jurisdictions: cases (alphabetical)

Abbreviations

Bull. EC	Bulletin of the European Communities
CEE	Charge having equivalent effect
CFSP	Common Foreign and Security Policy
Coreper	Committee of Permanent Representatives
CST	Civil Service Tribunal
DR	European Commission on Human Rights Decisions and Reports
EC	European Community (Treaty)
ECHR	European Convention on Human Rights
ECJ	European Court of Justice
ECR	European Court Reports
ECSC	European Coal and Steel Community
ECtHR	European Court of Human Rights
EEC	European Economic Community (Treaty)
EU (old)	European Union (Maastricht Treaty)
Euratom	European Atomic Energy Community
GATT	General Agreement on Tariffs and Trade
GC	General Court
MEEQR	Measure having an Equivalent Effect to Quantitative Restrictions
MEP	Member of the European Parliament
OJ	Official Journal of the European Union
QMV	Qualified Majority Voting
SEA	Single European Act
TEU	Treaty on European Union (post-Lisbon)
TFEU	Treaty on the Functioning of the European Union
UN	United Nations
US	United States
WTO	World Trade Organization

Introduction

The idea of European union is as old as the European idea of the sovereign State.[1] Yet the spectacular rise of the latter overshadowed the idea of a European Union for centuries. Within the twentieth century, two ruinous world wars and the social forces of globalization have however increasingly discredited the idea of the sovereign State. The decline of the – isolationist – State found expression in the spread of inter-state cooperation. The various efforts at European cooperation after the Second World War formed part of that transition from an international law of coexistence to an international law of cooperation.[2] Yet European "integration" would go far beyond the traditional forms of international "cooperation".

The European Union was born in 1952 with the coming into being of the European Coal and Steel Community (ECSC). Its original members were six European States: Belgium, France, Germany, Italy, Luxembourg, and the Netherlands. The Community had been created to integrate one industrial sector; and the very concept of *integration* indicated the wish of the contracting States "to break with the ordinary forms of international treaties and organizations".[3] The 1957 Treaties of Rome created two additional Communities: the European Atomic Energy Community and the European (Economic) Community. The "three Communities" were partly "merged" in 1967,[4] but continued to exist in relative independence. A first major treaty reform was effected in 1987 through the Single European Act, but an even bigger organizational leap was taken by the 1992

---

[1] R. H. Foerster, *Die Idee Europa 1300–1946, Quellen zur Geschichte der politischen Einigung* (Deutscher Taschenbuchverlag, 1963).

[2] W. G. Friedmann, *The Changing Structure of International Law* (Stevens, 1964).

[3] For a detailed discussion of the negotiations leading up to the signature of the ECSC Treaty, see: H. Mosler, "Der Vertrag über die Europäische Gemeinschaft für Kohle und Stahl", 14 (1951/2) *Zeitschrift für ausländisches öffentliches Recht und Völkerrecht*, 24 (translation – RS).

[4] This was achieved through the 1965 "Merger Treaty" (see Treaty establishing a Single Council and a Single Commission of the European Communities).

Table 0.1 European Treaties – Chronology

Signed	Name	Published	Entry
1951	Treaty establishing the European Coal and Steel Community	Founding Treaty[5]	1952
1957	Treaty establishing the European (Economic) Community	Founding Treaty[6]	1958
1957	Treaty establishing the European Atomic Energy Community	Founding Treaty	1958
1965	Treaty establishing a Single Council and a Single Commission	[1967] OJ 152	1967
1986	Single European Act	[1987] OJ L169	1987
1992	Treaty on European Union	[1992] OJ C191[7]	1993
1997	Treaty of Amsterdam	[1997] OJ C340	1999
2001	Treaty of Nice	[2001] OJ C80	2003
2004	Treaty establishing a Constitution for Europe	[2004] OJ C310	Failed
2007	Treaty of Lisbon amending the Treaty on European Union and the Treaty establishing the European Community	[2007] OJ C306	2009

Maastricht Treaty. The latter integrated the three Communities into the (Maastricht) European Union.

But for a decade, this European Union was under constant constitutional construction (Table 0.1). Treaty amendment followed treaty amendment! And in an attempt to get away from the ever-repeating minor treaty amendments, a European Convention was charged to prepare a major reform that would result in the "Constitutional Treaty". The 2004 Constitutional Treaty would have effected the biggest structural change in the history of the European Union. Yet the Treaty failed when Dutch and French referenda were lost; and it took almost another decade to rescue the reform effort into the 2007 Reform (Lisbon) Treaty. The Lisbon Treaty replicates nearly 90 per cent of the (failed) Constitutional Treaty and came into force on 1 December 2009. Despite its modest name, the Lisbon Treaty constitutes a radical new chapter in the history of the European Union. For while it formally builds on one of the original "Founding Treaties"

---

[5] The Treaty expired in 2002.

[6] For a consolidated version of the Treaty establishing the European Community, see: [2002] OJ C325.

[7] For a consolidated version of the Treaty on European Union, see: *ibid.*

Table 0.2 Structure of the TEU and TFEU

European Union			
EU Treaty		FEU Treaty	
Title I	Common Provisions	Part I	Principles
Title II	Democratic Principles	Part II	Citizenship (Non-Discrimination)
Title III	Institutions	Part III	Union (Internal) Policies
Title IV	Enhanced Cooperation	Part IV	Overseas Associations
Title V	External Action, and CFSP	Part V	External Action
Title VI	Final Provisions	Part VI	Institutions & Finances
		Part VII	General & Final Provisions

Protocols (37)
Charter of Fundamental Rights

and the 1992 Treaty on European Union, it has nonetheless "merged" the old "Community" legal order with the old "Union" legal order. The textual foundations of the "new" European Union are indeed dramatically different from anything that existed before the 2007 Reform Treaty.

What is the structure of the present European Union? The Union is based on two treaties: the Treaty on European Union (TEU) and the Treaty on the Functioning of the European Union (TFEU). The division into two EU Treaties follows a functional criterion. The Treaty on European Union contains the *general* provisions defining the Union, while the Treaty on the Functioning of the European Union contains the specific provisions with regard to the Union institutions and policies. Depending on their length, the Treaties are divided into "Parts", "Titles", "Chapters", "Sections" and "Articles". Numerous Protocols and the "Charter of Fundamental Rights" moreover join the Treaties. According to Article 51 TEU, Protocols to the Treaties "shall form an integral part thereof"; and the best way to make sense of them is to see them as legally binding "footnotes" to a particular article or section of the Treaties. By contrast, the Charter is "external" to the Treaties; yet it also has "the same legal value as the Treaties".[8] The structure of the Treaties is shown in Table 0.2.

Despite their impressive wordiness, the EU Treaties are designed to be "framework treaties". They are treaties whose substance is mainly made up from institutional provisions that are to provide the "framework" for

---

[8] Article 6 (1) (new) TEU.

Figure 0.1 Structure of the Book

subsequent secondary law. The policy areas in which the Union can act are thereby set out in Parts III and V of the TFEU. The former sets out twenty-four "internal" policies, while the latter lists a much smaller number of external areas of Union action. In order to legislate within one of these policy areas, the Union must have a legislative competence. These competences will generally be found in the specific policy title within Parts III or V of the TFEU; and they will constitute the principal legislative fountain for a particular part of European Union law.

What is the structure of this book on European Union law? The book is divided into three parts, which correspond to the three themes of "creation", "enforcement", and "substance" of European law.

Part I analyses the Union as an institutional "creature", and considers the creation of European (secondary) law. It starts with an overview of the four major Union institutions: the European Parliament, the Council, the Commission, and the European Court in Chapter 1. Chapter 2 investigates how these institutions cooperate in the creation of European legislation. The Union cannot legislate in all areas of social life; and Chapters 3 and 4 look at two constitutional limits to Union legislation. Based on the principle of conferral, the Union must act within the scope of competences conferred upon it by the Member States. The scope of these competences – and their nature – will be discussed in Chapter 3. The final Chapter within this part analyses a second constitutional limit to the exercise of Union competences: European fundamental rights. These rights first emerged as general principles of Union law, but have now been codified in the Union's Charter of Fundamental Rights.

Part II concentrates on the "enforcement" of European law in the courts. We shall see that European law establishes rights and obligations that directly affect individuals. The direct effect of European law in the national legal orders will be discussed in Chapter 5. Where a

European norm is directly effective, it will also be "supreme" over national law. The "supremacy" of European law is the subject of Chapter 6. But how will individuals enforce their "supreme" European rights? Chapters 7 and 8 look at the dual enforcement machinery within the Union legal order. Individuals will typically enforce their European rights in national courts. The Union legal order has thereby required national courts to provide effective remedies for the enforcement of European rights; and in order to assist national courts in the interpretation and application of European law, the Union envisages a preliminary reference procedure. The indirect enforcement of European law through the national courts is discussed in Chapter 7. It is complemented by the direct enforcement of European law in the European Courts, and Chapter 8 explores these direct actions.

Part III analyses the substantive heart of European law, that is: the law governing the internal market and European competition law. From the very beginning, *the* central economic task of the European Union was the creation of a "common market". The Rome Treaty had thereby not solely provided for a common market in goods. It equally required the abolition of obstacles to the free movement of persons, services, and capital. Europe's "internal market" was thus to comprise four fundamental freedoms. Two of these freedoms will be discussed in turn. The free movement of goods is the "classic" freedom of the Union, and Chapters 9 and 10 explore two strategies of market integration in this context. Chapter 11 subsequently examines the free movement of persons. The final Chapter provides a brief overview of EU competition law through the lens of Article 101 TFEU. European competition law is thereby traditionally seen as a functional complement to the internal market. It would – primarily – protect the internal market from *private* power.

This book is (relatively) short for a book on European law. But brevity is the spice of language; and in order to keep this book as spicy as possible, many selective choices had to be made. Inevitably, some aspects will not be covered, others only marginally. Nevertheless, this "Introduction to European Law" will deal with all essential aspects of this complex area. And by concentrating on the "essence" of the subject, the book aims to help seeing the proverbial "wood" instead of the trees. For these European trees are ever growing and multiplying, and it is no wonder that many a student might get lost in the legal undergrowth! But if there is a second wish which this "Introduction to European Law" has, it is also to make the reader "thirsty" for more. Yet this thirst will have to be quenched by one of the larger generalist textbooks,[9] or one of the major textbooks dedicated to a specialized branch of European law.[10]

---

[9] The three traditional textbooks in English are: D. Chalmers *et al.*, *European Union Law* (Cambridge University Press, 2014), P. Craig and G. de Búrca, *EU Law: Text, Cases, and Materials* (Oxford University Press, 2011), and A. Dashwood *et al.*, *European Union Law* (Hart, 2011). These have now been joined by my own *European Union Law* (Cambridge University Press, 2015).

[10] European law is traditionally divided into three major branches: European *constitutional* law (see T. Hartley, *The Foundations of European Union Law* (Oxford University Press, 2014); and: R. Schütze, *European Constitutional Law* (Cambridge University Press, 2012)), European *internal market* law (see C. Barnard, *The Substantive Law of the EU* (Oxford University Press, 2013); and: F. Weiss and C. Kaupa, *European Union Internal Market Law* (Cambridge University Press, 2014)), and European *competition* law (see J. Goyder and A. Albors-Llorens, *EC Competition Law* (Oxford University Press, 2009), and: A. Jones and B. Sufrin, *EU Competition Law* (Oxford University Press, 2014)). In addition to these three principal branches, the last two decades have seen the emergence of many smaller branches, such as European *external relations* law (see P. Eeckhout, *EU External Relations Law* (Oxford University Press, 2011), and: P. Koutrakos, *EU International Relations Law* (Hart, 2006)), and European *environmental* law (see J. H. Jans and H. Vedder, *European Environmental Law* (Europa Law Publishing, 2011), and: L. Krämer, *EC Environmental Law* (Sweet & Maxwell, 2012)).

Part I

European Law: Creation

This Part analyses the Union as an institutional "creature", and it equally considers the creation of European (secondary) law. It starts in Chapter 1 with an overview of the four major Union institutions: the European Parliament, the Council, the Commission, and the European Court. Chapter 2 investigates how these institutions cooperate in the creation of European legislation. The Union cannot legislate in all areas of social life; and Chapters 3 and 4 look at two constitutional limits to Union legislation. Based on the principle of conferral, the Union must act within the scope of competences conferred upon it by the Member States. The scope of these competences – and their nature – will be discussed in Chapter 3. Chapter 4 analyses a second constitutional limit to the exercise of Union competences: European fundamental rights. These rights first emerged as general principles of Union law, but have now been codified in the Union's Charter of Fundamental Rights.

Union Institutions 1

Introduction

The creation of governmental institutions is *the* central task of all constitutions. Each political community needs institutions to govern its society;
as each society needs common rules and a method for their making,
execution, and adjudication. The European Treaties establish a number
of European institutions to make, execute, and adjudicate European law.
The Union's institutions and their core tasks are defined in Title III of the

Treaty on European Union (TEU). The central provision here is Article 13 TEU:

> The Union shall have an institutional framework which shall aim to promote its values, advance its objectives, serve its interests, those of its citizens and those of the Member States, and ensure the consistency, effectiveness and continuity of its policies and actions.
>
> The Union's institutions shall be:
>
> – the European Parliament,
> – the European Council,
> – the Council,
> – the European Commission (hereinafter referred to as 'the Commission'),
> – the Court of Justice of the European Union,
> – the European Central Bank,
> – the Court of Auditors.[1]

The provision lists seven governmental institutions of the European Union. They constitute the core "players" in the Union legal order.[2] What strikes the attentive eye first is the number of institutions: unlike a tripartite institutional structure, the Union offers more than twice that number. The two institutions that do not – at first sight – seem to directly correspond to "national" institutions are the (European) Council and the Commission. The name "Council" represents a reminder of the "international" origins of the European Union, but the institution can equally be found in the governmental structure of Federal States. It will be harder to find the name "Commission" among the public institutions of States, where the executive is typically referred to as the "government". By contrast, central banks and courts of auditors exist in many national legal orders.

---

[1] Article 13(1) TEU. Paragraph 2 adds: "Each institution shall act within the limits of the powers conferred on it in the Treaties, and in conformity with the procedures, conditions and objectives set out in them. The institutions shall practise mutual sincere cooperation".

[2] While the Treaties set up seven "institutions", they do acknowledge the existence of other "bodies". First, according to Article 13(4) TEU, the Parliament, the Council and the Commission "shall be assisted by an Economic and Social Committee and a Committee of the Regions acting in an advisory capacity". The composition and powers of the "Economic and Social Committee" are set out in Articles 301–4 TFEU. The composition and powers of the "Committee of the Regions" are defined by Articles 305–7 TFEU. In addition to the Union's "Advisory Bodies", the Treaties also acknowledge the existence of a "European Investment Bank" (Articles 308–9 TFEU; as well as Protocol No. 5 on the Statute of the European Investment Bank).

Table 1.1 Treaty Provisions on the Institutions

EU Treaty – Title III		FEU Treaty – Part VI – Title I – Chapter 1	
Article 13	Institutional Framework	Section 1	European Parliament (Arts. 223–34)
Article 14	European Parliament	Section 2	European Council (Arts. 235–6)
Article 15	European Council	Section 3	Council (Arts. 237–43)
Article 16	Council	Section 4	Commission (Arts. 244–50)
Article 17	Commission	Section 5	Court of Justice (Arts. 251–81)
Article 18	High Representative	Section 6	European Central Bank (Arts. 282–4)
Article 19	Court of Justice	Section 7	Court of Auditors (Arts. 285–7)

Protocol (No. 3): Statute of the Court of Justice
Protocol (No. 4): Statute of the ESCB and the ECB
Protocol (No. 6): Location of the Seats of the Institutions etc.
(Internal) Rules of Procedure of the Institution

Where do the Treaties define the Union institutions? The provisions on the Union institutions are split between the Treaty on European Union and the Treaty on the Functioning of the European Union (Table 1.1).

The four sections of this Chapter will concentrate on the classic four Union institutions: the Parliament, the Council, the Commission, and the Court.[3]

1. The European Parliament

Despite its formal place in the Treaties, the European Parliament has never been the Union's "first" institution. For a long time it followed, in rank, behind the Council and the Commission. Parliament's original powers were indeed minimal. It was an "auxiliary" organ that was to assist the institutional duopoly of Council and Commission. This minimal role gradually increased from the 1970s onwards. Today the Parliament constitutes – with the Council – a chamber of the Union legislature.

---

[3] For an analysis of the three other Union institutions, see R. Schütze, *European Union Law* (Cambridge University Press, 2015), Chapters 5 and 6.

Directly elected by the European citizens,[4] Parliament constitutes not only the most democratic institution; in light of its elective "appointment", it is also the most supranational institution of the European Union.

This section will analyse two aspects of the European Parliament. First, we shall look at its formation through European elections. A second subsection provides an overview of Parliament's powers in the various governmental functions of the Union.

(a) Formation: Electing Parliament

When the European Union was born, the European Treaties envisaged that its Parliament was to be composed of "representatives of the peoples of the States".[5] This characterization corresponded to its formation. For the European Parliament was not directly elected. It was to "consist of delegates who shall be designated by the respective Parliaments from among their members in accordance with the procedure laid down by each Member State".[6] European parliamentarians were thus – delegated – *national* parliamentarians. This formation method brought Parliament close to an (international) "assembly". The founding Treaties had nonetheless breached the classic international law logic already in two ways. First, they had abandoned the idea of sovereign equality of the Member States by recognizing different sizes for national parliamentary delegations.[7] Second, and more importantly, the Treaties already envisaged that Parliament would eventually be formed through "elections by direct universal suffrage in accordance with a uniform procedure in all Member States".[8]

When did the transformation of the European Parliament from an "assembly" of national parliamentarians into a directly elected Parliament take place? It took two decades before the Union's 1976 "Election Act" was adopted.[9] And ever since the first parliamentary elections in 1979, the European Parliament ceased to be composed of "representatives of the

---

[4] Article 10(2) TEU: "Citizens are directly represented at Union level in the European Parliament".

[5] Article 137 EEC. See also Article 20 ECSC.

[6] Article 138 EEC. See also Article 21 ECSC.

[7] Originally, the EEC Treaty granted thirty-six delegates to Germany, France and Italy; fourteen delegates to Belgium and the Netherlands; and six delegates to Luxembourg.

[8] Article 138(3) EEC. See also Article 21(3) ECSC.

[9] "Act concerning the Election of the Members of the European Parliament by direct universal Suffrage". The Act was adopted in 1976 ([1976] OJ L278/5).

peoples of the States". It constituted henceforth the representative of a European people. The Treaties have – belatedly – recognized this dramatic constitutional change. They now characterize the European Parliament as being "composed of representatives of the Union's citizens".[10]

What is the size and composition of the European Parliament? How are elections conducted? The Treaties stipulate the following on the size and composition of the European Parliament:

> The European Parliament shall be composed of representatives of the Union's citizens. They shall not exceed seven hundred and fifty in number, plus the President. Representation of citizens shall be degressively proportional, with a minimum threshold of six members per Member State. No Member State shall be allocated more than ninety-six seats.
>
> The European Council shall adopt by unanimity, on the initiative of the European Parliament and with its consent, a decision establishing the composition of the European Parliament, respecting the principles referred to in the first subparagraph.[11]

The European Parliament has a maximum size of 751 members. While relatively big in comparison with the (American) House of Representatives, it is still smaller than the (British) House of Lords.[12] The Treaties themselves no longer determine its composition.[13] It is the European Council that decides on the national "quotas" for the Union's parliamentary representatives. The distribution of seats must however be "degressively proportional" within a range spanning from six to ninety-six seats. The European Council has recently taken a formal decision on the principles governing the allocation of national "quotas" within Parliament.[14] The concrete distribution of seats among Member States can be seen in Table 1.2.

The national "quotas" for European parliamentary seats constitute a compromise between the democratic principle and the federal principle. For while the democratic principle would demand that each citizen in the Union has equal voting power ("one person, one vote"), the federal

---

[10] Article 14(2) TEU.   [11] *Ibid.*

[12] To compare: the (American) House of Representatives has 435 seats. The (British) House of Commons has 650 seats, while the (British) House of Lords has about 800 seats.

[13] This had been the case prior to the 2007 reforms brought by the Lisbon Treaty.

[14] European Council, Decision establishing the Composition of the European Parliament (OJ [2013] L181/57), esp. Article 1.

Table 1.2 Distribution of Seats in the European Parliament
(Member States)

Member State (Seats)		
Belgium (21)	Ireland (11)	Austria (18)
Bulgaria (17)	Italy (72+1[15])	Poland (51)
Croatia (11)	Cyprus (6)	Portugal (21)
Czech Republic (21)	Latvia (8)	Romania (32)
Denmark (13)	Lithuania (11)	Slovenia (8)
Germany (96)	Luxembourg (6)	Slovakia (13)
Estonia (6)	Hungary (21)	Finland (13)
Greece (21)	Malta (6)	Sweden (20)
Spain (54)	Netherlands (26)	United Kingdom (73)
France (74)		

principle insists on the political existence of States. The result of this compromise was the rejection of a *purely* proportional distribution in favour
of a *degressively* proportional system. The degressive element within that
system unfortunately means that a Luxembourg citizen has ten times
more voting power than a British, French, or German citizen.

How are the *individual* members of Parliament elected? The Treaties
solely provide us with the most general of rules: "The members of the
European Parliament shall be elected for a term of five years by direct
universal suffrage in a free and secret ballot."[16] More precise rules are
set out in the (amended) 1976 Election Act. Article 1 of the Act commands that the elections must be conducted "on the basis of proportional
representation".[17] This outlaws the traditionally British election method of
first-past-the-post.[18] The specifics of the election procedure are however
principally left to the Member States.[19] European parliamentary elections

---

[15] This additional seat was added, because of Italian intransigence, by the Lisbon Inter-
governmental Council, see: Declaration (No. 4) on the composition of the European
Parliament: 'The additional seat in the European Parliament will be attributed to Italy.'
This is why the European Parliament has 751 and not 750 seats.

[16] Article 14(3) TEU.   [17] Article 1(1) and (3) of the 1976 Election Act (supra n. 9).

[18] This condition had not been part of the original 1976 Election Act, but was added through
a 2002 amendment. This amendment was considered necessary as, hitherto, the British
majority voting system "could alone alter the entire political balance in the European
Parliament" (F. Jacobs *et al.*, *The European Parliament* (Harper Publishing, 2005), 17). The
best example of this distorting effect was the 1979 election to the European Parliament
in which the British Conservatives won 60 out of 78 seats with merely 50 per cent of the
vote (*ibid.*).

[19] Article 8 of the 1976 Election Act: "Subject to the provisions of this Act, the electoral
procedure shall be governed in each Member State by its national provisions." Under the

thus still do not follow "a uniform electoral procedure in all Member States", but are rather conducted "in accordance with principles common to all Member States".[20] The Treaties nonetheless insist on one common constitutional rule: "every citizen of the Union residing in a Member State of which he is not a national shall have the right to vote and to stand as a candidate in elections to the European Parliament in the Member State in which he resides, under the same conditions as nationals of that State."[21]

(b) Parliamentary Powers

When the 1951 ECSC Treaty set up the European Parliament, its sole function was to exercise "supervisory powers".[22] Parliament was indeed a passive onlooker on the decision-making process within the first Community. The 1957 EEC Treaty expanded Parliament's functions to "advisory and supervisory powers".[23] This recognized the active power of Parliament to be consulted on Commission proposals before their adoption by the Council.[24] After sixty years of evolution and numerous amendments, the Treaty on European Union today defines the powers of the European Parliament in Article 14 TEU as follows:

> The European Parliament shall, jointly with the Council, exercise legislative and budgetary functions. It shall exercise functions of political control and consultation as laid down in the Treaties. It shall elect the President of the Commission.[25]

This definition distinguishes between four types of powers: legislative and budgetary powers as well as supervisory and elective powers.

(i) Legislative Powers

The European Parliament's primary power lies in the making of European laws. In the recent past, it has evolved into a "legislative powerhouse".[26]

Act, Member States are free to decide whether to establish national or local constituencies for elections to the European Parliament (*ibid.*, Article 2), and whether to set a minimum threshold for the allocation of seats (*ibid.*, Article 3).

[20] Both alternatives are provided for in Article 223(1) TFEU.   [21] Article 22(2) TFEU.

[22] Article 20 ECSC.   [23] Article 137 EEC.

[24] *Roquette Frères* v. *Council (Isoglucose)*, Case 138/79, [1980] ECR 3333.

[25] Article 14(1) TEU.

[26] M. Kohler, "European Governance and the European Parliament: From Talking Shop to Legislative Powerhouse", (2014) 52 *Journal of Common Market Studies* 600.

Its participation in the legislative process may take place at two moments in time. Parliament may informally propose new legislation.[27] However, it is not – unlike many national parliaments – entitled to formally propose bills. The task of making legislative proposals is, with minor exceptions, a constitutional prerogative of the Commission.[28]

The principal legislative involvement of Parliament starts therefore later, namely after the Commission has submitted a proposal to the European legislature. Like other federal legal orders, the European legal order acknowledges a number of different legislative procedures. The Treaties now textually distinguish between the "ordinary" legislative procedure and a number of "special" legislative procedures. The former is defined as "the joint adoption by the European Parliament and the Council" on a proposal from the Commission.[29] Special legislative procedures cover various degrees of parliamentary participation. Under the "consent procedure" Parliament must give its consent before the Council can adopt European legislation.[30] This is a cruder form of legislative participation that essentially grants a negative power. Parliament cannot suggest positive amendments, but must take-or-leave the Council's position. Under the "consultation procedure", by contrast, Parliament is not even entitled to do that. It merely needs to be consulted – a role that is closer to an advisory function than to a legislative one.[31] Exceptionally, a special legislative procedure may make Parliament the dominant legislative chamber.[32]

---

[27] Article 225 TFEU: "The European Parliament may, acting by a majority of its component Members, request the Commission to submit any appropriate proposal on matters on which it considers that a Union act is required for the purpose of implementing the Treaties. If the Commission does not submit a proposal, it shall inform the European Parliament of the reasons."

[28] On this power, see Chapter 2 – Section 1(a) below.   [29] Article 289(1) TFEU.

[30] For example: Article 19 TFEU, according to which "the Council, acting unanimously in accordance with a special legislative procedure and after obtaining the consent of the European Parliament, may take appropriate action to combat discrimination based on sex, racial or ethnic origin, religion or belief, disability, age or sexual orientation".

[31] For example: Article 22(1) TFEU, which states: "Every citizen of the Union residing in a Member State of which he is not a national shall have the right to vote and to stand as a candidate at municipal elections in the Member State in which he resides, under the same conditions as nationals of that State. This right shall be exercised subject to detailed arrangements adopted by the Council, acting unanimously in accordance with a special legislative procedure and after consulting the European Parliament[.]"

[32] For example: Article 223(2) TFEU – granting Parliament the power, with the consent of the Council, to adopt a Statute for its Members.

Importantly, the Parliament's "legislative" powers may also extend to the external relations sphere. After the 2007 reforms, Parliament has indeed become an important player in the conclusion of the Union's international agreements.

(ii) Budgetary Powers

Parliaments have historically been involved in the adoption of national budgets. For they were seen as legitimating the *raising* of revenue. In the words of the American colonists: "No taxation, without representation." In the European Union, this picture is somewhat inverted. For since Union revenue is fixed by the Council and the Member States,[33] the European Parliament's budgetary powers have not focused on the income side but on the expenditure side. Its powers have consequently been described as the "reverse of those traditionally exercised by parliaments".[34]

Be that as it may, Parliament's formal involvement in the Union budget started with the 1970 and 1975 Budget Treaties. They distinguished between compulsory and non-compulsory expenditure, with the latter being expenditure that would not result from compulsory financial commitments flowing from the application of European law. Parliament's powers were originally confined to this second category. The 2007 reforms have however abandoned the distinction between compulsory and non-compulsory expenditure, and Parliament has thus become an equal partner, with the Council, in establishing the Union's annual budget.[35]

(iii) Supervisory Powers

A third parliamentary power is that of holding the executive to account. Parliamentary supervisory powers typically involve the power to debate, question, and investigate.

A soft parliamentary power is the power to *debate*. To that effect, the European Parliament is entitled to receive the "general report on the activities of the Union" from the Commission,[36] which it "shall discuss in open session".[37] And as regards the European Council, the Treaties require its President to "present a report to the European Parliament after each of the meetings of the European Council".[38] (Similar obligations apply to the

---

[33] See Article 311 TFEU on the "Union's own resources".
[34] D. Judge and D. Earnshaw, *The European Parliament* (Palgrave, 2008), 198.
[35] Article 314 TFEU.   [36] Article 249(2) TFEU.   [37] Article 233 TFEU.
[38] Article 15(6)(d) TEU.

European Central Bank.[39]) The power to *question* the European executive is formally enshrined only for the Commission: "The Commission shall reply orally or in writing to questions put to it by the European Parliament or by its Members."[40] However, both the European Council and the Council have confirmed their willingness to be questioned by Parliament.[41] Early on, Parliament introduced the institution of "Question Time" – modelled on the procedure within the British Parliament.[42] And under its own Rules of Procedure, Parliament is entitled to hold "an extraordinary debate" on "a matter of major interest relating to European Union Policy".[43]

Parliament also enjoys the formal power to *investigate*. It is constitutionally entitled to set up temporary Committees of Inquiry to investigate alleged contraventions or maladministration in the implementation of European law.[44] These (temporary) committees complement Parliament's standing committees. They have been used, inter alia, to investigate the (mis)handling of the BSE crisis.

Finally, European citizens have the general right to "petition" the European Parliament.[45] And according to a Scandinavian constitutional tradition, the European Parliament will also elect an "ombudsman". The European Ombudsman "shall be empowered to receive complaints" from any citizen or Union resident "concerning instances of maladministration in the activities of the Union institutions, bodies or agencies". S/he "shall conduct inquiries" on the basis of complaints addressed to her or him directly or through a member of the European Parliament.[46]

(iv) Elective Powers

Modern constitutionalism distinguishes between "presidential" and "parliamentary" systems. Within the former, the executive officers are

---

[39] Article 284(3) TFEU.   [40] Article 230 TFEU – second indent.

[41] The Council accepted this political obligation in 1973; see Jacobs, *The European Parliament* (supra n. 18), 284.

[42] Rule 129 Parliament Rules of Procedure. For acceptance of that obligation by the Commission, see Framework Agreement on relations between the European Parliament and the European Commission, [2010] OJ L304/47, para. 46.

[43] Rule 153 Parliament Rules of Procedure.

[44] Article 226(1) TFEU. For a good overview of the history of these committees, see M. Shackleton, "The European Parliament's New Committees of Inquiry: Tiger or Paper Tiger?", 36 (1998) *Journal of Common Market Studies*, 115.

[45] According to Article 227 TFEU, any citizen or Union resident has the right to petition the European Parliament "on any matter which comes within the Union's field or activity and which affects him, her or it directly". See also Article 20(2)(d) TFEU.

[46] Article 228 TFEU.

independent from Parliament, whereas in the latter the executive is elected by Parliament. The European constitutional order sits somewhere "in between". Its executive was for a long time selected without any parliamentary involvement. However, as regards the Commission, the European Parliament has increasingly come to be involved in the appointment process. Today, Article 17 TEU describes the involvement of the European Parliament in the appointment of the Commission as follows:

> Taking into account the elections to the European Parliament and after having held the appropriate consultations, the European Council, acting by a qualified majority, shall propose to the European Parliament a candidate for President of the Commission. This candidate shall be elected by the European Parliament by a majority of its component members...The Council, by common accord with the President-elect, shall adopt the list of the other persons whom it proposes for appointment as members of the Commission. They shall be selected, on the basis of the suggestions made by Member States...The President, the High Representative of the Union for Foreign Affairs and Security Policy and the other members of the Commission shall be subject as a body to a vote of consent by the European Parliament. On the basis of this consent the Commission shall be appointed by the European Council, acting by a qualified majority.[47]

The appointment of the European executive thus requires a dual parliamentary consent. First, Parliament must "elect" the President of the Commission. Second, it must confirm the Commission as a collective body. (Apart from the Commission's President, the European Parliament has consequently not got the power to confirm each and every Commissioner.)[48] In light of this elective power given to Parliament, one is justified in characterizing the Union's governmental system as a "semi-parliamentary democracy".[49]

Once appointed, the Commission continues to "be responsible to the European Parliament".[50] Where its trust is lost, Parliament may vote on a motion of censure. If this vote of mistrust is carried, the Commission must resign as a body. The motion of collective censure mirrors Parliament's

---

[47] Article 17(7) TEU.
[48] However, Parliament may request each nominated Commissioner to appear before Parliament and to "present" his views. This practice thus comes close to "confirmation hearings" (Judge and Earnshaw, *The European Parliament* (supra n. 34), 205).
[49] P. Dann, "European Parliament and Executive Federalism: Approaching a Parliament in a Semi-Parliamentary Democracy", 9 (2003) *European Law Journal*, 549.
[50] Article 17(8) TEU.

appointment power, which is also focused on the Commission *as a collective body*. This blunt "nuclear option" has never been used.[51] However, unlike the appointment power, Parliament has been able to sharpen its tools of censure significantly by concluding a political agreement with the Commission. Accordingly, if Parliament expresses lack of confidence in an *individual* member of the Commission, the President of the Commission "shall either require the resignation of that Member" or, after "serious" consideration, explain the refusal to do so before Parliament.[52] While this is a much "smarter sanction", it has also never been used due to the demanding voting requirements in Parliament.

Parliament is also involved in the appointment of other European officers. This holds true for the Court of Auditors,[53] the European Central Bank,[54] and the European Ombudsman.[55] However, it is not involved in the appointment of judges to the Court of Justice of the European Union.

2. The Council of Ministers

The 1957 EEC Treaty had originally charged the Council of Ministers with the task "to ensure that the objectives set out in this Treaty are attained".[56] This task involved the exercise of legislative as well as executive functions. And while other institutions would also be involved in these functions, the Council was to be the central institution within the European Union.

This has – over time – dramatically changed with the rise of two rival institutions. On one side, the ascendancy of the European Parliament has limited the Council's legislative role within the Union. On the other side, the rise of the *European* Council has restricted the Council's executive powers. (Importantly: the European Council is not identical with the Council. It constitutes a separate Union institution composed of the Heads

---

[51] Once, however, the European Parliament came close to using this power when in 1999 it decided to censure the Santer Commission. However, that Commission chose collectively to resign instead.

[52] Framework Agreement (supra n. 42), para. 5. However, this rule had been contested by the Council; see Council Statement concerning the Framework Agreement on relations between the European Parliament and the Commission ([2010] OJ C287/1).

[53] Article 286(2) TFEU.   [54] Article 283(2) TFEU.

[55] Article 228(2) TFEU.   [56] Article 145 EEC.

of State or Government of the Member States.)[57] Today, the Council is best characterized as the "federal" chamber within the Union legislature. It is the organ in which national governments meet.

What is the composition of this federal chamber, and what is its internal structure? How will the Council decide – by unanimity or qualified majority? And what are the powers enjoyed by the Council? This second section addresses these questions in four subsections.

(a) Composition and Configurations

Within the European Union, the Council is the institution of the Member States. Its intergovernmental character lies in its composition. The Treaty on European Union defines it as follows:

> The Council shall consist of a representative of each Member State at ministerial level, who may commit the government of the Member State in question and cast its vote.[58]

Within the Council, each national minister thus represents the interests of "his" Member State. These interests may vary depending on the subject matter decided in the Council. And indeed, depending on the subject matter at issue, there are different Council configurations.[59] And for each configuration, a different national minister will be representing "his" State. While there is thus – legally – but one single Council, there are – politically – ten different Councils. The existing Council configurations are shown in Table 1.3.

What is the mandate of each Council configuration? The Treaties only define the tasks of the first two Council configurations.[60] The "General Affairs Council" is charged to "ensure consistency in the work of the different Council configurations" below the General Affairs Council.[61] The "Foreign Affairs Council", on the other hand, is required to "elaborate the Union's external action on the basis of strategic guidelines laid down by

---

[57] Article 15(2) TEU. For an analysis of the European Council, see Schütze, *European Union Law* (supra n. 3), Chapter 5 – Section 3.

[58] Article 16(2) TEU.

[59] Article 16(6) TEU: "The Council shall meet in different configurations, the list of which shall be adopted in accordance with Article 236 of the Treaty on the Functioning of the European Union."

[60] Article 16(6) TEU.   [61] *Ibid.*

Table 1.3 Council Configurations

Council Configurations
1   General Affairs
2   Foreign Affairs
3   Economic and Financial Affairs
4   Justice and Home Affairs
5   Employment, Social Policy, Health and Consumer Affairs
6   Competitiveness (Internal Market, Industry, Research and Space)
7   Transport, Telecommunications and Energy
8   Agriculture and Fisheries
9   Environment
10   Education, Youth, Culture and Sport

the European Council and ensure that the Union's action is consistent".[62] The thematic scope and functional tasks of the remaining Council configurations are constitutionally open. They will generally deal with the subjects falling within their nominal ambit.

(b) Internal Structure and Organs

The Council has developed committees to assist it. From the very beginning, a committee composed of representatives of the Member States would support the Council.[63] That committee was made permanent under the 1957 EEC Treaty.[64] The resultant "Committee of *Permanent* Representatives" became known under its French acronym: "Coreper". The Permanent Representative is the ambassador of a Member State at the European Union. S/he is based in the national "Permanent Representation to the European Union". Coreper has two parts: Coreper II represents the meeting of the ambassadors, while Coreper I – against all intuition – represents

---

[62] *Ibid.*

[63] The Committee beneath the ECSC Council was called "Commission de Coordination du Conseil des Ministres" (Cocor). Its members were not permanently residing in Brussels.

[64] The Rome Treaty contained, unlike the 1951 Paris Treaty, an express legal basis for a Council Committee in Article 151 EEC. While the provision did not expressly mention that these representatives would be permanent representatives, this had been the intention of the Member States (E. Noel, "The Committee of Permanent Representatives", 5 (1967) *Journal of Common Market Studies*, 219). The Merger Treaty formally established the Committee of Permanent Representatives (*ibid.*, Article 4).

the meetings of their deputies. Both parts correspond to particular Council configurations. Coreper II prepares the first four Council configurations – the more important political decisions; whereas Coreper I prepares the more technical remainder.

The function of Coreper is vaguely defined in the Treaties: "A Committee of Permanent Representatives of the Governments of the Member States shall be responsible for preparing the work of the Council."[65] The abstract definition has been – somewhat – specified in the following way: "All items on the agenda for a Council meeting shall be examined in advance by Coreper unless the latter decides otherwise. Coreper shall endeavour to reach agreement at its level to be submitted to the Council for adoption."[66] In order to achieve that task, Coreper has set up "working parties" below it.[67] (These working parties are composed of national civil servants operating on instructions from national ministries.) Where Coreper reaches agreement, the point will be classed as an "A item" that will be rubber-stamped by the Council. Where it fails to agree in advance, a "B item" will need to be expressly discussed by the ministers in the Council. (But importantly, even for "A items" Coreper is not formally entitled to take decisions itself. It merely "prepares" and facilitates formal decision-making in the Council.)

(c) Decision-making and Voting

The Council will – physically – meet in Brussels to decide. The meetings are divided into two parts: one dealing with legislative activities, the other with non-legislative activities. When discussing legislation, the Council must meet in public.[68] The Commission will attend Council meetings.[69] However, it is not a formal member of the Council and is thus not entitled to vote. The quorum within the Council is as low as it is theoretical: a

---

[65] Article 16(7) TEU and Article 240(1) TFEU. See also Article 19 of the Council Rules of Procedure.

[66] Article 19(2) Council Rules of Procedure.

[67] *Ibid.*, Article 19(3). Under this paragraph, the General Secretariat is under an obligation to produce a list of these preparatory bodies. For a recent version of this list, see General Secretariat of the Council of the European Union, 20 July 2010, POLGEN 115.

[68] Article 16(8) TEU.

[69] According to Article 5(2) Council Rules of Procedure, the Council may however decide to deliberate without the Commission.

majority of the members of the Council are required to enable the Council to vote.[70]

Decision-making in the Council will take place in two principal forms: *unanimity* voting and *majority* voting. Unanimity voting requires the consent of all national ministers and is provided in the Treaties for sensitive political questions.[71] Majority voting however represents the constitutional norm. The Treaties here distinguish between a simple and a qualified majority. "Where it is required to act by a simple majority, the Council shall act by a majority of its component members."[72] This form of majority vote is rare.[73] The constitutional default is indeed the qualified majority: "The Council shall act by a qualified majority except where the Treaties provide otherwise."[74]

What constitutes a qualified majority of Member States in the Council? This has been one of the most controversial constitutional questions in the European Union. From the very beginning, the Treaties had instituted a system of *weighted votes*. Member States would thus not be "sovereign equals" in the Council, but would possess a number of votes that correlated with the size of their population. Table 1.4 shows the traditional system of weighted votes.

The weighting of votes is to some extent "degressively proportional". The voting ratio between the biggest and the smallest State is ten to one – a ratio that is roughly similar to the degressively proportional system for the European Parliament. However, the voting system also represents a system of symbolic compromises. For example, the four biggest Member States are all given the same number of votes – despite Germany's significantly greater demographic magnitude.[75]

In the past, this system of weighted votes has been attacked from two sides: from the smaller Member States as well as the bigger Member States. The smaller Member States have claimed that it favours the bigger

---

[70] *Ibid.*, Article 11(4).

[71] Important examples of sensitive political issues still requiring unanimity are foreign affairs (see Article 31 TEU), and "the harmonisation of legislation concerning turnover taxes, excise duties and other forms of indirect taxation" (see Article 113 TFEU).

[72] Article 238(1) TFEU.

[73] For example: Article 150 TFEU. Most matters that allow for simple majority are (internal) procedural or institutional matters.

[74] Article 16(3) TEU.

[75] The German population exceeds that of France – the second most populous State of the Union – by about 17 million people.

Table 1.4 Weighted Votes System within the Council

Member States: Votes	
Germany, France, Italy, United Kingdom	29
Spain, Poland	27
Romania	14
Netherlands	13
Belgium, Czech Republic, Greece, Hungary, Portugal	12
Austria, Bulgaria, Sweden	10
Croatia, Denmark, Ireland, Lithuania, Slovakia, Finland	7
Cyprus, Estonia, Latvia, Luxembourg, Slovenia	4
Malta	3

Qualified Majority: 260/352

Member States and have insisted that the 260 votes must be cast by a majority of the States. The bigger Member States, by contrast, have complained that the weighting unduly favours smaller Member States and have insisted on the political safeguard that the 260 votes cast in the Council correspond to 62 per cent of the total population of the Union. With these two qualifications taken into account, decision-making in the Council traditionally demands a *triple* majority: a *majority* of the weighted votes must be cast by a *majority* of the Member States representing a *majority* of the Union population.

This triple majority system exclusively governed decision-making in the Union until 1 November 2014. From that date, a completely new system of voting applies in the Council. (However, until 31 March 2017, any Member State can insist on using the old system of voting in the Council; and until this time, both voting systems will thus coexist.)[76] This revolutionary change is set out in Article 16(4) TEU, which states:

> As from 1 November 2014, a qualified majority shall be defined as at least 55% of the members of the Council, comprising at least fifteen of them and representing Member States comprising at least 65% of the population of the Union. A blocking minority must include at least four Council members, failing which the qualified majority shall be deemed attained. The

[76] Protocol (No 36) on Transitional Provisions, Article 3(2).

other arrangements governing the qualified majority are laid down in Article 238(2) of the Treaty on the Functioning of the European Union.[77]

This new Lisbon voting system abolishes the system of weighted votes in favour of a system that grants each State a single vote. In a Union of 28 States, 55 per cent of the Council members correspond to 16 States. But this majority is again qualified from two sides. The bigger Member States have insisted on a relatively high population majority behind the State majority. The population threshold of 65 per cent of the Union population would mean that any three of the four biggest States of the Union could block a Council decision. The smaller Member States have thus insisted on a qualification of the second majority. A qualified majority will be "deemed attained" where fewer than four States try to block a Council decision.

The new Lisbon system of qualified majority voting was designed to replace the triple majority with a simpler double majority. And yet the Member States – always fearful of abrupt changes – have agreed on two constitutional compromises that cushion the new system of qualified majority voting. First, the Member States have revived the "Ioannina Compromise".[78] The latter was envisaged in a "Declaration on Article 16(4)",[79] and is now codified in a Council Decision.[80] According to the Ioannina Compromise, the Council is under an obligation – despite the formal existence of the double majority in Article 16(4) TEU – to continue deliberations, where a fourth of the States or States representing a fifth of the Union population oppose a decision.[81] The Council is here under the procedural duty to "do all in its power" to reach – within a

---

[77] The Treaty recognizes an express exception to this in Article 238(2) TFEU which states: "By way of derogation from Article 16(4) of the Treaty on European Union, as from 1 November 2014 and subject to the provisions laid down in the Protocol on transitional provisions, where the Council does not act on a proposal from the Commission or from the High Representative of the Union for Foreign Affairs and Security Policy, the qualified majority shall be defined as at least 72 % of the members of the Council, representing Member States comprising at least 65 % of the population of the Union."

[78] The compromise was negotiated by the Member States' foreign ministers in Ioannina (Greece) – from where it takes its name. The compromise was designed to smooth the transition from the Union of twelve to a Union of fifteen Member States.

[79] Declaration (No. 7) on Article 16(4) is attached to the Treaties and contains a draft Council Decision.

[80] The Council formally adopted the decision in 2007 (see Council Decision 2009/857, [2009] OJ L314/73).

[81] *Ibid.*, Article 4.

reasonable time – "a satisfactory solution" to address the concerns of the blocking Member States.[82]

This soft mechanism is complemented by a hard mechanism to limit qualified majority voting in the Council. For the Treaties also recognize – regionally limited – versions of the "Luxembourg Compromise".[83] A patent illustration of this can be found in the context of the Union's Common Foreign and Security Policy which contains the following provision: "If a member of the Council declares that, for vital and stated reasons of national policy, it intends to oppose the adoption of a decision to be taken by qualified majority, a vote shall not be taken".[84] A Member State can here unilaterally block a Union decision on what it deems to be its vital interest.

(d) Functions and Powers

The Treaties summarize the functions and powers of the Council as follows:

> The Council shall, jointly with the European Parliament, exercise legislative and budgetary functions. It shall carry out policy-making and coordinating functions as laid down in the Treaties.[85]

Let us look at each of these four functions. First, the Council has traditionally been at the core of the Union's legislative function. Prior to the rise of the European Parliament, the Council indeed was the Union "legislator". The Council is today only a co-legislator, that is: a branch of the bicameral Union legislature.[86] And like Parliament, it must exercise its legislative powers in public.[87] Second, Council and Parliament also share in the exercise of the budgetary function. Third, what about the policy-making function? In this respect, the *European* Council has overtaken the Council. The former now decides on the general policy choices, and the role of the Council has consequently been limited to specific policy choices that implement the general ones. Yet, these choices remain significant and the Council Presidency will set "its" agenda. Fourth, the Council

---

[82] *Ibid.*, Article 5.
[83] On the "Luxembourg Compromise", see Schütze, *European Union Law* (supra n. 3), Chapter 1 – Section 2(b).
[84] Article 31(2) TEU.   [85] Article 16(1) TEU.
[86] On this point, see Chapter 2 – Section 1(a) below.   [87] Article 16(8) TEU.

has significant coordinating functions within the European Union. Thus, in the context of general economic policy, the Member States are required to "regard their economic policies as a matter of common concern and shall coordinate them within the Council".[88] The idea of an "open method of coordination" experienced a renaissance in the last decade.[89]

3. The Commission

The technocratic character of the early European Union expressed itself in the name of a third institution: the Commission. The Commission constituted the centre of the European Coal and Steel Community, where it was "to ensure that the objectives set out in [that] Treaty [were] attained".[90] In the European Union, the role of the Commission was, however, gradually "marginalized" by the Parliament and the Council. With these two institutions constituting the Union legislature, the Commission is today firmly located in the executive branch. In guiding the European Union, it – partly – acts like the Union's government. This third section analyses the composition of the Commission first, before exploring the relationship between the President and "his" college. A final subsection looks at the functions and powers of the Commission.

(a) Composition and Election

The Commission consists of one national of each Member State.[91] Its members are chosen "on the ground of their general competence and European commitment from persons whose independence is beyond

---

[88] Article 121(1) TFEU.
[89] On the "open method of coordination", see G. de Búrca, "The Constitutional Challenge of New Governance in the European Union", 28 (2003) *European Law Review*, 814.
[90] Article 8 ECSC.
[91] Article 17(4) TEU. The Lisbon Treaty textually limits this principle in a temporal sense: it will theoretically only apply from the date of entry into force of the Treaty of Lisbon to 31 October 2014. Thereafter, Article 17(5) TEU states: "As from 1 November 2014, the Commission shall consist of a number of members, including its President and the High Representative of the Union for Foreign Affairs and Security Policy, corresponding to two thirds of the number of Member States, unless the European Council, acting unanimously, decides to alter this number." This provision had been a centrepiece of the Lisbon Treaty, as it was designed to increase the effectiveness of the Commission by decreasing its membership. However, after the failure of the first Irish referendum on the Lisbon Treaty, the European Council decided to abandon this constitutional reform in order to please the Irish electorate; see Presidency Conclusions of 11–12 December 2008 (Document 17271/1/08 Rev 1).

doubt".[92] The Commission's term of office is five years.[93] During this term, it must be "completely independent". Its members "shall neither seek nor take instructions from any Government or other institution, body, office or entity".[94] The Member States are under a duty to respect this independence.[95] Breach of the duty of independence may lead to a Commissioner being "compulsorily retired".[96]

How is the Commission selected? Originally, the Commission was "appointed".[97] The appointment procedure has subsequently given way to an election procedure. This election procedure has two stages. In a first stage, the President of the Commission will be elected. The President will have been nominated by the European Council "[t]aking into account the elections to the European Parliament", that is: in accordance with the latter's political majority.[98] The nominated candidate must then be "elected" by the European Parliament. If not confirmed by Parliament, a new candidate needs to be found by the European Council.[99] After the election of the Commission President begins the second stage of the selection process. In accord with the President, the Council will adopt a list of candidate Commissioners on the basis of suggestions made by the Member States.[100] With the list being agreed, the proposed Commission is subjected "as a body to a vote of consent by the European Parliament", and on the basis of this election, the Commission shall be appointed by the European Council.[101]

This complex and compound selection process constitutes a mixture of "international" and "national" elements. The Commission's democratic legitimacy thus derives partly from the Member States, and partly from the European Parliament.

(b) The President and "his" College

The Commission President helps in the selection of "his" institution. This position as the "Chief" Commissioner *above* "his" college is clearly

---

[92] Article 17(3) TEU.   [93] *Ibid.*   [94] *Ibid.*   [95] Article 245 TFEU – first indent.
[96] Article 245 TFEU – second indent. See also Article 247 TFEU: "If any Member of the Commission no longer fulfils the conditions required for the performance of his duties or if he has been guilty of serious misconduct, the Court of Justice may, on application by the Council acting by a simple majority or the Commission, compulsorily retire him." On the replacement procedure, see Article 246 TFEU.
[97] Articles 9 and 10 ECSC.
[98] The term of the Commission runs in parallel with that of the Parliament.
[99] Article 17(7) TEU – first indent.   [100] Article 17(7) TEU – second indent.
[101] Article 17(7) TFEU – third indent.

established by the Treaties.[102] "The Members of the Commission shall carry out the duties devolved upon them by the President *under his authority*."[103] In light of this political authority, the Commission is typically named after its President.[104]

The powers of the President are identified in Article 17(6) TEU, which reads:

> The President of the Commission shall:
>
> (a) lay down guidelines within which the Commission is to work;
> (b) decide on the internal organization of the Commission, ensuring that it acts consistently, efficiently and as a collegiate body;
> (c) appoint Vice-Presidents, other than the High Representative of the Union for Foreign Affairs and Security Policy, from among the members of the Commission.
>
> A member of the Commission shall resign if the President so requests. The High Representative of the Union for Foreign Affairs and Security Policy shall resign, in accordance with the procedure set out in Article 18(1), if the President so requests.

The three powers of the President mentioned above are formidable. First, s/he can lay down the political direction of the Commission in the form of strategic guidelines. The Presidential guidelines will subsequently be translated into the Commission's Annual Work Programme. Second, the President is entitled to decide on the internal organization of the Commission.[105] In the words of the Treaties: "[T]he responsibilities incumbent upon the Commission shall be structured and allocated among

---

[102] N. Nugent, *The European Commission* (Palgrave, 2000), 68: "The Commission President used to be thought of as *primus inter pares* in the College. Now, however, he is very much *primus*."

[103] Article 248 TFEU (emphasis added).

[104] For example: the last Commission was called the "Barroso Commission", while the current Commission is called the "Juncker Commission".

[105] Due to its dual constitutional role, some special rules apply to the High Representative of the Union. Not only do the Treaties determine the latter's role within the Commission, the President will not be able *unilaterally* to ask for her resignation. (See Article 18(4) TEU: "The High Representative shall be one of the Vice-Presidents of the Commission. He shall ensure the consistency of the Union's external action. He shall be responsible within the Commission for responsibilities incumbent on it in external relations and for coordinating other aspects of the Union's external action.") On the role of the High Representative, see Schütze, *European Union Law* (supra n. 3), Chapter 5 – Section 4(b)(iii).

Figure 1.1 Commission President: Jean-Claude Juncker

its members by its President." The President is authorized to "reshuffle the allocation of those responsibilities during the Commission's term of office",[106] and may even ask a Commissioner to resign. Third, the President can appoint Vice-Presidents from "within" the Commission. Finally, there is a fourth power not expressly mentioned in Article 17(6) TEU: "The President shall represent the Commission."[107]

What are the "ministerial" responsibilities into which the present Commission is structured? Due to the requirement of one Commissioner per Member State, the "Juncker Commission" had to divide the tasks of the European Union into twenty-seven (!) "portfolios". Reflecting the priorities of the current President, they are as set out in Table 1.5.

Each Commissioner is thereby responsible for "his" portfolio, and will be assisted in this by his own cabinet.[108] However, an organizational novelty

---

[106] Article 248 TFEU.   [107] Article 3(5) Commission Rules of Procedure.
[108] Article 19(1) Commission Rules of Procedure: "Members of the Commission shall have their own cabinet to assist them in their work and in preparing Commission decisions.

Table 1.5 Commission College: President and Portfolios

President
High Representative for Foreign Affairs and Security Policy

Agriculture and Rural Development	Euro and Social Dialogue
Better Regulation and Rule of Law	Financial Services and Capital Markets
Budget and Human Resources	Health and Food Safety
Climate Action and Energy	Humanitarian Aid and Crisis
Competition	Management
Digital Economy and Society	Internal Market and Industry
Digital Single Market	International Cooperation and
Economic and Financial Affairs	Development
Education, Culture, Youth	Jobs, Growth and Investment
Employment and Social Affairs	Justice, Consumers and Gender
Energy Union	Migration and Home Affairs
Environment and Fisheries	Regional Policy
European Neighbourhood and	Research and Science
Enlargement	Trade
	Transport and Space

of the 2014 Commission is the idea of "Project Teams" – combining various portfolios under the authority of a Vice-President of the Commission. The aim behind this administrative grouping seems to be the desire to set policy priorities from the very start, and to create more cohesion between various ministerial portfolios.[109]

(c) Functions and Powers

What are the functions and corresponding powers of the Commission in the governmental structure of the European Union? The Treaties provide a concise constitutional overview of its tasks in Article 17 TEU:

> The rules governing the composition and operation of the cabinets shall be laid down by the President."
[109] The "Project Teams" currently suggested are: "A Connected Digital Single Market"; "A Deeper and Fairer Economic and Monetary Union"; "A New Boost for Jobs, Growth and Investment"; "A Resilient Energy Union with a Forward-Looking Climate Change Policy". In addition to these themes, the High Representative is also to head the "team" of external relations DGs. For an overview, see: http://ec.europa.eu/about/juncker-commission/structure/index_en.htm.

> The Commission shall promote the general interest of the Union and take appropriate initiatives to that end. It shall ensure the application of the Treaties, and of measures adopted by the institutions pursuant to them. It shall oversee the application of Union law under the control of the Court of Justice of the European Union. It shall execute the budget and manage programmes. It shall exercise coordinating, executive and management functions, as laid down in the Treaties. With the exception of the common foreign and security policy, and other cases provided for in the Treaties, it shall ensure the Union's external representation. It shall initiate the Union's annual and multiannual programming with a view to achieving interinstitutional agreements.[110]

The provision distinguishes six different functions. The first three functions constitute the Commission's core functions. First, the Commission is tasked to "*promote* the general interests of the Union" through initiatives. It is thus to act as a "motor" of European integration. In order to fulfil this – governmental – function, the Commission is given the (almost) exclusive right to formally propose legislative bills.[111] "Union acts may only be adopted on the basis of a Commission proposal, except where the Treaties provide otherwise."[112] The Commission's prerogative to propose legislation is a fundamental characteristic of the European constitutional order. The right of initiative extends to (multi)annual programming of the Union,[113] and embraces the power to make proposals for law reform.[114]

The second function of the Commission is to "*ensure* the application" of the Treaties. This function covers a number of powers – legislative and executive in nature. The Commission may thus be entitled to apply the Treaties by adopting secondary legislation. These acts may be adopted

---

[110] Article 17(1) TEU.

[111] The Parliament or the Council can *informally* suggest legislative bills to the Commission (see Nugent, *The European Commission* (supra n. 102), 236).

[112] Article 17(2) TEU. For an exception, see Article 76 TFEU on legislative measures in the field of police and judicial cooperation in criminal matters.

[113] Under Article 314(2) TFEU, the Commission is entitled to propose the draft budget: "The Commission shall submit a proposal containing the draft budget to the European Parliament and to the Council not later than 1 September of the year preceding that in which the budget is to be implemented."

[114] This is normally done through "White Papers" or "Green Papers". For a famous "White Paper", see EU Commission, Completing the Internal Market: White Paper from the Commission to the European Council (COM(85) 310). For a famous "Green Paper", see EU Commission, Damages Actions for Breach of the EC Antitrust Rules (COM(2005) 672).

directly under the Treaties;[115] or, under powers delegated to the Commission from the Union legislature.[116] In some areas the Commission may also be granted the executive power to apply the Treaties itself. The direct enforcement of European law can best be seen in the context of European competition law,[117] where the Commission enjoys significant powers to fine – private or public – wrongdoers. These administrative penalties sanction the non-application of European law.

The third function of the Commission is to act as guardian of the Union. It shall thus *"oversee* the application" of European law. The Treaties indeed grant the Commission significant powers to act as "police" and "prosecutor" of the Union. The policing of European law involves the power to monitor and to investigate infringements of European law. The powers are – again – best defined in the context of European competition law.[118] Where an infringement of European law has been identified, the Commission may bring the matter before the Court of Justice. The Treaties thus give the Commission the power to bring infringement proceedings against Member States,[119] and other Union institutions.[120]

4. The Court of Justice of the European Union

"Tucked away in the fairyland Duchy of Luxembourg",[121] and housed in its "palace", lies the Court of Justice of the European Union. The Court

---

[115] See Article 106(3) TFEU: "The Commission shall ensure the application of the provisions of this Article and shall, where necessary, address appropriate directives or decisions to Member States."

[116] On delegated legislation, see Schütze, *European Union Law* (supra n. 3), Chapter 9 – Section 2.

[117] See Article 105(1) TFEU: "[T]he Commission shall ensure the application of the principles laid down in Articles 101 and 102. On application by a Member State or on its own initiative, and in cooperation with the competent authorities in the Member States, which shall give it their assistance, the Commission shall investigate cases of suspected infringement of these principles. If it finds that there has been an infringement, it shall propose appropriate measures to bring it to an end."

[118] See Regulation 1/2003 on the implementation of the rules on competition laid down in Articles [101] and [102] of the Treaty ([2003] OJ L1/1), Chapter V: "Powers of Investigation".

[119] Article 258 TFEU. For an extensive discussion of this, see Chapter 8 – Section 1 below.

[120] On this point, see Chapter 8 – Sections 2–4 below.

[121] E. Stein, "Lawyers, Judges, and the Making of a Transnational Constitution", 75 (1981) *American Journal of International Law*, 1.

constitutes the judicial branch of the European Union. It is composed of various courts that are linguistically roofed under the name "Court of Justice of the European Union" and includes the "Court of Justice", the "General Court" and "specialized courts".[122] The Court's task is to "ensure that in the interpretation and application of the Treaties the law is observed".[123]

This fourth section starts by analysing the Union's judicial architecture, before surveying the judicial powers of the Court of Justice of the European Union.

(a) Judicial Architecture: the European Court System

When the European Union was born, its judicial branch consisted of a single court: the "Court of Justice". The (then) Court was a "one stop shop". All judicial affairs of the Union would need to pass through its corridors.

With its workload having risen to dizzying heights, the Court pressed the Member States to provide for a judicial "assistant". And the Member States agreed to create a second court in the Single European Act. The latter granted the Council the power to "attach to the Court of Justice a court with jurisdiction to hear and determine at first instance", that was "subject to a right of appeal to the Court of Justice".[124] Thanks to this definition, the newly created court was baptized the "Court of First Instance".[125] With the Lisbon Treaty, the Court has now been renamed the "General Court". The reason for this change of name lies in the fact that the Court is no longer confined to first instance cases. Instead, "[t]he General Court shall have jurisdiction to hear and determine actions or proceedings brought against decisions of the specialized courts".[126] What are the "specialized courts" in the European Union? The Union has currently only one specialized court: the "Civil Service Tribunal".[127]

---

[122] Article 19(1) TEU.   [123] *Ibid.*   [124] Article 11(1) Single European Act.
[125] The Court was set up by Council Decision 88/591 establishing a Court of First Instance of the European Communities ([1988] OJ L319/1).
[126] Article 256(2) TFEU.
[127] Council Decision 2004/752 establishing the European Union Civil Service Tribunal ([2004] OJ L333/7). See also N. Lavranos, "The New Specialised Courts within the European Judicial System", 30 (2005) *European Law Review*, 261.

Figure 1.2 Structure of the Court of Justice of the European Union

The Court of Justice of the European Union thus represents a three-tiered system of courts.[128] The architecture of the Union's judicial branch can be seen in Figure 1.2.

(b) Jurisdiction and Judicial Powers

The traditional role of courts in modern societies is to act as independent adjudicators between competing interests. Their jurisdiction may be compulsory, or not. The jurisdiction of the Court of Justice of the European Union is compulsory "within the limits of the powers conferred on it in the Treaties".[129] While compulsory, the Court's jurisdiction is thus limited. Based on the principle of conferral, the Court has no "inherent" jurisdiction.

The functions and powers of the Court are classified in Article 19(3) TEU:

> The Court of Justice of the European Union shall, in accordance with the Treaties:
>
> (a) rule on actions brought by a Member State, an institution or a natural or legal person;

---

[128] In terms of the European Union's judicial reports, there are thus three different prefixes before a case. Cases before the Court of Justice are C-Cases, cases before the General Court are T-Cases (as the French name for the General Court is "Tribunal"), and cases before the Civil Service Tribunal are F-Cases (stemming from the French "fonction publique" for civil service).

[129] Article 13(2) TEU.

> (b) give preliminary rulings, at the request of courts or tribunals of the Member States, on the interpretation of Union law or the validity of acts adopted by the institutions;
>
> (c) rule in other cases provided for in the Treaties.

The provision classifies the judicial tasks by distinguishing between direct and indirect actions. The former are brought directly before the European Court. The latter arrive at the Court indirectly through preliminary references from national courts. The powers of the Court under the preliminary reference procedure are set out in a single Article.[130] By contrast, there exist a number of direct actions set out in the Treaty on the Functioning of the European Union. The TFEU distinguishes between enforcement actions brought by the Commission or a Member State,[131] judicial review proceedings for actions and inactions of the Union institutions,[132] damages actions for the (non-)contractual liability of the Union,[133] as well as a few minor jurisdictional heads.[134]

In light of its broad jurisdiction, the Court of Justice of the European Union can be characterized as a "constitutional", "administrative", and an "international" court as well as an "industrial tribunal". Its jurisdiction includes public and private matters. And while the Court claims to act like a "continental" civil law court, it has been fundamental in shaping the structure and powers of the European Union as well as the nature of European law. The (activist) jurisprudence of the Court will thus be regularly encountered in the subsequent chapters of this book.

Conclusion

This Chapter analysed the governmental structure of the European Union. The Union has seven "institutions" – four of which were looked at in some detail, namely: the European Parliament, the Council of Ministers, the Commission, and the Court of Justice of the European Union. Each of these institutions is characterized by its distinct composition and its

---

[130] Article 267 TFEU. The provision is analysed in Chapter 7 – Sections 3 and 4 below.
[131] Articles 258–60 TFEU. The provisions are analysed in Chapter 8 – Section 1 below.
[132] Articles 263–6 TFEU. The provisions are analysed in Chapter 8 – Sections 2 and 3 below.
[133] Articles 268 and 340 TFEU. The provisions are analysed in Chapter 8 – Section 4 below.
[134] Articles 269–74 TFEU.

decision-making mode. Importantly, the Union is not based on a strict separation of functions between its institutions but follows a "checks-and-balances" version of the separation-of-powers principle.[135] This means that various Union institutions share in the exercise of various governmental functions. This institutional power-sharing can clearly be seen with regard to the legislative function, which will be discussed in the next Chapter.

---

[135] For a discussion of this point, see: R. Schütze, *European Union Law* (supra n. 3), Chapter 5 – Section 1.

Introduction

British constitutionalism defines (primary) legislation as an act adopted by the Queen-in-Parliament. Behind this "compound" legislator stands a legislative procedure. This legal procedure links the House of Commons, the House of Lords and the monarchy. European constitutionalism also adopts a procedural definition of legislative power. However, unlike British constitutional law, the Treaties distinguish two types of legislative procedures: an ordinary legislative procedure and special legislative procedures. Article 289 TFEU states:

> 1. The ordinary legislative procedure shall consist in the joint adoption by the European Parliament and the Council of a regulation, directive or decision on a proposal from the Commission. This procedure is defined in Article 294.

> 2. In the specific cases provided for by the Treaties, the adoption of a regulation, directive or decision by the European Parliament with the participation of the Council, or by the latter with the participation of the European Parliament, shall constitute a special legislative procedure.[1]

European "legislation" is thus – formally – defined as an act adopted by the bicameral Union legislator. According to the *ordinary* legislative procedure, the European Parliament and the Council act as co-legislators with *symmetric* procedural rights. European legislation is therefore seen as the product of a "joint adoption" by both institutions. But the Treaties also recognize *special* legislative procedures. The defining characteristic of these special procedures is that they abandon the institutional equality between the European Parliament and the Council. Logically, then, Article 289(2) TFEU recognizes two variants. In the first variant, the European Parliament acts as the dominant institution, with the mere "participation" of the Council in the form of "consent".[2] The second variant inverts this relationship. The Council is here the dominant institution, with the Parliament either participating through its "consent",[3] or in the form of "consultation".[4]

Having analysed the various Union institutions in Chapter 1, this Chapter explores their interaction in the creation of European (secondary) law. Sections 1 and 2 respectively discuss the ordinary and special legislative procedures in more detail. Section 3 looks at the principle of subsidiarity – a constitutional principle that prevents the Union legislator from exercising its competences where the Member States would be able to achieve the desirable social aim themselves. Within the Union legal order, this principle has been primarily understood as a procedural safeguard that – indirectly – involves the national parliaments prior to the adoption of a legislative act. Finally, an excursus looks at the procedure for the conclusion of international agreements. These agreements, while not formally concluded under a legislative procedure, nonetheless constitute a rich (external) source of European secondary law.

---

[1] Article 289(1) and (2) TFEU.

[2] See Articles 223(2), 226 and 228 TFEU. The procedure for the adoption of the Union budget is laid down in Art. 314 TFEU and will not be discussed here.

[3] See Articles 19(1), 25, 86(1), 223(1), 311, 312 and 352 TFEU.

[4] See Articles 21(3), 22(1), 22(2), 23, 64(3), 77(3), 81(3), 87(3), 89, 113, 115, 118, 126, 127(6), 153(2), 182(4), 192(2), 203, 262, 308, 311, 349 TFEU.

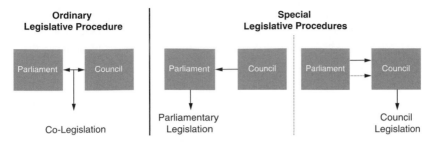

Figure 2.1 Structure of the Union Legislator

1. The "Ordinary" Legislative Procedure

(a) Constitutional Theory: Formal Text

The ordinary legislative procedure has seven stages. Article 294 TFEU defines five stages; two additional stages are set out in Article 297 TFEU.

Proposal stage. Under the ordinary legislative procedure, the Commission enjoys – with minor exceptions – the exclusive right to submit a legislative proposal.[5] This (executive) prerogative guarantees a significant agenda-setting power to the Commission. The Treaties – partly – protect this power from "external" interferences by insisting that any amendment that the Commission dislikes will require unanimity in the Council – an extremely high decisional hurdle.[6]

First reading. The Commission proposal goes to the European Parliament. The Parliament will act by a majority of the votes cast,[7] that is: the majority of physically present parliamentarians. It can reject the proposal,[8] approve it, or – as a middle path – amend it. The bill then moves to the

---

[5] Article 294(2) TFEU. Paragraph 15 recognizes exceptions to this rule in cases provided for in the Treaties. Perhaps the most significant exception is Article 76 TFEU referring to legislative measures in the field of police and judicial cooperation in criminal matters.

[6] Article 293(1) TFEU, as well as Article 284(9) TFEU. Moreover, until the conciliation stage the Commission may unilaterally alter or withdraw the proposal: Article 293(2) TFEU.

[7] Article 294(3) TFEU is silent on the voting regime within Parliament, and therefore Article 231 TFEU applies: "Save as otherwise provided in the Treaties, the European Parliament shall act by a majority of the votes cast. The rules of procedure shall determine the quorum."

[8] This option is not expressly recognized in the text of Article 294(3) TFEU, but it is indirectly recognized in Rule 60 of the Parliament's Rules of Procedure.

Council, which will act by a qualified majority of its members.[9] Where the Council agrees with Parliament's position, the bill is adopted after the first reading. Where it disagrees, the Council is called to provide its own position and communicate it, with reasons, to Parliament.

Second reading. The (amended) bill lies for the second time in Parliament's court; and Parliament has three choices as to what to do with it. Parliament may positively approve the Council's position by a majority of the votes cast;[10] or reject it by a majority of its component members.[11] Approval is thus easier than rejection. (This tendency is reinforced by assimilating passivity to approval.)[12] However, Parliament has a third choice: it may propose, by a majority of its component members, amendments to the Council position.[13] The amended bill will be forwarded to the Council and to the Commission (that must deliver an opinion on the amendments). The bill is thus back in the Council's court, and the Council has two options. Where it approves all (!) of Parliament's amendments, the legislative act is adopted.[14] (The Council thereby acts by a qualified majority, unless the Commission disagrees with any of the amendments suggested by the Council or the Parliament.)[15] But where the Council cannot approve all of Parliament's amendments, the bill enters into the conciliation stage.[16]

Conciliation stage. This stage presents the last chance to rescue the legislative bill. As agreement within the "formal" legislature has proved impossible, the Union legal order "delegates" the power to draft a "joint text" to a committee. This committee is called the "Conciliation Committee".[17] The mandate of the Committee is restricted to reaching agreement on a joint text "on the basis of the positions of the European

---

[9] Article 294(4) and (5) TFEU are silent on the voting regime, and therefore Article 16(4) TEU applies: "The Council shall act by a qualified majority except where the Treaties provide otherwise."

[10] Article 294(7)(a) TFEU.   [11] Article 294(7)(b) TFEU.

[12] According to Article 294(7)(a) TFEU – second alternative, where the Parliament does not act within three months, "the act shall be deemed to have been adopted in the wording which corresponds to the position of the Council".

[13] Article 294(7)(c) TFEU. For an (internal) limitation on what types of amendments can be made, see Rule 69(2) of the Parliament's Rules of Procedure.

[14] Article 294(8)(a) TFEU.   [15] Article 294(9) TFEU.   [16] Article 294(8)(b) TFEU.

[17] The Conciliation Committee is not a standing committee, but an ad hoc committee that "is constituted separately for each legislative proposal requiring conciliation" (European Parliament, "Codecision and Conciliation" at: www.europarl.europa.eu/code/infor-mation/ guide_en.pdf, 15).

Parliament and the Council at second reading".[18] The Committee is composed of members representing the Council,[19] and an equal number of members representing the European Parliament.[20] (The Commission will take part "in" the committee, but is not a part "of" the Committee. Its function is to act as a catalyst for conciliation.)[21] The Committee thus represents a "miniature legislature"; and like its constitutional model, the Committee co-decides by a qualified majority of the Council representatives, and a majority of the representatives sent by Parliament. Where the Committee does not adopt a joint text, the legislative bill has failed. Where the Committee has managed to approve a joint text, the latter returns to the "formal" Union legislator for a third reading.

Third reading. The "formal" Union legislature must positively approve the joint text (without the power of amending it). The Parliament needs to endorse the joint text by a majority of the votes cast, whereas the Council must confirm the text by a qualified majority. Where one of the two chambers disagrees with the proposal made by the Conciliation Committee, the bill finally flounders. Where both chambers approve the text, the bill is adopted and only needs to be "signed" and "published".

Signing and publication. The last two stages before a bill becomes law are set out in Article 297 TFEU which states: "Legislative acts adopted under the ordinary legislative procedure shall be signed by the President of the European Parliament and by the President of the Council"; and they shall subsequently "be published in the Official Journal of the European Union".[22] The publication requirement is a fundamental element of modern societies governed by the rule of law. Only "public" legislative

---

[18] Article 294(10) TFEU. However, the Court of Justice has been flexible and allowed the Conciliation Committee to find a joint text that goes beyond the common position after the second reading (see *The Queen on the Application of International Air Transport Association et al.* v. *Department of Transport,* Case C-344/04, [2006] ECR I-403).

[19] The Permanent Representative or his Deputy will typically represent the national ministers in the Council.

[20] The parliamentary delegation must reflect the political composition of the formal Parliament (see Rule 71 (2) of the Parliament's Rules of Procedure). It will normally include the three Vice-Presidents responsible for conciliation, the Rapporteur and Chair of the responsible parliamentary committee.

[21] Article 294(11) TFEU. Formally, it will be the Commissioner responsible for the subject matter of the legislative bill who will take part in the Conciliation Committee.

[22] Article 297(1) TFEU. For legislation, this will be the "L" Series.

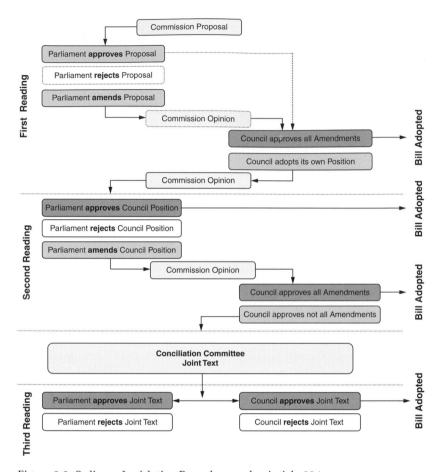

Figure 2.2 Ordinary Legislative Procedure under Article 294

acts will have the force of law. The Union legal order also requires that all legislative acts "shall state the reasons on which they are based and shall refer to any proposals, initiatives, recommendations, request or opinions required by the Treaties".[23] This formal "duty to state reasons" can be judicially reviewed, and represents a hallmark of legislative rationality.

(b) Constitutional Practice: Informal Trilogues

Constitutional texts often only provide a stylized sketch of the formal relations between institutions. And this formal picture will need

---

[23] Article 296 TFEU – second indent.

to be coloured and revised by informal constitutional practices. This is very much the case for the constitutional text governing the ordinary legislative procedure. The rudimentary status of the constitutional text is indeed recognized by the Treaties themselves,[24] and the importance of informal practices has been expressly acknowledged by the European institutions.[25] The primary expression of these informal institutional arrangements are tripartite meetings ("trilogues"). They combine the representatives of the three institutions in an "informal framework".[26]

What is the task of institutional trilogues? The trilogues system is designed to create informal bridges during the formal co-decision procedure that open up "possibilities for agreements at first and second reading stages, as well as contributing to the preparation of the work of the Conciliation Committee".[27] Trilogues may thus be held "at all stages of the [ordinary legislative] procedure".[28] Indeed, a "Joint Declaration" of the Union institutions contains respective commitments for each procedural stage. In order to facilitate a formal agreement within the Union legislator during the first reading, informal agreements between the institutional representatives will thus be forwarded to Parliament or Council respectively.[29] This equally applies to the second reading,[30] and to the conciliation stage.[31] The strategy of informality has proved extremely successful.[32] And yet, there are serious constitutional problems. For informal trilogues should not be allowed to short-circuit the formal legislative procedure. Were this to happen, democratic deliberation within a fairly

---

[24] Article 295 TFEU states: "The European Parliament, the Council and the Commission shall consult each other and by common agreement make arrangements for their cooperation. To that end, they may, in compliance with the Treaties, conclude interinstitutional agreements which may be of a binding nature."

[25] See "Joint Declaration on Practical Arrangements for the Codecision Procedure", [2007] OJ C145/5.

[26] *Ibid.*, para. 8.   [27] *Ibid.*, para. 7.   [28] *Ibid.*, para. 8.

[29] *Ibid.*, para. 14: "Where an agreement is reached through informal negotiations in trilogues, the chair of Coreper shall forward, in a letter to the chair of the relevant parliamentary committee, details of the substance of the agreement, in the form of amendments to the Commission proposal. That letter shall indicate the Council's willingness to accept that outcome, subject to legal-linguistic verification, should it be confirmed by the vote in plenary. A copy of that letter shall be forwarded to the Commission." For the inverted obligation, see para. 18.

[30] *Ibid.*, para. 23.   [31] *Ibid.*, paras. 24–5.

[32] According to the European Parliament, "Codecision and Conciliation" (supra n. 17), 14, in the period between 2004 and 2009, 72 per cent of legislative acts were agreed at first reading, and 23 per cent at second reading. This leaves only 5 per cent to pass through conciliation and the third reading.

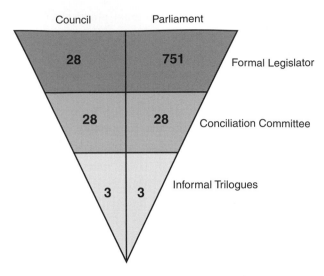

Figure 2.3 Declining Democratic Representation

representative European Union would be replaced by the informal government of a dozen representatives of the three institutions. And indeed, the democratic deficit of the Union would not lie in the *formal* structure of the Union legislator, but in its *informal* bypassing.

2. The "Special" Legislative Procedures

In addition to the ordinary legislative procedure, the Treaties recognize three special legislative procedures. Unlike the ordinary procedure, the Union act will here not be the result of a "joint adoption" of the European Parliament and the Council. It will be adopted by *one* of the two institutions. In the first variant of Article 289(2) TFEU, this will be the Parliament; yet the Treaties generally require the "consent" of the Council. In the second variant of Article 289(2) TFEU, the Council will adopt the legislative act; yet the Treaties require either the "consent" or "consultation" of the Parliament. The first two special procedures may be characterized as the "consent procedure", while the third special procedure can be referred to as the "consultation procedure".

What are the characteristics of the "consent procedure" and the "consultation procedure"? The former requires one institution to consent to the legislative bill of the other. Consent is less than co-decision, for only the dominant institution will be able to determine the substantive content of the bill. The non-dominant institution will be forced to "take-it-or-leave-it". But this veto power is still – much – stronger than mere consultation. For while the Court has recognized that consultation is "an essential factor in the institutional balance intended by the Treaty",[33] consultation is nonetheless a mere "formality".[34] The formal obligation to consult will *not* mean that the adopting institution must take into account the substantive views of the other.[35]

3. The Principle of Subsidiarity

Subsidiarity – the quality of being "subsidiary" – derives from *subsidium*. The Latin concept evolved in the military context. It represented an "assistance" or "aid" that stayed in the background. Figuratively, an entity is subsidiary where it provides a "subsidy" – an assistance of subordinate or secondary importance. In political philosophy, the principle of subsidiarity came to represent the idea "that a central authority should have a subsidiary function, performing only those tasks which cannot be performed effectively at a more immediate or local level".[36] The principle thus has a positive and a negative aspect.[37] It positively encourages "large associations" to assist smaller ones, where they need help; and it negatively discourages "to assign to a greater and higher association what lesser and subordinate organizations can do". It is this dual character that has given the principle of subsidiarity its "Janus-like" character.[38]

---

[33] *Roquette Frères* v. *Council (Isoglucose)*, Case 138/79, [1980] ECR 3333, para. 33.

[34] The "formality" still requires that the Council has to wait until Parliament has provided its opinion (see *ibid.*, para. 34): "In that respect it is pertinent to point out that observance of that requirement implies that the Parliament has expressed its opinion. It is impossible to take the view that the requirement is satisfied by the Council's simply asking for the opinion." On this point, see also *Parliament* v. *Council* Case C-65/93, [1995] ECR I-643; however, this case also established implied limitations on Parliament's prerogative (*ibid.*, paras. 27–8).

[35] This was confirmed in *Parliament* v. *Council*, Case C-417/93, [1995] ECR I-1185, esp. paras. 10 and 11.

[36] See *Oxford English Dictionary*: "subsidiary" and "subsidiarity".

[37] C. Calliess, *Subsidiaritäts- und Solidaritätsprinzip in der Europäischen Union* (Nomos, 1999), 26.

[38] V. Constantinesco, "Who's Afraid of Subsidiarity?," 11 (1991) *Yearbook of European Law*, 33 at 35.

When did the subsidiarity principle become a constitutional principle of the European Union? The principle of subsidiarity surfaced in 1975,[39] but it would only find official expression in the context of the Union's environmental policy after the Single European Act (1986).[40] The Maastricht Treaty on European Union (1992) finally lifted the subsidiarity principle beyond its environmental confines. It became a general constitutional principle of the European Union. Today, the Treaty on European Union defines it in Article 5, whose third paragraph states:

> Under the principle of subsidiarity, in areas which do not fall within its exclusive competence, the Union shall act only if and in so far as the objectives of the proposed action cannot be sufficiently achieved by the Member States, either at central level or at regional and local level, but can rather, by reason of the scale or effects of the proposed action, be better achieved at Union level.

The definition clarifies that subsidiarity is only to apply within the sphere of the Union's non-exclusive powers and thus confirms that the European principle of subsidiarity is a principle of *cooperative* federalism.[41]

The Treaty definition of subsidiarity thereby builds on *two* tests. The first may be called the *national insufficiency test*. The Union can only act where the objectives of the proposed action could not be sufficiently achieved by the Member States (centrally or regionally). This appears to be an absolute standard. By contrast, a second test is a *comparative efficiency test*. The Union should not act unless it can *better* achieve the objectives of the proposed action. This appears to be a relative standard. The question that therefore arises is this: will the combination of these two tests mean that the Union would not be entitled to act where it is – in relative terms – better able to tackle a social problem, but where the Member States could – in absolute terms – still achieve the desired result?

This is indeed not the only textual problem with Article 5(3). For the formulation "if and in so far" potentially offered *two* versions of the

---

[39] For a detailed textual genealogy of the subsidiarity principle in the European legal order, see R. Schütze, *From Dual to Cooperative Federalism: The Changing Structure of European Law* (Oxford University Press, 2009), 247 et seq.

[40] The (then) newly inserted Article 130r(4) EEC restricted Community environmental legislation to those actions whose objectives could "be attained better at Community level than at the level of the individual Member States".

[41] On the meaning of that concept, see Schütze, *From Dual to Cooperative Federalism* (supra n. 39), 4 et seq.

subsidiarity principle. The first version concentrates on the "if" question by asking *whether* the Union should act. This has been defined as the principle of subsidiarity *in a strict sense*. The second version concentrates on the "in-so-far" question by asking *how* the Union should act. This has been referred to as the principle of subsidiarity *in a wide sense*.[42]

The wording of Article 5(3) TEU is thus a terrible textual failure. Too many political cooks seem to have spoiled the legal broth! In the past two decades, two – parallel – approaches therefore evolved to give meaning to the subsidiarity principle. The first approach concentrates on the political safeguards of federalism. The second approach focuses on subsidiarity as an objective judicial standard.

(a) Subsidiarity as a Political Safeguard

Despite its literary presence,[43] the principle of subsidiarity has remained a subsidiary principle of European constitutionalism. The reason for its shadowy existence has been its lack of conceptual contours. If subsidiarity was everything to everyone, how should the Union apply it? To limit this semantic uncertainty, constitutional clarifications have tried to "procedur-alize" the principle. This attempt to develop subsidiarity into a political safeguard of federalism can be seen in Protocol (No. 2) "On the Application of the Principles of Subsidiarity and Proportionality". Importantly, the Protocol only applies to "draft legislative acts",[44] that is: acts to be adopted under the ordinary or a special legislative procedure.

The Protocol aims to establish "a system of monitoring" the application of the principle. Each Union institution is called upon to ensure constant respect for the principle of subsidiarity.[45] And this means in particular that they must forward draft legislative acts to national parliaments.[46]

---

[42] K. Lenaerts, "The Principle of Subsidiarity and the Environment in the European Union: Keeping the Balance of Federalism", 17 (1994) *Fordham International Law Journal*, 846 at 875.

[43] From the – abundant – literature, see G. Berman, "Taking Subsidiarity Seriously: Federalism in the European Community and the United States", 94 (1994) *Columbia Law Review*, 331; G. de Búrca, "Reappraising Subsidiarity Significance after Amsterdam", Harvard Jean Monnet Working Paper 1999/07; D. Z. Cass, "The Word that Saves Maastricht? The Principle of Subsidiarity and the Division of Powers within the European Community", 29 (1992) *Common Market Law Review*, 1107; Constantinesco, "Who's Afraid" (supra n. 38).

[44] Article 3 of the Protocol.   [45] *Ibid.*, Article 1.   [46] *Ibid.*, Article 4.

These draft legislative acts must "be justified" with regard to the principle of subsidiarity and proportionality.[47]

This (procedural) duty to provide reasons is defined as follows:

> Any draft legislative act should contain a detailed statement making it possible to appraise compliance with the principles of subsidiarity and proportionality. This statement should contain some assessment of the proposal's financial impact and, in the case of a directive, of its implications for the rules to be put in place by Member States, including, where necessary, the regional legislation. The reasons for concluding that a Union objective can be better achieved at Union level shall be substantiated by qualitative and, wherever possible, quantitative indicators. Draft legislative acts shall take account of the need for any burden, whether financial or administrative, falling upon the Union, national governments, regional or local authorities, economic operators and citizens, to be minimised and commensurate with the objective to be achieved.[48]

But how is this duty enforced? One solution would point to the European Court;[49] yet, the Protocol prefers a second solution: the active involvement of national parliaments in the legislative procedure of the European Union.[50] It was hoped that this idea would kill two birds with one stone. The procedural involvement of national parliaments promised to strengthen the federal *and* the democratic safeguards within Europe.

But if national parliaments are to be the Union's "watchdogs of subsidiarity",[51] would they enjoy a veto right (hard legislative solution) or only a monitoring right (soft legislative solution)? According to the Subsidiarity Protocol, each national parliament may within eight weeks produce a reasoned opinion stating why it considers that a European

---

[47] *Ibid.*, Article 5.   [48] *Ibid.*

[49] *Ibid.*, Article 8: "The Court of Justice of the European Union shall have jurisdiction in actions on grounds of infringement of the principle of subsidiarity by a legislative act, brought in accordance with the rules laid down in Article 263 of the Treaty on the Functioning of the European Union by Member States, or notified by them in accordance with their legal order on behalf of their national Parliament or a chamber thereof." For a discussion of the Court's deferential stance, see Section 3(b) below.

[50] This function is acknowledged in Article 12(b) TEU, which requests national parliaments to contribute to the good functioning of the Union "by seeing to it that the principle of subsidiarity is respected in accordance with the procedures provided for in the Protocol on the application of the principles of subsidiarity and proportionality".

[51] I. Cooper, "The Watchdogs of Subsidiarity: National Parliaments and the Logic of Arguing in the EU", 44 (2006) *Journal of Common Market Studies*, 281.

legislative draft does not comply with the principle of subsidiarity.[52] Each Parliament will thereby have two votes.[53] Where the negative votes amount to one-third of all the votes allocated to the national parliaments, the European Union draft "must be reviewed". This is called the "yellow card" mechanism, since the Union legislator "may decide to maintain, amend or withdraw the draft".[54]

The yellow card mechanism is slightly strengthened in relation to proposals under the ordinary legislative procedure; albeit, here, only a majority of the votes allocated to the national parliaments will trigger it.[55] Under this "orange card" mechanism, the Commission's justification for maintaining the proposal, as well as the reasoned opinions of the national parliaments, will be submitted to the Union legislator. And the Union legislator will have to consider whether the proposal is compatible with the principle of subsidiarity. Where one of its chambers finds that the proposal violates the principle of subsidiarity, the proposal is rejected.[56] While this arrangement makes it – slightly – easier for the European Parliament to reject a legislative proposal on subsidiarity grounds, it makes it – ironically – more difficult for the Council to block a proposal on the basis of subsidiarity than on the basis of a proposal's lack of substantive merit.[57]

Importantly, the Subsidiarity Protocol has rejected the idea of a "red card" mechanism. This rejection of a hard legislative solution has been bemoaned. The proposed procedural safeguards are said to "add very little"

---

[52] Article 6 Protocol (No. 2) "On the Application of the Principles of Subsidiarity and Proportionality".

[53] *Ibid.*, Article 7(1).

[54] *Ibid.*, Article 7(2). For an analysis of the first activation of the yellow card mechanism, see: F. Fabbrini and K. Granat, "'Yellow Card, but no Foul': The Role of the National Parliaments under the Subsidiarity Protocol and the Commission Proposal for an EU Regulation on the Right to Strike", (2013) 50 *C.M.L. Rev.* 115.

[55] *Ibid.*, Article 7(3).

[56] *Ibid.*, Article 7(3)(b): "if, by a majority of 55% of the members of the Council or a majority of the votes cast in the European Parliament, the legislator is of the opinion that the proposal is not compatible with the principle of subsidiarity, the legislative proposal shall not be given further consideration."

[57] For an analysis of this point, see G. Barrett, "'The King is Dead, Long live the King': the Recasting by the Treaty of Lisbon of the Provisions of the Constitutional Treaty concerning National Parliaments", 33 (2008) *European Law Review*, 66 at 80–1. In the light of the voting threshold, "it seems fair to predict that blockade of legislative proposals under Article 7(2) is likely to be a highly exceptional and unusual situation".

to the federal control of the Union legislator.[58] Others have – rightly – greeted the fact that the subsidiarity mechanism will leave the political decision to adopt the legislative act ultimately to the *European* legislator. "[T]o give national parliaments what would amount to a veto over proposals would be incompatible with the Commission's constitutionally protected independence."[59] "[A] veto power vested in national Parliaments would distort the proper distribution of power and responsibility in the EU's complex but remarkably successful system of transnational governance by conceding too much to State control."[60] Indeed, to have turned national parliaments into "co-legislators" in the making of European law would have aggravated the "political interweaving" of the European and the national level and thereby deepened joint-decision traps.[61] The rejection of the hard veto solution is thus to be welcomed. The soft legislative solution will indeed allow national parliaments to channel their scrutiny to where it can be most useful and effective: on their respective national governments.

(b) Subsidiarity as a Judicial Safeguard

Any substantive meaning of the subsidiarity principle is in the hands of the European Court of Justice. How has the Court defined the relationship between the national insufficiency test and the comparative efficiency test? And has the Court favoured the restrictive or the wide meaning of subsidiarity?

There are surprisingly few judgments that address the principle of subsidiarity. In *United Kingdom* v. *Council (Working Time Directive)*,[62] the United Kingdom had applied for the annulment of the Working Time Directive. The applicant claimed that

---

[58] See House of Commons, European Scrutiny Committee (Thirty-third Report: 2001–02): Subsidiarity, National Parliaments and the Lisbon Treaty, www.parliament .the-stationery-office.com/pa/cm200708/cmselect/cmeuleg/563/563.pdf, para. 35.

[59] A. Dashwood, "The Relationship between the Member States and the European Union/Community", 41 (2004) *Common Market Law Review*, 355 at 369.

[60] S. Weatherill, "Using National Parliaments to Improve Scrutiny of the Limits of EU Action", 28 (2003) *European Law Review*, 909 at 912.

[61] On the concept and shortfalls of "political interweaving" (*Politikverflechtung*), see: F. Scharpf, "The Joint-Decision Trap: Lessons from German Federalism and European Integration", 66 (1988), *Public Administration*, 239.

[62] *United Kingdom* v. *Council*, Case C-84/94, [1996] ECR I-5755.

> [The Union] legislature neither fully considered nor adequately demonstrated whether there were transnational aspects which could not be satisfactorily regulated by national measures, whether such measures would conflict with the requirements of the [Treaties] or significantly damage the interests of Member States or, finally, whether action at [European] level would provide clear benefits compared with action at national level ... [The principle of subsidiarity would] not allow the adoption of a directive in such wide and prescriptive terms as the contested directive, given that the extent and the nature of legislative regulation of working time vary very widely between Member States.[63]

How did the Court respond? The Court offered an interpretation of subsidiarity that has structured the judicial vision of the principle ever since:

> Once the Council has found that it is necessary to improve the existing level of protection as regards the health and safety of workers and to harmonize the conditions in this area while maintaining the improvements made, achievement of that objective through the imposition of minimum requirements necessarily presupposes [Union]-wide action, which otherwise, as in this case, leaves the enactment of the detailed implementing provisions required largely to the Member States. The argument that the Council could not properly adopt measures as general and mandatory as those forming the subject-matter of the directive will be examined below in the context of the plea alleging infringement of the principle of proportionality.[64]

This judicial definition contained two fundamental choices. First, the Court assumed that where the Union had decided to "harmonize" national laws, that objective necessarily presupposed Union legislation. This view answers the national insufficiency test with a mistaken tautology: only the Union can harmonize laws, and therefore the Member States already fail the first test. But assuming the "whether" of European action had been affirmatively established, could the European law go "as far" as it had? This was the second crucial choice of the Court. It decided against the idea of subsidiarity in a wider sense. For instead of analysing the intensity of the European law under Article 5(3) TEU, it chose to review it under the auspices of the principle of proportionality under Article 5(4) TEU.

It is there that the Court made a third important choice. In analysing the proportionality of the European law, it ruled that "the Council must be

[63] *Ibid.*, para. 46.
[64] *Ibid.*, para. 47.

allowed a wide discretion in an area which, as here, involves the legislature in making social policy choices and requires it to carry out complex assessments". Judicial review would therefore be limited to examining "whether it has been vitiated by *manifest error or misuse of powers, or whether the institution concerned has manifestly exceeded the limits of its discretion*".[65] The Court would thus apply a *low* degree of judicial scrutiny.

In subsequent jurisprudence, the Court drew a fourth – procedural – conclusion from choices one and three. In *Germany* v. *Parliament and Council (Deposit Guarantee Scheme)*,[66] the German Government had claimed that the Union act violated the *procedural* obligation to state reasons.[67] The European law had not explained how it was compatible with the principle of subsidiarity; and Germany insisted that it was necessary that "the [Union] institutions must give detailed reasons to explain why only the [Union], to the exclusion of the Member States, is empowered to act in the area in question". "In the present case, the Directive does not indicate in what respects its objectives could not have been sufficiently attained by action at Member State level or the grounds which militated in favour of [Union] action."[68]

The Court gave short shrift to that accusation. Looking at the recitals of the European law, it found that the Union legislator had given some "consideration" to the principle of subsidiarity. Believing previous actions by the Member States insufficient, the European legislator had found it indispensable to ensure a harmonized minimum level. This was enough to satisfy the procedural obligations under the subsidiarity enquiry.[69] It was a low explanatory threshold indeed.

Choices one, three, and four have been confirmed in subsequent jurisprudence. By concentrating on the national insufficiency test, the Court has thus short-circuited the comparative efficiency test.[70] It has

---

[65] *Ibid.*, para. 58 (emphasis added).

[66] *Germany* v. *Parliament and Council (Deposit Guarantee Scheme)*, Case C-233/94, [1997] ECR I-2405.

[67] On that duty to give reasons, see Section 1(a) above. Germany made it an express point that it was this provision – and not the principle of subsidiarity as such – that it claimed had been violated (*ibid.*, para. 24).

[68] *Ibid.*, para. 23.   [69] *Ibid.*, paras. 26–8.

[70] See *The Queen* v. *Secretary of State for Health, ex parte British American Tobacco (Investments) Ltd and Imperial Tobacco Ltd*, Case C-491/01, [2002] ECR I-11453, paras. 181–3: "[T]he Directive's objective is to eliminate the barriers raised by the differences which

not searched for qualitative or quantitative benefits of Union laws,[71] but confirmed its manifest error test – thus leaving subsidiarity to the political safeguards of federalism.[72] This is reflected in the low justificatory standard imposed on the Union legislator.[73] By contrast, as regards the second choice, the Court has remained ambivalent. While in some cases it has incorporated the intensity question into its subsidiarity analysis,[74] other jurisprudence has kept the subsidiarity and the proportionality principles at arm's length.[75]

What is the better option here? It has been argued that subsidiarity should be understood "in a wider sense".[76] For it is indeed impossible to reduce subsidiarity to "whether" the Union should exercise one of its competences. The distinction between "competence" and "subsidiarity" – between Article 5(2) and 5(3) TEU – will only make sense if the subsidiarity principle concentrates on the "whether" of *the specific act at issue*. But the "whether" and the "how" of the specific action are inherently tied together. The principle of subsidiarity will thus ask *whether* the European legislator has *unnecessarily* restricted national autonomy. A subsidiarity analysis that will not question the *federal* proportionality of a European

still exist between the Member States' laws, regulations and administrative provisions on the manufacture, presentation and sale of tobacco products, while ensuring a high level of health protection, in accordance with Article [114(3) TFEU]. Such an objective cannot be sufficiently achieved by the Member States individually and calls for action at [European] level, as demonstrated by the multifarious development of national laws in this case."

71 See Article 5 Protocol (No. 2) "On the Application of the Principles of Subsidiarity and Proportionality".

72 See *Germany* v. *Parliament*, Case C-233/94 (supra n. 66), para. 56.

73 See *Netherlands* v. *Parliament*, Case C-377/98, [2001] ECR I-7079, para. 33: "Compliance with the principle of subsidiarity is necessarily implicit in the fifth, sixth and seventh recitals of the preamble to the Directive, which state that, in the absence of action at [European] level, the development of the laws and practices of the different Member States impedes the proper functioning of the internal market. It thus appears that the Directive states sufficient reasons on that point."

74 In *The Queen* v. *Secretary of State for Health*, Case C-491/01 (supra n. 70), the Court identified the "intensity of the action undertaken by the [Union]" with the principle of subsidiarity and not the principle of proportionality (*ibid.*, para. 184). This acceptance of subsidiarity *sensu lato* can also be seen at work in *Arcor* v. *Germany*, Case C-55/06, [2008] ECR I-2931, where the Court identified the principle of subsidiarity with the idea that "the Member States retain the possibility to establish specific rules on the field in question" (*ibid.*, para. 144).

75 See *United Kingdom* v. *Council (Working Time Directive)*, Case C-84/94 (supra n. 62).

76 Schütze, *From Dual to Cooperative Federalism* (supra n. 39), 263 et seq.

law is, by contrast, bound to remain an empty formalism. Subsidiarity properly understood *is* federal proportionality.[77]

4. Excursus: The (Ordinary) Treaty-Making Procedure

How will the Union act externally, and through which procedures? This depends on the type of act adopted. An analysis of decision-making procedures within the Union's external powers must distinguish between unilateral acts and international agreements.[78] International agreements concluded by the Union have come to constitute a rich source of European law. The "ordinary" treaty-making procedure for them is found in Article 218 TFEU.[79]

What is the interinstitutional balance within this procedure? The central institution within this procedure is the Council – not just as *primus inter pares* with Parliament, but simply as *primus*. Article 218 acknowledges the central role of the Council in all stages of the procedure: "The Council shall authorize the opening of negotiations, adopt negotiating directives, authorize the signing of agreements and conclude them."[80] The Council hereby acts by a qualified majority, except in four situations. It shall act unanimously: when the agreement covers a field for which unanimity is required; for association agreements; with regard to Article 212 agreements with States that are candidates for Union accession; and, in respect of the Union's accession agreement to the European Convention on Human Rights (ECHR).[81]

Having recognized the primary role of the Council, Article 218 then defines the secondary roles of the other EU institutions in the various procedural stages of treaty-making. The provision distinguishes between the initiation and negotiation of the agreement, its signing and

---

[77] On the – liberal – principle of proportionality, see Chapter 8 – Section 3(b/ii) below.

[78] For an analysis of this point, see R. Schütze, *European Union Law* (Cambridge University Press, 2015), Chapter 8 – Section 3.

[79] Two special procedures are found in Articles 207 and 219 TFEU. The former deals with trade agreements within the context of the Union's common commercial policy. The latter expresses a derogation from the "ordinary" procedure for "formal agreements on an exchange-rate system for the euro in relation to the currencies of third states" (see Article 219(1) TFEU).

[80] Article 218(2) TFEU.   [81] Article 218(8) TFEU.

conclusion, and also provides special rules for its modification and suspension. Exceptionally, the Union can even become a party to an international agreement without having concluded it. This – rare – phenomenon occurs where the Union "inherits" international agreements from its Member States through the doctrine of functional succession.

(a) Initiation and Negotiation

Under Article 218(3), the Commission holds the exclusive right to make recommendations for agreements that principally deal with matters that do not fall within the Common Foreign and Security Policy (CFSP). By contrast, as regards subjects that exclusively or principally fall into the CFSP, it is the High Representative who will submit recommendations to the Council. For matters falling partly within the CFSP and partly outside it, there is also the possibility of "joint proposals".[82]

On the recommendation, the Council may decide to open negotiations and nominate the Union negotiator "depending on the subject matter of the agreement envisaged".[83] This formulation is ambivalent. Textually, the phrase suggests a liberal meaning. The Council can – but need not necessarily – appoint the Commission as Union negotiator for an agreement. According to this reading the Commission will not enjoy a prerogative to be the Union's negotiator. However, a systematic reading of the phrase leads to a different meaning. For if read in light of the jurisdictional division between the Commission and the High Representative at the recommendation stage, the Commission should be constitutionally entitled to be the Union negotiator for all Union agreements that "exclusively or principally" fall into the Treaty on the Functioning of the European Union.[84]

The Council will be able to address directives to the negotiator and subject its powers to consultation with a special committee. Where the Commission is chosen as Union negotiator, it thus still needs to be "authorized" by the Council and would conduct the negotiations under the control of the Council. The Commission's powers here are therefore between "autonomous" and "delegated" powers. The lower degree of institutional

---

[82] See Articles 22(2) and 30(1) TEU.   [83] Article 218(3) TFEU.
[84] In this sense see also P. Eeckhout, *EU External Relations Law* (Oxford University Press, 2011), 196.

autonomy is justified by the fact that third parties are involved. (The subsequent rejection of a negotiated agreement by the Council would indeed have "external" negative repercussions, and for that reason the *ex ante* involvement of the Council is a useful constitutional device.) On the other hand, the existence of an internal safeguard checking the Union negotiator creates, to some extent, a "two-front war". For the Union negotiator has not only to negotiate externally with the third party, but it also needs to deal internally with the Council.

Parliament is not formally involved in the negotiation. However, Article 218(10) constitutionalizes its right to be informed during all stages of the procedure. And this right has the potential of becoming an informal political safeguard that anticipates the interest of Parliament at the negotiation stage.[85]

Finally, any Union institution and the Member States are entitled to challenge the "constitutionality" of a draft agreement *prior* to its conclusion. This judicial safeguard can be found in Article 218(11), which creates the jurisdiction of the Court for an "Opinion".[86] Where this "Opinion" leads to a finding that the envisaged agreement is not compatible with the Treaties, the agreement may not enter into force – unless the Treaties themselves are amended.[87] The possibility of an *ex ante* "review" of a draft agreement contrasts with the Court's ordinary *ex post* review powers.[88] However, the exception is – again – justified by the fact that third party rights under international law are involved. Indeed, it is a rule of international law that, once an agreement is validly concluded under international law, a contracting party generally cannot subsequently invoke internal constitutional problems to deny its binding effect.[89] *Ex post*

---

[85] See Framework Agreement on Relations between the European Parliament and the European Commission, [2010] OJ L304/47, especially Annex III. According to para. 3 of the Annex, "[t]he Commission shall take due account of Parliament's comments throughout the negotiations".

[86] Article 218(11) TFEU.

[87] This happened, for example, with regard to the European Convention on Human Rights in 1996; see *Opinion 2/94 (Accession to ECHR)*, [1996] ECR I-1759. Prior to the Lisbon Treaty, accession to the Convention was thus unconstitutional. The Lisbon Treaty has amended the original Treaties, which now contain an express competence to accede to the ECHR in Article 6(2) TEU.

[88] On (*ex post*) judicial review in the Union legal order, see Chapter 8 – Section 3 below.

[89] See Article 46 Vienna Convention on the Law of Treaties: "(1) A State may not invoke the fact that its consent to be bound by a treaty has been expressed in violation of a

review of an international agreement will thus be too late to negate the external effects of an international agreement.

(b) Signing and Conclusion

The Council will sign and conclude the agreement on a proposal by the negotiator.[90]

Prior to the formal conclusion of the agreement, the European Parliament must be actively involved, except where the agreement *exclusively* relates to the CFSP. When compared with the Commission's involvement at the proposal stage,[91] the TFEU here seems more generous when it textually expands parliamentary involvement to agreements that even principally relate to CFSP matters. Yet in *Parliament* v. *Council (Pirates)*,[92] the Court clarified that this is not the case. Insisting that Article 218 "establishes symmetry between the procedure for adopting EU measures internally and the procedure for adopting international agreements in order to guarantee that the Parliament and the Council enjoy the same powers in relation to a given field",[93] the Court ruled that "exclusively" actually means "principally". The fact that an agreement touched upon some matters within the TFEU was not enough to establish Parliament's right to be involved.[94]

For matters outside the CFSP, Article 218(6) then distinguishes between two forms of parliamentary participation in the conclusion procedure: consultation and consent. The former is the residual category and applies to all agreements that do not require consent. The types of agreements where the Council needs to obtain parliamentary consent are enumerated in the form of five situations listed under Article 218(6)(a): (i) association agreements; (ii) the agreement on Union accession to the European Convention on Human Rights; (iii) agreements establishing a specific

provision of its internal law regarding competence to conclude treaties as invalidating its consent unless that violation was manifest and concerned a rule of its internal law of fundamental importance. (2) A violation is manifest if it would be objectively evident to any State conducting itself in the matter in accordance with normal practice and in good faith."

[90] Article 218(5) and (6) TFEU. The conclusion will usually be done by means of a Council Decision.

[91] Article 218(3) TFEU: agreements relating "exclusively *or principally*" (emphasis added) to the CFSP.

[92] *Parliament* v. *Council (Pirates)*, Case C-658/11, EU: C: 2014: 2025.

[93] Ibid., para. 56.   [94] Ibid., paras. 58–62.

institutional framework; (iv) agreements with important budgetary implications for the Union; (v) agreements covering fields to which either the ordinary legislative procedure applies, or the special legislative procedure where consent by the European Parliament is required.

The first, second and third categories may be explained by the constitutional idea of "political treaties".[95] For association agreements as well as institutional framework agreements, such as the ECHR, will by definition express an important *political* choice with long-term consequences. For these fundamental political choices Parliament – the representative of the European citizens – must give its democratic consent. The fourth category represents a constitutional reflex that protects the special role the European Parliament enjoys in establishing the Union budget.[96] The fifth category makes profound sense from the perspective of procedural parallelism. Under paragraph 6(a)(v), Parliament is entitled to veto "agreements covering fields" that internally require parliamentary co-decision or consent. The parallelism between the internal and external sphere is however not complete: Parliament will indeed *not* enjoy the power of co-conclusion in areas in which the "ordinary" legislative procedure applies. Its internal power to co-decision is here reduced to a mere power of "consent". It must "take-or-leave" the negotiated international agreement. This structural "democratic deficit" in the procedural regime for international agreements is not a *sui generis* characteristic of the European Union, but can be found in other constitutional orders of the world.[97] It is generally justified by reference to the "exceptional" nature of foreign affairs and, in particular: their "volatile" and "secretive" nature.

(c) Modification and Suspension (Termination)

Article 218(7) deals with *modifications* of international agreements that have been successfully concluded. The Council may "authorize the negotiator to approve on the Union's behalf modifications to the agreement where it provides for them to be adopted by a simplified procedure

---

[95] R. Jennings and S. Watts (eds.), *Oppenheim's International Law* (Oxford University Press, 2008), 211.

[96] For an extensive discussion of this category, see *Parliament* v. *Council (Mauritania Fisheries Agreement)*, Case 189/97, [1999] ECR I-4741.

[97] For example: in the United States. For a comparison between the EU and the US in this context, see: R. Schütze, "The 'Treaty Power' and Parliamentary Democracy: Comparative Perspectives", in *Foreign Affairs and the EU Constitution* (Cambridge University Press, 2014), Chapter 11.

or by a body set up by the agreement". (The Council can attach specific conditions to such an authorization.) In the absence of such a specific authorization for a simplified revision procedure, the ordinary treaty-making procedure will apply. This follows from a constitutional principle called *actus contrarius*. In order to modify an act or international agreement the same procedure needs to be followed that led to the conclusion of the international agreement in the first place.

Article 218(9) deals with the *suspension* of an international agreement. The provision specifies that the Commission or the High Representative may propose to the Council the suspension of the agreement. (And while the provision does not expressly refer to the jurisdictional division between the two actors, as mentioned in Article 218(3) for the proposal stage, we should assume that this rule would apply analogously. The High Representative should thus solely be entitled to recommend the suspension for international agreements that relate "exclusively or principally" to the CFSP.) Parliament is not expressly mentioned and will thus only have to be informed of the Council decision. This truncated procedure allows the Union quickly to decide on the (temporary) suspension of an agreement. However, this "executive" decision without parliamentary consent distorts to some extent the institutional balance in the external relations field.

How are Union agreements *terminated*? Unfortunately, Article 218 does not expressly set out a procedural regime for the termination of a Union agreement. Two views are possible. The first view is again based on the idea of *actus contrarius*: the termination of an agreement would need to follow the very same procedure for its conclusion. This procedural parallelism has been contested by reference to the common constitutional traditions of the Union's Member States, which leave the termination decision principally in the hands of the executive.[98] A second view therefore reverts to the suspension procedure applied analogously.

(d) Union Succession to Member State Agreements

Can the Union be bound by agreements that it has not formally concluded? The counterintuitive answer is positive: under European law, the Union

---

[98] C. Tomuschat, "Artikel 300 EG" in H. von der Groeben and J. Schwarze (eds.), *Kommentar zum Vertrag über die Europäische Union und zur Gründung der Europäischen Gemeinschaft* (Nomos, 2004), vol. IV, para. 61.

can be bound by agreements of its Member States where the Union has succeeded the latter.[99]

The doctrine of Union succession to international agreements of the Member States is thereby a doctrine of *functional* succession.[100] It is not based on a transfer of territory, but on a transfer of *functions*. The European Court announced this European doctrine in relation to the General Agreement on Tariffs and Trade in *International Fruit*.[101] Formally, the Union was not a party to the international treaty, but the Court found that "in so far as under the [European] Treat[ies] the [Union] has *assumed the powers previously exercised by Member States* in the area covered by the General Agreement, the provisions of that agreement have the effect of binding the [Union]".[102] Functional succession thus emanated from the exclusive nature of the Union's powers under the Common Commercial Policy (CCP). Since the Union had assumed the "functions" previously exercised by the Member States in this area, it was entitled and obliged to also assume their international obligations.

For a long time after *International Fruit,* the succession doctrine remained quiet. But in the last decade it has experienced a constitutional revival. This allowed the Court better to define the doctrine's contours. Three principles seem to govern functional succession in the European legal order. First, for the succession doctrine to come into operation *all* the Member States must be parties to an international treaty.[103] Second, *when* the international treaty is concluded is irrelevant. It will thus not matter whether the international treaty was concluded before or after the creation of the European Community in 1958.[104] Third, the Union will only succeed to international treaties, where there is a *"full transfer of the powers* previously exercised by the Member States".[105] The

---

[99] For an overview, see R. Schütze, "The 'Succession Doctrine' and the European Union" in *Foreign Affairs and the EU Constitution* (supra n. 97), Chapter 3.

[100] See P. Pescatore, *L'ordre juridique des Communautés Européennes* (Presse universitaire de Liège, 1975), 147–8 (the author's translation): "[B]y taking over, by virtue of the Treaties, certain competences and certain powers previously exercised by the Member States, the [Union] equally had to assume the international obligations that controlled the exercise of these competences and powers[.]"

[101] *International Fruit Company NV* v. *Produktschap voor Groenten en Fruit,* Joined Cases 21–24/72, [1972] ECR 1219.

[102] *Ibid.,* paras. 14–18 (emphasis added).

[103] *Commune deMesquer* v. *Total* Case C-188/07, [2008] ECR I-4501.

[104] *Intertanko and others* v. *Secretary of State for Transport,* Case 308/06, [2008] ECR I-4057.

[105] *Ibid.,* para. 4 (emphasis added).

Union will thus not succeed to all international agreements concluded by all the Member States, but only to those where it has assumed an exclusive competence. Would the European succession doctrine thereby be confined to the sphere of the Union's *constitutionally* exclusive powers; or would *legislative* exclusivity generated by Article 3(2) TFEU be sufficient?[106] The Court has shown a preference for a succession doctrine that includes legislative exclusivity. In *Bogiatzi*,[107] the Court indeed found that a "full transfer" could take place where European legislation completely preempted the Member States from the substantive scope of the international treaty.

Conclusion

Who is the Union legislator? The Union legislator is a compound legislator. However, depending on its composition, there exists an "ordinary" and three "special" legislative procedures. All four procedures combine the European Parliament and the Council, yet only under the ordinary legislative procedure do both enjoy symmetric constitutional rights.

Ordinary legislation must be adopted following a complex formal procedure that may, in the most extreme situation, comprise three readings. In the past, the Union has nonetheless tried to adopt legislation after its first and the second reading. In order to achieve this result, it has used informal trilogues between the Parliament, the Council and the Commission. And while these trilogues have been very successful, they do contain the danger of short-circuiting the democratic representation underpinning the ordinary legislative procedure.

The Union legislator is – generally – a subsidiary legislator. For the exercise of its non-exclusive competences is restricted by the principle of subsidiarity. The latter grants a constitutional advantage to national legislation; and in order to protect that constitutional advantage, the Union has pursued two mechanisms. The first mechanism concentrates on the procedural involvement of national parliaments in the (political) principle of subsidiarity. The second mechanism focuses on judicial limits imposed by the (legal) principle of subsidiarity.

---

[106] On the idea of legislative exclusivity, see: Chapter 3 – Section 4(a).
[107] *Bogiatzi* v. *Deutscher Luftpool and others*, Case C-301/08, [2009] CR I-10185.

A final section within the Chapter explored the (ordinary) treaty-making procedure. The negotiation of international treaties is thereby principally left in the hands of the Commission (and the High Representative). The conclusion of the agreement, by contrast, is the task of the Council. However, Parliament will need to give its consent on a wide range of agreements; yet, as we saw above, the external powers of the Parliament are lower than its internal powers.

Introduction

When the British Parliament legislates, it need not "justify" its acts. It is traditionally considered to enjoy a competence to do all things.[1] This "omnipotence" is seen as inherent in the idea of a sovereign parliament in a "sovereign state". The European Union is neither "sovereign" nor a "state". Its powers are *not inherent* powers. They must be *conferred* by its foundational charter: the European Treaties. This constitutional principle is called the "principle of conferral". The Treaty on European Union defines it as follows:

[1] In the words of A. V. Dicey, *Introduction to the Study of the Law of the Constitution* (Liberty Fund, 1982), 37–8: "The principle of Parliamentary sovereignty means neither more nor less than this, namely that Parliament thus defined has, under the English constitution, the right to make or unmake any law whatever: and, further, that no person or body is recognized by the law of England as having a right to override or set aside the legislation of Parliament."

> Under the principle of conferral, the Union shall act only within the limits of the competences conferred upon it by the Member States in the Treaties to attain the objectives set out therein. Competences not conferred upon the Union in the Treaties remain with the Member States.[2]

The Treaties employ the notion of competence in various provisions. Nevertheless, there is no positive definition of the concept. So what is a legislative competence? The best definition is this: a legislative competence is the *material field* within which an authority is entitled to legislate.

What are these material fields in which the Union is entitled to legislate? The Treaties do *not* enumerate the Union's "competences" in a single list. Instead, the Treaties pursue a different technique: they attribute legal competence for each and every Union activity in the respective Treaty title. Each policy area contains a provision – sometimes more than one – on which Union legislation can be based. The various "Union policies and internal actions" of the Union are set out in Part III of the Treaty on the Functioning of the European Union (Table 3.1).[3]

The Treaties thus present a picture of thematically limited competences in distinct policy areas. This picture is however – partly – misleading. Three legal developments have posed serious threats to the principle of conferral. First, the rise of teleological interpretation that will be discussed in Section 1 below. The Union's competences are interpreted in such a way that they potentially "spill over" into other policy areas. This "spillover" effect can be particularly observed with regard to a second development: the rise of the Union's general competences. For in addition to its thematic competences in specific areas, the Union enjoys two legal bases that horizontally cut across the various policy titles within the Treaties. These two competences are Articles 114 and 352 TFEU and will be discussed in Section 2. Lastly, there is a third development that would qualify the principle of conferral significantly: the doctrine of implied external powers (see Section 3 below).

What types of competences are recognized by the Treaties? The original Treaties did not specify the relationship between European and national

---

[2] Article 5(2) TEU.

[3] And yet, there exist some legal bases outside Part III of the TFEU, such as Article 16(2) TFEU "on rules relating to the protection of individuals with regard to the processing of personal data by Union institutions", and Article 352 TFEU – the Union's most famous legal base.

Table 3.1 Union Policies and Internal Actions

Part III TFEU – Union Policies and Internal Actions			
Title I	The Internal Market	Title XIII	Culture
Title II	Free Movement of Goods	Title XIV	Public Health
Title III	Agriculture and Fisheries	Title XV	Consumer Protection
Title IV	Free Movement of Persons, Services and Capital	Title XVI	Trans-European Networks
		Title XVII	Industry
Title V	Area of Freedom, Security and Justice	Title XVIII	Economic, Social and Territorial Cohesion
Title VI	Transport	Title XIX	Research and Technological Development and Space
Title VII	Common Rules on Competition, Taxation and Approximation of Laws	Title XX	Environment
Title VIII	Economic and Monetary Policy	Title XXI	Energy
		Title XXII	Tourism
Title IX	Employment	Title XXIII	Civil Protection
Title X	Social Policy	Title XXIV	Administrative Cooperation
Title XI	The European Social Fund		
Title XII	Education, Vocational Training, Youth and Sport		

Article 192	Title XX – Environment
The European Parliament and the Council, acting in accordance with the ordinary legislative procedure ... shall decide what action is to be taken by the Union in order to achieve the objectives referred to in Article 191.	Article 191 Aims and Objectives
	Article 192 Legislative Competence
	Article 193 Powers of the Member States

competences. They betrayed no sign of a distinction between different competence categories. This has however changed. Different competence categories were "discovered" by the European Court of Justice, and the Lisbon Treaty has now codified them. These competence categories will be discussed in Section 4.

1. Union Competences: Teleological Interpretation

The Union must act "within the limits of the competences conferred upon it *by the Member States*".[4] Did this mean that the Member States would be able to determine the scope of the Union's competences? A *strict* principle of conferral would indeed deny the Union the power autonomously

---

[4] Article 5(2) TEU (emphasis added).

to interpret its competences. But this solution encounters serious practical problems: how is the Union to work if every legislative bill would need to gain the consent of every national parliament? Classic international organizations solve this dilemma between theory and practice by insisting that the interpretation of international treaties must be in line with the clear intentions of the Member States.[5] Legal competences will thus be interpreted restrictively. This restrictive interpretation is designed to preserve the sovereign rights of the States by preserving the historical meaning of the founding treaty.

By contrast, a *soft* principle of conferral allows for teleological interpretation of competences. Instead of looking at the historical will of the founders, teleological interpretation asks what is the purpose – or *telos* – of a rule. It thus looks behind the legal text in search of a legal solution to a social problem that may not have been anticipated when the text was drafted. Teleological interpretation can therefore – partly – constitute a "small" amendment of the original rule. It is potentially a method of incremental change that complements the – rare – qualitative changes following "big" Treaty amendments.

Has the Union been able autonomously to interpret the scope of its competences, and if so how? After a brief period of following international law logic,[6] the Union embraced the constitutional technique of teleological interpretation. This technique can be seen in relation to the interpretation of the Union's *competences*, as well as in relation to the interpretation of European *legislation*.

The first situation is famously illustrated in the controversy surrounding the adoption of the (first) Working Time Directive.[7] The Directive had been based on a provision within Title X on "Social Policy". That provision allowed the Union to "encourage improvements, especially in the working environment, as regards the health and safety of workers".[8] Would

---

[5] In international law, this principle is called the "in dubio mitius" principle. In case of doubt, the "milder" interpretation should be preferred.

[6] See *Fédération Charbonnière de Belgique* v. *High Authority of the European Coal and Steel Community,* Case 8/55, [1954–56] ECR 245.

[7] *United Kingdom of Great Britain and Northern Ireland* v. *Council,* Case C-84/94, [1996] ECR I-5755.

[8] Ex-Article 118a(1) EEC. This competence is today Article 153(1)(a) TFEU, which allows the Union to support and implement the activities of the Member States as regards the "improvement in particular of the working environment to protect workers' health and safety".

this competence entitle the Union to adopt legislation on the general organization of working time?[9] The United Kingdom strongly contested this teleological reading. It claimed that there was no thematic link to health and safety, and that the Union legislator had therefore acted *ultra vires*. The Court, however, backed up the Union legislator. Its teleological reasoning was as follows:

> There is nothing in the wording of Article [153 TFEU] to indicate that the concepts of "working environment", "safety" and "health" as used in that provision should, in the absence of other indications, be interpreted restrictively, and not as embracing all factors, physical or otherwise, capable of affecting the health and safety of the worker in his working environment, including in particular certain aspects of the organization of working time.[10]

Famous exceptions aside,[11] the European Court has indeed accepted almost all teleological interpretations of Union competences by the Union legislator.

But more than that: the Court itself interprets Union legislation in a teleological manner. The classic case in this context is *Casagrande*.[12] In order to facilitate the free movement of persons in the internal market, the Union had adopted legislation designed to abolish discrimination between workers of different Member States as regards employment, remuneration, and other conditions of work.[13] And to facilitate the integration of the

---

[9] Section II of Directive 93/104 regulated minimum rest periods. Member States were obliged to introduce national laws to ensure that every worker is entitled to a minimum daily rest period of eleven consecutive hours per twenty-four hour period (*ibid.*, Article 3) and to a rest break where the working day is longer than six hours (*ibid.*, Article 4). Article 5 granted a minimum uninterrupted rest period of twenty-four hours in each seven-day period and determined that this period should in principle include Sunday. Article 6 established a maximum weekly working time of 48 hours; and finally, the Directive established a four weeks' paid annual leave (*ibid.*, Article 7).

[10] *United Kingdom* v. *Council*, Case C-84/94 (supra n. 7), para. 15. The Court, however, annulled the second sentence of Article 5 of the Directive that had tried to protect, in principle, Sunday as a weekly rest period. In the opinion of the Court, the Council had "failed to explain why Sunday, as a weekly rest day, is more closely connected with the health and safety of workers than any other day of the week" (*ibid.*, para. 37).

[11] *Germany* v. *Parliament and Council (Tobacco Advertising)*, Case C-376/98, [2000] ECR I-8419. This exception will be discussed below in Section 2(a) of this Chapter and more extensively still in Chapter 10 – Section 1.

[12] *Casagrande* v. *Landeshauptstadt München*, Case 9/74, [1974] ECR 773.

[13] Regulation 1612/68 on freedom of movement for workers within the Community, [1968] OJ (Special English Edition) 475.

worker and his family into the host state, the Union legislation contained the following provision:

> The children of a national of a Member State who is or has been employed in the territory of another Member State *shall be admitted* to that State's general educational, apprenticeship and vocational training courses under the same conditions as the nationals of that State, if such children are residing in its territory. Member States shall encourage all efforts to enable such children to attend these courses under the best possible conditions.[14]

Would this provision entitle the son of an Italian worker employed in Germany to receive an educational grant for his studies? Literally interpreted, the provision exclusively covers the "admission" of workers' children to the educational system of the host state. But the Court favoured a teleological interpretation that would maximize the useful effect behind the Union legislation. And since the purpose of the provision was "to ensure that the children may take advantage on an equal footing of the educational and training facilities available", it followed that the provision referred "*not only to rules relating to admission,* but also to general measures intended to facilitate educational attendance".[15] Thus, despite the fact that the (then) Treaties did not confer an express competence in educational matters on the Union, the Court considered that national educational grants fell within the scope of European legislation. The teleological interpretation of Union legislation had thus "spilled over" into spheres that the Member States had believed to have remained within their exclusive competences.

2. General Competences of the Union

In principle, the Treaties grant special competences within each policy area.[16] Yet in addition to these thematic competences, the Union legislator enjoys two general competences: Article 114 and Article 352 TFEU.

---

[14] *Ibid.*, Article 12 (emphasis added).
[15] *Casagrande* v. *Landeshauptstadt München*, Case 9/74, (supra n. 12) paras. 8–9 (emphasis added).
[16] We thus find the Union's competence on environmental protection (Article 192 TFEU), in the Treaties' title dedicated to the environment (Title XX of Part III of the TFEU). On this point, see Table 3.1 above.

The former represents the Union's "harmonization competence"; the latter constitutes its "residual competence". Both competences cut – horizontally – through the Union's sectoral policies, and have even been used – or some might say: abused – to develop policies not expressly mentioned in the Treaties.

(a) The Harmonization Competence: Article 114

On the basis of Article 114 TFEU, the European Union is entitled to adopt measures for the approximation of national laws "which have as their object the establishment and functioning of the internal market".

What is the scope of Article 114? In the past, the Union legislator has employed an extremely wide reading of this general competence. Its potentially unlimited scope is illustrated by *Spain* v. *Council*.[17] The European legislator had created a supplementary protection certificate for medicinal products, which could be granted under the same conditions as national patents by each of the Member States.[18] Three major constitutional hurdles seemed to oppose the constitutionality of this European law. First, Article 114 could theoretically not be used to create *new European* rights as it should only harmonize *existing national* rights. Second, the European law should theoretically further the creation of a single European market; yet, the supplementary certificate extended the duration of national patents and thus prolonged the compartmentalization of the common market into distinct national markets. Finally, at the time of its adoption only *two* Member States had legislation concerning a supplementary certificate. Was this enough to trigger the Union's *harmonization* power?

The Court took the first hurdle by force. It simply rejected the claim that the European law created a new right.[19] The same blind force would be applied to the second argument. The Court did not discuss whether the European law hindered the free circulation of pharmaceutical goods between Member States. Instead, the Court concentrated on the third hurdle in the form of the question, whether Article 114 required the pre-existence of diverse national laws. In the eyes of the Court, this was not

---

[17] *Spain* v. *Council*, Case C-350/92, [1995] ECR I-1985.
[18] Regulation 1768/92 concerning the creation of a supplementary protection certificate for medicinal products, [1992] OJ L182/1.
[19] *Spain* v. *Council*, Case C-350/92, (supra n. 17) para. 27.

the case. The Court accepted that the contested law aimed "*to prevent the heterogeneous development of national laws* leading to further disparities which would be likely to create obstacles to the free movement of medicinal products within the [Union] and thus directly affect the establishment and the functioning of the internal market".[20] The European legislator was thus entitled to use its harmonization power to prevent *future* obstacles to trade or a *potential* fragmentation of the internal market.

For a long time, the scope of the Union's harmonization power appeared devoid of constitutional boundaries. Yet, the existence of constitutional limits was confirmed in *Germany* v. *Parliament and Council (Tobacco Advertising)*.[21] The bone of contention had been a European law that banned the advertising and sponsorship of tobacco products.[22] Could a prohibition or ban be based on the Union's internal market competence? Germany objected to the idea. It argued that the Union's harmonization power could only be used to promote the internal market; and this was not so in the event, where the Union legislation constituted, in practice, a total prohibition of tobacco advertising.[23] The Court accepted – to the surprise of many – the argument. And it annulled, for the first time in its history, a European law on the ground that it went beyond the Union's harmonization power. Emphatically, the Court pointed out that the harmonization power could not grant the Union an unlimited power to regulate the internal market:

> To construe that article as meaning that it vests in the [Union] legislature a general power to regulate the internal market would not only be contrary to the express wording of the provisions cited above but would also be incompatible with the principle embodied in Article [5 TEU] that the powers of the [Union] are limited to those specifically conferred on it. Moreover, a measure adopted on the basis of Article [114] of the [FEU] Treaty must genuinely have as its object the improvement of the conditions for the establishment and functioning of the internal market. If a mere finding of disparities between national rules and of the abstract

---

[20] *Ibid.*, para. 35 (emphasis added).

[21] *Germany* v. *Parliament and Council (Tobacco Advertising)*, Case C-376/98 (supra n. 11).

[22] Directive 98/43/EC on the approximation of the laws, regulations and administrative provisions of the Member States relating to the advertising and sponsorship of tobacco products, [1998] OJ L213/9.

[23] Germany had pointed out that the sole form of advertising allowed under the Directive was advertising at the point of sale, which only accounted for 2 per cent of the tobacco industry's advertising expenditure (*Tobacco Advertising*, (supra n. 11) para. 24).

> risk of obstacles to the exercise of fundamental freedoms or of distortions of competition liable to result therefrom were sufficient to justify the choice of Article [114] as a legal basis, judicial review of compliance with the proper legal basis might be rendered nugatory.[24]

With *Tobacco Advertising*, the Court insisted on *three* constitutional limits to the Union's harmonization power. First, the European law must *harmonize* national laws. Thus Union legislation "which leaves unchanged the different national laws already in existence, cannot be regarded as aiming to approximate the laws of the Member States".[25] Second, a simple disparity in national laws will not be enough to trigger the Union's harmonization competence. The disparity must give rise to obstacles in trade or appreciable distortions in competition. Thus: while Article 114 can be used to "harmonize" *future* disparities in national laws, it must be "likely" that the divergent development of national laws will lead to obstacles in trade.[26] Third, the Union legislation must actually contribute to the elimination of obstacles to free movement or distortions of competition.[27] These three constitutional limits to the Union's "harmonization power" have been confirmed *in abstracto*;[28] yet subsequent jurisprudence has led to fresh accusations that Article 114 grants the Union an (almost) unlimited competence.[29]

(b) The Residual Competence: Article 352

Article 352 TFEU constitutes the most general competence within the Treaties. Comparable to the "Necessary and Proper Clause" in the American Constitution,[30] it allows the Union to legislate or act as follows:

---

[24] *Ibid.*, paras. 83–4.

[25] *Parliament & Council*, Case C-436/03, [2006] ECR I-3733, para. 44.

[26] *Germany* v. *Parliament and Council (Tobacco Advertising)*, Case C-376/98, (supra n. 11) para. 86.

[27] *British American Tobacco*, Case C-491/01, [2002] ECR I-11453, para. 60.

[28] On this point, see *ibid.*, as well as *Swedish Match*, Case C-210/03, [2004] ECR I-11893; and *Germany* v. *Parliament and Council (Tobacco Advertising II)*, Case C-3 80/03, [2006] ECR I-11573.

[29] The Union's harmonization competences are subject to a closer analysis in Chapter 10 below.

[30] According to Article I, Section 8, Clause 18 of the US Constitution, the American Union shall have the power "[t]o make all Laws which shall be necessary and proper for carrying into Execution the foregoing Powers, and all other Powers vested by this Constitution in the Government of the United States, or in any Department or Officer thereof".

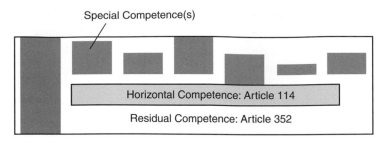

Figure 3.1 General and Special Competences

If action by the Union should prove necessary, within the framework of the policies defined in the Treaties, to attain one of the objectives set out in the Treaties, and the Treaties have not provided the necessary powers, the Council, acting unanimously on a proposal from the Commission and after obtaining the consent of the European Parliament, shall adopt the appropriate measures.

The competence under Article 352 may be used in two ways. First, it can be employed in a policy title in which the Union is already given a specific competence, but where the latter is deemed insufficient to achieve a specific objective. Second, the residual competence can be used to develop a policy area that has no specific title within the Treaties.

The textbook illustration for the second – and more dangerous – potential of Article 352 is provided by the development of a Union environmental policy *prior* to the Single European Act. Indeed: stimulated by the political enthusiasm to "create" such a European policy after the 1972 Paris Summit, the Commission and the Council developed such a policy *without* a specific competence title offered by the Treaties! The Member States themselves here called on the Union institutions to make the widest possible use of all provisions of the Treaties, especially Article 352.[31] The Member States thus favoured an extensive interpretation of the provision to cause a "small amendment" of the Treaties. This "indirect" development of a EU environmental competence in the following years was indeed impressive.[32]

---

[31] European Council, *First Summit Conference of the Enlarged Community*; Bulletin of the European Communities, EC 10–1972, 9 at 23.

[32] Prior to the entry into force of the Single European Act (SEA), a significant number of environment-related measures were adopted on the basis of Articles [115] and [352], thus "laying the foundation for the formation of a very specific [Union] environmental

Are there conceptual limits to Article 352? The provision expressly establishes two textual limitations. First, "[m]easures based on this Article shall not entail harmonization of Member States' laws or regulations in cases where the Treaties exclude such harmonization".[33] This precludes the use of the Union's residual competence in specific policy areas in which the Union is limited to merely "complementing" national action.[34] Second, Article 352 "cannot serve as a basis for attaining objectives pertaining to the common foreign and security policy".[35] This codifies past jurisprudence,[36] and is designed to protect the constitutional boundary drawn between the Treaty on European Union and the Treaty on the Functioning of the European Union.[37]

In addition to these two express constitutional boundaries, the European Court has also recognized an *implied* limitation to the Union's residual competence. While accepting that Article 352 could be used for "small" amendments to the Treaties, the Court has insisted that it could not be used to effect "qualitative leaps" that constitute big changes to the constitutional identity of the European Union.[38] This was confirmed in Opinion 2/94.[39] The European Court had been requested to preview the Union's power to accede to the European Convention on Human Rights (ECHR) – at a time when there was no express power to do so in the Treaties.[40] The Court here characterized the relationship between the Union's residual competence and the principle of conferral as follows:

> Article [352] is designed to fill the gap where no specific provisions of the Treaty confer on the [Union] institutions express or implied powers to act, if such powers appear none the less to be necessary to enable the [Union]

policy" (see F. Tschofen, "Article 235 of the Treaty Establishing the European Economic Community: Potential Conflicts between the Dynamics of Lawmaking in the Community and National Constitutional Principles", 12 (1991) *Michigan Journal of International Law*, 471 at 477).

[33] Article 352(3) TFEU.

[34] On "complementary" competences in the Union legal order that exclude all harmonization, see Section 4(d) below.

[35] Article 352(4) TFEU.

[36] See *Kadi* v. *Council and Commission*, Case C-402/05P, [2008] ECR I-6351, paras. 198–9.

[37] See Article 40 TEU – second indent.

[38] A. Tizzano, "The Powers of the Community", in Commission (ed.), *Thirty Years of Community Law* (Office for Official Publications of the EC, 1981), 43.

[39] Opinion 2/94 (*Accession by the European Community to the European Convention on Human Rights*), [1996] ECR I-1759.

[40] After the Lisbon Treaty, the Union is now given the express competence to accede to the Convention (see Article 6(2) TEU). On this point, see Chapter 4 – Section 4 below.

> to carry out its functions with a view to attaining one of the objectives laid down by the Treaty. That provision, being an integral part of an institutional system based on the principle of conferred powers, cannot serve as a basis for widening the scope of [Union] powers *beyond the general framework* created by the provisions of the Treaty as a whole and, in particular, by those that define the *tasks* and the *activities* of the [Union]. On any view, Article [352] cannot be used as a basis for the adoption of provisions whose effect would, in substance, be to amend the Treaty without following the procedure which it provides for that purpose.[41]

The framework of the Treaty was here defined by the Union's tasks and activities. They would form an outer jurisdictional boundary within which any legislative activity of the Union had to take place. The judicial reasoning in the second part of the judgment was then as follows. The Court found that the accession of the Union to the ECHR was not confined to a small (informal) amendment of the Union legal order, but one with "*fundamental institutional implications* for the [Union] and for the Member States"; and since accession "would be of *constitutional significance*", it "would therefore be such as to go beyond the scope of Article [352]".[42] Article 352 thus encounters an external border in the constitutional identity of the European legal order.

3. The Doctrine of Implied (External) Powers

The European Treaties do acknowledge the international personality of the European Union.[43] But what about the Union's treaty-making powers? The powers of the Union are enumerated powers; and under the 1957 EEC Treaty, these treaty-making powers were originally confined to international agreements under the Common Commercial Policy and Association Agreements with third countries or international organizations.[44] This restrictive attribution of treaty-making powers to the Union protected a status quo in which the Member States were to remain the protagonists on the international relations scene. This picture has changed dramatically through the doctrine of implied external powers. In the past four

---

[41] Opinion 2/94, paras. 29–30 (emphasis added).   [42] Opinion 2/94, para. 35.
[43] Article 47 TEU: "The Union shall have legal personality."
[44] See Articles 207 and 217 TFEU.

decades, the European Court has led – and won – a remarkable campaign to expand the Union's treaty-making powers.[45]

(a) *ERTA* and the Doctrine of Parallel Powers

The battle over external competences began with *ERTA*.[46] The European Road Transport Agreement ("ERTA") had been drafted to harmonize certain social aspects of international road transport and involved a number of Member States as potential signatories. The negotiations were conducted without formal involvement of the Union. The Commission felt excluded from its role as Europe's external broker. It unsuccessfully insisted on being involved in the negotiations and eventually brought the matter before the European Court. There, the Commission argued that the Union competence under its transport policy included a treaty-making power (and that this power had become exclusive after the adoption of Union legislation).[47]

With regard to the scope of the Union's external powers, the Commission specifically argued that Article 91 TFEU "conferred on the [Union] powers defined in wide terms with a view to implementing the common transport policy [which] must apply to external relations just as much as to domestic measures".[48] This wide teleological interpretation of the wording of the Union's transport competence was justified, for "the full effect of this provision would be jeopardized if the powers which it confers, particularly that of laying down 'any appropriate provisions', within the meaning of subparagraph (1) [d] of the article cited, did not extend to the conclusion of agreements with third countries".[49] The Council opposed this teleological interpretation, contending that "Article [91] relates only to measures *internal* to the [Union], and cannot be interpreted as authorizing the conclusion of international agreements". The power to enter into agreements with third countries "cannot be assumed in the absence of an express provision in the Treaty".[50]

---

[45] R. Schütze, "Parallel External Powers in the European Union: From 'Cubist' Perspectives Towards 'Naturalist' Constitutional Principles?", in *Foreign Affairs and the EU Constitution* (Cambridge University Press, 2014), Chapter 7.

[46] *Commission* v. *Council (ERTA)*, Case 22/70, [1971] ECR 263.

[47] On this point, see Section 4(a) below.   [48] *ERTA* (supra n. 46), para. 6.

[49] *Ibid.*, para. 7.   [50] *Ibid.*, paras. 9–10 (emphasis added).

In its judgment, the European Court famously sided with the Commission's extensive stance:

> To determine in a particular case the [Union's] authority to enter into international agreements, regard must be had to the whole scheme of the Treaty no less than to its substantive provisions. Such authority arises not only from an express conferment by the Treaty – as is the case with [Article 207] and [ex-]Article 114 [EEC] for tariff and trade agreements and with [Article 217] for association agreements – but may equally flow from other provisions of the Treaty and from measures adopted, within the framework of those provisions, by the [Union] institutions...
>
> According to [Article 90], the objectives of the Treaty in matters of transport are to be pursued within the framework of a common policy. With this in view, [Article 91 (1)] directs the Council to lay down common rules and, in addition, "any other appropriate provisions". By the terms of subparagraph (a) of the same provision, those common rules are applicable "to international transport to or from the territory of a Member State or passing across the territory of one or more Member States". This provision is equally concerned with transport from or to third countries, as regards that part of the journey which takes place on [Union] territory. It thus assumes that the powers of the [Union] extend to relationships arising from international law, and hence involve the need in the sphere in question for agreements with the third countries concerned.[51]

The passage spoke the language of teleological interpretation: in the light of the general scheme of the Treaty, the Union's power to adopt "any other appropriate provision" to give effect to the Union's transport policy objectives was interpreted to include the legal power to conclude international agreements.[52]

This doctrine of implied external powers was confirmed in Opinion 1/76.[53] However, its ultimate triumph would be celebrated in Opinion 2/91.[54] The European Court had here been requested to give an opinion on the conclusion of Convention No. 170 of the International Labour Organization. The Court's brief reasoning was as follows: the field covered by the relevant Convention fell within the Union's internal competence,

---

[51] *Ibid.*, paras. 15–16 and 23–7.

[52] In the words of the *ERTA* Court: "With regard to the implementation of the Treaty the system of internal [Union] measures may not therefore be separated from that of external relations" (*ibid.*, para. 19).

[53] Opinion 1/76 (*Laying-up Fund*), [1977] ECR 741.

[54] Opinion 2/91 (*ILO Convention No. 170*), [1993] ECR I-1061.

"[c]onsequently", the adoption of Convention No. 170 "falls within the [Union's] area of [external] competence".[55] From the very fact that the Union has an internal power – in this case the competence to adopt social provisions – the Court thus implied an external power to conclude international treaties for all matters falling within the scope of the Union's internal competence. The reasoning of the Court was based on the idea of a parallel treaty-making power running alongside internal legislative power. The European Court here confirmed a doctrine according to which "treaty power is coextensive with its internal domestic powers", and which thus "cuts across all areas of its internal domestic competence".[56]

(b) Article 216: Codifying *ERTA*?

The Lisbon Treaty has tried to codify the implied powers doctrine in Article 216 TFEU.[57] The provision states:

> The Union may conclude an agreement with one or more third countries or international organizations where the Treaties so provide or where the conclusion of an agreement is necessary in order to achieve, within the framework of the Union's policies, one of the objectives referred to in the Treaties, or is provided for in a legally binding Union act or is likely to affect common rules or alter their scope.[58]

While recognizing the express treaty-making competences of the Union elsewhere conferred by the Treaties, the provision grants the Union a residual competence to conclude international agreements in three situations.

The first alternative mentioned in Article 216 confers a treaty power to the Union "where the conclusion of an agreement is necessary in order to achieve, within the framework of the Union's policies, one of the objectives referred to in the Treaties". This formulation is – strikingly – similar to the one found in the Union's general competence in Article 352. And if the Court decides to confirm this parallelism, the Union will have

---

[55] *Ibid.*, paras. 15–17.

[56] E. Stein, "External Relations of the European Community: Structure and Process" in *Collected Courses of the Academy of European Law* (Martinus Nijhoff, 1990), vol. I-1, 115 at 146.

[57] See European Convention, Final Report Working Group VII – External Action (CONV 459/ 02), para. 18: "The Group saw merit in making explicit the jurisprudence of the Court[.]"

[58] Article 216(1) TFEU.

a residual competence to conclude international agreements that cuts across the jurisdictional scope of the entire Treaty on the Functioning of the Union.[59] This competence would even be wider than the judicial doctrine of parallel external powers. For past doctrine insisted that an implied external competence derived from an internal *competence* – and thus did not confer a treaty power to pursue any internal *objective*.[60] Yet the first alternative in Article 216 textually disconnects the Union's external competences from its internal competences. The latter might therefore no longer represent a constitutional limit to the Union's treaty powers.

Regardless of what the Court will eventually make of this first alternative, Article 216 mentions two additional situations. The Union will also be entitled to conclude international agreements, where this "is provided for in a legally binding act or is likely to affect common rules or alter their scope". Both alternatives make the existence of an external competence dependent on the existence of secondary Union law. Two objections may be launched against this view. Theoretically, it is difficult to accept that the Union can expand its competences without Treaty amendment through the simple adoption of internal Union acts. Practically, it is also hard to see how either alternative will ever go beyond the first alternative.

4. Categories of Union Competences

Different types of competences constitutionally pitch the *relative degree of responsibility* of public authorities within a material policy field. The

---

[59] It is true that Article 216 TFEU – unlike Article 352 TFEU – has no fourth paragraph excluding its use "for attaining objectives pertaining to the Common Foreign and Security Policy". The problem therefore has been raised whether Article 216 is even wider than Article 352 in that it may also be used to pursue a CFSP objective (see M. Cremona, "External Relations and External Competence of the European Union: the Emergence of an Integrated Policy" in P. Craig and G. de Búrca, *The Evolution of EU Law* (Oxford University Press, 2011), 217 at 226).

[60] The classic doctrine of implied external powers, as defined in Opinion 1/76, thus stated that "whenever [European] law has created for the institutions of the [Union] *powers* within its internal system for the purposes of attaining a specific objective, the [Union] has authority to enter into the international commitments necessary for the attainment of that objective even in the absence of an express provision in that connexion" (Opinion 1/76 (*Laying-up Fund*), [1977] ECR 741, para. 3 – emphasis added). And to make it even clearer, the Court went on to state that the external powers flowed "by implication from the provisions of the Treaty creating the internal *power*" (*ibid.*, para. 4 – emphasis added).

respective differences are of a relational kind: exclusive competences "exclude" the other authority from acting within the same policy area, while non-exclusive competences permit the co-existence of two legislators. Importantly, in order to provide a clear picture of the federal division of powers, each policy area should ideally correspond to one competence category.

What then are the competence categories developed in the European legal order? The distinction between exclusive and non-exclusive competences had emerged early on.[61] The Treaties today distinguish between various categories of Union competence in Article 2 TFEU. The provision reads as follows:

1. When the Treaties confer on the Union exclusive competence in a specific area, only the Union may legislate and adopt legally binding acts, the Member States being able to do so themselves only if so empowered by the Union or for the implementation of Union acts.

2. When the Treaties confer on the Union a competence shared with the Member States in a specific area, the Union and the Member States may legislate and adopt legally binding acts in that area. The Member States shall exercise their competence to the extent that the Union has not exercised its competence. The Member States shall again exercise their competence to the extent that the Union has decided to cease exercising its competence.

3. The Member States shall coordinate their economic and employment policies within arrangements as determined by this Treaty, which the Union shall have competence to provide.

4. The Union shall have competence, in accordance with the provisions of the Treaty on European Union, to define and implement a common foreign and security policy, including the progressive framing of a common defence policy.

5. In certain areas and under the conditions laid down in the Treaties, the Union shall have competence to carry out actions to support, coordinate or supplement the actions of the Member States, without thereby superseding their competence in these areas. Legally binding acts of the Union adopted on the basis of the provisions of the Treaties relating to these areas shall not entail harmonization of Member States' laws or regulations.

---

[61] See R. Schütze, "Dual Federalism Constitutionalised: The Emergence of Exclusive Competences in the EC Legal Order", 32 (2007) *European Law Review*, 3.

Exclusive   Shared   Coordinating   Complementary

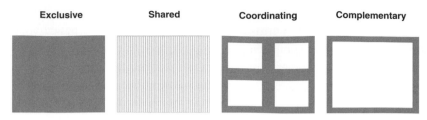

Figure 3.2 Competence Categories

Outside the Common Foreign and Security Policy,[62] the Treaties thus expressly recognize four general competence categories: exclusive competences, shared competences, coordinating competences, and complementary competences. And Articles 3 to 6 TFEU correlate the various Union policies to a particular competence category. Let us look at each competence category in turn.

(a) Exclusive Competences: Article 3

Exclusive powers are constitutionally guaranteed monopolies. Only one governmental level is entitled to act autonomously. Exclusive competences are thus double-edged provisions. Their positive side entitles one authority to act, while their negative side "excludes" anybody else from acting autonomously within its scope. For the European legal order, exclusive competences are defined as areas in which "only the Union may legislate and adopt legally binding acts". The Member States will only be enabled to act "if so empowered by the Union or for the implementation of Union acts".[63]

What are the policy areas of constitutional exclusivity? In the past, the Court has accepted a number of competences to qualify under this type. The first exclusive competence was discovered in the context of the Common Commercial Policy (CCP). In Opinion 1/75,[64] the Court found that the existence of a merely shared competence within the field would "compromise[ ] the effective defence of the common interests of the [Union]".[65]

---

[62] For an analysis of this *sui generis* category, see R. Schütze, *European Union Law* (Cambridge University Press, 2015), Chapter 8 – Section 2(a).
[63] Article 2(1) TFEU.
[64] Opinion 1/75 *(Draft Understanding on a Local Cost Standard)*, [1975] ECR 1355.
[65] *Ibid.*, para. 13.

A second area of exclusive competence was soon discovered in relation to the conservation of biological resources of the sea. In *Commission* v. *United Kingdom*,[66] the Court found that Member States would be "no longer entitled to exercise any power of their own in the matter of conservation measures in the waters under their jurisdiction".[67]

Article 3(1) TFEU now expressly mentions five policy areas: (a) the customs union; (b) the establishment of the competition rules necessary for the functioning of the internal market; (c) monetary policy for the Member States whose currency is the euro; (d) the conservation of marine biological resources under the common fisheries policy; and (e) the common commercial policy. In light of the judicial status quo, this enumeration poses some definitional problems.[68]

Much greater constitutional confusion is however created by Article 3(2) TFEU which states:

> The Union shall also have exclusive competence for the conclusion of an international agreement when its conclusion is provided for in a legislative act of the Union or is necessary to enable the Union to exercise its internal competence, or in so far as its conclusion may affect common rules or alter their scope.

In addition to the constitutionally fixed exclusive competences – mentioned in Article 3(1) – the Union legal order thus acknowledges the possibility of a *dynamic* growth of its exclusive competences in the external sphere. According to Article 3(2), the Union may subsequently obtain exclusive treaty-making power, where one of three situations is fulfilled. These three situations are said to codify three famous judicial doctrines. These doctrines were developed in the jurisprudence of the European Court prior to the Lisbon Treaty.[69]

According to the first situation, the Union will obtain a subsequently exclusive treaty-making power when the conclusion of an international agreement "is provided for in a legislative act". This formulation corresponds to the "WTO Doctrine". In Opinion 1/94 on the compatibility of the WTO Agreement with the Treaties,[70] the Court had indeed stated: "[w]henever the [Union] has concluded in its internal legislative acts

---

[66] *Commission* v. *United Kingdom*, Case 804/79, [1981] ECR 1045.
[67] *Ibid.*, para. 18.   [68] See Schütze, "Dual Federalism Constitutionalised" (supra n. 61).
[69] On the three judicial doctrines, see Schütze, "Parallel External Powers" (supra n. 45).
[70] Opinion 1/94 *(WTO Agreement)*, [1994] ECR I-5267.

provisions relating to the treatment of nationals of non-member countries or expressly conferred on the institutions powers to negotiate with non-member countries, it acquires exclusive external competence in the spheres covered by those acts".[71] Article 3(2) codifies this judicial doctrine. However, the codification is more restrictive, as it excludes the first alternative ("provisions relating to the treatment of nationals of non-member countries") from its scope.

The second situation mentioned in Article 3(2) grants the Union an exclusive treaty power, where this "is necessary to enable the Union to exercise its internal competence". This formulation appears to codify the "Opinion 1/76 Doctrine",[72] albeit in a much *less* restrictive form. In its jurisprudence the Court had confined this second line of subsequent exclusivity to situations "where the conclusion of an international agreement is necessary in order to achieve Treaty objectives *which cannot be attained by the adoption of autonomous rules*",[73] and where the achievement of an internal objective is "inextricably linked" with the external sphere.[74] None of these restrictions can be found in Article 3(2). And in its unqualified openness, the second situation comes close to the wording of the Union's "residual" legislative competence: Article 352 TFEU. The almost identical wording of Article 3(2) and Article 216 TFEU moreover suggests that "implied shared competence would disappear"; yet, this would be "a wholly undesirable departure from the case law".[75]

Finally, the third situation in Article 3(2) appears to refer to the Court's "*ERTA* doctrine". Under the *ERTA* doctrine,[76] the Member States are deprived of their treaty-making power to the extent that their exercise affects internal European law. Each time the Union "adopts provisions laying down common rules, whatever form these may take, the Member States no longer have the right, acting individually or even collectively, to undertake obligations with third countries *which affect those rules*".[77]

---

[71] *Ibid.*, para. 95.

[72] Opinion 1/76 *(Laying-Up Fund)*, [1977] ECR 741. On the evolution of the "Opinion 1/76 Doctrine", see Schütze, "Parallel External Powers" (supra n. 45), 258 et seq.

[73] Opinion 2/92 *(Third Revised Decision of the OECD on National Treatment)*, [1995] ECR I-521, Part V – para. 4 (emphasis added).

[74] *Commission* v. *Germany (Open Skies)*, Case C-476/98, [2002] ECR I-9855, para. 87.

[75] M. Cremona, "A Constitutional Basis for Effective External Action? An Assessment of the Provisions on EU External Action in the Constitutional Treaty", EUI Working Paper 2006/30, 10.

[76] *Commission* v. *Council (ERTA)* (supra n. 46).   [77] *Ibid.*, para. 18 (emphasis added).

The principle behind *ERTA* is to prevent an international agreement concluded by the Member States from undermining "the uniform and consistent application of the [Union] rules and the proper functioning of the system which they establish".[78] Has Article 3(2) properly codified this third judicial line of subsequently exclusive powers? The third alternative in Article 3(2) – strangely – breaks the link between a *Member State* agreement and internal European law, and replaces it with an analysis of the effect of a *Union* agreement on European rules. This simply must be an "editorial mistake" on the part of the Treaty-makers, and it is hoped that the Court will correct this as soon as possible.[79]

(b) Shared Competences: Article 4

Shared competences are the "ordinary" competences of the European Union. Unless the Treaties expressly provide otherwise, a Union competence will be shared.[80]

Within a shared competence, "the Union and the Member States may legislate".[81] However, according to the formulation in Article 2(2) TFEU both appear to be prohibited from acting at the same time: "[t]he Member States shall exercise their competence to the extent that the Union has not exercised its competence." This formulation invokes the geometrical image of a divided field: the Member States may only legislate in that part which the European Union has not (yet) entered. Within one field, *either* the European Union *or* the Member States can exercise their shared competence.[82]

When viewed against the constitutional status quo ante, this is a mystifying conception of shared competences. For in the past fifty years, shared

---

[78] Opinion 1/03 *(Lugano Convention)*, [2006] ECR I-1145, para. 133.

[79] The Court has indeed recently confirmed the pre-Lisbon status quo in *Commission* v. *Council*, Case C-114/12, EU: C: 2014: 2151.

[80] Article 4 TFEU states that EU competences will be shared "where the Treaties confer on it a competence which does not relate to the areas referred to in Articles 3 and 6", that is: areas of exclusive or complementary EU competence.

[81] Article 2(2) TFEU.

[82] The Union may, however, decide to "cease exercising its competence". This reopening of legislative space arises "when the relevant EU institutions decide to repeal a legislative act, in particular better to ensure constant respect for the principles of subsidiarity and proportionality". See Declaration (No. 18) "In Relation to the Delimitation of Competences".

competences allowed the Union and the Member States to act in the same field at the same time. The (exceptional) exception to that rule concerned situations where the Union field preempted the Member States.[83] The formulation in Article 2(2) TFEU is – sadly – based on that exception. It appears to demand "automatic [field] pre-emption of Member State action where the Union has exercised its power".[84] Will the technique of European minimum harmonization – allowing for higher national standards – thus be in danger? This seems doubtful, since the Treaties expressly identify minimum harmonization competences as shared competences.[85]

This preemption problem is not the only textual problem. For Article 4 TFEU recognizes a special type of shared competence in paragraphs 3 and 4. Both paragraphs separate the policy areas of research, technological development and space, as well as development cooperation and humanitarian aid from the "normal" shared competences. What is so special about these areas? According to paragraphs 3 and 4, the "exercise of that competence shall not result in Member States being prevented from exercising theirs". But since that qualification actually undermines the very essence of what constitutes a "shared" competence, set out in Article 2(2) TFEU, these policy areas should never have been placed there. This special type of shared competence has been described as parallel competence.

(c) Coordinating Competences: Article 5

Coordinating competences are defined in the third paragraph of Article 2 TFEU; and Article 5 TFEU places "economic policy", "employment policy", and "social policy" within this category. The inspiration for this third competence category was the absence of a political consensus in the European Convention (drafting the 2004 Constitutional Treaty). Whereas

---

[83] On the various preemption types, see Schütze, *European Union Law* (supra n. 62), Chapter 4 – Section 3.

[84] P. Craig, "Competence: Clarity, Conferral, Containment and Consideration", 29 (2004) *European Law Review* 323, 334. The Treaties, however, clarify that such field preemption would "only" be in relation to the legislative act (see Protocol (No. 25) "On the Exercise of Shared Competence": "With reference to Article 2 of the Treaty on the Functioning of the European Union on shared competence, when the Union has taken action in a certain area, the scope of this exercise of competence only covers those elements governed by the Union act in question and therefore does not cover the whole [competence] area.")

[85] See Article 4(2)(e) TFEU on the shared "environment" competence.

one group wished to place economic and employment coordination within the category of shared competences, an opposing view advocated their classification as complementary competence. The Presidium of the Convention thus came to feel that "the specific nature of the coordination of Member States' economic and employment policies merits a separate provision".[86]

The constitutional character of coordinating competences remains largely undefined. From Articles 2 and 5 TFEU, we may solely deduce that the European Union has a competence to provide "arrangements" for the Member States to exercise their competences in a coordinated manner. The Union's coordination effort may include the adoption of "guidelines" and "initiatives to ensure coordination". It has been argued that the political genesis for this competence category should place it, on the normative spectrum, between shared and complementary competences.[87] If this systematic interpretation is accepted, coordinating competences would have to be normatively stronger than complementary competences.

(d) Complementary Competences: Article 6

The term "complementary competence" is not used in Article 2(5) TFEU. However, it appears to be the best way generically to refer to "actions to support, coordinate or supplement the actions of the Member States".[88] Article 6 TFEU lists seven areas: the protection and improvement of human health; industry; culture; tourism; education, vocational training, youth, and sport; civil protection; and administrative co-operation. Is this an exhaustive list? This should be the case in the light of the residual character of shared competences.

The contours of this competence type are – again – largely unexplored by jurisprudence. However, after the Lisbon reform, it appears to be a

---

[86] The Presidium CONV 724/03 (Annex 2), 68. Arguably, the addition of a new competence type was unnecessary in the light of Article 2(6) TFEU. That provision states: "The scope of and arrangements for exercising the Union's competences shall be determined by the provisions of the Treaties relating to each area."

[87] See in this sense, Craig, "Competence" (supra n. 84), 338.   [88] Article 2(5) TFEU.

defining characteristic of complementary competences that they do "not entail harmonization of Member States' laws or regulations".[89]

But what exactly is the prohibition of "harmonization" supposed to mean? Two views can be put forward. According to the first, the exclusion of harmonization means that Union legislation must not modify *existing* national legislation. However, considering the wide definition given to the concept of "harmonization" by the Court of Justice in *Spain* v. *Council*, any legislative intervention on the part of the Union will unfold a de facto harmonizing effect within the national legal orders.[90] From this strict reading, the exclusion of harmonization would consequently deny all preemptive effect to European legislation.[91] A second and less restrictive view argues that the Union's legislative powers are only trimmed so as to prevent the *de jure* harmonization of national legislation.[92]

Conclusion

The Union is not a sovereign State that enjoys "inherent" competences. Its competences are "enumerated" competences that are "conferred" by the European Treaties. The majority of the Union's competences are spread across Part III of the Treaty on the Functioning of the European Union. In each of its policy areas, the Union will typically be given a specific competence. Its competences are thus thematically limited; yet, as we saw above, the Union legislator has made wide use of its powers by interpreting them teleologically.

---

[89] Article 2(5) TFEU – second indent.

[90] *Spain* v. *Council*, Case C-350/92, [1995] ECRI-1985. In that judgment, the Court found the adoption of a Regulation not beyond the scope of Article [114 TFEU] because it aimed "to prevent the heterogeneous development of national laws leading to further disparities" in the internal market (*ibid.*, para. 35). The case was discussed in Section 2(a) above.

[91] See A. Bardenhewer-Rating and F. Niggermeier, "Artikel 152", para. 20, in H. von der Groeben and J. Schwarze, *Kommentar zum Vertrag über die EU* (Nomos, 2003).

[92] For K. Lenaerts "incentive measures can be adopted in the form of Regulations, Directives, Decisions or atypical legal acts and are thus normal legislative acts of the [Union]". "[T]he fact that a [European] incentive measure may have the indirect effect of harmonizing ... does not necessarily mean that it conflicts with the prohibition on harmonization" (K. Lenaerts, "Subsidiarity and Community Competence in the Field of Education", 1 (1994–1995) *Columbia Journal of European Law*, 1 at 13 and 15).

In the past, the Union has also extensively used its general competences. Articles 114 and 352 TFEU indeed grant the Union two competences that horizontally cut across (almost) all substantive policy areas. In their most dramatic form, they have even allowed the Union to develop policies that were not expressly mentioned in the Treaties. Within the external relations field, the Union has developed a doctrine of implied parallel external powers. This was codified in Article 216 TFEU – a provision that now comes close to Article 352 TFEU.

Importantly, however, not all competences of the Union provide it with the same power. The Union legal order recognizes various competence categories. The Treaties distinguish between exclusive, shared, coordinating, and complementary competences. Each competence category constitutionally distributes power between the Union and the Member States. Within its exclusive competences, the Union is exclusively competent to legislate; whereas it shares this power with the Member States under its non-exclusive powers.

4 Fundamental Rights

Introduction

The protection of human rights is a central task of many modern constitutions.[1] Fundamental rights are here designed to set protective limits to governmental action(s). This protective task is principally transferred onto the judiciary and involves the judicial review of governmental action.[2] The protection of human rights may be limited to judicial review of the executive.[3] But in its expansive form, it extends to the review of parliamentary legislation.[4]

---

[1] On human rights as constitutional rights, see A. Sajó, *Limiting Government* (Central European University Press, 1999), Chapter 8.

[2] See M. Cappelletti, *Judicial Review in the Contemporary World* (Bobbs-Merrill, 1971).

[3] For the classic doctrine of parliamentary sovereignty in the United Kingdom, see A. V. Dicey, *Introduction to the Study of the Law of the Constitution* (Liberty Fund, 1982).

[4] On the idea of human rights as "outside" majoritarian (democratic) politics, see Sajó, *Limiting Government* (supra n. 1), Chapter 2, esp. 57 et seq.

The European Union follows this wider constitutional tradition.[5] It considers itself to be "founded on the values of respect for human dignity, freedom, democracy, equality, the rule of law and respect for human rights".[6] Human rights are thus given a "foundational" status and constitutionally limit the exercise of all Union competences.

What are the sources of human rights in the Union legal order? While there was no "Bill of Rights" in the original Treaties, three sources for European fundamental rights were subsequently developed. The European Court first began distilling general principles protecting fundamental rights from the constitutional traditions of the Member States. This *unwritten* bill of rights was inspired and informed by a second bill of rights: the European Convention on Human Rights. This *external* bill of rights was, decades later, matched by a *written* bill of rights specifically for the European Union: the Charter of Fundamental Rights. These three sources of European human rights are now expressly referred to – in reverse order – in Article 6 of the Treaty on European Union:

1. The Union recognises the rights, freedoms and principles set out in the Charter of Fundamental Rights of the European Union of 7 December 2000, as adapted at Strasbourg, on 12 December 2007, which shall have the same legal value as the Treaties . . .

2. The Union shall accede to the European Convention for the Protection of Human Rights and Fundamental Freedoms. Such accession shall not affect the Union's competences as defined in the Treaties.

3. Fundamental rights, as guaranteed by the European Convention for the Protection of Human Rights and Fundamental Freedoms and as they result from the constitutional traditions common to the Member States, shall constitute general principles of the Union's law.

What is the nature and effect of each source of fundamental rights? And to what extent will they limit the Union? This Chapter investigates the three bills of rights of the Union. Section 1 starts with the discovery of an

---

[5] On this point, see *Parti Écologiste "Les Verts"* v. *European Parliament*, Case 294/83 [1986] ECR 1339, para. 23: "a [Union] based on the rule of law, inasmuch as neither its Member States nor its institutions can avoid a review of the question whether the measures adopted by them are in conformity with the basic constitutional charter, the Treaty". For an extensive discussion of judicial review in the Union legal order, see Chapter 8 – Section 3.

[6] Article 2(1) TEU.

"unwritten" bill of rights in the form of general principles of European law. Section 2 subsequently discusses possible structural limits to European human rights in the form of international obligations flowing from the United Nations Charter. Section 3 analyses the Union's "written" bill of rights in the form of its Charter of Fundamental Rights. Finally, Section 4 explores the European Convention on Human Rights as an external bill of rights for the European Union.

1. The Birth of European Fundamental Rights

Originally, the European Treaties contained no express reference to human rights.[7] Nor did the birth of European fundamental rights happen overnight. The Court had been invited – as long ago as 1958 – to review the constitutionality of a European act in light of fundamental rights. In *Stork*,[8] the applicant challenged a European decision on the ground that the Commission had infringed *German* fundamental rights. In the absence of a European bill of rights, this claim drew on the so-called "mortgage theory". According to this theory, the powers conferred on the European Union were tied to a human rights "mortgage". *National* fundamental rights would bind the *European* Union, since the Member States could not have created an organization with more powers than themselves.[9] This argument was – correctly[10] – rejected by the Court. The task of the European institutions was to apply European laws "without regard for their validity under national law".[11] National fundamental rights could be *no direct* source of European human rights.

---

[7] For speculations on the historical reasons for this absence, see P. Pescatore, "The Context and Significance of Fundamental Rights in the Law of the European Communities", 2 (1981) *Human Rights Journal*, 295.

[8] *Stork* v. *High Authority of the European Coal and Steel Community*, Case 1/58, [1958] ECR (English Special Edition) 17.

[9] In Latin the legal proverb is clear: *Nemo dat quod non habet.*

[10] For a criticism of the "mortgage theory", see H. G. Schermers, "The European Communities Bound by Fundamental Rights", 27 (1980) *Common Market Law Review*, 249 at 251.

[11] *Stork* v. *High Authority*, Case 1/58 (supra n. 8), 26: "Under Article 8 of the [ECSC] Treaty the [Commission] is only required to apply Community law. It is not competent to apply the national law of the Member States. Similarly, under Article 31 the Court is only required to ensure that in the interpretation and application of the Treaty, and of rules laid down for implementation thereof, the law is observed. It is not normally required to rule on provisions of national law. Consequently, the [Commission] is not empowered to examine a ground of complaint which maintains that, when it adopted its decision, it

This position of the European Union towards national fundamental rights never changed. However, the Court's view evolved with regard to the existence of implied *EU* fundamental rights. Having originally found that European law did "not contain any general principle, *express or otherwise*, guaranteeing the maintenance of vested rights",[12] the Court subsequently discovered "fundamental human rights enshrined in the general principles of [European] law".[13]

This new position was spelled out in *Internationale Handelsgesellschaft*.[14] The Court here – again – rejected the applicability of national fundamental rights to European law. But the judgment now confirmed the existence of an "analogous guarantee inherent in [European] law".[15] Accordingly, "respect for fundamental rights forms an integral part of the general principles of law protected by the Court of Justice".[16] Whence did the Court derive these fundamental rights? The famous answer was that the Union's (unwritten) bill of rights would be "*inspired* by the constitutional traditions *common* to the Member States".[17] While thus not a direct source, national constitutional rights constituted an *indirect* source for the Union's fundamental rights.

What was the nature of this indirect relationship between national rights and European rights? How would the former influence the latter? A constitutional clarification was offered in *Nold*.[18] Drawing on its previous jurisprudence, the Court held:

> [F]undamental rights form an integral part of the general principles of law, the observance of which it ensures. In safeguarding these rights, the Court is bound to draw *inspiration* from constitutional traditions common to the Member States, and it cannot therefore uphold measures which are incompatible with fundamental rights recognized and protected by the constitutions of those States. Similarly, international treaties for the protection of human rights on which the Member States have collaborated

infringed principles of German constitutional law (in particular Articles 2 and 12 of the Basic Law)."
[12] *Geitling Ruhrkohlen-Verkaufsgesellschaft mbH, Mausegatt Ruhrkohlen-Verkaufsgesellschaft mbH and I. Nold KG* v. *High Authority of the European Coal and Steel Community*, Joined Cases 36, 37, 38/59 and 40/59, [1959] ECR (English Special Edition) 423 at 439 (emphasis added).
[13] *Stauder* v. *City of Ulm*, Case 29/69, [1969] ECR 419, para. 7.
[14] *Internationale Handelsgesellschaft mbH* v. *Einfuhr- und Vorratsstelle für Getreide und Futtermittel*, Case 11/70, [1979] ECR 1125.
[15] *Ibid.*, para. 4.   [16] *Ibid.*   [17] *Ibid.* (emphasis added).
[18] *Nold* v. *Commission*, Case 4/73, [1974] ECR 491.

> or of which they are signatories, can supply *guidelines* which should be
> followed within the framework of [European] law.[19]

In searching for fundamental rights inside the general principles of European law, the Court would thus draw "inspiration" from the common constitutional traditions of the Member States. One – ingenious – way of identifying a common "agreement" between the various national constitutional traditions was to use international *agreements* of the Member States. And one such international agreement was the European Convention on Human Rights. Having been ratified by all Member States and dealing specially with human rights,[20] the Convention would soon assume a "particular significance" in identifying fundamental rights for the European Union.[21] And yet none of this conclusively characterized the legal relationship between European human rights, national human rights and the European Convention on Human Rights.

Let us therefore look at the question of the Union human rights standard first, before analysing the constitutional doctrines on limits to EU human rights.

(a) The European Standard – an "Autonomous" Standard

Human rights express the fundamental values of a society. Each society may wish to protect distinct values and give them a distinct level of protection.[22] Not all societies may thus choose to protect a constitutional

---

[19] *Ibid.*, para. 13 (emphasis added).

[20] When the E(E)C Treaty entered into force on 1 January 1958, five of its Member States were already parties to the European Convention for the Protection of Human Rights and Fundamental Freedoms, signed in Rome on 4 November 1950. Ever since France joined the Convention system in 1974, all Member States have also been members of the European Convention legal order. For an early reference to the Convention in the jurisprudence of the Court, see *Rutili* v. *Ministre de l'intérieur*, Case 36/75, [1975] ECR 1219, para. 32.

[21] See *Höchst* v. *Commission*, Joined Cases 46/87 and 227/88, [1989] ECR 2859, para. 13: "The Court has consistently held that fundamental rights are an integral part of the general principles of law the observance of which the Court ensures, in accordance with constitutional traditions common to the Member States, and the international treaties on which the Member States have collaborated or of which they are signatories. The European Convention for the Protection of Human Rights and Fundamental Freedoms of 4 November 1950 (hereinafter referred to as 'the European Convention on Human Rights') is of particular significance in that regard."

[22] "Constitutions are not mere copies of a universalist ideal, they also reflect the idiosyncratic choices and preferences of the constituents and are the highest legal expression of

"right to work",[23] while most liberal societies will protect "liberty"; yet, the level at which liberty is protected might vary.[24]

Which fundamental rights exist in the European Union, and what is their level of protection? From the very beginning, the Court of Justice was not completely free to invent an unwritten bill of rights. Instead, and in the words of the famous *Nold* passage, the Court was "*bound to draw inspiration from constitutional traditions common to the Member States*."[25] But how binding would that inspiration be? Could the Court discover human rights that not all Member States recognize as a national human right? And would the Court consider itself under the obligation to use a particular standard for a human right, where a right's "scope and the criteria for applying it vary"?[26]

The relationship between the European and the various national standards is indeed not an easy one. Would the obligation to draw inspiration from the constitutional traditions *common* to the States imply a common *minimum* standard? Serious practical problems follow from this view. For if the European Union consistently adopted the lowest common denominator to assess the legality of its acts, this would inevitably lead to charges that the European Court refuses to take human rights seriously. Should the Union thus favour the *maximum* standard among the Member States,[27] as "the most liberal interpretation must prevail"?[28] This time, there are serious theoretical problems with this view. For the maximalist approach assumes that courts always balance private rights against public interests. But this is not necessarily the case;[29] and, in any event, the

---

the country's value system." See B. de Witte, "Community Law and National Constitutional Values", 2 (1991/2) *Legal Issues of Economic Integration*, 1 at 7.

[23] Article 4 of the Italian Constitution states: "The Republic recognises the right of all citizens to work and promotes those conditions which render this right effective."

[24] To illustrate this point with a famous joke: "In Germany everything is forbidden, unless something is specifically allowed, whereas in Britain everything which is not specifically forbidden, is allowed." (The joke goes on to claim that: "In France everything is allowed, even if it is forbidden; and in Italy everything is allowed, especially when it is forbidden.")

[25] *Nold* (supra n. 18), para. 13 (emphasis added).

[26] *AM & S Europe Limited* v. *Commission,* Case 155/79, [1982] ECR 1575, para. 19.

[27] In favour of a maximalist approach, see L. Besselink, "Entrapped by the Maximum Standard: On Fundamental Rights, Pluralism and Subsidiarity in the European Union", 35 (1998) *Common Market Law Review*, 629.

[28] This "Dworkinian" language comes from *Stauder* (supra n. 13), para. 4.

[29] The Court of Justice was faced with such a right–right conflict in *Society for the Protection of Unborn Children Ireland Ltd* v. *Stephen Grogan and others,* Case C-159/90, [1991] ECR I-4685, but (in)famously refused to decide the case for lack of jurisdiction.

maximum standard is subject to a communitarian critique that insists that the public interest should also be taken seriously.[30] The Court has consequently rejected both approaches.[31]

What about the European Convention on Human Rights as a – common – Union standard? What indeed is the status of the Convention in the Union legal order? The relationship between the Union and the European Convention has remained ambivalent. The Court of Justice has not found the ECHR to be formally binding on the Union through the mechanism of treaty succession. The European Court has also never considered itself materially bound by the interpretation given to the Convention by the European Court of Human Rights. This interpretative freedom has created the possibility of a distinct *Union* standard.[32]

Yet the 2007 Lisbon amendments might have changed this overnight. Today, there are strong textual reasons for claiming that the European Convention is *materially* binding on the Union. For according to the (new) Article 6(3) TEU, fundamental rights as guaranteed by the Convention "*shall constitute general principles of the Union's law*".[33] Will this formulation not mean that all Convention rights *are* general principles of Union law? If so, the Convention standard would henceforth provide a direct standard for the Union. But if this route were chosen, the Convention standard would – presumably – only provide a *minimum* standard for the Union's general principles.

In conclusion, the Union standard for the protection of fundamental rights is an *autonomous* standard. While drawing inspiration from the constitutional traditions common to the Member States and the European Convention on Human Rights, the Court of Justice has – so far – not

---

[30] J. Weiler, "Fundamental Rights and Fundamental Boundaries: On Standards and Values in the Protection of Human Rights" in N. Neuwahl and A. Rosas (eds.), *The European Union and Human Rights* (Brill, 1995), 51 at 61: "If the ECJ were to adopt a maximalist approach this would simply mean that for the [Union] in each and every area the balance would be most restrictive on the public and general interest. A maximalist approach to human rights would result in a minimalist approach to [Union] government."

[31] For the early (implicit) rejection of the minimalist approach, see *Hauer* v. *Land Rheinland-Pfalz*, Case 44/79, [1979] ECR 3727, para. 32 – suggesting that a fundamental right only needs to be protected in "*several* Member States" (emphasis added).

[32] For an excellent analysis of this point see: R. Lawson, "Confusion and Conflict? Diverging Interpretations of the Europe Convention on Human Rights in Strasbourg and Luxembourg" in R. Lawson and M. de Blois (eds.), *The Dynamics of the Protection of the Rights in Europe* (Martinus Nijhoff, 1994), vol. III, 219 and esp. 234–50.

[33] Article 6(3) TEU (emphasis added).

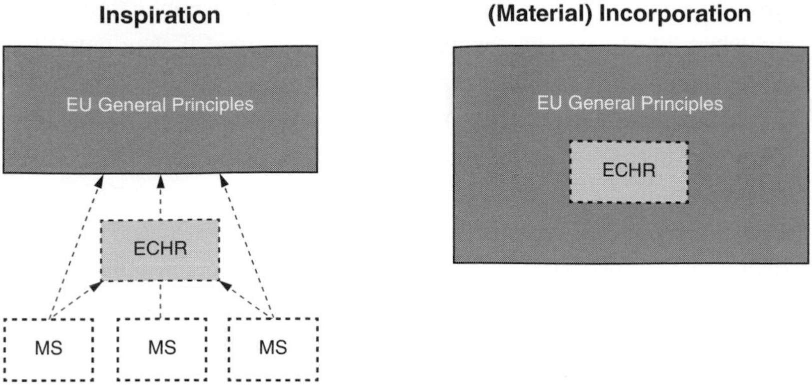

Inspiration

(Material) Incorporation

Figure 4.1 Inspiration Theory versus Incorporation Theory

considered itself directly bound by a particular national or international standard. The Court has thus been free to distil and protect what it sees as the shared values among the majority of people(s) within the Union and has thereby assisted – dialectically – in the establishment of a shared identity for the people(s) of Europe.[34]

(b) Limitations, and "Limitations on Limitations"

Within the European constitutional tradition, some rights are absolute rights. They cannot – under any circumstances – be legitimately limited.[35] However, most fundamental rights are *relative* rights that may be limited in accordance with the public interest. Private property may thus be taxed and individual freedom be restricted – *if* such actions are justified by the common good.

Has the European legal order recognized limits to human rights? From the very beginning, the Court clarified that human rights are "far from constituting unfettered prerogatives",[36] and that they may thus be

---

[34] T. Tridimas, "Judicial Federalism and the European Court of Justice", in J. Fedtke and B. S. Markesinis (eds.), *Patterns of Federalism and Regionalism: Lessons for the UK* (Hart, 2006), 149 at 150 – referring to the contribution of the judicial process "to the emergence of a European *demos*".

[35] The European Court of Justice followed this tradition and recognized the existence of absolute rights in *Schmidberger* v. *Austria*, Case C-112/00, [2003] ECR I-5659, para. 80: "the right to life or the prohibition of torture and inhuman or degrading treatment or punishment, which admit of no restriction".

[36] Case 4/73, *Nold* v. *Commission* (supra n. 18), para. 14.

subject "to limitations laid down in accordance with the public interest".[37] Nonetheless, liberal societies would cease to be liberal if they permitted unlimited limitations to human rights in pursuit of the public interest. Many legal orders consequently recognize limitations on public interest limitations. These "limitations on limitations" to fundamental rights can be relative or absolute in nature.

According to the principle of proportionality, each restriction of a fundamental right must be "proportionate" in relation to the public interest pursued.[38] The principle of proportionality is thus a relative principle. It balances interests: the greater the public interest protected, the greater the right restrictions permitted. And in order to limit this relativist logic, a second principle may come into play. For according to the "essential core" doctrine,[39] any limitation of human rights – even proportionate ones – must never undermine the "very substance" of a fundamental right. This sets an absolute limit to all governmental power by identifying an "untouchable" core within a fundamental right. Yet while the principle of proportionality is almost omnipresent in the jurisprudence of the Court,[40] the existence of an "essential core" doctrine is still unclear. True, the Court had used formulations that came – very – close to the doctrine,[41] but its relationship to the proportionality principle has long remained ambivalent.[42]

---

[37] *Ibid.*

[38] *Hauer*, Case 44/79 (supra n. 31), para. 23. On the proportionality principle in the Union legal order, see Chapter 8 – Section 3 (b/ii) below.

[39] For the German constitutional order, see Article 19(2) German Constitution: "The essence of a basic right must never be violated."

[40] See T. Tridimas, *The General Principles of EU Law* (Oxford University Press, 2007), Chapters 3–5.

[41] The European Courts appear to accept the doctrine implicitly; see e.g., *Nold* (supra n. 18, para. 14): "Within the [Union] legal order it likewise seems legitimate that these rights should, of necessity, be subject to certain limits justified by the overall objectives pursued by the [Union], on condition that the substance of these rights is left untouched"; as well as *Wachauf* v. *Bundesamt für Ernährung und Forstwirtschaft*, Case 5/88, [1989] ECR 2609, para. 18: "[R]estrictions may be imposed on the exercise of those rights, in particular in the context of a common organization of a market, provided that those restrictions in fact correspond to objectives of general interest pursued by the [Union] and do not constitute, with regard to the aim pursued, a disproportionate and intolerable interference, impairing the very substance of those rights."

[42] This point is made by P. Craig, *The Lisbon Treaty: Law, Politics, and Treaty Reform* (Oxford University Press, 2010), 224, who points out that the Court often merges the doctrine of proportionality and the "essential core" doctrine.

The Court however appears to have finally confirmed the existence of an "essential core" doctrine in *Zambrano*.[43] Two Colombian parents had challenged the rejection of their Belgian residency permits on the ground that their children had been born in Belgium and thereby assumed Belgian and – thus – European citizenship.[44] And since minor children would inevitably have to follow their parents, the question arose whether the latter's deportation would violate their children's fundamental status as Union citizens. The Court indeed held that the Belgian measures violated the Treaties, as they would "have the effect of depriving citizens of the Union of the genuine enjoyment of the substance of the rights conferred by virtue of their status as citizens of the Union".[45] The recognition of an untouchable "substance" of a fundamental right here functioned like an essential core doctrine. Yet in subsequent jurisprudence, the Court has clarified that it will give a narrow construction of what constitutes the "substance" of Union citizenship.[46]

2. United Nations Law: External Limits to European Human Rights?

The European legal order is a constitutional order based on the rule of law.[47] This implies that an individual, where legitimately concerned,[48] must be able to challenge the legality of a European act on the basis that his or her human rights have been violated. Should there be exceptions to this constitutional rule? This question is controversially debated in comparative constitutionalism. And it has lately received much attention in a

---

[43] *Zambrano* v. *Office national de l'emploi*, Case C-34/09, [2001] ECR I-1177. Admittedly, there are many questions that this – excessively – short case raises (see "Editorial: Seven Questions for Seven Paragraphs", 36 (2011) *European Law Review* 161).

[44] According to Article 20(1) TFEU: "Citizenship of the Union is hereby established. Every person holding the nationality of a Member State shall be a citizen of the Union. Citizenship of the Union shall be additional to and not replace national citizenship."

[45] *Zambrano* (supra n. 43), para. 42; and see also para. 44: "In those circumstances, those citizens of the Union would, as a result, be unable to exercise the substance of the rights conferred on them by virtue of their status as citizens of the Union."

[46] Cf. *McCarthy* v. *Secretary of State for the Home Department*, Case C-434/09, (2011) ECR I-3375 as well as *Dereci* v. *Bundesministerium für Inneres*, Case C-256/11, (2011) ECR I-11315.

[47] See *Parti Écologiste*, Case 294/83 (supra n. 5).

[48] On the judicial standing of private parties in the Union legal order, see Chapter 8 – Section 3 (c).

special form: will European fundamental rights be limited by international obligations flowing from the United Nations Charter?

The classic answer to this question was offered by *Bosphorus*.[49] The case dealt with a European regulation implementing the United Nations embargo against the Federal Republic of Yugoslavia. Protesting that its fundamental right to property was violated, the plaintiff challenged the European legislation. And the Court had no qualms in judicially reviewing the European legislation – even if a lower review standard was applied.[50] The constitutional message behind the classic approach was clear: where the Member States decided to fulfil their international obligations under the United Nations *qua* European law, they would have to comply with the constitutional principles of the Union legal order, and in particular: European human rights.

This classic approach was challenged by the General Court in *Kadi*.[51] The applicant was a suspected Taliban terrorist, whose financial assets had been frozen as a result of European legislation that reproduced United Nations Security Council Resolutions. Kadi claimed that his fundamental rights of due process and property had been violated. The Union organs intervened in the proceedings and argued – to the surprise of many – that "the Charter of the United Nations prevail[s] over every other obligation of international, [European] or domestic law" with the effect that European human rights should be inoperative.[52] To the even greater surprise – if not shock – of European constitutional scholars,[53] the General Court accepted this argument. How did the Court come to this conclusion? It had recourse to a version of the "succession doctrine",[54] according to which the Union may be bound by the international obligations of its Member States.[55]

---

[49] *Bosphorus Hava Yollari Turizm ve Ticaret AS* v. *Minister for Transport, Energy and Communications and others*, Case C-84/95, [1996] ECR I-3953.

[50] For a critique of the standard of review, see I. Canor, "'Can Two Walk Together, Except They Be Agreed?' The Relationship between International Law and European Law: The Incorporation of United Nations Sanctions against Yugoslavia into European Community Law through the Perspective of the European Court of Justice", 35 (1998) *Common Market Law Review*, 137 at 162.

[51] *Kadi* v. *Council and Commission*, Case T-315/01, [2005] ECR II-3649.

[52] *Ibid.*, paras. 156 and 177.

[53] P. Eeckhout, *Does Europe's Constitution Stop at the Water's Edge? Law and Policy in the EU's External Relations* (Europa Law Publishing, 2005); as well as R. Schütze, "On 'Middle Ground': The European Community and Public International Law", *EUI Working Paper* 2007/13.

[54] *Kadi*, Case T-315/01 (supra n. 51), paras. 193 et seq.

[55] On the doctrine, see Chapter 2 – Section 4(d) above.

While this conclusion was in itself highly controversial, the dangerous part of the judgment related to the consequences of that conclusion. For the General Court recognized "structural limits, imposed by general international law" on the judicial review powers of the European Court.[56] In the words of the Court:

> Any review of the internal lawfulness of the contested regulation, especially having regard to the provisions or general principles of [European] law relating to the protection of fundamental rights, would therefore imply that the Court is to consider, indirectly, the lawfulness of those [United Nations] resolutions. In that hypothetical situation, in fact, the origin of the illegality alleged by the applicant would have to be sought, not in the adoption of the contested regulation but in the resolutions of the Security Council which imposed the sanctions. In particular, if the Court were to annul the contested regulation, as the applicant claims it should, although that regulation seems to be imposed by international law, on the ground that that act infringes his fundamental rights which are protected by the [Union] legal order, such annulment would indirectly mean that the resolutions of the Security Council concerned themselves infringe those fundamental rights.[57]

The General Court thus declined jurisdiction to directly review European legislation *because it would entail an indirect review of the United Nations resolutions*. The justification for this self-abdication was that United Nations law was binding on all Union institutions, including the European Courts.

From a constitutional perspective, this reasoning was prisoner to a number of serious mistakes.[58] And in its appeal judgment,[59] the Court of Justice remedied these constitutional blunders and safely returned to the traditional *Bosphorus* approach. The Court held:

> [T]he obligations imposed by an international agreement cannot have the effect of prejudicing the constitutional principles of the [European Treaties], which include the principle that all [Union] acts must respect fundamental rights, that respect constituting a condition of their

---

[56] *Kadi*, Case T-315/01 (supra n. 51), para. 212.
[57] *Ibid.*, paras. 215–16 (references omitted).
[58] On this point, see: R. Schütze, "On 'Middle Ground': The European Union and Public International Law" (supra n. 53), 19 et seq.
[59] *Kadi and Al Barakaat International Foundation* v. *Council and Commission*, Case C-402/05P, [2008] ECR I-6351.

> lawfulness which it is for the Court to review in the framework of the complete system of legal remedies established by the Treat[ies].[60]

The United Nations Charter, while having special importance within the European legal order,[61] would – in this respect – not be different from other international agreements.[62] Like "ordinary" international agreements, the United Nations Charter might – if materially binding – have primacy over European legislation but "[t]hat primacy at the level of [European] law would not, however, extend to primary law, in particular to the general principles of which fundamental rights form part".[63] European human rights would thus *not* find an external structural limit in the international obligations stemming from the United Nations.[64] The Union was firmly based on the rule of law, and this meant that all European legislation – regardless of its "domestic" or international origin – would be limited by the respect for fundamental human rights.[65]

3. The Charter of Fundamental Rights

The desire for a *written* bill of rights for the European Union first expressed itself in arguments favouring accession to the European Convention on Human Rights.[66] Yet an alternative strategy became prominent in the late twentieth century: the Union's own written bill of rights. The initiative for a "Charter of Fundamental Rights" came from the European Council,[67] and the idea behind an internal codification was to strengthen the protection of fundamental rights in Europe "by making those rights more visible in a Charter".[68] The Charter was proclaimed in 2000, but it was *not* legally binding. Its status was similar to the European Convention on Human

---

[60] *Ibid.*, para. 285.   [61] *Ibid.*, para. 294 ("special importance").
[62] *Ibid.*, para. 300.   [63] *Ibid.*, para. 308.   [64] *Ibid.*, para. 327.
[65] The Court in fact identified a breach of the right of defence, especially the right to be heard (*ibid.*, para. 353), as well as an unjustified violation of the right to property (*ibid.*, para. 370).
[66] Commission, Memorandum on the Accession of the European Communities to the European Convention for the Protection of Human Rights and Fundamental Freedoms, [1979] Bulletin of the European Communities – Supplement 2/79, esp. 11 et seq.
[67] On the drafting process, see G. de Búrca, "The Drafting of the European Union Charter of Fundamental Rights", 26 (2001) *European Law Review*, 126. For a criticism of the idea of codification, see J. Weiler, "Does the European Union Truly Need a Charter of Rights?", 6 (2000) *European Law Journal*, 95 at 96.
[68] Charter, Preamble 4.

Rights: it provided a valuable *inspiration* but imposed no formal obligation on the European institutions.[69] This ambivalent status was immediately perceived as a constitutional problem. But it took almost a decade before the 2007 Lisbon Treaty recognized the Charter as having "the same legal value as the Treaties".

The Charter "reaffirms" the rights that result "in particular" from the constitutional traditions common to the Member States, the European Convention on Human Rights and the general principles of European law.[70] This formulation suggested two things. First, the Charter aims to codify existing fundamental rights and was thus not intended to create "new" ones.[71] And, second, it codified European rights from *various* sources – and thus not solely the general principles found in the European Treaties. To help identify the sources behind individual Charter articles, the Member States decided to give the Charter its own commentary. These "Explanations" are not strictly legally binding, but they must be given "due regard" in the interpretation of the Charter.[72]

The Charter divides the Union's fundamental rights into six classes. The classic liberal rights are covered by Titles I to III as well as Title VI. The controversial Title IV codifies the rights of workers; yet, provision is also made for the protection of the family and the right to health care.[73] Title V deals with "citizens' rights", that is: rights that a polity provides exclusively to its members. This includes the right to vote and to stand as a candidate in elections.[74] The general principles on the interpretation and application of the Charter are finally set out in Title VII. These general provisions establish four fundamental principles. First, the Charter is addressed to the Union and will only exceptionally apply to the Member States.[75] Second, not all provisions within the Charter are "rights"; that is:

---

[69] See *Parliament* v. *Council* Case C-540/03, [2006] ECRI-5769, para. 38: "the Charter is not a legally binding instrument."

[70] Charter, Preamble 5.

[71] See Protocol (No. 30) "On the Application of the Charter of Fundamental Rights of the European Union to Poland and to the United Kingdom," Preamble 6: "the Charter reaffirms the rights, freedoms and principles recognised in the Union and makes those rights more visible, but does not create new rights or principles".

[72] Article 6(1) TEU, and Article 52(7) Charter: "The explanations drawn up as a way of providing guidance in the interpretation of this Charter shall be given due regard by the courts of the Union of the Member States." These "Explanations" are published in [2007] OJ C303/17.

[73] See, respectively, Articles 33 and 35 of the Charter.   [74] Article 39 Charter.

[75] Article 51 Charter. On the application of the Charter to the Member States, see R. Schütze, "European Fundamental Rights and the Member States: From 'Selective' to 'Total' Incorporation?", 14 (2011/12) *Cambridge Yearbook of European Legal Studies* 337.

Table 4.1 Structure of the Charter of Fundamental Rights

EU Charter of Fundamental Rights
Preamble
Title I – Dignity
Title II – Freedoms
Title III – Equality
Title IV – Solidarity
Title V – Citizens' Rights
Title VI – Justice
Title VII – General Provisions
Article 51 – Field of Application
Article 52 – Scope and Interpretation of Rights and Principles
Article 53 – Level of Protection
Article 54 – Prohibition of Abuse of Rights
Protocol No. 30 on Poland and the United Kingdom
Explanations

directly effective entitlements to individuals.[76] Third, the rights within the Charter can, within limits, be restricted by Union legislation.[77] Fourth, the Charter tries to establish harmonious relations with the European Treaties and the European Convention, as well as with constitutional traditions common to the Member States.[78]

In the context of the present section, only principles two and three warrant special attention.

(a) (Hard) Rights and (Soft) Principles

It is important to note that the Charter makes a distinction between (hard) rights and (soft) principles.[79] Hard rights are rights that will have direct effect and can, as such, be invoked before a court. Not all provisions

---

[76] Article 51(1) and 52(5) Charter.   [77] Article 52(1) Charter.

[78] Article 52(2)–(4) as well as (6) of the Charter. But see also Article 53 on the "Level of Protection".

[79] The distinction seems to contradict the jurisprudence of the Court with regard to fundamental *rights* as general *principles* in the context of the European Treaties. However, the best way to understand the distinction between "rights" and "principles" is not to see them as mutually exclusive; see M. A. Dauses, "The Protection of Fundamental Rights in the Community Legal Order", 10 (1985), *European Law Review*, 399 at 406 and below.

within the Charter are rights in this strict sense. Indeed, the Charter also recognizes the existence of "principles" in its Title VII.[80]

What are these principles in the Charter, and what is their effect? The "Explanations" offer a number of illustrations, in particular Article 37 of the Charter dealing with "Environmental Protection". The provision reads: "A high level of environmental protection and the improvement of the quality of the environment *must be integrated into the policies of the Union* and ensured in accordance with the principle of sustainable development."[81] This wording contrasts strikingly with that of a classic right provision.[82] For it constitutes less a *limit* to governmental action than an *aim* for governmental action. Principles indeed come close to orienting objectives, which "do not however give rise to direct claims for positive action by the Union institutions".[83] They are not subjective rights, but objective guidelines. In the words of the Charter:

> The provisions of this Charter which contain principles may be implemented by legislative and executive acts taken by institutions...They shall be judicially cognisable only in the interpretation of such acts and in the ruling on their legality.[84]

The difference between rights and principles is thus between a hard and a soft judicial claim. An individual will not have an (individual) right to a high level of environmental protection. In line with the classic task of legal principles,[85] the courts must however generally draw "inspiration" from Union principles when interpreting European law.

But how is one to distinguish between "rights" and "principles"? Sadly, the Charter offers no catalogue of principles. Nor are its principles neatly grouped into a section within each substantive title. And even the wording of a particular article will not conclusively reveal whether it contains a right or a principle. But, most confusingly, even a single article "may contain both elements of a right and of a principle".[86] How is this possible? The best way to make sense of this is to see rights and principles

---

[80] Articles 51(1) and 52(5) of the Charter.   [81] Emphasis added.
[82] See Article 2 of the Charter: "Everyone has the right to life."
[83] "Explanations" (supra n. 72), 35.   [84] Article 52(5) of the Charter.
[85] See R. Dworkin, *Taking Rights Seriously* (Duckworth, 1996).
[86] "Explanations" (supra n. 72), 35.

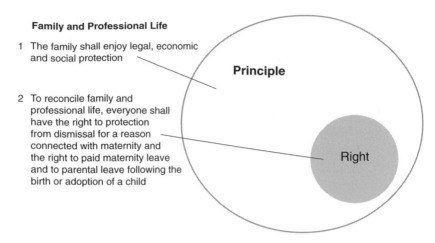

Family and Professional Life

1 The family shall enjoy legal, economic
   and social protection

2 To reconcile family and
   professional life, everyone shall
   have the right to protection
   from dismissal for a reason
   connected with maternity and
   the right to paid maternity leave
   and to parental leave following the
   birth or adoption of a child

Figure 4.2 Principles and Rights within the Charter

not as mutually exclusive concepts, but as distinct but overlapping legal constructs.[87] "Rights" are situational crystallizations of principles, and therefore derive from principles. A good illustration may be offered by Figure 4.2 and Article 33 of the Charter on the status of the family and its relation to professional life.

(b) Limitations, and "Limitations on Limitations"

Every legal order protecting fundamental rights recognizes that some rights can be limited to safeguard the general interest. For written bills of rights, these limitations are often recognized for each constitutional right. While the Charter follows this technique for some articles,[88] it also contains a provision that defines legitimate limitations to all fundamental rights. The "limitations on limitations" are set out in Article 52 of the Charter. The provision states:

> Any limitation on the exercise of the rights and freedoms recognised by this Charter must be *provided for by law* and *respect the essence of those*

---

[87] In this sense see R. Alexy, *A Theory of Constitutional Rights* (Oxford University Press, 2002), 47 – using the Wittgensteinian concept of "family resemblance" to describe the relation between "rights" and "principles".

[88] Article 17 (Right to Property) of the Charter states in paragraph 1: "No one may be deprived of his or her possessions, except in the public interest and in the cases and under the conditions provided for by law, subject to fair compensation being paid in good time for their loss. The use of property may be regulated by law in so far as is necessary for the general interest."

rights and freedoms. Subject to the principle of *proportionality,* limitations
may be made only if they are necessary and genuinely meet objectives of
general interest recognised by the Union or the need to protect the rights
and freedoms of others.[89]

The provision subjects all limitations to EU Charter rights to three constitutional principles. First, any limitation of a fundamental right must be
provided for "by law". This requirement seems to prohibit, out of hand,
human rights violations that are the result of individual acts based on
autonomous executive powers.[90] However, the problem is still this: will a
limitation of someone's fundamental rights require the (democratic) legitimacy behind formal legislation? Put differently: must every "law" limiting a fundamental right be adopted under a "legislative procedure"?[91]
This view would significantly affect the balance between fundamental rights and the pursuit of the common good of the Union. For if
Article 52 outlaws all limitations of fundamental rights that are the result
of *delegated* executive acts, much of the governmental machinery of the
Union would come to a halt. In order to prevent such a petrification of
the executive branch, the Court has thus favoured a material concept of
"law".[92]

However, Article 52(1) of the Charter mentions, of course, two further
constitutional limitations on right limitations. According to the principle
of proportionality, each restriction of fundamental rights must be necessary in light of the general interest of the Union or the rights of others. This
imposes an obligation on the Union institutions to balance their various
rights and interest at stake. And importantly, Article 52 has also confirmed
the independent existence of an absolute limit to public interferences into
fundamental rights by insisting that each limitation must always "respect
the essence" of the right in question. The codification of the "essential
core" doctrine is to be much welcomed. Its independence from the principle of proportionality has indeed recently been confirmed.[93]

---

[89] Article 52(1) Charter (emphasis added).
[90] See *Knauf Gips* v. *Commission,* Case C-407/08 P, (2010) ECR I-6371.
[91] In favour of this view see D. Triantafyllou, "The European Charter of Fundamental Rights
and the 'Rule of Law': Restricting Fundamental Rights by Reference", 39 (2002) *Common
Market Law Review,* 53–64 at 61: "Accordingly, references to 'law' made by the Charter
should ideally require a co-deciding participation of the European Parliament[.]"
[92] Such a material reading of the phrase "provided for by law" was confirmed in *Schecke
& Eifert* v. *Land Hessen,* Joined Cases C-92&93/09, (2010) ECR I-11063.
[93] *Digital Rights Ireland Ltd* v. *Minister for Communications, Marine and Natural Resources,*
Case C-293/12, EU: C: 2014: 238. The Court here clearly distinguished between a violation

4. The "External" Bill of Rights: the European Convention on Human Rights

The discovery of an unwritten bill of rights and the creation of a written bill of rights for the Union had been "internal" achievements. They did "not result in any form of external supervision being exercised over the Union's institutions".[94] And by preferring *its* internal human rights over any external international standard, the Court has even been accused of a "chauvinist" and "parochial" attitude.[95] This bleak picture *is* distorted – at the very least, when it comes to one international human rights treaty that has always provided an external standard to the European Union: the European Convention on Human Rights. From the very beginning, the Court of Justice took the Convention very seriously,[96] sometimes even too seriously.[97] This final section will look at the external standard imposed by the Convention prior to and after an eventual accession by the Union.

(a) Before Accession: Indirect Review of Union Law

The Union is (still) not a formal party to the European Convention. Could the Member States thus escape their international obligations under the Convention by transferring decision-making powers to the European Union? In order to avoid a normative vacuum, the European Convention system has accepted the *indirect* review of Union acts by establishing the doctrine of (limited) direct responsibility of Member States for acts of the Union.

Having originally found that the Union constituted an autonomous subject of international law whose actions could not be attributed to its Member States,[98] the European Commission on Human Rights and its

---

of the essential core doctrine (*ibid.*, paras. 39–40) and a breach of the principle of proportionality (*ibid.*, paras. 45–69).

[94] I. de Jesús Butler and O. de Schutter, "Binding the EU to International Human Rights Law", 27 (2008) *Yearbook of European Law*, 277 at 278. This statement is correct only if limited to *direct* external supervision.

[95] G. de Búrca, "The European Court of Justice and the International Legal Order After *Kadi*", 51 (2010) *Harvard International Law Journal*, 1 at 4.

[96] See S. Douglas-Scott, "A Tale of Two Courts: Luxembourg, Strasbourg and the Growing European Human Rights Acquis", 43 (2006) *Common Market Law Review*, 629.

[97] See *Spain* v. *United Kingdom*, Case C-145/04, [2006] ECR I-7917.

[98] *Ibid.* The Convention Commission held that the complaint was "outside its jurisdiction ratione personae since the [Member] States by taking part in the decision of the Council

Court subsequently changed views. In *M & Co* v. *Germany*,[99] the Commission found that, whereas "the Convention does not prohibit a Member State from transferring powers to international organisations", "a transfer of powers does not necessarily exclude a State's responsibility under the Convention with regard to the exercise of the transferred powers".[100] This would not, however, mean that the State was to be held responsible for all actions of the Union: "it would be contrary to the very idea of transferring powers to an international organisation to hold the Member States responsible for examining [possible violations] in each individual case."[101]

What, then, were the conditions for this limited indirect review of Union acts? Consistent with its chosen emphasis on state responsibility, the Convention system would not concentrate on the concrete decision of the Union, but on the State's decision to transfer powers to the Union. This transfer of powers was deemed "not incompatible with the Convention provided that within that organisation fundamental rights will receive an *equivalent protection*".[102] Member States would consequently not be responsible for every – compulsory – European Union act that violated the European Convention.

This was confirmed in *Bosphorus*.[103] Where the Union protected human rights in an "equivalent" manner to that of the Convention, the European Court of Human Rights would operate a "presumption" that the States had not violated the Convention by transferring powers to the European Union. This presumption translates into a lower review standard for acts adopted by the European Union,[104] since the presumption of equivalent protection could only be rebutted where the actual treatment of human rights within the Union was "manifestly deficient".[105] The lower review standard represented a compromise between two extremes: no control, as the Union was not a member, and full control even in situations in which the Member States acted as mere agents of the Union. This compromise

of the European [Union] had not in the circumstances of the instant case exercised their 'jurisdiction' within the meaning of Art 1 of the Convention".

[99] *M & Co* v. *Federal Republic of Germany* (1990) 64 DR 138.
[100] *Ibid.*, 145.   [101] *Ibid.*, 146.   [102] *Ibid.*, 145 (emphasis added).
[103] *Bosphorus Hava* v. *Minister*, Case 84/95 (supra n. 49).
[104] J. Callewaert, "The European Convention on Human Rights and European Union Law: A Long Way to Harmony", (2009) *European Human Rights Law Review* 768, 773: "through the Bosphorus-presumption and its tolerance as regards 'non manifest' deficiencies, the protection of fundamental rights under [European] law is policed with less strictness than under the Convention."
[105] *Bosphorus Hava* v. *Minister*, Case 84/95 (supra n. 49), paras. 156–7.

was "the price for Strasbourg achieving a level of control over the EU, while respecting its autonomy as a separate legal order".[106]

(b) After Accession: Direct Review of Union Law

The present Strasbourg jurisprudence privileges the Union legal order in not subjecting it to the full external review by the European Court of Human Rights. However, this privilege is not the result of the Union being a "model" member. Instead it results from the Union *not* being a formal member of the European Convention system.

Will the presumption that the Union – in principle – complies with the European Convention on Human Rights disappear with accession? It seems compelling that the *Bosphorus* presumption will cease once the Union accedes to the Convention. For "[b]y acceding to the Convention, the European Union will have agreed to have its legal system measured by the human rights standards of the ECHR", and will "therefore no longer deserve special treatment".[107] The replacement of an *indirect* review by a *direct* review should also – at least in theory – lead to the replacement of a *limited* review by a *full* review. Yet the life of law is not always logical, and the Strasbourg Court may well decide to cherish past experiences by applying a lower review standard to the (acceded) European Union. We must wait and see whether or not logic will trump experience.

However, what is certain already is that accession will widen the scope of application of the European Convention to include direct Union action. For in the past, the indirect review of Union acts was based on the direct review of Member State acts implementing Union acts. And this, by definition, required that a *Member State* had acted in some way.[108] Thus in situations where the Union institutions had acted directly upon an individual without any mediating Member State measures, this Union act could not – even indirectly – be reviewed.[109] In the absence of a connecting factor to one of the signatory States, the Union act was thus outside the Convention's jurisdiction. This will definitely change once the Union accedes

---

[106] Douglas-Scott, "A Tale of Two Courts" (supra n. 96), 639.
[107] T. Lock, "EU Accession to the ECHR: Implications for Judicial Review in Strasbourg", 35 (2010) *European Law Review*, 777 at 798.
[108] *Ibid.*, 779.
[109] See *Connolly* v. *Fifteen Member States of the European Union* (Application No. 73274/01).

to the Convention. Henceforth all *direct* Union actions would fall within the jurisdiction of the Strasbourg Court. Thus even if a lower external standard were to continue, it would henceforth apply to all Union acts – and not just acts executed by the Member States.

Conclusion

Fundamental rights constitute a central constitutional limit to all Union legislative and executive action. They are principally enforced by the judiciary in the form of judicial review.

The Union has, unfortunately, not reserved one place for human rights, but has instead developed three bills of rights. Its unwritten bill of rights results from the general principles of Union law. The Court here indirectly developed European Union fundamental rights from the constitutional traditions of the Member States. The Charter of Fundamental Rights adds a written bill of rights for the Union. The relationship between this written bill and the unwritten bill of rights within the EU Treaties remains however ambivalent. The same is true for the relationship between the two internal bills of EU rights and the European Convention on Human Rights. The latter has always provided an external bill of rights – yet the exact status of the European Convention in the Union legal order and its influence on the substance of EU fundamental rights remains to be settled.

Part II

European Law: Enforcement

This Part concentrates on the "enforcement" of Union law in the courts. We shall see that European law establishes rights and obligations that directly affect individuals. The direct effect of European law in the national legal orders will be discussed in Chapter 5. Where a European norm is directly effective, it will also be "supreme" over national law. The "supremacy" of European law is the subject of Chapter 6. How will individuals enforce their "supreme" European rights? Chapters 7 and 8 look at the dual enforcement machinery within the Union legal order. Individuals will typically enforce their European rights in national courts. The Union legal order has here required national courts to provide effective remedies for the enforcement of European rights; in order to assist these courts in the interpretation and application of European law, the Union envisages a preliminary reference procedure. Having the indirect enforcement of European law through the national courts discussed in Chapter 7, the direct enforcement of European law in the European Courts will be explored in Chapter 8.

Introduction

Classic international law holds that each State can choose the relationship between its "domestic" law and "international" law. Two – constitutional – theories thereby exist: monism and dualism. Monist States make international law part of their domestic legal order. International law will here directly apply *as if* it were domestic law.[1] By contrast, dualist States consider international law separate from domestic law. International law is viewed as the law *between* States; national law is the law *within* a State. While international treaties are thus binding "on" States, they cannot be

---

[1] Article VI, Clause 2 of the United States Constitution (emphasis added): "[A]ll Treaties made, or which shall be made, under the Authority of the United States, shall be the supreme Law of the Land; and the *Judges in every State shall be bound thereby, any Thing in the Constitution or Laws of any State to the Contrary notwithstanding.*"

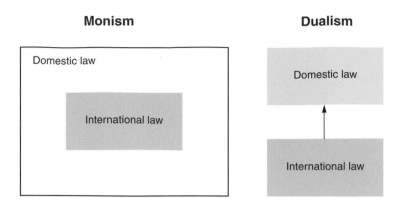

Figure 5.1 Monism and dualism

binding "in" States. International law here needs to be "transposed" or "incorporated" into domestic law and will here only have *indirect* effects through the medium of national law. The dualist theory is based on a basic division of labour: international institutions apply international law, while national institutions apply national law.

Did the European Union leave the choice between monism and dualism to its Member States?[2] Section 1 examines this question in greater detail, before the remainder of this Chapter explores the doctrine of direct effect for European law. Section 2 starts out with the direct effect of the European Treaties. The European Court indeed confirmed that some Treaty provisions would be self-executing in the national legal orders. Nonetheless, the European Treaties are framework treaties; that is: they primarily envisage the adoption of European *secondary* law. This secondary law may take various forms. These forms are set out in Article 288 TFEU. The provision defines the Union's legal instruments, and states:

---

[2] The choice between monism and dualism is traditionally a "national" choice. Thus, even where a State chooses the monist approach, monism in this sense only means that international norms are *constitutionally* recognized as an autonomous legal source of domestic law. Dualism, by contrast, means that international norms will not automatically (that is: through a constitutional incorporation) become part of the national legal order. Each international treaty demands a separate legislative act "incorporating" the international norm into domestic law. The difference between monism and dualism thus boils down to whether international law is incorporated via the constitution – such as in the United States; or whether international treaties need to be validated by a special parliamentary command – as in the United Kingdom. The idea that monism means that States have no choice but to apply international law is not accepted in international law.

[1] To exercise the Union's competences, the institutions shall adopt regulations, directives, decisions, recommendations and opinions.

[2] A regulation shall have general application. It shall be binding in its entirety and directly applicable in all Member States.

[3] A directive shall be binding, as to the result to be achieved, upon each Member State to which it is addressed, but shall leave to the national authorities the choice of form and methods.

[4] A decision shall be binding in its entirety. A decision which specifies those to whom it is addressed shall be binding only on them.

[5] Recommendations and opinions shall have no binding force.

The provision acknowledges three binding legal instruments – regulations, directives, and decisions – and two non-binding instruments. Why was there a need for three distinct binding instruments? The answer seems to lie in their specific – direct or indirect – effects in the national legal orders. While regulations and decisions were considered to be Union acts that would contain directly effective legal norms, directives appeared to lack this capacity. Much of the constitutional discussion on the direct effect of European secondary law has consequently concentrated on the direct effect of directives. Section 3 will therefore look at them in much detail. Finally, Section 4 analyses the doctrine of indirect effects within the Union legal order.

1. Direct Applicability and Direct Effect

Would the Union legal order permit a dualist approach towards European law on the part of the Member States? The European Treaties contained a signal in favour of this permissive approach. For there existed an "international" enforcement machinery in the form of infringement actions before the Court of Justice.[3] However, the Treaties also contained strong signals against the "ordinary" international reading of European law. Not only was the Union entitled to adopt legal acts that were to be "directly applicable *in* all Member States".[4] From the very beginning, the Treaties also established a constitutional mechanism that envisaged the direct application of European law by the national courts.[5]

---

[3] On this point, see Chapter 8 – Section 1 below.   [4] Article 288(2) TFEU.
[5] Article 267 TFEU. On the provision, see Chapter 7 – Sections 3 and 4 below.

But regardless of whether a monist view had or had not been intended by the founding Member States, the European Court discarded any dualist leanings in the most important case of European law: *Van Gend en Loos*.[6] The Court here expressly cut the umbilical cord with classic international law by insisting that the European legal order was a "new legal order". In the famous words of the Court:

> The objective of the E[U] Treaty, which is to establish a common market, the functioning of which is of direct concern to interested parties in the [Union], implies that this Treaty is *more than an agreement which merely creates mutual obligations between the contracting States*. This view is confirmed by the preamble to the Treaty which refers not only to the governments but to peoples. It is also confirmed more specifically by the establishment of institutions endowed with sovereign rights, the exercise of which affects Member States and also their citizens. Furthermore, it must be noted that the nations of the States brought together in the [Union] are called upon to cooperate in the functioning of this [Union] through the intermediary of the European Parliament and the Economic and Social Committee.
>
> In addition the task assigned to the Court of Justice under Article [267], the object of which is to secure uniform interpretation of the Treaty by national courts and tribunals, confirms that the States have acknowledged that [European] law has an authority which can be invoked by their nationals before those courts and tribunals. The conclusion to be drawn from this is that the [Union] constitutes a *new legal order of international law* for the benefit of which the States have limited their sovereign rights, albeit within limited fields, and the subjects of which comprise not only Member States but also their nationals. *Independently of the legislation of Member States,* [European] law therefore not only imposes obligations on individuals but is also intended to confer upon them rights which become part of their legal heritage.[7]

All judicial arguments here marshalled to justify a monistic reading of European law are debatable.[8] But with a stroke of the pen, the Court confirmed the independence of the European legal order from classic international law. Unlike ordinary international law, the European Treaties were

---

[6] *Van Gend en Loos* v. *Netherlands Inland Revenue Administration*, Case 26/62, [1963] ECR (Special English Edition) 1.

[7] *Ibid.*, 12 (emphasis added).

[8] For a critical overview, see T. Arnull, *The European Union and its Court of Justice* (Oxford University Press, 2006), 168 et seq.

more than agreements creating mutual obligations between States. All European law would be directly applicable in the national legal orders; and it was to be enforced in national courts – despite the parallel existence of an international enforcement machinery.[9] Individuals were subjects of European law, and individual rights and obligations could consequently derive *directly* from European law.

Importantly, because European law is directly applicable law, the European Union could also *itself* determine the effect and nature of European law within the national legal orders. The direct applicability of European law thus allowed the Union *centrally* to develop two foundational doctrines of the European legal order: the doctrine of direct effect and the doctrine of supremacy. The present Chapter analyses the doctrine of direct effect; Chapter 6 deals with the doctrine of supremacy.

What is the doctrine of direct effect? It is vital to understand that the Court's decision in favour of a monistic relationship between the European and the national legal orders did not mean that all European law would be directly effective, that is enforceable by national courts. To be enforceable, a norm must be "justiciable"; that is, it must be capable of being applied by a public authority in a specific case. But not all legal norms have this quality. For example, where a European norm requires Member States to establish a public fund to guarantee unpaid wages for insolvent private companies, yet leaves a wide margin of discretion to the Member States on how to achieve that end, this norm is not intended to have direct effects in a specific situation. While it binds the national legislator, the

---

[9] *Van Gend en Loos*, Case 26/62 (supra n. 6), 13: "In addition the argument based on Articles [258] and [259] of the [FEU] Treaty put forward by the three Governments which have submitted observations to the Court in their statements of [the] case is misconceived. The fact that these Articles of the Treaty enable the Commission and the Member States to bring before the Court a State which has not fulfilled its obligations does not mean that individuals cannot plead these obligations, should the occasion arise, before a national court, any more than the fact that the Treaty places at the disposal of the Commission ways of ensuring that obligations imposed upon those subject to the Treaty are observed, precludes the possibility, in actions between individuals before a national court, of pleading infringements of these obligations. A restriction of the guarantees against an infringement of [ex] Article 12 [EEC] by Member States to the procedures under Articles [258 and 259] would remove all direct legal protection of the individual rights of their nationals. There is the risk that recourse to the procedure under these Articles would be ineffective if it were to occur after the implementation of a national decision taken contrary to the provisions of the Treaty. The vigilance of individuals concerned to protect their rights amounts to an effective supervision in addition to the supervision entrusted by Articles [258 and 259] to the diligence of the Commission and of the Member States."

norm is not self-executing. The concept of direct applicability is thus wider than the concept of direct effect. Whereas the former refers to the *internal* effect of a European norm within national legal orders, the latter refers to the *individual* effect of a binding norm in specific cases.[10] Direct effect requires direct applicability, but not the other way around. The direct applicability of a norm only makes its direct effect *possible*.

2. Direct Effect of Primary Law

The European Treaties are framework treaties. They establish the objectives of the European Union, and endow it with the powers to achieve these objectives. Many of the European policies in Part III of the TFEU thus simply set out the competences and procedures for future Union secondary law. The Treaties, as primary European law, thereby offer the constitutional bones. But could this constitutional "skeleton" itself have direct effect? Would there be Treaty provisions that were sufficiently precise to give rise to rights or obligations that national courts could apply in specific situations?

The European Court affirmatively answered this question in *Van Gend en Loos*.[11] The case concerned a central objective of the European Union: the internal market. According to that central plank of the Treaties, the Union was to create a customs union between the Member States. Within a customs union, goods can move freely without any pecuniary charges being levied when crossing borders. The Treaties had chosen to establish the customs union gradually; and to this effect ex-Article 12 EEC contained a standstill obligation: "Member States shall refrain from introducing between themselves any new customs duties on imports or exports or any charges having equivalent effect, and from increasing those which they already apply in their trade with each other."[12] The Netherlands appeared to have violated this provision; and believing this to be the

---

[10] In this sense direct applicability is a "federal" question as it relates to the effect of a "foreign" norm in a domestic legal system, whereas direct effect is a "separation-of-powers" question as it relates to the issue of whether a norm must be applied by the legislature or the executive and judiciary.

[11] *Van Gend en Loos*, Case 26/62 (supra n. 6).

[12] The provision has been repealed. Strictly speaking, it is therefore not correct to identify Article 30 TEU as the successor provision, for that Article is based on ex-Articles 13 and 16 EEC. The normative content of ex-Article 12 EEC solely concerned the introduction of *new* customs duties; and therefore did not cover the abolition of existing tariff restrictions.

case, Van Gend & Loos – a Dutch import company – brought proceedings in a Dutch court against the National Inland Revenue. The Dutch court had doubts about the admissibility and the substance of the case and referred a number of preliminary questions to the European Court of Justice.

Could a private party enforce an international treaty in a national court? And if so, was this a question of national or European law? In the course of the proceedings before the European Court, the Netherlands government heavily disputed that an individual could enforce an international Treaty provision against its own government in a national court. Any alleged infringements had to be submitted to the European Court by the Commission or a Member State under the "international" infringement procedures set out in Articles 258 and 259 TFEU.[13] The Belgian government, having intervened in the case, equally claimed that the question of what effects an international treaty had within the national legal order "falls exclusively within the jurisdiction of the Netherlands court".[14] Conversely, the Commission countered that "the effects of the provisions of the Treaty on the national law of Member States cannot be determined by the actual national law of each of them but by the Treaty itself".[15] And since ex-Article 12 EEC was "clear and complete", it was "a rule of law capable of being effectively applied by the national court".[16] The fact that the European provision was addressed to the States did "not of itself take away from individuals who have an interest in it the right to require it to be applied in the national courts".[17]

Two views thus competed before the European Court. According to the "international" view, legal rights of private parties could "not derive from the [Treaties] or the legal measures taken by the institutions, but [solely] from legal measures enacted by Member States".[18] According to the "constitutional" view, by contrast, European law was capable of directly creating individual rights. The Court famously favoured the second view. It followed from the "spirit" of Treaties that European law was no "ordinary" international law. It would thus of itself be directly applicable in the national legal orders.

But when would a provision have direct effect, and thus entitle private parties to seek its application by a national court? Having briefly presented

---

[13] *Van Gend en Loos*, Case 26/62 (supra n. 6), 6. On enforcement actions by the Commission, see Chapter 8 – Section 1 below.
[14] *Van Gend en Loos*, Case 26/62 (supra n. 6), 6.   [15] *Ibid.*
[16] *Ibid.*, 7.   [17] *Ibid.*   [18] This was the view of the German government (*ibid.*, 8).

the general scheme of the Treaty in relation to customs duties,[19] the Court concentrated on the wording of ex-Article 12 EEC and found as follows:

> The wording of [ex-]Article 12 [EEC] contains a *clear and unconditional prohibition* which is not a positive but a *negative obligation*. This obligation, moreover, is not qualified by any reservation on the part of the States, *which would make its implementation conditional upon a positive legislative measure enacted under national law*. The very nature of this prohibition makes it ideally adapted to produce direct effects in the legal relationship between Member States and their subjects. The implementation of [ex-]Article 12 [EEC] does not require any legislative intervention on the part of the States. The fact that under this Article it is the Member States who are made the subject of the negative obligation does not imply that their nationals cannot benefit from this obligation.[20]

While somewhat repetitive, the test for direct effect is here clearly presented: wherever the Treaties contain a "prohibition" that was "clear" and "unconditional" it will have direct effect. Being an unconditional prohibition thereby required two things. First, the European provision had to be an *automatic* prohibition, that is: it should not depend on subsequent positive legislation by the European Union. And second, the prohibition should ideally be *absolute,* that is: "not qualified by any reservation on the part of the States".

This was a – very – strict test. But ex-Article 12 EEC was indeed "ideally adapted" to satisfy this triple test. It was a clear prohibition and unconditional in the double sense. However, if the Court had insisted on a strict application of all three criteria, very few provisions within the Treaties would have had direct effect. Yet the Court subsequently loosened the test considerably. And as we shall see below, it made it clear that the Treaties could be vertically and horizontally directly effective.

(a) Direct Effect: From Strict to Lenient Test

The direct effect test set out in *Van Gend* was informed by three criteria. First, a provision had to be clear. Second, it had to be unconditional in the sense of being an automatic prohibition. And third, this prohibition would

---

[19]   The Court considered ex-Article 12 EEC as an "essential provision" in the general scheme of the Treaty as it relates to customs duties (*ibid.*, 12).

[20]   *Ibid.*, 13 (emphasis added).

need to be absolute, that is: not allow for reservations. In its subsequent jurisprudence, the Court expanded the concept of direct effect on all three fronts.

First, how clear would a prohibition have to be to be directly effective? Within the Treaties' title on the free movement of goods, we find the following famous prohibition: "Quantitative restrictions on imports and all measures having equivalent effect shall be prohibited between Member States."[21] Was this a clear prohibition? While the notion of "quantitative restrictions" might have been – relatively – clear, what about "measures having equivalent effect"? The Commission had realized the open-ended nature of the concept and offered some early semantic help.[22] And yet, despite all the uncertainty involved, the Court found that the provision had direct effect.[23]

The same lenient interpretation of what "clear" meant was soon applied to even wider provisions. In *Defrenne*,[24] the Court analysed the following prohibition: "[e]ach Member State shall ensure that the principle of equal pay for male and female workers for equal work or work of equal value is applied."[25] Was this a clear prohibition of discrimination? Confusingly, the Court found that the provision may and may not have direct effect. With regard to indirect discrimination, the Court considered the prohibition indeterminate, since it required "the elaboration of criteria whose implementation necessitates the taking of appropriate measures at [European] and national level".[26] Yet in respect of direct discrimination, the prohibition was directly effective.[27]

What about the second part of the direct effect test? When was a prohibition automatic? Would this be the case, where the Treaties expressly

---

[21] Article 34 TFEU.
[22] Directive 70/50/EEC on the abolition of measures which have an effect equivalent to quantitative restrictions on imports and are not covered by other provisions adopted in pursuance of the EEC Treaty, [1970] OJ English Special Edition 17.
[23] *Iannelli & Volpi SpA* v. *Ditta Paolo Meroni*, Case 74/76, [1977] ECR 557, para. 13: "The prohibition of quantitative restrictions and measures having equivalent effect laid down in Article [34] of the [FEU] Treaty is mandatory and explicit and its implementation does not require any subsequent intervention of the Member States or [Union] institutions. The prohibition therefore has direct effect and creates individual rights which national courts must protect[.]"
[24] *Defrenne* v. *Sabena*, Case 43/75, [1976] ECR 455, para. 19.   [25] Article 157(1) TFEU.
[26] *Defrenne* v. *Sabena*, Case 43/75 (supra n. 24), para. 19.
[27] *Ibid.*, para. 24. This generous reading was subsequently extended to the yet wider prohibition on "any discrimination on grounds of nationality"; see *Martínez Sala* v. *Freistaat Bayern*, Case C-85/96, [1998] ECR I-2691, para. 63.

acknowledged the need for positive legislative action by the Union to achieve a Union objective? For example, the Treaty chapter on the right of establishment contains not just a prohibition addressed to the Member States in Article 49 TFEU;[28] the subsequent article states: "In order to attain freedom of establishment as regards a particular activity, the European Parliament and the Council, acting in accordance with the ordinary legislative procedure and after consulting the Economic and Social Committee, shall act by means of directives." Would this not mean that the freedom of establishment was conditional on legislative action? In *Reyners*,[29] the Court rejected this argument. Despite the fact that the general scheme within the chapter on freedom of establishment contained a set of provisions that sought to achieve free movement through positive Union legislation,[30] the Court declared the European right of establishment in Article 49 TFEU to be directly effective. And the Court had no qualms about giving direct effect to the general prohibition on "any discrimination on grounds of nationality" – despite the fact that Article 18 TFEU expressly called on the Union legislator to adopt rules "designed to prohibit such discrimination".[31]

Finally, what about the third requirement? Could relative prohibitions, even if clear, ever be directly effective? The prohibition on quantitative restrictions on imports, discussed above, is subject to a number of legitimate exceptions according to which it "shall not preclude [national] prohibitions or restrictions on imports, exports or goods in transit justified on grounds of public morality, public policy or public security".[32] Was this then a prohibition that was "not qualified by any reservation on the part of the States"? The Court found that this was indeed the case. For although these derogations would "attach particular importance to the interests of Member States, it must be observed that they deal with exceptional cases which are clearly defined and which do not lend themselves to any wide interpretation".[33] And since the application of these

---

[28] Article 49(1) TFEU states: "Within the framework of the provisions set out below, restrictions on the freedom of establishment of nationals of a Member State in the territory of another Member State shall be prohibited."

[29] *Reyners* v. *Belgian State*, Case 2/74, [1974] ECR 631. For an excellent discussion of this question, see P. Craig, "Once Upon a Time in the West: Direct Effect and the Federalization of EEC Law", 12 (1992) *Oxford Journal of Legal Studies*, 453 at 463–70.

[30] *Reyners*, Case 2/74 (supra n. 29) para. 32.

[31] *Martínez Sala* v. *Freistaat Bayern*, Case C-85/96 (supra n. 27).   [32] Article 36 TFEU.

[33] *Salgoil* v. *Italian Ministry of Foreign Trade*, Case 13/68, [1968] ECR 453 at 463.

exceptions was "subject to judicial control", a Member State's right to invoke them did not prevent the general prohibition "from conferring on individuals rights which are enforceable by them and which the national courts must protect".[34]

What, then, is the test for the direct effect of Treaty provisions in light of these – relaxing – developments? Today, the simple test is this: a provision has direct effect when it is capable of being applied by a national court. Importantly, direct effect does *not* depend on a European norm granting a subjective right; but on the contrary, the subjective right is a result of a directly effective norm.[35] Direct effect simply means that a norm can be "invoked" in and applied by a court. And this is the case, when the Court of Justice says it is! Today, almost all Treaty *prohibitions* have direct effect – even the most general ones. Indeed, in *Mangold*,[36] the Court held that an – unwritten and vague – *general* principle of European law could have direct effect.

Should we embrace this development? We should, for the direct effect of a legal rule "must be considered as being the normal condition of any rule of law". The very questioning of the direct effect of European law was an "infant disease" of the young European legal order.[37] And this infant disease has today – largely – been cured but for one area: the Common Foreign and Security Policy.

(b) Vertical and Horizontal Direct Effect

Where a Treaty provision is directly effective, an individual can invoke European law in a national court (or administration). This will normally be as against the State. This situation is called "vertical" effect, since the State is "above" its subjects. But whereas a private party is in a subordinate position vis-à-vis public authorities, it is in a coordinate position vis-à-vis other private parties. The legal effect of a norm between private parties is thus called "horizontal" effect. And while there has never been any doubt that Treaty provisions can be invoked in a vertical situation, there has been some discussion on their horizontal direct effects.

[34] *Van Duyn* v. *Home Office*, Case 41/74, [1974] ECR 1337, para. 7.
[35] M. Ruffert, "Rights and Remedies in European Community Law: A Comparative View", 34 (1997) *Common Market Law Review*, 307 at 315.
[36] *Mangold* v. *Helm*, Case C-144/04, [2005] ECR I-9981.
[37] P. Pescatore, "The Doctrine of 'Direct Effect': An Infant Disease of Community Law", 8 (1983) *European Law Review*, 155.

Should it make a difference whether European law is invoked in proceedings against the Inland Revenue or in a civil dispute between two
private parties? Should the Treaties be allowed to impose obligations
on individuals? The Court in *Van Gend* had accepted this theoretical
possibility.[38] And indeed, the horizontal direct effect of Treaty provisions
has never been in doubt for the Court.[39]

A good illustration of the horizontal direct effect of Treaty provisions
can be found in *Familiapress* v. *Bauer.*[40] The case concerned the
interpretation of Article 34 TFEU prohibiting unjustified restriction on
the free movement of goods. It arose in a *civil* dispute before the Vienna
Commercial Court between Familiapress and a German competitor, Bauer.
The latter was accused of violating the Austrian Law on Unfair Competition by publishing prize crossword puzzles – a sales technique that was
deemed unfair under Austrian law. Bauer defended itself in the national
court by invoking Article 34 TFEU – claiming that the directly effective
European right to free movement prevailed over the Austrian law. And
the Court of Justice found indeed that a national law that constituted an
unjustified restriction of trade would have to be disapplied in the – civil –
proceedings.

The question of whether a Treaty prohibition has horizontal direct effect
must however be distinguished from the question of whether it also outlaws private party actions. For example: imagine that the rule prohibiting
prize crossword puzzles had not been adopted by the Austrian legislature
but by the Austrian Press Association – a private body regulating Austrian
newspapers. Would this "private" rule equally breach Article 34 TFEU?
The latter is not a question of the *effect* of a provision, but rather of its
personal scope.

Many Treaty prohibitions are – expressly or impliedly – addressed to the
State.[41] Yet the Treaties equally contain some provisions that expressly

---

[38] *Van Gend en Loos*, Case 26/62 (supra n. 6), 12: "[European] law therefore not only
imposes obligations on individuals[.]"

[39] The direct effect of Article 34 TFEU was announced in a "horizontal" case between two
private parties; see *Iannelli & Volpi* v. *Meroni*, Case 74/76 (supra n. 23).

[40] *Vereinigte Familiapress Zeitungsverlags- und vertriebs GmbH* v. *Bauer Verlag*, Case C-
368/95, [1997] ECR I-3689.

[41] For example, Article 157 TFEU states (emphasis added) that "[e]ach *Member State* shall
ensure that the principle of equal pay for male and female workers for equal work or
work of equal value is applied"; and Article 34 TFEU prohibits restrictions on the free
movement of goods "between Member States".

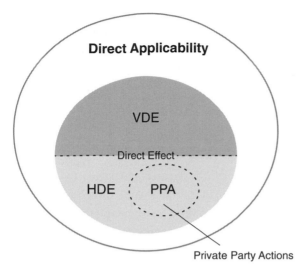

Figure 5.2 Direct Applicability, Direct Effect and Private Party Actions

address private parties.[42] The question of whether a Treaty prohibition
covers public as well as private actions is often controversial. Should the
"equal pay for equal work" principle or the free movement rules – both
expressly addressed to the Member States – also *impliedly* apply to private
associations and their actions? If so, the application of the Treaty will not
just impose *indirect* obligations on individuals (when they lose their right
to rely on a national law that violates European law); they will be *directly*
prohibited from engaging in an activity.

The Court has – in principle – confirmed that Treaty provisions, albeit
addressed to the Member States, might cover private actions.[43] Thus in
Defrenne, the Court found that the prohibition on pay discrimination
between men and women could equally apply to private employers.[44] And
while the exact conditions remain uncertain,[45] the Court has confirmed

---

[42] Article 102 TFEU prohibits "all agreements between undertakings" that restrict competition within the internal market, and is thus addressed to private parties.

[43] *Walrave and Koch* v. *Association Union Cycliste Internationale*, Case 36/74, [1974] ECR
1405, para. 19: "to limit the prohibitions in question to acts of a public authority would
risk creating inequality in their application".

[44] *Defrenne*, Case 43/75 (supra n. 24), para. 39: "In fact, since Article [157 TFEU] is mandatory in nature, the prohibition on discrimination between men and women applies not
only to the action of public authorities, but also extends to all agreements which are
intended to regulate paid labour collectively, as well as to contracts between individuals."

[45] The Court generally limits this application to "private" rules that aim to regulate "in a
collective manner" (*ibid.*, para. 17). See also *Union royale belge des sociétés de football
association ASBL* v. *Jean-Marc Bosman*, Case C-415/93, [1995] ECRI-4921.

and reconfirmed the inclusion of private actions within the free move-ment provisions.[46] To distinguish the logical relations between the various constitutional concepts of direct applicability, direct effect – both vertical (VDE) and horizontal (HDE), and private party actions (PPA) – Figure 5.2 may be useful.

3. Direct Effect of Secondary Law: Directives

When the European Union was born, the Treaties envisaged two instru-ments that were designed to contain norms that were directly effective: regulations and decisions. By contrast, a third instrument – the directive – appeared to lack this capacity. For according to Article 288(3) TFEU, a directive is defined as follows:

> A directive shall be binding, as to the result to be achieved, upon each Member State to which it is addressed, but shall leave to the national authorities the choice of form and methods.

This formulation suggested that directives were binding *on* States – not *within* States. And on the basis of such a "dualist" reading, directives would have no validity in the national legal orders. They seemed *not* to be directly applicable, and would thus need to be "incorporated" or "implemented" through national legislation. This dualist view was under-lined by the fact that Member States were only bound as to the result to be achieved – as obligations of result are common in classic international law.[47]

But could this indirect Union law have direct effects? In a coura-geous line of jurisprudence, the Court confirmed that directives could – under certain circumstances – have direct effect and thus entitle individ-uals to have their European rights applied in national courts. However, the Court subjected this finding to two limitations: one temporal, one normative. Direct effect would only arise *after* a Member State had failed properly to "implement" the directive, and then only in relation to the State authorities themselves. The second limitation is known as the

---

[46] On the complex case law, see: R. Schütze, *European Union Law* (Cambridge University Press, 2015), Chapter 13 – Section 1 (a).

[47] For this view, see L.-J. Constantinesco, *Das Recht der Europäischen Gemeinschaften* (Nomos, 1977), 614.

"no-horizontal-direct-effect rule". And while this constitutional rule has been confirmed, it has itself been limited and qualified.

(a) Direct Effect of Directives: Conditions and Limits

That directives could directly give rise to rights that individuals could claim in national courts was accepted in *Van Duyn* v. *Home Office*.[48] The case concerned a Dutch secretary, whose entry into the United Kingdom had been denied on the ground that she was a member of the Church of Scientology. Britain had tried to justify this limitation on the free movement of persons by reference to an express derogation that allowed such restrictions on grounds of public policy and public security.[49] However, in an effort to harmonize national derogations from free movement, the Union had adopted a directive according to which "[m]easures taken on grounds of public policy or of public security shall be based exclusively on the personal conduct of the individual concerned".[50] This outlawed national measures that limited free movement for generic reasons, such as membership of a disliked organization. Unfortunately, the United Kingdom had not "implemented" the directive into national law. Could Van Duyn nonetheless directly invoke the directive against the British authorities? The Court of Justice found that this was possible by emphasizing the distinction between direct applicability and direct effect:

> [B]y virtue of the provisions of Article [288] regulations are directly applicable and, consequently, may by their very nature have direct effects, it does not follow from this that other categories of acts mentioned in that Article can never have similar effects. It would be incompatible with the binding effect attributed to a directive by Article [288] to exclude, in principle, the possibility that the obligation which it imposes may be invoked by those concerned. In particular, where the [Union] authorities have, by directive, imposed on Member States the obligation to pursue a particular course of conduct, the useful effect of such an act would be weakened if the individuals were prevented from relying on it before their national courts and if the latter were prevented from taking it into consideration as an element of [European] law. Article [267], which empowers national courts

---

[48] *Van Duyn* v. *Home Office*, Case 41/74 (supra n. 34).   [49] Article 45(1) and (3) TFEU.

[50] Article 3(1) Directive 64/221 on the coordination of special measures concerning the movement and residence of foreign nationals which are justified on grounds of public policy, public security or public health, OJ (English Special Edition): Chapter 1963–1964/117.

> to refer to the Court questions concerning the validity and interpretation of all acts of the [Union] institutions, without distinction, implies furthermore that these acts may be invoked by individuals in the national courts.[51]

The Court – rightly – emphasized the distinction between direct applicability and direct effect, yet – wrongly – defined the relationship between these two concepts in order to justify its conclusion. To brush aside the textual argument that regulations are directly applicable while directives are not, it wrongly alluded to the idea that direct effect without direct application was possible.[52] And the direct effect of directives was justified by three different and distinct arguments. First, to exclude direct effect would be incompatible with the "binding effect" of directives. Second, their "useful effect" would be weakened if individuals could not invoke them in national courts. Third, since the preliminary reference procedure did not exclude directives, the latter must be capable of being invoked in national courts.

What was the constitutional value of these arguments? Argument one is a sleight of hand: the fact that a directive is not binding in *national law* is not "incompatible" with its binding effect under *international law*. The second argument is strong, but not of a legal nature: to enhance the useful effect of a rule by making it more binding is a political argument. Finally, the third argument only begs the question: while it is true that the preliminary reference procedure generically refers to all "acts of the institutions", it could be argued that only those acts that are directly effective can be referred. The decision in *Van Duyn* was right, but sadly without reason.

The lack of a convincing *legal* argument to justify the direct effect of directives soon prompted the Court to propose a fourth argument. "A Member State which has not adopted the implementing measures required by the Directive in the prescribed periods may not rely, as against individuals, on its own failure to perform the obligations which the directive entails."[53] This fourth reason has become known as the "estoppel

---

[51] *Van Duyn*, Case 41/74 (supra n. 34), para. 12.

[52] In the words of J. Steiner: "How can a law be enforceable by individuals within a Member State if it is not regarded as incorporated in that State?" (J. Steiner, "Direct Applicability in EEC Law – A Chameleon Concept", 98 (1982) *Law Quarterly Review*, 229–48 at 234). The direct effect of a directive presupposes its direct application. And indeed, ever since *Van Gend en Loos*, all directives must be regarded as directly applicable (see S. Prechal, *Directives in EC Law* (Oxford University Press, 2005), 92 and 229).

[53] *Ratti*, Case 148/78, [1979] ECR 1629, para. 22.

argument" – acknowledging its intellectual debt to English "equity" law. A Member State that fails to implement its European obligations is "estopped" from invoking that failure as a defence, and individuals are consequently and collaterally entitled to rely on the directive as against the State. Unlike the three original arguments, this fourth argument is *State*-centric. It locates the rationale for the direct effect of directives not in the nature of the instrument itself, but in the behaviour of the State.

This (behavioural) rationale would result in two important limitations on the direct effect of directives. Even if provisions within a directive were "unconditional and sufficiently precise" "those provisions may [only] be *relied upon by an individual against the State* where that State fails to implement the Directive in national law *by the end of the period prescribed or where it fails to implement the directive correctly*".[54] This direct effect test for directives differed from that for ordinary Union law, as it added a temporal and a normative limitation. *Temporally*, the direct effect of directives could only arise after the failure of the State to implement the directive had occurred. Thus, before the end of the implementation period granted to Member States, no direct effect can take place. And even once this temporal condition has been satisfied, the direct effect would operate only as against the State. This *normative* limitation on the direct effect of directives has become famous as the "no-horizontal-direct-effect rule".

(b) The No-Horizontal-Direct-Effect Rule

The Court's jurisprudence of the 1970s had extended the direct effect of Union law to directives. An individual could claim her European rights against a State that had failed to implement a directive into national law. This situation was one of "vertical" direct effect. Could an individual equally invoke a directive against another private party? This "horizontal" direct effect existed for direct Union law; yet should it be extended to directives? The Court's famous answer is a resolute "no": directives could not have horizontal direct effects.

The "no-horizontal-direct-effect rule" was first expressed in *Marshall*.[55] The Court based its negative conclusion on a textual argument:

---

[54] *Kolpinghuis Nijmegen BV*, Case 80/86, [1987] ECR 3969, para. 7 (emphasis added).
[55] *Marshall* v. *Southampton and South-West Hampshire Area Health Authority*, Case 152/84, [1986] ECR 723.

> [A]ccording to Article [288 TFEU] the binding nature of a directive, which constitutes the basis for the possibility of relying on the directive before a national court, exists only in relation to "each Member State to which it is addressed". It follows that a directive may not of itself impose obligations on an individual and that a provision of a directive may not be relied upon as such against such a person.[56]

The absence of horizontal direct effect was subsequently confirmed in *Dori*.[57] A private company had approached Ms Dori for an English language correspondence course. The contract had been concluded in Milan's busy central railway station. A few days later, she changed her mind and tried to cancel the contract. A right of cancellation had been provided by the European directive on consumer contracts concluded outside business premises,[58] but Italy had not implemented the directive into national law. Could a private party nonetheless directly rely on the unimplemented directive against another private party? The Court was firm:

> [A]s is clear from the judgment in *Marshall* . . . the case-law on the possibility of relying on directives against State entities is based on the fact that under Article [288] a directive is binding only in relation to "each Member State to which it is addressed". That case-law seeks to prevent "the State from taking advantage of its own failure to comply with [European] law" . . . The effect of extending that case-law to the sphere of relations between individuals would be to recognize a power in the [Union] to enact obligations for individuals with immediate effect, whereas it has competence to do so only where it is empowered to adopt regulations. It follows that, in the absence of measures transposing the directive within the prescribed time-limit, consumers cannot derive from the directive itself a right of cancellation as against traders with whom they have concluded a contract or enforce such a right in a national court.[59]

This denial of the direct effect of directives in horizontal situations was grounded in three arguments.[60] First, a textual argument: a directive is binding in relation to each Member State to which it is addressed. But

---

[56] *Ibid.*, para. 48.   [57] *Faccini Dori* v. *Recreb*, Case C-91/92, [1994] ECR I-3325.

[58] Directive 85/577 concerning protection of the consumer in respect of contracts negotiated away from business premises (OJ 1985 L372/31).

[59] *Dori* (supra n. 57), paras. 22–5.

[60] The Court silently dropped the "useful effect argument" as it would have worked towards the opposite conclusion.

had the Court not used this very same argument to establish the direct effect of directives in the first place? Second, the estoppel argument: the direct effect for directives exists to prevent a State from taking advantage of its own failure to comply with European law. And since individuals were not responsible for the non-implementation of a directive, direct effect should not be extended to them. Third, a systematic argument: if horizontal direct effect was given to directives, the distinction between directives and regulations would disappear. This was a weak argument, for a directive's distinct character could be preserved in different ways.[61] In order to bolster its reasoning, the Court added a fourth argument in subsequent jurisprudence: legal certainty.[62] Since directives were not published, they must not impose obligations on those to whom they are not addressed. This argument has lost some of its force,[63] but continues to be very influential today.

All these arguments may be criticized.[64] But the Court of Justice has stuck to its conclusion: directives cannot *directly* impose obligations on individuals. They lack horizontal direct effect. This constitutional rule of European law has nonetheless been qualified by one limitation and one exception.

(c) The Limitation to the Rule: The Wide Definition of State (Actions)

One way to minimize the no-horizontal-direct-effect rule is to maximize the vertical direct effect of directives. The Court has done this by giving extremely extensive definitions to what constitutes the "State", and what constitute "public actions".

---

[61] On this point, see R. Schütze, "The Morphology of Legislative Power in the European Community: Legal Instruments and Federal Division of Powers", 25 (2006) *Yearbook of European Law*, 91.

[62] See *The Queen on the Application of Delena Wells* v. *Secretary of State for Transport, Local Government and the Regions*, C-201/02, [2004] ECR 723, para. 56: "the principle of legal certainty prevents directives from creating obligations for individuals".

[63] The publication of directives is now, in principle, required by Article 297 TFEU.

[64] For an excellent overview of the principal arguments, see P. Craig, "The Legal Effect of Directives: Policy, Rules and Exceptions", 34 (2009) *European Law Review*, 349. But why does Professor Craig concentrate on arguments one and four, instead of paying attention to the strongest of the Court's reasons in the form of argument two?

What public authorities count as the "State"? A minimal definition restricts the concept to a State's central organs. Because they failed to implement the directive, the estoppel argument suggested them to be vertically bound by the directive. Yet the Court has never accepted this consequence, and has endorsed a maximal definition of the State. It thus held that directly effective obligations "are binding upon *all authorities of the Member States*"; and this included "all organs of the administration, including decentralised authorities, such as municipalities",[65] even "constitutionally independent" authorities.[66]

The best formulation of this maximalist approach was given in *Foster*.[67] Was the "British Gas Corporation" – a statutory corporation for developing and maintaining gas supply – part of the British "State"? The Court held this to be the case. Vertical direct effect would apply to any body "whatever its legal form, which has been made responsible, pursuant to a measure adopted by the State, *for providing a public service under the control of the State and has for that purpose special powers* beyond those which result from the normal rules applicable in relations between individuals".[68] This wide definition of the State consequently covers *private* bodies endowed with *public* functions.

This functional definition of the State, however, suggested that only "public acts", that is: acts adopted in pursuit of a public function, would be covered. Yet there are situations where the State acts horizontally like a private person: it might conclude private contracts and employ private personnel. Would these "private actions" be covered by the doctrine of vertical direct effect?

In *Marshall*, the plaintiff argued that the United Kingdom had not properly implemented the Equal Treatment Directive. But could an *employee* of the South-West Hampshire Area Health Authority invoke the direct effect of a directive against this State authority in this horizontal situation? The British government argued that direct effect would only apply

---

[65] *Costanzo SpA* v. *Comune di Milano*, Case 103/88, [1989] ECR 1839, para. 31 (emphasis added).

[66] *Johnston* v. *Chief Constable of the Royal Ulster Constabulary*, Case 222/84, [1986] ECR 1651, para. 49.

[67] *Foster and others* v. *British Gas*, Case C-188/89, [1990] ECR I-3313.

[68] *Ibid.*, para. 20 (emphasis added). For a more recent confirmation of that test, see *Vassallo* v. *Azienda Ospedaliera Ospedale San Martino di Genova et al.*, Case C-180/04, [2006] ECR I-7251, para. 26.

> against a Member State *qua* public authority and not against a Member
> State *qua* employer... As an employer a State is no different from a private
> employer... [I]t would not therefore be proper to put persons employed
> by the State in a better position than those who are employed by a private
> employer.[69]

This was an excellent argument, but the Court would have none of it.
According to the Court, an individual could rely on a directive as against
the State "regardless of the capacity in which the latter is acting, whether
employer or public authority".[70]

Vertical direct effect would thus not only apply to *private* parties exercising public functions, but also to public authorities engaged in *private*
activities.[71] This double extension of the doctrine of vertical direct effect
can be criticized for treating similar situations dissimilarly. For it creates
a discriminatory limitation to the no-horizontal-direct-effect rule.

(d) The Exception to the Rule: Incidental Horizontal Direct Effect

In the two previous situations, the Court respected the rule that directives
could not have direct horizontal effects, but limited the rule's scope of
application. Yet in some cases, the Court has found a directive *directly* to
affect the horizontal relations between private parties. This "incidental"
horizontal effect of directives must, despite some scholastic effort to the
contrary,[72] be seen as an *exception* to the rule. The incidental direct horizontal effect cases violate the rule that directives cannot directly impose
obligations on private parties. The two "incidents" chiefly responsible for
the doctrine of incidental horizontal direct effects are *CIA Security* and
Unilever Italia.

In *CIA Security* v. *Signalson and Securitel*,[73] the Court dealt with
a dispute between three Belgian competitors whose business was the

---

[69] *Marshall*, Case 152/84 (supra n. 55), para. 43.
[70] *Ibid.*, para. 49.   [71] *Ibid.*, para. 51.
[72] This phenomenon has been variously referred to as the "incidental" horizontal effect
of directives (see P. Craig and G. de Búrca, *EU Law* (Oxford University Press, 2007),
296 et seq.); the "horizontal side effects of direct effect" (see Prechal, *Directives in EC
Law* (supra n. 52), 261–70); or the "disguised" vertical effect of directives (M. Dougan,
"The 'Disguised' Vertical Direct Effect of Directives", 59 (2000) *Cambridge Law Journal*,
586–612).
[73] *CIA Security* v. *Signalson and Securitel*, Case C-194/94, [1996] ECR I-2201.

manufacture and sale of security systems. CIA Security had applied to a commercial court for orders requiring Signalson and Securitel to cease libel. The defendants had alleged that the plaintiff's alarm system did not satisfy Belgian security standards. This was indeed the case, but the Belgian legislation itself violated a European notification requirement established by Directive 83/189. But because the European norm was in a directive, this violation could – theoretically – not be invoked in a horizontal dispute between private parties. Or could it? The Court implicitly rejected the no-horizontal-direct-effect rule by holding the notification requirement to be "unconditional and sufficiently precise" and finding that "[t]he *effectiveness of [Union] control will be that much greater if the directive is interpreted as meaning that breach of the obligation to notify constitutes a substantial procedural defect such as to render the technical regulations in question inapplicable to individuals*".[74] CIA Security could thus rely on the directive as against its private competitors. And the national court "must decline to apply a national technical regulation which has not been notified in accordance with the directive".[75] What else was this but horizontal direct effect?

The Court confirmed the decision in *Unilever Italia* v. *Central Food*.[76] In both cases, then, the national courts were indeed required to disapply national legislation in *civil* proceedings between *private* parties. Did CIA Security not "win" a right from the directive to have national legislation disapplied? And did Signalson not "lose" the right to have national law applied? It seems impossible to deny that the directive *did* directly affect the rights and obligations of individuals. It imposed an obligation on the defendants to accept the forfeiting of their national rights. The Court thus *did* create an exception to the principle that a directly effective directive "cannot of itself apply in proceedings exclusively between private parties".[77] However, the exception to the no-horizontal-direct-effect rule has remained an exceptional exception. But even so, there are – strong – arguments for the Court to abandon its constitutional rule altogether.[78]

---

[74] *Ibid.*, para. 48 (emphasis added).   [75] *Ibid.*, para. 55.
[76] *Unilever Italia* v. *Central Food*, Case C-443/98, [2000] ECR I-7535.
[77] *Pfeiffer et al.* v. *Deutsches Rotes Kreuz, Kreisverband Waldshut*, Joined Cases C-397/01 to C-403/01, [2004] ECR I-8835, para. 109.
[78] See Craig, "Legal Effect of Directives" (supra n. 64), 390: "The rationales for the core rule that Directives do not have horizontal direct effect based on the Treaty text, legal certainty and the Regulations/Directives divide are unconvincing."

4. Indirect Effects: The Doctrine of Consistent Interpretation

Norms may have direct and indirect effects. A European provision lacking direct effect may still have certain indirect effects in the national legal orders. The lack of direct effect means exactly that: the norm cannot itself - that is *directly* - be invoked. However, European law may still have indirect effects on the interpretation of national law. For the European Court has created a general duty on national courts (and administrations)[79] to interpret national law as far as possible in light of all European law. The doctrine of consistent interpretation applies as a structural principle to all sources of European law.[80] However, the doctrine has been mainly developed in the context of directives, and many of the cases will thus refer to this particular Union instrument.

The doctrine of consistent interpretation was given an elaborate definition in *Von Colson*:

> [T]he Member States' obligation arising from a Directive to achieve the result envisaged by the Directive and their duty under Article [4(3) TEU] to take all appropriate measures, whether general or particular, to ensure the fulfilment of that obligation, is binding on all the authorities of Member States including, for matters within their jurisdiction, the courts. It follows that, in applying the national law, in particular the provisions of a national law specifically introduced in order to implement [a Directive], national courts are required to interpret their national law in the light of the wording and the purpose of the directive in order to achieve the result referred to in the third paragraph of Article [288].[81]

The duty of consistent interpretation is a duty to achieve the desired result by indirect means. Where a directive is not sufficiently precise to have

---

[79] *Henkel* v. *Deutsches Patent- und Markenamt*, Case C-218/01, [2004] ECR I-1725.

[80] In the - brilliant - summary of Advocate General Tizzano in *Mangold*, Case C-144/04 (supra n. 36), para. 117: "It must first be recalled that the duty of consistent interpretation is one of the 'structural' effects of [European] law which, together with the more 'invasive' device of direct effect, enables national law to be brought into line with the substance and aims of [European] law. Because it is structural in nature, the duty applies with respect to all sources of [European] law, whether constituted by primary or secondary legislation, and whether embodied in acts whose legal effects are binding or not. Even in the case of recommendations, the Court has held, 'national courts *are bound* to take [them] into consideration in order to decide disputes submitted to them'."

[81] *Von Colson and Elisabeth Kamann* v. *Land Nordrhein-Westfalen*, Case 14/83, [1984] ECR 1891, para. 26. Because this paragraph was so important in defining the duty of consistent interpretation, it is sometimes referred to as the "Von Colson Principle".

direct effect, it is – theoretically – addressed to the national legislator. It is the national legislator's prerogative to "concretize" the directive's indeterminate content in line with its own national views. But where the legislator has failed to do so, the task will be partly transferred to the national judiciary. For after the expiry of the implementation period,[82] national courts are under an obligation to "implement" the directive judicially through a "European" interpretation of national law. The duty of consistent interpretation applies regardless of "whether the [national] provisions in question *were adopted before or after the directive*".[83] The duty to interpret national law as far as possible in light of European law thereby extends to all national law – irrespective of whether the national law was intended to implement the directive. However, where domestic law had been specifically enacted to implement the directive, the national courts must even operate under the presumption "that the Member State, following its exercise of the discretion afforded to it under that provision, had the intention of fulfilling entirely the obligations arising from the directive".[84]

The duty of consistent interpretation may lead to the *indirect* implementation of a directive. For it can *indirectly* impose new obligations – both vertically and horizontally. An illustration of the horizontal *indirect* effect of directives can be seen in *Webb*.[85] The case concerned a claim by Mrs Webb against her employer. The latter had hired the plaintiff to replace a pregnant co-worker during her maternity leave. Two weeks after she had started work, Mrs Webb discovered that she was pregnant herself, and was dismissed for that reason. She brought proceedings before the

---

[82] National authorities are not required to interpret their national law in the light of Union directives *before* the expiry of the implementation deadline. After *Adeneler and Others* v. *Ellinikos Organismos Galaktos (ELOG)*, Case C-212/04, [2006] ECR I-6057, there is no room for speculation on this issue: "[W]here a directive is transposed belatedly, the general obligation owed by national courts to interpret domestic law in conformity with the directive exists only once the period for its transposition has expired" (*ibid.*, para. 115). However, once a directive has been adopted, a Member State will be under the (softer) obligation to "refrain from taking any measures liable seriously to compromise the result prescribed" in the directive: see *Inter-Environnement Wallonie ASBL* v. *Région Wallonne*, C-129/96, [1997] ECR 7411, para. 45. This obligation is, however, independent of the doctrine of indirect effects.

[83] *Marleasing* v. *La Comercial Internacional de Alimentación*, Case C-106/89, [1990] ECR I-4135, para. 8 (emphasis added).

[84] *Pfeiffer*, Cases C-397/01 to C-403/01 (supra n. 77), para. 112.

[85] *Webb* v. *EMO Air Cargo*, Case C-32/93, [1994] ECR I-3567.

Industrial Tribunal, pleading sex discrimination. The Industrial Tribunal rejected this on the ground that the reason for her dismissal had not been her sex but her inability to fulfil the primary task for which she had been recruited. The case went on appeal to the House of Lords, which confirmed the interpretation of national law but nonetheless harboured doubts about Britain's European obligations under the Equal Treatment Directive.

On a preliminary reference, the European Court indeed found that there was sex discrimination under the directive and that the fact that Mrs Webb had been employed to replace another employee was irrelevant.[86] On receipt of the preliminary ruling, the House of Lords was thus required to change its previous interpretation of national law. Mrs Webb *won* a right, while her employer *lost* the right to dismiss her. The doctrine of indirect effect thus changed the horizontal relations between two private parties. The duty of consistent interpretation has consequently been said to amount to "*de facto* (horizontal) direct effect of the directive".[87] This *de facto* horizontal effect is however an *indirect* effect. For it operates through the medium of national law.

Are there limits to the indirect effect of directives through the doctrine of consistent interpretation? The duty is very demanding: national courts are required to interpret their national law "*as far as possible, in the light of the wording and the purpose of the directive*".[88] But what will "as far as possible" mean? Should national courts be required to behave as if they were the national legislature? This might seriously undermine the (relatively) passive place reserved for judiciaries in many national constitutional orders. And the European legal order has indeed only asked national courts to adjust the interpretation of national law "in so far as it is given discretion to do so *under national law*".[89] The European Court thus accepts that there exist established national judicial methodologies and has permitted national courts to limit themselves to "the application of interpretative methods recognised by national law".[90] National courts are thus not obliged to "invent" or "import" novel interpretative methods.[91]

---

[86] *Ibid.*, paras. 26–8.   [87] See Prechal, *Directives in EC Law* (supra n. 52), 211.

[88] *Marleasing*, Case C-106/89 (supra n. 83), para. 8 (emphasis added).

[89] *Von Colson*, Case 14/83 (supra n. 81), para. 28 (emphasis added).

[90] *Pfeiffer*, Cases C-397/01 to C-403/01 (supra n. 77), para. 116.

[91] See M. Klammert, "Judicial Implementation of Directives and Anticipatory Indirect Effect: Connecting the Dots", 43 (2006) *Common Market Law Review*, 1251 at 1259. For the opposite view, see Prechal, *Directives in EC Law* (supra n. 52), 213.

However, within the discretion given to the judiciary under national law, the European doctrine of consistent interpretation requires the referring court "to do whatever lies within its jurisdiction, having regard to the whole body of rules of national law".[92]

But there are also European limits to the duty of consistent interpretation. The Court has clarified that the duty "is limited by the general principles of law which form part of [European] law and in particular the principles of legal certainty and non-retroactivity".[93] This has been taken to imply that the indirect effect of directives cannot aggravate the criminal liability of a private party, as criminal law is subject to particularly strict rules of interpretation.[94] But more importantly, the Court recognizes that the clear and unambiguous wording of a national provision constitutes an absolute limit to its interpretation.[95] National courts are thus not required to interpret national law *contra legem*.[96] The duty of consistent interpretation would thus find a boundary in the clear wording of a provision. In giving indirect effect to Union law, national courts are therefore not required to stretch the medium of national law beyond breaking point. They are only required to *interpret* the text – and not to *amend* it! The latter continues to be the task of the national legislatures – and not the national judiciaries.

The indirect horizontal effect of European law is consequently *limited* through the medium of national law. The duty of consistent interpretation is thus a milder incursion on the legislative powers of the Member States than the doctrine of horizontal *direct* effect. For this doctrine may lead to the doctrine of supremacy, which requires national courts to disapply national laws that conflict with directly effective European rules – regardless of their wording.[97]

---

[92] *Pfeiffer*, Case C-397/01 to C-403/01 (supra n. 77), para. 118.
[93] *Kolpinghuis*, Case 80/86 (supra n. 54), para. 13.
[94] *Arcaro*, Case C-168/95, [1996] ECR I-4705.
[95] *Kücükdeveci* v. *Swedex*, Case C-555/07, [2010] ECR I-365, para. 49.
[96] *Adeneler* v. *Ellinikos*, Case C-212/04 (supra n. 82), para. 110: "It is true that the obligation on a national court to refer to the content of a directive when interpreting and applying the relevant rules of domestic law is limited by general principles of law, particularly those of legal certainty and non-retroactivity, and that obligation cannot serve as the basis for an interpretation of national law *contra legem*."
[97] See Schütze, "Morphology" (supra n. 61), 126: "While the doctrine of consistent interpretation is a method to avoid conflicts, the doctrine of supremacy is a method to *solve* – unavoidable – conflicts."

Conclusion

For a norm to be a legal norm it must be enforceable.[98] The very questioning of the direct effect of European law was thus an "infant disease" of a young legal order.[99] "But now that [European] law has reached maturity, direct effect should be taken for granted, as a normal incident of an advanced constitutional order."[100]

The evolution of the doctrine of direct effect, discussed in this Chapter, indeed mirrors this maturation. Today's test for the direct effect of European law is an extremely lenient test. A provision has direct effect, where it is "unconditional" and thus "sufficiently clear and precise" – two conditions that probe whether a norm can be enforced in court. All sources of European law have been considered capable of producing law with direct effects. And this direct effect normally applies vertically as well as horizontally.

The exception to this rule is the "directive". For directives, the Union legal order prefers their indirect effects.[101] The directive thus represents a form of "background" or "indirect" European law.[102]

---

[98] On the difference between (merely) "moral" and (enforceable) "legal" norms, see: H. L. A. Hart, *The Concept of Law* (Clarendon Press, 1997).

[99] Pescatore, "The Doctrine of 'Direct Effect'" (supra n. 37).

[100] A. Dashwood, "From Van Duyn to Mangold via Marshall: Reducing Direct Effect to Absurdity" [2006/07] 9 *Cambridge Yearbook of European Legal Studies* 81.

[101] Case 80/86, *Kolpinghuis* (supra n. 54), para. 15: "The question whether the provisions of a directive may be relied upon as such before a national court arises only if the Member State concerned has not implemented the directive in national law within the prescribed period or has implemented the directive incorrectly."

[102] Case C-298/89, *Gibraltar* v. *Council*, [1993] ECR I-3605, para. 16 (emphasis added): "normally a form of *indirect regulatory or legislative measure*".

6 (Legal) Supremacy

Introduction

Since European law is directly applicable in the Member States, it must be recognised alongside national law by national authorities. And since European law may have direct effect, it might come into conflict with national law in a specific situation.

Where two legislative wills come into conflict, each legal order must determine *how* these conflicts are to be resolved. The resolution of legislative conflicts requires a hierarchy of norms. Modern federal States typically resolve conflicts between federal and state legislation in favour of the former: federal law is supreme over State law.[1] This "centralised solution" has become so engrained in our constitutional mentalities that we tend to forget that the "decentralized solution" is also possible: local

---

[1] Article VI(2) of the US Constitution, for example, states: "This Constitution, and the Laws of the United States which shall be made in pursuance thereof; and all treaties made, or which shall be made, under the Authority of the United States, *shall be the supreme Law of the Land*."

law may reign supreme over central law.[2] Supremacy and direct effect are thus *not* different sides of the same coin. While the supremacy of a norm implies its direct effect, the direct effect of a norm will *not* imply its supremacy.[3] Each federal legal order must thus determine which law prevails. The simplest supremacy format is one that is absolute: all law from one legal order is superior to all law from the other. Absolute supremacy may however be given to the legal system of the smaller *or* the bigger political community. Between these two extremes lies a range of possible nuances.

When the Union was born, the European Treaties did not expressly state the supremacy of European law.[4] Did this mean that supremacy was a matter to be determined by the national legal orders; or was there a *Union* doctrine of supremacy? We shall see that there are *two* perspectives on the supremacy question. According to the *European* perspective, all Union law prevails over all national law. This "absolute" view is not shared by the Member States. Indeed, according to the *national* perspective, the supremacy of European law is relative: some national law is considered to be beyond the supremacy of European law. National challenges to the absolute supremacy of European law are traditionally expressed in two contexts. First, some Member States – in particular their Supreme Courts – have fought a battle over human rights within the Union legal order. They claim that European law cannot violate *national* fundamental rights. The most famous battle over the supremacy of European law in this context is the conflict between the European Court of Justice and the German Constitutional Court.[5] A similar contestation occurred in a

---

[2] For a long time, the "subsidiarity solution" structured federal relationships during the Middle Ages. Its constitutional spirit is best preserved in the old legal proverb: "Town law breaks county law, county law breaks common law." In the event of a legislative conflict, supremacy was thus given to the rule of the smaller political entity.

[3] We can see direct effect without supremacy in the status given to customary international law in the British legal order.

[4] The Constitutional Treaty *would* have added an express provision (Article I-6 CT): "The Constitution and law adopted by the institutions of the Union in exercising competences conferred on it shall have primacy over the law of the Member States." However, the provision was not taken over by the Lisbon Treaty. Yet the Lisbon Treaty has added Declaration 17 which states: "The Conference recalls that, in accordance with well settled case law of the Court of Justice of the European Union, the Treaties and the law adopted by the Union on the basis of the Treaties have primacy over the law of Member States, under the conditions laid down by the said case law."

[5] The following Chapter concentrates on the jurisprudence of the German Constitutional Court. The latter has long been the most pressing and – perhaps – prestigious national

second context: ultra vires control. In denying the Union an unlimited competence,[6] Member States here insist that they have the last word with regard to the competences of the Union.

This Chapter analyses the supremacy doctrine within the Union legal order in four steps. We shall start with the European doctrine of absolute supremacy in Section 1, before looking at the effect of the principle on national law in Section 2. The subsequent sections, by contrast, analyse the national perspective on the supremacy principle in the form of two challenges to the supremacy of European law. Section 3 explores the national claim asserting the relative supremacy of European law in the context of fundamental human rights. Section 4 extends this analysis to the contested question of who is the ultimate arbiter of the scope of the Union's competences.

1. The European Perspective: Absolute Supremacy

The strong dualist traditions within two of the Member States in 1958 posed a serious legal threat to the unity of the Union legal order.[7] Within dualist States, the status of European law is seen as depending on the national act "transposing" the European Treaties. Where this was a parliamentary act, any subsequent parliamentary acts could – expressly or impliedly – repeal the transposition law. Within the British tradition, this follows from the classic doctrine of parliamentary sovereignty: an "old" parliament cannot bind a "new" one. Any "newer" parliamentary act will thus theoretically prevail over the "older" European Union act. But the supremacy of European law could even be threatened in monist States. For even in monist States, the supremacy of European law will find a limit in the State's constitutional structures.

Would the European legal order insist that its law was to prevail over national law, including national constitutions? The Court of Justice did

court in the Union legal order. For the reaction of the French Supreme Courts, see R. Mehdi, "French Supreme Courts and European Union Law: Between Historical Compromise and Accepted Loyalty", 48 (2011) *Common Market Law Review*, 439. For the views of the Central European Constitutional Courts, see W. Sadurski, "'Solange, Chapter 3': Constitutional Courts in Central Europe – Democracy – European Union", 14 (2008) *European Law Journal*, 1.

[6] On the – strange – (German) notion of *Kompetenz-Kompetenz*, see R. Schütze, *European Union Law* (Cambridge University Press, 2015), Chapter 2 – Section 2(a).

[7] C. Sasse, "The Common Market: Between International and Municipal Law", 75 (1965–6) *Yale Law Journal*, 696–753.

just that in a series of foundational cases. But while the establishment of the supremacy over internal national law was swift, its extension to the international treaties of the Member States was much slower.

(a) Supremacy over Internal Law of the Member States

Frightened by the decentralized solution to the supremacy issue, the Court centralized the question of supremacy by turning it into a principle of European law. In *Costa* v. *ENEL*,[8] the European judiciary was asked whether national legislation adopted *after* 1958 could prevail over the original Treaties. The litigation involved an unsettled energy bill owed by Costa to the Italian "National Electricity Board". The latter had been created by the 1962 Electricity Nationalization Act, which was challenged by the plaintiff as a violation of the 1957 Treaty. The Italian dualist tradition responded that the European Treaty – like ordinary international law – had been transposed by national legislation that could – following international law logic – be derogated by subsequent national legislation. Could the Member States thus unilaterally determine the status of European law in their national legal order? The Court rejected this reading and distanced itself from the international law thesis:

> By contrast with ordinary international treaties, the E[U] Treaty has created its own legal system which, on the entry into force of the Treaty, became an integral part of the legal systems of the Member States and which their courts are bound to apply . . . The integration into the laws of each Member State of provisions which derive from the [Union], and more generally the terms and the spirit of the Treaty, make it impossible for the States, as a corollary, to accord precedence to a unilateral and subsequent measure over a legal system accepted by them on a basis of reciprocity. Such a measure cannot therefore be inconsistent with that legal system. The *executive force* of [European] law cannot vary from one State to another in deference to subsequent domestic laws, without jeopardizing the attainment of the objectives of the Treaty . . . It follows from all these observations that the law stemming from the Treaty, an independent source of law, could not, because of its special and original nature, be overridden by domestic legal provisions, however framed, without being deprived of its character as [European] law and without the legal basis of the [Union] itself being called into question.[9]

European law would reign supreme over national law, since its "executive force" must not vary from one State to another. The supremacy of Union

---

[8] *Costa* v. *ENEL*, Case 6/64, [1964] ECR 585.   [9] *Ibid.*, 593–4.

law could not be derived from classic international law;[10] and for that reason the Court had to declare the Union legal order autonomous from ordinary international law. But, how supreme was European law? The fact that the European *Treaties* prevailed over national legislation did not automatically imply that *all* secondary law would prevail over *all* national law. Would the Court accept a "nuanced" solution for certain national norms, such as national constitutional law?

The European Court never accepted the relative scope of the supremacy doctrine. This was clarified in *Internationale Handelsgesellschaft*.[11] A German administrative court had doubted that European legislation could violate fundamental rights as granted by the German Constitution and raised this very question with the European Court of Justice. Were the fundamental structural principles of national constitutions, including human rights, beyond the scope of Union supremacy? The Court disagreed:

> Recourse to the legal rules or concepts of national law in order to judge the validity of measures adopted by the institutions of the [Union] would have an adverse effect on the uniformity and efficiency of [European] law. The validity of such measures can only be judged in the light of [European] law.[12]

The validity of European laws could thus not be affected – even by the most fundamental norms within the Member States. The Court's vision of

---

[10] Some legal scholars refer to the "supremacy" of international law vis-à-vis national law (see F. Morgenstern, "Judicial Practice and the Supremacy of International Law", 27 (1950) *British Yearbook of International Law*, 42). However, the concept of supremacy is here used in an imprecise way. Legal supremacy stands for the priority of one norm over another. For this, two norms must conflict and, therefore, form part of the same legal order. However, classic international law is based on the sovereignty of States and that implies a dualist relation with national law. The dualist veil protected national laws from being overridden by norms adopted by such "supranational" authorities as the Catholic Church or the Holy Roman Empire. When a State opens up to international law, this "monistic" stance is a *national* choice. International law as such has never imposed monism on a State. Reference to the international law doctrine of *pacta sunt servanda* will here hardly help. The fact that a State cannot invoke its internal law to justify a breach of international obligations is not supremacy. Behind the doctrine of *pacta sunt servanda* stands the concept of legal responsibility: a State cannot – without legal responsibility – escape its international obligations. The duality of internal and international law is thereby maintained: the former cannot affect the latter (as the latter cannot affect the former).

[11] *Internationale Handelsgesellschaft mbH* v. *Einfuhr- und Vorratsstelle für Getreide und Futtermittel*, Case 11/70, [1970] ECR 1125.

[12] *Ibid.*, para. 3.

the supremacy of European law over national law was an absolute one: "The whole of [European] law prevails over the whole of national law."[13]

(b) Supremacy over International Treaties of the Member States

While the European doctrine of supremacy had quickly emerged with regard to national legislation,[14] its extension to international agreements of the Member States was much slower. From the very beginning, the Treaties here recognized an express exception to the supremacy of European law. According to Article 351 TFEU:

> The rights and obligations arising from agreements concluded before 1 January 1958 or, for acceding States, before the date of their accession, between one or more Member States on the one hand, and one or more third countries on the other, shall not be affected by the provisions of the Treaties.[15]

Article 351 codified the "supremacy" of *prior* international agreements of the Member States over conflicting European law. In the event of a conflict between the two, it was European law that could be disapplied *within the national legal orders*. Indeed, Article 351 "would not achieve its purpose if it did not imply a duty on the part of the institutions of the [Union] not to impede the performance of the obligations of Member States which stem from a prior agreement".[16] This was a severe incursion into the integrity of the European legal order, and as such had to be interpreted restrictively.[17]

But would there be internal or external limits to the "supremacy" of prior international treaties of the Member States? The Court indeed clarified that there existed internal limits to the provision. Article 351(1) would

---

[13] R. Kovar, "The Relationship between Community Law and National Law", in EC Commission (ed.), *Thirty Years of Community Law* (EC Commission, 1981), 109, at 112–13.

[14] On the establishment of the *social* acceptance of the doctrine, see: K. Alter, *Establishing the Supremacy of European Law: the Making of an International Rule of Law in Europe* (Oxford University Press, 2001).

[15] Paragraph 1. The provision continues (para. 2): "To the extent that such agreements are not compatible with the Treaties, the Member State or States concerned shall take all appropriate steps to eliminate the incompatibilities established. Member States shall, where necessary, assist each other to this end and shall, where appropriate, adopt a common attitude."

[16] *Attorney General* v. *Burgoa*, Case 812/79, [1980] ECR 2787, para. 9. This was confirmed in *Criminal Proceedings against Jean-Claude Levy*, Case C-158/91, [1993] ECR I-4287.

[17] *The Queen* v. *Secretary of State for Home Department, ex parte Evans Medical Ltd and Macfarlan Smith Ltd*, Case C-324/93, [1995] ECR I-563, para. 32.

only allow Member States to implement their *obligations* towards *third*
states.[18] Member States could thus not rely on Article 351 to enforce their
rights; nor could they rely on the provision to fulfil their international
obligations between themselves.

These internal limitations are complemented by external limitations.
The Court clarified their existence in *Kadi*.[19] While admitting that
Article 351 TFEU would justify derogations from primary Union law,
the Court insisted that the provision "cannot, however, be understood
to authorize any derogation from the principles of liberty, democracy
and respect for human rights and fundamental freedoms enshrined in
Article [2] [T]EU as a foundation of the Union".[20] In the opinion of the
Court, "Article [351 TFEU] may in no circumstances permit any challenge
to the principles that form part of the very foundations of the [Union]
legal order."[21] The Union's constitutional core constituted a limit to the
supremacy of prior international treaties concluded by the Member States.

But should the – limited – application of Article 351 TFEU be extended,
by analogy, to *subsequent* international agreements?[22] The main constitutional thrust behind the argument is that it protects the effective exercise
of the treaty-making powers of the Member States. For "otherwise the
Member States could not conclude any international treaty without running the risk of a subsequent conflict with [European] law".[23] This idea
has been criticized: there would be no reason why the "normal" constitutional principles characterizing the relationship between European
law and unilateral national acts should not also apply to subsequently
concluded international agreements.[24] A middle position has proposed

---

[18] *Commission* v. *Italy*, Case 10/61, [1962] ECR 1, 10–11: "[T]he terms 'rights and obligations' in Article [351] refer, as regards the 'rights', to the rights of third countries and,
as regards the 'obligations', to the obligations of Member States and that, by virtue of
the principles of international law, by assuming a new obligation which is incompatible
with rights held under a prior treaty, a State ipso facto gives up the exercise of these
rights to the extent necessary for the performance of its new obligation."

[19] *Kadi and Al Barakaat International Foundation* v. *Council and Commission*, Case
C-402/05P, [2008] ECR I-6351. The facts of the case were discussed in Chapter 4 –
Section 2 above.

[20] *Ibid.*, para. 303.   [21] *Ibid.*, para. 304.

[22] J. H. F. van Panhuys, "Conflicts between the Law of the European Communities and
Other Rules of International Law", 3 (1965-6) *Common Market Law Review*, 420, 434.

[23] E. Pache and J. Bielitz, "Das Verhältnis der EG zu den völkerrechtlichen Verträgen ihrer
Mitgliedstaaten", 41 (2006), *Europarecht*, 316 at 327 (my translation).

[24] E. Bülow, "Die Anwendung des Gemeinschaftsrechts im Verhältnis zu Drittländern" in
A. Clauder (ed.), *Einführung in die Rechtsfragen der europäischen Integration* (Europa-
Union Verlag, 1972), 52 at 54.

limiting the analogous application of Article 351 to situations where the conflict between post-accession international treaties of Member States and subsequently adopted European legislation was "objectively unforeseeable" and could therefore not be expected.[25]

None of the proposals to extend Article 351 by analogy has however been mirrored in the jurisprudence of the European Court of Justice.[26] The Court has unconditionally upheld the supremacy of European law over international agreements concluded by the Member States after 1958. In light of the potential international responsibility of the Member States, is this a fair constitutional solution? Should it indeed make a difference whether a rule is adopted by means of a unilateral national measure or by means of an international agreement with a third State? Constitutional solutions still need to be found to solve the Member States' dilemma of choosing between the Scylla of liability under the European Treaties and the Charybdis of international responsibility for breach of contract. Should the Union legal order, therefore, be given an *ex ante* authorization mechanism for Member States' international agreements? Or, should the Union share financial responsibility for breach of contract with the Member State concerned?

These are difficult constitutional questions. They await future constitutional answers.

2. Supremacy's "Executive" Nature: Disapplication, not Invalidation

What are the legal consequences of the supremacy of European law over conflicting national law? Must a national court "hold such provisions inapplicable to the extent to which they are incompatible with [European] law", or must it "declare them void"?[27] This question concerns the constitutional effect of the supremacy doctrine in the Member States.

The classic answer to these questions is found in *Simmenthal II*.[28] The issue raised in the national proceedings was this: "What consequences

---

[25] E.-U. Petersmann, "Artikel 234" in H. von der Groeben, J. Thiesing and C.-D. Ehlermann (eds.), *Kommentar zum EWG-Vertrag* (Nomos, 1991), 5725 at 5731 (para. 6).

[26] See *Commission* v. *Belgium & Luxembourg*, Joined Cases C-176 and 177/97, [1998] ECR I-3557.

[27] This very question was raised in *Firma Gebrüder Luck* v. *Hauptzollamt Köln-Rheinau*, Case 34/67, [1968] ECR 245.

[28] *Amministrazione delle Finanze dello Stato* v. *Simmenthal SpA*, Case 106/77, [1978] ECR 629.

flow from the direct applicability of a provision of [Union] law in the event of incompatibility with a subsequent legislative provision of a Member State?"[29] Within the Italian constitutional order, national legislation could be *repealed* solely by Parliament or the Supreme Court. Would lower national courts thus have to wait until this happened and, in the meantime, apply national laws that violate Union laws? Unsurprisingly, the European Court rejected such a reading. Appealing to the "very foundations of the [Union]", national courts were under a direct obligation to give immediate effect to European law. The supremacy of European law meant that "rules of [European] law must be fully and uniformly applied in all the Member States from the date of their entry into force and for so long as they continue in force".[30] But did this mean that the national court had to *repeal* the national law? According to one view, supremacy indeed meant that national courts must declare conflicting national laws void. European law would "break" national law.[31] Yet the Court preferred a milder – second – view:

> [I]n accordance with the *principle of precedence* of [European] law, the relationship between provisions of the Treaty and directly applicable measures of the institutions on the one hand and the national law of the Member States on the other is such that those provisions and measures not only by their entry into force render *automatically inapplicable* any conflicting provision of current national law but – in so far as they are an integral part of, and take precedence in, the legal order applicable in the territory of each of the Member States – also preclude the valid adoption of new legislative measures to the extent to which they would be incompatible with [European] provisions.[32]

Where national measures conflicted with European law, the supremacy of European law would thus not render them void, but only "inapplicable". Not "invalidation" but "disapplication" was required of national courts,

---

[29] *Ibid.*, para. 13.   [30] *Ibid.*, para. 14.

[31] This is the very title of a German monograph by E. Grabitz, *Gemeinschaftsrecht bricht nationales Recht* (L. Appel, 1966). This position was shared by Hallstein: "[T]he supremacy of [European] law means essentially two things: its rules take precedence irrespective of the level of the two orders at which the conflict occurs, and further, [European] law *not only invalidates previous national law but also limits subsequent national legislation*" (W. Hallstein quoted in Sasse, "The Common Market" (supra n. 7), 696–753 at 717 (emphasis added)).

[32] *Simmenthal*, Case 106/77 (supra n. 28), para. 17 (emphasis added).

where European laws came into conflict with pre-existing national laws. Yet, in the above passage, the effect of the supremacy doctrine appeared stronger in relation to future national legislation. Here, the Court said that the supremacy of European law would "preclude the *valid adoption* of new legislative measures to the extent to which they would be incompatible with [European] provisions".[33] Was this to imply that national legislators were not even *competent* to adopt national laws that would run counter to *existing* European law? Were these national laws void *ab initio*?[34]

In *Ministero delle Finanze* v. *IN.CO.GE.'90*,[35] the Commission picked up this second prong of the *Simmenthal* ruling and argued that "a Member State has *no power whatever to [subsequently] adopt* a fiscal provision that is incompatible with [European] law, with the result that such a provision . . . must be treated as *non-existent*".[36] But the European Court of Justice disagreed with this interpretation. Pointing out that *Simmenthal* "did not draw any distinction between pre-existing and subsequently adopted national law",[37] it held that the incompatibility of subsequently adopted rules of national law with European law did not have the effect of rendering these rules non-existent.[38] National courts were thus only under an obligation to disapply a conflicting provision of national law – be it prior *or* subsequent to the Union law.

What will this tell us about the nature of the supremacy doctrine? It tells us that the supremacy doctrine is about the "executive force" of European law. The Union legal order, while integrated with the national legal orders, is not a "unitary" legal order. European law leaves the "validity" of national norms untouched; and will not negate the underlying legislative competence of the Member States. The supremacy principle is thus

---

[33] *Ibid.*, para. 17 (emphasis added).

[34] A. Barav, "Les Effets du Droit Communautaire Directement Applicable", 14 (1978) *Cahiers de Droit Européen*, 265 at 275–6. See also Grabitz, *Gemeinschaftsrecht*, and Hallstein, quoted in Sasse (both supra n. 31).

[35] *Ministero delle Finanze* v. *IN.CO.GE.'90 Srl and others*, Joined Cases C-10-22/97, [1998] ECR I-6307.

[36] *Ibid.*, para. 18 (emphasis added).

[37] Arguably, the *Simmenthal* Court had indeed not envisaged two different consequences for the supremacy principle. While para. 17 (supra text and n. 33) appears to make a distinction depending on whether national legislation existed or not, the operative part of the judgment referred to both variants. It stated that a national court should refuse of its own motion to "apply any conflicting provision of national legislation" (*Simmenthal*, dictum).

[38] *Ministero delle Finanze*, Cases C-10-22/97 (supra n. 35), paras. 20–1.

not addressed to the State legislatures, but to the national executive and judicial branches. (And while in some situations the national *legislator* will be required to amend or repeal national provisions that give rise to legal uncertainty,[39] this secondary obligation is not a direct result of the supremacy doctrine but derives from Article 4(3) TEU.)[40] The executive force of European law thus generally leaves the normative validity of national law intact. National courts are not obliged to "break" national law. They must only not apply it when in conflict with European law in a specific case. Supremacy may then best be characterized as a "remedy". Indeed, it "is the most general remedy which individuals whose rights have been infringed may institute before a national court of law".[41]

This remedial supremacy doctrine has a number of advantages. First, some national legal orders may not grant their (lower) courts the power to invalidate parliamentary laws. The question of who may invalidate national laws is thus left to the national legal order.[42] Second, comprehensive national laws must only be disapplied to the extent to which they conflict with European law.[43] They will remain operable in purely internal situations. Third, once the Union act is repealed, national legislation may become fully operational again.[44]

3. National Challenges I: Fundamental Rights

The European Union is not a federal State in which the sovereignty question is solved. The European Union is a federal union of States; and

---

[39] *Commission* v. *France* Case 167/73, [1974] ECR 359. The Court now appears generally to assume that the presence of a national provision that conflicts with European law will *ipso facto* "give... rise to an ambiguous state of affairs in so far as it leaves persons concerned in a state of uncertainty as to the possibilities available to them relying on [European] law"; see *Commission* v. *Italy*, Case 104/86, [1988] ECR 1799, para. 12.

[40] See e.g. *ibid.*, para. 13.

[41] W. van Gerven, "Of Rights, Remedies and Procedures", 37 (2000) *Common Market Law Review*, 501 at 506.

[42] *Filipiak* v. *Dyrektor Izby Skarbowej w Poznaniu*, Case C-314/08, [2009] ECR I-11049, para. 82: "Pursuant to the principle of the primacy of [European] law, a conflict between a provision of national law and a directly applicable provision of the Treaty is to be resolved by a national court applying [European] law, if necessary by refusing to apply the conflicting national provision, and not by a declaration that the national provision is invalid, the powers of authorities, courts and tribunals in that regard being a matter to be determined by each Member State."

[43] B. de Witte, "Direct Effect, Supremacy and the Nature of the Legal Order" in P. Craig and G. de Búrca (eds.), *The Evolution of EU Law* (Oxford University Press, 1999), 177 at 190.

[44] *Ibid.*

each federal union is characterized by a political dualism. Each citizen is indeed a member of *two* political bodies which will compete for loyalty and, sometimes, the "national" view on a political question may not correspond with the "European" view on the matter.

What happens when the political views of a Member State clash with that of the federal Union? Controversies over the supremacy of federal law are as old as the (modern) idea of federalism.[45] And while the previous sections espoused the European answer to the supremacy doctrine, this absolute vision is – unsurprisingly – not shared by all the Member States. There indeed exists a competing national view – or better: national views – on the supremacy issue. The extreme version of such a national view can be found in the (British) 2011 European Union Act. The latter unambiguously states as follows:

> Directly applicable or directly effective EU law (that is, the rights, powers, liabilities, obligations, restrictions, remedies and procedures referred to in section 2(1) of the European Communities Act 1972) falls to be recognised and available in law in the United Kingdom only by virtue of that Act or where it is required to be recognised and available in law by virtue of any other Act.[46]

A milder national perspective, on the other hand, accepts the supremacy of European law over national *legislation*; yet the supremacy of European law is still relative, since it is granted and limited by national *constitutional* law.

A first national challenge to the absolute supremacy of European law crystallized around *Internationale Handelsgesellschaft*.[47] For after the European Court of Justice had given its absolute view on the supremacy of European law, the case moved back to the German Constitutional Court.[48] And the German Court here defined its perspective on the question. Could

---

[45] R. Schütze, "Federalism as Constitutional Pluralism: Letter from America" in J. Kommarek and M. Avbelj (eds.), *Constitutional Pluralism in the European Union and Beyond* (Hart, 2012), Chapter 8.

[46] 2011 European Union Act, Section 18. For an analysis of the 2011 Act, see: M. Gordon and M. Dougan, "The United Kingdom's European Union Act 2011: 'Who won the bloody war anyway?'", (2012) 37 *European Law Review* 3 esp. at 8: "It may be that, some two decades after the decision of the House of Lords in *Factortame* (No.2), there is some virtue in s.18 reminding use that the domestic supremacy of EU law rests alone on its continuing statutory basis."

[47] *Internationale Handelsgesellschaft*, Case 11/70 (supra n. 11).

[48] BVerfGE 37, 271 *(Solange I (Re Internationale Handelsgesellschaft))*. For an English translation, see [1974] 2 CMLR 540.

national constitutional law, especially national fundamental rights, affect the application of European law in the domestic legal order? Famously, the German Constitutional Court rejected the European Court's vision and replaced it with its counter-theory of the *relative* supremacy of European law. The reasoning of the German Court was as follows: while the German Constitution expressly allowed for the transfer of sovereign powers to the European Union in its Article 24,[49] such a transfer was itself limited by the "constitutional identity" of the German State. Fundamental constitutional structures were thus beyond the supremacy of European law:

> The part of the Constitution dealing with fundamental rights is an *inalienable essential feature of the valid Constitution of the Federal Republic of Germany and one which forms part of the constitutional structure of the Constitution*. Article 24 of the Constitution does not without reservation allow it to be subjected to qualifications. In this, the present state of integration of the [Union] is of crucial importance. The [Union] still lacks ... in particular a codified catalogue of fundamental rights, the substance of which is reliably and unambiguously fixed for the future in the same way as the substance of the Constitution ...
>
> *So long as* this legal certainty, which is not guaranteed merely by the decisions of the European Court of Justice, favourable though these have been to fundamental rights, is not achieved in the course of the further integration of the [Union], the reservation derived from Article 24 of the Constitution applies ... *Provisionally, therefore, in the hypothetical case of a conflict between [European] law and a part of national constitutional law or, more precisely, of the guarantees of fundamental rights in the Constitution, there arises the question of which system of law takes precedence, that is, ousts the other. In this conflict of norms, the guarantee of fundamental rights in the Constitution prevails* so long as the *competent organs of the [Union] have not removed the conflict of norms in accordance with the Treaty mechanism.*[50]

"So long" as the European legal order had not developed an adequate standard of fundamental rights, the German Constitutional Court would "disapply" European law that conflicted with the fundamental rights guaranteed in the German legal order. There were thus *national* limits to the

---

[49] Article 24(1) of the German Constitution states: "The Federation may by a law transfer sovereign powers to international organizations." A new article was subsequently inserted into the German Constitution expressly dealing with the European Union (see Article 23 German Constitution).

[50] *Solange I*, [1974] 2 CMLR 540 at 550-1 (paras. 23–4, emphasis added).

supremacy of European law. However, these national limits were also *relative,* as they depended on the evolution and nature of European law. This was the very essence of the "so-long" formula. For once the Union legal order had developed equivalent human rights guarantees, the German Constitutional Court would no longer challenge the supremacy of European law.

The Union legal order did indeed subsequently develop extensive human rights bill(s),[51] and the dispute over the supremacy doctrine was significantly softened in the aftermath of a second famous European case with a national coda. In *Wünsche Handelsgesellschaft,*[52] the German Constitutional Court not only recognized the creation of "substantially similar" fundamental right guarantees, it drew a remarkably self-effacing conclusion from this:

> In view of those developments it must be held that, *so long* as the European [Union], and in particular in the case law of the European Court, generally ensures an effective protection of fundamental rights as against the sovereign powers of the [Union] which is to be regarded as substantially similar to the protection of fundamental rights required unconditionally by the Constitution, and in so far as they generally safeguard the essential content of fundamental rights, the Federal Constitutional Court will no longer exercise its jurisdiction to decide on the applicability of secondary [Union] legislation cited as the legal basis for any acts of German courts or authorities within the sovereign jurisdiction of the Federal Republic of Germany, and it will no longer review such legislation by the standard of the fundamental rights contained in the Constitution[.][53]

This judgment became known as "So-Long II", for the German Constitutional Court had again recourse to this famous formulation in determining its relationship with European law. But importantly, this time, the "so-long" condition was inverted. The German Court promised not to question the supremacy of European law "so long" as the latter guaranteed substantially similar fundamental rights to those recognized by the German constitution. This was not an absolute promise to respect the absolute supremacy of European law, but a result of the Court's own relative

---

[51] On this point, see Chapter 4 above.
[52] BVerfGE 73, 339 *(Solange II (Re Wünsche Handelsgesellschaft)).* For an English translation, see: [1987] 3 CMLR 225.
[53] *Ibid.,* 265 (para. 48) (emphasis added).

supremacy doctrine having been fulfilled. "So-Long II" thus only refined the national perspective on the limited supremacy of European law in "So-Long I".

4. National Challenges II: Competence Limits

With the constitutional conflict over fundamental rights (temporarily) settled, a second concern emerged: the ever-growing competences of the European Union.

Who was to control and limit the scope of European law? Was it enough to have the *European* legislator centrally controlled by the *European* Court of Justice? Or should the national constitutional courts be entitled to a decentralized ultra vires review? The European view on this is crystal clear: national courts cannot disapply – let alone invalidate – European law.[54] Yet unsurprisingly, this absolute view has not been shared by all Member States. And it was again the German Constitutional Court that set the tone and the vocabulary of the academic debate. The ultra vires question was at the heart of its (in)famous *Maastricht Decision* and would be refined in *Honeywell*.

The German Court set out its ultra vires doctrine in *Maastricht*.[55] Starting from the premise that the European Treaties adhere to the principle of conferred powers, the Court found that the Union ought not to be able to extend its own competences. While the Treaties allowed for teleological interpretation, there existed a clear dividing line "between a legal development within the terms of the Treaties and a making of legal rules which breaks through its boundaries and is not covered by valid Treaty law".[56] This led to the following conclusion:

> Thus, if European institutions or agencies were to treat or develop the Union Treaty in a way that was no longer covered by the Treaty in the form that is the basis for the Act of Accession, the resultant legislative

---

[54] On this point see Section 1 above, and in particular the *Foto-Frost* doctrine, according to which only the Court of Justice of the European Union can judicially review Union acts (see: *Foto-Frost* v. *Hauptzollamt Lübeck-Ost*, Case 314/85, [1987] ECR 4199).

[55] BVerfGE 89, 155 *(Maastricht Decision)*. For an English translation, see [1994] 1 CMLR 57.

[56] *Ibid.*, 105 (para. 98).

instruments would not be legally binding within the sphere of German sovereignty. The German state organs would be prevented for constitutional reasons from applying them in Germany. Accordingly the Federal Constitutional Court will review legal instruments of European institutions and agencies to see whether they remain within the limits of the sovereign rights conferred on them or transgress them...

Whereas a dynamic extension of the existing Treaties has so far been supported on the basis of an open-handed treatment of Article [352] of the [FEU] Treaty as a "competence to round-off the Treaty" as a whole, and on the basis of considerations relating to the "implied powers" of the [Union], and of Treaty interpretation as allowing maximum exploitation of [Union] powers ("effet utile"), in future it will have to be noted as regards interpretation of enabling provisions by [Union] institutions and agencies that the Union Treaty as a matter of principle distinguishes between the exercise of a sovereign power conferred for limited purposes and the amending of the Treaty, so that its interpretation may not have effects that are equivalent to an extension of the Treaty. Such an interpretation of enabling rules would not produce any binding effects for Germany.[57]

The German Constitutional Court thus threatened to disapply European law that it considered to have been adopted ultra vires.

This national review power was subsequently confirmed.[58] Yet, the doctrine was limited and refined in *Honeywell*.[59] The case resulted from a constitutional complaint that targeted the European Court's ruling in *Mangold*.[60] The plaintiff argued that the European Court's "discovery" of a European principle that prohibited discrimination on grounds of age was ultra vires as it read something into the Treaties that was not there. In its decision, the German Constitutional Court confirmed its relative supremacy doctrine. It claimed the power to disapply European law that it

---

[57] *Ibid.*, 105 (para. 99).

[58] BVerfGE 123, 267 *(Lisbon Decision)*. For an English translation, see [2010] 3 CMLR 276. The Court here added a third sequel to its "So-Long" jurisprudence *(ibid.*, 343): "As long as, and insofar as, the principle of conferral is adhered to in an association of sovereign states with clear elements of executive and governmental co-operation, the legitimation provided by national parliaments and governments complemented and sustained by the directly elected European Parliament is sufficient in principle."

[59] 2 BvR 2661/06 *(Re Honeywell)*. For an English translation, see [2011] 1 CMLR 1067. For a discussion of the case, see M. Paydandeh, "Constitutional Review of EU Law after *Honeywell*: Contextualizing the Relationship between the German Constitutional Court and the EU Court of Justice", 48 (2011), *Common Market Law Review*, 9.

[60] *Mangold* v. *Helm*, Case C-144/04, [2005] ECR I-9981.

considered not to be covered by the principle of conferral. The principle of supremacy was thus not unlimited.[61] However, reminiscent of its judicial deference in *So-Long II*, the Court accepted a presumption that the Union would generally act within the scope of its competences:

> If each Member State claimed to be able to decide through their own courts on the validity of legal acts by the Union, the primacy of application could be circumvented in practice, and the uniform application of Union law would be placed at risk. If however, on the other hand the Member States were completely to forgo ultra vires review, disposal of the treaty basis would be transferred to the Union bodies alone, even if their understanding of the law led in the practical outcome to an amendment of a Treaty or an expansion of competences. That in the borderline cases of possible transgression of competences on the part of the Union bodies – which is infrequent, as should be expected according to the institutional and procedural precautions of Union law – the [national] constitutional and the Union law perspective do not completely harmonise, is due to the circumstance that the Member States of the European Union also remain the masters of the Treaties...
>
> Ultra vires review by the Federal Constitutional Court can moreover *only be considered if it is manifest* that acts of the European bodies and institutions have taken place outside the transferred competences. A breach of the principle of conferral is only manifest if the European bodies and institutions have transgressed the boundaries of their competences *in a manner specifically violating the principle of conferral*, the breach of competences is in other words sufficiently qualified. This means that the act of the authority of the European Union *must be manifestly in violation of competences* and that the impugned act is highly significant in the structure of competences between the Member States and the Union with regard to the principle of conferral and to the binding nature of the statute under the rule of law.[62]

This limits the national review of European law to "specific" and "manifest" violations of the principle of conferral. There was thus a presumption that the Union institutions would generally act intra vires; and only for clear and exceptional violations would the German Constitutional Court

---

[61] *Honeywell* [2011] 1 CMLR 1067 at 1084: "Unlike the primacy of application of federal law, as provided for by Article 31 of the Basic Law for the German legal system, the primacy of application of Union law cannot be comprehensive." (It is ironic that this is said by the German Federal(!) Constitutional Court.)

[62] *Ibid.*, 1085–6 (paras. 42 and 46 (emphasis added)).

challenge the supremacy of European law. This has – so far – never happened. But even if the German court's behaviour was again "all bark and no bite",[63] the very speech act of articulating national limits to the supremacy of European law was an expression of the continued existence of a dual or plural perspective on the locus of sovereignty in the European Union. It proves the continued existence of two political levels that compete for the loyalty of their citizens. Sovereignty within the Union thus continues to be contested.[64]

Conclusion

The doctrine of direct effect demands that a national court *applies* European law. And the doctrine of supremacy demands that a national court *disapplies* national law that conflicts with European law.

For the European legal order, the absolute supremacy of European law means that all Union law prevails over all national law. The absolute nature of the supremacy doctrine is, however, contested by the Member States. While they generally acknowledge the supremacy of European law, they have insisted on national constitutional limits. Is this relative nature of supremacy a "novelty" or "aberration"?[65] This view

---

[63] C. U. Schmid, "All Bark and No Bite: Notes on the Federal Constitutional Court's 'Banana Decision'", 7 (2001) *European Law Journal*, 95.

[64] In its *"Lisbon Decision"*, the German Constitutional Court even added a third constitutional limit to European integration: the "State identity limit". Claiming that European unification could not be achieved in such a way "that not sufficient space is left to the Member States for the political formation of the economic, cultural and social living conditions", the Court identified "[e]ssential areas of democratic formative action". "Particularly sensitive for the ability of a constitutional state to democratically shape itself are decisions on substantive and formal criminal law (1), on the disposition of the monopoly on the use of force by the police within the state and by the military towards the exterior (2), fundamental fiscal decisions on public revenue and public expenditure, the latter being particularly motivated, *inter alia,* by social policy considerations (3), decisions on the shaping of living conditions in a social state (4) and decisions of particular cultural importance, for example on family law, the school and education system and on dealing with religious communities (5)." (See *ibid.,* paras. 249 and 252.)

[65] See N. Walker, 'The Idea of Constitutional Pluralism' [2002] 65 *Modern Law Review* 317 at 338. This – "Eurocentric" – view shockingly ignores the American experience, in which the Union and the States were seen to have "constitutional" claims and in which the "Union" was – traditionally – not (!) conceived in statist terms (see E. Zoeller, "Aspects Internationaux du Droit Constitutionnel. Contribution à la Théorie de la Féderation d'états", [2002] 194 *Recueil des Cours de l'Académie de la Haye* 43).

is introverted and unhistorical when compared with the constitutional experiences of the United States.[66] Indeed, the normative ambivalence surrounding the supremacy principle in the European Union is part and parcel of Europe's *federal* nature.[67]

---

[66] Schütze, "Federalism as Constitutional Pluralism" (supra n. 45).
[67] On this point, see: R. Schütze, *European Union Law* (Cambridge University Press, 2015), Chapter 2.

Introduction

National courts are the principal judicial enforcers of European law. "Ever since *Van Gend en Loos* the Court has maintained that it is the task of the national courts to protect the rights of individuals under [Union] law and to give full effect to [Union] law provisions."[1] Indeed, whenever European law is directly effective, national courts must apply it; and wherever a Union norm comes into conflict with national law, each national court must disapply the latter. The Union legal order thereby insists that nothing within the national judicial system must prevent national courts from

---

[1] S. Prechal, "National Courts in EU Judicial Structures" (2006) 25 *Yearbook of European Law* 429.

exercising their functions as "guardians" of the European judicial order.[2] In *Simmenthal*,[3] the Court thus held that each national court must be able to disapply national law – even where the national judicial system traditionally reserves that power to a central constitutional court:

> [E]very national court must, in a case within its jurisdiction, apply [Union] law in its entirety and protect rights which the latter confers on individuals and must accordingly set aside any provision of national law which may conflict with it, whether prior or subsequent to the [Union] rule. Accordingly any provision of a national legal system and any legislative, administrative or judicial practice which might impair the effectiveness of [European] law by withholding from the national court having jurisdiction to apply such law the power to do everything necessary at the moment of its application to set aside national legislative provisions which might prevent [Union] rules from having full force and effect are incompatible with those requirements which are the very essence of [Union] law.[4]

Functionally, the direct effect (and supremacy) of European law thus transforms every single national court into a "European" court. This decentralized system differs from the judicial system in the United States in which the application of federal law is principally left to "federal" courts. Federal courts here apply federal law, while State courts apply State law. The European system, by contrast, is based on a philosophy of cooperative federalism: *all* national courts are entitled and obliged to apply European law to disputes before them. In opting for the decentralized judicial enforcement via State courts, the EU judicial system comes thereby close to German judicial federalism; yet unlike the latter, State courts are

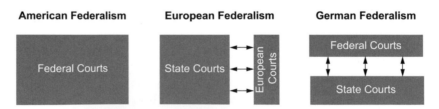

Figure 7.1 Judicial Federalism in Comparative Perspective

---

[2] Opinion 1/09 (Draft Agreement on the Creation of European and Community Patent Court) (2011) ECR I-1137, para. 66.

[3] Case 106/77, *Amministrazione delle Finanze dello Stato* v. *Simmenthal* [1978] ECR 629.

[4] *Ibid.*, paras. 21–2. For a recent confirmation, see e.g. Joined Cases C-188–9/10, *Melki & Abdeli* EU: C: 2010: 363, esp. para. 44.

not hierarchically subordinated. Indeed, there is no compulsory appeal procedure from the national to the European Courts; and the relationship between national courts and the European Court is thus based on their *voluntary* cooperation. National courts are consequently only functionally – but not institutionally – Union courts.

Has the Union therefore had to take State courts as it finds them? The Union has indeed traditionally recognized the "procedural autonomy" of the judicial authorities of the Member States:

> Where national authorities are responsible for implementing [European law] it must be recognised that in principle this implementation takes place with due respect for the forms and procedures of national law.[5]

This formulation has become known as the principle of "national procedural autonomy".[6] It essentially means that in the judicial enforcement of European law, the Union "piggybacks" on the national judicial systems.[7] Yet the danger of such "piggybacking" is that there is a *European right* but no *national remedy* to enforce that right.

But rights without remedies are "pie in the sky": a metaphysical meal. Each right should have its remed(ies);[8] and for that reason, the autonomy of national enforcement procedures was never absolute. The Union has indeed imposed a number of obligations on national courts. The core duty governing the decentralized enforcement of European law by national courts is thereby rooted in Article 4(3) TEU: the duty of "sincere cooperation".[9] It is today complemented by Article 19(1), which states:

---

[5] Case 39/70, *Norddeutsches Vieh- und Fleischkontor GmbH* v. *Hauptzollamt Hamburg-St. Annen* [1971] ECR 49, para. 4.

[6] For a criticism of the notion, see C. N. Kakouris, "Do the Member States Possess Judicial Procedural 'Autonomy'?" (1997) 34 *Common Market Law Review* 1389.

[7] K. Lenaerts *et al.*, *EU Procedural Law* (Oxford University Press, 2014), 107.

[8] Remedies might be said to fall into two broad categories. *Ex ante* remedies are to prevent the violation of a right (interim relief, injunctions), while *ex post* remedies are used to "remedy" a violation that has already occurred (damages liability). On the many (unclear) meanings of "remedy", see P. Birks, "Rights, Wrongs, and Remedies" (2000) 20 *Oxford Journal of Legal Studies* 1 at 9 et seq.

[9] Article 4(3) TEU states: "Pursuant to the principle of sincere cooperation, the Union and the Member States shall, in full mutual respect, assist each other in carrying out tasks which flow from the Treaties. The Member States shall take any appropriate measure, general or particular, to ensure fulfilment of the obligations arising out of the Treaties or resulting from the acts of the institutions of the Union. The Member States shall facilitate the achievement of the Union's tasks and refrain from any measure which could jeopardise the attainment of the Union's objectives."

"Member States shall provide remedies sufficient to ensure effective legal protection in the fields covered by Union law."

But what does this mean? And to what extent does it limit the procedural autonomy of the Member States? The European Court has derived two concrete obligations on national courts: the principle of equivalence and the principle of effectiveness.[10] Both principles have led to a significant *judicial* harmonization of national procedural laws, and this Chapter analyses their evolution in Section 1. Section 2 then turns to a second – and very intrusive – incursion of the procedural autonomy of the Member States: the liability principle. Had the principles of equivalence and effectiveness relied on the existence of *national* remedies for the enforcement of European law, this principle establishes a *European* remedy. An individual could here, under certain conditions, claim compensatory damages resulting from a breach of European law.

Finally, we shall explore an interpretative bridge that exists between national courts and the European Court of Justice. For in the absence of an "institutional" connection between the European Court and the national courts, how has the Union legal order guaranteed a degree of uniformity in the decentralized judicial enforcement of European law? From the very beginning, the Treaties contained a mechanism for the interpretative assistance of national courts: the preliminary reference procedure. The general and specific aspects of the procedure will be discussed in Sections 3 and 4. Suffice to say here that the European Court is only *indirectly* involved in the judgment delivered by the national court. It cannot "decide" the case, as the principal action continues to be a "national action".

1. National Remedies: Equivalence and Effectiveness

The general duty governing the decentralized enforcement of European law by national courts is Article 4(3) TEU.[11] This duty of "sincere cooperation" has traditionally imposed two limitations on the procedural autonomy of the Member States: the principle of equivalence and the principle of effectiveness. The classic expression of both limitations can be found in *Rewe*:

---

[10] The Court expressly refers to both principles: see Joined Cases C-392/04 and C-422/04 *i-21 Germany & Arcor* v. *Germany*, [2006] ECR I-8559, para. 57.

[11] For the text of Article 4(3) TEU, see supra n. 9.

> [I]n the absence of [European] rules on this subject, it is for the domestic legal system of each Member State to designate the courts having jurisdiction and to determine the procedural conditions governing actions at law intended to ensure the protection of the rights which citizens have from the direct effect of [European] law, it being understood that such conditions cannot be less favourable than those relating to similar actions of a domestic nature . . . In the absence of such measures of harmonization the right conferred by [European] law must [thus] be exercised before the national courts in accordance with the conditions laid down by national rules. The position would be different only if the [national rules] made it impossible in practice to exercise the rights which the national courts are obliged to protect.[12]

The procedural autonomy of the Member States is thus *relative*. First, national procedural rules cannot make the enforcement of European rights less favourable than the enforcement of similar national rights. This prohibition of procedural discrimination is the principle of equivalence. Second, national procedural rules – even if not discriminatory – ought not to make the enforcement of European rights "impossible in practice". This would become known as the principle of effectiveness. Both principles have led to a *judicial* harmonization of national procedural laws, and this third Section analyses their evolution.

(a) The Equivalence Principle

The idea behind the principle of equivalence is straightforward: national procedures and remedies for the enforcement of European rights "cannot be less favourable than those relating to similar actions of a domestic nature".[13] When applying European law, national courts must act *as if* they were applying national law. National procedures and remedies must not discriminate between national and European rights. The principle of equivalence will consequently not affect the substance of national remedies. It only requires the formal extension of those remedies to "similar" or "equivalent" actions under European law.

The logic of non-discrimination requires that similar actions be treated similarly. But what are "equivalent" or "similar" actions? The devil always

---

[12] *Rewe*, Case 33/76, [1976] ECR 1989, para. 5. See also *Comet BV* v. *Produktschap voor Siergewassen*, Case 45/76, [1976] ECR 2043. For the modern version, see *Peterbroeck, Van Campenhout & Cie* v. *Belgian State*, Case C-312/93, (1995) ECR I-4599.

[13] *Rewe*, Case 33/76 (supra n. 12), para. 5.

lies in the detail, and much case law on the equivalence principle has concentrated on this devilish question. In *Edis*,[14] a company had been required to pay a registration charge. Believing the charge to be contrary to European law, the plaintiff applied for a refund from the State that was rejected by the Italian courts on the ground that the limitation period for such refunds had expired. However, Italian law recognized various limitation periods – depending on whether the refund was due to be paid by public or private parties. The limitation period for public authorities was shorter than that for private parties. And this posed the following question: was the national court entitled to simply extend the national public refund procedure to charges in breach of European law; or was it required to apply the more generous *private* refund procedure? The Court answered as follows:

> Observance of the principle of equivalence implies, for its part, that the procedural rule at issue applies without distinction to actions alleging infringements of [Union] law and to those alleging infringements of national law, with respect to the same kind of charges or dues. *That principle cannot, however, be interpreted as obliging a Member State to extend its most favourable rules governing recovery under national law to all actions for repayment of charges or dues levied in breach of [European] law.* Thus, [European] law does not preclude the legislation of a Member State from laying down, alongside a limitation period applicable under the ordinary law to actions between private individuals for the recovery of sums paid but not due, special detailed rules, which are less favourable, governing claims and legal proceedings to challenge the imposition of charges and other levies. The position would be different only if those detailed rules applied solely to actions based on [European] law for the repayment of such charges or levies.[15]

In the present case, the "equivalent" action was thus to be based on the national remedies that existed for refunds from *public* bodies. The existence of a more favourable limitation period for refunds from private parties was irrelevant, since the equivalence principle only required treating like actions alike. And the "like" action in this case was the refund procedure applicable to a public body. The national procedural rules thus did not violate the principle of equivalence.

---

[14] *Edilizia Industriale Siderurgica Srl (Edis)* v. *Ministero delle Finanze*, Case C-231/96, [1998] ECR I-4951.

[15] *Ibid.*, paras. 36–7 (emphasis added).

However, matters might not be so straightforward.[16] For the equivalence principle requires national courts to evaluate "whether the actions concerned are similar as regards their purpose, cause of action and essential characteristics".[17] And this teleological comparability test might require them to look beyond the specific procedural regime for a national right.

(b) The Effectiveness Principle

The power of the effectiveness principle to interfere with the principle of national procedural autonomy was – from the start – much greater. However, the Court's jurisprudence on the principle is disastrously unclear. The best way to analyse the cases is to identify general historical periods and a variety of specific thematic lines.[18] The academic literature on the effectiveness principle thereby typically distinguishes between three periods of evolution. A first period of *restraint* is replaced by a period of *intervention,* which in turn gives way to a period of *balance.*[19]

Each of these periods corresponds to a particular effectiveness standard. The European Court began to develop the principle from a minimal standard. National remedies would solely be found ineffective, where they "made it *impossible* in practice to exercise the rights which the national courts are obliged to protect".[20] With time, the Court however increasingly moved to a maximum standard insisting on the "full effectiveness" of European law.[21] This maximum standard was eventually replaced by a medium standard in a third period.

Originally, the European Court showed much restraint towards the procedural autonomy of the Member States. The Court indeed pursued a

---

[16] *Levez* v. *Jennings (Harlow Pools) Ltd,* Case C-326/96, [1998] ECR I-7835.

[17] *Preston et al.* v. *Wolverhampton Healthcare NHS Trust and Others,* Case C-78/98, [2000] ECR I-3201, para. 57.

[18] For illustrations of this – brilliant and necessary – approach, see M. Dougan, *National Remedies before the Court of Justice: Issues of Harmonisation and Differentiation* (Hart, 2004), Chapters 5 and 6; as well as T. Tridimas, *The General Principles of EU Law* (Oxford University Press, 2006), Chapter 9.

[19] A. Arnull, *The European Union and its Court of Justice* (Oxford University Press, 2006), 268; as well as Dougan, *National Remedies* (supra n. 18) 227, and Tridimas, *General Principles* (supra n. 18), 420 et seq.

[20] *Rewe,* Case 33/76 (supra n. 12), para. 5 (emphasis added).

[21] *The Queen* v. *Secretary of State for Transport, ex parte: Factortame Ltd and others,* Case C-213/89, [1990] ECR I-2433, para. 21.

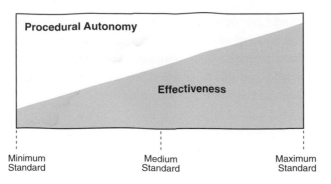

Figure 7.2 Standards of Effectiveness

policy of judicial minimalism.[22] The standard for an "effective remedy" was low and simply required that the national procedures must not make the enforcement of European rights (virtually) impossible. This minimalist approach is exemplified by *Rewe*.[23] In that case, the plaintiff had applied for a refund of monies that had been charged in contravention of the European Treaties. The defendant accepted the illegality of the charges, but counterclaimed that the limitation period for a refund had expired. The Court accepted that the existence of a limitation period did not make the enforcement of European rights impossible and found for the defendant.

In subsequent jurisprudence, the Court however developed a more demanding standard of "effectiveness". In *Von Colson*,[24] two female candidates for becoming warden in an all-male prison had been rejected. The State prison had indisputably discriminated against them on the ground that they were women. Their European right to equal treatment had thus been violated, and the question arose how this violation could be remedied. The remedy under German law restricted the claim for damages to the plaintiffs' travel expenses. Was this an effective remedy for the enforcement of their European rights? The Court here clarified that the effectiveness principle required that the national remedy "be such as to guarantee real and effective judicial protection".[25] The remedy would need to have "a real deterrent effect on the employer", and in the context of a compensation claim this meant that the latter "must in any event be *adequate* in relation to the damage sustained".[26]

---

[22] A. Ward, *Judicial Review and the Rights of Private Parties in EC Law* (Oxford University Press, 2007), 87.

[23] *Rewe*, Case 33/76 (supra n. 12).

[24] *Von Colson and Elisabeth Kamann* v. *Land Nordrhein-Westfalen* Case 14/83, [1984] ECR 1891.

[25] *Ibid.*, para. 23.   [26] *Ibid.* (emphasis added).

The most famous intervention into the procedural autonomy of a Member State in this second period is however to be found in an English case: *Factortame.*[27] The case concerned a violation of the Union's internal market law through a British nationality requirement imposed on fishing vessels. The case went to the House of Lords, and the Lords found that the substantive conditions for granting interim relief were in place, but held "that the grant of such relief was precluded by the old common-law rule that an interim injunction may not be granted against the Crown, that is to say against the government, in conjunction with the presumption that an Act of Parliament is in conformity with [European] law until such time as a decision on its compatibility with that law has been given".[28] Unsure whether this common law rule itself violated the effectiveness principle under European law, the House of Lords referred the case to Luxembourg. And the European Court answered as follows:

> [A]ny provision of a national legal system and any legislative, administrative or judicial practice which might impair the effectiveness of [European] law by withholding from the national court having jurisdiction to apply such law the power to do everything necessary at the moment of its application to set aside national legislative provisions which might prevent, even temporarily, [European] rules from having full force and effect are incompatible with those requirements, which are the very essence of [European] law. It must be added that the *full effectiveness* of [European] law would be just as much impaired if a rule of national law could prevent a court seized of a dispute governed by [European] law from granting interim relief in order to ensure the full effectiveness of the judgment to be given on the existence of the rights claimed under [European] law. It follows that a court which in those circumstances would grant interim relief, if it were not for a rule of national law, is obliged to set aside that rule.[29]

While short of creating a new remedy, this came very close to demanding a maximum standard of effectiveness. Yet the Court soon withdrew from this highly interventionist stance and thereby entered into a third period in the evolution of the effectiveness principle.

In this third period, the Court tried – and still tries – to find a balance between the minimum and the maximum standard of effectiveness.[30]

---

[27] *The Queen* v. *Secretary of State for Transport, ex parte Factortame Ltd and others*, Case C-213/89 (supra n. 21).

[28] *Ibid.*, para. 13.   [29] *Ibid.*, paras. 20–1 (emphasis added).

[30] F. G. Jacobs, "Enforcing Community Rights and Obligations in National Courts: Striking the Balance" in A. Biondi and J. Lonbay (eds.), *Remedies for Breach of EC Law* (Wiley,

The retreat from the second period of high intervention can be seen in *Steenhorst-Neerings*,[31] where the Court developed a distinction between national procedural rules whose effect was to totally *preclude* individuals from enforcing European rights and those national rules that merely *restrict* their remedies.[32] In *Preston*,[33] the Court had to deal with the 1970 Equal Pay Act whose Section 2(4) barred any claim that was not brought within a period of six months following cessation of employment. And instead of concentrating on the "full effectiveness" or "adequacy" of the national remedy, the Court stated that "[s]uch a limitation period does not render impossible *or excessively difficult* the exercise of rights conferred by the [European] legal order and is not therefore liable to strike at the very essence of those rights".[34] The Court here had recourse to a – stronger – alternative to the (minimal) impossibility standard: national procedures that would make the exercise of European rights "excessively difficult" would equally fall foul of the principle of effectiveness. This medium standard lies in between the minimum and the maximum standard.[35]

2. State Liability: The *Francovich* Doctrine

Even if the Court had pushed for a degree of uniformity in the decentralized enforcement of European law via the principles of equivalence and effectiveness, it would still be *national* remedies whose scope or substance was extended. But what would happen if no national remedy

---

1996). See also Dougan, *National Remedies* (supra n. 18), 29: "There has been a definite retreat back towards the orthodox presumption of national autonomy in the provision of judicial protection. But the contemporary principle of effectiveness surely remains more intrusive than the case law of the 1970s and early 1980s."

[31] *Steenhorst-Neerings* v. *Bestuur van de Bedrijfsvereniging voor Detailhandel, Ambachten en Huisvrouwen*, Case C-338/91, [1993] ECR I-5475.

[32] On the distinction, see Ward, *Judicial Review* (supra n. 22), 131. The distinction was elaborated in *Johnson* v. *Chief Adjudication Officer*, Case C-31/90, [1991] ECR I-3723.

[33] *Preston* v. *Wolverhampton*, Case C-78/98 (supra n. 17).

[34] *Ibid.*, para. 34 (emphasis added).

[35] When would this medium standard of effectiveness be violated? Instead of providing hard and fast rules, the Court has come to prefer a contextual test spelled out for the first time in *Peterbroeck*, Case C-312/93 (supra n. 12). In order to discover whether a national procedural rule makes the enforcement of European rights "excessively difficult", the Court analyses each case "by reference to the role of that provision in the procedure, its progress and its special features, viewed as a whole, before the various national instances" (*ibid.*, para. 14).

existed? Would the non-existence of a national remedy not be an absolute barrier to the enforcement of European law? For a long time, the Court appeared to insist that the European Treaties were "not intended to create new remedies in the national courts to ensure the observance of [Union] law other than those already laid down by national law".[36]

In what was perceived as a dramatic turn of events, the European Court renounced this position and proclaimed the existence of a *European* remedy for breaches of European law in *Francovich*.[37] The Court here held that in certain situations the State was liable to compensate losses caused by its violation of European law. This section will look at the birth of the state liability doctrine first, before analysing its conditions.

(a) The Birth of the *Francovich* Doctrine

For a clairvoyant observer there was "little doubt that one future day the European Court will be asked to say, straightforwardly, whether [European] law requires a remedy in damages to be made available in the national courts".[38] This day came on 8 January 1990. On this day, the Court received a series of preliminary questions in *Francovich and others* v. *Italy*.[39]

The facts of the case are memorably sad.[40] Italy had flagrantly flouted its obligations under the Treaty by failing to implement a European directive designed to protect employees in the event of their employer's insolvency.[41] The Directive had required Member States to pass national legislation guaranteeing the payment of outstanding wages. Francovich had been employed by an Italian company, but had hardly received any wages. He brought proceedings against his employer; yet the employer had gone into insolvency, and for that reason Francovich brought a

---

[36] *Rewe Handelsgesellschaft et al.* v. *Hamptzollamt Kiel (Butter-Cruises)*, Case 158/80, [1981] ECR 1805.

[37] *Francovich and Bonifaci et al* v. *Italy*, Joined Cases C-6/90 and C-9/90, [1991] ECR I-5357.

[38] A. Barav, "Damages in the Domestic Courts for Breach of Community Law by National Public Authorities" in H. G. Schermers *et al.* (eds.), *Non-Contractual Liability of the European Communities* (Nijhoff, 1988), 149 at 165.

[39] *Francovich and Bonifaci*, Joined Cases C-6/90 and C-9/90 (supra n. 37).

[40] Opinion of Mr Advocate General Mischo (*ibid.*, para. 1): "Rarely has the Court been called upon to decide a case in which the adverse consequences for the individuals concerned of failure to implement a directive were as shocking as in the case now before us."

[41] The Court had already expressly condemned this failure in *Commission* v. *Italian Republic*, Case 22/87, [1989] ECR 143.

separate action against the Italian State to cover his losses. In the course of these second proceedings, the national court asked the European Court whether the State itself would be obliged to cover the losses of employees. The European Court found that the Directive had left the Member States a "broad discretion with regard to the organization, operation and financing of the guarantee institutions", and it therefore lacked direct effect.[42] It followed that "the persons concerned cannot enforce those rights against the State before the national courts where no implementing measures are adopted within the prescribed period".[43]

But this was not the end of the story! The Court – unhappy with the negative result flowing from the lack of direct effect – continued:

> [T]he principle whereby a State must be liable for loss and damage caused to individuals as a result of breaches of [European] law for which the State can be held responsible is inherent in the system of the Treaty. A further basis for the obligation of Member States to make good such loss and damage is to be found in Article [4(3)] of the Treaty [on European Union], under which the Member States are required to take all appropriate measures, whether general or particular, to ensure fulfilment of their obligations under [European] law. Among these is the obligation to nullify the unlawful consequences of a breach of [European] law. It follows from all the foregoing that it is a principle of [European] law that the Member States are obliged to make good loss and damage caused to individuals by breaches of [European] law for which they can be held responsible.[44]

The European Court here took a qualitative leap in the context of remedies. Up to this point, it could still legitimately be argued that the principle of national procedural autonomy precluded the creation of European remedies as the principles of equivalence and effectiveness solely required the extension of *national* remedies to violations of European law. With *Francovich* the Court clarified that the right to reparation for such violations was "a right founded directly on [European] law".[45] The action for State liability was thus a *European* remedy that had to be made available in the national courts.[46] How did the Court justify this

---

[42] *Francovich and Bonifaci*, Joined Cases C-6/90 and C-9/90 (supra n. 37), para. 25.
[43] *Ibid.*, para. 27.
[44] *Ibid.*, paras. 33–7.   [45] *Ibid.*, para. 41.
[46] On the application of this principle in the United Kingdom, see J. Convery, "State Liability in the United Kingdom after *Brasserie du Pêcheur*", 34 (1997) *Common Market Law Review*, 603.

"revolutionary" result? It had recourse to the usual constitutional sus-
pects: the very nature of the European Treaties and the general duty
under Article 4(3) TEU. A more sophisticated justification was added by a
later judgment. In *Brasserie du Pecheur,*[47] the Court found:

> Since the Treaty contains no provision expressly and specifically govern-
> ing the consequences of breaches of [European] law by Member States, it
> is for the Court, in pursuance of the task conferred on it by Article [19] of
> the [EU] Treaty of ensuring that in the interpretation and application of
> the Treaty the law is observed, to rule on such a question in accordance
> with generally accepted methods of interpretation, in particular by
> reference to the fundamental principles of the [Union] legal system and,
> where necessary, general principles common to the legal systems of the
> Member States. Indeed, it is to the general principles common to the laws
> of the Member States that the second paragraph of Article [340] of the
> [FEU] Treaty refers as the basis of the non-contractual liability of the
> [Union] for damage caused by its institutions or by its servants in the
> performance of their duties. The principle of the non-contractual liability
> of the [Union] expressly laid down in Article [340] of the [FEU] Treaty is
> simply an expression of the general principle familiar to the legal systems
> of the Member States that an unlawful act or omission gives rise to an
> obligation to make good the damage caused. That provision also reflects
> the obligation on public authorities to make good damage caused in the
> performance of their duties.[48]

The principle of State liability was thus rooted in the constitutional traditions common to the Member States and was equally recognized in the
principle of *Union* liability for breaches of European law.[49] There was
consequently a parallel between *State* liability and *Union* liability for tor-
tious acts of public authorities. And this parallelism would have a decisive
effect on the conditions for State liability for breaches of European law.

(b) The Three Conditions for State Liability

Having created the liability principle for State actions, the *Francovich*
Court nonetheless made the principle dependent on the fulfilment of three
conditions:

---

[47] *Brasserie du Pêcheur SA* v. *Bundesrepublik Deutschland* and *The Queen* v. *Secretary
of State for Transport, ex parte Factortame Ltd and others,* Joined Cases C-46/93 and
C-48/93, [1996] ECR I-1029.
[48] *Ibid.,* paras. 27–9.   [49] On this point, see Chapter 8 – Section 4 below.

> The first of those conditions is that the result prescribed by the directive should entail the grant of rights to individuals. The second condition is that it should be possible to identify the content of those rights on the basis of the provisions of the directive. Finally, the third condition is the existence of a causal link between the breach of the State's obligation and the loss and damage suffered by the injured parties. Those conditions are sufficient to give rise to a right on the part of individuals to obtain reparation, a right founded directly on [European] law.[50]

The original liability test was thus as follows: the European Act must have been intended to grant individual rights, and these rights would – even if they lacked direct effect – have to be identifiable.[51] If this was the case, and if European law was breached by a Member State not guaranteeing these rights, any loss that was caused by that breach could be claimed by the individual.[52] On its face, this test appeared to be complete and was thus one of *strict* liability: any breach of an identifiable European right would give rise to State liability. But the Court subsequently clarified that this was *not* the case, for the *Francovich* test was to be confined to the specific context of a flagrant non-implementation of a European Directive.

Drawing on its jurisprudence on *Union* liability, the Court subsequently introduced a more restrictive principle of State liability in *Brasserie du Pêcheur*.[53] The Court here clarified that State liability was to be confined to "sufficiently serious" breaches. To cover up the fact that it had implicitly added a "fourth" condition to its *Francovich* test, the Court replaced the new condition with the second criterion of its "old" test. The new liability test could thus continue to insist on three – necessary and sufficient – conditions, but now read as follows:

---

[50] *Francovich and Bonifaci*, Joined Cases C-6/90 and C-9/90 (supra n. 37) paras. 40–1.

[51] For an analysis of this criterion, see Dougan, *National Remedies* (supra n. 18), 238 et seq. For a case in which the European Court found that a Directive did not grant rights, see *Paul et al.* v. *Germany*, Case C-222/02, [2004] ECR I-9425.

[52] For an analysis of this criterion, see Tridimas, *General Principles* (supra n. 18), 529–33. See particularly *Brinkmann Tabakfabriken GmbH* v. *Skatteministeriet*, Case C-319/96, [1998] ECR I-5255.

[53] *Brasserie du Pêcheur*, Joined Cases C-46/93 and C-48/93 (supra n. 47), para. 42: "The protection of the rights which individuals derive from [European] law cannot vary depending on whether a national authority or a [Union] authority is responsible for the damage." On the constitutional principles governing Union liability, see Chapter 8 – Section 4 below.

> [European] law confers a right to reparation where three conditions are met: the rule of law infringed must be intended to confer rights on individuals; the breach must be sufficiently serious; and there must be a direct causal link between the breach of the obligation resting on the State and the damage sustained by the injured parties.[54]

The Court justified its limitation of State liability to "sufficiently serious" breaches by reference to the wide discretion that Member States might enjoy, especially when exercising legislative powers. The "limited liability" of the legislature is indeed a common constitutional tradition of the Member States and equally applies to the Union legislature. Where legislative functions are concerned, Member States "must not be hindered by the prospect of actions for damages".[55] The special democratic legitimacy attached to parliamentary legislation provided thus an argument against public liability for breaches of private rights, "unless the institution concerned has manifestly and gravely disregarded the limits on the exercise of its powers".[56] And in analysing whether a breach was sufficiently serious in the sense of a "manifest... and grave... disregard", the Court would balance a number of diverse factors,[57] such as the degree of discretion enjoyed by the Member States as well as the clarity of the Union norm breached.

Unfortunately, there are very few hard and fast rules to determine when a breach is sufficiently serious. Indeed, the second criterion of the *Brasserie* test has been subject to much uncertainty. Would the manifest and grave disregard test only apply to the legislative function? The Court appears to have answered this question in *Hedley Lomas*,[58] when dealing

---

[54] *Ibid.*, para. 51.   [55] *Ibid.*, para. 45.

[56] *Ibid.* See also *The Queen* v. *H.M. Treasury, ex parte British Telecommunications*, Case C-392/93, (1996) ECR I-10631, para. 42.

[57] *Brasserie du Pêcheur*, Joined Cases C-46/93 and C-48/93 (supra n. 53), para. 56: "The factors which the competent court may take into consideration include the clarity and precision of the rule breached, the measure of discretion left by that rule to the national or [Union] authorities, whether the infringement and the damage caused was intentional or involuntary, whether any error of law was excusable or inexcusable, the fact that the position taken by a [Union] institution may have contributed towards the omission, and the adoption or retention of national measures or practices contrary to [European] law."

[58] *The Queen* v. *Ministry of Agriculture, Fisheries and Food, ex parte Hedley Lomas*, Case C-5/94, [1996] ECR I-2553.

with the failure of the national *executive* to correctly apply European law. The Court found:

> [W]here, at the time when it committed the infringement, the Member State in question was not called upon to make any legislative choices and had only considerably reduced, or even no, discretion, the mere infringement of [European] law may be sufficient to establish the existence of a sufficiently serious breach[.][59]

While thus affirming that all breaches must be sufficiently serious to trigger State liability, the less discretion, the less limited would the liability of a State be.[60] The Court here seemed to acknowledge two alternatives within the second *Brasserie* condition – depending on whether the State violated European law via its legislative or executive branch. The existence of these two alternatives would find expression in *Larsy*,[61] where the Court found:

> [A] breach of [European] law is sufficiently serious where a Member State, in the exercise of its legislative powers, has manifestly and gravely disregarded the limits on its powers and, secondly, that where, at the time when it committed the infringement, the Member State in question had only considerably reduced, or even no, discretion, the mere infringement of [European] law may be sufficient to establish the existence of a sufficiently serious breach.[62]

For an executive failure, the threshold for establishing State liability is thus much lower than the liability threshold for legislative actions. While the incorrect *application* of a clear European norm by the national executive will incur automatic liability, the incorrect implementation of a directive by the national legislature may not.[63] Nonetheless, the European Court distinguishes the *incorrect* implementation of a directive from its *non*-implementation. The use of a stricter liability regime for legislative *non*-action makes much sense, for the failure of the State cannot be excused by reference to the exercise of legislative discretion. The Court

---

[59] *Ibid.*, para. 28.
[60] *Haim* v. *Kassenzahnärztliche Vereinigung Nordrhein*, Case C-424/97, [2000] ECR I-5123, para. 38.
[61] *Larsy* v. *Institut national d'assurances sociales pour travailleurs indépendants*, Case C-118/00, [2001] ECR I-5063.
[62] *Ibid.*, para. 38.
[63] *Denkavit et al.* v. *Bundesamt für Finanzen*, Cases C-283 and 291-2/94, [1996] ECR I-4845.

has consequently held that the non-implementation of a directive could *per se* constitute a sufficiently serious breach.[64]

3. Preliminary Rulings I: General Aspects

Where national courts encounter problems relating to the interpretation of European law, they can refer "preliminary questions" to the European Court. The questions are "preliminary", since they *precede* the application of European law by the national court. The preliminary rulings procedure constitutes the cornerstone of the Union's judicial federalism. This federalism is *cooperative* in nature: the European Court and the national courts collaborate in the adjudication of a single case.

The procedure for preliminary rulings is set out in Article 267 TFEU, which reads:

> [1] The Court of Justice of the European Union shall have jurisdiction to give preliminary rulings concerning:
>   (a) the interpretation of the Treaties;
>   (b) the validity and interpretation of acts of the institutions, bodies, offices or agencies of the Union.
> [2] Where such a question is raised before any court or tribunal of a Member State, that court or tribunal may, if it considers that a decision on the question is necessary to enable it to give judgment, request the Court to give a ruling thereon.
> [3] Where any such question is raised in a case pending before a court or tribunal of a Member State against whose decisions there is no judicial remedy under national law, that court or tribunal shall bring the matter before the Court.[65]

---

[64] *Dillenkofer* v. *Germany*, Case C-178/94, [1996] ECR I-4845, para. 29: "[F]ailure to take any measure to transpose a directive in order to achieve the result it prescribes within the period laid down for that purpose constitutes per se a serious breach of [European] law and consequently gives rise to a right of reparation for individuals suffering injury if the result prescribed by the directive entails the grant to individuals of rights whose content is identifiable and a causal link exists between the breach of the State's obligation and the loss and damage suffered."

[65] The (omitted) fourth paragraph states: "If such a question is raised in a case pending before a court or tribunal of a Member State with regard to a person in custody, the Court of Justice of the European Union shall act with the minimum of delay."

The provision establishes a constitutional nexus between the European and the national courts. This section looks at the general aspects of preliminary rulings. We start by analysing the jurisdiction of the European Court under the procedure, and then move to the nature and effect of preliminary rulings in the Union legal order.

(a) The Jurisdiction of the European Court

The European Court's jurisdiction, set out in paragraph 1 of Article 267, covers all Union law – including international agreements of the Union.[66] It is however limited to *European* law. "The Court is not entitled, within the framework of Article [267 TFEU], to interpret rules pertaining to national law."[67] Nor can it theoretically give a ruling on the compatibility of national rules with Union law.

The Court's competence with regard to European law extends to questions on the "validity and interpretation" of that law. Preliminary references may thus be made in relation to *two* judicial functions. They can concern the *validity* of European law; and in exercising its judicial review function, the European Court will be confined to providing a ruling on the validity of Union acts below the Treaties. National courts can equally ask about the *interpretation* of European law. This includes all types of European law – ranging from the deepest constitutional foundations to the loftiest soft law.

The *application* of European law is – theoretically – not within the power of the Court. Article 267 "gives the Court no jurisdiction to apply the Treat[ies] to a specific case".[68] However, the distinction between "interpretation" and "application" is sometimes hard to make. The Court has tried to explain it as follows:

> When it gives an interpretation of the Treat[ies] in a specific action pending before a national court, the Court limits itself to deducing the meaning of the [European] rules from the wording and spirit of the Treat[ies], it being left to the national court to apply in the particular case the rules which are thus interpreted.[69]

---

[66] *Haegemann*, Case 181/73, (1974) ECR 449.
[67] *Hoekstra (née Unger)*, Case 75/63, [1964] ECR 177, para. 3.
[68] *Costa* v. *ENEL*, Case 6/64, [1964] ECR 585 at 592.
[69] *Da Costa et al.* v. *Netherlands Inland Revenue Administration*, Joined Cases 28-30/62, [1963] ECR 31 at 38.

Theoretically, this should mean that the Court of Justice cannot decide whether or not a national law, in fact, violates EU law. And yet, the Court has often made this very assessment.[70]

A famous illustration of the blurred line between "interpretation" and "application" is provided by the "Sunday trading cases".[71] Would the national prohibition on trading on Sundays conflict with the Union's internal market provisions? Preliminary references had been made by a number of English courts to obtain an interpretation on the Treaties' free movement of goods provisions. The Court found that national rules governing opening hours could be justified on public interest grounds, but asked the referring national courts "to ascertain whether the effects of such national rules exceed what is necessary to achieve the aim in view".[72] Yet the decentralized application of this proportionality test led to a judicial fragmentation of the United Kingdom. Simply put, different national courts decided differently. The Court thus ultimately took matters into its own hands and centrally applied the proportionality test.[73] And in holding that the British Sunday trading rules were not disproportionate interferences with the internal market, the Court crossed the line between "interpretation" and "application" of the Treaties.

(b) The Legal Nature of Preliminary Rulings

What is the nature of preliminary rulings from the European Court? Preliminary references are not appeals. They are – principally – discretionary acts of a national court asking for interpretative help from the European Court. The decision to refer to the European Court of Justice thus lies entirely with the national court – not the parties to the dispute.[74] But

---

[70] For two excellent analyses of this category of cases, see G. Davies, "The Division of Powers between the European Court of Justice and National Courts", *Constitutionalism Web-Papers* 3/2004 (SSRN Network: www.ssrn.com); as well as T. Tridimas, "Constitutional Review of Member State Action: The Virtues and Vices of an Incomplete Jurisdiction", 9 (2011) *International Journal of Constitutional Law*, 737.

[71] See M. Jarvis, "The Sunday Trading Episode: In Defence of the Euro-defence", 44 (1995) *International and Comparative Law Quarterly*, 451.

[72] *Torfaen Borough Council*, Case C-145/88, [1989] ECR I-3851, para. 15.

[73] *Stoke-on-Trent City Council* v. *B&Q*, Case C-169/91, [1992] ECR I-6635.

[74] *Kempter* v. *Hauptzollamt Hamburg-Jonas*, Case C-2/06, [2008] ECR I-411, para. 41: "the system established by Article [267 TFEU] with a view to ensuring that [European] law is interpreted uniformly in the Member States instituted direct cooperation between the

once the European Court has given a preliminary ruling, this ruling will be binding. But *whom* will it bind – the parties to the national dispute or the national court(s)?

Preliminary rulings cannot bind the parties in the national dispute, since the European Court will not "decide" their case. It is therefore misleading to even speak of a binding effect *inter partes* in the context of preliminary rulings.[75] The Court's rulings are addressed to the national court requesting the reference; and the Court has clarified that "that ruling is binding on the national court as to the interpretation of the [Union] provisions and acts in question".[76] Yet, will the binding effect of a preliminary ruling extend beyond the referring national court? In other words, is a preliminary ruling equivalent to a "decision" addressed to a single court; or will the European Court's interpretation be generally binding on all national courts?

The Court has long clarified that a preliminary ruling is *not* a "decision"; indeed, it is not even seen as an (external) act of a Union institution.[77] What then is the nature of preliminary rulings? The question has been hotly debated in the academic literature. And we may contrast two views competing with each other. According to the common law view, preliminary rulings are legal precedents that generally bind all national courts. Judgments of the European Court are binding *erga omnes*.[78]

The problem with this – masterful yet mistaken – theory is that the European Court subscribes to a second constitutional view: the civil law tradition. Accordingly, its judgments do not create "new" legal rules but only clarify "old" ones. In the words of the Court:

> The interpretation which, in the exercise of the jurisdiction conferred upon it by Article [267 TFEU], the Court of Justice gives to a rule of [European] law clarifies and defines where necessary the meaning and scope of that

---

Court of Justice and the national courts by means of a procedure which is completely independent of any initiative by the parties".

[75] Contra, see A. Toth, "The Authority of Judgments of the European Court of Justice: Binding Force and Legal Effects", 4 (1984) *Yearbook of European Law*, 1.

[76] *Benedetti* v. *Munari*, Case 52/76, [1977] ECR 163, para. 26.

[77] *Wünsche Handelsgesellschaft* v. *Germany*, Case 69/85 (Order), [1986] ECR 947, para. 16.

[78] See A. Trabucchi, "L'Effet 'erga omnes' des Décision Préjudicielles rendus par la Cour de Justice des Communautés Européennes", 10 (1974) *Revue Trimestrielle de Droit Européen*, 56.

> rule as it must be or ought to have been understood and applied from the
> time of its coming into force[.]⁷⁹

The Court of Justice thus adopts the – (in)famous – "declaration theory". In light of the "civilian" judicial philosophy of the European Court, its judgments are *not* generally binding.⁸⁰ There is no vertical or multilateral effect of judicial decisions, as "judgments of the European Courts are *not sources* but *authoritative evidences* of [European] law": "[A]n interpretation given by the Court becomes an integral part of the provision interpreted and cannot fail to affect the legal position of all those who may derive rights and obligations from that provision."⁸¹

Are there constitutional problems with the Union's civil law philosophy? There indeed are "temporal" problems. For the "declaratory" effect of preliminary rulings generally generates "retroactive" effects.⁸² In *Kühne & Heitz,*⁸³ the Court thus held that a (new) interpretation of European law must be applied "even to legal relationships which arose or were formed before the Court gave its ruling on the question on interpretation".⁸⁴ The Court has nonetheless recognized that its civil law philosophy must – occasionally – be tempered by the principles of legal certainty and financial equity.⁸⁵ It has therefore – exceptionally – limited the temporal effects of its preliminary rulings to an effect *ex nunc,* that is: an effect from the time of the ruling. However, the Court has equally clarified that legal certainty will not prevent the retroactive application of a (new) interpretation, where the judgment of a national court of final instance "was, in the light of a decision given by the Court subsequent to it, based on a misinterpretation of [European] law which was adopted without a

---

⁷⁹ *Amministrazione delle Finanze dello Stato* v. *Denkavit,* Case 61/79, [1980] ECR 1205, para. 16; and more recently *Kühne & Heitz* v. *Productschap voor Pluimvee en Eieren,* Case C-453/00, [2004] ECR I-837, para. 21.

⁸⁰ In this sense, see Toth, "The Authority of Judgments" (supra n. 75), 60: "in the cases under discussion the Court itself has never meant to attribute, as is sometimes suggested, a general binding force to interpretative preliminary rulings."

⁸¹ *Ibid.,* 70 and 74 (emphasis added).

⁸² On this point, see G. Bebr, "Preliminary Rulings of the Court of Justice: Their Authority and Temporal Effect", 18 (1981) *Common Market Law Review,* 475, esp. 491: "The retroactive effect of a preliminary interpretative ruling is, according to the Court, the general rule."

⁸³ *Kühne & Heitz,* Case C-453/00 (supra n. 79).   ⁸⁴ *Ibid.,* para. 22.

⁸⁵ For the former rationale, see *Kempter,* Case C-2/06 (supra n. 74); for the latter rationale, see *Defrenne* v. *Sabena,* Case 43/75, [1976] ECR 455.

question being referred to the Court for a preliminary ruling under the third paragraph of Article [267]".[86]

4. Preliminary Rulings II: Special Aspects

Article 267(2) defines the competence of national courts to ask preliminary questions. The provision allows "any court or tribunal of a Member State" to ask a European law question that "is necessary to enable it to give judgment". And while any national courts "may" refer a question to the European Court under paragraph 2, Article 267(3) imposes an obligation on certain courts. Article 267(3) defines these as courts "against whose decisions there is no judicial remedy under national law".

Let us look at each of these special aspects of the preliminary reference procedure in turn.

(a) "Who": National Courts and Tribunals

The formulation "court or tribunal" in Article 267 directly refers to *judicial* authorities. This removes *administrative* authorities, which have indeed been systematically excluded from the scope of the judicial cooperation procedure.[87]

But what exactly is a "court or tribunal" that can refer questions to the Court of Justice? The Treaties provide no positive definition. Would the concept therefore fall within the competence of the Member States? Unsurprisingly, the European Court has not accepted this idea and has provided a European definition of the phrase. Its definition is extremely wide. In *Dorsch Consult*,[88] the Court thus held:

> In order to determine whether a body making a reference is a court or tribunal for the purposes of Article [267] of the Treaty, which is a question governed by [Union] law alone, the Court takes account of a number of factors, such as whether the body is established by law, whether it is

---

[86]   *Kempter*, Case C-2/06 (supra, n. 74), para. 39. For a critical analysis of this case, see A. Ward, "Do unto Others as you would have them do unto you: 'Willy Kempter' and the Duty to Raise EC Law in National Litigation", 33 (2008) *European Law Review*, 739.

[87]   See only: *Corbiau*, Case C-24/92, (1993) ECR I-1277; as well as: Case C-53/03, *Syfait et al.* v. *GlaxoSmithKline*, [2005] ECR I-4609.

[88]   *Dorsch Consult Ingenieurgesellschaft* v. *Bundesbaugesellschaft Berlin*, Case C-54/96, [1997] ECR I-4961.

> permanent, whether its jurisdiction is compulsory, whether its procedure is inter partes, whether it applies rules of law and whether it is independent.[89]

The last criterion is often controlling. Therefore, an authority that is not independent from the State's administrative branch is not a court or tribunal in the meaning of European law.[90]

The enormous breadth of this European definition is illustrated in *Broekmeulen*.[91] The plaintiff had obtained a medical degree from Belgium and tried to register as a "General Practitioner" in the Netherlands. The registration was refused on the ground that Dutch professional qualifications were not satisfied. The plaintiff appealed before the "Appeals Committee for General Medicine" – a professional body set up under private law. This Appeals Committee was not a court or tribunal under Dutch law. Would it nonetheless be a "court or tribunal" under European law, and, as such, be entitled to make a preliminary reference? The European Court found as follows:

> In order to deal with the question of the applicability in the present case of Article [267 TFEU], it should be noted that it is incumbent upon Member States to take the necessary steps to ensure that within their territory the provisions adopted by the [Union] institutions are implemented in their entirety. If, under the legal system of a Member State, the task of implementing such provisions is assigned to a professional body acting under a degree of governmental supervision, and if that body, in conjunction with the public authorities concerned, creates appeal procedures which may affect the exercise of rights granted by [European] law, it is imperative, in order to ensure the proper functioning of [Union] law, that the Court should have an opportunity of ruling on issues of interpretation and validity arising out of such proceedings. As a result of all the foregoing considerations and in the absence, in practice, of any right of appeal to the ordinary courts, the Appeals Committee, which operates with the consent of the public authorities and with their cooperation, and which, after an adversarial procedure, delivers decisions which are recognized as final, must, in a matter involving the application of [European] law, be

---

[89] *Ibid.*, para. 23.

[90] *Syfait et al.* v. *GlaxoSmithKline*, Case C-53/03, [2005] ECR I-4609. On the general question, whether national competition authorities should be considered "courts or tribunals" in the sense of Article 267 TFEU, see A. Komninos, "Article 234 EC and National Competition Authorities in the Era of Decentralisation", 29 (2004) *European Law Review*, 106.

[91] *Broekmeulen* v. *Huisarts Registratie Commissie*, Case 246/80, [1981] ECR 2311.

> considered as a court or tribunal of a Member State within the meaning of Article [267 TFEU].[92]

Can higher national courts limit the power of a lower national court to refer preliminary questions? The European legal order has given short shrift to the attempt to break the cooperative nexus between the European Court and *each level of the national judiciary*. In *Rheinmühlen*,[93] the Court thus held that "a rule of national law whereby a court is bound on points of law by the rulings of a superior court cannot deprive the inferior courts of their power to refer to the Court questions of interpretation of [Union] law involving such rulings".[94] For if inferior courts could not refer to the Court of Justice, "the jurisdiction of the latter to give preliminary rulings and the application of [European] law *at all levels of the judicial systems* of the Member States would be compromised".[95]

Any national court or tribunal, at any level of the national judicial hierarchy, and at any stage of its judicial procedure, is thus entitled to refer a preliminary question to the European Court of Justice. National rules allowing for an appeal against the decision of a national court to refer a preliminary question to the European Court will thus violate "the autonomous jurisdiction which Article [267 TFEU] confers on the referring court".[96] For the English judicial hierarchy, the judicial federalism constructed by the European Court thus looks as Figure 7.3.

(b) "What": Necessary Questions

National courts are entitled to request a preliminary ruling, where – within a pending case – there is a "question" on which they consider it "necessary" for judgment to be given. In the past, the European Court has been eager to encourage national courts to ask preliminary questions. For these questions offered the Court formidable opportunities to say what the European constitution "is". Thus, even where questions were "imperfectly formulated", the Court was willing to extract the "right" ones.[97] Moreover, the Court will generally not "criticize the grounds and

---

[92] *Ibid.*, paras. 16–17.   [93] *Rheinmühlen-Düsseldorf,* Case 166/73, [1974] ECR 33.
[94] *Ibid.*, para. 4.
[95] *Ibid.* (emphasis added). For a recent confirmation, see *Elchinov* v. *Natsionalna zdravno-osiguritelnakasa,* Case C-173/09, [2010] ECR I-8889, para. 27.
[96] *Cartesio,* Case C-210/06, [2008] ECR I-9641 para. 95.
[97] *Costa* v. *ENEL,* Case 6/64, (supra n. 68) 593: "[T]he Court has the power to extract from a question imperfectly formulated by the national court those questions which alone pertain to the interpretation of the Treaty."

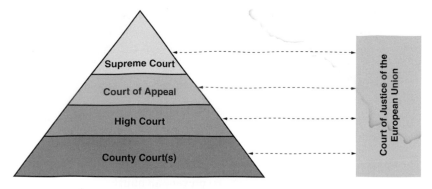

Figure 7.3 Preliminary Rulings under Article 267

purpose of the request for interpretation".[98] In the words of a seminal judgment on the issue:

> As regards the division of jurisdiction between national courts and the Court of Justice under Article [267] of the [FEU] Treaty the national court, which is alone in having a direct knowledge of the facts of the case and of the arguments put forward by the parties, and which will have to give judgment in the case, is in the best position to appreciate, with full knowledge of the matter before it, the relevance of the questions of law raised by the dispute before it and the necessity for a preliminary ruling so as to enable it to give judgment.[99]

Nonetheless, in – very – exceptional circumstances the Court may reject a request for a preliminary ruling. This happened in *Foglia* v. *Novello (No.1)*,[100] where the Court insisted that questions referred to it must be raised in a "genuine" dispute.[101] Where the parties to the national dispute agreed, in advance, on the desirable outcome, the Court will decline jurisdiction.[102] In a sequel to this case, the Court justified this jurisdictional limitation as follows:

---

[98] *Ibid.*

[99] *Pigs Marketing Board* v. *Raymond Redmond*, Case 83/78, (1978) ECR 2347, para. 25.

[100] *Foglia* v. *Novello*, Case 104/79, [1980] ECR 745.

[101] G. Bebr, "The Existence of a Genuine Dispute: an Indispensable Precondition for the Jurisdiction of the Court under Article 177 EEC?", 17 (1980) *Common Market Law Review*, 525.

[102] *Foglia* v. *Novello*, Case 104/79, (supra n. 100) paras. 11–13 (emphasis added): "The duty of the Court of Justice under Article [267] of the [FEU] Treaty is to supply all courts in the [Union] with the information on the interpretation of [European] law which is necessary to enable them to settle *genuine* disputes which are brought before them."

> [T]he duty assigned to the Court by Article [267] is not that of delivering advisory opinions on general or hypothetical questions but of assisting in the administration of justice in the Member States. It accordingly does not have jurisdiction to reply to questions of interpretation which are submitted to it within the framework of procedural devices arranged by the parties in order to induce the Court to give its views on certain problems of [European] law which do not correspond to an objective requirement inherent in the resolution of a dispute.[103]

The Court of Justice has consequently imposed *some* jurisdictional control on requests for preliminary rulings. To prevent an abuse of the Article 267 procedure, the European Court will "check, as all courts must, whether it has jurisdiction".[104] Yet, the Court was also eager to emphasize that it wished "not in any way [to] trespass upon the prerogatives of the national courts".[105] The Court thus renewed its pledge to "place as much reliance as possible upon the assessment by the national court of the extent to which the questions submitted are essential".[106] The Court will therefore decline jurisdiction "only if it is manifest that the interpretation of [European] law or the examination of the validity of a rule of [European] law sought by that court bears no relation to the true facts or the subject-matter of the main proceedings".[107]

(c) The Obligation to Refer and *"Acte Clair"*

While any national court "may" refer a question to the European Court under paragraph 2, Article 267(3) imposes an obligation:

> Where any such question is raised in a case pending before a court or tribunal of a Member State against whose decisions there is no judicial remedy under national law, that court or tribunal shall bring the matter before the Court.

What is the scope of this obligation? Two theoretical options exist. Under the "institutional" theory, the formulation refers to the highest judicial *institution* in the country. This would restrict the obligation to refer preliminary questions to a single court in a Member State – in

---

[103] *Foglia* v. *Novello (No. 2)*, Case 244/80 [1981] ECR 3045, para.18.
[104] *Ibid.*, para. 19.　　[105] *Ibid.*, para. 18.　　[106] *Ibid.*, para. 19.
[107] *Imperial Chemical Industries (ICI)* v. *Kenneth Hall Colmer (Her Majesty's Inspector of Taxes)*, Case C-264/96, [1998] ECR I-4695, para. 15.

the United Kingdom: the Supreme Court. By contrast, the "procedural" theory links the definition of the court of last instance to the judicial *procedure* in the particular case. This broadens the obligation to refer to every national court whose decision cannot be appealed in the particular case.

The Court of Justice has – from the very beginning – favoured the second theory.[108] The key concept in Article 267(3) is thereby the "appeal*ability*" of a judicial decision. What counts is the *ability* of the parties to appeal to a higher court. The fact that the merits of the appeal are subject to a prior declaration of admissibility by the superior court may therefore not deprive the parties of a judicial remedy.[109] Where an appeal is *procedurally* possible, the obligation under Article 267(3) will not apply.

Apart from the uncertainty concerning what are courts "against whose decisions there is no judicial remedy under national law", the wording of Article 267(3) appears relatively clear. Yet, this picture is – misleadingly – deceptive. For the European Court has judicially "amended" the provision in two very significant ways.

The first "amendment" relates to references on the validity of European law. Despite the restrictive wording of paragraph 3, the European Court has here insisted that *all* national courts – even courts that are not courts of last resort – are under an obligation to refer *when they are in doubt about the validity of a Union act.*[110] This *expansion* of the scope of Article 267(3) follows from the structure of the Union's judicial federalism, which grants the exclusive power to invalidate European law to the Court of Justice.[111]

---

[108] The procedural theory received support in *Costa* v. *ENEL*, Case 6/64 (supra n. 68), where the ECJ treated an Italian court of *first* instance as a court against whose decision there was no judicial remedy.

[109] *Lyckeskog*, Case C-99/00, [2002] ECR I-4839, paras. 16–17: "Decisions of a national appellate court which can be challenged by the parties before a supreme court are not decisions of a court or tribunal of a Member State against whose decisions there is no judicial remedy under national law within the meaning of Article [267 TFEU]. The fact that examination of the merits of such appeals is subject to a prior declaration of admissibility by the Supreme Court does not have the effect of depriving the parties of a judicial remedy."

[110] See *The Queen on the Application of International Air Transport Association et al.* v. *Department for Transport*, Case C-344/04, [2006] ECR I-403 para. 30.

[111] Within the Union legal order, the power to annul a Union act is an *exclusive* competence of the European Court: Case 314/85, *Foto-Frost* v. *Hauptzollamt Lübeck-Ost* [1987] ECR 4199. On this power, see: Chapter 8 – Section 3 below.

By contrast, a second "amendment" has limited the obligation to refer preliminary questions. This *limitation* followed from constitutional common sense. For to ask a question implies uncertainty as to the answer. And where the answer is "clear", there may be no need to raise a question. Yet on its textual face, Article 267(3) treats national courts "as perpetual children": they are forbidden from interpreting European law – even if the answers are crystal clear.[112] And in order to counter this, the Union legal order imported a French legal doctrine under the name of *acte clair*. The doctrine simply means that where it is *clear* how to *act,* a national court need not ask a preliminary question.

The doctrine of *acte clair* began its European career in *Da Costa*.[113] In this case, the Court held:

> [T]he authority of an interpretation under Article [267] already given by the Court may deprive the obligation of its purpose and thus empty it of its substance... Such is the case especially when the question raised is *materially identical* with a question which has already been the subject of a preliminary ruling in a similar case.[114]

The Court subsequently clarified that this covered a second situation. Where the European Court had already given a negative answer to a question relating to the *validity* of a Union act, another national court need not raise the same question again.[115] But general guidelines on the constitutional scope of the *acte clair* doctrine were only offered in *CILFIT*.[116] The Court here generally widened the doctrine to all situations "where previous decisions of the Court have already dealt with the *point of law* in question, irrespective of the nature of the proceedings which led to those decisions, even though the questions at issue are not strictly identical".[117]

However, national courts will only be released from their obligation to refer questions under Article 267(3) TFEU, where the correct application of

---

[112] J. C. Cohen, "The European Preliminary Reference and U.S. Court Review of State Court Judgments: A Study in Comparative Judicial Federalism", 44 (1996) *American Journal of Comparative Law*, 421 at 438.

[113] *Da Costa et al* v. *Netherlands Inland Revenue Administration*, Joined 28–30/62, [1963] ECR 31.

[114] *Ibid.*, 38 (emphasis added).

[115] *International Chemical Corporation*, Case 66/80 [1981] ECR 1191, paras. 12–13.

[116] *CILFIT and others* v. *Ministry of Health*, Case 283/81, [1982] ECR 3415.

[117] *Ibid.*, para. 14 (emphasis added).

European law is "so obvious as to leave no scope for any reasonable doubt as to the matter in which the question raised is to be resolved".[118] This is an extremely high threshold, which the Court linked to the fulfilment of a number of very (!) restrictive conditions.[119] These *CILFIT* conditions "were designed to prevent national courts from abusing the doctrine in order to evade their obligation to seek a preliminary ruling where they are disinclined to adhere to the Court's case-law".[120]

Conclusion

Functionally, national courts are Union courts; yet the decentralized application of European law by national courts means that the procedural regime for the enforcement of European rights is principally left to the Member States.

This rule of "national procedural autonomy" is however qualified. The two constitutional principles judicially developed by the Court here are the equivalence and the effectiveness principle. The former requests national courts to extend existing national remedies to similar European actions. The latter demands that these national remedies must not make the enforcement of European law "excessively difficult". There is a third important qualification: the liability principle. The *Francovich* doctrine

---

[118] *Ibid.*, para. 16.

[119] *Ibid.*, paras. 16–20: "Before it comes to the conclusion that such is the case, the national court or tribunal must be convinced that the matter is equally obvious to the courts of the other Member States and to the Court of Justice. Only if those conditions are satisfied, may the national court or tribunal refrain from submitting the question to the Court of Justice and take upon itself the responsibility for resolving it. However, the existence of such a possibility must be assessed on the basis of the characteristic features of [European] law and the particular difficulties to which its interpretation gives rise. To begin with, it must be borne in mind that [Union] legislation is drafted in several languages and that the different language versions are all equally authentic. An interpretation of a provision of [European] law thus involves a comparison of the different language versions. It must also be borne in mind, even where the different language versions are entirely in accord with one another, that [European] law uses terminology which is peculiar to it. Furthermore, it must be emphasized that legal concepts do not necessarily have the same meaning in [European] law and in the law of the various Member States. Finally, every provision of [European] law must be placed in its context and interpreted in the light of the provisions of [European] law as a whole, regard being had to the objectives thereof and to its state of evolution at the date on which the provision in question is to be applied."

[120] K. Lenaerts *et al.*, *EU Procedural Law* (supra n. 7), 100.

obliges national courts to provide for damages actions that compensate for losses resulting from (sufficiently serious) breaches of European law by a Member State.

In order to guarantee a degree of uniformity in the interpretation of European law, the Treaties provide for a "preliminary reference proce-dure". This is not an appeal procedure, but allows national courts to ask – if they want to – questions relating to the interpretation of European law. This – voluntary – cooperative arrangement is replaced by a constitutional obligation for national courts of last resort.

Introduction

The European Treaties establish a dual enforcement mechanism for European Union law. Apart from the decentralized enforcement by national courts, the Union legal order equally envisages the centralized enforcement of European law in the European Courts. The judicial competences of the European Courts are enumerated in the section of the TFEU dealing with the Court of Justice of the European Union.

Four classes of judicial actions will be discussed in this Chapter. The first class is typically labelled an "enforcement action" in the strict sense of

Table 8.1 Judicial Competences and Procedures

Judicial Competences and Procedures (Articles 258–81 TFEU)	
Article 258	Enforcement Action brought by the Commission
Article 259	Enforcement Action brought by another Member State
Article 260	Action for a Failure to Comply with a Court judgment
Article 261	Jurisdiction for Penalties in Regulations
Article 262	(Potential) Jurisdiction for disputes relating to European intellectual property rights
Article 263	Action for Judicial Review
Article 265	(Enforcement) Action for the Union's Failure to Act
Article 267	Preliminary Rulings
Article 268	Jurisdiction in Damages Actions under Article 340
Article 269	Jurisdiction for Article 7 TEU
Article 270	Jurisdiction in Staff Cases
Article 271	Jurisdiction for Cases involving the European Investment Bank and the European Central Bank
Article 272	Jurisdiction granted by Arbitration Clauses
Article 273	Jurisdiction granted by special agreement between the Member States
Article 274	Jurisdiction of national courts involving the Union
Article 275	Non-Jurisdiction for the Union's Common Foreign and Security Policy
Article 276	Jurisdictional Limits within the Area of Freedom, Security and Justice
Article 277	Collateral (Judicial) Review for acts of general application

the term. This action is set out in Articles 258 and 259 TFEU and concerns the failure of a Member State to act in accordance with European law (Section 1). The three remaining actions "enforce" the European Treaties against the Union itself. These actions can be brought for a failure to act (Section 2), for judicial review (Section 3), and for damages (Section 4).

1. Enforcement Actions against Member States

Where a Member State breaches European law, the central way to "enforce" the Treaties is to bring that State before the European Court. The European legal order envisages two potential applicants for enforcement actions against a failing Member State: the Commission and another

Member State. The procedure governing the former scenario is set out in Article 258; and the – almost – identical procedure governing the second scenario is set out in Article 259. Both procedures are inspired by international law logic. For not only are individuals excluded from enforcing their rights under that procedure, the European Court also cannot repeal national laws that violate European law. Its judgment will simply "declare" that a violation of European law has taken place. However, as we shall see below, this declaration may now be backed up by financial sanctions.

(a) The Procedural Conditions under Article 258

Enforcement actions against a Member State are "the *ultima ratio* enabling the [Union] interests enshrined in the Treat[ies] to prevail over the inertia and resistance of Member States".[1] They are typically brought by the Commission.[2] For it is the Commission, acting in the general interest of the Union, that is charged to ensure that the Member States give effect to European law.[3] The procedural regime for enforcement actions brought by the Commission is set out in Article 258 TFEU, which states:

> If the Commission considers that a Member State has failed to fulfil an obligation under the Treaties, it shall deliver a reasoned opinion on the matter after giving the State concerned the opportunity to submit its observations. If the State concerned does not comply with the opinion within the period laid down by the Commission, the latter may bring the matter before the Court of Justice of the European Union.

The provision clarifies that before the Commission can bring the matter to the Court, it must pass through an administrative stage. The purpose of this pre-litigation stage is "to give the Member State concerned an opportunity, on the one hand, to comply with its obligations under [European] law and, on the other, to avail itself of its right to defend itself against the complaints made by the Commission".[4] This administrative stage expressly requires a "reasoned opinion", and before that – even if

---

[1] *Italy* v. *High Authority*, Case 20/59, [1960] ECR 325 at 339.
[2] The following section therefore concentrates on proceedings brought by the Commission. Member States do very rarely bring actions against another Member State; but see *Spain* v. *United Kingdom*, Case C-145/04, [2006] ECR I-7917.
[3] See *Commission* v. *Germany*, [1995] ECR I-2189. On the Commission's powers in this context, see Chapter 1 – Section 3(c).
[4] *Commission* v. *Belgium*, Case 293/85, [1988] ECR 305, para. 13.

not expressly mentioned in Article 258 – a "letter of formal notice". In the "letter of formal notice" the Commission will notify the State that it believes it to violate European law, and ask it to submit its observations. Where the Commission is not convinced by the explanations offered by a Member State, it will issue a "reasoned opinion"; and after that second administrative stage,[5] it will go to court.

What violations of European law may be litigated under the enforcement procedure? With the general exceptions mentioned above,[6] the Commission can raise any violation of European law, including breaches of the Union's international agreements.[7] However, the breach must be committed by the "State". This includes its legislature, its executive and – in theory – its judiciary. The Member State might also be responsible for violations of the Treaties by territorially autonomous regions.[8] And even the behaviour of its nationals may – exceptionally – be attributed to the Member State.[9]

Are there any defences that a State may raise to justify its breach of European law? Early on, the Court clarified that breaches of European law by one Member State cannot justify breaches by another. In *Commission* v. *Luxembourg and Belgium*,[10] the defendants had argued that "since international law allows a party, injured by the failure of another party to perform its obligations, to withhold performance of its own, the Commission has lost the right to plead infringement of the Treaty".[11] The Court did not accept this "international law" reading of the European Treaties. The latter were "not limited to creating reciprocal obligations between the different natural and legal persons to whom it is applicable, but establish . . . a new legal order, which governs the powers, rights and obligations of the said persons, as well as the necessary procedures for taking cognizance of and penalizing any breach of it".[12] The binding effect of European law was thus comparable to the effect of "national" or "institutional" law.[13] The Court has also denied the availability of "internal"

---

[5] The Court has insisted that the Member State must – again – be given a reasonable period to correct its behaviour; see *Commission* v. *Belgium*, Case 293/85 (supra n. 4).

[6] See Articles 275 and 276 TFEU.

[7] *Commission* v. *Germany (IDA)*, Case C-61/94, [1996] ECR I-3989.

[8] See *Commission* v. *Germany*, Case C-383/00, [2002] ECR I-4219.

[9] *Commission* v. *Ireland (Buy Irish)*, Case 249/81, [1982] ECR 4005.

[10] *Commission* v. *Luxembourg and Belgium*, Case 90–91/63, [1964] ECR 625.

[11] *Ibid.*, 631.   [12] *Ibid.*

[13] P. Pescatore, *The Law of Integration: Emergence of a New Phenomenon in International Relations Based on the Experience of the European Communities* (Sijthoff, 1974), 67 and 69.

constitutional problems,[14] or budgetary restraints, as justifications.[15] However, one of the arguments that the Court has accepted in the past is the idea of *force majeure* in an emergency situation.[16]

(b) Judicial Enforcement through Financial Sanctions

The European Court is not entitled to void national laws that violate European law. It may only declare national laws or practices incompatible with European law.[17] Where the Court has found that a Member State has failed to fulfil an obligation under the Treaties, "the State shall be required to take the necessary measures to comply with the judgment of the Court".[18] Inspired by international law logic, the European legal order here builds on the normative distinctiveness of European and national law. It remains within the competence of the Member States to remove national laws or practices that are incompatible with European law.

Nonetheless, the Union legal order may "punish" violations by imposing financial sanctions on a recalcitrant State. The sanction regime for breaches by a Member State is set out in Article 260(2) and (3) TFEU. Importantly, financial sanctions will not automatically follow from every breach of European law. According to Article 260(2), the Commission may only apply for a "lump sum or penalty payment",[19] where a Member State has failed to comply with a *judgment of the Court*. And even in this limited situation, the Commission must bring a second (!) case before the Court.[20] There is only one exception to the requirement of a second judgment. This "exceptional" treatment corresponds to a not too exceptional situation:

---

[14] See *Commission* v. *Ireland*, Case C-39/88, [1990] ECR I-4271, para. 11: "a Member State may not plead internal circumstances in order to justify a failure to comply with obligations and time-limits resulting from [European] law."

[15] See *Commission* v. *Italy*, Case 30/72, [1973] ECR 161.

[16] For an excellent discussion of the case law, see L. Prete and B. Smulders, "The Coming of Age of Infringement Proceedings", 47 (2010) *Common Market Law Review*, 9 at 44.

[17] *France* v. *Commission*, Cases 15 & 16/76, [1979] ECR 32.

[18] Article 260(1) TFEU.

[19] The Court has held that Article 265 TFEU allows it to impose a "lump sum" *and* a "penalty payment" at the same time (see *Commission* v. *France (French Fisheries II)*, Case C-304/02, [2005] ECR I-6262).

[20] The Court has softened this procedural requirement somewhat by specifically punishing "general and persistent infringements"; see *Commission* v. *Ireland (Irish Waste)*, Case C-494/01 [2005] ECR I-3331. For an extensive discussion of this type of infringement, see P. Wennerås, "A New Dawn for Commission Enforcement under Articles 226 and 228 EC: General and Persistent (GAP) Infringements, Lump Sums and Penalty Payments", 43 (2006) *Common Market Law Review*, 31 at 33–50.

the failure of a Member State properly to transpose a "directive".[21] Where a Member State fails to fulfil its obligation "to notify measures transposing a directive adopted under a legislative procedure",[22] the Commission can apply for a financial sanction in the first enforcement action. The payment must take effect on the date set by the Court in its judgment, and is thus directed at the specific breach of European law.

2. Actions Against the Union: Failure to Act

Enforcement actions primarily target a Member State's failure to act (properly). However, infringement proceedings may also be brought against Union institutions. Actions for failure to act are thereby governed by Article 265 TFEU, which states:

> Should the European Parliament, the European Council, the Council, the Commission or the European Central Bank, in infringement of the Treaties, fail to act, the Member States and the other institutions of the Union may bring an action before the Court of Justice of the European Union to have the infringement established. This Article shall apply, under the same conditions, to bodies, offices and agencies of the Union which fail to act.
>
> The action shall be admissible only if the institution, body, office or agency concerned has first been called upon to act. If, within two months of being so called upon, the institution, body, office or agency concerned has not defined its position, the action may be brought within a further period of two months.
>
> Any natural or legal person may, under the conditions laid down in the preceding paragraphs, complain to the Court that an institution, body, office or agency of the Union has failed to address to that person any act other than a recommendation or an opinion.

An action for failure to act may thus be brought against any Union institution or body – with the exception of the Court of Auditors and the European Court. It can be brought by another Union institution or body, a Member State, and even a private party.[23]

---

[21] On the legal instrument "Directive", see Chapter 5 – Section 3 above.

[22] Article 260(3) TFEU.

[23] However, with regard to private parties, the Court appears to read a "direct and individual concern" criterion into Article 265 TFEU; see *T. Port GmbH & Co.* v. *Bundesanstalt für Landwirtschaft und Ernährung*, Case C-68/95, [1996] ECR I-6065.

What are the procedural stages of this action? As with enforcement actions against a Member State, the procedure is divided into an administrative and a judicial stage. The judicial stage will only commence once the relevant institution has been "called upon to act", and has not "defined its position" within two months.[24]

What types of "inactions" can be challenged? In its early jurisprudence, the Court appeared to interpret the scope of Article 265 in parallel with the scope of Article 263 (to be discussed below).[25] This suggested that only those inactions with (external) legal effects might be challenged. However, the wording of the provision points the other way – at least for non-private applicants. And this wider reading was indeed confirmed in *Parliament* v. *Council (Comitology)*,[26] where the Court found that "[t]here is no necessary link between the action for annulment and the action for failure to act".[27] Actions for failure to act can thus also be brought in relation to "preparatory acts".[28] The material scope of Article 265 is, in this respect, wider than that of Article 263.

However, in one important respect the scope of Article 265 is much smaller than that of Article 263. For the European Court has added an "unwritten" limitation that cannot be found in the text of Article 265. It insists that a finding of a failure to act requires the existence of an *obligation to act*. Where an institution has "the right, but not the duty" to act, no failure to act can be established.[29] This is, for example, the case with regard to the Commission's competence to bring enforcement actions under Article 258. Under this article "the Commission is not bound to commence the proceedings provided for in that provision but in this regard has a discretion which excludes the right for individuals to require that institution to adopt a specific position".[30] The existence of institutional discretion thus excludes an obligation to act.

In *Parliament* v. *Council (Common Transport Policy)*,[31] the Court offered further commentary on what the existence of an obligation to act requires.

---

[24] On what may count as a "defined" position, see *Parliament* v. *Council*, Case 377/87, [1988] ECR 4017, and *Pesqueras Echebastar* v. *Commission*, Case C-25/91, [1993] ECR I-1719.

[25] *Chevallery* v. *Commission*, Case 15/70, [1970] ECR 975, para. 6: "[T]he concept of a measure capable of giving rise to an action is identical in Articles [263] and [265], as both provisions merely prescribe one and the same method of recourse".

[26] *Parliament* v. *Council*, Case 302/87, [1988] ECR 5615.   [27] *Ibid.*, para. 1.

[28] *Parliament* v. *Council*, Case 377/87 (supra n. 24).

[29] *Star Fruit Co* v. *Commission*, Case 247/87, [1989] ECR 291, esp. para. 12.

[30] *Ibid.*, para. 11.   [31] *Parliament* v. *Council*, Case 13/83, [1985] ECR 1513.

Parliament had brought proceedings against the Council claiming that it had failed to lay down a framework for the common transport policy. The Council responded by arguing that a failure to act under Article 265 "was designed for cases where the institution in question has a legal obligation to adopt a *specific* measure and that it is an inappropriate instrument for resolving cases involving the introduction of a whole system of measures within the framework of a complex legislative process".[32] The Court joined the Council and rejected the idea that enforcement proceedings could be brought for the failure to fulfil the *general* obligation to develop a Union policy. The failure to act would have to be "sufficiently defined"; and this would only be the case, where the missing Union act could be "identified individually".[33]

What are the consequences of an established failure to act on the part of the Union? According to Article 266, the institution "whose failure to act has been declared contrary to the Treaties shall be required to take the necessary measures to comply with the judgment of the Court of Justice of the European Union". And in the absence of an express time-limit for such compliance, the Court acknowledges that the institution "has a reasonable period for that purpose".[34]

3. Annulment Actions: Judicial Review

The action for judicial review in the European Union legal order is set out in Article 263 TFEU. The provision reads:

> [1] The Court of Justice of the European Union shall review the legality of legislative acts, of acts of the Council, of the Commission and of the European Central Bank, other than recommendations and opinions, and of acts of the European Parliament and of the European Council intended to produce legal effects vis-à-vis third parties. It shall also review the legality of acts of bodies, offices or agencies of the Union intended to produce legal effects vis-à-vis third parties.

---

[32] *Ibid.*, para. 29 (emphasis added).

[33] *Ibid.*, para. 37. The Court thus held in para. 53 that "the absence of a common policy which the Treaty requires to be brought into being does not in itself necessarily constitute a failure to act sufficiently specific in nature to form the subject of an action under Article [265]".

[34] *Ibid.*, para. 69.

[2] It shall for this purpose have jurisdiction in actions brought by a Member State, the European Parliament, the Council or the Commission on grounds of lack of competence, infringement of an essential procedural requirement, infringement of the Treaties or of any rule of law relating to their application, or misuse of powers.

[3] The Court shall have jurisdiction under the same conditions in actions brought by the Court of Auditors, by the European Central Bank and by the Committee of the Regions for the purpose of protecting their prerogatives.

[4] Any natural or legal person may, under the conditions laid down in the first and second paragraphs, institute proceedings against an act addressed to that person or which is of direct and individual concern to them, and against a regulatory act which is of direct concern to them and does not entail implementing measures...

[6] The proceedings provided for in this Article shall be instituted within two months of the publication of the measure, or of its notification to the plaintiff, or, in the absence thereof, of the day on which it came to the knowledge of the latter, as the case may be.[35]

Where an action for judicial review is well founded, the Court of Justice "shall declare the acts concerned to be void".[36] The Union will henceforth "be required to take the necessary measures to comply with the judgment of the Court of Justice of the European Union";[37] and may even be subject to paying compensation for damage caused by the illegal act.[38] But what are the procedural requirements for a judicial review action? Article 263 follows a complex structure; and the easiest way to understand its logic is to break it down into four constituent components. Paragraph 1 concerns the question *whether* the Court has the power to review particular types of Union acts. Paragraph 2 tells us *why* there can be judicial review, that is: on what grounds one can challenge the legality of a European act. Paragraphs 2–4 concern the question of *who* may ask for judicial review

---

[35] The omitted paragraph 5 lays down special rules for Union agencies and bodies. It states: "Acts setting up bodies, offices and agencies of the Union may lay down specific conditions and arrangements concerning actions brought by natural or legal persons against acts of these bodies, offices or agencies intended to produce legal effects in relation to them." The following Section will not deal with this special aspect of judicial review.

[36] Article 264(1) TFEU. However, according to Article 264(2) TFEU, the Court can – exceptionally – "if it considers this necessary, state which of the effects of the act which it has declared void shall be considered as definitive".

[37] Article 266 TFEU.   [38] Articles 268 and 340 TFEU. On this point, see Section 4 below.

and thereby distinguish between three classes of applicants. Finally, paragraph 6 tells us *when* an application for review must be made, namely: within two months.

(a) "Whether": The Existence of a "Reviewable" Act

Paragraph 1 determines whether there can be judicial review. This question has two dimensions. The first dimension relates to *whose* acts may be challenged; the second dimension clarifies *which* acts might be reviewed.

Whose acts can be challenged in judicial review proceedings? According to Article 263(1), the Court is entitled to review "legislative acts"; that is: acts whose joint authors are the European Parliament and the Council. It can also review unilateral acts of all Union institutions and bodies, except for the Court of Auditors. By contrast, the Court cannot judicially review acts of the Member States. And this prohibition includes unilateral national acts, as well as international agreements of the Member States. The European Treaties thus cannot – despite their being the foundation of European law – be reviewed by the Court. For as collective acts of the Member States, they cannot be attributed to the Union institutions, and as such are beyond the review powers of the European Court.

Which acts of the Union institutions can be reviewed? Instead of a positive definition, Article 263(1) only negatively tells us which acts cannot be reviewed. Accordingly, there will be no judicial review for "recommendations" or "opinions". The reason for this exclusion is that both instruments "have no binding force",[39] and there is thus no need to challenge their *legality*.

The provision equally excludes judicial review for acts of the European Parliament, the European Council, and of other Union bodies not "intended to produce legal effects vis-à-vis third parties". The rationale behind this limitation is that it excludes acts that are "internal" to an institution. And despite being textually limited to *some* Union institutions, the requirement of an "external" effect has been extended to all Union acts. The Court has thus clarified that purely preparatory acts of the Commission or the Council cannot be challenged. "[A]n act is open to review only if it is a measure definitely laying down the position of

---

[39]   Article 288(5) TFEU.

the Commission or the Council."[40] In a legislative or executive procedure involving several stages, all preparatory acts are consequently considered "internal" acts; and as such cannot be reviewed.

But apart from this insistence on a legal effect outside the Union institution(s), the Court has embraced a wide definition of which acts may be reviewed. The nature of the act would thereby be irrelevant. In *ERTA*,[41] the Court thus found:

> Since the only matters excluded from the scope of the action for annulment open to the Member States and the institutions are "recommendations or opinions" – which by the final paragraph of Article [288 TFEU] are declared to have no binding force – Article [263 TFEU] treats as acts open to review by the Court all measures adopted by the institutions which are intended to have legal force. The objective of this review is to ensure, as required by Article [19 TEU], observance of the law in the interpretation and application of the Treaty. It would be inconsistent with this objective to interpret the conditions under which the action is admissible so restrictively as to limit the availability of this procedure merely to the categories of measures referred to by Article [288 TFEU]. *An action for annulment must therefore be available in the case of all measures adopted by the institutions, whatever their nature or form, which are intended to have legal effects.*[42]

The Court's wide review jurisdiction is however externally limited by Articles 275 and 276 TFEU.[43]

(b) "Why": Legitimate Grounds for Review

Not every reason is a sufficient reason to request judicial review. While the existence of judicial review is an essential element of all political

---

[40] *International Business Machines (IBM)* v. *Commission*, Case 60/81, [1981] ECR 2639, para. 10.

[41] *Commission* v. *Council (ERTA)*, Case 22/70, [1971] ECR 263.

[42] *Ibid.*, paras. 39–42 (emphasis added).

[43] The Treaties acknowledge two general limitations on the jurisdiction of the European Court: Articles 275 and 276 TFEU. The former declares that the European Court "shall not have jurisdiction with respect to the provisions relating to the common foreign and security policy nor with respect to acts adopted on the basis of those provisions" (Article 275(1) TFEU). And Article 276 TFEU decrees that the European Court "shall have no jurisdiction to review the validity or proportionality of operations carried out by the police or other law-enforcement services of a Member State or the exercise of the responsibilities incumbent upon Member States with regard to the maintenance of law and order and the safeguarding of internal security".

orders subject to the "rule of law", the extent of judicial review will differ depending on whether a procedural or a substantive version is chosen.

The British legal order has traditionally followed a *procedural* definition of the rule of law. Accordingly, courts are (chiefly) entitled to review whether in the adoption of an act the respective legislative or executive procedures have been followed.[44] The "merit" or "substance" of a legislative act is here beyond the review powers of the courts. By contrast, the American constitutional order has traditionally followed a substantive definition of the rule of law. Courts are here obliged to review the content of a legislative act, in particular: whether it violates fundamental human rights as guaranteed in the Constitution. A substantive rule of law entails the danger of a "government of judges"; that is: the government of philosophical guardians whose views might not reflect the democratic will of the political majority. Yet, many modern States recognize the need for non-majoritarian institutions to protect individual rights against the "tyranny of the multitude".[45]

For the European legal order, Article 263(2) TFEU limits judicial review to four legitimate grounds: "lack of competence", "infringement of an essential procedural requirement", "infringement of the Treaties or any rule of law relating to their application", and "misuse of powers". Do these reasons indicate whether the Union subscribes to a formal or substantive rule of law?

Let us look at this general question first, before analysing the principle of proportionality as a specific ground of review.

(i) "Formal" and "Substantive" Grounds

The Union legal order recognizes three "formal" grounds of review.

First, a European act can be challenged on the ground that the Union lacked the competence to adopt it. The ultra vires review of European law thereby extends to primary and secondary legislation. The review of the former originates in the principle of conferral.[46] Since the Union may only exercise those powers conferred on it by the Treaties, any action beyond

---

[44] A. W. Bradley and K. D. Ewing, *Constitutional and Administrative Law* (Pearson, 2003), Chapters 30 and 31.

[45] The phrase is attributed to E. Burke. For an overview of Burke's thought, see L. Gottschalk, "Reflections on Burke's Reflections on the French Revolution", 100 (1956) *Proceedings of the American Philosophical Society*, 417.

[46] On the principle of conferral, see Chapter 3 – Introduction above.

these powers is ultra vires and thus voidable. With regard to secondary legislation, this follows not from the (vertical) principal of conferral, but from the (horizontal) principle protecting the institutional balance within the Union.[47]

Second, a Union act can be challenged if it infringes an essential procedural requirement. According to this second ground of review, not all procedural irregularities may invalidate a Union act but only those that are "essential". When are "essential" procedural requirements breached? The constitutional principles developed under this jurisdictional head are the result of an extensive "legal basis litigation".[48] An essential procedural step is breached when the Union adopts an act under a procedure that leaves out an institution that was entitled to be involved.[49] Alternatively, the Union may have adopted an act on the basis of a wrong voting arrangement *within* one institution. Thus, where the Council voted by unanimity instead of a qualified majority, an essential procedural requirement is breached.[50] By contrast, no essential procedural requirement is infringed when the Union acts under a "wrong" competence, which nonetheless envisages an identical legislative procedure.[51]

The third formal ground of review is "misuse of powers", which has remained relatively obscure.[52] The subjective rationale behind it is the prohibition on pursuing a different objective from the one underpinning a legal competence.[53]

Finally, a Union act can be challenged on the ground that it represents an "infringement of the Treaties or any other rule of law relating to their application". This constitutes a "residual" ground of review. And the European Court has used it as a constitutional gate to import a range of

---

[47] On the delegation doctrine in the Union legal order, see R. Schütze, *European Union Law* (Cambridge University Press, 2012), Chapter 9 – Section 2(a).

[48] On the phenomenon of "legal basis litigation" in the Union legal order, see H. Cullen and A. Worth, "Diplomacy by Other Means: the Use of Legal Basis Litigation as a Political Strategy by the European Parliament and Member States", 36 (1999) *Common Market Law Review*, 1243.

[49] See *Commission* v. *Council (ERTA)*, Case 22/70, (supra n. 41), as well as *Parliament* v. *Council (Chernobyl)*, Case C-70/88, [1990] ECR I-2041.

[50] See *United Kingdom* v. *Council*, Case 68/86, [1988] ECR 855, as well as *Commission* v. *Council*, Case C-300/89, [1991] ECR I-2867.

[51] *Commission* v. *Council*, Case 165/87, [1988] ECR 5545, para. 19: "only a purely formal defect which cannot make the measure void".

[52] For a more extensive discussion of this ground of review, see H. Schermers and D. Waelbroeck, *Judicial Protection in the European Union* (Kluwer, 2001), 402 et seq.

[53] See *Gutmann* v. *Commission*, Joined Cases 18 and 35/65, [1965] ECR 103.

"unwritten" general principles into the Union legal order.[54] These principles include, inter alia, the principles of legal certainty and legitimate expectations. And the introduction of these principles has added a *substantive* dimension to the rule of law in the European Union. For it has been used to review the content of Union legislation against fundamental rights.[55] One expression of the Union's choice in favour of the substantive dimension of the rule of law is the principle of proportionality.

(ii) Proportionality: A Substantive Ground

The constitutional function of the proportionality principle is to protect liberal values.[56] It constitutes one of the "oldest" general principles of the Union legal order.[57] Beginning its career as an unwritten principle, the proportionality principle is now codified in Article 5(4) TEU:

> Under the principle of proportionality, the content and form of Union action shall not exceed what is necessary to achieve the objectives of the Treaties.[58]

The proportionality principle has been characterized as "the most far-reaching ground for review", and "the most potent weapon in the arsenal of the public law judge".[59] However, the Treaties expressly limit its pervasive power in Article 276 TFEU with regard to police operations in the area of freedom, security and justice.

How will the Court assess the proportionality of a Union act? The Court has developed a proportionality test. In its most elaborate form, the test follows a tripartite structure.[60] It analyses the *suitability, necessity,* and

---

[54] On the general principles in the Union legal order see T. Tridimas, *General Principles* (Oxford University Press, 2007).

[55] On the emergence of fundamental rights as general principles of Union law, see Chapter 4 – Section 1 above.

[56] On the origins of the proportionality principle, see J. Schwarze, *European Administrative Law* (Sweet & Marwell, 2006), 678–9.

[57] An implicit acknowledgement of the principle may be found in *Fédération Charbonnière de Belgique* v. *High Authority of the ECSC*, Case 8/55, [1954–56] ECR 245 at 306: "not exceed the limits of what is strictly necessary".

[58] The provision continues: "The institutions of the Union shall apply the principle of proportionality as laid down in the Protocol on the application of the principles of subsidiarity and proportionality".

[59] Tridimas, *General Principles* (supra n. 54), 140.

[60] See *The Queen* v. *Minister of Agriculture, Fisheries and Food and Secretary of State for Health, ex parte Fedesa and others*, Case C-331/88, [1990] ECR I-4023, para. 13: "[T]he principle of proportionality is one of the general principles of [Union] law. By virtue

proportionality (in the strict sense) of a Union act. (However, the Court does not always distinguish between the second and third prong.) Within its suitability review, the Court will check whether the European measure was suitable to achieve a given objective. This might be extremely straightforward.[61] The necessity test is, on the other hand, more demanding. The Union will have to show that the act adopted represents the *least restrictive means* to achieve a given objective. Finally, even the *least* restrictive means to achieve a public policy objective might disproportionately interfere with individual rights. Proportionality in a strict sense thus weighs whether the burden imposed on an individual is excessive or not.

While this tripartite test may – in theory – be hard to satisfy, the Court has granted the Union a wide margin of appreciation wherever it enjoys a sphere of discretion. The legality of a discretionary Union act will only be affected "if the measure is manifestly inappropriate".[62] This relaxed standard of review has meant that the European Court rarely finds a Union measure to be disproportionately interfering with fundamental rights.

However, we find a good illustration of a disproportionate Union act in *Kadi*.[63] In its fight against international terrorism, the Union had adopted a Regulation freezing the assets of people suspected to be associated with Al-Qaeda. The applicant alleged, inter alia, that the Union act disproportionately restricted his right to property. The Court held that the right to property was not absolute and "the exercise of the right to property may be restricted, provided that those restrictions in fact correspond to objectives of public interest pursued by the [Union] and do not constitute, in relation to the aim pursued, a disproportionate and intolerable interference, impairing the very substance of the right so guaranteed".[64] And

of that principle, the lawfulness of the prohibition of an economic activity is subject to the condition that the prohibitory measures are appropriate and necessary in order to achieve the objectives legitimately pursued by the legislation in question; when there is a choice between several appropriate measures recourse must be had to the least onerous, and the disadvantages caused must not be disproportionate to the aims pursued."

[61] For a – rare – example where the test was not satisfied, see *Crispoltoni* v. *Fattoria autonoma tabacchi di Città di Castello*, Case C-368/89, [1991] ECR I-3695, esp. para. 20.

[62] *Fedesa*, Case C-331/88 (supra n. 60), para. 14. See also *Germany* v. *Council (Bananas)*, Case C-122/95, [1998] ECR I-973, para. 79.

[63] *Kadi and Al Barakaat International Foundation* v. *Council and Commission*, Case C-402P, [2008] ECR I-6351.

[64] *Ibid.*, para. 355.

this required that "a fair balance has been struck between the demands of the public interest and the interest of the individuals concerned".[65] This fair balance had not been struck for the applicant;[66] and the Union act would, so far as it concerned the applicant,[67] have to be annulled.

(c) "Who": Legal Standing before the European Courts

The Treaties distinguish between three types of applicants in three distinct paragraphs of Article 263 TFEU.

Paragraph 2 mentions the applicants that can always bring an action for judicial review. These "privileged" applicants are: the Member States, the European Parliament,[68] the Council, and the Commission. The reason for their privileged status is that they are *ex officio* deemed to be affected by the adoption of a Union act.

Paragraph 3 lists applicants that are "semi-privileged". These are the Court of Auditors, the European Central Bank, and the Committee of the Regions. They are "partly privileged", as they may solely bring review proceedings "for the purpose of protecting their prerogatives".[69]

Paragraph 4 – finally – addresses the standing of natural or legal persons. These applicants are "non-privileged" applicants, as they must demonstrate that the Union act affects them specifically. This fourth paragraph has been highly contested in the past fifty years. And in order to make sense of the Court's jurisprudence, we must start with a historical analysis of its "Rome formulation", before moving to the current "Lisbon formulation" of that paragraph.

---

[65] *Ibid.*, para. 360.   [66] *Ibid.*, para. 371.

[67] *Ibid.*, para. 372. However, the Court found that the Union act as such could, in principle, be justified (*ibid.*, para. 366).

[68] Under the original Rome Treaty, the European Parliament was not a privileged applicant. The reason for this lay in its mere "consultative" role in the adoption of Union law. With the rise of parliamentary involvement after the Single European Act, this position became constitutionally problematic. How could Parliament cooperate or even co-decide in the legislative process, yet not be able to challenge an act that infringed its procedural prerogatives? To close this constitutional gap, the Court judicially "amended" ex-Article 173 EEC by giving the Parliament the status of a "semi-privileged" applicant (see *Parliament* v. *Council (Chernobyl)*, Case 70/88 (supra n. 49)). This status was codified in the Maastricht Treaty; and the Nice Treaty finally recognized Parliament's status as a fully privileged applicant under ex-Article 230(2) EC.

[69] For a definition of this phrase in the context of Parliament's struggle to protect its prerogatives before the Nice Treaty, see *Parliament* v. *Council*, Case C-316/91, [1994] ECR I-625, as well as *Parliament* v. *Council*, Case C-187/93, [1994] ECR I-2857.

(i) The Rome Formulation and its Judicial Interpretation

The Rome Treaty granted individual applicants the right to apply for judicial review in ex-Article 230 EC. Paragraph 4 of that provision stated:

> Any natural or legal person may . . . institute proceedings against a *decision* addressed to that person or against a *decision* which, although in the form of a regulation or *decision* addressed to another person, is of *direct and individual concern* to the former.[70]

This "Roman" formulation must be understood against the background of two constitutional choices. First, the drafters of the Rome Treaty had wished to confine the standing of private parties to challenges of individual "decisions", that is: administrative acts. The Rome Treaty thereby distinguished between three types of decisions: decisions addressed to the applicant, decisions addressed to another person, and decisions "in the form of a regulation". This third decision was a decision "in substance", which had been put into the wrong legal form.[71] Judicial review was here desirable to avert an abuse of powers.

Second, not every challenge of a decision by private parties was permitted. Only those decisions that were of "direct and individual concern" to a private party could be challenged. And while this concern was presumed for decisions addressed to the applicant, it had to be proven for all other decisions. Private applicants were thus "non-privileged" applicants in a dual sense. Not only could they *not* challenge all legal acts, they were – with the exception of decisions addressed to them – not presumed to have a legitimate interest in challenging the act.

Both constitutional choices severely restricted the standing of private parties and were heavily disputed. In the Union legal order prior to Lisbon, they were subject to an extensive judicial and academic commentary.[72]

---

[70] Ex-Article 230(4) EC (emphasis added).

[71] On the various instruments in the European legal order, see Chapter 5 – Introduction above. On the material distinction between "decisions" and "regulations", see *Confédération nationale des producteurs de fruits et légumes and others* v. *Council*, Case 16–17/62, [1962] ECR 471, where the Court found that the Treaty "makes a clear distinction between the concept of a 'decision' and that of a 'regulation'" (*ibid.*, 478). Regulations were originally considered the sole "generally applicable" instrument of the European Union, and their general character distinguished them from individual decisions.

[72] For the academic controversy (in chronological order), see A. Barav, "Direct and Individual Concern: an Almost Insurmountable Barrier to the Admissibility of Individual Appeal to the EEC Court", 11 (1974), *Common Market Law Review*, 191; H. Rasmussen, "Why is Article 173 Interpreted Against Private Plaintiffs?", 5 (1980) *European Law Review*,

In a first line of jurisprudence, the Court succeeded significantly in "re-writing" ex-Article 230(4) EC by deserting the text's insistence on a "decision". While it had originally paid homage to that text in denying private party review of generally applicable acts,[73] the Court famously abandoned its classic test and clarified that the general nature of a Union act was irrelevant. In *Codorniu*,[74] the Court thus found:

> Although it is true that according to the criteria in the [fourth] paragraph of [ex-]Article [230] of the [EC] Treaty the contested provision is, by nature and by virtue of its sphere of application, of a legislative nature in that it applies to the traders concerned in general, that does not prevent it from being of individual concern to some of them.[75]

This judicial "amendment" cut the Gordian knot between the "individual" nature of an act and ex-Article 230(4) EC. Private parties could henceforth challenge single provisions within *any* legal act – even generally applicable acts like regulations or directives – as long as they could demonstrate "direct and individual concern".

This brings us to the second famous battleground under ex-Article 230(4) EC. What was the meaning of the "direct and individual concern" formula? The criterion of direct concern was taken to mean that the contested measure *as such* would have to affect the position of the applicant.[76] This would not be the case, where the contested measure envisaged any form of discretionary implementation that would breach the "direct" link between the measure and the applicant. (In this case, the Union legal order would require the applicant to challenge the implementing measure – and not the "parent" act.)

112; N. Neuwahl, "Article 173 Paragraph 4 EC: Past, Present and Possible Future", 21 (1996) *European Law*, 17; A. Arnull, "Private Applicants and the Action for Annulment since *Codorniu*", 38 (2001), *Common Market Law*, 8; and A. Ward, *Judicial Review and the Rights of Private Parties in EU Law* (Oxford University Press, 2007).

[73] The Court's classic test concentrated on whether – from a material point of view – the challenged act was a "real" regulation. The "test" is spelled out in *Calpak* v. *Commission*, Case 790/79, [1980] ECR 1949, paras. 8–9: "By virtue of the second paragraph of Article [288] of the Treaty [on the Functioning of the European Union] the criterion for distinguishing between a regulation and a decision is whether the measure at issue is of general application or not."

[74] *Codorniu* v. *Council*, Case C-309/89, [1994] ECR I-1853.   [75] *Ibid.*, para. 19.

[76] See *Parti écologiste "Les Verts"* v. *European Parliament*, Case 294/83, [1986] ECR 1339 para. 31: "The contested measures are of direct concern to the applicant association. They constitute a complete set of rules which are sufficient in themselves and which require no implementing provisions."

Sadly, the criterion of "individual concern" was less straightforward. It was given an authoritative interpretation in *the* seminal case on the standing of private parties under ex-Article 230(4) EC: the *Plaumann* case. Plaumann, an importer of clementines, had challenged a Commission decision refusing to lower European customs duties on that fruit. But since the decision was not addressed to him – it was addressed to his Member State: Germany – he had to demonstrate that the decision was of "individual concern" to him. The European Court defined the criterion as follows:

> Persons other than those to whom a decision is addressed may only claim to be individually concerned if that decision affects them by reason of certain attributes which are peculiar to them or by reason of circumstances in which they are differentiated from all other persons and by virtue of these factors distinguishes them individually just as in the case of the person addressed.[77]

This formulation became famous as the "*Plaumann* test". If private applicants wish to challenge an act not addressed to them, it is not sufficient to rely on the adverse – absolute – effects that the act has on them. Instead, they must show that – relative to everybody else – the effects of the act are "peculiar to them". This *relational* standard insists that they must be "differentiated from all other persons". The applicants must be *singled* out as if they were specifically addressed. In the present case, the Court denied this *individual* concern, as Plaumann was seen to be only *generally* concerned "as an importer of clementines, that is to say, by reason of a commercial activity which may at any time be practised by any person".[78] The *Plaumann* test is therefore *very* strict: whenever a private party is a member of an "open group" of persons – anybody could decide to become an importer of clementines tomorrow – legal standing under ex-Article 230(4) EC will be denied.[79] A person must thus belong to a "closed group" so as to be entitled to challenge a Union act.

---

[77] *Plaumann* v. *Commission*, Case 25/62, [1963] ECR 95 at 107.   [78] *Ibid.*

[79] Even assuming that Plaumann was the only clementine importer in Germany at the time of the decision, the category of "clementine importers" was open: future German importers could wish to get involved in the clementine trade. Will there ever be "closed groups" in light of this definition? For the Court's approach in this respect, see *CAM* v. *Commission*, Case 100/74, [1975] ECR 1393, as well as *Piraiki-Patraiki and others* v. *Commission*, Case 11/82, [1985] ECR 207.

Unsurprisingly, this restrictive reading of private party standing was heavily criticized as an illiberal limitation of an individual's fundamental right to judicial review.[80] And the Court would partly soften its stance in specific areas of European law.[81] However, it generally refused to introduce a more liberal approach to the standing of private applicants. In *Unión de Pequeños Agricultores (UPA)*,[82] the Court indeed expressly rejected the invitation to overrule its own jurisprudence on the – disingenuous[83] – ground that

> [w]hile it is, admittedly, possible to envisage a system of judicial review of the legality of [Union] measures of general application different from that established by the founding Treaty and never amended as to its principles, it is for the Member States, if necessary, in accordance with Article 48 TEU, to reform the system currently in force.[84]

Has this – requested – constitutional amendment taken place? Let us look at the Lisbon formulation dealing with the standing of private parties.

(ii) The Lisbon Formulation and its Interpretative Problems

The Lisbon Treaty has substantially amended the Rome formulation. The standing of private parties is now enshrined in Article 263(4) TFEU. The provision states:

> Any natural or legal person may... institute proceedings against an *act* addressed to that person or which is of *direct and individual concern* to them, and against a *regulatory act* which is of direct concern to them and does not entail implementing measures.[85]

The new formulation of paragraph 4 textually recognizes the decoupling of private party standing from the nature of the Union act challenged.

---

[80] See Article 47 EU Charter of Fundamental Rights: "Everyone whose rights and freedoms guaranteed by the law of the Union are violated has the right to an effective remedy before a tribunal in compliance with the conditions laid down in this Article."

[81] This had happened – for example – in the area of European competition law; see *Metro-SB-Großmärkte* v. *Commission*, Case 26/76, [1977] ECR 1875.

[82] *Unión de Pequeños Agricultores, (UPA)* v. *Council*, Case C-50/00, [2002] ECR I-6677.

[83] The *Plaumann* test is a result of the Court's own interpretation of what "individual concern" means, and the Court could have therefore – theoretically – "overruled" itself. This has happened in other areas of European law; see *Criminal Proceedings against Keck and Mithouard*, Joined Cases C-267/91 and C-268/91, [1993] ECR I-6097.

[84] *Unión de Pequeños Agricultores (UPA)* v. *Council*, Case C-50/00 (supra n. 82), para. 45.

[85] Article 263(4) TFEU (emphasis added).

In codifying *Codorniu*, an individual can thus potentially challenge any Union "act" with legal effects. However, depending on the nature of the act, Article 263(4) TFEU still distinguishes three scenarios. First, decisions addressed to the applicant can automatically be challenged. Second, with regard to regulatory acts, a private party must prove "direct concern" and that the regulatory act does not need implementing measures.[86] Third, for all other acts, the applicant must continue to show "direct *and individual concern*". The Lisbon amendment thus abandons the requirement of an "individual concern" only for the second but not the third category of acts. The dividing line between the second and third category is thus poised to become *the* post-Lisbon interpretative battlefield within Article 263(4) TFEU; and this line is determined by the concept of "regulatory act".

What are "regulatory acts"? The term is not defined in the Treaties. Two constitutional options exist. According to a first view, "regulatory acts" are defined as all "generally applicable acts".[87] This reading liberalizes the standing of private applicants significantly, as the second category would cover all legislative as well as executive acts of a general nature. According to a second view, on the other hand, the concept should be defined in contradistinction to "legislative acts". Regulatory acts are here understood as non-legislative acts.[88] This view places acts adopted under the – ordinary or special – legislative procedure outside the second category. The judicial review of formal legislation would consequently

---

[86] "Direct concern" should theoretically mean that no implementing act is needed. Why then does Article 263(4) TFEU repeat this expressly? The answer might lie in the prior jurisprudence of the Court (see *Regione Siciliana* v. *Commission*, Case C-417/04 P, [2006] ECR I-3881). The Court was here not concerned whether there was a formal need for implementing measures. It was only interested in whether the act materially determined the situation of the applicant as such. Thus, even a Directive could be potentially of direct concern; see *Union Européenne de l'artisanat et des petites et moyennes entreprises (UEAPME)* v. *Council*, Case T-135/96, [1998] ECR II-02335. From this perspective, the new Article 263(4) TFEU, and its insistence on the absence of an implementing act, might signal the wish of the Lisbon Treaty-makers for a return to a more restrictive – formal – position.

[87] See M. Dougan, "The Treaty of Lisbon 2007: Winning Minds, not Hearts", 45 (2008) *Common Market Law Review*, 617; and J. Bast, "Legal Instruments and Judicial Protection", in A. von Bogdandy and J. Bast (eds.), *Principles of European Constitutional Law* (Hart, 2009), 345 at 396.

[88] A. Ward, "The Draft EU Constitution and Private Party Access to Judicial Review of EU Measures", in T. Tridimas and P. Nebbia (eds.), *European Union Law for the Twenty-First Century* (Hart, 2005), 201 at 221; as well as A. Dashwood and A. Johnston, "The Institutions of the Enlarged EU under the Regime of the Constitutional Treaty", 41 (2004) *Common Market Law Review*, 1481 at 1509.

require "direct *and* individual concern", and would thus remain largely immune from private party challenges.

How have the European Courts decided? In *Inuit I*,[89] the General Court sided with the second – narrower – view. The case involved a challenge by seal products traders to a Union Regulation (almost) completely banning the marketing of such products in the internal market. Having been adopted on the basis of Article 114 TFEU, under the ordinary legislative procedure, the question arose to what extent Union legislation could be challenged by interested private parties. After a comprehensive analysis of the various arguments for and against the inclusion of legislative acts into the category of regulatory acts, the General Court found the two classes of acts to be mutually exclusive. In the word of the General Court:

> [I]t must be held that the meaning of "regulatory act" for the purposes of the fourth paragraph of Article 263 TFEU must be understood as covering all acts of general application *apart from legislative acts.*[90]

The judgment was confirmed on appeal,[91] where the Court of Justice held as follows:

> [T]he purpose of the alteration to the right of natural and legal persons to institute legal proceedings, laid down in the fourth paragraph of [ex-]Article 230 EC, was to enable those persons to bring, under less stringent conditions, actions for annulment of acts of general application other than legislative acts. The General Court was therefore correct to conclude that the concept of "regulatory act" provided for in the fourth paragraph of Article 263 TFEU does not encompass legislative acts.[92]

For private party challenges to legislative acts (as well as decisions not addressed to the applicant), the Union legal order thus continues to require proof of a "direct *and individual* concern". And any reports on the death of *Plaumann* have also turned out to be greatly exaggerated. For the Court in *Inuit I* expressly identified "individual concern" under Article 263(4) TFEU with the *Plaumann* test:

> In that regard, it can be seen that the second limb of the fourth paragraph of Article 263 TFEU corresponds... to the second limb of the fourth paragraph of [ex-]Article 230 EC. The wording of that provision has not

---

[89] *Inuit* v. *Parliament & Council*, Case T–18/10, (2011) ECR II-5599.
[90] *Ibid.*, para. 56 (emphasis added).
[91] *Inuit* v. *Parliament & Council*, Case C–583/11 P, EU: C: 2013: 625.
[92] *Ibid.*, paras. 60–61.

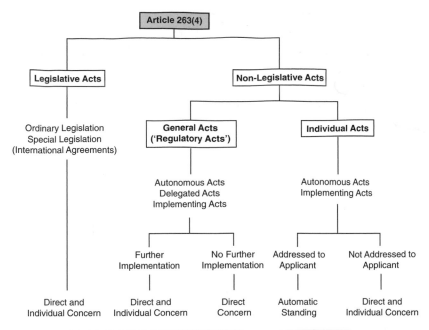

Figure 8.1 Types of Acts under Article 263(4)

been altered. Further, there is nothing to suggest that the authors of the Treaty of Lisbon had any intention of altering the scope of the conditions of admissibility already laid down in the fourth paragraph of [ex-]Article 230 EC... In those circumstances, it must be held that the content of the condition that the act of which annulment is sought should be of individual concern, as interpreted by the Court in its settled case-law since *Plaumann v Commission*, was not altered by the Treaty of Lisbon... According to that case-law, natural or legal persons satisfy the condition of individual concern only if the contested act affects them by reason of certain attributes which are peculiar to them or by reason of circumstances in which they are differentiated from all other persons, and by virtue of these factors distinguishes them individually just as in the case of the person addressed[.][93]

The Court thus refused to replace the "old" *Plaumann* test with a "new" less restrictive test; yet there are nonetheless good reasons for this change. The strongest critique of the *Plaumann* test has thereby come from the pen of Advocate General Jacobs. In *Unión de Pequeños Agricultores (UPA)*,[94]

---

[93] *Inuit*, Case C-583/11 P, paras. 70–72.
[94] *Unión de Pequeños Agricultores*, Case C-50/00 (supra n. 82).

his learned opinion pointed to the test's anomalous logic. It is indeed absurd that "the greater the number of persons affected the less likely it is that effective judicial review is available".[95] But what alternative test might then be suitable? "The only satisfactory solution is therefore to recognise that an applicant is individually concerned by a [Union] measure where the measure has, or is liable to have, a *substantial adverse effect* on his interests."[96] But as we saw in the previous subsection, the Court has rejected this reinterpretation on the formal ground that abandoning *Plaumann* would require Treaty amendment.

4. Damages Actions: Union Liability

Where the Union has acted illegally, may the Court grant damages for losses incurred? The European Treaties do acknowledge an action for damages in Article 268 TFEU;[97] yet, for a strange reason the article refers to another provision: Article 340 TFEU. This provision reads:

> The contractual liability of the Union shall be governed by the law applicable to the contract in question.
>
> In the case of non-contractual liability, the Union shall, in accordance with the general principles common to the laws of the Member States, make good any damage caused by its institutions or by its servants in the performance of their duties.[98]

The provision distinguishes between contractual liability in paragraph 1, and non-contractual liability in paragraph 2. While the former is governed by national law, the latter is governed by European law. Paragraph 2 recognizes that the Union can do "wrong" either as an institution or through its servants,[99] and that it will be under an obligation to make good damage incurred. What are the European constitutional principles

---

[95] Opinion of Advocate General Jacobs, in *ibid.*, para. 59.

[96] *Ibid.*, para. 102 (emphasis added).

[97] Article 268 TFEU: "The Court of Justice of the European Union shall have jurisdiction in disputes relating to compensation for damage provided for in the second and third paragraphs of Article 340."

[98] Article 340(1) and (2) TFEU.

[99] As regards the Union's civil servants, only their "official acts" will be attributed to the Union. With regard to their personal liability, Article 340(4) TFEU states: "The personal liability of its servants towards the Union shall be governed by the provisions laid down in their Staff Regulations or in the Conditions of Employment applicable to them."

underpinning an action for the non-contractual liability of the Union? Article 340(2) has had a colourful and complex constitutional history. It has not only been transformed from a dependent action to an independent action; its substantial conditions have changed significantly. This final section will briefly analyse the procedural and substantive conditions of Union liability actions.

(a) Procedural Conditions: From Dependent to Independent Action

The action for damages under Article 340(2) started its life as a dependent action, that is: an action that hinged on the prior success of another action. In *Plaumann* – a case discussed in the previous section – a clementine importer had brought an annulment action against a Union decision, while at the same time asking for compensation equivalent to the customs duties that had been paid as a consequence of the European decision. However, as we saw above, the action for annulment failed due to the restrictive standing requirements under Article 263(4). And the Court found that this would equally end the liability action for damages:

> In the present case, the contested decision has not been annulled. An administrative measure which has not been annulled cannot of itself constitute a wrongful act on the part of the administration inflicting damage upon those whom it affects. The latter cannot therefore claim damages by reason of that measure. The Court cannot by way of an action for compensation take steps which would nullify the legal effects of a decision which, as stated, has not been annulled.[100]

A liability action thus had to be preceded by a (successful) annulment action. The *Plaumann* Court insisted on a "certificate of illegality" before even considering the substantive merits of Union liability. This dramatically changed in *Lütticke*.[101] The case constitutes the "declaration of independence" for liability actions:

> Article [340] was established by the Treaty as an independent form of action with a particular purpose to fulfil within the system of actions and subject to conditions for its use, conceived with a view to its specific purpose.[102]

---

[100] *Plaumann*, Case 25/62 (supra n. 77), 108.
[101] *Lütticke et al.* v. *Commission*, Joined Cases 31/62 and 33/62, [1962] ECR 501.
[102] *Ibid.*, para. 6.

According to the Court, it would be contrary to "the independent nature" of this action as well as to "the efficacy of the general system of forms of action created by the Treaty" to deny admissibility of the damages action on the ground that it might lead to a similar result as an annulment action.[103]

What are the procedural requirements for liability actions? The proceedings may be brought against any Union action or inaction that is claimed to have caused damage. The act (or omission) must however be an "official act", that is: it must be attributable to the Union.[104] Unlike Article 263 TFEU, there are no limitations on the potential applicants: anyone who feels "wronged" by a Union (in)action may bring proceedings under Article 340(2).[105] And against whom? With the exception of the European Central Bank,[106] the provision only generically identifies the Union as the potential defendant. However, the Court has clarified that "in the interests of a good administration of justice", the Union "should be represented before the Court by the institution or institutions against which the matter giving rise to liability is alleged".[107]

When will the action have to be brought? Unlike the strict two-months' limitation period for annulment actions, liability actions can be brought within a five-year period.[108] The procedural requirements for liability actions are thus much more liberal than the procedural regime governing annulment actions.

(b) Substantive Conditions: From *Schöppenstedt* to *Bergaderm*

The constitutional regime governing the substantive conditions for liability actions may be divided into two historical phases. In a first phase, the European Court distinguished between "administrative" and "legislative"

---

[103] *Ibid.* In the present case, the Court dealt with an infringement action for failure to act under Article 265 TFEU (see Section 2 above), but the same result applies to annulment actions; see *Schöppenstedt* v. *Council*, Case 5/71, [1971] ECR 975.

[104] The Union must be the author of the act, and this means that the Treaties themselves – as collective acts of the Member States – cannot be the basis of a liability action (see *Compagnie Continentale France* v. *Council*, Case 169/ 73, [1975] ECR 117, para. 16).

[105] See *CMC Cooperativa muratori e cementisti and others* v. *Commission*, Case 118/83, [1985] ECR 2325.

[106] Article 340(3) TFEU.

[107] *Werhahn Hansamühle and others* v. *Council*, Case 63–69/72, [1973] ECR 1229, para. 7.

[108] Article 46 Statute of the Court.

Union acts.[109] The former were subject to a relatively low liability threshold. The Union would be liable for (almost) any illegal action that had caused damage.[110] By contrast, legislative acts were subject to the so-called "*Schöppenstedt* formula".[111] The latter stated:

> [W]here *legislative* action involving measures of economic policy is concerned, the [Union] does not incur non-contractual liability for damage suffered by individuals as a consequence of that action, by virtue of the provisions contained in Article [340], second paragraph, of the Treaty, *unless a sufficiently flagrant violation of a superior rule of law for the protection of the individual has occurred.*[112]

This formula made Union liability for legislative acts dependent on the breach of a "superior rule" of Union law – whatever that meant[113] – which aimed to grant rights to individuals.[114] And the breach of that rule would have to be sufficiently serious.[115]

This test was significantly "reformed" in *Bergaderm*.[116] The reason for this reform was the Court's wish to align the liability regime for breaches of European law by the Union with the liability regime governing the Member States.[117] Today, European law confers a right to reparation

> where three conditions are met: the rule of law infringed must be intended to confer rights on individuals; the breach must be sufficiently serious; and there must be a direct causal link between the breach of the obligation resting on the State and the damage sustained by the injured parties.[118]

Two important changes were reflected in the "*Bergaderm* formula". First, the Court abandoned the distinction between "administrative" and

---

[109] Tridimas, *General Principles* (supra n. 54), 478 et seq.

[110] See *Adams* v. *Commission*, Case 145/83, [1985] ECR 3539, para. 44: "[B]y failing to make all reasonable efforts . . . the Commission has incurred liability towards the applicant in respect of that damage."

[111] *Schöppenstedt* v. *Council*, Case 5/71 (supra n. 103).

[112] *Ibid.*, para. 11 (emphasis added).

[113] On the concept of a "superior rule", see Tridimas, *General Principles* (supra n. 54), 480–2.

[114] *Vreugdenhil BV* v. *Commission*, Case C-282/90, [1992] ECR I-1937.

[115] See *Bayerische HNL Vermehrungsbetriebe and others* v. *Council and Commission*, Joined Cases 83 and 94/76, 4, 15 and 40/77, [1978] ECR 1209.

[116] *Bergaderm et al.* v. *Commission*, Case C-352/98P, [2000] ECR I-5291.

[117] *Ibid.*, para. 41. This inspiration was "mutual". For as we saw in Chapter 7 – Section 4, the Court used Article 340(2) TFEU as a rationale for the creation of a liability regime for the Member States.

[118] *Ibid.*, para. 42.

"legislative" acts. The new test would apply to all Union acts regardless of their nature.[119] Second, the Court dropped the idea that a "superior rule" had to be infringed. Henceforth, it was only necessary to show that the Union had caused damage by breaching a rule intended to confer individual rights, and that the breach was sufficiently serious. And the decisive test for finding that a breach of European law was sufficiently serious was whether the Union "manifestly and gravely disregarded the limits on its discretion".[120]

Conclusion

This Chapter looked at four judicial actions that can be brought directly before the Court of Justice of the European Union. Three of these actions are relatively straightforward. The Treaties distinguish between infringement actions against the Member States, and proceedings against the Union for a failure to act. Proceedings against the Union can also be brought where the Union is liable for non-contractual damages.

The European Court is also empowered to review the legality of European (secondary) law. The Union legal order has thereby opted for a strong "rule of law" version. It allows the Court to review the formal and substantive legality of European law. However, in the past, there existed severe procedural limitations on the right of individual applicants to request judicial review proceedings. The Lisbon Treaty has partly liberalized these procedural restrictions for "regulatory" acts; yet the *Plaumann* test continues to apply for all legislative acts.

---

[119] *Bergaderm*, Case C-352/98P (supra n. 116), para. 46. See also *Holcim* v. *Commission*, Case C-282/05P, [2007] ECR I-2941.

[120] *Bergaderm*, Case C-352/98P (supra n. 116), para. 43. However, where there was no discretion, "the mere infringement of [Union] law may be sufficient to establish the existence of a sufficiently serious breach" (*ibid.*, para. 44).

Part III

European Law: Substance

This final Part analyses the substantive heart of European law. When the Union was founded, its central aim was the creation of a "common" or "internal" market between the Member States. Such an internal market was to go well beyond a free trade area or a customs union. Its aim was to create an area without internal frontiers to the free movement of goods, persons, services, and capital. To guarantee these four fundamental freedoms, the EU Treaties pursue a dual strategy: negative and positive integration. Negative integration refers to the removal of illegal national barriers to trade, whereas positive integration means Union legislation that "harmonizes" national laws. Chapters 9 and 10 will explore both strategies in the context of the free movement of goods. Chapter 11 then analyses the free movement of persons. Finally, Chapter 12 wishes to offer an "introduction" to EU competition law. The latter is traditionally seen as a functional complement to the internal market.

Chapter 9 Internal Market: Goods I

Chapter 10 Internal Market: Goods II

Chapter 11 Internal Market: Persons

Chapter 12 Competition Law: Cartels

Introduction

How could the Union create a "single" market out of "diverse" national markets? To create an internal market, the EU Treaties pursue a dual strategy: negative and positive integration.[1] The Union is first charged to "free" the internal market from national barriers to trade in goods. And in order to do so, the Treaties contain a number of constitutional prohibitions "negating" illegitimate obstacles to intra-Union trade. This strategy of *negative* integration is complemented by a – second – strategy of *positive* integration. The Union is here charged to adopt positive

---

[1] J. Pinder, "Positive and Negative Integration: Some Problems of Economic Union in the EEC", (1968) 24 *The World Today* 88.

legislation to harmonize the diverse national laws. For that purpose, the Treaties confer a number of "harmonization" competences to the Union. The most famous provision here is Article 114, which entitles the Union to adopt harmonization measures that "have as their object the establishment and functioning of the internal market".[2] This Chapter explores the Union's negative integration tools in the context of the free movement of goods, while the next Chapter investigates the Union harmonization competences.

What is the "negative integration" regime governing goods? In order to create an internal market in goods, the Union legal order insists that illegal barriers to intra-Union trade must be removed. Its constitutional regime is however split over two sites within Part III of the TFEU. It finds its principal place in Title II governing the free movement of goods, and is complemented by a chapter on "Tax Provisions" within Title VII. Within these two sites, we find three constitutional prohibitions. Section 1 examines the prohibition on customs duties. These are fiscal duties charged when goods cross national borders. Section 2 moves to the second type of fiscal charge: discriminatory taxes imposed on foreign goods. Section 3 then investigates the legality of regulatory restrictions to the free movement of goods. Regulatory restrictions are not, unlike fiscal duties, pecuniary charges. They simply "regulate" access to the national market by – for example – establishing product or labelling requirements. Finally, Section 4 will look at possible justifications for regulatory restrictions to trade in goods.

1. Fiscal Barriers I: Customs Duties

Customs duties are the classic commercial weapon of the protectionist state. They are traditionally employed to "protect" domestic goods against cheaper imports. Customs duties operate like a "countervailing" charge, which is typically demanded at the national border. Within a customs union, these pecuniary charges are prohibited. Within the European Union, they are outlawed by Article 30 TFEU. The provision states:

> Customs duties on imports and exports and charges having equivalent effect shall be prohibited between Member States. The prohibition shall also apply to customs duties of a fiscal nature.

Textually, the prohibition applies to charges on imports and exports; and no exceptions are made. But these textual commands were only partly

[2] Article 114 TFEU.

Table 9.1 Treaty Provisions on the Free Movement of Goods

Title II: Free Movement of Goods	Title VII: Competition, Taxation, Approximation
Chapter 1: Customs Union	**Chapter 1: Rules on Competition**
Article 30: Prohibition on CD and CEE	
Article 31: Common Customs Tariff	**Chapter 2: Tax Provisions**
Article 32: Commission Duties	Article 110: Prohibition of Discriminatory Taxes
Chapter 2: Customs Cooperation	Article 111: Repayment of Internal Taxes
Chapter 3: Quantitative Restrictions	Article 112: Countervailing Charges
Article 34: Prohibition of QR and MEE on Imports	Article 113: Harmonisation of Indirect Taxes
Article 35: Prohibition of QR and MEE on Exports	**Chapter 3: Approximation of Laws**
Article 36: Justifications	
Article 37: State Monopolies of a Commercial Character	

followed. For while the European Court would indeed develop a single constitutional regime for imports and exports, it has allowed for objective justifications within Article 30.

(a) Article 30: An Absolute Prohibition

What is a customs duty? With no definition in the EU Treaties, the Court has defined the concept in a general way. It is "any pecuniary charge" that is "imposed on goods by reason of the fact that they cross a frontier".[3] Yet the Treaty not only outlaws customs duties in this strict sense. For Article 30 extends the prohibition to "charges having equivalent effect" (CEE). This wording betrayed "a general intention to prohibit not only measures which obviously take the form of the classic customs duty".[4] Article 30 was also to cover all those charges with an equivalent result. And in *Commission* v. *Italy*,[5] the Court thus defined a CEE as "any charge which, by altering the price of an article exported, has the same restrictive

---

[3] *Commission* v. *Italy (Statistical Lery)*, Case 24/68, [1969] ECR 193, para. 7.
[4] *Commission* v. *Luxembourg and Belgium*, Case 2 and 3/62, [1962] ECR 425, 432.
[5] *Commission* v. *Italy*, Case 7/68, [1968] ECR 423.

effect on the free circulation of that article as a customs duty".[6] The purpose of the charge would thereby be irrelevant, as Article 30 "ma[de] no distinction based on the purpose of the duties and charges the abolition of which it requires".[7] All that mattered was the effect of a charge, and even the smallest of effects would matter.[8]

Would Article 30 nonetheless require a *protectionist* effect, that is: an effect that protected domestic goods? Despite a brief flirtation with a protectionist rationale,[9] the Court has chosen a different standard. The mere presence of a *restricting* effect on the free movement of goods will trigger Article 30. This constitutional choice was made in *Statistical Levy*.[10] Italy had imposed a levy on goods leaving (or entering) Italy for the purpose of collecting statistical data. Since the levy applied universally to all goods crossing the national border, it argued that the measure could not constitute a CEE "since any protection of domestic production or discrimination is eliminated".[11] The Court disagreed:

> [T]he purpose of the abolition of customs barriers is not merely to eliminate their protective nature, as the Treaty sought on the contrary to give general scope and effect to the rule on the elimination of customs duties and charges having equivalent effect, in order to ensure the free movement of goods. It follows from the system as a whole and from the general and absolute nature of the prohibition of any customs duty applicable to goods moving between Member States that customs duties are prohibited independently of any consideration of the purpose for which they were introduced and the destination of the revenue obtained there from.[12]

Statistical Levy clarified that Article 30 outlawed *all* restrictions – including non-discriminatory restrictions devoid of a protectionist effect.[13] The "general and absolute nature of the prohibition of any customs duties" was confirmed in subsequent jurisprudence.[14] "[A]ny pecuniary charge – however small – imposed on goods by reason of the fact that they cross a frontier constitutes an obstacle to the movement of such goods."[15] And such an obstacle remained an obstacle "even if it is not imposed for the

---

[6] *Ibid.*, 429.   [7] *Ibid.*

[8] *Commission* v. *Italy (Statistical Levy)*, Case 24/68 (supra n. 3) para. 14: "The very low rate of the charge cannot change its character with regard to the principles of the Treaty[.]"

[9] *Commission* v. *Luxembourg and Belgium*, Case 2 and 3/62 (supra n. 4), 432.

[10] *Commission* v. *Italy (Statistical Levy)*, Case 24/68 (supra n. 3).

[11] *Ibid.*, para. 12.   [12] *Ibid.*, paras. 6–7.   [13] *Ibid.*, para. 9.

[14] *Sociaal Fonds voor de Diamantarbeiders* v. *S.A. Ch. Brachfeld & Sons and Chougol Diamond Co*, Case 2/69, [1969] ECR 211, para. 11/14.

[15] *Ibid.*

benefit of the State, is not discriminatory or protective in effect or if the product on which the charge is imposed is not in competition with any domestic product".[16]

The restriction rationale underlying Article 30 thereby stems from the material scope of Article 30. For the prohibition only outlaws national measures that impose a charge on the frontier-crossing of goods. These measures are – by definition – not applicable to goods never leaving the domestic market.[17] A discrimination rationale would here simply not work.

This explains an important conceptual limit to the scope of Article 30. For if it only applies to *frontier* measures it cannot cover measures qualifying as *internal* taxation. The question thus arises as to when a fiscal charge constitutes a measure having an effect equivalent to a customs duty, and when it constitutes an internal tax.[18] In its past jurisprudence, the Court demarcated the respective spheres of Articles 30 and 110 by treating the latter as a *lex specialis*. It has thus found that "financial charges within a general system of internal taxation *applying systematically to domestic and imported products according to the same criteria* are not to be considered as charges having equivalent effect".[19] Equally applicable fiscal charges that apply the "same criteria" to domestic and imported goods will thus not fall under Article 30.[20]

(b) Objective "Justifications"

May a State exceptionally impose customs duties in certain situations? There are no express justifications for fiscal barriers to trade in goods.

---

[16] *Ibid.*, paras. 15/18.

[17] The reference to borders should theoretically mean "national" borders as Article 30 prohibits charges "between Member States". However, the Court has extended the scope of the prohibition to include some charges imposed on goods crossing *regional* frontiers; see *Administration des Douanes et Droits Indirects* v. *Léopold Legros and others*, Case C-163/90, [1992] ECR I-4625.

[18] And since the Treaty only outlaws *discriminatory* internal taxes, the answer to this question will conclusively determine the legality of non-discriminatory fiscal charges. On this point, see Section 2 below.

[19] *Capolongo* v. *Azienda Agricole*, Case 77/72, [1973] ECR 611, para. 12 (emphasis added).

[20] The Court has interpreted the requirement of an application of the "same criteria" strictly. In *Denkavit Loire* v. *France*, Case 132/78, [1979] ECR 1923, the Court had to deal with a French health measure that generally imposed a financial charge on meat. However, the calculation base of the charge differed depending on whether the meat had been slaughtered on French territory or whether it had been imported. The Court held that such a differential system would not apply the "same criteria" to domestic and imported products *(ibid.*, para. 8).

This absence contrasts with the presence of such express justifications for regulatory barriers under Article 36.[21]

Could the latter provision nonetheless apply by analogy to fiscal barriers? In *Commission* v. *Italy*,[22] the defendant tried to justify a charge on the export of goods with artistic or historical value by pointing to Article 36. Yet the Court rejected this reasoning. Exceptions to the free movement of goods had to be interpreted restrictively. And with regard to Article 36 this meant that it "is not possible to apply the exception laid down in the latter provision to measures which fall outside the scope of the prohibitions referred to in the chapter relating to the elimination of quantitative restrictions between Member States".[23] Article 36 was thus confined to *regulatory* restrictions and could not be extended to *fiscal* charges. And since there were no specific justifications for measures falling into Article 30, the Court concluded that the provision "does not permit of any exceptions".[24]

The Court however subsequently recognized two *implied* exceptions. The first exception relates to the situation where a fiscal charge constitutes consideration for a service rendered. In *Statistical Levy*,[25] the Italian government thus argued that its wish to create statistical data for imports and exports benefited individual traders, and that this commercial advantage "justifies their paying for this public service" as a *quid pro quo*.[26] The Court indeed accepted the abstract idea;[27] yet it nonetheless found against Italy, since the charge was not consideration for a *specific service* benefiting *individual traders*. The statistical information was only "beneficial to the economy as a whole", and the advantage was thus "so general" that the charge could not be regarded "as the consideration for a *specific* benefit".[28]

The second (implied) justification from the absolute prohibition of fiscal charges are charges that a Member State levies as compensation for

---

[21] See Table 9.1 above. For the text of Article 36 and its interpretation, see Section 4 below.
[22] *Commission* v. *Italy (Art Treasures)*, Case 7/68 (supra n. 5).   [23] *Ibid.*, 430.
[24] *Commission* v. *Italy (Statistical Levy)*, Case 24/68 (supra n. 3), para. 10; and see also *Sociaal Fonds voor de Diamantarbeiders* v. *S.A. Ch. Brachfeld*, Case 2/69 (supra n. 14), paras. 19/21.
[25] *Commission* v. *Italy (Statistical Levy)*, Case 24/68 (supra n. 3).   [26] *Ibid.*, para. 15.
[27] *Ibid.*, para. 11: "Although it is not impossible that in certain circumstances a specific service actually rendered may form consideration for a possible proportional payment for the service in question, this may only apply in specific cases which cannot lead to the circumvention of the provisions of [Article 30] of the Treaty."
[28] *Ibid.*, para. 16 (emphasis added).

frontier checks that are required under European law.[29] The rationale behind this exception is that the Member States here act on behalf of the Union, and in a way that facilitates the free movement of goods.

2. Fiscal Barriers II: Discriminatory Internal Taxation

The prohibition of customs duties and the prohibition of protectionist taxation are two sides of the same coin. The prohibition established in Article 110 TFEU indeed complements Article 30 TFEU:

> Article [110] supplements the provision[] on the abolition of customs duties and charges having equivalent effect. Its aim is to ensure free movement of goods between the Member States in normal conditions of competition by the elimination of all forms of protection which may result from the application of internal taxation.[30]

Despite their complementary aims, the material scopes of Articles 30 and 110 are nonetheless fundamentally different. The former catches national measures that impose a charge on goods when crossing a frontier. By contrast, Article 110 applies where foreign goods are subject – with domestic goods – to internal taxation. The scopes of Articles 30 and 110 are thus mutually exclusive.[31]

Article 110 deals with measures that apply to foreign *and* domestic goods. The provision is therefore – unlike Article 30 – not formulated as an absolute prohibition. Instead it states:

> [1] No Member State shall impose, directly or indirectly, on the products of other Member States any internal taxation of any kind *in excess of* that imposed directly or indirectly on similar domestic products.

---

[29] In *Bauhuis* v. *The Netherlands*, Case 46/76, [1977] ECR 5, the Court had been asked to deal with a Union law that required veterinary and public health inspections by the exporting Member State so as to make multiple frontier inspections unnecessary. The health inspections were thus not unilaterally imposed by a Member State but reflected "the general interest of the [Union]" (*ibid.*, para. 29); and as such, they would not hinder trade in goods (*ibid.*, para. 30). National charges for these "Union" inspections were thus legal (*ibid.*, para. 31). For a subsequent codification of the *Bauhuis* test, see *Commission* v. *Germany*, Case 18/87, [1988] ECR 5427.

[30] *Bergandi* v. *Directeur général des impôts*, Case 252/86, [1988] ECR 1342, para. 17.

[31] *Compagnie Commerciale de l'Ouest and others* v. *Receveur Principal des Douanes de La Pallice Port*, Case C-78/90, [1992] ECR I-1847, para. 22: "The provisions on charges having equivalent effect and those on discriminatory internal taxation cannot be applied together. The scope of each of those provisions must therefore be defined."

> [2] Furthermore, no Member State shall impose on the products of other Member States any internal taxation of such a nature to afford *indirect protection* to other products.

The aim behind Article 110 is to outlaw domestic tax systems that protect national goods. It thereby distinguishes between two types of protectionist taxes. Paragraph 1 declares illegal all national tax laws that *discriminate* between foreign and domestic goods. Discrimination here means that "similar" foreign goods are treated dissimilarly. This might occur through direct or indirect means. Direct discrimination takes place where national tax legislation *legally* disadvantages foreign goods by – for example – imposing a higher tax rate than that for domestic goods.[32] Indirect discrimination occurs where the same national tax formally applies to both foreign and domestic goods, but materially imposes a *heavier* fiscal burden on the former.[33]

Paragraph 2 covers a second variant of fiscal protectionism. Strictly speaking, it is not based on a discrimination rationale. For its scope is wider than outlawing the dissimilar treatment of "similar" goods.[34] Yet by insisting on proof of a protectionist effect it is stricter than paragraph 1,[35] since the latter will not require evidence of such an effect.

Let us look at both protectionist variants in turn.

(a) Paragraph 1: Discrimination Against "Similar" Foreign Goods

Article 110(1) prohibits foreign goods to be taxed "in excess of" similar domestic goods. This outlaws internal taxes that discriminate between national and imported products. Discrimination will thereby cover direct discrimination,[36] as well as indirect discrimination.[37]

The key to this prohibition lies in the concept of "similarity". When are domestic and foreign goods *similar*? Early on, the Court clarified

---

[32] See *Lütticke GmbH* v. *Hauptzollamt Sarrelouis*, Case 57/65, [1966] ECR 205; as well as *Hansen & Balle* v. *Hauptzollamt de Flensburg*, Case 148/77, [1978] ECR 1787.

[33] On this point, see my discussion of *Humblot* v. *Directeur des services fiscaux*, Case 112/84 in Section 2(a) below.

[34] On the two distinct tests for Article 110(1) and 110(2) TFEU, see *Fink-Frucht GmbH* v. *Hauptzollamt München-Landsbergerstrasse*, Case 27/67, [1967] ECR 223.

[35] See *Commission* v. *Sweden*, C-167/05, [2008] ECR I-2127.

[36] Cf. Case 57/65 *Lütticke* (supra n. 32).

[37] *Humblot* v. *Directeur des services fiscaux*, Case 112/84, [1985] ECR 1367.

that similarity is wider than identity;[38] and that similarity relates to comparability.[39] Comparability thereby means that two goods "have similar characteristics and meet the same needs from the point of view of consumers".[40] But are "whisky" and "cognac" comparable drinks?[41] Or should it make a difference that the former is seen as an *apéritif*, while the latter constitutes a *digestif*?[42]

The Court has endorsed a "broad interpretation of the concept of similarity",[43] which however takes account of "objective" differences between two seemingly similar products. An excellent illustration of this approach is *Humblot*.[44] Monsieur Humblot had acquired a (German) Mercedes car in France. The car possessed 36 CV (fiscal horsepower) and he had to pay a special tax imposed by the French Revenue Code, which distinguished between a progressive annual tax for cars up to 16 CV and a single special tax for cars above this rate. The special tax was nearly five times higher than the highest rate of the general progressive tax. And as France did not produce any cars above 16 CV, the question arose whether the special tax was "in excess of" the national tax on domestic goods. But are small (French) cars comparable to big (German) cars? The French government defended its internal tax regime by arguing that "the special tax is charged solely on luxury vehicles, which are *not similar*, within the meaning of the first paragraph of Article [110] to cars liable to the differential tax".[45] The Court disagreed. For while it acknowledged the power of the Member States to "subject products such as cars to a system of road tax which increases progressively in amount depending on an *objective criterion*, such as the power rating",[46] the French tax system did not do so and thus indirectly discriminated against foreign cars.[47]

---

[38] See *Hansen & Balle*, Case 148/77 (supra n. 32), para. 19: "The application of that provision is based not on a strict requirement that the products should be identical but on their 'similarity'."

[39] See *Commission* v. *France (Whisky v Cognac)*, Case 168/78, [1980] ECR 347, para. 5.

[40] *Rewe-Zentrale des Lebensmittel-Großhandels GmbH* v. *Hauptzollamt Landau/Pfalz*, Case 45/75, [1976] ECR 181.

[41] *Commission* v. *France (Whisky v. Cognac)*, Case 168/78 (supra n. 39).

[42] *Ibid.*, para. 33.

[43] *John Walker* v. *Ministeriet for Skatter og Afgifter*, Case 243/84, [1986] ECR 875, para. 11.

[44] *Humblot* v. *Directeur des Services Fiscaux*, Case 112/84, [1985] ECR 1367.

[45] *Ibid.*, para. 9.   [46] *Ibid.*, para. 12.

[47] While the Court was coy with regard to the exact violation, the case appears to acknowledge a partial violation of Article 110(1) in para. 14. For a subsequent case on

What "objective" criteria may however be used fiscally to distinguish between seemingly similar products?[48] This question is – misleadingly – called the question of "objective justification".[49] What stands behind this misnomer is the idea that while a national tax system must be neutral towards foreign goods, it can discriminate between goods "on the basis of objective criteria".[50] Thus, where a Member State discriminates on the basis of a regional policy objective, such a public policy objective will not amount to protectionist discrimination. The discrimination is here "justified" by "objective" criteria that distinguish two products. This can be seen in *Commission* v. *France (Natural Sweet Wines)*.[51] The Commission had brought proceedings against a French tax scheme that exempted naturally sweet wines from the higher consumption duty on liqueur wines. The French Government defended this differential treatment by pointing to the fact that "natural sweet wines are made in regions characterized by low rainfall and relatively poor soil, in which the difficulty of growing other crops means that the local economy depends heavily on their production".[52] This regional policy objective gave preferential treatment to a "traditional and customary production" over similar goods resulting from industrial production. And this "objective" criterion was not discriminating against foreign goods.[53]

(b) Paragraph 2: Protection Against "Competing" Foreign Goods

Strictly speaking, the rationale behind Article 110(2) is not a prohibition on discriminatory taxation. For the idea of discrimination implies treating similar products dissimilarly. And where there are no similar domestic products, there cannot be discrimination.[54] The scope of Article 110(2) is thus wider. It outlaws all internal taxes that grant "indirect protection" to domestic goods. Unlike national taxes that are discriminatory, the provision targets national taxes that generally disadvantage foreign goods. However, the Court has held that such indirect protection only occurs where domestic goods are *in competition* with imported

---

the – reformed – French car tax system, see *Feldain* v. *Directeur des services fiscaux du département du Haut-Rhin* Case 433/85, [1987] ECR 3521.

[48] *Commission* v. *Italy (Regenerated Oil)* Case 21/79, [1980] ECR 1.

[49] The term is used in *ibid.*, para. 16: "objectively justified".

[50] *John Walker* v. *Ministeriet for Skatter og Afgifter*, Case 243/84 (supra n. 43), para. 23.

[51] *Commission* v. *France (Natural Sweet Wines)*, Case 196/85, [1987] ECR 1597.

[52] *Ibid.*, para. 9.   [53] *Ibid.*, para. 10.

[54] *Commission* v. *Italy (Bananas)*, Case 184/85, [1987] ECR 2013.

goods.[55] Article 110(2) consequently requires two elements to be fulfilled before a national tax is found to hinder the free movement of goods. First, the national law will tax *competing* goods differently. And second, this differentiation indirectly protects *national* goods.

When will two goods be in competition? Within Article 110(2), the Court has generally adopted a flexible approach. This can be seen in *Commission* v. *United Kingdom (Beer & Wine)*.[56] The Commission had brought infringement proceedings against Great Britain in the belief that its tax regime for wine granted indirect protection to British beer. The excise tax on wine was indeed significantly higher than that on beer, and as Britain produced very little wine but a lot of beer, the suspicion of indirect protectionism arose. Britain counterclaimed that there was no competitive relationship between beer and wine, and that there could thus be no such protectionist effect. Not only were the two products "entirely different" with regard to their production and price structure,[57] the goods would hardly ever be substituted by consumers.[58] The Court was not impressed with this line of argument, and espoused its dynamic understanding of product substitution:

> In order to determine the existence of a competitive relationship under the second paragraph of Article [110], it is necessary to consider not only the present state of the market but also the possibilities for development within the context of the free movement of goods at the [Union] level and the further potential for the substitution of products for one another which may be revealed by intensification of trade, so as fully to develop the complementary features of the economies of the Member States in accordance with the objectives laid down by Article [3] of the [EU] Treaty...For the purpose of measuring the degree of substitution, it is impossible to restrict oneself to consumer habits in a Member State or in a given region. In fact, those habits, which are essentially variable in time and space, cannot be considered to be a fixed rule; the tax policy of a Member State

[55] Where this is not the case, Article 110(2) will indeed not apply; see *Commission* v. *Denmark*, Case 47/88, [1990] ECR I-4509; as well as *De Danske Bilimportorer* v. *Skatteministeriet, Toldog Skattestyrelsen*, Case C-383/01, [2003] ECR I-6065.

[56] *Commission* v. *United Kingdom (Beer & Wine, Interim Judgment)*, Case 170/78, [1980] ECR 417.

[57] *Ibid.*, para. 13.

[58] *Ibid.*: "As regards consumer habits, the Government of the United Kingdom states that in accordance with long-established tradition in the United Kingdom, beer is a popular drink consumed preferably in public-houses or in connexion with work; domestic consumption and consumption with meals is negligible. In contrast, the consumption of wine is more unusual and special from the point of view of social custom."

must not therefore crystallize given consumer habits so as to consolidate an advantage acquired by national industries concerned to comply with them.[59]

The Court here brilliantly attacked the chicken-and-egg problem within Article 110(2). For two goods might not presently be in competition *because* of the artificial price differences created by internal taxation. The British argument that its tax policy only reflected a social habit in which beer was mass-consumed, while wine was an "elitist" drink, disregarded the fact that the social habit might itself – at least partly – be the product of its fiscal policy. And once this fiscal policy disappeared, beer and wine *could* be in competition. This *dynamic* understanding of product substitutability acknowledges the ability of fiscal regimes to *dynamically* shape consumer preferences.

Once a foreign product has been found to be in competition with a domestic product, the Court will investigate whether the national tax regime generates a protectionist effect. In the above case, the Court indeed found that the higher tax burden on wine would afford protection to domestic beer production.[60] And in another case involving "drinks in Luxembourg",[61] the Court considered a clear protectionist effect to exist where "an essential part of domestic production" came within the most favourable tax category whereas competing products – "almost all of which [were] imported from other Member States" – were subject to higher taxation.[62]

3. Regulatory Barriers: Quantitative Restrictions

Regulatory barriers are legal obstacles to trade which cannot be overcome by the payment of money.[63] They potentially range from a complete ban on (foreign) products to the partial restriction of a product's use.

---

[59] *Ibid.*, paras. 6 and 14.

[60] *Commission* v. *United Kingdom (Beer & Wine, Final Judgment)*, Case 170/78, [1983] ECR 2265, para. 27.

[61] G. Rodrigues Iglesias, "Drinks in Luxembourg: Alcoholic Beverages and the Case Law of the European Court of Justice", in D. O'Keeffe (ed.), *Judicial Review in European Union Law: Liber Amicorum in Honour of Lord Slynn of Hadley* (Kluwer, 2000), 523.

[62] *Commission* v. *France (Whisky v. Cognac)*, Case 168/78 (supra n. 39), para. 41.

[63] This general rule was expressed in *Iannelli & Volpi* v. *Meroni*, Case 74/76, [1977] ECR 557, para. 9: "[O]bstacles which are of a fiscal nature or have equivalent effect and are covered by Articles [30 and 110] of the Treaty do not fall within the prohibition in Article [34]."

What types of legal barriers to the free movement of goods do the Treaties outlaw? The Treaty regime for regulatory barriers is set out in Chapter 3 of Title II. The chapter outlaws quantitative restrictions on imports (Article 34) and exports (Article 35); yet it also contains a provision according to which restrictions on imports or exports can be justified (Article 36). Two systemic features of this constitutional arrangement strike the attentive eye. First, unlike the legal regime governing customs duties, the Treaties expressly distinguish between *two* prohibitions: one for imports, and one for exports. And second, the constitutional regime for regulatory barriers expressly allows for exceptions. This section deals with the first feature and analyses the – respective – prohibitions for quantitative restrictions on imports and exports. Section 4 will then examine the express (and implied) justifications for regulatory restrictions on the free movement of goods.

(a) Quantitative Restrictions on Imports: Article 34

The central provision governing regulatory barriers to imports is Article 34 TFEU. It states:

> Quantitative restrictions on imports and all measures having equivalent effect shall be prohibited between Member States.

The core of this prohibition consists of the concept of "quantitative restrictions". These are restrictions that legally limit the quantity of imported goods to a fixed amount.[64] Quantitative restrictions are quotas, which – in their most extreme form – amount to a total ban.[65] Import quotas operate as absolute frontier barriers: once a quota for a product is exhausted, foreign imports cannot enter the domestic market. However, the text of Article 34 covers – like that of Article 30 on customs duties – a second category of measures, namely "Measures having an Equivalent Effect to Quantitative Restrictions" (MEEQRs). And it is this category that has been at the centre of judicial and academic attention in the past half-century.

---

[64] See *Geddo* v. *Ente Nazionale Risi*, Case 2/73, [1973] ECR 865, para. 7: "The prohibition on quantitative restrictions covers measures which amount to a total or a partial restraint of, according to the circumstances, imports, exports, or goods in transit."
[65] *Regina* v. *Henn and Darby*, Case 34/79, [1979] ECR 3795, para. 12: "[P]rohibition on imports ... is the most extreme form of restriction."

What are these mysterious MEEQRs? We find a first (legislative) definition of these measures in Directive 70/50.[66] The Directive distinguishes between two types of MEEQRs. National measures that are *not* "applicable equally" to domestic and foreign products and "which hinder imports which could otherwise take place" are dealt with in its Article 2. They are seen as MEEQR. By contrast, measures that are "applicable equally" are not generally seen as equivalent to those of quantitative restrictions.[67] Yet Article 3 of the Directive nonetheless extends the concept of MEEQR to certain equally applicable measures:

> This Directive also covers measures governing the marketing of products which deal, in particular, with shape, size, weight, composition, presentation, identification or putting up and which are equally applicable to domestic and imported products, *where the restrictive effect of such measures on the free movement of goods exceeds the effects intrinsic to trade rules.*
>
> This is the case, in particular, where:
>
> – the restrictive effects on the free movement of goods are out of proportion to their purpose;
> – the same objective can be attained by other means which are less of a hindrance to trade.[68]

This provision was informed by a fundamental constitutional choice. Product requirements that were equally applicable to domestic and imported goods were – in principle – considered outside the scope of Article 34. For their restrictive effects on the free movement of goods were seen as "*inherent in the disparities* between rules applied by Member States".[69] And these legislative disparities would need to be removed through the Union's harmonization powers.[70] Equally applicable marketing measures would thus only *exceptionally* fall within the scope of Article 34, when they had "a restrictive effect on the free movement of goods over and above that which is intrinsic to such rules".[71]

---

[66] Commission Directive 70/50 on the abolition of measures which have an effect equivalent to quantitative restrictions on imports and are not covered by other provisions adopted in pursuance of the EEC Treaty, [1970] OJ L13/29.

[67] *Ibid.*, recital 8.   [68] *Ibid.*, Article 3 (emphasis added).

[69] *Ibid.* (emphasis added).

[70] On the scope of Article 114 TFEU, see Chapter 10 – Section 1 below.

[71] Directive 70/50 (supra n. 66), recital 9.

Despite the Directive's strong impact on the early case law,[72] the Court eventually developed a second definition in *Dassonville*.[73] The case involved the legality of Belgian rules that made the sale of Scotch whisky dependent on having a "certificate of origin" from the British customs authorities. Was this certification requirement an MEEQR? The Court thought so, and gave the following famous definition:

> All trading rules enacted by Member States which are capable of hindering, directly or indirectly, actually or potentially, intra-[Union] trade are to be considered as measures having an effect equivalent to quantitative restrictions.[74]

This formulation became known as the "*Dassonville* formula". On its surface, the formula did not distinguish between equally and non-equally applicable rules; yet like Directive 70/50, it seemed to focus on unreasonable restrictions to the free movement of goods.[75]

But what were unreasonable restrictions? Whatever the original intentions behind *Dassonville*, a lasting answer to this question was given in *Cassis de Dijon*.[76] The case concerned a German marketing rule that fixed the minimum alcohol strength of liqueurs at 25 per cent. This national rule prohibited the sale of Cassis de Dijon as a liqueur in Germany, for the distinguished French drink only had an alcohol content below 20 per cent. Formally, the national measure applied equally to foreign and domestic goods. Would the Court thus search for a disproportionate restrictive effect? The Court gave the following famous answer:

> Obstacles to movement within the [Union] resulting from disparities between national laws relating to the marketing of the products in question must be accepted in so far as those provisions may be recognized as being necessary in order to satisfy mandatory requirements relating in particular

---

[72] See *Commission* v. *Germany*, Case 12/74, [1975] ECR 181.
[73] *Procureur du Roi* v. *Dassonville*, Case 8/74, [1974] ECR 837.
[74] *Ibid.*, para. 5.
[75] *Ibid.*, para. 6: "In the absence of a [Union] system guaranteeing for consumers the authenticity of a product's designation of origin, if a Member State takes measures to prevent unfair practices in this connexion, it is however subject to the condition that these measures should be reasonable and that the means of proof required should not act as a hindrance to trade between Member States[.]"
[76] *Rewe-Zentral AG* v. *Bundesmonopolverwaltung für Branntwein*, Case 120/78, [1979] ECR 649.

> to the effectiveness of fiscal supervision, the protection of public health, the fairness of commercial transactions and the defence of the consumer ...
>
> [T]he requirements relating to the minimum alcohol content of alcoholic beverages do not serve a purpose which is in the general interest and such as to take precedence over the requirements of the free movement of goods, which constitutes one of the fundamental rules of the [Union]... There is therefore no valid reason why, provided that they have been lawfully produced and marketed in one of the Member States, alcoholic beverages should not be introduced into any other Member State; the sale of such products may not be subject to a legal prohibition on the marketing of beverages with an alcohol content lower than the limit set by the national rules.[77]

Formally, the judgment can superficially be aligned with the logic behind Directive 70/50. Yet substantively, the Court here implicitly overruled the presumption that trade restrictions flowing from disparities between equally applicable product requirements will only *exceptionally* qualify as MEEQRs. *Cassis* inverts this presumption of legality, and transforms it into a presumption of illegality. Thus: *unless* there are mandatory requirements in the general interest, Member States are *not* entitled to impose their domestic product standards on imported goods. This presumption of illegality would become known as the "principle of mutual recognition". Member States must – in principle – mutually recognize each other's product standards.[78]

After *Cassis*, the idea of a discrimination rationale behind Article 34 appeared to be sidelined. And in a subsequent period, the Court indeed cultivated an absolute prohibition for all regulatory restrictions to trade in goods. A striking illustration of this anti-regulatory philosophy is *Torfaen*.[79] The case formed part of the *Sunday Trading* cases.[80] It had been brought by Torfaen Borough Council, which alleged that B&Q had infringed the 1950 (British) Shops Act by trading on Sunday. The defendant counterclaimed that the British restriction on opening times of shops

---

[77] *Ibid.*, paras. 8 and 14.

[78] This constitutional principle would, in turn, influence the scope of positive integration under the harmonization competences of the Union. On this point, see R. Schütze, *European Union Law* (Cambridge University Press, 2015), Chapter 14 – Section 3(c).

[79] *Torfaen Borough Council* v. *B&Q*, Case 145/88, [1989] ECR 3851.

[80] For an analysis of these cases, see C. Barnard, "Sunday Trading: A Drama in Five Acts", 57 (1994) *Modern Law Review*, 449.

was an MEEQR. The national law reduced the absolute amount of total sales; and since a percentage of these sales were foreign goods, the Sunday trading ban constituted a restriction on imports. The European Court, drawing on its jurisprudential line on sales restrictions,[81] indeed held that the Shops Act would constitute an MEEQR if "the effects of such national rules exceed what is necessary to achieve the aim in view".[82]

This judicial signal was fatally effective. For it encouraged commercial traders to challenge virtually all national laws that somehow restricted the marketing of goods on the basis of the *Dassonville* formula.[83] It soon dawned on the Court that its jurisprudence had gone too far. And it therefore announced a judicial retreat in *Keck*.[84] In this case criminal proceedings had been brought against a supermarket manager who had allowed products to be sold at a loss. This form of sales promotion was prohibited in France, but Keck argued that the prohibition constituted an MEEQR because it restricted intra-Union trade in goods.[85] The Court disagreed. While confirming the *Dassonville* formula, it held that certain measures would only fall foul of Article 34 if they were discriminatory:

> National legislation imposing a general prohibition on resale at a loss is not designed to regulate trade in goods between Member States. Such legislation may, admittedly, restrict the volume of sales, and hence the volume of sales of products from other Member States, in so far as it deprives traders of a method of sales promotion. But the question remains whether such a possibility is sufficient to characterize the legislation in question as a measure having equivalent effect to a quantitative restriction on imports …
>
> It is established by the case-law beginning with "Cassis de Dijon" that, in the absence of harmonization of legislation, obstacles to free movement of goods which are the consequence of applying, to goods coming from other Member States where they are lawfully manufactured and marketed, rules

---

[81] The two judicial precedents in this respect were *Oebel*, Case 155/80, [1981] ECR 1993, and *Cinéthèque and others* v. *Fédération nationale des cinémas français*, Case 60 and 61/84, [1985] ECR 2605.

[82] *Torfaen*, Case 145/88 (supra n. 79), para. 15. The Court expressly referred to Article 3 of Directive 70/50 (supra n. 66) as inspiration for this test.

[83] See D. Chalmers, "Free Movement of Goods within the European Community: An Unhealthy Addiction to Scotch Whisky", 42 (1993) *International and Comparative Law Quarterly*, 269.

[84] *Criminal Proceedings against Keck and Mithouard*, Joined Cases C-267 and C-268/91, [1993] ECR I-6097.

[85] *Ibid.*, para. 3.

> that lay down requirements to be met by such goods (such as those relating to designation, form, size, weight, composition, presentation, labelling, packaging) constitute measures of equivalent effect prohibited by Article [34]. This is so even if those rules apply without distinction to all products unless their application can be justified by a public-interest objective taking precedence over the free movement of goods. *By contrast, contrary to what has previously been decided, the application to products from other Member States of national provisions restricting or prohibiting certain selling arrangements is not such as to hinder directly or indirectly, actually or potentially, trade between Member States within the meaning of the* Dassonville *judgment, so long as those provisions apply to all relevant traders operating within the national territory and so long as they affect in the same manner, in law and in fact, the marketing of domestic products and of those from other Member States.*[86]

The case constitutes a symbolic watershed. Drawing a distinction between product requirements and "selling arrangements",[87] *Keck* clarified that the latter would only constitute MEEQRs where they *discriminated* against the marketing of foreign goods.[88] Only discriminatory selling arrangements would violate the free movement of goods provisions.[89] Product requirements, by contrast, would still not need to be discriminatory to fall within the scope of Article 34. And in light of the two distinct constitutional tests, the distinction between product requirements and selling arrangements has become *the* classificatory battle in the post-*Keck* jurisprudence.[90]

One must however bear in mind that "product requirements" and "selling arrangements" are only two specific categories of measures that potentially constitute MEEQRs. Other categories may equally fall foul of Article 34. However, for a very long time it seemed that all MEEQRs would need to be rules that somehow interfered with the commercial chain leading from production and trading to the selling of a good. Rules that limited the *consumer* use of a good appeared to be outside the scope of Article 34.

---

[86] *Ibid.*, paras. 12–16 (emphasis added).

[87] The distinction had been – academically – suggested by E. White, "In Search of the Limits of Article 30 of the EEC Treaty", 26 (1989) *Common Market Law Review*, 235.

[88] For an important first evaluation of *Keck*, see S. Weatherill, "After Keck: Some Thoughts on How to Clarify the Clarification", 33 (1996), *Common Market Law Review*, 885.

[89] See *Konsumentombudsmannen (KO)* v. *Gourmet*, Case C-405/98, [2001] ECR I-1795, esp. para. 25.

[90] See *Familiapress* v. *Bauer Verlag*, Case C-368/95, [1997] ECR I-3689. On the general classification of advertising restrictions as selling arrangements, see *Hünermund and others* v. *Landesapothekerkammer Baden-Württemberg*, Case C-292/92, [1993] ECR 6787.

But even this implied limitation has recently been challenged in *Italian Trailers*.[91]

The case involved a provision within the Italian Highway Code that prohibited the use of trailers on motorcycles and mopeds. The Commission considered the provision to constitute an MEEQR and brought proceedings against Italy. Italy defended itself by insisting that "a rule concerning use is covered by Article [34 TFEU] only if it prohibits all uses of a product or its only use, if the product only has one", whereas "if there is a discretion as to the possible uses of the product, the situation no longer falls under Article [34]."[92] In its ruling, the Court picked up this distinction and differentiated between trailers for general use and trailers specifically designed for motorcycles.[93] With regard to the latter, the question was this: would the *prohibition* on using motor trailers on a public highway constitute an MEEQR?

The Court answered this question positively:

It should be noted in that regard that a prohibition on the use of a product in the territory of a Member State has a considerable influence on the behaviour of consumers, which, in its turn, affects the access of that product to the market of that Member State. Consumers, knowing that they are not permitted to use their motorcycle with a trailer specially designed for it, have practically no interest in buying such a trailer. Thus, Article 56 of the Highway Code prevents a demand from existing in the market at issue for such trailers and therefore hinders their importation. It follows that the prohibition laid down in Article 56 of the Highway Code, to the extent that its effect is to hinder access to the Italian market for trailers which are specially designed for motorcycles and are lawfully produced and marketed in Member States other than the Italian Republic, constitutes a measure having equivalent effect to quantitative restrictions on imports within the meaning of Article [34 TFEU], unless it can be justified objectively.[94]

This extension of the scope of Article 34 to national measures that limit consumer use has been confirmed in *Mickelsson*.[95] The Court here clarified that there was no need to show discrimination. Its sole concern was whether the rules totally or "greatly" prevented consumers from using products that were lawfully produced in another Member State; and if this was the case, the national measure would negatively influence consumers

---

[91] *Commission* v. *Italy (Italian Trailers)*, Case C-110/05, (2009) ECR I-519.
[92] *Ibid.*, para. 19.   [93] *Ibid.*, paras. 51 et seq.   [94] *Ibid.*, paras. 56–8.
[95] *Åklagaren* v. *Mickelsson and Roos*, Case C-142/05, (2009) ECR I-4273.

and thus hinder "access to the domestic market" of foreign products. And in limiting market access, these rules violated Article 34.[96]

(b) Quantitative Restrictions on Exports: Article 35

The wording in Article 35 mirrors that of Article 34: "Quantitative restrictions on exports, and all measures having equivalent effect, shall be prohibited between Member States."

Would it not be "logical" if the legal principles governing quantitative restrictions on exports mirrored those on imports? This argument will work for some measures;[97] yet – importantly – not for others, as the scope of Article 35 is indirectly limited by the scope of Article 34. For if the *Cassis* principle of mutual recognition is to work, the product standards of the exporting state must be presumed legitimate. With regard to product requirements, the Court has consequently interpreted Article 35 to include only those national laws that specifically discriminate against exports.

This logical extension of *Cassis* was made in *Groenveld*.[98] A wholesaler of horsemeat had challenged the legality of a Dutch law prohibiting the (industrial) production of horsemeat sausages. The law had been adopted in order to protect Dutch meat exports in light of the fact that the consumption of horsemeat was not allowed in the national markets of some important trading partners. The Court held that the prohibition on the (industrial) production of horsemeat sausages did not constitute an MEEQR on exports:

> [Article 35] concerns national measures which have as their specific object or effect the restriction of patterns of exports and thereby the establishment of a difference in treatment between the domestic trade of a Member State and its export trade in such a way as to provide a particular advantage for national production or for the domestic market of the State in question at the expense of the production or of the trade of other Member States. This is not so in the case of a prohibition like that in question which is applied objectively to the production of goods of a certain kind without drawing a distinction depending on whether such goods are intended for the national market or for export.[99]

Equally applicable product requirements would thus *not* constitute MEEQR on exports. But did this mean that Article 35 would never apply to equally

---

[96] *Ibid.*, para. 28.
[97] See *Procureur de la République de Besançon* v. *Les Sieurs Bouhelier and others*, Case 53/76, [1977] ECR 197.
[98] *Groenveld* v. *Produktschap voor Vee en Vlees*, Case 15/79, [1979] ECR 3409.
[99] *Ibid.*, para. 7.

applicable national laws? It took almost thirty years before the Court gave a decisive answer to this question in *Gysbrechts*.[100] The case involved a Belgian law that prohibited distant selling contracts from requiring the consumer to provide his or her credit card number before a period of seven working days (within which withdrawal from the contract was possible).[101] Was this an MEEQR on exports? The Court found that the national measure indeed "deprive[d] the traders concerned of an efficient tool with which to guard against the risk of non-payment", and thus restricted trade. But in light of the equally applicable nature of the measure, did it fulfil the *Groenveld* formula?[102] The Court found that this was indeed the case, since "its actual effect is none the less greater on goods leaving the market of the exporting Member State than on the marketing of goods in the domestic market of that Member State".[103] Equally applicable measures may thus constitute MEEQRs on exports, where they indirectly discriminate. And the discriminatory selling arrangement in the present case would thus need to be justified.

4. Justifying Regulatory Barriers: Article 36 and Mandatory Requirements

From the very beginning, the Treaty acknowledged that some quantitative restrictions or measures having equivalent effect could be justified on certain grounds. This express acknowledgement reflected the fact that regulatory barriers to trade often pursue a legitimate *regulatory* interest. These legitimate interests are set out in Article 36, which states:

> The provisions of Articles 34 and 35 shall not preclude prohibitions or restrictions on imports, exports or goods in transit justified on grounds of public morality, public policy or public security; the protection of health

---

[100] *Gysbrechts and Santurel Inter*, Case C-205/07, [2008] ECR I-9947. For an analysis of this case, see M. Szydlo, "Export Restrictions within the Structure of Free Movement of Goods. Reconsideration of an Old Paradigm", 47 (2010) *Common Market Law Review*, 753.

[101] *Gysbrechts*, Case C-205/07 (supra n. 100), para. 13.

[102] The Court expressly confirmed *Groenveld*, Case 15/79 (supra n. 98) in *Gysbrechts*, Case C-205/07 (supra n. 100), para. 40.

[103] *Ibid.*, para. 43. This point was explained in para. 42: "As is clear from the order for reference, the consequences of such a prohibition are generally more significant in cross-border sales made directly to consumers, in particular, in sales made by means of the internet, by reason, inter alia, of the obstacles to bringing any legal proceedings in another Member State against consumers who default, especially when the sales involve relatively small sums."

> and life of humans, animals or plants; the protection of national treasures
> possessing artistic, historic or archaeological value; or the protection of
> industrial and commercial property. Such prohibitions or restrictions shall
> not, however, constitute a means of arbitrary discrimination or a disguised
> restriction on trade between Member States.

The provision exempts restrictions on the free movement of goods, where they are justified on grounds of public morality,[104] public policy,[105] public security,[106] public health,[107] national treasures,[108] and the protection of intellectual property.[109] The Court has found this list to be exhaustive: the exceptions listed in Article 36 "cannot be extended to cases other than those specifically laid down".[110] The Court has further found that since Article 36 "constitutes a derogation from the basic rule that all obstacles to the free movement of goods between Member States shall be eliminated", it "must be interpreted strictly".[111] And yet, despite limiting the scope of the Treaty's express derogations, the Court has allowed for implied derogations. These implied justifications for restrictions to the free movement of goods are called "mandatory requirements".

(a) Implied Justifications: Mandatory Requirements

Despite having found the *express* exceptions in Article 36 to be exhaustive, the Court has recognized the existence of *implied* justifications. In *Cassis de Dijon*,[112] the Court thus exempted obstacles to the free movement of goods that were "necessary in order to satisfy *mandatory requirements* relating in particular to the effectiveness of fiscal supervision, the protection of public health, the fairness of commercial transactions and the defence of the consumer".[113] The best explanation for the

---

[104] See *Regina* v. *Henn and Darby*, Case 34/79 (supra n. 65).

[105] See *R.* v. *Thompson, Johnson & Woodiwiss*, Case 7/78, [1978] ECR 2247.

[106] See *Campus Oil and others* v. *Minister for Industry and Energy and others*, Case 72/83, [1984] ECR 2727.

[107] See *Commission* v. *United Kingdom*, Case 40/82, [1982] ECR 2793.

[108] According to P. Oliver et al., *Free Movement of Goods in the European Union* (Hart, 2010), 281 there is no case law on the direct application of this ground.

[109] See *Van Zuylen frères* v. *Hag AG*, Case 192/73, [1974] ECR 731.

[110] *Commission* v. *Ireland (Irish Souvenirs)*, Case 113/80, [1981] ECR 1625, para. 7.

[111] *Bauhuis*, Case 46/76 (supra n. 29), para. 12.

[112] *Rewe-Zentral AG* v. *Bundesmonopolverwaltung für Branntwein*, Case 120/78 (supra n. 76).

[113] *Ibid.*, para. 8 (emphasis added).

acceptance of implied justifications may be the dramatically expanded scope of Article 34, which – after *Cassis* – henceforth outlawed all non-discriminatory obstacles to trade that resulted from national disparities in product requirements. Subsequently, the Court indeed clarified that these mandatory requirements could solely justify national laws "which apply without discrimination to both domestic and imported products".[114]

The nature of a national restriction – whether discriminatory or not – thus determines which justifications are available to a Member State. Discriminatory national measures can only be justified by reference to the express – and exhaustive – list of public interest grounds in Article 36.[115] By contrast, national measures that do not discriminate will benefit from an open-ended list of implied "mandatory requirements".[116] This distinction has been criticized;[117] and the Court has sometimes tried to evade it by sharp scholastic means,[118] or by bluntly fudging the issue of the (non-)discriminatory character of a national measure.[119] One of the interesting questions in this context is whether selling arrangements that fall within the scope of Article 34 may ever be justified by mandatory requirements. Theoretically, this should not be the case if constitutional logic is followed.[120] However, the Court has given reason to believe that a softer rule might apply in practice.[121]

---

[114] *Criminal Proceedings against Gilli and Andres*, Case 788/79, [1980] ECR 2071, para. 6.

[115] *Commission* v. *Ireland (Irish Souvenirs)*, Case 113/80 (supra n. 110), esp. para.11.

[116] This list is very long and includes, inter alia: consumer protection (see *Commission* v. *Germany*, Case 178/84, [1987] ECR 1227); the prevention of unfair competition (*Cassis de Dijon*, Case 120/78 (supra n. 76)); the protection of the environment (see *Commission* v. *Denmark*, Case 302/86, [1988] ECR 4607); the improvement of working conditions (see *Oebel*, Case 155/80 (supra n. 81); the diversity of the press (see *Familiapress* v. *Bauer*, Case C-368/95 (supra n. 90) and many others.

[117] See Advocate General F. Jacobs in *Preussen Elektra* v. *Schleswag*, Case C-379/98, [2001] ECR I-2099, paras. 227 et seq.

[118] See *Commission* v. *Belgium (Walloon Waste)*, Case C-2/90, [1992] ECR I-4431.

[119] *Preussen Elektra* v. *Schleswag*, Case C-379/98 (supra n. 117).

[120] We saw above that solely discriminatory selling arrangements can constitute MEEQRs, and therefore these national measures could, in theory, solely be justified on the grounds mentioned in Article 36.

[121] See *Konsumentombudsmannen* v. *De Agostini*, Case C-34/95, [1997] ECR I-3843, paras. 39–45 (emphasis added): "[T]he Court held that legislation which prohibits television advertising in a particular sector concerns *selling arrangements* for products belonging to that sector in that it prohibits a particular form of promotion of a particular method of marketing products … Consequently, an outright ban on advertising aimed at children less than 12 years of age and of misleading advertising, as provided for by the Swedish legislation, is not covered by Article [34] of the Treaty, unless it is shown that the ban

(b) The Proportionality Principle and National Standards

Even if a legitimate public interest can be found to justify a national measure, restrictions on the free movement of goods will be subject to a proportionality test. The Court has insisted that national laws authorized by Article 36 "only comply with the Treaty in so far as they are justified, that is to say, *necessary* for the attainment of the objectives referred to by this provision".[122] And this proportionality test has been extended to mandatory requirements.[123]

What will proportionality in this context mean? Proportionality generally means "that national legislation which restricts or is liable to restrict intra-[Union] trade must be proportionate to the objectives pursued and that those objectives must not be attainable by measures which are less restrictive of such trade".[124] This least-restrictive-means test constitutes the cornerstone of the proportionality inquiry. But behind this test stands an important question: what standard of protection will it be based on? If the British legislature favours a high level of public morality and bans all imports of pornography, should it matter that other Member States do not prefer to stand on such high moral ground? Or, should Germany be allowed to insist on "beer purity" as the highest standard of consumer protection, while other Member States allow their beer to be brewed with artificial ingredients? The question of proportionality is thus intrinsically linked to the desirable standard of protection. And unfortunately, this is a question to which the Court has not given consistent answers.[125]

We find acceptance of a State's (high) national standard in *Henn & Darby*.[126] The case concerned the importation of pornographic films and

---

does not affect in the same way, in fact and in law, the marketing of national products and of products from other Member States. In the latter case, it is for the national court to determine whether the ban is necessary to satisfy *overriding requirements of general public importance* or one of the aims listed in Article 36 of the [FEU] Treaty if it is proportionate to that purpose and if those aims or requirements could not have been attained or fulfilled by measures less restrictive of intra-[Union] trade."

[122] *Simmenthal* v. *Ministero delle Finanze italiano*, Case 35/76, [1976] ECR 1871, para. 10 (emphasis added).

[123] *Rewe-Zentral* v. *Bundesmonopolverwaltung für Branntwein*, Case 120/78 (supra n. 76); as well as *Rau Lebensmittelwerke* v. *De Smedt*, Case 261/81, [1982] ECR 3961, para. 12: "It is also necessary for such rules to be proportionate to the aim in view."

[124] See *Aher-Waggon GmbH* v. *Germany*, Case C-389/96, [1998] ECR I-4473, para. 20.

[125] On this point, see G. De Búrca, "The Principle of Proportionality and its Application in EC Law", 13 (1993) *Yearbook of European Law*, 105.

[126] *Regina* v. *Henn and Darby*, Case 34/79 (supra n. 65).

magazines from Denmark, which violated the British import ban for such goods. Could this national law be justified on grounds of public morality, or would the "lower" Danish standard provide an argument that public morality can survive in a society that is more permissive of pornography? The Court chose the higher British standard as its baseline. It held that it was, as a rule, "for each Member State to determine in accordance with its own scale of values and in the form selected by it the requirements of public morality in its territory".[127] However, the Court subsequently clarified that "a Member State may not rely on grounds of public morality in order to prohibit the importation of goods from other Member States when its legislation contains no prohibition on the manufacture or marketing of the same goods on its territory".[128] Yet this qualification did not "preclude the authorities of the Member State concerned from applying to those goods, once imported, the same restrictions on marketing which are applied to similar products manufactured and marketed within the country".[129] It indeed did not undermine the legality of a (high) national standard, but only eliminated "arbitrary discriminations" that led to a "disguised restriction on trade between Member States".[130]

In other areas, by contrast, the Court has not deferred to a high national standard. In *Commission* v. *Germany (Beer Purity)*,[131] the Court thus rejected the claim that a German law confining the designation "beer" to beverages brewed without artificial additives was a proportionate means to protect consumers.[132] Pointing to its dynamic consumer perception – developed in another context[133] – it found that German consumers could be sufficiently protected by suitable labelling requirements.[134] In the Court's view, a high national standard must thus not "crystallize given consumer habits so as to consolidate an advantage acquired by national industries concerned to comply with them".[135] The Court consequently did

---

[127] *Ibid.*, para. 15.
[128] *Conegate* v. *HM Customs & Excise*, Case 121/85, [1986] ECR 1007, para. 16. In this respect *Conegate* overruled *Henn & Darby*.
[129] *Conegate* v. *HM Customs & Excise*, Case 121/85 (supra n. 128), para. 21.
[130] Article 36 TFEU – second sentence.
[131] *Commission* v. *Germany*, Case 178/84, [1987] ECR 1227.
[132] *Ibid.*, para. 53: "[I]n so far as the German rules on additives in beer entail a general ban on additives, their application to beers imported from other Member States is contrary to the requirements of [Union] law as laid down in the case-law of the Court, since that prohibition is contrary to the principle of proportionality."
[133] On this point, see Section 2(b) above.
[134] *Commission* v. *Germany*, Case 178/84 (supra n. 131), para. 35.   [135] *Ibid.*, para. 32.

not allow Germany to choose its own "scale of values" and insisted on the European standard of the "reasonably circumspect consumer".[136] And it is against this Court-chosen standard that the necessity of a national restriction on the free movement of goods is often judged.

Conclusion

The aim of this Chapter has been to explore the degree of negative integration in the context of the free movement of goods. The constitutional regime governing this "first" fundamental freedom is more complex than that for the other three freedoms. For instead of one single prohibition of illegal trade barriers, the EU Treaties distinguish between fiscal and regulatory barriers; and for fiscal barriers, the Treaties further distinguish between customs charges and internal taxation. For customs charges, the Court has traditionally constructed Article 30 as an absolute prohibition that applies to all charges between Member States. By contrast, the prohibition of discriminatory tax measures under Article 110 is still informed by a discrimination rationale.

For regulatory measures adopted by the Member States, the Court's rationale has changed over time, and Article 34 now seems to comprise a number of tests that apply to different categories of national measures. This differential approach also applies to justifications to regulatory restrictions. Express justifications only exist with regard to regulatory barriers to trade and are found in Article 36. These grounds have been enriched by implied justifications called "mandatory requirements". The latter will however – in theory – only apply to non-discriminatory restrictions; yet the Court seems to have also played with the idea of extending them to discriminatory measures. The central problem with regard to justifying national restrictions is however not so much the grounds of justification but the standard against which national restrictions are reviewed.

[136] See *Verband Sozialer Wettbewerb eV* v. *Clinique Laboratoires and Estée Lauder Cosmetics*, Case C-315/92, [1994] ECR I-317, para. 24; and *Verein gegen Unwesen in Handel und Gewerbe Köln eV* v. *Mars*, Case C-470/93, [1995] ECR I-1923, para. 24.

Introduction

The gradual integration of national markets into a "common" or "internal" market can be achieved by two complementary mechanisms. First, the Treaties may themselves "negate" certain national barriers to intra-European trade. For the free movement of goods, this form of negative integration was discussed in the previous Chapter. A second constitutional technique is "positive integration". The Union here adopts positive legislation to – partly or exhaustively – remove the diversity of national laws. The idea of integration through legislation stands behind Article 26 TFEU. It states:

> The Union shall adopt measures with the aim of establishing or ensuring the functioning of the internal market, in accordance with the relevant provisions of the Treaties.[1]

Legislative competences for positive integration are often found within the specific policy areas of the Union.[2] However, the Treaties also contain a number of horizontal harmonization competences that allow the Union

---

[1] Article 26(1) TFEU.   [2] On this point, see Chapter 3 – *Introduction* – above.

Table 10.1 Harmonization Competences

Chapter 2: Tax Provisions		Chapter 3: Approximation of Laws	
Article 110	Discriminatory Taxation	Article 114	General Competence I
Article 111	Export Repayments	Article 115	General Competence II
Article 112	Export Repayments Approval	Article 116	Specific Competence: Competition
Article 113	Specific Competence: Taxes	Article 117	Commission Consultation
		Article 118	Specific Competence: Intellectual Property

to create an "internal market". These "internal market" competences can be found in Chapter 3 of Title VII of the TFEU. They have been the bedrock of the Union's positive integration programme. Articles 114 and 115 here provide the Union with a harmonization competence "for the approximation of the provisions laid down by law, regulation or administrative action in Member States *which have as their object the establishment and functioning of the internal market*".[3]

These two general harmonization competences apply to all four fundamental freedoms.[4] They are complemented by more "specific" harmonization competences. With regard to fiscal measures, Article 113 allows the Union to harmonize legislation on "forms of indirect taxation to the extent that such harmonisation is necessary to ensure the establishment and functioning of the internal market and to avoid distortions of competition". By contrast, Article 116 specifically targets distortions of competition, while Article 118 empowers the Union "[i]n the context of the establishment and functioning of the internal market" to "establish measures for the creation of European intellectual property rights".[5]

This Chapter explores the legal principles and constitutional limits governing positive integration in the context of the free movement of goods. Section 1 analyses the scope and nature of the general harmonization competence(s): Articles 114 and 115 TFEU. We shall see there that the Union has an – almost – unlimited competence to harmonize national laws that affect the establishment or functioning of the internal market.

---

[3] Article 114(1) TFEU (emphasis added).

[4] According to Article 26(2) TFEU: "[t]he internal market shall comprise an area without internal frontiers in which the free movement of goods, persons, services and capital is ensured in accordance with the provisions of the Treaties."

[5] Article 118(1) TFEU.

Section 2 looks at the relationship between Article 114 and other legislative competences within the Union legal order. Section 3 investigates the extent to which Member States can derogate from harmonized Union standards; and, finally, Section 4 is dedicated to a specific area of Union harmonization: tax harmonization.

1. Harmonization Competences: General Issues

Originally, the sole harmonization competences for the "internal market" were Articles 115 and 116 TFEU. The former entitled the European Union to "issue directives for the approximation of such provisions laid down by law, regulation or administrative action in Member States as directly affect the establishment or functioning of the common market". Article 116 was more specific. It allowed the Union to issue directives, where the differences between national laws "is distorting the conditions of competition in the internal market". The competence was designed as the positive integration platform for the EU's competition policy; yet despite its more specific focus, it soon declined into oblivion.[6]

Article 115, by contrast, turned out to be "quite simply unlimited".[7] Yet the competence had a *political* hurdle: it required unanimity in the Council; and this political safeguard of federalism would substantially limit the exercise of the Union's harmonization competence in its early life.[8] This however dramatically changed after the Single European Act, which provided Article 115 with a "brilliant assistant": Article 114.[9] The new constitutional neighbour textually widened the Union's internal market competence;[10] and – importantly – it no longer required a unanimous decision of all Member States. Today Article 114 states:

---

[6] U. Everling, "Zur Funktion der Rechtsangleichung in der Europäischen Gemeinschaft: vom Abbau der Verzerrungen zur Schaffung des Binnenmarktes", in F. Capotorti *et al.* (eds.), *Du droit international au droit de l'intégration: liber amicorum Pierre Pescatore* (Nomos, 1987), 227 at 232.

[7] P. Leleux, "Le rapprochement des législations dans la communauté economique européenne", (1968) 4 *Cahiers De Droit Européen* 129 at 138.

[8] On this point, see: A. Dashwood, "Hastening Slowly: The Community's Path Towards Harmonization", in: H. Wallace, W. Wallace and C. Webb (eds.), *Policy-Making in the European Community* (Wiley & Sons Ltd, 1983), 177.

[9] D. Vignes, "The Harmonisation of National Legislation and the EEC", (1990) 15 *European Law Review* 358 at 367.

[10] Constitutionally, Article 114 TFEU no longer contained the – by now obsolete – references to "directives" as instruments of harmonization; nor did it mention the "direct [e]ffect" of national laws on the internal market.

1. Save where otherwise provided in the Treaties, the following provisions shall apply for the achievement of the objectives set out in Article 26. The European Parliament and the Council shall, acting in accordance with the ordinary legislative procedure and after consulting the Economic and Social Committee, adopt the measures for the approximation of the provisions laid down by law, regulation or administrative action in Member States which have as their object the establishment and functioning of the internal market.

2. Paragraph 1 shall not apply to fiscal provisions, to those relating to the free movement of persons nor to those relating to the rights and interests of employed persons.

3. The Commission, in its proposals envisaged in paragraph 1 concerning health, safety, environmental protection and consumer protection, will take as a base a high level of protection, taking account in particular of any new development based on scientific facts. Within their respective powers, the European Parliament and the Council will also seek to achieve this objective.[11]

This gave the Union legislator a horizontal competence, save where otherwise provided,[12] to harmonize national laws that affected the internal market. Positive harmonization could thereby be achieved by means of qualified majority within the Council. This departure from the unanimity requirement within the Council would however not extend to all areas within the internal market. Indeed Article 114(2) expressly states that Article 114(1) would "not apply to fiscal provisions, to these relating to the free movement of persons nor to those relating to the rights and interests of employed persons". (These politically "sensitive" matters would thus continue to fall under Article 115 TFEU or one of the specific legal competences within the relevant Treaty titles.) The fear of "unqualified" qualified majority voting also led to the inclusion of two further qualifications. First, Article 114(3) obliges the Commission to base its legislative proposals on a "high level of protection" with regard to these interests. And second: Article 114(4–5) TFEU – quoted below – allowed, for the first time in the Union's history, for differential positive integration.[13]

Despite these qualifications, Article 114 is, apart from Article 352 TFEU, the broadest competence of the Union. Indeed: its horizontal and

---

[11] Article 114(1–3) TFEU. For the text of paragraphs 4 and 5, see Section 3 below.

[12] On the "residual" nature of Article 114, see Section 2 below.

[13] For the historical justification of these paragraphs, see: A. G. G. Tesauro in *France* v. *Commission*, Case C-41/93, (1994) ECR I-1829, para.4.

supranational nature have turned Article 114 into "the" preferred constitutional base for the Union's positive integration programme. This section explores the scope of Article 114 by analysing the concept of "harmonization" and the substantive conditions that need to be satisfied before the Union is entitled to activate its "internal market" competence.

(a) The Concept of "Approximation" or "Harmonization"

All internal market competences are based on the idea of harmonization. Would the idea of "approximation" or "harmonization" thereby require the existence of national laws before and after the Union legislation? Is it correct to assert that the concept of approximation "would appear necessarily to imply that the matter in question is governed by national rules in the first place, and remains governed by national rules after they have been harmonized"?[14]

For a long time, European constitutional thought indeed strongly linked the concept of harmonization to the *subsequent* existence of national laws. Originally, this was the result of the harmonization instrument of the "directive".[15] Directives require Member States to adopt national legislation that will implement the Union command. The result of a directive are thus "harmonized" *national* rules; and it consequently seemed that the *subsequent* existence of national rules was a conceptual characteristic of the notion of harmonization. This however changed with the Single European Act. For Article 114 TFEU "decoupled" the idea of harmonization from the directive. The Union could henceforth adopt any measure under its internal market competence – and this included "regulations" as instruments of *direct* Union legislation.[16]

But could harmonization of national laws take place through a Union *decision*? Serious doubts should be in order. For how could an individual decision – an executive act – ever harmonize national laws? In *Germany* v. *Council*,[17] this constitutional delicacy was placed on the judicial table.

---

[14] In this sense: J. Usher, "Harmonisation of Legislation", in: D. Lasok *et al.* (eds.), *Les Communautés Européennes en Fonctionnement* (Bruylant, 1981), 171 at 174.

[15] According to Article 288(3) TFEU, "[a] directive shall be binding, as to the result to be achieved, upon each Member State to which it is addressed, but shall leave to the national authorities the choice of form and methods". On the Union instrument of "directive", see Chapter 5 – Section 3 above.

[16] On the Union instrument of "regulation", see: R. Schütze, *European Union Law* (Cambridge University Press, 2015), Chapter 3 – Section 2(a).

[17] *Germany* v. *Council*, Case C-359/92, [1994] ECR I-3681.

Germany argued that the power to "harmonize" did not entitle the Union to adopt decisions (dis)approving certain products.[18] And since the Product Safety Directive granted just such a power in certain situations, the relevant provision had to be void.[19] The Court held otherwise:

> The measures which the Council is empowered to take under that provision are aimed at "the establishment and functioning of the internal market". In certain fields, and particularly in that of product safety, the approximation of general laws alone may not be sufficient to ensure the unity of the market. *Consequently, the concept of "measures for the approximation" of legislation must be interpreted as encompassing the Council's power to lay down measures relating to a specific product or class of products and, if necessary, individual measures concerning those products.*[20]

Despite its reference to harmonization, Article 114 TFEU would thus entitle the Union to adopt specific decisions that did not formally harmonize national laws.

But could Article 114 also be employed for the establishment of a centralized authorization procedure operated by the Commission, or even the creation of the Union's own executive infrastructure? Subsequent jurisprudence clarified that Article 114 could indeed be used for both purposes.

The cause célèbre here is *United Kingdom* v. *Parliament and Council.*[21] It concerned the validity of Regulation 2065/2003 that tried to ensure the

---

[18] Germany's principal claim in this respect is quoted in para. 17: "The German Government objects to that argument essentially on the ground that the sole aim of Article [114] et seq. of the [FEU] Treaty, and of Article [114(1)] in particular, is the approximation of laws and that those articles do not therefore confer power to apply the law to individual cases in the place of the national authorities, as permitted by Article 9 of the directive."

[19] Directive 92/59 on general product safety (OJ 1992 L228, 24), which is today replaced by Directive 2001/95 on general product safety (OJ 2002 L11, 4). Article 9 here provided as follows: "If the Commission becomes aware, through notification given by the Member States or through information provided by them, in particular under Article 7 or Article 8, of the existence of a serious and immediate risk from a product to the health and safety of consumers in various Member States and if: [(a) ... (d)] the Commission, after consulting the Member States and at the request of at least one of them, may adopt a decision, in accordance with the procedure laid down in Article 11, requiring Member States to take temporary measures from among those listed in Article 6(1)(d) to (h)."

[20] *Germany* v. *Council*, Case C-359/92 (supra n. 17), paras. 37–8 (emphasis added).

[21] *United Kingdom* v. *Parliament and Council*, Case C-66/04, (2005) ECR I-10553. In relation to Article 114 TFEU's use to create a Union body, see: *United Kingdom* v. *Parliament and Council (ENISA)*, Case C-217/04, [2006] ECR I-3771, especially para. 44: "The legislature may deem it necessary to provide for the establishment of a [Union] body responsible for

effective functioning of the internal market through a Union authorization procedure for food products.[22] The British government protested: "The legislative power conferred by Article [114 TFEU] is a power to *harmonise national laws, not a power to establish [Union] bodies or to confer tasks on such bodies, or to establish procedures for the approval of lists of authorised products.*"[23] Yet in its judgment, the Court confirmed this very power.[24] The Union legislator would indeed enjoy "a discretion, depending on the general context and the specific circumstances of the matter to be harmonised, as regards the harmonisation technique".[25] The Union was thus entitled to create a Union agency and endow it with the power to adopt – binding – individual decisions.

In sum: the Union enjoys an (almost) total freedom with regard to the formal type of harmonization act. This freedom of form is matched by a freedom of substance. For the Court has never identified the concept of harmonization with a "medium" regulatory standard, and indeed grants the Union legislator a wide substantive discretion.[26]

What about the *prior* existence of national laws as a precondition for Article 114 TFEU? This question was the subject of *Spain* v. *Council.*[27] The European legislator here believed the national patent protection for medicinal products to be insufficient, and saw this insufficiency as penalizing European pharmaceutical research. It therefore created a supplementary protection certificate that could be granted under the same conditions as national patents by each of the Member States.[28] Two major constitutional hurdles however seemed to oppose the legality of this European

---

contributing to the implementation of a process of harmonisation in situations where, in order to facilitate the uniform implementation and application of acts based on that provision, the adoption of non-binding supporting and framework measures seems appropriate."

[22] Regulation 2065/2003 on smoke flavourings used or intended for use in or on foods, (2003) OJ L309/1, Article 9(1)(b) as well as Article 11(1).

[23] *United Kingdom* v. *Parliament and Council*, Case C-66/04 (supra n. 21), para. 18 (emphasis added).

[24] *Ibid.*, para. 64.

[25] *Ibid.*, para. 45. This was recently confirmed in *United Kingdom* v. *Parliament and Council (ESMA)*, Case C-270/12, EU: C: 2014: 18.

[26] For an early version of this argument, see: T. Vogelaar, "The Approximation of the Laws of the Member States under the Treaty of Rome", [1975] 12 *Common Market Law Review*, 211 at 213.

[27] *Spain* v. *Council*, Case C-350/92, [1995] ECR I-1985.

[28] Regulation 1768/92 concerning the creation of a supplementary protection certificate for medicinal products, [1992] OJ L182/1.

law. First, Article 114 TFEU could theoretically not be used to create *new* rights as it could only harmonize *existing* rights.[29] Second, at the time of the adoption of the Union law only *two* Member States had legislation concerning a supplementary certificate.

Were these hurdles insurmountable for the use of Article 114? The Court took the first hurdle by force. It simply rejected the claim that the European law created a new right.[30] Concentrating on the second hurdle, the Court then addressed the question, whether Article 114 required the *pre*-existence of diverse national laws before Union harmonization could take place. In the eyes of the Court, this was not the case! The Union could also use its internal market competence "to *prevent the heterogeneous development of national laws* leading to further disparities which would be likely to create obstacles to the free movement of medicinal products within the [Union] and thus directly affect the establishment and the functioning of the internal market".[31] The Union was thus entitled – even in the absence of national laws on a specific point at a specific time – to use its harmonization power to prevent the *future* fragmentation of the internal market.[32]

This judicial ruling was confirmed in *Vodafone*;[33] and it seems to have emptied the concept of harmonization of any content. If there indeed were conceptual limits to Article 114, they would have to be found somewhere else.

(b) The "Establishment" or "Functioning" of the Internal Market

The Union's internal market competence is a horizontal competence. It is horizontal because it is not thematically limited. Article 114 applies to *any* national measure that affects the establishment or functioning of the internal market.[34] Its horizontal scope thereby refers to two

---

[29] Union legislation that creates "new" rights will have to be based on Article 352 TFEU, cf. *Spain* v. *Council* (supra n. 27), para. 23 (with reference to Opinion 1/94 (Competence of the Community to conclude international agreements concerning services and the protection of intellectual property), [1994] ECR I-5267, para. 59).

[30] *Spain* v. *Council* (supra n. 27), para. 27.   [31] *Ibid.*, para. 35 (emphasis added).

[32] On the idea of "preventive" harmonization in the internal market, see: M. Seidel, "Präventive Rechtsangleichung im Bereich des Gemeinsamen Marktes", (2006) 41 *Europarecht* 26.

[33] *Vodafone and others* v. *Secretary of State for Business, Enterprise and Regulatory Reform*, Case C-58/08, (2010) ECR I-4999.

[34] Cf. S. Weatherill, "The Limits of Legislative Harmonization Ten Years after *Tobacco Advertising*: How the Court's Case Law has become a 'Drafting Guide'", (2011) 12 *German*

alternative objectives. The first alternative deals with the "establishment" of the internal market and concerns obstacles to free movement. The second alternative refers to the "functioning" of the internal market and addresses distortions of competition resulting from disparities between national laws. The combination of these two alternatives means that the scope of positive integration under Article 114 TFEU is wider than the scope of negative integration under Article 34 TFEU.[35]

To what extent would Union legislation have to serve the "establishment" or "functioning" of the internal market? Until the end of the twentieth century, the jurisprudence of the Court unequivocally confirmed the widest possible reading of the Union's general harmonization competence: almost anything, it seemed, could be based on Article 114!

This perception significantly changed with *Germany* v. *Parliament and Council (Tobacco Advertising)*.[36] The judgment famously confirmed the existence of constitutional limits for the competence. The bone of contention was a Union law that banned the advertising and sponsorship of tobacco products.[37] Germany disliked the idea and claimed that a prohibition or even a ban of a product could never be based on the Union's *internal market* competence. Article 114 could only be used to "establish" trade and this was not the case, where Union legislation *prohibited* trade in tobacco products.[38] And while admitting that Article 114 could still be used to ensure the functioning of the internal market, this second alternative within Article 114 should only apply to cases where the distortion of competition was "considerable".[39]

Law Journal 827 at 831: "[Article 114] is functionally driven: any national measure may be harmonized provided that leads to an improvement in the functioning of the internal market envisaged by Article 26 TFEU[.]"

[35] This means that even where a national law is outside the scope of Article 34 TFEU – such as non-discriminatory selling arrangements after *Keck* (see: Chapter 9 – Section 3(a) above), these selling arrangements could be harmonized under Article 114 TFEU if they affect the functioning of the internal market. For an overview of the debate on the (only partial) connection between Articles 34 and 114 TFEU, see: G. Davies, "Can Selling Arrangements be Harmonised?", (2005) 30 *European Law Review*, 370.

[36] *Germany* v. *Parliament and Council (Tobacco Advertising)*, Case C-376/98, [2000] ECR I-8419.

[37] Directive 98/43 on the approximation of the laws, regulations and administrative provisions of the Member States relating to the advertising and sponsorship of tobacco products, [1998] OJ L213/9.

[38] Germany had pointed out that the sole form of advertising allowed under the Directive was advertising at the point of sale, which only accounted for 2 per cent of the tobacco industry's advertising expenditure (*Tobacco Advertising* (supra n. 36), para. 24).

[39] *Ibid.*, para. 29.

To the surprise of many academic observers, the Court accepted these arguments and annulled, for the first time in its history, a Union law on the grounds that it went beyond the internal market competence. Emphatically, the Court underlined that Article 114 could not grant the Union a general power to regulate the internal market:

> *To construe that article as meaning that it vests in the [Union] legisla-*
> *ture a general power to regulate the internal market would not only be*
> *contrary to the express wording of the provisions cited above but would*
> *also be incompatible with the principle embodied in Article [5 TEU] that*
> *the powers of the [Union] are limited to those specifically conferred on it.*
> Moreover, a measure adopted on the basis of Article [114] of the Treaty
> must genuinely have as its object the improvement of the conditions for
> the establishment and functioning of the internal market. If a mere finding
> of disparities between national rules and of the abstract risk of obstacles
> to the exercise of fundamental freedoms or of distortions of competition
> liable to result therefrom were sufficient to justify the choice of Article
> [114] as a legal basis, judicial review of compliance with the proper legal
> basis might be rendered nugatory.[40]

What consequences did the Court draw from this statement of principle? The Court split its ruling into an "establishment" and "functioning" part and analysed, in turn, the two alternative applications of the Union's harmonization competence.

Regarding the elimination of obstacles to free movement, the Court qualified its generous ruling in *Spain* v. *Council*.[41] While accepting that "recourse to Article [114] as a legal basis is possible if the aim is to prevent the emergence of future obstacles to trade resulting from mul-tifarious development of national laws", the Court nonetheless insisted that "*the emergence of such obstacles must be likely* and the measure in question must be designed to prevent them".[42] Were future obstacles to intra-Union trade in tobacco advertising likely? The Court accepted this for press products; yet "for numerous types of advertising of tobacco products", the prohibition within the Directive "cannot be justified by the need to eliminate obstacles to the free movement of advertising media or the freedom to provide services in the field of advertising".[43] The Union legislature had thus not been entitled to rely on its internal market

---

[40] *Ibid.*, paras. 83–4 (emphasis added).
[41] *Spain* v. *Council*, Case C-350/92 (supra n. 27).
[42] *Tobacco Advertising* (supra n. 36), para. 86 (emphasis added).
[43] *Ibid.*, paras. 97 and 99.

power on the grounds that the measure would eliminate obstacles to free movement.

But recourse to the competence could still be justified by means of the second alternative in Article 114: the elimination of distortions of competition. In previous jurisprudence, the Court had interpreted this condition widely by allowing all harmonizing measures that "deal with disparities between the laws of the Member States in areas where such disparities are liable to create or maintain distorted conditions of competition".[44] This had suggested that *any* disparities in national laws liable to create *any* distortion of competition could be harmonized.

Tobacco Advertising now corrected this excessive reading of the "functioning" part of the internal market competence. For the Court here accepted Germany's invitation: distortions of competition would have to be *appreciable* to entitle the Union to act under Article 114: "In the absence of such a requirement, the powers of the [Union] legislature would be practically unlimited." Constitutionally, the Union legislator was thus not entitled to pass laws under Article 114 "with a view to eliminating the smallest distortions of competition".[45] And since the national laws at issue had only a "remote and indirect" effect on competition, disparities between them could not lead to distortions that were appreciable.[46] The Directive could thus not have been legitimately based on the second prong of the internal market competence, and the Court consequently annulled the European directive.

In conclusion: with *Tobacco Advertising*, the Court expressly accepted *some* effects-related constitutional limits to the Union's internal market power. First, a simple disparity in national laws will not be enough to trigger the Union's harmonization competence. The disparity must give rise to obstacles in trade or appreciable distortions in competition. And while Article 114 TFEU may be used to harmonize *future* disparities in national laws, it must be "likely" that the divergent development of national laws leads to such obstacles in trade or appreciable distortions of competition. (The Court has – strangely – come to verbalize this requirement by extending the constitutional criterion of a "direct effect" – textually mandated only in Article 115 TFEU – to Article 114 TFEU.[47]) Second, the

---

[44] Cf. *Commission* v. *Council (Titanium dioxide)*, Case C-300/89, (1991) ECR I-2867, para. 15.

[45] *Tobacco Advertising*, para. 107.   [46] *Tobacco Advertising*, para. 109.

[47] Cf. *Swedish Match*, Case C-210/03, [2004] ECR I-11893, para. 29; *Germany* v. *Parliament and Council (Tobacco Advertising II)*, Case C-380/03, [2006] ECR I-11573, para. 37; and

Union measure must *actually contribute* to the elimination of obstacles to free movement or distortions of competition,[48] and where this is not the case the Union measure is not a measure of positive integration and will thus be annulled.

These two constitutional limits to the Union's "internal market" competence have been confirmed *in abstracto* by subsequent jurisprudence;[49] yet, their concrete application has led to renewed accusations that Article 114 grants the Union a general competence for the internal market.[50]

2. Relationship to "Sectoral" Legislative Competences

Article 114 TFEU presents itself with an understatement. With false modesty, it states that it only applies "save where otherwise provided in the Treaties". This is deeply misleading. For it suggests that the provision is but a residual competence that only applies where no more specific legal competence is available.[51] The question thus arises whether the Union may use its general harmonization competence under Article 114 or rather – say – the Union's special environmental competence if it wishes to set environmental standards for industrial machinery.

Had the Court taken a strict view on the residual nature of Article 114, hardly any matters may have fallen within its scope. Yet the Court has rejected this view and treats Article 114 TFEU like a "normal" legislative

see also: *The Queen, on the application of Vodafone Ltd and Others* v. *Secretary of State for Business, Enterprise and Regulatory Reform*, Case C-58/08, (2010) ECR I-4999, para. 32: "While a mere finding of disparities between national rules and the abstract risk of infringements of fundamental freedoms or distortion of competition is not sufficient to justify the choice of Article [114 TFEU] as a legal basis, the [Union] legislature may have recourse to it in particular where there are differences between national rules which are such as to obstruct the fundamental freedoms and thus have a direct effect on the functioning of the internal market."

[48] *British American Tobacco*, Case C-491/01, [2002] ECR I-11453, para. 60.

[49] For the relevant case law, see supra n. 47.

[50] This has led D. Wyatt, "Community Competence to Regulate the Internal Market", Oxford Faculty of Law Research Paper 9/2007, to query whether *Tobacco Advertising* was a "false dawn" (*ibid.*, 23). For an analysis of legislative and judicial practice after *Tobacco Advertising*, see also the excellent analysis by S. Weatherill, "The Limits of Legislative Harmonization Ten Years after *Tobacco Advertising*" (supra n. 34).

[51] This is however the case for Article 352 TFEU. For an analysis of this point, see: R. Schütze, "Organized Change towards an 'Ever Closer Union': Article 308 EC and the Limits of the Community's Legislative Competence", (2003) 22 *Yearbook of European Law* 79 at 99 et seq.

competence. This was confirmed in *Titanium Dioxide*.[52] The Court here acknowledged that harmonization measures would typically have a dual aim, namely an internal market aim as well as a specific *substantive* policy aim.[53] And in deciding whether or not Article 114 or a specific legal competence applies, the Court would have recourse to the "centre of gravity" doctrine.[54] The latter makes the choice of competence dependent on whether the Union measure principally deals with the internal market or with the more specific substantive interest. And where a Union law's "weight" falls more heavily on the internal market side, Article 114 will apply.

There are however two qualifications to this picture. First, Article 114 itself expressly excludes three matters from its legislative scope. For it states in paragraph 2 that the harmonization competence "shall not apply to *fiscal* provisions, to those relating to the *free movement of persons* nor to those relating to the *rights and interests of employed persons*". These three areas can thus never be harmonized on the basis of Article 114. If Union harmonization is here deemed necessary, this will have to be done either under Article 115 TFEU – requiring unanimity – or one of the special substantive competences dealing with taxation, the free movement of persons, or employment. In the past, the Court has given a broad interpretation to the scope of the excluded policy fields in Article 114(2).[55]

Is the list in Article 114(2) exhaustive, or has the Court added a number of "implied" exclusions? The Court has not. The Member States have

---

[52] *Commission* v. *Council (Titanium dioxide)*, Case C-300/89 (supra n. 44).

[53] *Ibid.*, para. 11.

[54] Cf. *Commission* v. *Council (Waste)*, Case C-155/91, (1993) ECR I-939; as well as: *Parliament* v. *Council (Waste II)*, Case C-187/93, (1994) ECR I-2857. For an academic analysis of the phenomenon of legal basis litigation, esp. in relation to Article 114 TFEU, see: R. Barents, "The Internal Market Unlimited: Some Observations on the Legal Basis of Community Legislation", (1993) 30 *Common Market Law Review* 85; as well as: H. Cullen and A. Charlesworth, "Diplomacy by Other Means: The Use of Legal Basis Litigation as a Political Strategy by the European Parliament and Member States", (1999) 36 *Common Market Law Review* 1243.

[55] For a wide and teleological interpretation of the phrase "fiscal provisions" in Article 114(2) TFEU, see: *Commission* v. *Council*, Case C-338/01, (2004) ECR I-4829, para. 63: "With regard to the interpretation of the words 'fiscal provisions', there is nothing in the Treaty to indicate how that concept should be construed. It is, however, necessary to point out that, by reason of their general character, those words cover not only all areas of taxation, without drawing any distinction between the types of duties or taxes concerned, but also all aspects of taxation, whether material rules or procedural rules."

nonetheless tried to "shield" some special Union competences from the "creeping" scope of the general harmonization competence. How so? In their capacity as Masters of the Treaties, they have increasingly included clauses within specific policy areas that expressly exclude the harmonization of national laws within a specific policy area. For example: under its "public health" competence in Article 168, the Union is entitled to adopt health measures but only "*excluding any harmonisation* of the laws and regulations of the Member States".[56]

But while these clauses may limit the ability of the Union legislator to adopt harmonization measures under these special competences, do they also limit the scope of Article 114? The European Court appears to have expressed a negative inclination in *Tobacco Advertising*.[57] Germany had challenged the use of Article 114 for the Tobacco Advertising Directive on the ground that the Directive was a "health measure" and should therefore have been based on Article 168 TFEU; and since the latter excluded any harmonization, the Directive should be annulled.

The Court however rejected this argument in full. While admitting that "[t]he national measures *affected* [were] to a large extent inspired by public health policy objectives",[58] the Court clarified that the exclusion of harmonization in Article 168(5) did "not mean that harmonising measures adopted on the basis of other provisions of the Treaty cannot have any impact on the protection of human health".[59] "[T]he [Union] legislature cannot be prevented from relying on [Article 114] on the ground that public health protection is a decisive factor in the choices to be made."[60]

In conclusion: the exclusion of harmonization in a specific (complementary) competence appears thus *not* to operate as a limitation on Article 114 TFEU. Yet the Court has also warned the Union legislator. The latter must not use its internal market power "to circumvent the express exclusion of harmonisation" that are laid down in the Treaties.[61] Such "abuses" of legislative power would be sanctioned in the future.

3. "Opting Up": Derogation Clauses in Article 114

Once the Union has adopted a harmonization measure, all national measures that conflict with the Union measure should – theoretically – have

---

[56] Article 168(5) TFEU (emphasis added).
[57] *Germany* v. *Council (Tobacco Advertising)*, Case C-376/98 (supra n. 36).
[58] *Ibid.*, para. 76 (emphasis added).   [59] *Ibid.*, para. 78.
[60] *Ibid.*, para. 88.   [61] *Ibid.*, para. 79.

to be disapplied. This follows from the supremacy of European law. When Article 114 TFEU was drafted, some Member States however feared that the introduction of qualified majority voting in the Council could undermine higher national standards in politically sensitive areas. They consequently insisted on a constitutional mechanism that allowed them to "justify" these – derogating – national laws. This was greeted with theoretical outrage;[62] yet the practical consequences of the "public policy" justifications in Article 114(4–5) have been very limited.

Drafted in parallel with Article 36 TFEU, the fourth and fifth paragraph of Article 114 state:

4. If, after the adoption of a harmonisation measure by the European Parliament and the Council, by the Council or by the Commission, a Member State deems it necessary to *maintain* national provisions *on grounds of major needs referred to in Article 36, or relating to the protection of the environment or the working environment*, it shall notify the Commission of these provisions as well as the grounds for maintaining them.

5. Moreover, without prejudice to paragraph 4, if, after the adoption of a harmonisation measure by the European Parliament and the Council, by the Council or by the Commission, a Member State deems it necessary to *introduce* national provisions based on *new scientific evidence relating to the protection of the environment or the working environment on grounds of a problem specific to that Member State arising after the adoption of the harmonisation measure*, it shall notify the Commission of the envisaged provisions as well as the grounds for introducing them.[63]

The two paragraphs allow a Member State to "maintain" or "introduce" national measures that "conflict" with the harmonized Union measure. Importantly, conflict here means that a Member State does *not comply with Union legislation adopted under Article 114*. (Articles 114(4) and (5) TFEU thus do not cover situations, where a Member State is entitled – under the harmonization measure – to adopt stricter or higher national norms.[64] They exclusively refer to the situation where a Member State

---

[62] P. Pescatore, "Some critical remarks on the 'Single European Act'", (1987) 24 *Common Market Law Review* 9; C.-D. Ehlermann, "The Internal Market following the Single European Act", (1987) 24 *Common Market Law Review* 361.

[63] Emphasis added.

[64] On the various harmonization techniques, see: R. Schütze, *European Union Law* (Cambridge University Press, 2015), Chapter 14 – Section 3.

would "breach" Union legislation by insisting on a standard that is *higher* than the – mandatory and exhaustive – Union standard.) Article 114(4) thereby covers the situation where a Member State wishes to "maintain" – existing – national laws, whereas Article 114(5) refers to the power of Member States to "introduce" – new – national laws. Both situations are subject to an administrative procedure conducted by the Commission,[65] which can subsequently be reviewed by the European Court.[66]

Article 114(4) entitles a Member State to apply to the Commission for the permission to maintain its higher laws "*on grounds of major needs referred to in Article 36, or relating to the protection of the environment or the working environment*".[67] The list of public interest grounds is here limited to the express public interest derogations for the free movement of goods and two – and only two – unwritten mandatory requirements recognized by the Court.[68] By contrast, Article 114(5) does not mention the public policy grounds in Article 36. It insists on new scientific evidence and even demands a problem specific to a Member State. Article 114(5) thus appeared from the very beginning much stricter than Article 114(4).

This view was judicially confirmed in *Denmark* v. *Commission*,[69] where the Court held as follows:

> The difference between the two situations envisaged in Article [114] is that, in the first, the national provisions predate the harmonisation measure. They are thus known to the [Union] legislature, but the legislature cannot or does not seek to be guided by them for the purpose of harmonisation. It is therefore considered acceptable for the Member State to request that its own rules remain in force...
>
> By contrast, in the second situation, the adoption of new national legislation *is more likely to jeopardise harmonisation*. The [Union] institutions could not, by definition, have taken account of the national text when drawing up the harmonisation measure. In that case, the requirements

---

[65] For the elaborate administrative and procedural regime, see: Article 114(6)–(8) TFEU. For an overview of these provisions, see: N. de Sadeleer, "Procedures for Derogation from the Principle of Approximation of Laws under Article 95 EC", (2003) 40 *Common Market Law Review* 889.

[66] Article 114(9) TFEU provides: "By way of derogation from the procedure laid down in Articles 258 and 259, the Commission and any Member State may bring the matter directly before the Court of Justice of the European Union if it considers that another Member State is making improper use of the powers provided for in this Article."

[67] Emphasis added.

[68] On these mandatory requirements, see Chapter 9 – Section 4(a) above.

[69] *Denmark* v. *Commission*, Case C-3/00, (2003) ECR I-2643.

referred to in Article [36 TFEU] are not taken into account, and only grounds relating to protection of the environment or the working environment are accepted, on condition that the Member State provides new scientific evidence and that the need to introduce new national provisions results from a problem specific to the Member State concerned arising after the adoption of the harmonisation measure.

It follows that neither the wording of Article [114(4) TFEU] nor the broad logic of that article as a whole entails a requirement that the applicant Member State prove that maintaining the national provisions which it notifies to the Commission is justified by a problem specific to that Member State... Analogous considerations apply to the requirement for new scientific evidence. That condition is imposed under Article [114(5) TFEU] for the introduction of new derogating national provisions, but it is not laid down in Article [114(4) TFEU] for the maintenance of existing derogating national provisions. It is not one of the conditions imposed for maintaining such provisions.[70]

The Court here found that the Commission was entitled, in the exercise of its administrative discretion, to be much stricter in granting derogations under Article 114(5).

This was confirmed in subsequent administrative and judicial practice. In *Upper Austria* v. *Commission*,[71] Austria had applied for a specific derogation under Article 114(5) in relation to the Union Directive on genetically modified organisms (GMOs). The Austrian measure intended to prohibit the cultivation of seed composed of or containing GMOs as well as the breeding of transgenic animals. The Commission however refused to allow the stricter national law on the ground that "Austria failed to provide new scientific evidence or demonstrate that a specific problem in [that country] arose".[72] Austria appealed to the General Court against that administrative decision, and this gave the Court an opportunity to explain the criteria in Article 114(5).

The Court unambiguously clarified that the criteria of "new scientific evidence" and the existence of "a problem specific to the Member State" were cumulative conditions;[73] and that the burden of proof for both criteria squarely lied with the Member State concerned.[74] Unhappy

---

[70] *Ibid.*, paras. 58–62 (emphasis added).
[71] *Land Oberösterreich and Republic of Austria* v. *Commission*, Joined Cases T-366/03 and T-235/04, (2005) ECR II-4005.
[72] *Ibid.*, para. 15.   [73] *Ibid.*, para. 54.   [74] *Ibid.*, para. 63.

with this ruling, Austria subsequently appealed to the Court of Justice. However, the Court equally confirmed the negative Commission decision; yet additionally alluded that the reference to a "specific" national problem would not require the existence of a "unique" problem within one Member State.[75]

4. Tax Harmonization, in particular: Article 113

From the very beginning, the Treaty contained one competence that expressly envisaged the harmonization of national taxation. It can today be found in Article 113 TFEU and states:

> The Council shall, acting unanimously in accordance with a special legislative procedure and after consulting the European Parliament and the Economic and Social Committee, adopt provisions for the *harmonisation of legislation concerning turnover taxes, excise duties and other forms of indirect taxation* to the extent that such harmonisation is necessary to ensure the establishment and the functioning of the internal market and to avoid distortion of competition.[76]

The provision allows the Union, when backed up by the unanimous consent of all national governments in the Council, to harmonize all forms of "indirect taxation". Indirect taxes are taxes that are imposed indirectly. (While direct taxes look at the value added by a production *activity*, indirect taxes impose a tax on a product's *price*. Indirect taxes are therefore consumption or consumer taxes. They are collected from the person who is not directly responsible for the economic change that is taxed.)

The two principal forms of indirect taxation expressly mentioned by Article 113 were turnover (sales) taxes and excise duties. The founding fathers indeed regarded these two indirect taxes as "a matter of primary importance",[77] because they posed a particularly serious danger for the establishment and functioning of the internal market.

---

[75] *Land Oberösterreich and Republic of Austria* v. *Commission*, Joined Cases C-439/05 P and C-454/05 P, (2007) ECR I-7141, paras. 65 et seq.

[76] Article 113 TFEU (emphasis added).

[77] European Communities, "The Value-Added Tax in the European Community", (European Communities, 1970), 3: "It seems clear from the marked difference between the approach to harmonisation of indirect taxes on the one hand, and of direct taxes on the other, that the authors of the Rome Treaty regarded harmonisation of turnover taxes and excise duties as a matter of primary importance."

In the past, the Union has engaged in the harmonization of both forms of indirect taxes. With regard to turnover taxation, it has thereby followed the French tradition and adopted a Union-wide system of "Value Added Tax" (VAT). This system is codified in Directive 2006/112 "on the common system of value added tax".[78] VAT is here defined as the application to goods (and services) of "a general tax on consumption exactly proportional to the price of the goods".[79] The standard rate for that tax is currently 15 per cent.[80] The rate is however a minimum rate that allows Member States to charge a higher VAT rate in their territory.[81]

In addition to VAT, the Union may also harmonize special consumer taxes. These excise duties are "a modern version of ancient taxes" ("excises").[82] They are typically imposed on "sensitive" or "luxury" goods like tobacco and alcohol. Traditionally, the level at which these taxes were pitched has differed significantly in the Member States. The Union has therefore adopted a number of harmonization measures.[83] These measures establish – again – only minimum tax rates.[84] They consequently allow Member States to exercise their "sovereign" right to impose higher duties if they consider this appropriate in light of their socio-economic choices.

The wording of Article 113 conceptually excludes the harmonization of *direct* taxes, such as income and corporation tax. It is nonetheless important to recall that the harmonization of direct taxes is not beyond

---

[78] Directive 2006/112 on the common system of value added tax, (2006) OJ L347/1.
[79] *Ibid.*, Article 1(2).
[80] *Ibid.*, Article 97: "From 1 January 2011 until 31 December 2015, the standard rate may not be lower than 15%." The Directive however also recognizes a number of reduced rates and also allows for exemptions.
[81] The highest VAT (standard) rate in a Member State is currently set at 25 per cent in Croatia, Denmark, and Sweden.
[82] D. W. Williams, *EC Tax Law* (Longman, 1998), 93.
[83] For alcoholic beverages, see: Directive 92/83 on the harmonisation of the structures of excise duties on alcohol and alcoholic beverages, (1992) OJ L316/21; for energy products, see: Directive 2003/96 restructuring the Community framework for the taxation of energy products and electricity, (2003) OJ L283/51; for manufactured tobacco, see: Directive 2011/64 on the structure and rates of excise duty applied to manufactured tobacco, (2011) OJ L176/24. Common rules for all three products are set out in Directive 2008/118 concerning the general arrangements for excise duty, (2009) OJ L9/12.
[84] These "minimum" levels can still be very high. For cigarettes, for example, the overall excise duty "shall represent at least 57% of the weighted average retail selling price of cigarettes released for consumption". Cf. Directive 2011/64 (supra n. 83), Article 10.

the scope of positive integration as such. For while the second paragraph of Article 114 TFEU excludes their harmonization by qualified majority, these taxes may still be harmonized by a unanimous Council on the basis of Article 115 TFEU. Importantly, all tax harmonization is therefore still subject to a "fiscal veto". Each Member State thus holds onto its political "sovereignty" over taxation. This fiscal veto has made the harmonization of taxation very difficult. EU legislation in this area is indeed piecemeal and thin.[85]

Conclusion

This Chapter has tried to explore the scope and nature of positive integration within the internal market. While focusing on the free movement of goods, the principles discussed within this Chapter will apply, *mutatis mutandis*, to all of the internal market.

What is the scope of positive integration? Section 1 explored the limits to the Union's internal market competences. We saw there that the Union has not been eager to limit its harmonization competences. It has refused to give a specific content to the technique of "harmonization", and it has traditionally interpreted the requirement that Union harmonization must serve the establishment or functioning of the internal market extremely widely. An important – symbolic – turning point did however occur with *Tobacco Advertising*. The Court here annulled for the first time a Union measure on the ground that it was not covered by the general competence under Article 114. Importantly, as we saw in Section 2, the Union's general harmonization competence in Article 114 is thereby not limited by specific legislative competences within the Treaties. Wherever the centre of gravity of a Union act falls onto the internal market side, legislative harmonization under Article 114 is possible.

Once harmonization has occurred, the Member States are, in principle, obliged to follow the Union standard; yet the Union legal order has also

---

[85] Cf. Directive 2003/48 on taxation of savings income in the form of interest payments, (2003) OJ L157/38; as well as: Directive 2011/96 on the common system of taxation applicable in the case of parent companies and subsidiaries of different Member States, (2011) OJ L345/8.

recognized a limited number of derogations in Articles 114(4) and (5). These derogations exceptionally allow a Member State to maintain or introduce a higher (!) national standard – even if this partly undermines the free movement of goods.

Finally, Section 4 looked at the – very – sensitive issue of tax harmonization. The Union's harmonization powers are here still subject to a "fiscal veto" by each Member State; and this political safeguard has blocked many harmonization efforts within this area.

11 Internal Market: Persons

Introduction

Apart from goods, the European Treaties also aim to ensure the free movement of certain categories of persons. The constitutional choice for an internal "market" in persons was originally informed by an economic rationale. The market-building philosophy behind the European Treaties thus limited the right to move to economically active persons.

The Treaties thereby distinguished between two classes of economic migrants, namely: "employed" and "self-employed" persons; and the Treaty title dealing with persons consequently addresses "Workers" in Chapter 1 and the "Right of Establishment" in Chapter 2. Each of the two chapters contains a central prohibition, whose wording outlaws restriction on the "import" of persons by the (host) State. Yet the Court has found that

Table 11.1 Treaty Provisions on the Free Movement of Persons

Free Movement of Persons			
Citizenship Rights (Articles 20–5)			
Free Movement of Workers		**Freedom of Establishment**	
Article 45	Prohibition on (unjustified) restrictions	Article 49	Prohibition on national restrictions
Article 46	Union Competence: Free movement of workers	Article 50	Union Competence: Freedom of establishment
Article 47	Duty to encourage the exchange of young workers	Article 51	Official Authority Exception for self-employed persons
Article 48	Union Competence: social security	Article 52	Legitimate justifications for national restrictions
		Article 53	Union Competence: Mutual Recognition
		Article 54	Legal persons (companies)
		Article 55	Establishment through participation in a company's capital

Secondary Law (Selection)
Regulation 492/2011 on Freedom of Movement of Workers
Directive 2004/38 on the Rights of Citizens (Citizenship Directive)

both provisions will equally apply to restrictions on the free movement of persons by the "exporting" (home) State.[1] Both chapters also contain a number of legislative competences for the Union. These competences have been widely exercised in the past; and for this reason, European law on the free movement of persons is a rich mixture of primary and secondary law. But the complexity within this area is due to a second factor: the existence of European citizenship rights.[2] Article 20 TFEU grants every European citizen the "right to move and reside freely within the territory

---

[1] The Court has expressed this constitutional choice by referring to the expanded personal scope of both provisions. With regard to workers, see *Scholz* v. *Opera Universitaria di Cagliari and Cinzia Porcedda*, Case C-419/92, [1994] ECR I-505; and with regard to self-employed persons, see: *Knoors* v. *Staatssecretaris van Economische Zaken*, Case 115/78, [1979] ECR 399.

[2] Part Two of the TFEU.

of the Member States".[3] This general movement right is however a residual right. It must "be exercised in accordance with the conditions and limits defined by the Treaties and by the measures adopted thereunder".[4] Yet the general provisions on European citizenship have themselves had an effect on the specific movement rights for economically active citizens. This symbiotic relationship is embodied in the "Citizenship Directive".[5]

This Chapter looks into the complex constitutional arrangements governing the free movement of persons in four sections. Sections 1 and 2 analyse the special free movement rights for economically active persons, that is: workers and the self-employed. Section 3 investigates the general rights to free movement granted to all European citizens. Finally, Section 4 explores the various possible justifications to restrictions on the free movement of persons.

1. Free Movement of Workers

The Treaty contains a single provision that governs national restrictions and possible justifications to the free movement of workers. The text of Article 45 TFEU reads as follows:

1. Freedom of movement for workers shall be secured within the Union.
2. Such freedom of movement shall entail the abolition of any discrimination based on nationality between workers of the Member States as regards employment, remuneration and other conditions of work and employment.
3. It shall entail the right, subject to limitations justified on grounds of public policy, public security or public health:
   (a) to accept offers of employment actually made;
   (b) to move freely within the territory of Member States for this purpose;
   (c) to stay in a Member State for the purpose of employment in accordance with the provisions governing the employment of nationals of that State laid down by law, regulation or administrative action;

---

[3] Article 20(2)(a) TFEU, which is elaborated in Article 21 TFEU. A similar right is enshrined in Article 45 EU Charter of Fundamental Rights.

[4] Article 20(2) TFEU – last indent.

[5] Directive 2004/38 on the right of citizens of the Union and their family members to move and reside freely within the territory of the Member States, [2004] OJ L158/77.

> (d) to remain in the territory of a Member State after having been
>   employed in that State, subject to conditions which shall be embod-
>   ied in regulations to be drawn up by the Commission.
> 4. The provisions of this Article shall not apply to employment in the
>   public service.

The article has been given direct effect.[6] It thus grants European rights
that individuals can invoke in national courts. Yet many of the rights
workers will enjoy under Article 45 are also codified in Union legislation.
The two pertinent pieces of legislation in this context are Regulation
492/2011 "on freedom of movement of workers within the Union",[7] and
Directive 2004/38 "on the right of citizens and their family members to
move and reside freely within the territory of the Member States".[8]

What is the personal and material scope of the rights granted by Article 45 and the relevant Union legislation? Who is considered to be a
"worker"? And what types of national restrictions are prohibited? Let us
look at both aspects in turn.

(a) Personal Scope: Workers and "Quasi-workers"

When is a person a "worker"? Is part-time work sufficient? And are
persons searching for work already "workers"? These questions concern
the personal scope of Article 45, which defines the categories of persons

---

[6] See *Van Duyn* v. *Home Office*, Case 41/74, [1974] ECR 1337, esp. paras. 6–7: "These
provisions impose on Member States a precise obligation which does not require the
adoption of any further measure on the part of the [Union] institutions or of the Member
States and which leaves them, in relation to its implementation, no discretionary power.
Paragraph 3, which defines the rights implied by the principle of freedom of movement
for workers, subjects them to limitations justified on grounds of public policy, public
security or public health. The application of these limitations is, however, subject to
judicial control, so that a Member State's right to invoke the limitations does not prevent
the provisions of Article [45], which enshrine the principle of freedom of movement for
workers, from conferring on individuals rights which are enforceable by them and which
the national courts must protect." Article 45 TFEU has also been held to apply to private
party actions: see *Walrave and Koch* v. *Association Union Cycliste Internationale*, Case
36/74, [1974] ECR 1405, as well as *Union royale belge des sociétés de football association
ASBL* v. *Jean-Marc Bosman*, Case C-415/93, [1995] ECR I-4921. On the doctrine of direct
effect with regard to Treaty provisions, see Chapter 5 – Section 2.
[7] Regulation 492/2011 on freedom of movement for workers within the Union, [2011] OJ
L141/1.
[8] Directive 2004/38 on the right of citizens of the Union and their family members to move
and reside freely within the territory of the Member States (supra n. 5).

falling within the scope of the provision.[9] The Court of Justice has thereby insisted that it alone enjoys the "hermeneutic monopoly" to determine the scope of the term "worker".[10] It held:

> [I]f the definition of this term were a matter within the competence of national law, it would therefore be possible for each Member State to modify the meaning of the concept of "migrant worker" and to eliminate at will the protection afforded by the Treaty to certain categories of persons.[11]

The concept of "worker" had to be a European legal concept, as "the Treaty would be frustrated if the meaning of such a term could be unilaterally fixed and modified by national law".[12]

What then is the European scope of the concept of "worker"? The Court has given an extremely broad definition in *Lawrie-Blum*.[13] The term was to be defined "in accordance with objective criteria which distinguish the employment relationship by reference to the rights and duties of the persons concerned". The essential feature was "that for a certain period of *time* a person performs services for and *under the direction of another person* in return for which he receives *remuneration*".[14] This definition contained three criteria. First, a person would have to be "settled".[15] Second, the person would have to be under the direction of someone else; and consideration for this subordination was – third – the payment of remuneration.[16]

But what form of remuneration would be required to trigger the scope of Article 45? In *Levin*,[17] a British national was refused a residence permit

---

[9] The section concentrates on the "worker" as the primary beneficiary of Article 45 TFEU. However, the provision, and in particular European legislation on the matter, equally entitles additional classes of persons and especially a worker's family.

[10] F. Mancini, "The Free Movement of Workers in the Case-Law of the European Court of Justice" in D. Curtin and D. O'Keeffe (eds.), *Constitutional Adjudication in the European Community and National Law* (Butterworths, 1992), 67.

[11] *Hoekstra (née Unger)* v. *Bestuur der Bedrijfsvereniging voor Detailhandel en Ambachten*, Case 75/63, [1964] ECR 177, 184.

[12] *Ibid.*   [13] *Lawrie-Blum* v. *Land Baden-Württemberg*, Case 66/85, [1986] ECR 2121.

[14] *Ibid.*, para. 17 (emphasis added).

[15] This requirement of "permanency" distinguishes "workers" under Article 45 TFEU from "posted workers" who fall within the scope of the free movement of services. On "posted workers" as a distinct category, see R. Schütze, *European Union Law* (Cambridge University Press, 2015), Chapter 16 – Section 2(a).

[16] In this sense, see *Trojani* v. *Centre public d'aide sociale de Bruxelles*, Case C-456/02, [2004] ECR I-7573, para. 22: "the constituent elements of any paid employment relationship, namely subordination and the payment of remuneration".

[17] *Levin* v. *Staatssecretaris van Justitie*, Case 53/81, [1982] ECR 1035.

in the Netherlands on the ground that she was not engaged in work that provided her with remuneration "commensurate with the means of subsistence considered as necessary by the legislation of the Member State".[18] Would the rights under Article 45 thus depend on receiving a minimum salary within the host Member State? The Court, anxious to avoid a definition that differed depending on the Member State involved, held otherwise:

> Since part-time employment, although it may provide an income lower than what is considered to be the minimum required for subsistence, constitutes for a large number of persons an effective means of improving their living conditions, the effectiveness of [Union] law would be impaired and the achievement of the objectives of the Treaty would be jeopardized if the enjoyment of rights conferred by the principle of freedom of movement for workers were reserved solely to persons engaged in full-time employment and earning, as a result, a wage at least equivalent to the guaranteed minimum wage in the sector under consideration...
>
> In this regard no distinction may be made between those who wish to make do with their income from such an activity and those who supplement that income with other income, whether the latter is derived from property or from the employment of a member of their family who accompanies them. *It should however be stated that whilst part-time employment is not excluded from the field of application of the rules on freedom of movement for workers, those rules cover only the pursuit of effective and genuine activities, to the exclusion of activities on such a small scale as to be regarded as purely marginal and ancillary.*[19]

The Court here defined a "worker" as a person remunerated for an "effective and genuine" activity. Under this minimalist definition, the number of working hours and the level of remuneration was irrelevant, except where the activity was so small that it was "purely marginal and ancillary". Subsequent jurisprudence has consolidated this minimalist standard.[20] It thus held that benefits in kind could be considered "remuneration" as long as the work done was "capable of being regarded as forming part of the normal labour market".[21] But what about people who could not support themselves in the host State? The Court here insisted that even where a

---

[18] *Ibid.*, para. 10.   [19] *Ibid.*, paras. 15–17 (emphasis added).

[20] See *Kempf* v. *Staatssecretaris van Justitie*, Case 139/85, [1986] ECR 1741; as well as *Trojani*, Case C-456/02 (supra n. 16).

[21] *Ibid.*, para. 24.

person needs financial assistance *from the State* to supplement his income, this would still be irrelevant for his status as a "worker" as long as he was engaged in an effective and genuine activity.[22]

The Court's minimalist definition of "worker" had given an extremely broad personal scope to Article 45. Yet it still hinged on the *presence* of a genuine employment relationship. But would Article 45 also cover people searching for *future* employment, or persons who had engaged in *past* employment? The Court has indeed found that these "quasi-workers" form part of the personal scope of Article 45. For former employees this solution is suggested by the provision itself;[23] and the Court emphatically confirmed this in *Lair*.[24] A French national had brought proceedings against a German University for refusing to award her a maintenance grant. This was a social advantage which a worker would have been entitled to claim under Article 45.[25] But could Mrs Lair claim this right *after* having ceased work in the host State? Three Member States intervened in the case and argued that "a person loses the status of worker, on which the social advantages depend, when, in the host State, [s]he gives up either [her] previous occupational activity or, if unemployed, [her] search for employment in order to pursue full-time studies".[26]

The Court disagreed, and found that "the rights guaranteed to migrant workers *do not necessarily depend on the actual or continuing existence of an employment relationship*".[27] Non-employed persons would thus continue to enjoy "certain rights linked to the status of worker even when they are no longer in an employment relationship".[28] However, these

---

[22] *Kempf* v. *Staatssecretaris van Justitie*, Case 139/85 (supra n. 20), para. 14: "It follows that the rules on this topic must be interpreted as meaning that a person in effective and genuine part-time employment cannot be excluded from their sphere of application merely because the remuneration he derives from it is below the level of the minimum means of subsistence and he seeks to supplement it by other lawful means of subsistence. In that regard it is irrelevant whether those supplementary means of subsistence are derived from property or from the employment of a member of his family, as was the case in *Levin*, or whether, as in this instance, they are obtained from financial assistance drawn from the public funds of the Member State in which he resides, provided that the effective and genuine nature of his work is established."

[23] Article 45(3)(d) TFEU expressly refers to the right "to remain in the territory of a Member State after having been employed in that State, subject to conditions which shall be embodied in regulations to be drawn up by the Commission."

[24] *Lair* v. *Universität Hannover*, Case 39/86, [1988] ECR 3161.

[25] *Ibid.*, para. 28. On the material scope of Article 45 TFEU and the notion of social advantage under Article 7(2) of Regulation 492/2011, see Section 1(b) below.

[26] *Ibid.*, para. 29.   [27] *Ibid.*, para. 31 (emphasis added).

[28] *Ibid.*, para. 36.

rights required "some continuity between the previous occupational activity and the course of study".[29] This qualification was to prevent abuses of the host State's social welfare system.[30]

What about persons seeking future employment? The Court expressly expanded the personal scope of Article 45 to job-seekers in *Antonissen*.[31] The case arose from a preliminary question by an English High Court on the compatibility of a British law permitting the deportation of foreigners after six months of unemployment. Was such a temporal limitation on the status of (potential) workers possible? While the Court confirmed that the personal scope of Article 45 included job-seekers, it accepted that the mobility of workers would not be undermined by national measures offering "a reasonable time" to find work.[32] And in the absence of Union harmonization on the matter, a period of six months was considered reasonable.[33] The Court was nonetheless eager to add that "if after the expiry of that period the person concerned provides evidence that he is continuing to seek employment and that he has genuine chances of being engaged", the job-seeker could not be forced to leave the territory of the host Member State.[34]

(b) Material Scope: Discrimination and Beyond

Which rights will workers enjoy on the basis of Article 45 TFEU and Union legislation? Article 45(2) expressly refers to "the abolition of any discrimination based on nationality between workers of the Member States as regards employment, remuneration and other conditions of work and employment"; and Article 45(3) clarifies that this "shall entail the right" to accept offers, to move freely and to stay within the territory of a Member State for that purpose.

---

[29] *Ibid.*, para. 37. The Court however qualified this qualification as follows: "Such continuity may not, however, be required where a migrant has involuntarily become unemployed and is obliged by conditions on the job market to undertake occupational retraining in another field of activity." For a broad definition of "involuntary", see *Ninni-Orasche* v. *Bundesminister für Wissenschaft, Verkehr und Kunst*, Case C-413/01, [2003] ECR I-13187.

[30] *Lair* v. *Universität Hannover*, Case 39/86 (supra n. 24), para. 43. In *Brown* v. *The Secretary of State for Scotland*, Case 197/86, [1988] ECR 3205, the Court thus imposed strict requirements when a former worker was entitled to educational rights, such as a grant for university studies.

[31] *The Queen* v. *Immigration Appeal Tribunal, ex parte Antonissen*, Case C-292/89, [1991] ECR I-745.

[32] *Ibid.*, para. 16.   [33] *Ibid.*, para. 21.   [34] *Ibid.*

These textual bones are given substantive flesh by Directive 2004/38 and Regulation 492/2011.[35] The latter sets out the specific rights for workers and their families.[36] In addition to outlawing access restrictions to the labour market of the host State,[37] the Regulation confirms the principle of equal treatment during an employment relationship. The central provision here is Article 7:

> 1. A worker who is a national of a Member State may not, in the territory of another Member State, be *treated differently from national workers by reason of his nationality* in respect of any conditions of employment and work, in particular as regards remuneration, dismissal, and, should he become unemployed, reinstatement or re-employment.
> 2. He shall enjoy the *same social and tax advantages* as national workers.[38]

Despite the direct effect of Article 45 TFEU, Article 7 of the Regulation – or, better: its predecessor – has had a profound impact on the material scope of the free movement of workers. It provides a negative expression of the equal treatment principle in paragraph 1, and a positive expression of that principle in paragraph 2.

Was Article 7(1) inspired by a discrimination rationale; and if so, which one? In *Sotgiu*,[39] the Court clarified that the formulation "by reason of his nationality" was not confined to direct discrimination:

> The rules regarding equality of treatment, both in the Treaty and in Article 7 of Regulation [492/2011], forbid not only overt discrimination by reason of nationality but also *all covert forms of discrimination* which, by the application of other criteria of differentiation, lead in fact to the same result.[40]

---

[35] Regulation 492/2011 on freedom of movement for workers within the Union, [2011] OJ L141/1. The Regulation has three Chapters. Chapter 1 deals with "Equality, Equal Treatment and Workers' Families". Chapter 2 concerns "Clearance of Vacancies and Applications for Employment". Finally, Chapter 3 sets up a "Committee for ensuring close cooperation between the Member States in matters concerning the freedom of movement of workers and their employment".

[36] These rights are set out in Chapter 1 of the Regulation. Chapter 1 is divided into three Sections: Section 1 is on "Eligibility for Employment" (Articles 1–6). Section 2 deals with "Employment and Equality of Treatment" (Articles 7–9), while Section 3 concerns "Workers' Families" (Article 10).

[37] See Article 4(1) of the Regulation: "Provisions laid down by law, regulation or administrative action of the Member States which restrict by number or percentage the employment of foreign nationals in any undertaking, branch of activity or region, or at a national level, shall not apply to nationals of the other Member States."

[38] Emphasis added.   [39] *Sotgiu* v. *Deutsche Bundespost*, Case 152/73, [1974] ECR 153.

[40] *Ibid.*, para. 11 (emphasis added).

Article 7(1) of the Regulation thus covers forms of direct and indirect discrimination. Where national legislation treated workers differently on grounds of their origin or residence, this *could* be "tantamount, as regards their practical effect, to discrimination on the grounds of nationality".[41] Subsequent jurisprudence thereby crystallized two situations in which national laws would appear to be *indirectly* discriminatory.[42] The first situation concerns national laws that "although applicable irrespective of nationality" nonetheless "affect essentially migrant workers or the great majority of those affected are migrant workers".[43] The second situation arises where national laws "are indistinctly applicable but can more easily be satisfied by national workers than by migrant workers or where there is a risk that they may operate to the particular detriment of migrant workers".[44] Unless the differential treatment can here be objectively justified, both types of national laws would violate Article 7(1) of the Regulation.

A positive expression of equal treatment rights for migrant workers is set out in Article 7(2) of the Regulation. Foreign workers are here granted "the same social and tax advantages as national workers".[45] The notion of "social advantage" has received a wide teleological meaning. In *Cristini*,[46] the Court found the phrase to refer to "all social and tax advantages, whether or not attached to the contract of employment";[47] and this included travel reductions in fares for large families offered by the State. This definition was confirmed in *Lair*,[48] where the Court further broadened the concept of social advantage to all advantages which entailed "the possibility of improving [a worker's] living and working conditions and promoting his social advancement".[49] This included all advantages that

---

[41] *Ibid.*   [42] See *O'Flynn* v. *Adjudication Officer*, Case C-237/94, [1996] ECR I-2617.

[43] *Ibid.*, para. 18 (with extensive references to the case law).

[44] *Ibid.* (with extensive references to the case law).

[45] Originally, the Court excluded job-seekers from the scope of the provision. In *Centre public d'aide sociale de Courcelles* v. *Lebon*, Case 316/85, [1987] ECR 2811, the Court held (*ibid.*, para. 26): "[T]he right to equal treatment with regard to social and tax advantages applies only to workers. Those who move in search of employment qualify for equal treatment only as regards access to employment in accordance with Article [45] of the [FEU] Treaty and Articles 2 and 5 of Regulation 1612/68." This judgment was qualified in *Collins* v. *Secretary of State for Work and Pensions*, Case C-138/02, [2004] ECR I-2703.

[46] *Cristini* v. *SNCF*, Case 32/75, [1975] ECR 1085.   [47] *Ibid.*, para. 13.

[48] *Lair* v. *Universität Hannover*, Case 39/86, (supra n. 24).   [49] *Ibid.*, para. 20.

> whether or not linked to a contract of employment, are generally granted to national workers primarily because of their status as workers or by virtue of the mere fact of their residence on the national territory and whose extension to workers who are nationals of other Member States therefore seems likely to facilitate the mobility of such workers within the [Union].[50]

However, as under Article 7(1) of the Regulation, Member States are entitled to justify differential treatment "if it is based on objective considerations that are independent of the nationality of the persons concerned and proportionate to the legitimate aim of the national provisions".[51] A residence requirement might thus be legitimate, where a Member State wishes "to ensure that there is a *genuine link* between an applicant for an allowance in the nature of a social advantage within the meaning of Article 7(2) of Regulation".[52]

Finally, what about *non*-discriminatory restrictions to the free movement of workers? While much of the case law on workers focuses on discriminatory national laws, the Court accepts that non-discriminatory measures might also fall within the scope of Article 45 TFEU. The famous confirmation of that possibility is *Bosman*.[53] The case concerned a professional football rule according to which a footballer could not be employed by another club unless the latter paid a transfer or training fee. This was a non-discriminatory rule that applied to nationals and non-nationals alike.[54] Nonetheless, the Court found that "those rules are likely to restrict the freedom of movement of players who wish to pursue their activity in another Member State by preventing or deterring them from leaving the clubs to which they belong even after the expiry of their contracts of employment with those clubs".[55] The said rules would thus "constitute an obstacle to freedom of movement for workers",[56] since they "*directly affect players' access to the employment market in other Member States*".[57]

Formulated as a general principle, this suggests that "[n]ational provisions which *preclude or deter a national of a Member State from leaving his country of origin* in order to exercise his right to freedom of movement

---

[50] *Ibid.*, para. 21.
[51] *Collins* v. *Secretary of State for Work and Pensions*, Case C-138/02 (supra n. 45), para. 66.
[52] *Ibid.*, para. 67.
[53] *Union royale belge des sociétés de football association ASBL* v. *Jean-Marc Bosman*, Case C-415/93 (supra n. 6).
[54] *Ibid.*, para. 98.   [55] *Ibid.*, para. 99.   [56] *Ibid.*, para. 100.
[57] *Ibid.*, para. 103 (emphasis added).

therefore constitute restrictions on that freedom even if they apply without regard to the nationality of the workers concerned".[58] Non-discriminatory restrictions are thus covered by Article 45 TFEU.

2. Freedom of Establishment

Freedom of establishment constitutes the second side of the European coin on the free movement of persons. It guarantees the free movement of self-employed persons. To achieve this aim, the relevant Treaty chapter contains a prohibition on illegal national barriers, and grants the Union two legislative competences.[59] This Section will concentrate on the prohibition in the form of Article 49,[60] which states:

> Within the framework of the provisions set out below, restrictions on the freedom of establishment of nationals of a Member State in the territory of another Member State shall be prohibited. Such prohibition shall also apply to restrictions on the setting-up of agencies, branches or subsidiaries by nationals of any Member State established in the territory of any Member State.
>
> Freedom of establishment shall include the right to take up and pursue activities as self-employed persons and to set up and manage undertakings, in particular companies or firms within the meaning of the second paragraph of Article 54, under the conditions laid down for its own nationals by the law of the country where such establishment is effected, subject to the provisions of the Chapter relating to capital.

(a) Personal Scope: Self-employed Persons (and Companies)

The personal scope of Article 49 captures "self-employed" persons. Like workers, self-employed persons will need to be engaged in a genuine

---

[58] *Olympique Lyonnais* v. *Bernard and Newcastle UFC*, Case C-325/08, [2010] ECR I-2177, para. 34 (emphasis added). See also *Commission* v. *Denmark*, Case 464/02, [2005] ECR I-7929, para. 45: "It is settled case-law that Article [45 TFEU] prohibits not only all discrimination, direct or indirect, based on nationality, but also national rules which are applicable irrespective of the nationality of the workers concerned but impede their freedom of movement."

[59] See Articles 50 and 53 TFEU. This section will not deal with the various legislative instruments in this context. The most important instrument adopted under Article 53 TFEU is Directive 2005/36 on the recognition of professional qualifications, [2005] OJ L255/22.

[60] The provision was given direct effect in *Reyners* v. *Belgium*, Case 2/74, [1974] ECR 631.

economic activity. However, unlike workers, self-employed persons do not work under the direction of an employer and will not receive a "salary" compensating for their subordination. The personal scopes of Articles 45 and 49 are thus "mutually exclusive".[61] The definition of "worker" thereby negatively determines the personal scope of the freedom of establishment. Importantly, self-employed persons might be natural *or* legal persons. For Article 54 TFEU expressly provides that the freedom of establishment covers companies and firms.[62]

Self-employed persons (and companies) will typically produce goods or perform services. And while there are no delineation problems with regard to goods, the Union legal order had to delimit the personal scope of Article 49 from the perspective of the free movement of services. For this third freedom protects, among other things, persons offering a service in another State.[63] What then is the characteristic feature underlying the personal scope of the freedom of establishment? The Court has identified it as follows:

> The right of establishment, provided for in Articles [49] to [54] of the Treaty, is granted both to legal persons within the meaning of Article [54] and to natural persons who are nationals of a Member State of the [Union]. Subject to the exceptions and conditions laid down, it allows all types of self-employed activity to be taken up and pursued on the territory of any other Member State, undertakings to be formed and operated, and agencies, branches or subsidiaries to be set up . . .
>
> The concept of establishment within the meaning of the Treaty is therefore a very broad one, allowing a [Union] national to participate, *on a stable and continuous basis, in the economic life of a Member State* other than his State of origin and to profit there from, so contributing to economic and social interpenetration within the [Union] in the sphere of activities as self-employed persons. In contrast, where the provider of services moves

---

[61] *Gebhard* v. *Consiglio dell'Ordine degli Avvocati e Procuratori di Milano*, Case 55/94, [1995] ECR I-4165, para. 20.

[62] Article 54 TFEU states: "Companies or firms formed in accordance with the law of a Member State and having their registered office, central administration or principal place of business within the Union shall, for the purposes of this Chapter, be treated in the same way as natural persons who are nationals of Member States. 'Companies or firms' means companies or firms constituted under civil or commercial law, including cooperative societies, and other legal persons governed by public or private law, save for those which are non-profit-making."

[63] According to Article 56 TFEU, "restrictions on freedom to provide services within the Union shall be prohibited in respect of nationals of Member States who are established in a Member State other than that of the person for whom the services are intended."

to another Member State, the provisions of the chapter on services, in particular the third paragraph of Article [57], envisage that he is to pursue his activity there on a temporary basis.[64]

The decisive criterion distinguishing "established" service providers from "temporary" service providers is thus the "stable and continuous basis" on which the former participate in the economy of the host Member State. A "stable and continuous" presence will trigger the personal scope of the freedom of establishment. However, the concept of establishment will not require exclusive presence in the host State (as this would rule out secondary establishment). The applicability of Article 49 however is determined by the "duration", "regularity, periodicity or continuity" of the services provided.[65] A continuous presence will not need to take the form of a "branch" or "agency" but may consist of an "office".[66] Yet the existence of some infrastructure – like an office – is not conclusive evidence in favour of establishment.[67]

(b) Material Scope: Discrimination and Beyond

Article 49 prohibits "restrictions on the freedom of establishment". The prohibition thereby expressly covers primary and secondary establishment. Primary establishment occurs where a natural or legal person establishes itself for the first time. The right to establishment is, however, "not confined to the right to create a single establishment within the [Union]", but includes "freedom to set up and maintain, subject to observance of the professional rules of conduct, more than one place of work within the [Union]".[68]

Secondary establishment indeed covers "the setting-up of agencies, branches or subsidiaries by nationals of any Member State [already] established in the territory of any Member State".[69] This right of secondary establishment is thereby given to every person or company

---

[64] *Gebhard*, Case 55/94 (supra n. 61), paras. 23–6 (emphasis added). The third paragraph of Article 57 TFEU states that "[w]ithout prejudice to the provisions of the Chapter relating to the right of establishment, the person providing a service may, in order to do so, temporarily pursue his activity in the Member State where the service is provided, under the same conditions as are imposed by that State on its own nationals".

[65] *Gebhard*, Case 55/94 (supra n. 61) para. 27.

[66] See *Commission* v. *Germany*, Case 205/84, [1986] ECR 3755, para. 21.

[67] *Gebhard*, Case 55/94 (supra n. 61), para. 27.

[68] *Ordre des avocats au Barreau de Paris* v. *Klopp*, Case 107/83, [1984] ECR 2971, para. 19.

[69] Article 49 TFEU – first indent.

lawfully established in a Member State of the Union, even if it has no business in the State of primary establishment.[70] This constitutional choice allows a company to freely choose its Member State of incorporation within the Union. (However, where a company moves to another Member State, it may lose its legal personality in its original home State.[71] This principle – which partly restricts the right of secondary establishment – follows from the right of each Member State to decide when a company is "primarily" established.)[72]

Which types of restrictions will Article 49 prohibit? The wording of the provision clearly covers discriminatory measures. This includes *directly* discriminatory national laws,[73] and equally prohibits *indirect* discrimination on grounds of nationality.[74] A good illustration for indirect discrimination can be found in *Klopp*.[75] The case involved a German barrister registered with the Düsseldorf (Germany) bar, who had applied for secondary registration at the Paris (France) bar. His application was however rejected by the Paris Bar Council on the ground that he did not satisfy the French law on barristers that required them to join or establish a set of chambers in one place only. This law was not directly discriminatory, since it also applied to French barristers; yet the Court had no problem in finding an indirect discrimination to have taken place:

> It should be emphasized that under the second paragraph of Article [49] freedom of establishment includes access to and the pursuit of the activities of self-employed persons "under the conditions laid down for its own nationals by the law of the county where such establishment is effected". It

---

[70] *Segers* v. *Bestuur van de Bedrijfsvereniging voor Bank- en Verzekeringswezen, Groothandel en Vrije Beroepen*, Case 79/85, [1986] ECR 2375. The *Segers* principle was confirmed in *Centros* v. *Erhvervs-og Selskabsstyrelsen*, Case C-212/97, [1999] ECR I-1459.

[71] *The Queen* v. *HM Treasury and Commissioners of Inland Revenue, ex parte Daily Mail*, Case 81/87, [1988] ECR 5483. This distinguishes legal persons from natural persons, as the latter will not lose their nationality when moving their primary establishment to another Member State.

[72] This is recognized in Article 54 TFEU, which defers to the laws of the Member States with regard to the formation of companies. National laws typically follow one of two theories. According to the "incorporation theory", a company is "established" through the simple act of formal registration. This contrasts with the "seat theory", which makes formal registration dependent on the company having its managerial and business centre within the State of registration.

[73] See *Reyners* v. *Belgium*, Case 2/74 (supra n. 60); as well as *The Queen* v. *Secretary of State for Transport, ex parte Factortame (Factortame II)*, Case C-221/89, [1991] ECR I-3905.

[74] *Thieffry* v. *Conseil de l'ordre des avocats à la cour de Paris*, Case 71/76, [1977] ECR 765; as well as *Engelmann*, Case C-64/08, [2010] ECR I-8219.

[75] *Ordre des avocats au Barreau de Paris* v. *Onno Klopp*, Case 107/83, (1984) ECR 2971.

> follows from that provision and its context that in the absence of specific [Union] rules on the matter each Member State is free to regulate the exercise of the legal profession in its territory. Nevertheless that rule does not mean that the legislation of a Member State may require a lawyer to have only one establishment throughout the [Union] territory. Such a restrictive interpretation would mean that a lawyer once established in a particular Member State would be able to enjoy the freedom of the Treaty to establish himself in another Member State only at the price of abandoning the establishment he already had.[76]

Whether the scope of Article 49 also covered non-discriminatory measures remained uncertain for some time.[77] This uncertainty was ultimately removed in *Gebhard*.[78] The case involved a German lawyer who had practised in Italy under the title "avvocato" without being formally admitted to the Italian Bar. This violated the relevant national rules on the organization of the legal profession. Yet despite their "non-discriminatory" character, the Court unambiguously found them to violate Article 49 because they were "liable to hinder or make less attractive" the freedom of establishment.[79] This *Dassonville*-like formula potentially included all types of regulatory barriers. However, the Court appears to limit its negative ambit to national measures that hinder "[a]ccess to the market" to foreign establishments.[80]

3. European Citizenship: A General Right to Move and Stay?

With the formal introduction of the provisions on European citizenship,[81] the European Treaties recognize a range of rights that pertain to all

---

[76] *Ibid.*, paras. 17–18.   [77] See *Commission* v. *Belgium*, Case 221/85, [1987] ECR 719.
[78] *Gebhard*, Case 55/94 (supra n. 61).   [79] *Ibid.*, para. 37.
[80] *Caixa Bank France* v. *Ministère de l'Économie, des Finances et de l'Industrie*, Case C-442/02, [2004] ECR I-8961, para. 14; as well as *Commission* v. *Spain*, Case C-400/08, [2011] ECR I-1915, para. 64: "In that context, it should be borne in mind that the concept of 'restriction' for the purposes of Article [49 TFEU] covers measures taken by a Member State which, although applicable without distinction, affect access to the market for undertakings from other Member States and thereby hinder intra-[Union] trade." For an analysis of the case law on persons in light of the market access test, see E. Spaventa, *Free Movement of Persons in the European Union: Barriers to Movement in Their Constitutional Context* (Kluwer, 2007), Chapter 5.
[81] The citizenship provisions were introduced by the (old) Treaty on European Union concluded in Maastricht. For an early analysis of these provisions, see C. Closa, "The Concept of Citizenship in the Treaty on European Union", 29 (1992) *Common Market Law Review*,

"Europeans" by virtue of being Union citizens.[82] These rights are generally set out in Article 20 TFEU, and are subsequently specified in the following articles. With regard to free movement, Article 21 TFEU states:

> 1. Every citizen of the Union shall have the right to move and reside freely within the territory of the Member States, subject to the limitations and conditions laid down in the Treaties and by the measures adopted to give them effect.
> 2. If action by the Union should prove necessary to attain this objective and the Treaties have not provided the necessary powers, the European Parliament and the Council, acting in accordance with the ordinary legislative procedure, may adopt provisions with a view to facilitating the exercise of the rights referred to in paragraph 1.[83]

Does paragraph 1 establish a general right for all Union citizens to move and reside anywhere within the Union? Was this a clear and unconditional provision? Paragraph 2 grants the Union a legislative competence to facilitate the exercise of the free movement rights mentioned in paragraph 1. The competence has been used – together with some special movement competences – for the adoption of Directive 2004/38 "on the right of citizens of the Union and their family members to move and reside freely within the territory of the Member States."[84]

(a) Article 21(1): A Direct Source of Movement Rights

Would Article 21(1) TFEU be directly effective, and therefore directly grant movement rights to European citizens? Having approached the matter in various indirect ways,[85] the Court finally gave a direct answer in

---

1137. And for an excellent re-evaluation, see D. Kochenov, "Ius Tractum of Many Faces: European Citizenship and the Difficult Relationship between Status and Rights", 15 (2009) *Columbia Journal of European Law*, 169.

[82] This European citizenship is "additional" to their national citizenship (see Article 20(1) TFEU).

[83] Article 21(3) TFEU provides a special Union competence for measures concerning social security or social protection.

[84] [2004] OJ L158/77.

[85] See *Martínez Sala* v. *Freistaat Bayern*, Case C-85/96, [1998] ECR I-2691; and *Grzelczyk* v. *Centre public d'aide sociale d'Ottignies-Louvain-la-Neuve*, Case C-184/99, [2001] ECR I-6193. In the latter case the Court famously held (*ibid.*, para. 31) that "Union citizenship is destined to be the fundamental status of nationals of the Member States".

Baumbast.[86] The case concerned the fight of a German father to stay with his daughters in the United Kingdom while they continued their education in a British school. The fundamental question put before the European Court was this: would a Union citizen, who no longer enjoyed a right of residence as a migrant worker, nonetheless enjoy an independent right of residence on the basis of Article 21(1) alone?

The United Kingdom government vehemently rejected this view. "[A] right of residence cannot be derived directly from Article [21(1) TFEU]", because "[t]he limitations and conditions referred to in that paragraph show that it is not intended to be a free-standing provision".[87] The Court famously found otherwise:

> [T]he Treaty on European Union does not require that citizens of the Union pursue a professional or trade activity, whether as an employed or self-employed person, in order to enjoy the rights provided in Part Two of the [FEU] Treaty, on citizenship of the Union. Furthermore, there is nothing in the text of that Treaty to permit the conclusion that citizens of the Union who have established themselves in another Member State in order to carry on an activity as an employed person there are deprived, where that activity comes to an end, of the rights which are conferred on them by the [FEU] Treaty by virtue of that citizenship. *As regards, in particular, the right to reside within the territory of the Member States under Article [21(1)] that right is conferred directly on every citizen of the Union by a clear and precise provision of [that] Treaty.*
>
> Purely as a national of a Member State, and consequently a citizen of the Union, Mr Baumbast therefore has the right to rely on Article [21(1)]. Admittedly, that right for citizens of the Union to reside within the territory of another Member State is conferred subject to the limitations and conditions laid down by the [Treaties] and by the measures adopted to give it effect. However, the application of the limitations and conditions acknowledged in Article [21(1)] in respect of the exercise of that right of residence is subject to judicial review. Consequently, any limitations and conditions imposed on that right do not prevent the provisions of Article [21(1)] from conferring on individuals rights which are enforceable by them and which the national courts must protect.[88]

---

[86] *Baumbast and R* v. *Secretary of State for the Home Department*, Case C-413/99, [2002] ECR I-7091.

[87] *Ibid.*, para. 78.

[88] *Ibid.*, paras. 83–6 (emphasis added) (with express reference to the reasoning in *Van Duyn* v. *Home Office*, Case 41/74 (supra n. 6)).

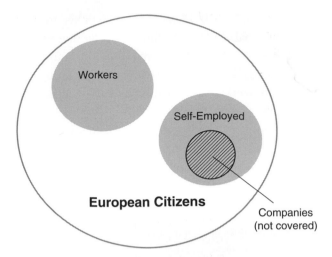

Figure 11.1 Relationship between Citizenship and Special Competences

The Court here clarified four things. First, Article 21(1) was directly effective and would thus grant general movement rights that can be invoked against national law. The fact that these rights were subject to limitations and conditions was no barrier to their direct effect. Second, the personal scope of the citizenship provisions did not depend on the economic status of a person. Europeans enjoyed free movement rights as *citizenship* rights; and citizenship was a "fundamental status" independent of someone's economic position.[89] Third, the citizenship provisions would be residual provisions. They would not apply whenever one of the specialized movement regimes was applicable. Fourth, any limitation on citizenship rights through European legislation would be subject to judicial review. And where these legislative limitations were disproportionate, the Court could strike them down on the basis of Article 21(1).[90]

(b) Directive 2004/38: Rights and Limitations

The Directive on the right of citizens to move and reside freely within the Union was adopted to codify in "a single legislative act" the various secondary sources governing the free movement of persons.[91] It lays down "the conditions governing the *exercise* of the right of free movement and

---

[89] *Ibid.*, para. 82 (with reference to *Grzelczyk*, Case C-184/99 (supra n. 85)).
[90] *Ibid.*, paras. 91–3.   [91] Directive 2004/38, Preamble 4.

residence within the territory of the Member States by Union citizens" (and their family members).[92] The Directive contains five substantive chapters. Chapter II concerns the rights of exit and entry (Articles 4–5). Chapter III details the rights of residence (Articles 6–15). Chapter IV lays down rules for the right of permanent residence (Articles 16–21). Chapter V assembles provisions that are common to the right of (temporary) residence and permanent residence (Articles 22–6). Finally, Chapter VI provides detailed rules on legitimate restrictions to the right of entry and residence on grounds of public policy, public security or public health (Articles 27–33).

What are the most important rights recognized in the Directive? Having spelled out the right to exit and enter a Member State on condition of a valid identity card or passport, the Directive distinguishes three classes of residency rights. According to Article 6, all Union citizens will have the short-term right to reside in the territory of another Member State for a period of up to three months "as long as they do not become an unreasonable burden on the social assistance system of the host Member State".[93] A second class of residency rights is established by Article 7, whose first paragraph states:

> All Union citizens shall have the right of residence on the territory of another Member State for a period of longer than three months if they:
>
> (a) are workers or self-employed persons in the host Member State; or
> (b) have sufficient resources for themselves and their family members not to become a burden on the social assistance system of the host Member State during their period of residence and have comprehensive sickness insurance cover in the host Member State; or
> (c) – are enrolled at a private or public establishment, accredited or financed by the host Member State on the basis of its legislation or administrative practice, for the principal purpose of following a course of study, including vocational training; and
>   – have comprehensive sickness insurance cover in the host Member State and assure the relevant national authority, by means of a declaration or by such equivalent means as they may choose, that they have sufficient resources for themselves and their family members not to

---

[92] Directive 2004/38, Article 1(a). Article 3 however restricts the personal scope to "Union citizens who move to or reside in a Member State *other than that of which they are a national*" (emphasis added).

[93] *Ibid.*, Article 14(1).

> become a burden on the social assistance system of the host Member
> State during their period of residence; or
> (d) are family members accompanying or joining a Union citizen who
> satisfies the conditions referred to in points (a), (b) or (c).

The provision acknowledges four categories of persons who will benefit
from mid-term residency rights. Subparagraph a refers to the economically active migrants expressly recognized by the Treaties. (Article 7(3)
of the Directive subsequently confirms that Union citizens who are no
longer working or self-employed "shall retain the status of worker or
self-employed" in certain circumstances.) This is extended to all persons
with "sufficient resources" and with "comprehensive sickness insurance"
(subparagraph b),[94] with students benefiting from a slightly more generous treatment (subparagraph c). Family members will be entitled to
accompany or join (subparagraph d).

Finally, the Directive grants a third class of right: the "right of permanent residence" in certain situations. The general rules for this are laid
down in Article 16, which confers such a right after lawful presence in
the host State "for a continuous period of five years".[95] Importantly, this
right of long-term residency is independent of the economic status and
the financial means of the person concerned.

Once a person is legally resident in another Member State, the Directive
expressly grants this person a right to equal treatment in Article 24. The
connection between lawful residence and equal treatment has been firmly
established in the jurisprudence of the European Court.[96] In principle, a
Member State must thus treat all legally resident Union citizens within its
territory like its own nationals.[97] This general principle is however subject

---

[94] Article 8(4) of the Directive thereby partly defines "sufficient resources" by stating:
"Member States may not lay down a fixed amount which they regard as 'sufficient
resources', but they must take into account the personal situation of the person concerned.
In all cases this amount shall not be higher than the threshold below which nationals of
the host Member State become eligible for social assistance, or, where this criterion is not
applicable, higher than the minimum social security pension paid by the host Member
State."

[95] Article 17 thereby establishes a more preferable regime for former workers or self-
employed persons, and Article 18 deals with the acquisition of the right of permanent
residence by certain family members.

[96] See *Martínez Sala*, Case C-85/96 and *Grzelczyk*, Case C-184/99 (both supra n. 85).

[97] See *Trojani* (supra n. 16), para. 40.

to such "specific provisions as are expressly provided for in the Treaty and secondary law".[98] Controversially, the equality principle has specifically been derogated by Article 24(2) with regard to social assistance and maintenance aid for studies.

4. Justifying Restrictions on (Self-)employed Persons

Restrictions on the free movement of persons might be justified on the basis of legitimate public interests. For workers, Article 45(3) expressly allows for "limitations justified on grounds of public policy, public security or public health". And for the freedom of establishment, Article 52 permits the "special treatment for foreign nationals on grounds of public policy, public security or public health". Finally, Article 21(1) TFEU subjects the free movement of EU citizens generally "to the limitations and conditions laid down in the Treaties and by the measures adopted to give them effect".

Many problems encountered in the context of goods will apply, *mutatis mutandis*, to justified restrictions on the free movement of persons.[99] However, unlike the provisions on goods, the Treaties recognize an additional justification for national restrictions: the public service exception.

(a) Express Justifications and (Implied) Imperative Requirements

The express justifications for restrictions on persons mentioned in the Treaties are substantially identical to those on goods. However, unlike the casuistic approach governing goods, Directive 2004/38 has partly codified the case law.[100] Article 27 of the Directive thereby confirms the power of the Member States to "restrict the freedom of movement and residence of Union citizens and their family members, irrespective of nationality, on grounds of public policy, public security or public health".

With regard to the first two public interest grounds, the Directive further clarifies that national restrictions must "be based exclusively on the

---

[98] Article 24(1) of Directive 2004/38.
[99] On justified restrictions to the free movement of goods, see Chapter 9 – Section 4.
[100] Directive 2004/38 (supra n. 5), Chapter VI (Articles 27–33).

personal conduct of the individual concerned",[101] and that this personal conduct "must represent a genuine, present and sufficiently serious threat affecting one of the fundamental interests of society".[102] With regard to public health, Article 29 of the Directive subsequently determines that only "diseases with epidemic potential" and the like will justify measures restricting free movement.[103]

Is the list of public interest justifications exhaustive? The Court has indeed held that discriminatory measures – whether direct or indirect – can solely be justified by reference to the express justifications recognized by the Treaty (and secondary law).[104] Yet as soon as the Court had acknowledged that non-discriminatory measures could potentially violate the free movement provisions, it simultaneously recognized the existence of additional – implied – justifications. Unfortunately, these implied justifications were not called "mandatory requirements", but rather "imperative requirements" or "overriding requirements" relating to the public interest.[105]

The Court accepts a whole range of such imperative requirements.[106] The constitutional principles governing these imperative requirements are set out in *Gebhard*,[107] where the Court held:

> [N]ational measures liable to hinder or make less attractive the exercise of fundamental freedoms guaranteed by the Treaty must fulfil four conditions: they must be applied in a non-discriminatory manner; they must be

---

[101] Article 27(2) of Directive 2004/38 – first indent. For an early judicial definition of what constitutes personal conduct, see *Van Duyn* v. *Home Office*, Case 41/74 (supra n. 6).

[102] Article 27(2) of Directive 2004/38 – second indent. For an early judicial definition of what constitutes a "present" threat, see *Régina* v. *Pierre Bouchereau*, Case 30/77, [1977] ECR 1999.

[103] Article 29(1) of Directive 2004/38.

[104] See *Engelmann*, Case C-64/08 (supra n. 74), para. 34.

[105] The terminology of the Court is – sadly – not uniform; see *Centros*, Case C-212/97 (supra n. 70), para. 32 ("imperative requirements"); *Caixa Bank France*, Case C-442/02 (supra n. 80) para. 17 ("overriding requirements"). Sometimes, the Court even replaces "requirements" with "reasons"; see *Marks & Spencer plc* v. *David Halsey (Her Majesty's Inspector of Taxes)*, Case C-446/03, [2005] ECR I-10837, para. 35 ("imperative reasons").

[106] Such imperative requirements include consumer protection (see *Commission* v. *France*, 220/83, [1986] ECR 3663), environmental protection (see *De Coster*, Case C-17/00, [2001] ECR I-9445), and many, many more. For an excellent overview, see C. Barnard, *The Substantial Law of the EU: The Four Freedoms* (Oxford University Press, 2013), 522 et seq.

[107] *Gebhard*, Case 55/94, (supra n. 61).

justified by imperative requirements in the general interest; they must be suitable for securing the attainment of the objective which they pursue; and they must not go beyond what is necessary in order to attain it.[108]

Imperative requirements offered by the Member States as potential justifications will thus only apply to non-discriminatory measures and will be subject to the principle of proportionality.[109]

(b) In particular: The Public Service Exception

Many States prefer to reserve "State jobs" for their nationals. And the Treaties concede a public service exception for restrictions on the free movement of persons. For workers, we find this special justification in Article 45(4) TFEU, which states that "[t]he provisions of this Article shall not apply to *employment in the public service*".[110] For the freedom of establishment this special limitation can be found in Article 51 excluding activities "connected, even occasionally, with the *exercise of official authority*".

On the surface, both provisions appear to exclude different activities from their respective scopes. For workers, the wording suggests employment by a State institution, that is: an *institutional* definition. By contrast, the provision on establishment seems to adopt a *functional* definition, as it links the exception to the exercise of official authority by a private party.[111] Yet despite these textual disparities, the Court has developed a uniform definition for both freedoms. Early on, the Court clarified that it was of "no interest whether a worker is engaged as a workman *(ouvrier)*, a clerk *(employé)* or an official *(fonctionnaire)* or even whether the terms on which he is employed come under public or private law".[112] Since these

---

[108] *Ibid.*, para. 37.
[109] On the principle of proportionality in the context of the free movement of goods, see Chapter 9 – Section 4(b) above.
[110] Emphasis added.
[111] This functional definition was confirmed by the Court in *Reyners*, Case 2/74 (supra n. 60), paras. 44–5 (emphasis added): "The first paragraph of Article [51] must enable Member States to exclude non-nationals from taking up *functions* involving the exercise of official authority, which are connected with one of the activities of self-employed persons provided for in Article [49]. This need is fully satisfied when the exclusion of nationals is limited to those activities which, taken on their own, constitute a direct and specific connection with the exercise of official authority."
[112] *Sotgiu* v. *Deutsche Bundespost*, Case 152/73 (supra n. 39), para. 5.

designations could "be varied at the whim of national legislatures", they could not provide a criterion for the interpretation of European law.[113] In *Commission* v. *Belgium*,[114] the Court explained this choice in favour of a single functional definition of "public service" as follows:

> [D]etermining the sphere of application of Article [45(4)] raises special difficulties since in the various Member States authorities acting under powers conferred by public law have assumed responsibilities of an economic and social nature or are involved in activities which are not identifiable with the functions which are typical of the public service yet which by their nature still come under the sphere of application of the Treaty. In these circumstances the effect of extending the exception contained in Article [45(4)] to posts which, whilst coming under the State or other organizations governed by public law, still do not involve any association with tasks belonging to the public service properly so called, would be to remove a considerable number of posts from the ambit of the principles set out in the Treaty and to create inequalities between Member States according to the different ways in which the state and certain sectors of economic life are organized.[115]

Because the meaning of the concept "public service" required a "uniform interpretation",[116] the Court here rejected an institutional definition and favoured a functional definition in Article 45(4). This functional classification thereby "depends on whether or not the posts in question are typical of the specific activities of the public service in so far as the exercise of powers conferred by public law and responsibility for safeguarding the general interest of the State are vested in it".[117] This definition of public service potentially includes employees of a private company, where the latter performs public functions.[118] The Court has however subjected its functional test to "very strict conditions".[119] The work must involve "a *special relationship of allegiance* to the State and reciprocity of rights and duties which form the foundation of the bond of nationality".[120] The simple transfer of some public powers to employees is not enough. It is necessary that these public powers are exercised "on a regular

---

[113] *Ibid.*   [114] *Commission* v. *Belgium*, Case 149/79, [1980] ECR 3881.
[115] *Ibid.*, para. 11.   [116] *Ibid.*, para. 12.   [117] *Ibid.*
[118] *Anker et al.* v. *Germany*, Case C-47/02, [2003] ECR I-10447.
[119] *Lawrie-Blum*, Case 66/85 (supra n. 13), para. 28.
[120] *Commission* v. *Belgium*, Case 149/79 (supra n. 114), para. 10 (emphasis added).

basis by those holders and do not represent a very minor part of their activities".[121]

In a separate jurisprudential line, the Court has moreover clarified that the public service exception only permits restrictions on the *access to* but not *discriminations inside* a position involving public power. Thus, where foreigners have been admitted to a public service post, they will benefit from the equal treatment principle. In the words of the Court:

> [Article 45(4)] cannot justify discriminatory measures with regard to remuneration or other conditions of employment against workers once they have been admitted to the public service. The very fact that they have been admitted shows indeed that those interests which justify the exceptions to the principle of non-discrimination permitted by Article [45(4)] are not at issue.[122]

The reasoning under Article 45(4) applies, *mutatis mutandis*, to Article 51 and restrictions to professions involving public power.

Conclusion

The free movement of persons is a complex fundamental freedom. It not only comprises the free movement of workers and the freedom of establishment for the self-employed as well as companies, but the European Treaties also grant a (limited) movement right to all citizens of the Union. These three distinct constitutional sources of free movement rights for persons were discussed in this Chapter. Each of the three sources is complemented by secondary law; and the interplay between negative and positive integration has resulted in a mixture of primary and secondary Union law that makes this area of European law rich in technical nuances.

In order to navigate these technical waters, two elements – one qualitative, one quantitative – should be kept in mind. Despite the introduction of

---

[121] *Anker et al.* v. *Germany*, Case C-47/02 (supra n. 118), para. 63. And despite the express reference to the lower threshold of "occasional" exercise of public powers in Article 51 TFEU, the case law on that provision appears to run in parallel to that on Article 45(4); see Barnard, *Substantial Law* (supra n. 106), 517 et seq.

[122] *Sotgiu* v. *Deutsche Bundespost*, Case 152/73 (supra n. 39), para. 4. And see also *Commission* v. *Belgium*, Case 149/79 (supra n. 114), esp. paras. 20–2.

the horizontal provisions on Union citizenship, the Union legal order continues to qualitatively distinguish between categories of person exercising movement rights. Economically active Union "workers" and "professionals" will thus generally be entitled to full assimilation into the host State, while non-economically active citizens will not. Within the latter category, the Union has moreover adopted a quantitative approach.[123] The number of rights that a migrant Union citizen can claim will depend on the degree of his or her integration into the host society.

[123] C. Barnard, *The Substantive Law* (supra n. 106), 468.

Introduction

Competitive markets are markets in which economic rivalry is to enhance efficiency. Market "forces" determine the winners and losers of this rivalry, and competition will – ultimately – force inefficient losers out of the market.

Who, then, forces the winner(s) to act efficiently? By the end of the nineteenth century, this question was first raised in the United States of America. After a period of intense competition "the winning firms were seeking instruments to assure themselves of an easier life";[1] and they started to use – among other things – the common law "trust" to coordinate their behaviour within the market. To counter the anti-competitive effects of these trusts, the American legislator adopted the first competition law of the modern world: the Sherman Antitrust Act (1890).[2] The Act attacked two cardinal sins within all competition law: anti-competitive agreements,[3] and monopolistic markets.[4]

The US experience has significantly shaped the competition law of the European Union.[5] However, the inclusion of a Treaty Chapter on EU competition law was originally rooted not so much in competition concerns as such. It was rather the "general agreement that the elimination of tariff barriers would not achieve its objectives if private agreements or economically powerful firms were permitted to be used to manipulate the flow of trade".[6] EU competition law was here – at first – primarily conceived as a complement to the internal market.[7] The principal provisions on EU competition law are found in Chapter 1 of Title VII of the TFEU. The Chapter is divided into two Sections – one dealing with classic competition law, that is: "[r]ules applying to undertakings"; the other with public interferences in the market through "[a]ids granted by States".

---

[1] G. Amato, *Antitrust and the Bounds of Power: The Dilemma of Liberal Democracy in the History of the Market* (Hart, 1997), 8.

[2] The Act was named after the Senator John Sherman, who proposed it.

[3] Cf. Sherman Act, Section 1: "Every contract, combination in the form of trust or otherwise, or conspiracy, in restraint of trade or commerce among the several States, or with foreign nations, is declared to be illegal[.]"

[4] Cf. Sherman Act, Section 2: "Every person who shall monopolize, or attempt to monopolize, or combine or conspire with any other person or persons, to monopolize any part of the trade or commerce among the several States, or with foreign nations, shall be deemed guilty of a felony[.]"

[5] On the direct relation of American law and its indirect influence via German law, see: D. Gerber, *Law and Competition in Twentieth-Century Europe: Protecting Prometheus* (Oxford University Press, 2001).

[6] *Ibid.*, 343.

[7] This link between the internal market and EU competition law continues to be textually anchored in the Treaties. According to Article 3(3) TEU (emphasis added), "[t]he Union shall establish an internal market. It shall work for the sustainable development of Europe based on balanced economic growth and price stability, [and] a highly *competitive* social market economy, aiming at full employment and social progress." The meaning of the provision is clarified in Protocol (No. 27) "On the Internal Market and Competition", according to which "the internal market as set out in Article 3 of the Treaty on European Union *includes a system ensuring that competition is not distorted*" (emphasis added).

Table 12.1 Competition Rules – Overview

FEU Treaty – Title VII – Chapter 1	
Section 1: Rules Applying to Undertakings	**Section 2: Aids Granted by States**
Article 101 Anticompetitive Agreements	Article 107 State Aid Prohibition
Article 102 Abuse of a Dominant Position	Article 108 Commission Powers
Article 103 Competition Legislation I	Article 109 Competition Legislation II
Article 104 "Transitional" Provisions	
Article 105 Commission Powers	
Article 106 Public Undertakings (and public services)	

EU competition law is thereby built on four pillars. The first pillar deals with anti-competitive cartels and can be found in Article 101. The second pillar concerns situations where a dominant undertaking abuses its market power and is covered in Article 102. The third pillar is unfortunately invisible: when the Treaties were concluded, they did not mention the control of mergers. This constitutional gap has never been closed by subsequent Treaty amendments; yet it has received a legislative filling in the form of the European Union Merger Regulation (EUMR). The fourth pillar of EU competition law concerns "public" interferences into free competition, and in particular state aids.

This final Chapter "introduces" EU competition law by exploring only the first pillar: Article 101. This Article is in many respects emblematic for the "European" approach to competition law. We start by considering the "jurisdictional" aspect of the provision in Section 1 and 2.[8] The "substantive" criteria within Article 101, and their relationship to each other, will then be discussed in Sections 3 and 4.

1. Article 101: Jurisdictional Aspects

Article 101 outlaws anti-competitive collusions between undertakings, that is: "cartels". Historically, this form of illegal behaviour has been the most dangerous anti-competitive practice. The prohibition on any

---

[8] In this sense: O. Odudu, *The Boundaries of EC Competition Law* (Oxford University Press, 2006), 58.

collusion between undertakings to restrict competition in the internal market is thereby set out in Article 101. It states:

1. The following shall be prohibited as incompatible with the internal market: all agreements between undertakings, decisions by associations of undertakings and concerted practices which may affect trade between Member States and which have as their object or effect the prevention, restriction or distortion of competition within the internal market...
2. Any agreements or decisions prohibited pursuant to this Article shall be automatically void.
3. The provisions of paragraph 1 may, however, be declared inapplicable in the case of:
   - any agreement or category of agreements between undertakings,
   - any decision or category of decisions by associations of undertakings,
   - any concerted practice or category of concerted practices,

   which contributes to improving the production or distribution of goods or to promoting technical or economic progress, while allowing consumers a fair share of the resulting benefit, and which does not:

   (a) impose on the undertakings concerned restrictions which are not indispensable to the attainment of these objectives;
   (b) afford such undertakings the possibility of eliminating competition in respect of a substantial part of the products in question.

Article 101 follows a tripartite structure. Paragraph 1 prohibits as incompatible with the internal market collusions between undertakings that are anti-competitive by object or effect if they affect trade between Member States. Paragraph 3 exonerates certain collusions that are justified by their overall pro-competitive effects for the Union economy. In between this dual structure of prohibition and justification – oddly – lies paragraph 2, which determines that illegal collusive practices are automatically void and thus cannot be enforced in court.[9]

This Section looks at two jurisdictional aspects of Article 101(1) – and all EU competition law generally; namely the kinds of undertakings

---

[9] This is not the sole consequence of a violation of Article 101 TFEU. The Union has typically used its powers to impose significant fines on undertakings violating the provision. On the enforcement of European competition law generally, see W. Wils, *Principles of European Antitrust Enforcement* (Hart, 2005).

caught as well as the requirement of an "effect on trade between Member States".

(a) The Concept of "Undertaking"

The English word "undertaking" has traditionally not meant what the EU Treaties want it to mean.[10] The word is a translation from the German and French equivalents, and was deliberately chosen to avoid pre-existing meanings in British company law.[11] According to *Höfner & Elser*, an undertaking is "every entity engaged in an economic activity, regardless of the legal status of the entity and the way in which it is financed".[12]

This definition ties the notion of undertaking to an *activity* instead of the institutional form of the actor. This *functional* definition broadens the personal scope of the competition rules to include entities that may – formally – not be regarded as companies. It catches natural persons,[13] and includes "professionals" – such as barristers.[14] Even the "State" and its public bodies may sometimes be regarded as an undertaking, where they engage in an economic activity.[15] The advantage of this broad functional definition is its flexibility; its disadvantage however is its uncertainty. Depending on its actions, an entity may or may not be an "undertaking" within the meaning of EU competition law in particular situations.[16]

What, then, are economic activities? The Court has consistently held that "any activity consisting in offering goods or services on a given market is an economic activity".[17] This offer-related definition has been held to exclude (final) consumption – "consumers" – from the scope of Article 101.[18]

---

[10] In its sinister and saddest form, the word refers to the preparations for a funeral service.

[11] R. Lane, *EC Competition Law* (Longman, 2001), 33.

[12] *Höfner and Elser* v. *Macrotron*, Case C-41/90, [1991] ECR I-1979, para. 21.

[13] Cf *Hydrotherm* v. *Compact*, Case 170/83, [1984] ECR 2999, para. 11.

[14] Cf. *Wouters et al.* v. *Algemene Raad van de Nederlandse Orde van Advocaten*, Case C-309/99, [2002] ECR I-1577, para. 49.

[15] See *Commission* v. *Italy*, Case 118/85, [1987] ECR 2599.

[16] Advocate General F. Jacobs, *Firma Ambulanz Glöckner* v. *Landkreis Südwestpfalz*, Case C-475/99, [2001] ECR I-8089, para. 72 "[T]he notion of undertaking is a relative concept in the sense that a given entity might be regarded as an undertaking for one part of its activities while the rest falls outside the competition rules."

[17] *Pavlov and Others* v. *Stichting Pensioenfonds Medische Specialisten*, Case C-180/98, (2000) ECR I-6451, para. 75.

[18] Cf. *FENIN* v. *Commission*, T-319/99, (2003) ECR II-357.

The market-orientated nature of economic activities has also been contrasted with the solidarity-orientated nature of public functions. In *Poucet & Pistre*,[19] the Court thus refused to consider organizations managing a public social security system as "undertakings", since their activities were "based on the principle of national solidarity" and "entirely non-profit-making".[20] A private body may thus not count as an undertaking, where it is engaged in "a task in the public interest which forms part of the essential functions of the State".[21] However, what counts as an essential public function is not always easy to tell. The Court has refused to be bound by a "historical" or "traditional" understanding of public services. In *Höfner & Elser* it consequently found that "[t]he fact that employment procurement activities are normally entrusted to public agencies cannot affect the economic nature of such activities", since "[e]mployment procurement has not always been, and is not necessarily, carried out by public entities".[22]

Sadly, then, the Court has so far not found a convincing definition of what counts as an economic activity.[23]

(b) Effect on Trade between Member States

Not all anti-competitive behaviour falls within the jurisdictional scope of EU competition law, and in particular Article 101. Article 101 only catches agreements that may "affect trade between Member States".[24]

What is the point behind this jurisdictional limitation around Article 101? The answer lies – partly – in the principle of subsidiarity.[25] The *European* Union will only concern itself with agreements that have a *European* dimension, which is manifested through a (potential) effect on trade *between* Member States. In the words of the European Court:

---

[19]   *Poucet & Pistre*, Joined Cases C-159/91 and C-160/91, (1993) ECR I-637.

[20]   *Ibid.*, paras. 18–19. This was confirmed in *Albany International BV* v. *Stichting Bedrijfspensioenfonds Textielindustrie*, Case C-67/96, (1999) ECR I-5751. The latter case has been particularly controversial.

[21]   *Cali & Figli Srl* v. *Servizi ecologici porto di Genova*, Case C-343/95, [1997] ECR I-1547, esp. paras. 22–3.

[22]   *Höfner & Elser* v. *Macrotron*, Case C-41/90 (supra n. 12).

[23]   For an academic analysis of the case law, see: O. Odudu, "The Meaning of Undertaking within 81 EC", (2006) 7 *Cambridge Yearbook of European Legal Studies* 211.

[24]   The following sections refer to "agreements", but the analysis applies, *mutatis mutandis*, to decisions of associations of undertakings, and concerted practices.

[25]   On the notion of "subsidiarity" in the Union legal order, see: Chapter 2 – Section 3 above.

> The concept of an agreement "which may affect trade between Member States" is intended to define, in the law governing cartels, the boundary between the areas respectively covered by [European] law and national law. It is only to the extent to which the agreement may affect trade between Member States that the deterioration in competition caused by the agreement falls under the prohibition of [European] law contained in Article [101]; otherwise it escapes that prohibition.[26]

Agreements must thus have an *inter-state* dimension – otherwise they will be outside the sphere of European competition law.

But what is this "European" sphere of competition law? The jurisdictional scope of Article 101 has been – very – expansively interpreted.[27] And the Court has developed a number of constitutional tests as to when inter-state trade has been affected. An agreement would need to be "capable of constituting a *threat, either direct or indirect, actual or potential, to freedom of trade between Member States* in a manner which might harm the attainment of the objectives of a single market between States".[28] This formula was amended in *Société Technique Minière*, where the Court held Article 101 to apply to any agreement that "may have an influence, direct or indirect, actual or potential, on the *pattern of trade between Member States*".[29] This "pattern-of-trade" test is extremely broad as it captures both quantitative as well as qualitative changes to trade.[30]

The fact that an agreement relates to a single Member State will not necessarily mean that Article 101 is not applicable.[31] What counts are the

---

[26] *Consten and Grundig* v. *Commission*, Case 56 and 58/64, [1964] ECR 299 at 341.

[27] Article 101 TFEU. For a general analysis of this criterion, see J. Faull, "Effect on Trade Between Member States", 26 (1999), *Fordham Corporate Law Institute*, 481; as well as Commission, "Guidelines on the effect on trade concept contained in Articles [101 and 102] of the Treaty", (2004) OJ C101/81.

[28] *Consten and Grundig* v. *Commission*, Case 56 and 58/64 (supra n. 26), 341 (emphasis added).

[29] *Société Technique Minière* v. *Maschinenbau Ulm*, Case 56/65, [1965] ECR 235 at 249 (emphasis added).

[30] On the substantive "neutrality" of the "pattern-of-trade" test, see also Commission, "Guidelines on the effect on trade concept" (supra n. 27), paras. 34–5: "The term 'pattern-of-trade' is neutral. It is not a condition that trade be restricted or reduced. Patterns of trade can also be affected when an agreement or practice causes an increase in trade."

[31] See *Belasco and others* v. *Commission*, Case 246/86, [1989] ECR 2117, para. 38: "Accordingly, although the contested agreement relates only to the marketing of products in a single Member State, it must be held to be capable of influencing intra-[Union] trade."

(potential) *effects* of a national agreement on the European markets.[32] And when measuring the effect of an agreement on trade between Member States, the Court will take into account whether or not the agreement forms part of a broader network of agreements.

> "The existence of similar contracts is a circumstance which, together with others, is capable of being a factor in the economic and legal context within which the contract must be judged."[33]

This "contextual" view of agreements was subsequently developed in *Delimitis*.[34] The case arose out of a dispute between the plaintiff publican and the brewery Henninger, and turned on the legality of a beer supply agreement. Could a single agreement concluded by a local pub with a local brewery have an effect in intra-Union trade? The Court here expressly placed the agreement within the network of agreements to which it belonged and held that "the *cumulative effect of several similar agreements* constitutes one factor amongst others in ascertaining whether, by way of a possible alteration of competition, trade between Member States is capable of being affected".[35] It was consequently necessary to analyse the effects of an all-beer supply agreement within the network to see if the single agreement contributed to a cumulative effect that had an inter-state dimension.

Nonetheless, not all effects on inter-state trade will lead to proceedings under Article 101. For the effects "must not be insignificant";[36] and the Union will only police agreements that *appreciably* affect intra-Union trade.[37] According to its "non-appreciably-affecting-trade" (NAAT) rule,[38] agreements will generally not fall within the jurisdictional scope of Article 101 if two cumulative conditions are met. First, "[t]he aggregate market

---

[32] See *Brasserie de Haecht* v. *Wilkin-Janssen (II)*, Case 48/72, [1973] ECR 77, paras. 26 et seq.

[33] *Brasserie de Haecht* v. *Consorts Wilkin-Janssen (I)*, Case 23/67, (1967) ECR 407 at 416.

[34] *Delimitis* v. *Henninger Bräu*, Case C-234/89, (1991), ECR I-9935.

[35] *Ibid.*, para. 14 (emphasis added).

[36] *Javico International and Javico AG* v. *Yves Saint Laurent Parfums SA (YSLP)*, Case C-306/96, [1998] ECR I-1983, para. 16 (with reference to *Völk* v. *Vervaecke*, Case 5/69, [1969] ECR 295).

[37] The Commission makes a clear distinction between an appreciable effect on inter-state *trade* on the one hand, and appreciable restrictions on *competition* on the other. The former will be discussed here, while the latter will be discussed in Section 3(d) below.

[38] "Guidelines on the effect on trade concept contained in Articles [101 and 102] of the Treaty" (supra n. 27), para. 50.

share of the parties on any relevant market within the [Union] affected by the agreement does not exceed 5%". And second, "the aggregate annual [Union] turnover of the undertakings concerned in the products covered by the agreement does not exceed 40 million euro".[39]

2. Forms of Collusion between Undertakings

Article 101 covers anti-competitive collusions *between* undertakings. The prohibited action must thus be *multilateral*. But what types of multilateral collusions are covered by the prohibition? Article 101 refers to three types of collusions: "agreements between undertakings, decisions by associations of undertakings and concerted practices".

Let us look at each collusive form in turn.

(a) Agreements I: Horizontal and Vertical Agreements

The European concept of "agreement" has been given an extremely wide conceptual scope.[40] The Union legal order is indeed not interested in whether the agreement formally constitutes a "contract" under national law.[41] What counts is "a concurrence of wills" between economic operators.[42] "Gentlemen's agreements" have thus been classified as agreements under Article 101, as long as the parties consider them binding.[43]

One of the central concerns within the early Union legal order was the question of whether Article 101 covers "horizontal" as well as "vertical" agreements. Horizontal agreements are agreements between undertakings that are competing with each other, that is: horizontally placed at the same commercial level. Vertical agreements, by contrast, are agreements between undertakings at different levels of the commercial chain. Since Article 101 prohibits anti-competitive agreements, would it not follow

---

[39] *Ibid.*, para. 52.
[40] For an analysis of the concept of "agreement", see J. Shaw, "The Concept of Agreement in Article 85 EEC", 16 (1991) *European Law Review*, 262.
[41] On the notion of contract under English law, see G. Treitel et al., *The Law of Contract* (Sweet & Maxwell, 2007).
[42] See *Bayer AG* v. *Commission*, Case T-41/96, [2000] ECR II-3383, para. 69; and *Bundesverband der Arzneimittel-Importeure and Commission* v. *Bayer*, Case C-2 and 3/01 P, [2004] ECR I-23, para. 97.
[43] See *ACF Chemiefarma* v. *Commission*, Case 41/69, [1979] ECR 661, paras. 106 et seq.

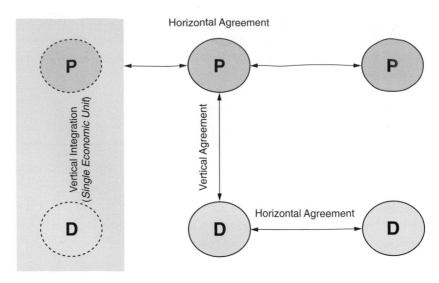

Figure 12.1 Horizontal and Vertical Agreements

that only "horizontal" agreements between *competitors* are covered? This logic is not without its problems. For while vertical agreements between a producer (P) and a distributor (D) may increase efficiency through a specialized division of labour,[44] they may also significantly harm the consumer through a restriction of price competition.[45]

Would vertical agreements fall within the jurisdictional scope of Article 101? The European Court has – famously – answered this question in *Consten* and *Grundig* v. *Commission*.[46] The German producer Grundig had concluded a distribution agreement for the French market with Consten. This agreement was said to breach European competition law. The applicants argued that the Union lacked jurisdiction under Article 101 as "distributorship contracts do not constitute 'agreements between undertakings' within the meaning of that provision, since the parties are not on a footing of equality".[47] The Court disagreed:

> Article [101] refers in a general way to all agreements which distort competition within the common market and does not lay down any distinction

---

[44] Lane, *EC Competition Law* (supra n. 11), 92: "Their prime advantage is that they allow for net economic efficiency: they enable the producer to concentrate upon production and relieve it of the obligation of shifting the goods on the market, for that will be the concern of the (specialist) distributor who is better suited to the task."

[45] *Ibid.*, 97: "Looking at the economics, it is not surprising: the factory gate value of goods is sometimes a fraction of their shop value[.]"

[46] *Consten and Grundig* v. *Commission*, Case 56 and 58/64 (supra n. 26).   [47] *Ibid.*, 339.

between those agreements based on whether they are made between competitors operating at the same level in the economic process or between non-competing persons operating at different levels. In principle, no distinction can be made where the Treaty does not make any distinction.

Furthermore, the possible application of Article [101] to a sole distributorship contract cannot be excluded merely because the grantor and the concessionaire are not competitors inter se and not on a footing of equality. Competition may be distorted within the meaning of Article [101(1)] not only by agreements which limit it as between the parties, but also by agreements which prevent or restrict competition which might take place between one of them and third parties. For this purpose, it is irrelevant whether the parties to the agreement are or are not on a footing of equality as regards their position and function in the economy. This applies all the more, since, by such an agreement, the parties might seek, by preventing or limiting the competition of third parties in respect of the products, to create or guarantee for their benefit an unjustified advantage at the expense of the consumer or user, contrary to the general aims of Article [101].[48]

The arguments in favour of including vertical agreements were thus textual and teleological. Within its text, Article 101 did not make a distinction between horizontal and vertical agreements, and thus seemed to cover both types generically. Teleologically, Article 101 was said not only to protect against restrictions of competition imposed on the distributor, but also to protect third parties, namely: consumers and competitors. And since vertical agreements could create unjustified disadvantages for these third parties, they would have to be within the jurisdiction of European competition law.[49]

(b) Agreements II: "Tacit Acquiescence" versus "Unilateral Conduct"

Every agreement – whether horizontal or vertical – must be concluded on the basis of common consent between the parties. It must be formed by a concurrence of *two* wills. The idea of an "agreement" will thus find a conceptual boundary where one party *unilaterally* imposes its will on

---

[48] *Ibid.*

[49] This second argument was an important one: vertical agreements would need to be within the scope of Article 101 TFEU because they could have an anti-competitive effect both with regard to intra-brand competition, that is: price competition between distributors, but also inter-brand competition between different producers. On the distinction between inter-brand and intra-brand competition, see Section 3(a) below.

the other. Yet there may sometimes be a fine line between tacit acceptance and unilateral imposition. And the European Courts have struggled to demarcate this line for the Union legal order.[50] The reason for this conceptual fuzziness lies in what the Courts call "apparently unilateral" behaviour in continuous contractual relations between two parties.

A good illustration of such "apparently unilateral behaviour" can be found in *Ford* v. *Commission*.[51] The American car manufacturer had established a selective distribution system in Europe, and in particular in Britain and Germany, on the basis of a "main dealer agreement". That agreement appeared not to violate Article 101, and originally allowed German distributors to order right-hand as well as left-hand drive cars. However, as the prices for Ford cars on the British market suddenly increased significantly, British customers began buying from German dealers. Afraid that its British distributor would suffer the consequences, Ford notified its German dealers that it would no longer accept their orders for right-hand drive cars. (These would now be exclusively reserved for the British market.) Was the decision to discontinue supplies to the German dealers an agreement? Ford claimed that the discontinuance decision was of a unilateral nature; and "a unilateral act cannot be included among agreements".[52] The Court however held otherwise:

> Such a decision on the part of the manufacturer does not constitute, on the part of the undertaking, a unilateral act which, as the applicants claim, would be exempt from the prohibition contained in Article [101(1)] of the Treaty. On the contrary, *it forms part of the contractual relations between the undertaking and its dealers.*[53]

This extremely generous interpretation of "consent" has however found some limits. In *Bayer* v. *Commission*,[54] the German pharmaceutical company used its distribution system to market "Adalat" – a medical product designed to treat cardiovascular disease. The price of the product differed significantly as it was indirectly fixed by the respective national health authorities. The prices fixed by the Spanish and French health services were thereby on average 40 per cent lower than prices in the United

---

[50] See *AEG* v. *Commission*, Case 107/82, [1983] ECR 3151; *Ford-Werke AG and Ford of Europe Inc.* v. *Commission*, Joined Cases 25 and 26/84, [1985] ECR 2725; and *BMW* v. *ALD Auto-Leasing*, Case C-70/93, [1995] ECR I-3439.

[51] *Ford-Werke AG and Ford of Europe Inc.* v. *Commission*, Joined Cases 25 and 26/84 (supra n. 50).

[52] *Ibid.*, para. 15.   [53] *Ibid.*, para. 21 (emphasis added).

[54] *Bayer AG* v. *Commission*, Case T-41/96 (supra n. 42).

Kingdom; and following commercial logic, Spanish and French whole-salers began exporting to the British market. With its British dealer regis-tering an enormous loss of turnover, Bayer decided to stop delivering large orders to Spanish and French wholesalers. Instead, it provided them with the quantities that it thought would only saturate their national markets. Was this indirect export restriction a consensual agreement? The Gen-eral Court rejected this view. While accepting that "apparently unilateral conduct" can qualify as an agreement, the latter required – as a con-ceptual minimum – the "existence of an acquiescence by the other part-ners, express or implied, in the attitude adopted by the manufacturer".[55] And in the present case, even tacit acquiescence was missing.[56] For the mere continuation of the business relationship could not as such be tacit acquiescence.[57]

The judgment was confirmed on appeal,[58] where the European Court concisely clarified the situation as follows: "The mere concomitant exis-tence of an agreement which is in itself neutral and a measure restricting competition that has been imposed unilaterally does not amount to an agreement prohibited by that provision."[59] Put the other way around: for an "apparently unilateral" measure to become part of a continuous contractual relationship, the other party must – at the very least – tac-itly acquiesce. And this tacit acquiescence must be shown through actual compliance with the "apparently unilateral" measure.

(c) Concerted Practices and Parallel Conduct

The conclusion of an agreement is but one form of collusion between undertakings. Another form mentioned in Article 101(1) is "concerted

---

[55] *Ibid.*, para. 72.

[56] *Ibid.*, paras. 151 et seq: "Examination of the attitude and actual conduct of the wholesalers shows that the Commission has no foundation for claiming that they aligned themselves on the applicant's policy designed to reduce parallel imports...[T]he wholesalers con-tinued to try to obtain packets of Adalat for export and persisted in that line of activity, even if, for that purpose, they considered it more productive to use different systems to obtain supplies, namely the system of distributing orders intended for export among the various agencies on the one hand, and that of placing orders indirectly through small wholesalers on the other."

[57] For this point, see I. Lianos, "Collusion in Vertical Relations under Article 81 EC", 45 (2008) *Common Market Law Review*, 1027 at 1044.

[58] *Bundesverband der Arzneimittel-Importeure and Commission* v. *Bayer*, Case C-2 & 3/01 P (supra n. 42).

[59] *Ibid.*, para. 141.

practices". The concept was designed as a safety net to catch all forms of collusive behaviour falling short of an agreement.[60] This has been confirmed by the European Court, which identifies the aim behind the concept of concerted practice as bringing "within the prohibition of that Article a form of coordination between undertakings which, without having reached the stage where an agreement properly so-called has been concluded, knowingly substitutes practical cooperation between them for the risk of competition".[61]

The heart of a concerted practice is seen in a "coordination" between undertakings "which becomes apparent from the behaviour of the participants".[62] Yet the Court was quick to point out that not all "parallel behaviour" between undertakings – such as the parallel raising of prices – can be identified with a concerted practice.[63] Article 101 would "not deprive economic operators of the right to adapt themselves intelligently to the existing and anticipated conduct of their competitors".[64] Parallel behaviour that follows from market forces would be beyond reproach. In the absence of any form of "practical cooperation" through "direct or indirect contact",[65] undertakings will thus be allowed to align their commercial behaviour to the "logic" of the market.[66]

(d) Cartel Decisions through Associations of Undertakings

This third category of collusion is designed to catch institutionalized cartels; and this may include professional bodies, such as the Bar Council.[67]

---

[60] For that reason, there may be no need for a categorical dividing line between an agreement and a concerted practice; see *Commission* v. *Anic Partecipazioni*, Case C-49/92 P, [1999] ECR I-4125, para. 132: "[W]hilst the concepts of an agreement and of a concerted practice have particularly different elements, they are not mutually incompatible."

[61] *Imperial Chemical Industries* v. *Commission*, Case 48/69, [1972] ECR 619, para. 64.

[62] *Ibid.*, para. 65.   [63] *Ibid.*, para. 66.

[64] *Coöperatieve Vereniging "Suiker Unie" UA and others* v. *Commission*, Joined Cases 40 to 48, 50, 54 to 56, 111, 113 and 114/73, [1975] ECR 1663, para. 174; as well as *Commission* v. *Anic Partecipazioni*, Case C-49/92 P (supra n. 60), para. 117.

[65] *"Suiker Unie"* v. *Commission*, para. 27 and para. 174 (supra n. 64); as well as *Commission* v. *Anic Partecipazioni*, Case C-49/92 P (supra n. 60), para. 117.

[66] The evidentiary burden on the Commission is very high; see *Ahlström Osakeyhtiö and others* v. *Commission*, Joined Cases C-89/85, C-104/85, C-114/85, C-116/85, C-117/85 and C-125/85 to C-129/85, [1993] ECR I-1307, para. 71: "[P]arallel conduct cannot be regarded as furnishing proof of concertation unless concertation is the only plausible explanation for such conduct."

[67] See *Wouters et al.* v. *Algemene Raad van de Nederlandse Orde van Advocaten*, Case C-309/99 (supra n. 14).

The inclusion of this form of collusion into Article 101 clarified that undertakings could not escape the scope of Article 101 by substituting *multilateral* collusion between them by establishing an association that would adopt *unilateral* decisions on their behalf. A cartel decision – even in the soft form of a "recommendation" – may thus be caught as collusive behaviour under Article 101(1).[68]

3. Restriction of Competition: Anti-competitive Object or Effect

In order for an agreement to violate the prohibition of Article 101(1), it must be anti-competitive; it must be a "prevention, restriction or distortion of competition".[69]

The meaning of "restriction of competition" in this context has been very controversial. If it simply referred to a restriction of the *individual* freedom to trade, then all binding agreements would be anti-competitive. For "[t]o bind, to restrain, is of their very essence".[70] This individualist definition of restriction has never been dominant in the Union legal order.[71] A second view has therefore argued that Article 101, while not protecting the individual freedom of a specific competitor, nonetheless protects the *structural* freedom offered by the market to – actual or potential – competitors. This view emphasizes the exclusionary effects of restrictions of competition and corresponds to the "Harvard School".[72] A third view has finally imported the "Chicago School" into the debate on the scope of Article 101(1). It argues that the prohibition should exclusively outlaw "exploitative effects" in the form of allocative inefficiencies to consumer

---

[68] See *Van Landewyck and others* v. *Commission*, Joined Cases 209 to 215 and 218/78, [1980] ECR 3125, para. 89.
[69] This formulation covers hypothetical, quantitative, and qualitative limitations of competition. In this Section, "restriction" of competition will be employed as a generic term.
[70] See *Chicago Board of Trade* v. *United States*, 246 US 231 (1918) 238.
[71] The early case law may however be read as unduly concentrating on the freedom of individuals; see E. Rousseva, *Rethinking Exclusionary Abuses in EU Competition Law* (Hart, 2010), 83 et seq.
[72] The "European" equivalent of the "Harvard School" is the "Freiberg School", which has become famous for its "ordoliberalism". For a concise overview of the philosophical positions of that school, see D. Gerber, "Constitutionalizing the Economy: German Neo-Liberalism, Competition Law and the 'New Europe'", 42 (1994) *American Journal of Comparative Law*, 25.

welfare.[73] The case law of the European Courts has been closest to the second view – even if the European administration has once tried hard to move towards the third view.[74]

This Section analyses four aspects of what constitutes a restriction of competition in the Union legal order. We start by looking at the various dimensions of competition, before examining the two modes of violating Article 101(1) – restrictions by "object or effect". This includes an analysis of whether the "ancillary restraints" doctrine represents a "rule of reason" in disguise. A final subsection offers a brief encounter with the *de minimis* limitation on restrictions of competition.

(a) Two Dimensions: Inter-brand and Intra-brand Competition

A restriction of competition is primarily a restriction between competitors. Early on, the European Court had however confirmed that competition could be restricted by horizontal as well as vertical agreements.[75] But was this solely an admission that vertical agreements could restrict inter-brand competition, that is: competition between producers of different brands? Or did the inclusion of vertical agreements into the scope of Article 101(1) signal that *intra*-brand competition – competition between distributors of the same brand – was independently protected?

The European Court has preferred the second reading. The Union legal order consequently recognizes two independent dimensions of competition: inter-brand and intra-brand competition. In *Consten and Grundig*,[76] the Court thus rejected the plaintiffs' argument that there could be no restriction of competition through vertical agreements:

> The principle of freedom of competition concerns the various stages and manifestations of competition. Although competition between producers is generally more noticeable than that between distributors of products of the same make, it does not thereby follow that an agreement tending

---

[73] Odudu, *The Boundaries* (supra n. 8), 102.

[74] See Commission, "Guidelines on the application of Article 81(3) [now: Article 101(3)] of the Treaty", [2004] OJ C101/97. However, see also *GlaxoSmithKline and others* v. *Commission*, Joined Cases C-501/06 P, C-513/06 P, C-515/06 P and C-519/06 P, [2009] ECR I-9291, where the Court rejected the "Chicagoization" of European competition law.

[75] For a discussion of this point, see Section 2(a) above.

[76] *Consten and Grundig* v. *Commission*, Case 56 and 58/64 (supra n. 26).

> to restrict the latter kind of competition should escape the prohibition of
> Article [101(1)] merely because it might increase the former.[77]

Would every restriction of competition through vertical agreements violate Article 101(1)? In a later decision, the Court recognized that a pro-competitive effect in inter-brand competition might come at the price of a restriction of intra-brand competition. This holistic approach can be seen in *Société Technique Minière*,[78] where the Court found an exclusive distribution agreement *not* to violate Article 101 on the following grounds:

> The competition in question must be understood within the actual context in which it would occur in the absence of the agreement in dispute. In particular it may be doubted whether there is an interference with competition if the said agreement seems really necessary for the penetration of a new area by an undertaking. Therefore, in order to decide whether an agreement containing a clause "granting an exclusive right of sale" is to be considered as prohibited by reason of its object or of its effect, it is appropriate to take into account in particular the nature and quantity, limited or otherwise, of the products covered by the agreement, [and] *the position and importance of the grantor and the concessionaire on the market for the products concerned*[.][79]

The existence of a restriction of competition will thus have to be evaluated alongside both "brand" dimensions, and by balancing both dimensions. The Commission appears to share this holistic approach.[80]

(b) Restrictions by Object: European "Per Se Rules"

An agreement may fall within Article 101(1) if it is anti-competitive by "object or effect". These are alternative conditions.[81] The fulfilment of one will fulfil Article 101(1).

---

[77] *Ibid.*, 342. And at a later part of the judgment (*ibid.*, 343), the Court provided the rationale for this choice: "Because of the considerable impact of distribution costs on the aggregate cost price, it seems important that competition between dealers should also be stimulated. The efforts of the dealer are stimulated by competition between distributors of products of the same make."

[78] *Société Technique Minière* v. *Maschinenbau Ulm*, Case 56/65 (supra n. 29).

[79] *Ibid.*, 250 (emphasis added).

[80] Commission, "Guidelines on Article [101](3)" (supra n. 74), para. 17 et seq.

[81] *Société Technique Minière* v. *Maschinenbau Ulm*, Case 56/65 (supra n. 29), 249.

The possibility of violating European competition law "by object" will not mean that purely imaginary restrictions intended by the parties are covered. The reference to the purpose of an agreement must not be misunderstood as referring to the subjective intentions of the parties. On the contrary, it refers to the objective content of the agreement. It is designed to identify certain "hardcore restrictions" within an agreement, which need not be subjected to a detailed effects analysis.[82] These hardcore restrictions can simply be presumed to be "sufficiently deleterious" to competition.[83] In this sense, restrictions by object operate as "per se rules", that is: rules whose breach "as such" constitutes a violation of competition law. (However, European competition law allows even hardcore restrictions to be potentially justified under Article 101(3); and for that reason they are not as absolute as American "per se" rules.)

What are the hardcore restrictions that the Union legal order considers restrictions by object? Various contractual clauses have been given this status – in both horizontal and vertical agreements. With regard to horizontal agreements, they have been said to include price-fixing clauses,[84] output-limiting clauses,[85] and market-sharing clauses.[86] With regard to vertical agreements, restrictions by object will be presumed to exist if the agreement contains a clause that imposed a fixed (minimum) resale price,[87] grants absolute territorial protection,[88] or is a "restriction of active

---

[82] *Consten and Grundig* v. *Commission*, Case 56 and 58/64 (supra n. 26), 342: "Besides, for the purpose of applying Article [101(1)], there is no need to take account of the concrete effects of an agreement once it appears that it has as its object the prevention, restriction or distortion of competition."

[83] *Société Technique Minière* v. *Maschinenbau Ulm*, Case 56/65 (supra n. 29), 249. And see also *T-Mobile Netherlands and others* v. *Raad van bestuur van de Nederlandse Mededingingsautoriteit*, Case C-8/08, [2009] ECR I-4529, para. 29: "by their very nature, as being injurious to the proper functioning of normal competition".

[84] See Article 101(1)(a): "directly or indirectly fix purchase or selling prices or any other trading conditions"; and see in particular *Imperial Chemical Industries* v. *Commission*, Case 48/69 (supra n. 61).

[85] See Article 101(1)(b): "limit or control production, markets, technical development, or investment", and see in particular *Chemiefarma* v. *Commission*, Case 41/69 (supra n. 43).

[86] See Article 101(1)(c): "share markets or sources of supply"; and see in particular *Coöperatieve Vereniging "Suiker Unie" UA and others* v. *Commission*, Joined Cases 40 to 48, 50, 54 to 56, 111, 113 and 114/73 (supra n. 64).

[87] Article 4(a) of (Commission) Regulation 330/2010 on the application of Article 101(3) of the Treaty on the Functioning of the European Union to categories of vertical agreements and concerted practices, [2010] OJ L102, 1.

[88] *Ibid.*, Article 4(b).

or passive sales to end users by members of a selective distribution system operating at the retail level of trade".[89]

The most contentious types of hardcore restriction have here been clauses that restrict parallel trade. And the classic case here is – once more – *Consten and Grundig*.[90] Grundig had appointed Consten its exclusive distributor in France. Consten had thereby promised to market and service the German products in France – a potentially costly commitment. In exchange, Grundig agreed not to deliver its goods to other traders on the French market, and also agreed to contractually prohibit its German wholesalers from exporting goods into France. This level of territorial protection was still *relative*, since it solely applied to Grundig's own distribution system. Yet in order to prevent "parallel traders" – third parties trading in parallel to the official distribution channel – from selling its products in France, Grundig granted an intellectual property right to Consten. This intellectual property right established *absolute* territorial protection for Consten: not a single trader within France could sell Grundig products without the official distributor's consent. In the eyes of the European Court, such an agreement establishing absolute territorial protection betrayed a clear wish of the parties "to eliminate any possibility of competition at the wholesale level",[91] and thus constituted an agreement that had as its *object* the restriction of competition.[92]

(c) Restrictions by Effect: A European "Rule of Reason"?

Where agreements do not contain clauses that are automatically deemed restrictions of competition, Article 101(1) requires proof of the agreement's anti-competitive *effect*.[93] The central question here is: will the

---

[89] *Ibid.*, Article 4(c).
[90] *Consten and Grundig* v. *Commission*, Case 56 and 58/64 (supra n. 26).   [91] *Ibid.*, 343.
[92] For a confirmation of this "tough" view on restrictions of parallel trade as a restriction by object, see *GlaxoSmithKline and others* v. *Commission*, Joined Cases C-501/06 P, C-513/06 P, C-515/06 P and C-519/06 P (supra n. 74) – which overruled the General Court's attempt to soften that principle of European competition law in *GlaxoSmithKline Services* v. *Commission*, Case T-168/01, [2006] ECR II-2969.
[93] In order to assess the effect of an individual agreement *on* the market, the Court will analyse the agreement's position *within* the market. It thereby applies a contextual approach that places an individual agreement within its economic context. Where an agreement forms part of a network of agreements, the Courts may thus look at the "cumulative" effects within the market. On this "economic" contextualism, see in particular *Delimitis* v. *Henninger Bräu*, Case C-234/89 (supra n. 34).

prohibition be triggered as soon as an agreement contains clauses that have *some* anti-competitive effects; or will it only apply to agreements that are *overall* anti-competitive? Put differently: should Article 101(1) catch agreements that limit – in absolute terms – production, yet enhance – in relative terms – competition through the development of a new product?

The wording of Article 101(1) suggests an absolute test, but the argument has been made that an absolute test is over-inclusive and should be replaced by a relative test that weighs the anti-competitive effects of an agreement against its pro-competitive effects. The debate on whether Article 101(1) follows an absolute or a relative test has been associated with the American doctrine of a "rule of reason". (According to the latter, the absolute prohibition of anti-competitive agreements in American competition law will not apply to reasonable restrictions of trade.) Should such an implied limitation also apply to Article 101(1) – even though the article already recognizes an express justification in Article 101(3)? The existence of a rule of reason doctrine has been hotly debated in European circles.[94] And the debate is not just theoretical: the constitutional choice concerning whether there exists an implicit rule of reason in Article 101(1) may have significant practical consequences.[95]

What have the European Courts said? They have given ambivalent signals. For while the Courts – in theory – deny the existence of a rule of reason under Article 101(1),[96] there are a number of jurisprudential lines that come very close to a practical application of the doctrine. Did the European Court not insist that a restriction of competition was not anti-competitive if "*necessary* for the penetration of a new area by an undertaking"?[97] Was this balancing of anti-competitive effects against pro-competitive effects not a rule of reason in disguise? The European Courts have denied this, and have instead developed alternative doctrines to explain their reasoning. The most famous doctrine in this respect is the doctrine of ancillary restraints.

---

[94] See Odudu, *The Boundaries* (supra n. 8); as well as R. Nazzini, "Article 81 EC between Time Present and Time Past: A Normative Critique of 'Restrictions of Competition' in EU Law", 43 (2006) *Common Market Law Review*, 497.

[95] It will be seen below that Article 101(3) is not a "neutral" exemption for pro-competitive agreements, since it makes the exemption dependent on the fulfilment of four conditions.

[96] See *Métropole Télévision (M6) and others* v. *Commission*, Case T-112/99, [2001] ECR II-2459; as well as *O2 (Germany)* v. *Commission*, T-328/03, [2006] ECR II-1231.

[97] See *Société Technique Minière* v. *Maschinenbau Ulm*, Case 56/65 (supra n. 29), 250 (emphasis added).

Is the doctrine of ancillary restraints a rule of reason doctrine in disguise? Three cases may assist us in answering this question. In *Remia & Nutricia*,[98] the Court had to deal with the legality of a "non-compete clause". These clauses prevent the seller of a business from competing with the buyer within a period of time after the sale. This is undoubtedly a restriction of competition on the part of the seller; yet very few undertakings would be willing to purchase a business without a guarantee that its previous owner will temporarily stay out of the market. Finding that transfer agreements generally "contribute to the promotion of competition because they lead to an increase in the number of undertakings in the market", the Court nonetheless recognized that without the non-compete clause, "the agreement for the transfer of the undertaking could not be given effect".[99] However, such ancillary restrictions within an overall pro-competitive agreement would fall outside the scope of Article 101(1). This ancillary restraints doctrine was confirmed in *Pronuptia* in the context of a franchise agreement,[100] and received its most elaborate form in *Métropole Télévision*.[101] The General Court here held as follows:

> In [European] competition law the concept of an "ancillary restriction" covers any restriction which is directly related and necessary to the implementation of a main operation... The condition that a restriction be necessary implies a two-fold examination. It is necessary to establish, first, whether the restriction is objectively necessary for the implementation of the main operation and, second, whether it is proportionate to it. As regards the objective necessity of a restriction, it must be observed that inasmuch as... the existence of a rule of reason in [European] competition law cannot be upheld, it would be wrong, when classifying ancillary restrictions, to interpret the requirement for objective necessity as implying a need to weigh the pro- and anti-competitive effects of an agreement. Such an analysis can take place only in the specific framework of Article [101(3)] of the [FEU] Treaty.[102]

---

[98] *Remia and others* v. *Commission*, Case 42/84, [1985] ECR 2545.   [99] *Ibid.*, para. 19.
[100] *Pronuptia de Paris* v. *Pronuptia de Paris Irmgard Schillgallis*, Case 161/84, [1986] ECR 353, paras. 16 et seq. and especially paras. 17 and 18: "[T]he franchisor must be able to take the measures necessary for maintaining the identity and reputation of the network bearing his business name or symbol. It follows that provisions which establish the means of control necessary for that purpose do not constitute restrictions on competition for the purposes of Article [101(1)]. The same is true of the franchisee's obligation to apply the business methods developed by the franchisor and to use the know-how provided."
[101] *Métropole Télévision (M6)* v. *Commission*, Case T-112/99 (supra n. 96).
[102] *Ibid.*, para. 104 (references omitted).

The doctrine of ancillary restraints thus differs from a rule of reason in that it does not involve a concrete balancing of the pro-competitive and anti-competitive effects of the agreement. The operation of the doctrine is, according to the Court, "relatively abstract".[103] It only tolerates contractual clauses restricting competition without which "the main agreement is difficult or even impossible to implement".[104] Only *objectively necessary restrictions* of competition within an overall pro-competitive agreement will thus be accepted. And these objectively necessary restrictions must be "ancillary", that is: "subordinate" to the object of the main agreement.[105]

(d) Non-appreciable Restrictions: The De Minimis Rule

According to the common law principle *de minimis non curat lex*, the law will not concern itself with trifles. Translated into the present context, the European Court has declared that it will not use Article 101 to establish "perfect competition" but only "workable competition" within the internal market.[106] Minor market imperfections will thus be tolerated. Restrictions of competition will only fall within Article 101(1) where they do so "to an appreciable extent".[107] This is called the *de minimis* rule.

According to the Court, *de minimis* is measured not in quantitative or qualitative trade terms, but depends on the relevant market share. This view is shared by the Commission, which has offered guidance in its "De Minimis Notice".[108] The Notice is designed to "quantif[y], with the help of market share thresholds, what is not an appreciable restriction of competition under Article [101] of the [FEU] Treaty".[109] With the exception of "hardcore" restrictions,[110] the Commission considers that a 10 per cent

---

[103] *Ibid.*, para. 109.   [104] *Ibid.*

[105] See Commission, "Guidelines on Article [101](3)" (supra n. 74), paras. 29 and 30.

[106] *Metro SB-Großmärkte GmbH & Co. KG* v. *Commission*, Case 26/76, [1977] ECR 1875, para. 20; and confirmed in *Metro SB-Großmärkte GmbH & Co. KG* v. *Commission*, Case 75/84, [1986] ECR 3021, para. 65.

[107] *Société Technique Minière* v. *Maschinenbau Ulm*, Case 56/65 (supra n. 29), 249.

[108] The exact title of the Notice is: "Commission Notice on agreements of minor importance which do not appreciably restrict competition under Article 81(1) of the Treaty establishing the European Community (de minimis)", [2001] OJ C 368/13.

[109] *Ibid.*, para. 2.

[110] *Ibid.*, para. 11. However, the exclusion of the hardcore restrictions from the Commission's *de minimis* test will not automatically mean that they are always appreciable restrictions. The better view holds that the market thresholds for these types of restrictions must here simply be significantly lower to compensate for the gravity of their restrictive character.

aggregate market share for the parties to horizontal agreements and a 15 per cent aggregate market share for parties to vertical agreements will not appreciably restrict competition within the meaning of Article 101(1).[111] Importantly, the Commission and the Courts thereby investigate an individual agreement's economic context.[112]

4. Article 101(3): Exemptions through Pro-competitive Effects

Where an agreement has been found to be anti-competitive under Article 101(1), it will be void – unless it is justified and exempted under Article 101(3). The provision theoretically applies to all agreements that violate Article 101(1) – and thus even restrictions per object. It is directly effective and can thus be invoked as a protective shield by any undertaking facing legal proceedings.[113] In an effort to enhance legal certainty, the Union has however adopted a variety of exemption regulations that provide detailed criteria when certain categories of agreements are exempted under Article 101(3).

(a) Direct Exemptions under Article 101(3)

Article 101(3) potentially covers any agreement – even agreements that have been found to restrict competition by object. However, it makes the exemption conditional on four cumulative criteria. The first two criteria are positive, the other two criteria negative in nature.[114]

---

[111] "Commission Notice on agreements of minor importance" (supra n. 108), para. 7.

[112] On this contextual examination of a single agreement, see text supra n. 33.

[113] The direct effect of Article 101(3) had not always been the case. Indeed it was one of the "revolutionary" changes brought by Regulation 1/2003 on the implementation of the rules on competition laid down in Articles [101 and 102] of the Treaty, [2003] OJ L1/1.

[114] There has been a spirited debate on whether these criteria – all of which are "economic" in nature – are exhaustive or not. The Commission considers them exhaustive (see Commission, "Guidelines on Article [101](3)" (supra n. 74), para. 42): "The four conditions of Article [101(3)] are also exhaustive. When they are met the exception is applicable and may not be made dependent on any other condition. Goals pursued by other Treaty provisions can be taken into account to the extent that they can be subsumed under the four conditions of Article [101(3)]." Nonetheless, it is important to note that the Treaties' competition rules cannot be completely isolated from other policies; and this is particularly true for those policies – like environmental policy – that contain an express horizontal clause (see Article 11 TFEU (emphasis added): "Environmental protection requirements must be integrated *into the definition and implementation of the Union's policies and activities,* in particular with a view to promoting sustainable development").

Positively, Article 101(3) stipulates that the agreement must "contribute[] to improving the production or distribution of goods or to promoting technical or economic progress, while allowing consumers a fair share of the resulting benefit".[115] Where the agreement thus generates *productive* or *dynamic* efficiencies,[116] these efficiency gains might outweigh the economic inefficiencies identified in Article 101(1) but only under the – second – condition that consumers get a fair share in the resulting overall benefit. What is a "fair share"? According to the Commission:

> The concept of "fair share" implies that the pass-on of benefits must at least compensate consumers for any actual or likely negative impact caused to them by the restriction of competition found under Article [101(1)]...If such consumers are worse off following the agreement, the second condition of Article [101(3)] is not fulfilled.[117]

But even if that is the case, Article 101(3) will not allow anti-competitive restrictions that are "not indispensable" for the pro-competitive effects of the agreement; or agreements which "eliminat[e] competition in respect of a substantial part of the products in question".[118] A violation of either one of these negative conditions will mean that an agreement cannot benefit from an exemption. With regard to the indispensability of a restriction, the Commission has developed a two-fold test: "First, the restrictive agreement as such must be reasonably necessary in order to achieve the efficiencies. Secondly, the individual restrictions of competition that flow from the agreement must also be reasonably necessary for the attainment of the efficiencies."[119] The first test thereby requires "that the efficiencies be specific to the agreement in question in the sense that there are no other economically practicable and less restrictive means of achieving the efficiencies".[120] Once this global test has been passed, the Commission will then analyse the indispensability of each individual restriction of competition. Here, it will assess "whether individual restrictions are reasonably necessary in order to produce the efficiencies".[121]

Finally, a specific restriction – even if indispensable for the pro-competitive effects of the agreement – must not substantially eliminate

---

[115] Article 101(3) TFEU.
[116] For an elaboration of this, see Commission, "Guidelines on Article [101](3)" (supra n. 74), paras. 48 et seq. The typical example for an agreement enhancing "productive efficiency" is a "specialization agreement". A "Research and Development" agreement is an example for an agreement that may enhance dynamic efficiency.
[117] *Ibid.*, para. 85.   [118] Article 101(3) TFEU.
[119] Commission, "Guidelines on Article [101](3)" (supra n. 74), para. 73.
[120] *Ibid.*, para. 75.   [121] *Ibid.*, para. 78.

competition. This absolute limit on the exemptability of an agreement will be a function of the structure of the market.[122]

(b) Exemptions by Category: Block Exemption Regulations

In order to enhance legal certainty, Article 101(3) envisaged from the very beginning that an entire "category of agreements" might be exempted.[123] Article 103 thereby allowed the Council to "lay down detailed rules for the application of Article 101(3)".[124] This legal base was used early on;[125] and in a way that delegated the power to exempt agreements "en bloc" by means of regulations to the Commission. The Commission has adopted a variety of so-called "block exemption regulations".[126] It however retains the power to withdraw the benefit of a block exemption from an individual agreement.[127]

Many block exemption regulations originally followed a formal "category" approach. They would contain a "white list" of desirable clauses, and a "black list" of hardcore restrictions for a type of agreement.[128] This sector-specific approach towards block exemptions has been overtaken by a more flexible and economic approach.

The flagship illustration of the new structure of block exemption regulations is the Regulation for vertical agreements.[129] The Regulation exempts

---

[122] *Ibid.*, para. 107: "Whether competition is being eliminated within the meaning of the last condition of Article [101(3)] depends on the degree of competition existing prior to the agreement and on the impact of the restrictive agreement on competition, i.e. the reduction in competition that the agreement brings about. The more competition is already weakened in the market concerned, the slighter the further reduction required for competition to be eliminated within the meaning of Article [101(3)]."

[123] For this excellent textual point, see Lane, *EC Competition Law* (supra n. 11), 125.

[124] Article 103(2)(b) TFEU.

[125] Council Regulation 19/65 on application of Article 85(3) [now: Article 101(3)] of the Treaty to certain categories of agreements and concerted practices, [1965] OJ L36/533; and Council Regulation 2821/71 on application of Article 85(3) [now: Article 101(3)] of the Treaty to categories of agreements, decisions and concerted practices, [1971] OJ L285/46.

[126] See e.g. Commission Regulation 330/2010 on the application of Article 101(3) of the Treaty on the Functioning of the European Union to categories of vertical agreements and concerted practices, [2010] OJ L102/1. For the numerous "sectoral" block exemption regulations, see: http://ec.europa.eu/competition/antitrust/legislation/legislation.html.

[127] See Article 29 of Regulation 1/2003 (Withdrawal in individual cases), [2003] OJ L1/1.

[128] For a criticism of this "formalist" approach in the context of vertical agreements, see B. Hawk, "System Failure: Vertical Restraints and EC Competition Law", 32 (1995) *Common Market Law Review*, 973.

[129] See Commission Regulation 330/2010 (supra n. 126). For a discussion of this Regulation, see R. Wish and D. Bailey, "Regulation 330/2010: The Commission's New Block Exemption for Vertical Agreements", 47 (2010) *Common Market Law Review*, 1757.

all vertical agreements,[130] provided that "the market share held by the supplier does not exceed 30% of the relevant market on which it sells the contract goods or services and the market share held by the buyer does not exceed 30% of the relevant market on which it purchases the contract goods or services".[131] The Regulation still contains a "black list" of hard-core restrictions.[132] Yet there no longer exists a white list of permissible contractual clauses, and the Regulation thus concentrates essentially on the economic effect of an agreement in following the liberal principle that all is allowed that is not prohibited.

Conclusion

EU competition law constitutes a cornerstone within the Union's internal policies. The Union is here entitled to "regulate" and "police" the internal market so as to ensure undistorted competition. The two sections within the Treaties' Competition Chapter thereby correspond to two forms of distortions within the internal market. Section 1 subjects private undertakings to the Union competition rules, whereas Section 2 establishes a Union regime governing State aids.

This Chapter looked at the first pillar of EU competition law: Article 101. The provision prohibits anti-competitive collusions between undertakings that distort competition and affect trade between Member States. We saw that the Union has given a wide jurisdictional scope to the provision (and EU competition rules generally); yet that it tries to find an appropriate balance between pro- and anti-competitive considerations for every agreement. Due to the Union's historic task to create an internal market, vertical agreements have been of particular importance to the Union; and distribution agreements indeed continue to occupy a prominent place within the case law of the Courts.

---

[130] Commission Regulation 330/2010 (supra n. 126), Article 2.
[131] *Ibid.*, Article 3(1).   [132] *Ibid.*, Article 4.

Appendices

Appendix I Academic Literature: Further Reading

The literature with regard to European Union law has exploded in the last thirty years. Today, there exists a forest of general EU law textbooks and journals. The list in Table 13.1 is by no means comprehensive. It is meant to point the interested reader to a gateway for an in-depth study of a particular part of European Union law.

Table 13.1 General Textbooks and Journals

General Textbooks	General Journals
D. Chalmers *et al.*, *European Union Law* (Cambridge University Press, 2014)	Cambridge Yearbook of European Legal Studies
P. Craig and G. de Búrca, *EU Law: Text, Cases and Materials* (Oxford University Press, 2011)	Common Market Law Review
A. Dashwood *et al.*, *Wyatt & Dashwood's European Union Law* (Hart, 2011)	European Law Review
R. Schütze, *European Union Law* (Cambridge University Press, 2015)	European Law Journal
S. Weatherill, *Cases & Materials on EU Law* (Oxford University Press, 2014)	Journal of Common Market Studies
L. Woods and P. Watson, *Steiner & Woods' EU Law* (Oxford University Press, 2014)	Yearbook of European Law

In order to provide the reader with some more specific literature suggestions, I have listed between six and nine books and articles for each chapter below. They could be considered "essential reading" for a course on EU law; yet the prior study of the relevant chapter in a bigger general EU law textbook might be useful before jumping to a particular journal article or book chapter on a potentially (very) specific aspect of EU law.

Introduction (History)

P. Craig, *The Lisbon Treaty: Law, Politics, and Treaty Reform* (Oxford University Press, 2010)

D. Curtin, "The Constitutional Structure of the Union: A Europe of Bits and Pieces", (1993) 30 *Common Market Law Review* 17

P. D. Dinan, *Europe Recast: A History of European Union* (Palgrave, 2004)

P. Pescatore, "Some Critical Remarks on the 'Single European Act'", (1987) 24 *Common Market Law Review* 9

J.-C. Piris, *The Lisbon Treaty: A Legal and Political Analysis* (Cambridge University Press, 2010)

D. Urwin, *The Community of Europe: A History of European Integration Since 1945* (Longman, 1994).

Chapter 1: Union Institutions

N. Brown and T. Kennedy, *The Court of Justice of the European Communities* (Sweet & Maxwell, 2000)

R. Corbett *et al.*, *The European Parliament* (Harper Publishing, 2011)

P. Dann, "European Parliament and Executive Federalism: Approaching a Parliament in a Semi-Parliamentary Democracy" [2003] 9 *European Law Journal* 549

F. Hayes-Renshaw and H. Wallace, *The Council of Ministers* (Palgrave, 2006)

J.-P. Jacque, "The Principle of Institutional Balance" [2004] 41 *Common Market Law Review* 383

S. Novak, "The Silence of Ministers: Consensus and Blame Avoidance in the Council of the European Union", (2013) 51 *Journal of Common Market Studies* 1091

N. Nugent, *The European Commission* (Palgrave, 2000)

Chapter 2: Union Legislation

L. Buonanno and N. Nugent, *Policies and Policy Processes of the European Union* (Palgrave, 2013)

I. Cooper, "The Watchdogs of Subsidiarity: National Parliaments and the Logic of Arguing in the EU" [2006] 44 *Journal of Common Market Studies* 281

F. Fabbrini and K. Granat, "'Yellow Card, but no Foul': The Role of the National Parliaments under the Subsidiary Protocol and the Commission Proposal for an EU Regulation on the Right to Strike", (2013) 50 *Common Market Law Review* 115

S. Hix and B. Høyland, *The Political System of the European Union* (Palgrave, 2005)

B. Kohler-Koch and B. Rittberger, *Debating the Democratic Legitimacy of the European Union* (Rowman & Littlefield Publishers, 2007)

C. Reh *et al.*, "The Informal Politics of Legislation: Explaining Secluded Decision Making in the European Union", (2013) 49 *Comparative Political Studies* 1112

Chapter 3: Union Competences

L. Azoulai (ed.), *The Question of Competence in the European Union* (Oxford University Press, 2014)

P. Craig, "Competence: Clarity, Conferral, Containment and Consideration" [2004] 29 *European Law Review* 323

A. Dashwood, "The Limits of European Community Powers", (1996) 21 *European Law Review* 113.

T. Konstadinides, "Drawing the Line between Circumvention and Gap-filling: an Exploration of the Conceptual Limits of the Treaty's Flexibility Clause", (2012) 31 *Yearbook of European Law* 227

R. Schütze, "Lisbon and the Federal Order of Competences: A Prospective Analysis" [2008] 33 *European Law Review* 709

S. Weatherill, "Competence Creep and Competence Control", (2004) 23 *Yearbook of European Law* 1

D. Wyatt, "Community Competence to Regulate the Internal Market" (Oxford University Faculty of Law Research Paper 9/2007)

Chapter 4: Fundamental Rights

P. Alston (ed.), *The EU and Human Rights* (Oxford University Press, 1999)

L. Besselink, "Entrapped by the Maximum Standard: on Fundamental Rights, Pluralism and Subsidiarity in the European Union" [1998] 35 *Common Market Law Review* 629

J. Coppel and A. O'Neill, "The European Court of Justice: Taking Rights Seriously?"' [1992] 29 *Common Market Law Review* 669

S. Douglas-Scott, "A Tale of Two Courts: Luxembourg, Strasbourg and the Growing European Human Rights Acquis" [2006] 43 *Common Market Law Review* 629

K. Lenaerts, "Exploring the Limits of the EU Charter of Fundamental Rights", (2012) 8 *European Constitutional Law Review* 375

S. Peers *et al.*, *The EU Charter of Fundamental Rights: A Commentary* (Hart, 2014)

J. Weiler, "Fundamental Rights and Fundamental Boundaries: On Standards and Values in the Protection of Human Rights", in N. Neuwahl and A. Rosas (eds.), *The European Union and Human Rights* (Brill, 1995), 51

Chapter 5: Direct Effect

P. Craig, "Once Upon a Time in the West: Direct Effect and the Federalisation of EEC Law" [1992] 12 *Oxford Journal of Legal Studies* 453

A. Dashwood, "From *Van Duyn* to *Mangold* via *Marshall*: Reducing Direct Effect to Absurdity" [2006/07] 9 *Cambridge Yearbook of European Legal Studies* 81

S. Drake, "Twenty Years after *Von Colson*: the Impact of 'Indirect Effect' on the Protection of the Individual's Community Rights" [2005] 30 *European Law Review* 329

P. Pescatore, "The Doctrine of 'Direct Effect': an Infant Disease of Community Law" [1983] 8 *European Law Review* 155

S. Prechal, *Directives in EC Law* (Oxford University Press, 2006)

A. Schrauwen and J. Prinssen, *Direct Effect: Rethinking a Classic of EC Legal Doctrine* (Europa Law Publishing, 2004)

R. Schütze, "The Morphology of Legislative Power in the European Community: Legal Instruments and Federal Division of Powers" [2006] 25 *Yearbook of European Law* 91

J. Steiner, "Direct Applicability in EEC Law – A Chameleon Concept" [1982] 98 *Law Quarterly Review* 229–48

Chapter 6: (Legal) Supremacy

K. Alter, *Establishing the Supremacy of European Law: the Making of an International Rule of Law in Europe* (Oxford University Press, 2001)

P. Craig, "Britain in the European Union", in J. Jowell and D. Oliver (eds.), *The Changing Constitution* (Oxford University Press, 2011), 102

B. Davies, *Resisting the European Court of Justice: West Germany's Confrontation with European Law, 1949–1979* (Cambridge University Press, 2014)

U. Everling, "The Maastricht Judgment of the German Federal Constitutional Court and its Significance for the Development of the European Union", (1994) 14 *Yearbook of European Law* 1

R. Kovar, "The Relationship between Community Law and National Law" in EC Commission (ed.), *Thirty Years of Community Law* (EC Commission, 1981), 109

M. Kumm, "Who is the Final Arbiter of Constitutionality in Europe?", (1999) 36 *Common Market Law Review* 351

W. Sadurski, "'Solange, Chapter 3': Constitutional Courts in Central Europe – Democracy – European Union" [2008] 14 *European Law Journal* 1

Chapter 7: National Actions

A. Arnull, "The Principle of Effective Judicial Protection in EU Law: an Unruly Horse?" (2011) 36 *European Law Review* 51.

M. Broberg and N. Fenger, *Preliminary References to the European Court of Justice* (Oxford University Press, 2014)

M. Broberg, "Acte Clair Revisited", (2008) 45 *Common Market Law Review* 1383

M. Claes, *The National Courts' Mandate in the European Constitution* (Hart, 2005)

M. Dougan, *National Remedies before the Court of Justice: Issues of Harmonisation and Differentiation* (Hart, 2004)

M. Dougan, "The Vicissitudes of Life at the Coalface: Remedies and Procedures for Enforcing Union Law Before the National Courts" in P. Craig and G. de Búrca, *The Evolution of EU Law* (Oxford University Press, 2011) 407

C. N. Kakouris, "Do the Member States possess Judicial Procedural 'Autonomy'?" [1997] 34 *Common Market Law Review* 1389

T. Tridimas, "Liability for Breach of Community Law: Growing Up and Mellowing Down?" (2001) 38 *Common Market Law Review* 301

Chapter 8: European Actions

A. Albors-Llorens, "Remedies against the EU Institutions after Lisbon: An Era of Opportunity", (2012) 71 *Cambridge Law Journal* 507

S. Andersen, *The Enforcement of EU Law* (Oxford University Press, 2012)

S. Balthasar, "Locus Standi Rules for Challenges to Regulatory Acts by Private Applicants: the New Article 263(4) TFEU" (2010) 35 *European Law Review* 542

K. Gutman, "The Evolution of the Action for Damages against the European Union and its Place in the System of Judicial Protection", (2011) 48 *Common Market Law Review* 695

K. Lenaerts, I. Maselis and K. Gutman, *EU Procedural Law* (Oxford University Press, 2014)

L. Prete and B. Smulders, "The Coming of Age of Infringement Proceedings" (2010) 47 *Common Market Law Review* 9

J. Usher, "Direct and Individual Concern: An Effective Remedy or a Conventional Solution?", (2003) 28 *European Law Review* 575

A. Ward, *Judicial Review and the Rights of Private Parties in EU Law* (Oxford University Press, 2007)

Chapter 9: Internal Market: Goods I

C. Barnard, *The Substantive Law of the EU: The Four Freedoms* (Oxford University Press, 2013), Chapters 2–7

D. Chalmers, "Free Movement of Goods within the European Community: An Unhealthy Addiction to Scotch Whisky?" (1993) 42 *International and Comparative Law Quarterly* 269

A. Easson, "Cheaper Wine or Dearer Beer? Article 95 Again", (1984) 9 *European Law Review* 57

P. Oliver (ed.), *Oliver on Free Movement of Goods in the European Union* (Hart, 2010)

M. Poiares Maduro, *We the Court* (Hart, 1998)

N. Nic Shuibhne, "The Free Movement of Goods and Article 28 EC: An Evolving Framework", (2002) 27 *European Law Review* 408

E. Spaventa, "Leaving *Keck* behind? The Free Movement of Goods after the Rulings in *Commission* v. *Italy and Mickelsson and Roos*", (2009) 34 *European Law Review* 914

F. Weiss and C. Kaupa, *European Union Internal Market Law* (Cambridge University Press, 2014), Chapter 3

Chapter 10: Internal Market: Goods II

R. Barents, "The Internal Market Unlimited: Some Observations on the Legal Basis of Community Legislation", (1993) 30 *Common Market Law Review* 85

C. Barnard and J. Scott, *The Law of the Single European Market: Unpacking the Premises* (Hart, 2002)

G. Davies, "Can Selling Arrangements be Harmonised?" (2005) 30 *European Law Review* 37

N. de Sadeleer, "Procedures for Derogation from the Principle of Approximation of Laws under Article 95 EC", (2003) 40 *Common Market Law Review* 889

R. Schütze, *From Dual to Cooperative Federalism: The Changing Structure of European Law* (Oxford University Press, 2009)

P. J. Slot, "Harmonisation", (1996) 21 *European Law Review* 378

S. Weatherill, *Law and Integration in the European Union* (Clarendon, 1995)

S. Weatherill, "The Limits of Legislative Harmonization Ten Years after *Tobacco Advertising*: How the Court's Case Law has become a 'Drafting Guide'", (2011) 12 *German Law Journal* 827

Chapter 11: Internal Market: Persons

C. Barnard, *The Substantive Law of the EU: The Four Freedoms* (Oxford University Press, 2013), Chapters 8–10 and 13

L. Daniele, "Non-Discriminatory Restrictions to the Free Movement of Persons", (1997) 22 *European Law Review* 191

M. Dougan, "The Constitutional Dimension to the Case Law on Union Citizenship", (2006) 31 *European Law Review* 613

J. Shaw, *The Transformation of Citizenship in the European Union* (Cambridge University Press, 2007)

E. Spaventa, *Free Movement of Persons in the European Union: Barriers to Movement in their Constitutional Context* (Kluwer, 2007)

E. Spaventa, "From 'Gebhard' to 'Carpenter': towards a (non-)economic European Constitution", (2004) 41 *Common Market Law Review* 743

A. Tryfonidou, "In search of the Aim of the EC Free Movement of Persons Provisions: Has the Court of Justice missed the Point?" (2009) 46 *Common Market Law Review* 1591

F. Weiss and C. Kaupa, *European Union Internal Market Law* (Cambridge University Press, 2014), Chapters 4–6

Chapter 12: Competition Law: Cartels

G. Amato, *Antitrust and the Bounds of Power: The Dilemma of Liberal Democracy in the History of the Market* (Hart, 1997)

J. Faull, "Effect on Trade Between Member States", (1999) 26 *Fordham Corporate Law Institute* 481

J. Goyder and A. Albors-Llorens, *EC Competition Law* (Oxford University Press, 2009)

A. Jones and B. Sufrin, *EU Competition Law: Text, Cases and Materials* (Oxford University Press, 2013)

I. Lianos, "Collusion in Vertical Relations under Article 81 EC", 45 (2008) *Common Market Law Review* 1027

O. Odudu, "The Meaning of Undertaking within Article 81 EC", (2006) 7 *Cambridge Yearbook of European Legal Studies* 211

A. Weitbrecht, "From Freiburg to Chicago and beyond: The first 50 years of European Competition Law", (2008) 29 *European Competition Law Review* 81

R. Wish and D. Bailey, *Competition Law* (Oxford University Press, 2012)

R. Wish and B. Sufrin, "Article 85 and the Rule of Reason", (1987) 7 *Yearbook of European Law* 1

Appendix II: How to Find (and Read) EU Judgments

All EU cases are traditionally identified by a number/year figure that is followed by the names of the parties. Cases before the Court of Justice are preceded by a C-, while cases decided before the General Court are preceded by a T- (for the French 'Tribunal').[1] The Civil Service Tribunal prefixes its cases with an F- (for the French 'Fonction publique').

In the past, all judgments of all EU Courts were published in paper form in the purple-bound 'European Court Reports' (ECR). Cases decided by the Court of Justice were published in the ECR-I series; cases decided by the General Court were published in the ECR-II series, while cases decided by the Civil Service Tribunal were published in the ECR-SC series. However, as of 2012, the entire Court of Justice of the European Union has decided to go "paperless" and now publishes its judgments only electronically.[2] The two principal websites here are the Court's own curia-website (http://curia.europa.eu/jcms/jcms/j_6/), and the Union's general EU lex-website (http://eur-lex.europa.eu/homepage.html). For judgments referred to in the main text of this book, the easiest way is however to go to <www.schutze.eu>, which contains the 'Lisbon' version of all classic EU Court judgments mentioned in this text.

Once upon a time, judgments issued by the European Court of Justice were – to paraphrase Hobbes – "nasty, brutish and short". Their shortness was partly due to a structural division the Court made between the "Issues of Fact and of Law" (or later: "Report for the Hearing") – which set out the facts, procedure and the arguments of the parties – and the "Grounds of Judgment". Only the latter constituted the judgment *sensu stricto* and was often very short indeed. The Court originally also tried to adopt the "French" judicial ideal of trying to put the entire judgment into a single "sentence"! A judgment like *Van Gend en Loos* contains about 2,000 words – not more than an undergraduate essay.

---

[1] Importantly: cases decided before the creation of the General Court will have no prefix at all. For there was only one court: the Court of Justice.

[2] In the absence of a "page number" in a printed book, the Union henceforth has recourse to a "European Case Law Identifier". This is composed of EU: C[T/F]: Year: Number.

This world of short judgments is – sadly or not – gone. A typical judgment issued today will, on average, be four to five times as long as *Van Gend*. (And in the worst case scenario, a judgment, especially in the area of EU competition law, may be as long as 100,000 words – the size of this book!) This new comprehensiveness is arguably the product of a more refined textualist methodology, but it also results from a change in the organisation and style of judgments. Modern judgments have come to integrate much of the facts and the parties' arguments into the main body of a "single" judgment, and this has especially made many direct actions much longer and much more repetitive!

The structure of a modern ECJ judgment given under the preliminary reference procedure may be studied by looking at *Mangold*.

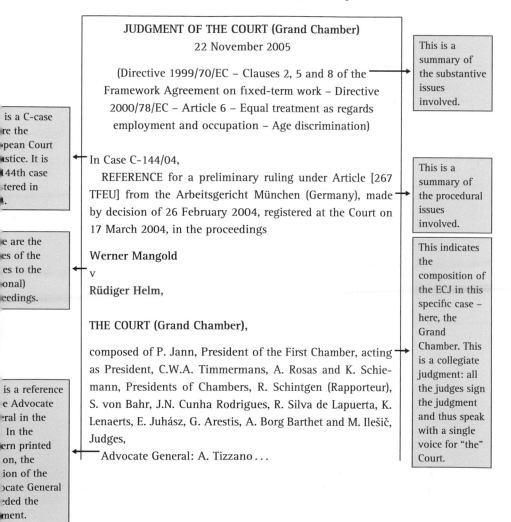

JUDGMENT OF THE COURT (Grand Chamber)
22 November 2005

(Directive 1999/70/EC – Clauses 2, 5 and 8 of the Framework Agreement on fixed-term work – Directive 2000/78/EC – Article 6 – Equal treatment as regards employment and occupation – Age discrimination)

This is a summary of the substantive issues involved.

is a C-case re the pean Court stice. It is 44th case tered in

In Case C-144/04,
REFERENCE for a preliminary ruling under Article [267 TFEU] from the Arbeitsgericht München (Germany), made by decision of 26 February 2004, registered at the Court on 17 March 2004, in the proceedings

This is a summary of the procedural issues involved.

e are the es of the es to the onal) eedings.

Werner Mangold

v

Rüdiger Helm,

This indicates the composition of the ECJ in this specific case – here, the Grand Chamber. This is a collegiate judgment: all the judges sign the judgment and thus speak with a single voice for "the" Court.

THE COURT (Grand Chamber),

is a reference e Advocate ral in the In the ern printed on, the ion of the cate General ded the ment.

composed of P. Jann, President of the First Chamber, acting as President, C.W.A. Timmermans, A. Rosas and K. Schiemann, Presidents of Chambers, R. Schintgen (Rapporteur), S. von Bahr, J.N. Cunha Rodrigues, R. Silva de Lapuerta, K. Lenaerts, E. Juhász, G. Arestis, A. Borg Barthet and M. Ilešič, Judges,
Advocate General: A. Tizzano . . .

Judgment

1. This reference for a preliminary ruling concerns the interpretation of Clauses 2, 5 and 8 of the Framework Agreement on fixed-term contracts concluded on 18 March 1999 ('the Framework Agreement'), put into effect by Council Directive 1999/70/EC of 28 June 1999 concerning the framework agreement on fixed-term work concluded by ETUC, UNICE and CEEP (OJ 1999 L 175, p. 43), and of Article 6 of Council Directive 2000/78/EC of 27 November 2000 establishing a general framework for equal treatment in employment and occupation (OJ 2000 L 303, p. 16).

2. The reference has been made in the course of proceedings brought by Mr Mangold against Mr Helm concerning a fixed-term contract by which the former was employed by the latter ('the contract').

Having given a brief synopsis of the issues involved, the court starts by presenting the legal context, that is: the relevant norms of European and national law.

Legal context

The relevant provisions of [Union] law

The Framework Agreement

3. According to Clause 1, '[t]he purpose of this Framework Agreement is to:
   (a) improve the quality of fixed-term work by ensuring the application of the principle of non-discrimination;
   (b) establish a framework to prevent abuse arising from the use of successive fixed-term employment contracts or relationships'...

The relevant provisions of national law

14 Paragraph 1 of the Beschäftigungsförderungsgesetz (Law to promote employment), as amended by the law of 25 September 1996 (BGBl. 1996 I, p. 1476) ('the BeschFG 1996'), provided...

The main proceedings and the questions referred for a preliminary ruling

20   On 26 June 2003 Mr Mangold, then 56 years old, concluded with Mr Helm, who practises as a lawyer, a contract that took effect on 1 July 2003.

This is one of the most important sections for the reader of the judgment. The Court here presents the facts and the procedure(s) of the specific case.

21   Article 5 of that contract provided that:

'1.   The employment relationship shall start on 1 July 2003 and last until 28 February 2004.

2.   The duration of the contract shall be based on the statutory provision which is intended to make it easier to conclude fixed-term contracts of employment with older workers (the provisions of the fourth sentence, in conjunction with those of the fourth sentence, of Paragraph 14(3) of the TzBfG . . .), since the employee is more than 52 years old . . . '

31   Those were the circumstances in which the Arbeitsgericht München decided to stay proceedings and to refer the following questions to the Court of Justice for a preliminary ruling:

'1(a)   Is Clause 8(3) of the Framework Agreement . . . to be interpreted, when transposed into domestic law, as prohibiting a reduction of protection following from the lowering of the age limit from 60 to 58? . . . '

Admissibility of the reference for a preliminary ruling

32   At the hearing the admissibility of the reference for a preliminary ruling was challenged by the Federal Republic of Germany, on the grounds that the dispute in the main proceedings was fictitious or contrived. Indeed, in the past Mr Helm has publicly argued a case identical to Mr Mangold's, to the effect that Paragraph 14(3) of the TzBfG is unlawful . . .

Concerning the questions referred for a preliminary ruling

On Question 1(b)

40   In Question 1(b), which it is appropriate to consider first, the national court asks whether, on a proper construction of Clause 5 of the Framework Agreement, it is contrary to that provision for rules of domestic law such as those at issue in the main proceedings to contain none of the restrictions provided for by that clause in respect of the use of fixed-term contracts of employment . . .

On those grounds, the Court (Grand Chamber) hereby rules:

1.   On a proper construction of Clause 8(3) of the Framework Agreement on fixed-term contracts concluded on

---

Side annotations:

Court quotes preliminary questions referred by the national court.

In the main part of the judgment, the Court will cover each of the preliminary questions, one by one. Sometimes, it may change the order – as in this case; or it may decide that one question was inadmissible, or that the answer to one question makes its response to another unnecessary. (In any direct actions, the Court will come to a wholly separate 'Arguments of the Parties' from the 'Findings of the Court' for each of the legal points raised.)

We saw in Chapter 7, Section 3 that the Court will first check if the national court was entitled to use the preliminary procedure under Article 267 TFEU.

This is the core '*ratio decidendi*' of the judgment.

18 March 1999, put into effect by Council Directive 1999/70/EC of 28 June 1999 concerning the framework agreement on fixed-term work concluded by ETUC, UNICE and CEEP, domestic legislation such as that at issue in the main proceedings, which for reasons connected with the need to encourage employment and irrespective of the implementation of that agreement, has lowered the age above which fixed-term contracts of employment may be concluded without restrictions, is not contrary to that provision . . .

Index